Letters of

RICHARD
WAGNER

The Burrell Collection

Letters of

RICHARD
WAGNER

The Burrell Collection
PRESENTED TO THE CURTIS INSTITUTE
OF MUSIC BY ITS FOUNDER
MRS. EFREM ZIMBALIST

Edited with notes by
JOHN N. BURK

NEW YORK
VIENNA HOUSE
1972

This 1972 VIENNA HOUSE edition is reprinted
by arrangement with The Macmillan Company.
International Standard Book Number: 0-8443-0031-4
Library of Congress Catalogue Number: 78-183325
Manufactured in the United States of America

My dear Mrs. Burrell:

It is one of the deep satisfactions of my life that it was possible, some nineteen years ago, to acquire the Collection of Wagneriana that so justly bears your name.

Your indefatigable labor in searching, finding and salvaging this treasure, and the altruism of your aim in so doing, had made an ineradicable impression upon me—as had the tragic fact of your death before your contemplated "Life of Richard Wagner" could be completed.

Over a period of years this material has been sorted and edited, and it is now presented in book form.

Time and space have little to do with the meeting of kindred spirits. Although we never met, I reach out my hand to you. It bears this book—compiled in homage to you.

Mary Curtis Zimbalist

This book is published with the permission
of the heirs of Richard Wagner.

PREFACE

The great mass of the literature by and about the most self-explanatory of composers falls into two sorts. The bulk of it was gathered at Bayreuth and published from there under Wagner's own eye, or under the careful supervision of Cosima Wagner after his death. Then there have been the letters which never returned to Wagner, nor came into the hands of his family at Villa Wahnfried, in some cases by the intent of their owners. A few of these have found their way into publication. But a larger number of them, by a curious chain of circumstances, have remained undisclosed until now.

The accumulation of the documents outside of Bayreuth was the almost single-handed work of the Honorable Mrs. Burrell. In the years immediately following Wagner's death, the English lady felt that the existing biographies were lamentably spotty and grossly inaccurate. She proceeded to gather what material she could and to write the "complete" *Life*. Her own death, in 1898, broke off her tale where Wagner was no more than out of school. Mrs. Burrell's husband and daughter at once published the fragment as "a worthy foundation for the monument she had hoped to erect to the genius of Richard Wagner." But she had already done her great labor in gathering the material. The Collection itself would have remained her "monument," even if she had been able to carry her writing efforts further. The matter rested for many years after her death. The Collection itself, as the property of her heirs, lay untouched, unavailable for inspection by Wagnerian research. In 1929 it was catalogued, whereby at least the dates and general nature of the contents were made known.

In 1931 the Collection became purchasable, and so came to the attention of Mrs. Mary Louise Curtis Bok (now Mrs. Efrem Zimbalist) in America. That a zealous lady had used her privilege of wealth to uncover buried truths and contribute to the enlightenment of the musical world, appealed to her. She considered it her good fortune to be able to bring about the continuation of the interrupted project. In donating the Collection to the Curtis Institute of Music, she combines with her endeavors in behalf of musical education another in behalf of recorded history.

The Collection contains 840 items, most of them letters, to which Mrs. Zimbalist has added 25 separately acquired. Except for the small handful of the letters which have escaped into print in one way or another, and which are so identified, the Burrell letters here appear for the first time.

The present editor, in his task of fulfillment, has had good reason to appreciate the pioneering enterprise, the prodigious labors of Mrs. Burrell in hunting out, tracking down, authenticating, and docketing her material. But admiration and good faith cannot extend to the carrying out of the biography as she began it. Her beginning of the *Life* as published on a presentation basis by her heirs is so large as to format that the pages must be turned at arm's length. An average apartment dweller of today could find no place for such a book, except perhaps under his bed. The reader, unless he were a linguist, would have trouble with the letters, which Mrs. Burrell presented in their original language only. She would have no translations. "I hold to reproducing letters exactly as I receive them," she wrote. This editor bows to practicability and necessary compromise, easing his conscience with Emerson's remark about translations that he would prefer not to swim a stream if a bridge were at hand.

In other respects there can be no question of carrying on in the vein of Mrs. Burrell's text. Her style and her point of view were her own, and also belonged to an earlier day when the attitude toward Wagner was far less objective than now, and far less informed. The material which has waited so long to be published is too voluminous to permit extended commentary, nor does the whole story need to be told again. The editor has tried to do no more than bring order and intelligibility into a mass of diverse material by what has seemed necessary in the way of connecting narrative and chapter division. This is the main body of the book. The second part (Appendix A) consists of a complete listing in chronological order, with each item quoted, described, or indicated by cross reference to the main text. Many letters are relegated to this section for the sole reason that they do not fit conveniently elsewhere. They will be found to clear up numerous points in that complex of circumstance which was Wagner's career.

It is hoped that the letters may before long be published in their own language and country. Meanwhile, it has not been found possible to include in this volume every letter in its complete form, nor to more than indicate the musical manuscripts. Such a fortuitous amassing of letters will always turn up useless matter. The editor declares himself innocent of so much as a temptation to suppress or manipulate any passage to support a case.

It has been Mrs. Zimbalist's desire not only to publish the Collection as completely as reason allows, but to make the documents fully available to Wagnerian scholarship. Because many of the original letters are fragile (the usually penniless Wagner of his younger days used thin paper to save postage), it has been necessary to photograph every item. There is a complete file, in photostatic copy, at the Curtis Institute of Music in Philadelphia.

The translation of the manuscripts has been accomplished by Hans Abraham, Henry Lea, and Dr. Richard Stoehr. Mr. Abraham has ably taken over the editor's chair to collate the original Uhlig correspondence with the published text and to condense the diary of the garrulous Fräulein, Susanne Weinert. Ernest Newman, to whom all Wagnerians are indebted, has given his gracious personal attention to the clearing up of some puzzles. Felix Wolfes has examined the quoted German texts. Dr. Hugo Leichtentritt and Ernst Krenek have solved problems in deciphering. Mrs. Margaret H. Burns has kept a firm hand on the flow of the many items in their metamorphoses from photostat to printed page, forestalling confusion.

CONTENTS

ILLUSTRATIONS

Letters of
RICHARD
WAGNER

The Burrell Collection

❧ I ❦

THE SEARCHES OF MRS. BURRELL

The Burrell Collection has had a strange history. Many years ago, while Wagner was still alive, a lady in England conceived an enormous admiration for his works. She was the wife of the Honorable Willoughby Burrell and the daughter of Sir John Banks, K.C.B., a prominent physicist of Trinity College, Dublin. As time went on, Mary Burrell ceased to be content with haunting Bayreuth and other operatic centers of Europe, applauding performances of the *Ring* or *Tristan*. She possessed, as well as a fund of romantic idealism, a sense of a wrong to be righted and a British passion for the truth at all costs. She undertook to comb the Continent for material and write the biography that would tell all.

Mrs. Burrell beheld on the one hand vicious attacks on Wagner by the hostile clans, and, emanating from the Villa Wahnfried in Bayreuth under the eye of his widow, a published record of his life that was sometimes handled with more caution than candor. Glasenapp's *Life*, written in close collaboration with Bayreuth, was open to this charge. The book by Houston Stewart Chamberlain that appeared in 1896, while she was working upon her own book, was obviously a close family document by one destined to marry Wagner's daughter Eva. Prager's *Wagner as I knew Him,* which had appeared in 1892, was exposed by Chamberlain as worse than unreliable. Mrs. Burrell had no use for the "scribblers," as she called them, who merely "touched up" the material of the *Autobiographical Sketch* (with the *Communication to My Friends* the only autobiographical material then available) to give it a fresh appearance. In other words, she found that the already considerable windy writing about Wagner added nothing of great importance to what he himself had told. This lady was no scribbler, nor did she pretend to be a virtuoso of the pen. What she wanted was to find matter that had been misstated or remained unknown (or had been kept unknown), and to order and publish it in the necessary narrative form. Least of all did she trust the collections of letters that came forth with the sanction of Wagner's widow: it must be said at once that she remained throughout her life ready to believe the worst of Frau Cosima.

Mrs. Burrell was qualified for this task (and it was no slight task at that time) by an enormous pertinacity, a plentiful supply of money, and, as motive power, a strong faith in Wagner and his works. She was rewarded—and no doubt astonished—by what she found. It would have been natural to suppose that after

I

Wagner, working on his prodigious *My Life* (*Mein Leben*), had made every effort to recapture the letters he had written to many people in many parts of Europe, and after his widow had long continued as the custodian of all that pertained to her famous husband, little would have been left for a self-appointed lady-historian in England to pick up. But it so happened that there were those who distrusted Cosima, or who for one reason or another had kept their Wagner letters or other relics to themselves. Mrs. Burrell spent with an open hand, and the "vendors," as she called them, came flocking. She traveled about freely, followed up clues, interviewed every imaginable friend or relative of Wagner, or their descendants, and carried away her evidence, wherever possible, in written and certified form. Her principal single find in the way of a descendant was Natalie Bilz-Planer, the supposed sister, but actually the illegitimate daughter, of Minna. Wagner's first wife had been a saver of letters and papers of various sorts, and on her death in 1866 these duly went to Natalie. It was twenty-four years later, in 1890, that Mrs. Burrell communicated with Natalie. Natalie looked upon Cosima, the supplanting wife, with much bitterness; and Mrs. Burrell had only to convince her that, far from being in league with Cosima, she was actually hostile to Bayreuth, to extract, bit by bit, and by the lure of payments, the bulk of the inherited papers, including 128 letters from Wagner to Minna.

But this was not Mrs. Burrell's most sensational discovery. An Italian printer in Basel, Switzerland, by the name of Bonfantini, had set in type, under Wagner's supervision, between 1870 and 1875, the first three volumes of the autobiography *My Life*. He had printed, as he was ordered, eighteen [1] copies which Wagner had entrusted, under vow of secrecy, to his intimate circle, and later called back or destroyed. In 1892 Mrs. Burrell found Bonfantini's widow, and discovered that Bonfantini, sensing something unusual in his mysterious consignment, had secretly struck off an extra copy for himself. Mrs. Burrell acquired this copy, together with letters of instruction to Bonfantini from Wagner and from Cosima. She held in her hand, in unbound sheets as they had come from the press, one of the longest and most revealing autobiographies ever written— a book that described episodes until then unknown or only hinted at, that made what had so far been written about Wagner little more than gropings in the dark. But the time had not come for these revelations. Nineteen years more were to pass before Cosima would publish them. Mrs. Burrell could not have published any part of her stolen book, whose contents presumably remained a double-locked secret at Wahnfried.[2] She was obviously teeming with knowledge she could not use, but which was bound to inform her narrative in a hundred indirect ways. The book also gave her an entirely fresh set of clues, which she lost no time in pursuing.

What Mrs. Burrell finally brought together was indeed remarkable. Besides

[1] See 484E.

[2] However, the title page and prefatory page were reproduced as illustrations in her book.

letters from various periods of Wagner's life, there were musical and literary sketches, completed manuscripts, printed scores, pictures, printed programs, birth and marriage certificates, contracts, passports. She had the material for an immense book, which she at length proceeded to write. The enormous difficulties of her task were increased by attacks of neuralgia, which kept her from reading, or holding a pen. In 1898, when the manuscript which had been her life's aim had reached Wagner's twenty-first year, she died. Those twenty-one years were accounted for with elaborate care. But they took her only to the threshold of his career as a provincial conductor and of his meeting with Minna: in other words, just to the point when her really special treasures were about to come into her story. Mrs. Burrell's heirs at once published her manuscript.

The Collection itself lay for years untouched and unseen. William Ashton Ellis bespoke other biographers when, with justifiable pique, he referred to one of the letters as having "plunged into the recesses of a secretive collector's portfolio." At length, in 1929, the Collection was examined and catalogued. The catalogue, which describes each item and gives in a few words the gist of many of the letters, has done vicarious service in Wagnerian literature since that time, the synopsis having been quoted where the original has been unavailable.

Another story must now be told. Through the long years when this Collection lay in darkness, mysteries, legends, and gossip have gathered about it. Mrs. Burrell made it plain in her book that she believed, presumably on the strength of her own gathered material, that Cosima had manipulated the Wagner documents to suit her ends. The anonymous compilers of the catalogue, thirty-one years after her death, roundly backed Mrs. Burrell's point of view. The authors of the catalogue devote the larger part of their preface to passing dark hints about the perfidious ways of Cosima as the custodian of the "Bayreuth tradition," or making open charges against her. Wagner was "set to work" to collect the letters he had written far and wide. He was also "set to work" to dictate his life to Cosima. Her "pen put it down, and every incident of it is clouded." In these ways was the "official view promulgated by his family," and it is "untrue."

Through the years that the Collection has remained a closed secret, these statements have necessarily been taken as an assurance that when it should be opened up, the misdeeds of Bayreuth and Wagner's widow would be laid bare. My Life has been the subject of the compilers' most ominous charges. If they had taken the trouble to compare the suppressed copy with the published one, they would have found that the amount of "doctoring" in the public print was negligible. This comparison, of course, the more thoroughgoing Mrs. Burrell would have made if she had lived to examine the published autobiography in 1911. But her suspicions were largely based on bewilderment. When she stumbled upon the bootlegged copy of My Life, she beheld her idol, her gleaming crusader for a glorious art, a very different sort of person at close view. Since this person was apparently describing himself of his own free will, she was unable to accept the words as his. She decided that "Richard Wagner was not responsible" for this "miserable book," that its unmistakable purpose was to "ruin everyone connected with Wagner." She believed that he "consented under pressure to the book being put together, that he yielded to the temptation of allowing everyone else's character to be blackened in order to make his own great fault pale before the iniquities, real or invented, of others." These were the words of an adorer who had opened the book of her hero and found there a stranger. Cosima bore the brunt of her disillusion.

The compilers have shown little judgment in standing behind Mrs. Burrell's desperate and emotional conclusion so many years later. They should rather have shown, with their advantage over her of a thirty years' perspective, a reasonable objectivity, instead of lapsing into the old partisan state of mind which must either blacken Cosima or whitewash her. It is obvious now, and should have been obvious then, that the Archegotist need not have been "set to work" to talk to the world about so absorbing a topic as himself, nor would he have subjected himself to petticoat control on so important a subject.

The publication of the catalogue, and its preface in particular, stirred up a considerable broil. The death of Cosima Wagner, in 1930, induced two literary adventurers by the names of Hurn and Root to capitalize on floating suspicions with a post-mortem attack on her, together with any baseless defamation of Wagner which happened to occur to them. I would not bring up the subject of a book long since nullified, except that the writers referred to the Burrell Collection as the source of almost all of their charges. It is now plain that they could have seen little more than the outside of the Collection, having succeeded in obtaining no more than three letters (Nos. 69, 213, and 306), which they quoted in part. Otherwise the catalogue, and nothing else, was their springboard, and they applied their leaping imaginations to the already irresponsible statements in its preface. They had the effrontery to call their book *The Truth About Wagner*, and indeed their effrontery served the good end of reducing much of the anti-Cosima agitation to absurdity, and so considerably deflating it.

The strangest part of the whole matter is that this prodigious fuss over Cosima is based on practically nothing at all. Most of the Collection is pre-Cosima, and does not touch her in any way. There are a few formal notes by her, in discharge of obligations, but otherwise she is scarcely even mentioned. If we dismiss the venomous epithets of Natalie Bilz-Planer, obviously worthless, the issue never rises at all, except in one place—the manuscript notebook of Wagner's letters to Uhlig, hand-copied by Uhlig's daughter Elsa, before she delivered the originals to Bayreuth for publication (256). In Appendix B these copies are compared with the published version and every discrepancy noted. The reader may at last, instead of relying upon the haphazard suppositions of others, see for himself exactly how Cosima went about her editing and the precise degree of her guilt.

❧ II ❧

WAGNER'S STEPDAUGHTER NATALIE

"The 'Little Natalie' really writes very confusedly, and, much as I hate to say so, I fear there is no place in which she will feel well! Though she now signs herself as 'Frau Bilz,' she is still a genuine old spinster. . . . Whether the best furniture of the 'poor seduced Richard' could bring her much is doubtful. It has lost too much of its presentability. The poor little old woman is to be pitied, for she won't find any peace in this life!"
—Marie Schmole to Mrs. Burrell, February 20, 1896 (163 B)

In Natalie Bilz-Planer, the surviving illegitimate daughter of Minna, Mrs. Burrell discovered her principal source of information, but also her principal witness, for Natalie had lived for years in the Wagner household. Natalie talked and wrote volubly, supplying Mrs. Burrell with rambling *"Notizen"*; her memory was good, considering the years which had elapsed, but her stories usually fell into bitter denunciations of the "rivals" her mother had hated, and whom she in turn had learned to hate. To be compelled to sift reliable data out of this prejudiced jumble was no doubt an embarrassment to Mrs. Burrell, as it is to the present editor. The reader, too, should be forewarned with a description of Natalie.

In her notations for the continuation of her *Life of Wagner* (2), Mrs. Burrell describes how she came upon "Wagner's love letters to his first wife," and their inheritor, Natalie herself, in 1890:

"The story of the quest is a romantic one. I was told that her [Minna's] sister, who lived in a home for old ladies at Leisnig in Saxony, possessed the piano which Wagner had used during the composition of *Tannhäuser*. Wishing to buy it I travelled with my husband and two children from Dresden through the Valley of the Mulde; on reaching the picturesque village of Leisnig we were driven up a steep and winding road like that to the Wartburg." She describes the landscape and the meager inn at which they stopped.

"We then inquired the way to our destination and reached not a 'home for old ladies' but a poorhouse of the poorest description and in it in a narrow dark room an aristocratic-looking little lady with fine and reserved manners; her deafness made it extremely difficult to communicate with her, and many hours on several days did I spend in proving to her that no one knew so much about

5

Richard as I did and that I was prepared to sacrifice myself and my life to making a biography of him such as had never been written for any musician, no, nor for any king, a literary monument to his genius.

"At last she gave me her confidence and said that being in absolute want she had sent piles of letters and other things to Richard after he had written her endless letters asking for them; in return for which he bought her into this institution for life. 'You were very foolish to part with them,' said I. 'Yes, but you know how he could write when he wanted anything.' (Yes I did and so will the reader very soon.) . . . I imagine that her helpless and friendless position forced her to tell him that she had sent him all she had.

"The poorhouse also did duty as a hospital, the room next hers was that in which the dead bodies were laid out, the food she got was almost uneatable, she had existed in this misery for years and yet it would scarcely be correct to say simply that I bought these letters from her for she would not have sold them to anyone else, and she must have destroyed an immense number before she made up her mind to let me have the remainder. Readers can judge of this by the number of letters he refers to which are not forthcoming. One of these love letters she had already torn into pieces, then repented, gave it to me, and a troublesome task it was to copy it." (68)

Mrs. Burrell's description of Natalie as "an aristocratic-looking little lady with fine and reserved manners" seems overgenerous. Her refinement is explainable only as the front of reduced gentility, at odds with her surroundings.

Natalie Bilz-Planer possessed a mass of papers—letters, music, and other relics —which she had inherited from her mother, Minna Wagner, who, in her time, had been a careful saver of letters by, or pertaining to, her husband. Further than this, Natalie was in a position to furnish rare first-hand information. She had lived with the Wagners intermittently through their married years together, passing for Minna's sister, while actually (though she herself did not know it) Minna's illegitimate daughter by an early encounter with an army officer.

This information Mrs. Burrell soon ferreted out. In her copy of *My Life* acquired from Bonfantini's widow, she must have read Wagner's brief statement: "A certain Herr von Einsiedel fell desperately in love with her, and abused the power of his passion to take advantage of the inexperienced girl in an unguarded moment." But Mrs. Burrell was on the trail of this Planer skeleton two years before she bought her copy of *My Life*. She obtained from the Lutheran church Zum Heiligen Kreuz in Dresden, a copy (testified July 13, 1891) of Natalie's baptismal certificate (6). The date of birth (and baptism) was February 22, 1826, which would mean that Minna was seduced at the age of fifteen. The father appears as Ernst Rudolph von Einsiedel, Captain of the Royal Saxon Guards. Since the child was baptized as Ernestine Natalie, and so named after her father, Minna's interest in him may have been more than momentary.

Mrs. Burrell lost no opportunity to make the most of Natalie. After Minna's

NATALIE BILZ-PLANER (7)

death, in 1866, Wagner had written to Natalie (453) requesting the letters he had written to Minna. Natalie sent him a large quantity of them, which were eventually published from Wahnfried in 1908. But Natalie had a way of not letting everything go out of her hands. Wagner, noticing that many of his letters to Minna, including all of his letters as her suitor, were not forthcoming, wrote that if these letters had been destroyed, well and good; but if not, they belonged to him as the writer. Natalie must have pretended that they had been lost.

There is no continuous record of Natalie's life. We know that she was with her mother at Magdeburg in 1834, when she would have been seven years old, and when Minna, the darling of the theater, could hardly have held her vogue and her position had she not passed her off as a sister. Natalie, or "Nette," as she was called, appears by incidental mention as living with Wagner and Minna from the time when they were first married until the flight from Königsberg. She was not with them at Riga, nor in Paris until November, 1840, when she lived with them through the worst of their poverty. When the Wagners went to Dresden, she stayed with Wagner's sister Cäcilie Avenarius in Paris until 1843, then returning to Saxony to stay with Minna's sister Charlotte Tröger, in Zwickau, joining the Wagners in Dresden in 1845. She was with them for most of the Zürich years, later returning to the Trögers. She seems to have been lumpish and dull-witted. Wagner accepted the girl without enthusiasm, but equably enough as an appendage to Minna. Since she had to be either included in the household or provided for elsewhere, it was cheaper to keep her and save a servant. Wagner later described her in *My Life* as "undeveloped in mind and body—awkward and silly. . . . Friction between her and her mother often led to disturbances of our domestic peace." Minna, who always showed a grudging attitude toward her, would nag her and order her about, and Natalie would refuse to take orders from her supposed "sister." Natalie had always earned her living and pocket money by being useful around the house, but this friction became insupportable when it was added to increasing marital friction. In the summer of 1843, when Natalie first made her home with the Trögers, there was a protracted effort to equip her with enough French, English, sketching, and piano playing to be a governess, but to this poor Natalie was never equal. Her mother despaired of finding a husband for her; but shortly after Minna's death she married and became Natalie Bilz-Planer, outlived her husband, and continued for years under contribution from Cosima.

When Mrs. Burrell first communicated with Natalie in her retreat at Leisnig, Natalie was suspicious that her English visitor might be a secret emissary of Cosima, whom she hated as bitterly as Minna had hated her. But she soon became convinced that Mrs. Burrell had little more use for Cosima than she had and yielded up her letters piecemeal, each time throwing the good English lady's notations for her book into fresh disorder. On the death of her benefactress, in 1898, there were still more to come, and these Mrs. Burrell's heirs duly acquired.

On September 19, 1890, Natalie writes (82 A): "If God had bestowed as many high gifts of the mind on me as on you, gracious lady, I would write Minna's memoir—but not as a sister—that would spoil everything." And a month later, October 12, she evidently expects that her notes will be used verbatim by Mrs. Burrell, for she asks her to attribute them to "an old friend," instead of "a sister," so that they may seem unbiased (82 C). Her letters continue to take this attitude, from which it appears that Mrs. Burrell, wishing to get as much as possible out of her, was allowing her to think that the forthcoming book would be a life of Minna as well as Wagner, a vindication of the wife as much as a glorification of the husband. So Natalie wrote, at great pains and in her sprawling hand, quantities of *Aufzeichnungen,* trying, with pitiable effect, to assume an elegant, literary style. Unfortunately, her writings were mostly wasted effort and must have been as useless to Mrs. Burrell as they are for present purposes. She would no sooner get well started than she would bog down in recriminations against the hated Cosima or Mathilde Wesendonck. What she wrote about these two is not testimony. She was not present at the Asyl during the unpleasantness over Mathilde; if she ever met Cosima it was either when Cosima was the young wife of von Bülow, still cordially regarded by Minna, or in later years, when she was the settled wife of Wagner and on terms of kindly but unapproachable courtesy with Natalie. Natalie's opinion of these two was therefore her memory of hysterical tirades by Minna, become after many years a habit of poisonous epithets. The letters of Natalie herself in her old age show the suspicion and cunning of persecution mania.

4 *(Natalie Bilz-Planer, in Leisnig, October 25, 1891, to Mrs. Burrell)*

"HIGHLY ESTEEMED MADAME:

"With my hearty thanks for the 250 marks sent to me, I herewith dispatch the desired reminiscences along with 3 letters which you may appreciate. O, I have still more of these costly pearls to adorn your great immortal work on Richard and Minna. They are in my little holy sanctuary for you and it would be a great pity if they should be lost for posterity. So I beg you, highly esteemed Madame, to let me know your address after your departure from Paris. I don't know whether I am mistaken in guessing that a little trap has been set for me by the clever Elisabeth Kietz, or whatever her married name may be; to escape this I tricked them out of asking me questions and gave them no satisfaction.

"Though I am shriveled and old, when it is necessary I can be as mum as a wax taper. Hoping that the notes and the beautiful letters will be appreciated, thanking you again and with deep respects to all of you, I remain yours faithfully

NATALIE BILZ

"Pardon me for not copying the reminiscences, but my eyes won't allow it."

Aside from Mrs. Burrell and her family, on whom she invariably fawns, it is hard to find anyone of her past or present whom Natalie looks upon with definite favor. Minna has never a reproachful word from her; and Wagner himself, except for his occasional ill treatment of Minna, is criticized only as the dupe of designing females. (This supports Wagner's record as always good-natured and tolerant toward the inmate of his household whom he is unable to respect.) August Röckel was Wagner's "evil spirit," his "deceitful corrupter, who, under jesuitical pretext of friendship, was Richard's greatest enemy." Gustav Kietz's daughter has "invented the unfounded lie" that Natalie has dickered with a dealer over Minna's portrait. The dealers in autograph letters, with whom, in spite of her indignant protests to the contrary, she seems to have done some trading, are all swindlers. She has no good word for her fellow inmates in the institution at Leisnig, and the superintendent is doing his best to rob and starve her. Natalie's venom on the subject of Cosima may well have been due to her bitter necessity of accepting charity from the second wife of Wagner after Wagner's death.[1]

It is easy to understand her bitterness, for Natalie was unloved and unwanted through her life. Wagner was an exception in that he always had a kind word for her, the ugly duckling who was never transformed, who was always more or less of a burden to her mother and stepfather. She was useful around the house but an aggravation to Minna. She was never quick enough to fend for herself. Primed (at some expense) to become a governess, she was too slow-witted to qualify at teaching anything. Minna was cruelly frank about the fact that she was too unattractive to capture a husband. Speaking of a candidate for whom she was "too old" (March 6, 1862), she adds: "don't make such ugly faces, otherwise you won't even get that poor wretch" (361 H); and on April 18, 1862: "You would not be amiable enough to hold a man permanently, that goes with the sort who has no brains but is naturally attractive" (361 I). These blunt allusions to Natalie's ungainliness and failure with men confirm Natalie's pathetic letter to Wagner's sister Cäcilie Avenarius after Minna's death:

"In what rough words, and with what wounding inconsiderateness the fact has been flung in my face a thousand times that God had not been kind to me in the matter of looks! I cannot tell you what bitter pain such reproaches often caused me. Believe me, such hard, cold lovelessness, such pitilessness can turn us ostensibly into something quite different from what we really are. One becomes, without wishing it, reserved and self-contained; servile fear takes the place of love in all that one does and says; in one's every attitude one becomes awkward, clumsy, stupid, a monstrosity to oneself and others." [2] In face of this treatment, and possibly aware of Minna's deception as to her origin, Natalie is surely to be praised for taking up Minna's cudgels as stoutly as she did in her old age.

A letter of November 24, 1892 (89), is a sample of Natalie's thorny memories.

[1] See 8.
[2] Friedrich Herzfeld, *Minna Planer und ihre Ehe mit Richard Wagner.*

She brings up (and not for the only time) the Richard-Minna-Mathilde triangle, and mentions certain "anonymous letters" to Minna which Natalie (of course with no justification) would like to attribute to Mathilde Wesendonck.

Natalie writes: "As for the base anonymous letters where the poor good Richard is so infamously besmirched in regard to Minna and doubtless outrageously slandered, and where his actions and way of living are immensely exaggerated, nobody but poor Minna and I ever saw those horrible letters, because Minna, after reading them, immediately burned them to ashes in the stove."

Although Minna refused to believe these letters, or let their contents be known, Natalie is here ready to divulge that their purpose was to induce Minna to divorce her husband, and "so publicly expose herself as a vulgar woman unworthy of him, and clear the field for her rivals. . . . And Minna, in her unspeakable sorrow and anguish of heart, considered Frau Wesendonck, that cold, slippery serpent, as the diabolical instigator of all this until she bitterly, with streaming eyes, accused her before God. And if all those nasty incriminations and reports about Richard could have been true," she continues, shifting her ground, "it was certainly the sole fault of that disloyal, coquettish, heartless creature Mathilde, who pulled Richard down from the path of honor and duty and manly self-esteem, and exposed him like a rudderless vessel to the winds and waves of seduction." After much more to this effect, she writes: "Indeed, most honored lady, that celebrated, lamblike, sweet little friend, the charming Mathilde, was careful not to tell you of all those diabolical deeds so efficiently and slyly inflicted upon Minna, in her efforts not to tear from her own head the crown of her matchlessness before your eyes." By this remark Natalie shows that she is aware of addressing a devoted friend of Mathilde, whom Mrs. Burrell then held in high esteem and increasing affection. Mrs. Burrell has noted on the envelope: "Only about anonymous letters to Minna, maligning Richard; trying to get Minna to divorce him. That Richard was in Dresden without meeting or visiting Minna, trying to get Louisa and Pusinelli to persuade her to consent to a divorce."

Mrs. Burrell is obviously none too ready to accept Natalie's outpourings without question. The reader will do well to follow her example.

⇘ III ⇙

WAGNER'S BOYHOOD

There is no need to reopen here the controversy over Wagner's paternity, except to submit the few indications (and they are no more than that) that Ludwig Geyer, the actor-poet who married Wagner's mother in the early stages of her widowhood, and less than a year after the composer's birth, was indeed his father. That the manuscript for the privately printed *My Life* (475) does *not* begin with the words "I am the son of Ludwig Geyer" (as Nietzsche once claimed, thereby causing much trouble), is now well known.

Geyer appears in the Collection in a few small items. One is a letter to Wagner's mother. It is dated January 14, 1814, when Frau Wagner was a widow of two months (15). It was published, in the original German only, in Mrs. Burrell's book (1), together with three others (of December 22, 1813, January 28 and February 11, 1814) which Mrs. Burrell had been allowed by Wagner's sister Cäcilie to see and copy.[1] Geyer speaks with affection of the various children, especially Albert, who has just recovered from a sickness. "To those faithful souls Jettchen and Luischen kindly express my wish: to be as high in their esteem as they are in mine. The Cossack's wildness can be nothing else than divine; for the first window he smashes he shall have a silver medal. God protect you! Greetings and kisses to all the friends and to my Albert from your ever faithful friend—Geyer."

"The Cossack" must refer to Richard Wagner, then eight months old. Mrs. Burrell ventures that "Cossack" must have been a current expression for anything unruly. The Cossacks, who had come in from Russia to combat Napoleon's troops and so protect the Saxons, were then regarded with terror by friend as well as foe. Geyer had written in his letter just before Christmas: "Light a beautiful tree for the Cossack—I should like to rough it up with that lad on the sofa." This amused perception of individual prowess in a baby who could not yet walk has surely the familiar ring of the fatuous parent!

[1] The rather elaborate phraseology in these letters, and the formal use of *Sie* has been remarked upon as surprising on the part of a suitor who, even though he were not the father of the infant Richard, would become, within four months, the progenitor of Cäcilie. Ernest Newman accounts for the *Sie* as a customary politeness of the period (see his *Life of Richard Wagner*, Vol. 1, p. 10).

21 (*MS Statement by H. Löscher, sexton, with stamp of the Kirche zum Heiligen Kreuz, Dresden, July 13, 1891*)

"It is here testified that Richard Geyer was confirmed in this church on Easter, 1827, according to the registry."

That Wagner was confirmed under the name of "Richard Geyer" is not conclusive evidence. As a matter of convenience, the name Geyer had been adopted by the family, the children included. Thus Wagner was entered in the books of the Kreuzschule in Leipzig, December, 1822, as "Wilhelm Richard Geyer, son of the Dresden Court player."

Natalie Bilz-Planer, making "Notations" for Mrs. Burrell (December 11, 1890–February 16, 1891), describes childhood experiences of Richard Wagner as Natalie might have heard them from Wagner himself, or from members of his family (19 A). On the first page she makes the statement that Ludwig Geyer married Wagner's mother "out of friendship for Richard's late father, to protect from want the helpless widow who was left with several children." Richard's "stepfather had a great antipathy for little Richard, who in his earliest years was a weak, sick child." This antipathy, she adds, "only later changed to deep affection." These remarks show at once how Natalie had a way of getting things wrong. Geyer's intimacy with the widow not only overstepped posthumous loyalty to his friend—his usual pennilessness could have offered her little support. Far from feeling any antipathy for the baby Richard, Geyer singled him out as a favorite.[2] Natalie's imagination is plainly directed against gossip about Wagner's paternity.

The first anecdote concerns a performance of Schiller's *William Tell* at the Court Theater in Dresden, in which Ludwig Geyer took the title part. When the child who was to portray Tell's youngest son fell sick, little Richard, aged four, was put in as substitute, while his sister Clärchen, already an experienced child actress, was to take the part of the older son of Tell. Richard was to be on the stage at the moment when Tell was parted from his wife, and was to go to her while delivering his single line, "And I'll stay with Mother."

The tale is told by Mrs. Burrell in her book.[3] Here is Natalie's account (19 A), from which hers is taken:

"When the great day of the performance arrived, Father Geyer, with both his stepchildren, betook himself to the theater and delivered the children to the woman in the dressing room, where they had a distressingly difficult time with Richard, since the shy boy wouldn't allow himself to be dressed and made up, and kept wiping his face with his hands, smearing the paint and tears together over his face; so in the end Father Geyer had to be called in to help; he advised them to dress and make Clärchen up first, so that the boy would see that his

[2] See 15.   [3] P. 42.

head wouldn't come off, besides which Clärchen talked him into being dressed and having nice red cheeks painted on himself too, so that he would look quite pretty, and if he kept still he would get many, many cream puffs (the pastry he liked most). And so, owing to these promises of treasures, the big work of dressing and making up ended successfully.

"In the course of the performance the scene, so much dreaded by Father Geyer, came when Tell in his home takes leave of his wife before starting off with the elder boy. During the whole scene so far little Richard had timidly nestled close to his sister and clung to her skirt so that she had to loosen his hands in order to make her exit with her father; but the child, uneasy at what was happening, broke into the cry of terror: 'Cläre, you're going? I'll go too,' and made hastily for the middle exit instead of rushing to his mother with the words, 'and I'll stay with Mother,' according to Schiller's drama. This unexpected, stormy, and effective exit, so contrary to Schiller's intention, was loudly applauded by the audience. So little Richard celebrated his first triumph on the Dresden Court stage, which induced Father Geyer, who had nearly fallen over the little chap, to say, half amused and half annoyed, 'Well, I must say, the boy has talent for improvising; either something quite important may become of him, or nothing at all.' "

The next anecdote takes place a few years later, and refers to Richard's friendship with his stepsister, Cäcilie Geyer:

"It happened on a bright summer afternoon that the mother, living in Lescheritz near Dresden during the summer months, had gone to town but was to return in the evening. Then the two children made up their minds to meet mother. Cäcilie, a small, pretty, rather vain girl, pulled off her shoes and stockings to show off her small dainty feet, and proudly started forth with brother Richard. But alas! Her happiness was of short duration. For, not toughened like the village children, she soon complained bitterly, crying that her feet hurt her so much and that she couldn't go any further.

"Richard, himself still a little fellow, also began to cry helplessly and was deeply touched by her distress. So, after their weeping had run its full course, hunger and thirst came; it grew dark, too, and mother hadn't returned. In spite of their plight it was time to think of going home, whereupon Richard, with his good sympathetic heart, pulled off one of his own small shoes and put it on Cäcilie, so that she could walk more easily if they firmly held on to each other, while each wore one shoe only."

The second installment is concerned with small Richard's fondness for sweets and his pirating ways. On one occasion he found himself alone in the kitchen with some meat cakes ready to be cooked and, not liking their taste, threw them one by one under the table. At another time he skimmed the cream from

the tops of several jars; at still another, he befriended the proprietor of a con-
fectionary shop, begged some *réglisse* or marshmallow paste, and when he had
worked this stratagem to its end, managed to run up a charge for more against
his parents. The following tale about his imaginative terrors as a child, also
recounted by Mrs. Burrell,[4] has its evident source in Natalie:

"A characteristic feature of his early years was his great nervous terrors which
even as a man he never quite got rid of. As he narrates himself, the special
objects of his fears were beer bottles of stone then commonly used. These bottles
in their polished glaze made such a dreadfully uncanny and ghost-like impression on his highly excited imagination that they appeared to him like laughing
devils, mocking and taunting him and changing their shape every moment.
Nothing would have induced him to go upstairs by himself in the dark, because
from the stair windows on each floor he could see these beer jugs on shelves
which had been put in front of the kitchen windows. It was bad enough in the
day-time when he need only quickly close his eyes and run past those windows
without seeing the terrifying things. How often was he scolded by the maid
when, as quite a big boy, coming from the *Kreuzschule*, he rang for her to come
down. But when she appeared, he pretended astonishment and innocence, as if
he had only been playing with the bell-pull."

Wagner has told in *My Life* how, as a schoolboy of fifteen, he wrote a tragedy
entitled *Leubald und Adelaïde*. "The manuscript of this drama," writes Wagner,
"has, unfortunately, been lost, but I can still see it in my mind's eye. The handwriting was most affected, and the backward-sloping tall characters with which
I had aimed at giving it an air of distinction had already been compared by one
of my teachers to Persian hieroglyphics." This all-absorbing literary plunge was
not looked upon with approval by Wagner's teachers, not even by his indulgent
Uncle Adolf. "In this composition," Wagner continues, "I had constructed a
drama in which I had drawn largely upon Shakespeare's *Hamlet, King Lear,*
and *Macbeth*, and Goethe's *Götz von Berlichingen*." And he describes from
memory years later his Leubald as a sort of Hamlet more thoroughgoing in
avenging the murder of his father. Not only the murderer but all his relatives
suffer under Leubald's sword, these returning to haunt him as ghosts. Only one
relative is missed—the murderer's daughter Adelaïde. Leubald falls in love with
a girl in distress who turns out to be none other than she. He goes mad, murders
her too, and dies with her, his head in her lap, Tristan-wise.

The manuscript which Wagner believed to have been lost was preserved by
Minna, left to Natalie, and so purchased by Mrs. Burrell in 1891 (23). It is
written in a painstakingly neat hand in double columns.[5]

---

[4] P. 43.

[5] Messrs. Hurn and Root, in *The Truth About Wagner,* have reproduced the reverse of
the title page (showing the cast), and a page of the text, having obtained photographs of

Mrs. Burrell's researches led her in Leipzig to Robert Sipp, with whom Wagner, at the age of sixteen, had studied violin. Sipp, born in Leipzig, July 5, 1806, became a violinist in the Gewandhaus orchestra, and taught Wagner that instrument for a short while at Leipzig in 1829. Wagner, looking back, considered that he had derived a "practical working knowledge" of the instrument, but supposed that he had "inflicted unutterable torture" on his mother and sisters by his practicing. When Mrs. Burrell visited Sipp in 1889, she found him a personable and "merry" old man. Questioned, he remarked about his pupil of sixty years before: "He caught on quickly, but was lazy and unwilling to practice. He was my very worst pupil." This last remark was made "with a peal of laughter, it was his standing joke." [6]

The next year, Mrs. Burrell corresponded with Sipp and his daughter, sending photographs of Wagner and a score of *Tannhäuser*; she evidently was after a written statement from him. Both father and daughter answer in grateful acknowledgment (24). But the writing of the old man of eighty-five is feeble. He can only say: "The favor I could do you by describing incidents from the life of my once small and later great pupil, Richard Wagner, was such a slight one that your gratitude almost puts me to shame." But no written information from Sipp appears in her biography.

The two letters of 1900 inform the daughter and heir of Mrs. Burrell of the death of Robert Sipp, who, seven years older than Wagner, had thus managed to outlive him by seventeen years.

---

these from the Burrell Collection. The authors state that the bottom of the first page was "torn off by an angry school teacher. . . ." This is another case of leaping to a false conclusion. The deed was done by an eccentric autograph collector to whom Natalie showed the manuscript. When Natalie refused to let him have the manuscript, he impudently tore off and pocketed Wagner's signature. Hugo Thärmann, for this was his name, was, incidentally, a teacher. Mrs. Burrell, learning of this from Natalie, made one of her tireless searches, and found Thärmann's widow, who told her he had died in a lunatic asylum. Mrs. Burrell describes the result of this fruitless quest in a note attached to the manuscript.

[6] Mrs. Burrell's biography.

❧ IV ❧

WAGNER'S FIRST LOVE

The letters hitherto published of Richard Wagner to his first wife begin in the year 1842, at the point where the young couple, having weathered tribulations in Paris bordering on starvation, had returned to Germany on the promise of the mounting of his new opera *Rienzi* in Dresden. The explanation, of course, is that all of the earlier letters and many later ones remained in Natalie's hands. Perhaps she feared that at Wahnfried, where Wagner's career was being carefully pieced together, letters favorable to Minna's case would be ignored, or that the frantic and abandoned outpourings of the suitor Richard might not survive the unsympathetic scrutiny of the second wife.

For an estimate of Minna and her relations with Wagner, the world has had to rely on what Cosima Wagner at Wahnfried was able to collect: mostly humdrum letters of the domesticated husband, sometimes chiding, sometimes mildly affectionate, usually chatting about everyday doings. But of the earlier Minna, Minna Planer the leading lady and heartbreaker of the theater, the object of Wagner's tempestuous pursuit, we have had nothing but the descriptions by Wagner himself, vivid and penetrating as they are, in his autobiography. Wagner's picture is not actually distorted; it is reasonably close to the truth, but it is necessarily prejudicial. For example, we have no more positive evidence of Minna's infidelities as Wagner's fiancée and young wife than the jealous suspicions at the time, and the statements later, of Wagner himself. The defendant has never a chance to raise her voice in her own behalf. No letters from Minna to Wagner in these years have survived. But there are 9 of a later period in the Burrell Collection. There are also in the Collection 18 letters written by Wagner to Minna as his fiancée and 110 written as her husband. To these are added the written testimony of Natalie (and here, for once, is bias in Minna's favor). So, Minna must still be viewed principally by reflected light; but the illumination is now considerably increased.

Until now it has been hard to understand Wagner's persistent attachment to Minna, why he made such strenuous and even frantic efforts to win her back long after their complete incompatibility had become obvious to everyone, including themselves, and after she, finding only an impossible disharmony with him, had broken away again and again. Her steadfast devotion to him through the lean years in Paris Wagner never forgot. But gratitude alone would not account for Wagner's continual returns to Minna, nor could his desire for a protecting and comforting domesticity account for his repeated attempts to build some sort of living arrangement on the ruins of their wedlock. It now appears that her attraction for Wagner was more deep-rooted than has been realized.

There were four times in his life that Wagner really lost his head over a woman. In the cases of Jessie Laussot and Mathilde Wesendonck, artistic sympathy drew them together and the circumstance of others involved soon tore them apart. With Cosima von Bülow there was a similar beginning, and a triumph over even worse involvements. Wagner's love for Minna Planer had no such involvements, but because it had no basis whatever of artistic sympathy, it could not last. Artistic sympathy can be the ingredient of permanence. It generates a controlled, outwardly renewing passion. Wagner's love for Minna was more violent. That it continued as long as it did was due to the prodigious strength of his infatuation, and to his retentive imagination, which indelibly preserved every experience, even when Minna's memories had turned to gall. His first great love was a tempest, the like of which was never again to occur in that storm center which was Wagner's heart.

Minna Wagner is probably thought of by most people as the middle-aged *Hausfrau* of a familiar photograph where she appears in heavy silks and uncompromising collar, features rather plain and quite unarresting—a portrait giving no lingering suggestion of the popular actress of her younger days, the object of high-flown poems, eager managers, and feature billings. The portrait in this Collection (81) made shortly before her marriage and showing her in what seems to be an elaborate theatrical coiffure, may hardly convey the word picture to be found in the pages of *My Life,* where Wagner could look back further than a love long since turned to ashes, and revive in his memory the once breathlessly cherished image. But the actual letters of courtship far outdo *My Life,* they show a Wagner so far gone in love that all other considerations, including the progress of his career, are for the moment set aside.

At the risk of trying the reader's patience, I shall review portions of the autobiography, with the double purpose of picturing the alluring young actress as Wagner saw her and directly comparing his account with the story the love letters tell. One would expect a disparity between the reminiscent Wagner of thirty years later, writing for posterity, and the immediate actor in the drama, writing for Minna alone. Not seeing his love letters, supposing them lost, he had nothing more than a notebook, kept at the time, to prompt his memory and fix his dates. The two accounts prove that he wrote his later story in complete good faith and confirm the astonishing accuracy of his memory. They agree in every essential.

Wagner's first glimpse of Minna Planer was one of those fateful moments which he was able to put down on paper in sharp detail many years later in *My Life*. It was on August 1, 1834. He had just arrived at the little town of Lauchstädt, a summer resort near Halle and Leipzig, to take his first job as conductor, joining the provincial Magdeburg troupe, which was then fulfilling an off-season tour. Seeking a lodging, he encountered in the hallway of his new quarters the leading lady of the theatrical contingent of the company.[1] "Looking very charming and fresh, the young actress's general manner and movements were full of a certain majesty and grave assurance which lent an agreeable and captivating air of dignity to her otherwise pleasant expression. Her scrupulously clean and tidy dress completed the startling effect of the unexpected encounter. After I had been introduced to her in the hall as the new conductor, and after she had done regarding with astonishment the stranger who seemed so young for such a title,[2] she recommended me kindly to the landlady of the house, and begged that I might be well looked after; whereupon she walked proudly and serenely across the street to her rehearsal."

Wagner continued to be attracted by the contrast between Minna's self-possession, her innate dignity, and the lax Bohemianism of her colleagues—the more so because she too was "broad-minded" in her own quiet way. She was gently tolerant of the attentions of the new young conductor, putting up barriers only when necessary. What seemed to the susceptible Wagner an innate and alluring sobriety, a refreshing refinement, standing out against the coarser ways of those about her, might more accurately be described as the indispensable armor of a much-pursued theatrical beauty, who indeed had learned her lesson. She had been compelled by her father's reverses to help support her family from childhood, and at fifteen she had been seduced. She had carefully covered her tracks; and while progressing from amateur theatricals into successful professional

---

[1] Minna's position has been referred to in English as the "juvenile lead." She was customarily called the *"erste Liebhaberin"* (Wagner uses the phrase in the autobiography), which made her the heroine and leading lady in youthful roles. A Bremen manager offered her, in May, 1834, the lead in comedy and the alternate second in drama (*Schauspiel*), an offer which she did not accept. Minna specifically states her position in a letter to her manager at Magdeburg (52 B) as *"erste tragische Liebhaberin,"* first tragic actress. Minna took many tragic parts; she protested in her letter that the leading parts in *Romeo and Juliet* and *Faust* were by right hers, and not for her rival, who was supposed to be the ingénue. We have no evidence that Minna ever attained either Juliet or Gretchen. The point is that she considered herself professionally entitled to those roles. Her last appearance on the stage (in Riga, April 18, 1839) was in the title part of Schiller's *Maria Stuart*.

[2] Wagner was then twenty-one; Minna was on the verge of twenty-five. The following account of their first meeting, given by Natalie to Mrs. Burrell (98), has the air of having been embroidered in the telling: "In the basement of the house was a small shop. Minna had gone down to buy cream and Richard was upstairs, looking for rooms to rent. He didn't like them and returned downstairs; there he saw Minna standing, and asked whether she lived in the house. In an instant he was upstairs again, rented the rooms, and soon love-poems fluttered past her window. But he was not able to make her acquaintance until they went to Magdeburg. 'Fair poems fluttered past her window'—on papers of all colors."

Mrs. Burrell has this to say: "Any amount of Idylls might be written about the meeting of the fiery young composer and the beautiful actress, their subsequent wanderings in lovely Thuringia and the summer evenings at romantic Rudolstadt. Readers conversant with German life, German literature, and German scenery can supply the idylls from their imagination" (2).

PORTRAIT OF MINNA PLANER, BY OTTERSTEDT, 1836 (81)

engagements in Dresden, she had concealed from everyone the extremely inconvenient fact that the little girl Natalie, whom she made known as her sister, was really her own child.[3] Minna was an artist by necessity. To her the stage was primarily a means for supporting her parents and sisters. Being before all else practical, she recognized that an aura of stage-door admiration increased an actress's following, and that to favor a manager's personal interest was a way to obtain and hold engagements. This was the usual currency of theatrical intercourse, and in allowing it, the watchful Minna was alert to preserve safe bounds against harmful scandal or the danger of a second disaster. Wagner was baffled and unhappy when his impulsiveness always encountered in her a cool, common-sense calculation. This was but one respect, one of many, in which the nature of each found the other diametrically opposed.

Minna seems to have been as highly esteemed for her abilities as an actress as she was admired for her physical charm. Wagner's remark in the autobiography that she had no real acting talent does not fit with a considerable evidence in her favor. Even allowed that she seldom rose above the provincial theaters, her trophies in the way of unconditional bids from various managers are impressive, as the Burrell Collection shows.[4] Wagner himself admits having been charmed by her acting of a fairy in love (*Fee Amorosa*) in a stage confection called *Lumpaci Vagabundus*.[5] The parts allotted to her (the Collection has some of her own working scripts) were sometimes in the high-flown language of their romantic day; mere good looks could never have sufficed when nothing less than a fine power in declamation was required. In such a part as Fenella in Auber's *The Dumb Girl of Portici,* which she played under Wagner's baton at a performance for their own benefit on their wedding eve, charm of face and figure were indispensable but not enough.[6] The part (sometimes taken by a ballerina) required not only skill in posture, but the ability to convey in pantomime various pathetic and decidedly complicated situations.

Among the papers saved by Minna were several poems addressed to her by anonymous admirers, such as the following, stronger in ardor than grammar:

[3] See 6.

[4] While she was at Magdeburg, from the beginning of 1834 to the spring of 1836, she had offers from various managers, inquiring her "pleasure as to which parts she would prefer to star in," and asking her to name her conditions and terms. These feelers came in the year 1834 from Brandenburg, Bremen, Lübeck, Leipzig; in 1835 from Schwerin, Brandenburg (again), Aachen, Bamberg. Besides the offers from Königsberg and from the Königstadt Theater in Berlin, which two she accepted, there came an offer from the Hoftheater in Berlin. Before her Magdeburg engagement she had appeared with some regularity at the Eumorphia Theater in Dresden from 1831 to 1833, and, as her treasured programs show, in this period she had appeared in Dessau, Altenburg, and the Karl XII Theater in Dresden.

[5] A comedy by Johann Nestroy, first performed in 1833, and long popular in Central Europe.

[6] This wordless part gave Minna, who of course was never a singer, her one opportunity to appear in opera.

32 D

"TO MINA P . . . . R

"Lend me, O Heaven, O truth, lend me inspiration, the colors of thy purer light that I might paint a picture of her form. Nay, I could paint no more than the outlines of the lovely one! Ah, this countenance in which reign, pure and lofty, the teeming abundance of happiness, the flowering color of health and the heavenly radiance which only innocence bestows, and the fair, yearning eyes, whose gaze, devout, innocent, frank, is the unwitting wounder of hearts; above, the dark brows' shadowy curve and on the noble forehead the brown, graceful hair, which when loosened gloriously flows around the shoulders, and lying in curls lends grandeur and allurement; friendly lips blooming as the dark bud of a rose, and the noble figure slender and light as the Graces, swift gliding as a Vestal priestess, yet hardly touching the ground! Dare I continue to paint the godlike charms of this maiden, and her smile which seems to hover on her lips? And then her whole form, woven from snowy lilies, and as if surrounded by the glow of roses? When Nature created you, O fair one, she broke the mold and never more may create so fair an image. Ah, I have known you long, you splendid creature, beautiful in youth, your lovely image flitting around in my dreams, when I knew nothing yet of love first stirring in my heart.

"But love awakened when I first saw her friendly image, often embraced in my dreams, but elusive to my grasp, dissolving into a shadow. What else is then Man's happiness: Seen from afar it glitters deceptively like gold, emanating radiance, as reflected by the arch of the sky in splendid colors, but seen closely, it becomes yielding, bodiless air. And my heart is filled with unsatisfied yearning, awakening the dreamer and robbing him of rest. This is celestial Love, not the heart's voluptuous beat, not the earthly flame of the swiftly rising blood, nor a sensuously venomous creation of the fantasy. No, the Love which fills my heart is true and pure; its dream is placid, with a still, nostalgic yearning, mingled with my waking, and my serious thoughts."

The following damaging reflection is written in pencil, presumably by Minna: "Poor in words is this suffering compared to my love and longing. *His* loving was not so great when he wrote these words."

Minna, the much-sought and ever tranquil leading lady, had no reason to bother herself especially about the new conductor. Wagner tells how, saying good night to her from his floor below at Lauchstädt, he reached up to her window and held her hand, because to forestall gossip she had directed that her door be locked nightly from the outside. He mentions a three months' falling out with her, which might have meant that she was unwilling to give him privileges over others, to put up with his exactions and extravagances. His hot blood was a signal for caution, but his plans for his new opera, *Das Liebesverbot*, were persuasive, and their narrator intriguing. If the twenty-one-year-old conductor were to be even half believed, a future as composer lay in store for him in every opera house of Germany, not to mention Paris, whence all success stemmed. Later events have proved that when Wagner gave his whole attention to a woman (this was the first time he had really put his heart into it), he was hard to resist. Minna developed a liking for him and gave him guarded encouragement. When he was confined to his room by the erysipelas which was to bother him intermittently throughout his life, Minna stole down to nurse and comfort him. Almost cured, Wagner made some light apology for his rough skin, and Minna, to reassure him, kissed him on the mouth.[7] Wagner tells us of this in his autobiography, and he adds, "This was all done with a friendly serenity and composure that had something almost motherly about it, and it was free from all suggestion of frivolity or heartlessness."

A change in their relations is conveniently dated by the event. At a New Year's Eve party, so he tells us, where there was a good deal of free behavior, she maintained her usual becoming restraint, while to his delight she was tacitly accepted as his special province. Wagner had apparently learned by now that how far Minna was willing to go in private was less significant than what she was ready to admit in public. "From that time onward," writes Wagner, "I remained permanently on the best terms with Minna. I do not believe that she ever felt any sort of passion or genuine love for me, or indeed that she was capable of such a thing, and I can therefore only describe her feeling for me as one of heartfelt good will, and the sincerest desire for my success and prosperity, inspired as she was with the kindest sympathy, and genuine delight at, and admiration for, my talents. All this at last became part of her nature." And he adds later, "without ever betraying any desire or ardor herself, she never met my impetuous advances with coldness."

Wagner was charmed by her gentle acquiescence, by what seemed to him a combination of maidenly delicacy and unintended voluptuous invitation. An outside observer, further removed than Wagner from Minna's radiance, might find a more cynical definition for her "reserve." The realist might call it nothing more than the inarticulate muteness of a little-schooled, self-made artisan of the theater, lacking the understanding and the mental alertness of the true artist. Wagner in his heart of hearts saw this clearly and later admitted it; but he chose to be blind and fatuous. The composure which Wagner describes in Minna did not discourage him, it only inflamed him, as did everything else about her. When she held him at a distance, he only found her the more desirable. When it appeared that she was considering other suitors, and was coolly balancing one opportunity against another, his fits of jealousy only increased his determination to have her for himself.

Ernest Newman inclines to the view that during the first months at Magde-

[7] A letter to Apel, dated Dec. 13, 1834, and dwelling on his ailment, gives a probable date to this episode.

burg, Wagner was not yet really absorbed in Minna; and he supports this by pointing out that in Wagner's frequent letters at this time to his young friend Theodor Apel, Minna is not even mentioned. But it should be remembered that Apel was his confidant and companion in the interchange of fine speculations, poetic or philosophical, according to the way of serious romantic young artists of that period.[8] Would he have been willing to confess to Apel that he was on the way to losing his head about what he elsewhere called "the daughter of a decent bourgeois in pursuit of a respectable living," while she was holding him at arm's length? Wagner was even more sensitive than most people about appearing in the role of the neglected and spurned, a position all the more equivocal for the composer of *Das Liebesverbot,* who had just been protesting a fine disregard for the bourgeois respectabilities. Any such confession would have been taken by Apel as a mockery of the bold, "modern" liberalism of that opera, which Wagner has described as the "victory of frank sensuality over Puritanical hypocrisy." This had been a favorite topic between the two friends on their excursion to Teplitz the summer before—a topic, by the way, which would have been quite beyond Minna. To her the conventions of moral censure would have been something to submit to when convenient, circumvent when necessary—certainly not something to defy on principle. Summer flirtations such as the two youths had pursued together in Bohemia were another matter, for these were pointedly considered as ephemeral, never encroaching upon their high-flown protestations, their solemn attitudes. Wagner betrays shamefacedness when he writes repeatedly to Apel of his "ennui" with the drab German Philistinism of the Magdeburg troupe. By throwing his lot with Minna, to whom lofty sentiments meant nothing more than the spoken lines which were her bread and butter, he was simply subsiding into this Philistinism. When Apel visited Magdeburg in February, 1835, for the performance of his drama *Columbus,* Wagner could no longer have concealed how matters stood. His letters from that point take the line, sincere but unconvincing, that his love for Minna was really beyond Apel's comprehension, and after all not debasing but ennobling.

Wagner repeatedly dwells upon the mood of wild recklessness which controlled his actions in this period of his life. He underscores this trait in his *Autobiographical Sketch* of 1843, again in his *Communication to My Friends* (1852), and again, years later, in *My Life.* The word he most uses to describe this mood in all three places is *Leichtsinnigkeit,* which has been variously translated as "frivolity" and "levity." But neither word is adequate. Even his worst enemies have never accused the ever intense Wagner of being a water fly, a skimmer of surfaces. The German word is often used in the sense of "irresponsibility" or "thoughtlessness," and Wagner was literally "thoughtless." He had for once abandoned thinking for feeling. As he tells us in his *Communication to My Friends,* he had for the time being forgotten his "reverent seriousness" (*heiligen Ernst*) in his thirst for "direct impressions, gained from life itself—a

---

[8] Cf. Schumann's letters to Emil Flechsig; Chopin's to Titus Woyciechowski.

bold eagerness for the turmoil of the senses, a defiant exuberance of gaiety." This mood had its artistic reflection in an actually warm espousal of the tonal opportunism of Meyerbeer, Spontini, and Auber, and a flirtation, soon rejected, with the *opéra comique* style. The defiance of convention in certain contemporary writers such as Heine, Heinse (*Ardinghello*), and Wagner's insurrectionary friend Laube (*Das junge Europa*) was the basis of much talk between Wagner and Apel about "modern" license in love—a philosophic bond between them. This mood led Wagner to welcome the free and easy Bohemianism of professional theatrical life, and its most alluring embodiment—Minna herself. His passion for Minna, pursued headlong, against the advice of his mother, his friends, and his own clear-sighted vision of disaster ahead, was, he would have us believe, the ultimate extravagance of this phase. He summed up his marriage with her as "modern retribution for modern *Leichtsinnigkeit*." [9]

Wagner had as yet no thought for ultimate consequences. Not progressing too well in his courtship at first, he soon began to penetrate by devious ways the armor of the resistant Minna. He talked, no doubt, of a rosy future, and although she could not have understood much of his lingo, there was something impressive about the respect he was winning in his new post as full conductor at Magdeburg. "She was surprised," wrote Wagner, "at the rapidity of my success." This, at least, was something tangible, something to be counted on the fingers. He dissipated wildly, especially when she held him off, and alarmed Minna for his health. He liked to think, and made her think, that nothing could restore him to sanity but her gentle, consoling hand. He has told how on a certain evening in her rooms he drank a good deal too much and "sank into a heavy slumber." Unable to move him, she "unhesitatingly resigned her bed" to his use. "There I slept until wakened by the wonderful grey of dawn. On recognizing where I was, I at once realized and grew ever more convinced of the fact that this morning's sunrise marked the starting point of an infinitely momentous period of my life. The spectre of care had at last entered into my existence. Without any light-hearted jests, without gaiety or joking of any description, we breakfasted quietly and decorously together, and at an hour when, in view of the compromising circumstances of the previous evening, we could set out without attracting undue notice, I went with Minna for a long walk beyond the city gates. So we parted, and from that day onward, as an openly acknowledged pair of lovers, we gave ourselves over, freely and without embarrassment, to our tender interests in each other."

But possession did not bring peace to Wagner, and principally because it was not really full spiritual possession. Minna would not surrender the interests of her career, kept always to herself a privilege of independence, a privacy about her plans and her male friendships. He had the overpowering feeling that he could not possibly live without Minna, and his uncertainty of being able to hold her was torture to him. A letter from Wagner to his brother Albert, dated

[9] "Communication to My Friends," *Prose Works*, Vol. I, p. 297.

February 4, 1835,[10] shows that the two had reached a definite understanding as an engaged couple, though without any agreement about so decisive a step as marriage.

The operatic season of 1835 came to an end. Bethmann, the director of the Magdeburg company, was in a state of bankruptcy, paying his troupe in promises, or not at all. The practical Minna managed to salvage something from this not unusual crisis of an uncertain profession. Wagner, of course, came out of it with an alarming crop of debts. His attempt to recover with a benefit concert at which Mme. Schroeder-Devrient kindly sang ended in a fiasco. And now the insistence of the buzzing crowd of creditors forced him to make a hasty departure in May for Leipzig, where he hoped to extract something from what he describes as his "affluent acquaintances" in his native town. But he had no doubt already tapped every source for what it would yield; even Apel had a bottom to his purse, and Wagner's family had learned by this time to be wary of the youngest brother, from whom the only sure answer to a loan was an eventual return for more. Two at Leipzig were consistently sympathetic: his mother (who nevertheless had little money to give him) and his unfailingly devoted sister Rosalie. Into her house the young bankrupt now walked, leading "an intelligent brown poodle," which he pointed out as "the only visible property" which the first year of his professional labors had brought him.

Since Minna had to stay behind for the completion of the dramatic season in Magdeburg, this needed journey brought about their first real separation and Wagner's first love letters.

[10] A synopsis of this letter is printed in Kapp and Kastner, *Gesammelte Briefe*; the actual text is not published in any collection.

❧ V ❧

WAGNER TO MINNA PLANER

(May, 1835)

49 (*Leipzig, May 6, 1835, to Fräulein Minna Planer, at the Theater,
3 Engelstrasse, Magdeburg*)

"MY DEAR, DEAR, MY OWN UNIQUE GIRL!

"Already more than twenty-four hours apart from you, after I have so often treasured every minute! What will come of this? I am lost in my misery and tears, and I can find joy in nothing, nothing whatever! You have become too dear to me, I am sure of that, you dear and lovely child! How can I become accustomed so soon to our separation? How can I bear your absence? You have become part of me, and without you I feel in all my limbs as if a part of me were missing. Alas, if you felt only half my longing, then you too would be filled with love and memories. I still wept after you had gone. Tell me, were you angry about the letter I sent you so late? Oh, I would almost have come to you myself, but then I knew that I would have stayed with you and would have given up my journey and everything. Alas, who could describe my state of loneliness? Yes, my Minna, I love you, and am a little vain about it; look, I imagine I have instilled life and soul into you which you didn't have before, so far as I knew. Besides, I often thought you didn't love me after all, but now I believe you do. Nay, when I gave you the last kiss, all your love overwhelmed me twice and a thousandfold. O my Life, don't forget, don't betray me ever, faithfully cling to me, remain my Minna, and if you ever felt love, so give it all to me and never let me share it with anyone else. Never forget that my whole heart is yours. Do you hear? Do you hear? Don't ever betray me! You can never know with what painful feelings I am thinking of you both.[1] It cuts me to the quick that I must know you in these miserable, depraved conditions. I'll take pains to do something for the Haas,[2] though you rejected my offer to do something for you. You must get away from there, that is clear. I now hate Leipzig and Magdeburg and everything, it's only you I love. Oh, join me soon

---

[1] *Euch*: Minna's mother was staying with her.
[2] Mme. Haas (see also letter following) was an older member of the troupe (see *My Life*, pp. 116–117). Julius Kapp describes her as a quasi-chaperon to the pair, disqualified by her own interest in Wagner (*The Women in Wagner's Life*).

so that I can see you and be convinced you love me still. Write by return mail if you still love me and still think of me. Write, write, and strengthen me, my angel. More soon! More soon! Adieu! Adieu! Think of me, think of your

RICHARD

"Reichels Garten (Rear)
Care of Rosalie Wagner"

*50 (Leipzig, May 10, 1835, to Fräulein Minna Planer,
at the Theater of Magdeburg, 3 Engelstrasse)*

"Tell me, my Angel, is this kind of you? Like a man thirsting for a drink I have been waiting for a few lines from you! Come, come, this is not right, you might have sent me a word or two to let me know that you still love me— which I often doubt. I am only half alive here or not at all. I am always restless, excited, and so full of a boundless impatience that I truly wonder at being able to sit calmly and write to you. It will take me a long time to feel at home here, and, strange to say, Magdeburg with you seems more desirable, with all its trouble, confusion and miserable conditions, than the uneventful leisure here, where I am without interest and love. Ah, come to me soon—you could never imagine how I long for you! I am always moved when I walk through the Grimma'sche Gasse. There is a shop with your name over it; and yesterday while walking through the Rosenthal I met a man whom I had known but never noticed. But when I saw him, it came to me that his name was Planer, and so I shook hands with him and walked with him for almost half an hour. I often imagine seeing you, but it's never you. So, do write to me! Look, I love you so much and you don't love me at all! Not at all! O God, when I stop to think that you may have already forgotten me, that I may have reason to be jealous, then I could just break everything [3]—even myself. Look, Minna, if you never felt for me before and if you really do so now, cling to this feeling, you may call it love or what you will, cling to it and don't forget that it is bound to ennoble you more than all vanities of convention; cling to it and don't give it up. If your love—God forbid—should cool toward me, never let its warmth die in your heart, and if you ever love again, love with your whole heart. Ah, what have I said? I have been speaking of cooling of love, of another love, but how could I stand it? You see, these thoughts come when you don't write to me, when I don't hear anything from you and have to be brooding and suspecting all the time. Write, write!

"How are things going with you, with your family? I'm afraid it is going badly with them. What do you intend to do—stick to your last plan? I haven't yet found any suitable occasion to see Ringelhardt about the Haas; maybe I'll do it today. If so, I'll write her at once. By the way, you need not show her our letters, not on account of the letters, but because of the complete distrust I have

---

[3] Specifically, *Löffel*: spoons.

for her. Through Apel I have learned here some of her utterances that make me ask you to withdraw your confidence from her as well. I'm sorry for her.

"Goodbye, my beloved girl, give my regards to anybody you deem worthy of them, say also to the widow Dähnert that I was thinking of her, not because I like her, but because she was fond of me. I kiss you a thousand times, but don't forward those kisses to anybody else, do you understand? To nobody else, no, no! But save them until you see me again. Oh, how much I have to atone for, for having been overexacting so often; I'm quite alone, quite alone! Goodbye, goodbye. I press you to my heart in desperation [als ob ich vergehen sollte].

"Adieu! Adieu! Your

RICHARD"

When Minna had completed her engagement, she went to Dresden to join her family and, according to a promise extracted by her lover in their moment of parting, joined him at Leipzig en route. Wagner introduced Minna to members of his family but without specific revelation of their status. Rosalie divined an "affair" and fondly teased her brother about "being in love." Minna went on to Dresden as planned, after staying three days at Leipzig. Wagner wrote later to Apel, on June 8, that she had made this visit, "in the vilest weather," purely to please him. "It is remarkable what an influence I have won over the girl; you should see her letters;—they burn with flame, and we both know that that is not her way." Since not one of her letters from this period has survived, we can only guess that Wagner's boasting led him into exaggeration; that the fire in his letters brought from her some passages of responsive warmth, and that he made the most of them.

Wagner wrote to her in Dresden the day after her departure (51):

"Unfortunately I must write in haste, my dear Angel, and not as I should like. You were with me in my dreams, at least so it seemed to me all day long yesterday. After having seen you off, I went home, and, full of sorrow, yearning, grief, and bad humor, I went back and lay on the bed in a melancholy mood. There I vividly dreamed of you once again, but I saw you also leaving me, walking farther and farther away. I was overcome with sadness, and with an anxious sigh I woke up! You may imagine my state at finding myself deserted and alone again. Ah, it is terrible! Goodbye, my beloved one. I'll write you soon more calmly and fully! Give my best regards to your family, whom I look forward to meeting. God protect you. Adieu, Adieu, my Minna.

"Your

RICHARD WAGNER"

Later, he intercepted her on the road as she was returning to Magdeburg, where Bethmann's enterprise, under the providential smile of royal patronage, was about to stagger to its feet once more for another season. Wagner on a sudden impulse carried off Minna and "one of her sisters" whom she had taken with her, for a holiday excursion into the Saxon Alps—-this on money borrowed for the purpose. To complete the party there trotted along "Rüpel" (Bounder), the brown poodle. Wagner describes this idyllic holiday as one of the happiest moments in his life. Perhaps he remembered it as the one point in all his court-ship when he succeeded in getting Minna really to himself, away from the theater affairs, which always seemed to come first, and from the attentions of other men (even a passing fit of jealousy was soon dismissed). This harmony could never be recaptured, once corrosive disputation came between them again. Now, with blue skies above them and a still fresh fervor in their hearts, they reached for a moment the blessed and rare state where there was nothing to argue about.

But their return to Magdeburg was also a return to problems. Minna's mother had joined her, and this shrewd lady failed to see in the young conductor a desirable addition to her daughter's career. Whether or not the question of marriage was openly discussed, it was evidently on the minds of all three. Wagner confesses in the autobiography that at this point the thought filled him "with dismay." This was the reasoning, the clear-sighted Wagner we know. But we know equally well the Wagner who desired mightily and went to every length to attain his desire. Minna was dismayed in her own way, and, as Wagner tells us, definitely reluctant. She was well aware that she was by far the better provider of the two, and that the money-making power of his music, such as a symphony which he had talked about but never finished, and *Das Liebes-verbot*, which he was just then completing, was nothing to count on. On the contrary, Wagner's pocketbook never caught up with his extravagances. Minna was very likely already experiencing the unpleasant surprises at her door which were to plague her later: the creditors of Wagner who turned hopefully from his penniless self to his more thriving mistress.[4]

But another problem confronted Minna: a problem more serious, more urgent, and more vexatious, so far as she was concerned. A new rival had appeared, a Mme. Grabowsky, who was the wife of the stage manager of the company and so directly threatened Minna's sacred privileges in the matter of roles. Minna was not accustomed to standing aside for anybody's wife. She expected to be asked without reservations what roles she would prefer. In fact, there were in her desk standing offers of just this sort, such as one from the intendant of the Court Theater in Berlin (62).[5] The following draft,[6] in Wagner's hand, scribbled on the back of a discarded letter, would indicate that she turned to him to help her word an ultimatum to Bethmann:

[4] See 70 and 71.
[5] Another letter (64) from Cerf, the manager of the Königstadt Theater, can evidently afford to be more high-handed. He postpones the question of roles until her arrival.
[6] 52B.

"To my greatest regret I learned today that the role of Christine in *Die Königin von Schweden* [?] was cast for Mad. Grabowsky, although it used to be assigned to me, and that you also gave to her the roles of Juliet in *Romeo and Juliet* and of Gretchen in *Faust*. There can be no doubt that I as the first tragic actress of your theater am entitled to the aforesaid roles; certainly not Mad. Grabowsky, who, as you yourself have assured me, is to be used for the ingénue parts.

"I see in this contradictory distribution of the roles a most obvious injustice which my honor forbids me to tolerate. Therefore I remind you of my most just claims for those roles and will never consent to being deprived to the slightest extent of what is due me as first tragic actress. I hope that you will agree to my reasonable and just demands, especially since I have certainly never yet neglected my obligations." [7]

Let us examine for a moment the discarded letter on the back of which Wagner has jotted his draft.[8] The writing is in Minna's hand and bears her signature but no salutation. It shows that to discourage suitors, even when she was Wagner's mistress, was a continuing necessity, and that this must have been done with Wagner's knowledge:

"I received both your letters and your request for an answer. As I have assured you by word of mouth, I shall enjoy your feelings of friendship for me and now I can only repeat this in writing. But if the mysterious intimations in your letters, which I fail to understand, should have a different meaning, I would sincerely regret it, since my position and my circumstances do not allow me to enter into any other relationship.

M. PLANER

"Magdeburg the 24th of August
You are not a good pen"

The added line, in slightly blurred script, explains why the letter was laid aside.

One infers from subsequent events that if Minna wrote and sent her protest to Bethmann, she did not wait for an answer. This time she suddenly made her own decision in her own way, and acted on it forthwith, consulting neither the

[7] In the remaining space Natalie has undertaken to explain Wagner's draft: "This concerns the affairs of the Magdeburg Theater, where Richard helped Minna to write to Director Beethmann [*sic*]. An actor—Grabowsky and his wife had started an intrigue against Minna behind her back, because he wanted to insinuate his wife as the first dramatic actress and heroine instead of Minna. This woman, however, was not able to play Minna's roles."

[8] 52 A.

manager to whom she was bound nor the lover who considered her beholden to him. She simply told Wagner of her intention to leave, and, giving him no time for lengthy protestations, did so on the following morning. She may have forestalled argument for the simple reason that she had decided to rid herself of both Magdeburg and Wagner—forever. At least Wagner strongly suspected this, as his letters will show.

❧ VI ❧

WAGNER TO MINNA IN BERLIN

(November, 1835)

It could not have been much after dawn on November 4 when Minna took coach for Berlin, there to fulfill her engagement with Cerf, with Königsberg as a later objective.

Wagner, needless to say, was wild. A hard-smitten young man speaks in the nine letters which he wrote to her on the first nine days of their separation. The autobiography says that "she thus plunged me, whom she did not appear to consider in the matter, into the depths of despair. . . . She departed leaving me behind overcome with grief and doubt as to the meaning of her conduct. At last, in passionate agitation, I wrote urging her to come back and, in order to move her not to separate her destiny from mine, I came forth with a specific declaration with a view to a possible early marriage."[1]

The letters confirm this account. The date of the first is that of Minna's departure; it must have been written even before the morning mists had lifted:

53 *(Magdeburg, November 4, 1835)*

"In the morning, 8:30—

"Minna, my state of mind can't be described—you are gone and my heart is broken. I'm sitting here hardly able to think and crying and sobbing like a child. Great God, what shall I do? How and where may I find consolation and peace! When I saw you leaving, all my feelings and sensations painfully broke loose in me; the morning mist in which I saw you drive away trembled through my tears; Minna, Minna, all at once I felt the terrible certainty that the coach was bearing you away from me for good. My dearest girl in doing this you are doing a terrible wrong—I am bound to you by chains a hundred thousand strong, and now I feel as if you would throw them around my neck and would strangle me with them. Minna, Minna, how you have changed me! I'm sitting now in my quarters, thoughts are whirling around me; a ghastly void—nothing but tears,

---

[1] In the English version of *Mein Leben,* this is mistranslated, "I . . . hinted at the hope of early marriage." As the letter of Nov. 4 will show, there was no mere "hinting" involved. What Wagner wrote was, *"Ich . . . trat . . . mit förmlichen, auf eine bald zu ermöglichende Heirath abzielenden, Erklärungen hervor."*

pity, and misery. How are you now, yourself? A large beautiful city—oh, I can't continue! But all the same, I have to continue, my heart is too full; what shakes me so deeply and gnaws at the core of my soul is that you miss the importance of this crisis in our fate so completely—Minna, look, we are still living in such a tender stage of our love; a mere gnat crossing our love's whims is enough to disturb us. Even to face the thought of a twelve days' separation is enough to shake me to the depths of my soul, and—good God—to you a separation for a full half-year is some slight affair that you slip into without any emotion. You didn't even make it a matter of an understanding [*Verständigung*] between us. Well, I must tell you again what I so earnestly told you before: I left Magdeburg in May of this year with a deep love for you in my heart. I felt no longer free, I felt bound to you. The short separation clearly proved to me that I couldn't live without you. How could I come to possess you? By marriage. To attain this goal, it was necessary to change the whole course of my life, all that I had outlined for my reputation as a composer. In accordance with my situation, I had arranged my career as follows: I wished first to remain in Leipzig to finish my new opera, which I planned to perform there in the winter. Then, having succeeded, I would have gone to Berlin, Dresden, Munich, Prague, Frankfurt, etc., in order to have my opera performed in those cities. If it had been successful everywhere, I would have gone on to Paris the following summer and from there I might have hastened to go to Italy in the winter together with Apel.[2] This was the definite plan for my career. But such a plan would allow no place at all for marriage with you. On this restless path a single person might manage, but the two of us would need a more tranquil life. To attain this I had to abandon all my plans and take up a practical career, the only one which could lead to our goal. So I gave up everything and procured a new engagement in Magdeburg, for the double purpose of starting my changed path of life and remaining permanently near you. How happy I was, my Minna! Now at last I believed I could propose to you and make our union the single goal of our life together. We have a full half-year ahead to prepare it. Either I shall succeed in getting in this time a sufficiently secure position by *myself* or if luck is not so good the two of us *together* should have enough to marry on. Minna, I sacrifice many other beautiful things to this beautiful plan. I am young; with the desired good fortune my future as a composer may not lack

2 Compare this with the plan he had outlined to Apel a year earlier (Oct. 27, 1834): "Yes, my dearest Theodor, my plan is now fixed and irrevocable. My *Feen,* by being performed at three or four good theaters, is to give honorable advertisement in advance to my *Liebesverbot,* which I am now completing. I shall make a hit with this opera, and win fame and money. If I am fortunate enough to acquire both, I shall take them both, and you, too, to Italy without fail in the spring of 1836. In Italy I shall then compose an Italian opera, and according as that goes, others too. Then, brown and strong, we shall go on to France. In Paris I shall compose a French opera—and God knows where I shall be then! And *who* I shall be—certainly no longer a German Philistine! This is my career, and it must be yours, too!"

glory—to possess you I sacrifice a colorful, happy life which I could attain only in a different way. And you? Minna, all my faith is leaving me; a pitiful theater-intrigue, sure to blow over soon, is important enough to you to destroy our living together, brought about by many sacrifices on my part. And don't you feel any grief or pain as you are heading toward this long separation which will necessarily keep us apart for good? Minna, didn't I implore you—'Give me this half-year, don't leave me, and I swear to you to consider this as a sacrifice on your part which irrevocably shall bind and oblige me to you; make this slight sacrifice to your vanity and I will give you in return my whole life'—And you were silent and then coldly answered: 'I can't act otherwise, I must have my roles.' Do you have a human heart? Have you *any* feeling for sublime love and fidelity? Minna, Minna, does not this voice penetrate your heart? My God, my God, what else can I tell you, my heart is breaking! Once more I say: I sacrifice all the conditions of my life for you and can you not sacrifice two roles for me? I am beside myself—I have once more laid bare my soul to you; if you don't want to accept it, I have spoken for the last time to you with such ardor. From now on you shall get only quite calm letters from me. I am at the end of my rope.

"Your
RICHARD"

On the following day Wagner wrote to Theodor Apel: "What a state I am in! My God! My God! If I wanted to be modern, this would be the very moment to effect a separation. But there you are. My heart is broken, in real bourgeois fashion—broken." Indeed it was, and with his heart had gone his pride, his ambition, his career. But he saw with great clarity. When he called his proposed marriage a "sacrifice," he was speaking with more truth than persuasion, and he was hardly being tactful when he wrote in effect: "I am giving up more than you are, and I am accepting marriage only because I cannot live without you, and can hold you in no other way."

Minna could have answered—and probably did—that his offered "sacrifice" was a very unproven future, while hers would be a very definite and productive present. If his logic did not move her, there was something far more moving than logic in his letters. Perhaps there lay some extraordinary future in this dynamo who was her lover. One thing was certain: He loved her—literally—to distraction, and in a way she had never been loved before. She had certainly never encountered anything like this in the furtive and greedy letters, sometimes disguised in metaphor, which came to her so often by way of the stage door.

54 (Magdeburg, November 5, 1835)

"No, Minna, it can't be, I can't believe that you have gone from me not to come back again! Oh, that last day! If only on account of the agony of that day, you ought to know what you must do. Like my own shadow I have been wandering about. Nothing matters to me any longer, nothing interests me. My aspirations—the opera—my affairs—they no longer exist for me when you desert me; for you have been the focus of all my striving, all my actions; here I accepted the job only for the sake of possessing you. Dear child, another week like this day and I shall be consumed with grief and sorrow; even on the street I haven't been able to hold back my tears; alas, and your apartment, when I enter it, I am torn with pain. O Minna, you fill me with misery, and you don't even pity me! My heart is broken, everything I'm facing is colorless and void of joy. And the future—what am I to do here—what? If you don't come back to me, and if I find that you have bound yourself in Berlin, I would have to consider it as a breach of our love, and then not even God could keep me here any longer, and I have firmly made up my mind that I would commit an act of despair. Where then? It would make no difference—I would deliberately seek my own ruin, for you cannot possibly love me if you coolly disregard these tears and these entreaties. I'll throw myself into a quite new life with the *wish* to lose myself in it. O Minna, my dearest, with all the fervor which the most intense love can command, see me embracing your knees and imploring you in an agony of despair: Return to me, come back! Then a happy and beautiful future will smile on us, but if you do not come my ruin is certain. Oh, come, come! Don't listen to the voice of vanity this time, whether your mother's or that of someone else, listen to the voice of Love! And why must I beseech you to do this? Have I not the right to speak in quite a different tone? I could summon the right of Love, and say: 'Minna, return—I offer you herewith, formally and according to custom, my hand and the ring, and you belong to me.' And by God, so I will speak now, and to your mother as well—and now listen: Bethmann was upset and wanted to consider the contract as broken, but I succeeded in persuading him to forgive you your unjust trick. He explained to me that *Romeo and Juliet* had not been cast by him, but by Grabowsky, and even if he himself should assign Juliet to Mme. Grabowsky, since he doesn't consider you quite suitable for that role, you ought in any case to have Gretchen and Lucia; this is the truth. By the way, *Der Glöckner* is to be restored so that you may retain your full rights. These are his own words as he wished them conveyed to you. And, Minna, even if you fail to come to an agreement with the theater— well, do you belong more to the theater than to *me*? We'll become betrothed, you'll stay with me, and the money still at my disposal will help us through until a secure position unites us entirely—Minna, *I can offer you no more, if you disdain all this and still abandon me, you must then understand that I can no longer believe in your love. God be with you! Amen!* And this is the end—I can do no more. I have spoken now as a lover and as a man and have considered everything. Do the same and speak as a woman.

"Your betrothed
RICHARD WAGNER"

Wagner was now for the first time directing upon a woman the full and imperious force of his desire. No woman in the future would be able to withstand that force. Nor could Minna withstand it now. It would eventually override, in its complete recklessness, her cautious thoughts of sober expediency.

55 (Magdeburg, November 6, 1835)

"My dear sweet Betrothed,

"So I greet you! And not a morning shall pass without this greeting. My pain and grief for you which are turning me to a shadow have made it irrevocably clear to me—though I had never a doubt—I can't live without you any longer. From the unshakable firmness of this thought I am finding new hope. For since I made up my mind to devote myself to you *entirely,* it can only be that you will devote yourself to me as well. This firm thought and irrevocable resolution brings me a certain reassurance, since I know that I do *everything, everything* to bind you to me; and you can't do otherwise, you must accept it— see, this is my conviction. May God in Heaven prevent you from believing, and writing to me, that all this could also happen if you remained in Berlin. For the sake of our love, reject such an idea. My two letters of yesterday and the day before should be enough to prove to you that the step you have taken would confirm the complete untruth of your love. I have nothing more to add, and for heaven's sake don't write another word about it; I take a solemn oath that *never again* will you hear the slightest harsh or hateful word from me, nor get the slightest chiding, if you convince me of your true love by accepting my suggestions; solemnly as I swear this, I shall rely on you not to write the slightest word about your alleged need for remaining in Berlin. I will not allow it now or ever—you *are my betrothed* and I have *a claim on you.* We shall *marry as early as Easter.* What, then, have you to do in Berlin?

"You will have somehow to arrange your reconciliation here; you certainly mixed things up thoroughly, and without reason. Frau Bethmann told me you might have said at least a word about having to leave as early as Wednesday and she might have done something about it. But whatever you may say now, you worked out everything—even in regard to me—in such a secretive way—whatever you may say now—that it was already too late to dissuade you when I learned about it. You were certainly fixed in your wicked intention not to return; otherwise you would not have been able to act so dishonestly toward the theater management and me. Properly, I ought to be very cross with you. But since it was through this that you became my fiancée, all resentment has faded away, and you never will hear another reproach. Bethmann, who now as director is in the position of having been offended, can't possibly make the first move, as you demanded. I beg you to write him first a few words of apology (without losing face)—You *had* to go on Wednesday, as otherwise your whole leave would have been purposeless; you knew that it wouldn't have been granted to you as early as Wednesday and so you made up your mind to retaliate in this way for a greater wrong done to you. Besides, you wanted to assure a guarantee for your roles, etc. Don't miss doing this, dear child, and come back; surely all will be adjusted. And even if the worst comes to the worst, and it fails—ought we to sacrifice our impending betrothal and marriage, as well as the sweet interval of our engagement, to theater troubles? God forbid! I hold to what I wrote yesterday. O Minna, Minna, everything would be dead around me unless this hope were alive in my soul. I am full of ambition and have made up the following plan: If you return and can't come to an understanding with Bethmann, which is in no case likely, we'll leave Magdeburg together in February, so that my luck may come by Easter. Trust me! I'm not reckless and I well realize what responsibility I am taking on for your fate. I will truly fulfill it! God be with you, my dear betrothed [*Braut*], and attune your heart to our happiness. *Leb'wohl! Leb'wohl!*

"Your
RICHARD"

56 *(Magdeburg, November 7, 1835)*

"MY SWEET BETROTHED!

"I have now made up my mind to bear no grudge against you any longer. Otherwise would not many. parts of your letter of yesterday justify such a grudge? One thing especially: You write: 'I *can't* return to Magdeburg; I'll tell you why by word of mouth.' So it becomes clear that you had already definitely resolved not to come back, and that you have other reasons, too, which you haven't yet confided to me and which probably induced you to take as a pretext that stage intrigue which would soon have been straightened out anyway. What a wrong you have done me! In any case, you have deceived and cheated me! When, as late as Tuesday noon, I got to know by accident that you were in for a complete break with the director, you had already made up your mind without taking me, your betrothed, into your confidence; when, in deep distress, I urged you to confess to me how matters stood, what your intentions were and what your reasons, you answered me with nothing more than an embarrassed smile. Oh, it is terrible! So you have still other reasons? You will tell them to me *by word of mouth?* I don't understand how you will manage that, if you continue as you intended. So I demand your reasons, with all severity, *in writing*. These reasons, too, can be disposed of, if it serves to bring us soon together. You write that in your opinion by staying in Berlin you could hasten our union after all. Minna, do you wish to deceive yourself or are you really deceiving yourself? First of all: my last lines must have made clear to you that by your continued staying away, despite all that I offered you in those letters, you would reveal the entire insincerity of your love; in the second place, how would this hasten our union? I don't understand you. Berlin is not the place for us, for there is no chance for *me* there *now*. I can't imagine what position I could take there. I can't yet figure out at all what your goal may be in Berlin, and how that would lead to our marriage. Do tell me your opinion on this point. For I would like to know whether you still connect thoughts of your marriage with your Berlin engagement in any way. You write that you, too, would not be able to live without me, since you would have given me your life if I had wished it, but when your honor is concerned, etc. . . . My dear, how are these things in keeping with each other? You can't live without me and you flee from me risking uncertainy? You will sacrifice to me your life but not your theatrical career—which I would tread upon to keep it from separating us. I swear to you, Minna, I don't care for your stage life at all, and before sacrificing our love to it I would rather remove you instantly and entirely from the theater, marrying you on the spot, with 600 thaler salary, to which I can add 200 thaler for a few years, and will earn so much more by works of all kinds that I may reach the sum of 1,000 thaler. The rest God will give; I would rather support you myself by the sweat of my brow than part with you on account of that infamous theater mess. This I swear to you. You write that I would have your fate on my conscience if I left you, and I tell you: 'Well, lay your fate entirely in my hands, and I will faithfully take it on my own conscience.' You write: 'Only remain good and faithful to me, I don't care for the rest.' But if you didn't care more for everything else than for me, would you desert me for such trifles? Look, dear Love, I could show all that you have planned and done to be senseless and pointless, but you yourself don't listen to the voice of reason. Oh, if you would recognize the unceasing strength and endurance of my love, your ice would melt and you would be compelled to throw yourself into my arms. I am becoming now quite frank and free-spoken toward your mother and she seems to feel herself how impossible it would be for me to bear being separated from you. Open your heart, Minna, if you don't I am going to compel you; by God, I shall come to Berlin and tear you away by force, and if that should pain you, tell me that you don't love me any longer, and so give me the death blow! My dear, my dear, no one was ever loved as much as you! I will prove my love to you by renewing now with unceasing strength my offers for our union; if you reject this union there will be other ways to convince you of the power of my love. This is sworn by your

RICHARD"

57 (*Magdeburg, November 8, 1835*)

"I didn't receive any letter from you yesterday, my dear Love. I pray and implore you, write to me every day as long as you are away; even if the gallant visitors take much of your time, if you really love me you will find half or a quarter of an hour for your poor Richard, who now knows this only refreshment and comfort in his terrible sufferings. Oh, don't withdraw this comfort from me; for your letters are my only hope, they must bring me at last an answer to my most urgent entreaties and demands. It cannot and will not be otherwise; I would sooner become accustomed to the thought of an early death, than to that of a separation from you. But I will play this chord no more today. What is there left to say after my previous letters, to the girl whose heart has not been touched by these entreaties, by these presentations, these offers? This girl would no longer be touched in her heart—only by a sharp knife. So now I will say no more—I will talk only about myself.

"How do I live! Great God, could there be a more mournful, miserable life! I am alone, alone, in this town, deserted as in death; there is no one, nothing, to interest me; everything is cold and unsympathetic. It was on your account that I came here and took this position; you were my reason for being here; and only because of you did these houses, these streets have an interest for me. It was with you in mind that I performed my duties, for I knew you were in the box above when I was conducting at my desk, I knew that this pleased you, and it did my vanity good. Now—everything has vanished! With what monstrous indifference I go to my place on the stage from where I see your dear face no longer; with what contempt I look upon my routine, and—alas— with what feelings I enter your house. I never open the door at the right, where there would be no dear 'Come in' to answer my knock. I turn to the room at the left, which I never liked; I see your sister in *your* dressing gown, and facing me Otterstedt's picture. I drink alone from the glass which was ours together. Your mother pours my coffee into your cup, so that I may not forget you. O heavens! And such stupid, indifferent people like Schreiber, who, as if taunting me, is becoming bolder and bolder with Amalie. I have to look on while they are kissing each other—Minna, Minna, must you make me bear this misery for so long? It is shameful! You know my sensitiveness, you often saw my tears, kissed them away from my eyes. Do I no longer move you? I am working hard to conquer my pain; as early as seven in the morning I sit down to write to you; then I work continuously until one o'clock at my opera, which now is reviving in me in its full power, and is closely connected with the possession of you. Then I go to eat, then a quick walk to my sister's, from there back home; after that I work again until seven o'clock, then I drop in to see your family, which is mine, and home again, to my sad, lonely bed. But how long can this go on? I shall break down in the end. I get dull, become diffident, forget how to love and hate, and so there is nothing left of me. This is my lot, a shameful lot which certainly I was never meant for. Never let yourself imagine that time will soothe and lessen that pain. Time affects me in a quite different way—Instead of gradually diminishing my love for you as a habit and dulling it, your absence has only made it stronger and more durable, and the same would happen with my agony of separation. I can already feel how it begins to gnaw at my heart.

"But you won't let me perish. You shall return to me, we are going to possess each other once more, this time never to separate again! It cannot, it must not be otherwise! I go on living only in this hope. God greet you, my angel!

"Your
RICHARD"

58 (*Magdeburg, November 9, 1835*)

"Minna, Minna, what is the matter? This is my sixth letter, and I wait in vain for a second one from you. Do you find my letters and their contents not worthy of an answer? Or do you still hesitate to give me the *right* answer? By God, if I had not far greater worries about you, I'd be jealous, believing that Otterstedt [3] prevents you from writing. No, I am engaged to you now, and so I assume infidelity is impossible, and it is right, too, that I have complete trust in you. But why do you not write? I demand a letter from you every day. From the time that you have read this demand, I shall consider each day that brings me no letter from you as a breach of faith. O my Minna, will you not so sweeten my misery? Is our separation not punishment enough for what you consider my transgressions? Must you wound me still further?

"There are many things I can't discuss with you now—because I don't know what your own point of view is at the moment. This only shall be brought home to you with flaming words—'Never abandon me, never degrade me by disregarding all my misery, my imploring, my admonitions and offers. You would lower me in my own estimation by treating as a trifle my holiest feelings, my manliest resolutions, while still persisting in your own selfish plans.' No, this cannot be. These are my first and last words, and so they shall remain, my dear betrothed—you will hear none other than these—or none at all!

"I greet and kiss you,

"Your
RICHARD"

59 (*Magdeburg, November 10, 1835*)

"Now tell me, Minna, what am I to think of you? Are you out of your mind, that you leave me in this state without a letter for so long a time? Must not all my thoughts, quieted by my great trust in you, be reawakened with double force when I know that you are in Berlin, and in what surroundings?

"My dear, if it is mere negligence on your part, you are doubly to be blamed

[3] This may well have been the mysterious "Herr von O.," the "young nobleman" mentioned by Wagner, in *My Life* (p. 112), as on "very intimate terms" with Minna in the Lauchstädt days, but whose interest could come to nothing because his parents, who held the money, intended for him a match according to his station.

or—have you really already forgotten me? I'm furious! You women really are more insensitive than stone!

"I read in the paper that you are to appear as Esmeralda today—otherwise I would have known nothing about it. I can easily imagine how people are after you in Berlin—behave worthily, though I must often have doubts about it when you fail to write to me at all.

"I have now completely won your mother over; she is more friendly toward me and more confiding than I would ever have believed; I told her quite plainly that I can't live without you, and that I must soon have you as my own. She took it very well and said to me (and this surprised me) that you will surely return when it becomes feasible; so that we may be together through the winter, and you can hold out well enough until Easter. She spoke this way yesterday, even though she has been against it until now. You may imagine how great my faith and love must be when I have been able to touch this cold woman and bring her around—besides, she said: 'She will arrange her relations with Berlin in such a way that, returning after starring there, she may have renewed terms here, if she is justly dealt with; if worst comes to worst—she could accept Berlin's offer!' These are her own words—how much hope and comfort they have given me! But I wish you not to think of Berlin again. It is not a question of one or the other, there is only *one* choice: You must choose *me*.

"People here say you were entirely in the right; only last night I met some from the familiar orchestra box, and all were agreed that the mixup with the Grabowskys should stop and shall be stopped; and it may also happen that they will be ousted very soon, since it is the general wish to engage the Pellerts. It was common talk that the Grabowsky was terrible in tragic roles and that you are indispensable. This is the real situation.

"O Minna, my sweet betrothed, come, come—you will nowhere feel so happy, so much at home, so well and cozy as in the arms of your

RICHARD"

Learning, so he tells us in *My Life* (p. 137), that Minna "was not inclined to renew her engagement at the Berlin Theater," Wagner took advantage of the moment to place her case before the theater committee, arguing that he loved Minna, and since he must have her back, they must take her back. He delivered this piece of logic so passionately and imperiously that they were astonished into agreement. Of course if they had not been feeling her loss, they would have been less ready to overlook her default.

60 (*Magdeburg, November 11, 1835*)

"My dear, dear Minna, how grateful I am, how can I thank you for your letter! The decisive moment had come, and your letter had to bring the decision. I held it in my hand for a long while unopened; anxiety filled my heart; if its

message had been: 'Dearest, I can't act otherwise, I *must* stay here, and therefore, much as it pains me, I can't accept your offer,' those words would have
quite killed me, Minna. But God in Heaven has heard me, and blessed you with
tenderness, gentleness, love, and strength. In return, take me for ever and ever!
Now everything, everything is all right and all is won; it needed only a firm
resolution; you have made this decision; you did it out of love for me; now—
leave the rest to me. Radiant joy still scatters all my planning thoughts; however, I really expected this, you had to be persuaded, it couldn't have been otherwise. Oh, how I shall love you for this, you will hear no more from me of evil
distrust or scolding, I will be your lifelong knight and protector. Now listen—

"I have already taken up on my own account, and without request from
you, several points of my last letter which you are inquiring about now. Things
stand well here, even better than you suppose. Yesterday I saw Bethmann about
it; he complained about the heartless way you left him in the lurch; but I—you
may blame me for this or not—tried to straighten things out. I explained it as a
rash step on your part, which you, in exasperation, quickly decided upon and
quickly acted upon. I told him that, if the conflict over your roles could be
straightened out, you would gladly return, although you are satisfied where you
are, but I frankly intimated to him that you would return rather for my sake
than for his. Please write him about this, my dearest; you will lose nothing by
it, for strictly speaking there is no defense for your running away. If you have
been treated unjustly in the matter of your roles, then you must bring your
complaint and demand your rights; but only after being refused are you justified
in canceling your agreement. You might also mention that it is for my sake that
you wish to return. Anyway, come back, and everything will be adjusted! What
I told you yesterday about the attitude of the public toward the Grabowskys is
perfectly true.

"Now about your mother! My dear, you have no longer anything to fear
about her attitude. We both agree. You know what I wrote to you yesterday.
Well, last night *Mother, Amalie, Schreiber*, and I drank a toast to their betrothal
and ours. Your mother is quite changed toward me; yesterday evening I explained to all three of them that you must return, that I can't live without you
any longer; I am to become engaged to you, so that we may soon be married.
Schreiber fell in at once, we all touched glasses, and Mother was full of joy.
Now we began to joke; I greeted Schreiber as 'brother-in-law'; Amalie said
that it would all be charming—one day they would say, "Today we are going
to the *Kapellmeister's,*' and I retorted, 'The next day we will go to the *Kammersänger's!*' Your mother would be the housekeeper for all of us, we would all
stay together in *one* house—and so it went on through the evening. Oh, if you
had only been there! Joy and hope revived mightily in my heart; as for your
mother, she couldn't contain her laughing. Amalie said: 'Well, I'll write to
Minna so that she will come soon.' Oh, do it soon, have done with your starring,
and come back never to leave me again!

"I am much too drunk with joy to answer in detail your misgivings about our income and livelihood. You mean to say, I'll have to face privations, and reproach you for it? *Pfui!* I feel quite differently. I don't even think of privations. I have brains and talent, and by possessing you I shall get a serious incentive to use them. By Easter much will have been decided, and we must count on luck. More of this tomorrow!

"My dear angel, my good, sweet betrothed, be as happy as we are; everything will work out in our favor.

"Your

Richard"

"And now," says *My Life*, "I set off by express post in the dead of night and in dreadful winter weather to meet my returning sweetheart. I greeted her with tears of deepest joy, and led her back in triumph to her cosy Magdeburg home already become so dear to me." As the season progressed, so Wagner tells us, he and Minna were "drawn more and more closely together." He completed *Das Liebesverbot* by the new year of 1836, and Minna shared his hopes for its successful performance. It was put on in March; but the company was again falling apart for lack of funds, and *Das Liebesverbot* became its tragic final gasp. Minna went to Königsberg to sign a favorable contract there, hoping also to have Wagner taken as conductor. Wagner's last weeks in Magdeburg were by his own account a depressing close to a futile chapter in his career. He had reaped nothing but debts; his creditors were so insistent that he could not return to his rooms without finding a summons nailed to his door. He went to Leipzig, but Leipzig would have none of *Das Liebesverbot*, and he soon left to avoid his relatives' questions about his "excitability and depression," and his mother's entreaties that he should "on no account be drawn into a marriage while so young." So far as Minna was concerned, the improvident Wagner was a very unlikely prospect indeed, at this moment, and Wagner was the more touched when she cast her lot with his and tried to make her terms with Königsberg depend upon his acceptance there. "Now Minna became," he wrote, "with truly comforting assurance and fortitude, my one remaining support in all matters."

❧ VII ❧

WAGNER TO MINNA IN KÖNIGSBERG
(May–July, 1836)

Wagner went to Berlin, arriving May 18, the day after Minna had gone on from there to Königsberg. His principal aim was to approach Cerf, at the Königstadt Theater with *Das Liebesverbot*. Since Cerf's main interest was in putting on light, money-making pieces, the encouragement he gave Wagner was probably not backed by any real intention of undertaking this unpromising opera. He spoke of engaging new singers for *Das Liebesverbot*, of enabling Wagner to replace Gläser, the present conductor, temporarily, or to succeed him later. As it was to turn out, Cerf did nothing. Wagner, desperately snatching at straws, was fooled by him for a while.

67 *(Berlin, May 21, 1836)*

"My poor, poor Minna! Oh, if you only could know the feeling I put into those words. See, the tears are flowing from my eyes, all my manliness is broken by grief. You are so far, so far, so far away, among strange, rough people, and all this is a sacrifice made for me. I read over your letters, the ones you wrote me from Berlin, and now I realize everything, everything. Yes, it is a sacrifice for me! Minna, if I am not able to make you very happy, then I am hardly worthy of you! So far away, alas, so far—ah, the very thought would crush me if I were to give up hope! Now you are everything, everything in this world to me—you know well that you have every claim upon me. And what, Minna, could ever make me forget this? What could induce or compel me to cease loving you, to give you up? Once more I swear to you: If fate should send us north and south, then my only thought would be how to overcome that separation. O my poor child, how is it with you now, so far removed from everything you knew and loved? Do you weep, are you sad, or are you as steady and courageous as ever? O my God, how troubled I am by the thought that you were misled by Königsberg, that you found everything there different from what you had expected, no prospect for us, etc., and to do this you have so completely cut yourself off from everyone. May God not punish me by letting it go on this way. I could never describe with what anguish of mind and soul I am looking forward to a letter from you. What will it reveal to me, what will

43

I learn from it? If you feel unhappy, if you see no hope I couldn't stand it! My Minna, Minna, Minna! I weep without restraint, and really I'm not ashamed of my tears. It is no usual state I am in, all the misery of my life culminates in the thought: There is a good, dear, wonderful girl who is suffering for my sake! Minna, my poor child, give me some comfort, some reassurance. Well, I am in Berlin, in the same hotel where you stayed half a year ago, but not in your room No. 19: Schwabe is still there—I couldn't find out where you stayed this last time, but I did find that you left on Tuesday. I am helpless here and deserted, but there may be a slight turn in my bad luck. My main effort here, above all else, is to secure something to fall back on, so that when I come to you in the far distant north, if we should run into difficulties later, we could make our retreat without feeling that our chances are cut off. I got an introduction to Cerf from a writer here called Glasbrenner; I found him in the best humor, and the long and short of it is that I have won his favor. He told me right away: 'If you have nothing now, I can do something for you. Gläser wants to take a leave of absence, and you can have his place for the time being.' I mentioned my opera at once, and he seemed willing, but there can be no question of doing it just now, because he hasn't got his new singers yet. I have spoken to him several times since, and we know each other better; he has told me that he likes me very much. He is going to advance Gläser's leave four weeks, so that perhaps I can begin soon. If I can take over even for a short time, it will be easy for me to start rehearsing my opera, the more so because yesterday he declared himself ready, on *Laube's* and Glasbrenner's intercession (these two are laboring in my cause here, and advertise me everywhere as a giant genius), to give my opera as early as possible, when he can find a cast (which he could do now, if necessary). Today I am definitely going to push the fellow. Your letter, which I am waiting for, shall decide everything! If I can't start with my job at Königsberg right away, I'll stay here in *Gläser's* place for the time being, and will personally conduct my opera, or perhaps make a contract with Cerf for later, perhaps in a year, when Gläser's contract is up—so I'll secure my return to the more cultivated Germany, and maybe some time come to Berlin with my dear wife and a fine youngster, to take Gläser's position; at that time you need no longer be at the theater. But if you should send me the contract now, I'd come to you in a moment, *that would be the best of all for me*; I would deliver my opera to Cerf, and I would get *Laube, Glasbrenner*, and the others to have an eye on its performance. But if Cerf has really fallen for me, I might, with a contract for Königsberg in my hands, corner him and perhaps induce him to make a permanent contract with me. Then perhaps I can get him to engage you in addition and, if not, I could marry you then, even if you are not at the theater. But these are at best beautiful plans, I can't yet count on anything with certainty, for you know what Cerf is like. So we won't yet delude ourselves with this hope; the principal thing and the most necessary one always remains a contract for Königsberg. Therefore let this be your main concern, my dear child, it is the most important thing, and try your utmost to get it as soon as possible, starting right away, for to see you *soon* is and remains my *greatest* and most inexpressible yearning. Work on it, and bring it about, my good angel. Ah, how glad I would be, if I could contribute something to our happiness, so that for once you would owe something to *me*, since *I* have you to thank so far for *everything, everything*. My poor, poor girl, what trouble and stress I have caused you already; I mean recently and still *now, now!* Minna, Minna, I am dying with misery and longing—my poor, poor child! So far, so far from me! Oh, it is terrible. Tell me, do you not also weep a great deal? Do you not have sorrow and grief? And do you love me even so? Even so? And now, nothing, nothing in this world must separate me from you, by God and Eternity, nothing, nothing, my Minna, can tear you from your

RICHARD

"I must close, I can say no more.
You know me, yes, you know me!"

The following letter has been torn across twice and one of these pieces torn in two. The catalogue says: "Natalie Planer, from whom Mrs. Burrell obtained this letter, told Mrs. Burrell that she tore it herself, preparatory to destroying it." [1]

68 *(Berlin, May 23, 1836)*

"Yesterday was my birthday. It was a wholly detestable day. No one, not one sympathetic person— Ah, Minna, I am entirely miserable, I wouldn't know what to do with myself if fate should long delay our union. I am dead to everything, inwardly I am wasting away and I am more aware than ever that only a *happy* life with *you* can restore my powers. Only then, I feel, will I be able to take hold and work as a vigorous and happy man; every hope that beckons to me when I am alone has simply no existence. My child, I just read through all your letters one by one, and rejoice as one blessed in our love; how it has developed and enfolded us ever more closely. I am touched to the depth of my being. See, Minna, I can yearn again, with all the youthfulness and longing of

---

[1] What disturbed Natalie in the contents of this particular letter may be left to a detective skilled in such matters. If it was the reference to Schwabe, there are certainly more damaging references to the same gentleman in later letters. Perhaps she started to destroy a number or all of the love letters, and paused to listen to the potent argument of Mrs. Burrell that when *My Life* appeared, Minna's infidelities would in any case be unmercifully laid out for the world to read. Schwabe, for example, is there presented as having courted Minna in Berlin. Minna probably discouraged him, so Wagner thought, but sinned by her silence when she allowed Wagner, unknowing, to accept his constant friendship and advice. In view of this and more damning revelations the love letters would weigh the scale in Minna's favor, presenting her as wholly desirable, as becomingly prudent, and at all times the pursued rather than the pursuing.

a year ago, so ardent, so young does my love remain. And what a love this is! What couple ever showed more fortitude than we? Suffering the most oppressive hardships of life, almost crushed by the weight of our worries, we have continued to love and long for each other, as if nothing else in life mattered to us. My love for you is so strong, stronger than it ever has been. Is this not beautiful? And what have we not gone through! Are we just a couple of lovers, are we not more proven and more inwardly bound together than many a married couple? Well, we will fight it through and give an example of what true love is able to do and to be. Recently I saw *Fidelio* in the opera house. Schwabe was sitting beside me. At the place where Leonore has saved her Florestan and embraces him, my eyes filled with tears. Schwabe [Schw.] supposed it was the drama that had moved me; but oh, what had happened in my soul! I thought: 'Like Leonore your Minna would give up her life for you, or accept any suffering, any hardship to save you, if she knew you were threatened with ruin. And this Minna I should abandon, as some cold-hearted people suggest? A wife who everywhere would follow me in steadfastness and love?' And is it not true, my Minna, that you would do this for me? I know it, you would do it, you have proved it to me, and I?—What am I talking about? Is it still possible that we are to be separated? Are we not already united, and what bond is stronger than ours: Can any bond be stronger than that which is forged by suffering and sympathy? It has made us one, you are my wife! [2]

"May 24th: I shall write you something every morning, my angel, so that you may have a complete diary from me. Never has my sleep been as restless as now—it drives me early out of my bed, the lonely bed which gives me no comfort. I can say that I dream only of you, but they are disquieting dreams—What is to happen? I am on the best imaginable terms with Cerf—He thinks so highly of me that he announced out loud in the Kronprinz yesterday that Gläser would leave soon and that during his absence I would take his position and might perform my opera. The opera, of course, is my main concern. For a long-term engagement is entirely out of the question here. At the utmost, my hope and my aim is that, if I were unable to begin my engagement in Königsberg right away, I might remain here about six weeks or two months in Gläser's position, which certainly would bring me much honor and reputation. During that period I'd perform my opera, and if people become favorably disposed toward me, which my writer friends will promote—I would conclude, before leaving, a contract with Cerf from next year on; for at that time Kugler's contract is to expire; but it goes without saying that I'll demand more authority than Kugler so as to alternate with Gläser and to get a higher salary than his [Kugler's]. Thus I would come to Königsberg at the end of the summer, and would marry you *speedily*, and return with you after a year to Berlin, where you may not need to be at the theater at all; for by that time, I expect also to

---

[2] *Weib*; here and elsewhere Wagner anticipates.

earn something by my compositions. All this is quite good, and better than I had anticipated. My real preference, however, would be to go to Königsberg at once—the Berlin opportunity will not escape me, and in Königsberg I know someone whom I prefer to Berlin and the whole world, and this someone is *you,* my own, my all. Berlin is less important to me at present than it is for the future. Ah, my Minna, could I leave you alone for so long a time, could I do it at all? You know how indispensable you are to me; you know what I am without you!—A restless, deserted, unhappy man, who, lacking you, lacks breath, air, and everything. And this is not an empty phrase; you know well how true and how obvious it is. O my Minna, my Minna. Are you cheerful now, or are you suffering too?

"The 25th. Every day from now on I shall be looking for a letter from you; it is torment for me. Can you believe that I have no further use for this whole, great city of Berlin, except to find a reminder of you? What an insignificant person this Schwabe is after all, but I am with him a good deal because he knows about our love, and I can always talk with him about you. Yesterday I rode to Charlottenburg with him, Dedel, and someone from Königsberg; our conversation was about nothing but you; I was also told that Herr Hübsch is said to be a handsome [*hübscher*] young man, and they wanted to make me jealous; but this time they didn't succeed, for I know well enough that though you did leave your picture with Herr von Barby, which you tried in every way to deny, a real faithlessness would be impossible for you *now*, because I know you to be true to me in your heart. Conditions and life in Königsberg were described to me by several people from there as being not so very unpleasant; on the contrary I am sure that, united with you, I would like it there as well as anywhere. I learnt from Wohlbrück in Riga that L. Schubert,[3] your director of music, is certainly to go to Riga by fall, and that therefore I could join you then in any case, if not earlier. But I couldn't stand being separated from you until then. Do everything you can to bring me to you soon—otherwise I can't bear it. As I told you, Berlin won't escape me. Cerf will finally put on my opera, even without me, and I'll get a contract out of him beginning next year. But someone has told me that we will like Königsberg so well that we won't leave it soon. Schwabe already has had set aside for me the most beautiful, heaviest white satin for your bridal gown, which I'm to bring along. Minna, Minna my angel, soon, soon! I die with longing.

"It is the 26th already and I have no letter yet from you. You probably have gotten my first letter long ago. O Minna, my restlessness is becoming unbearable. I am not only indifferent toward all other things, they even disgust me now. No, Minna, you could hardly imagine the strength of my love; I must be united with you or I shall be dead to everything. I have thoughts for nothing, desire for nothing, nothing has any meaning for me. I am young, but while I

[3] Schuberth.

am alone life has already ceased to have interest for me. When something turns out well for me, like my negotiations with Cerf, I find pleasure in it only in so far as it is a further step toward our happiness together. I know now that my opera is to be given here, and that is worth much. Even though we go far away from here I shall still have left something behind that may facilitate our return. If the opera pleases, and I have no fear about that, what a step forward that will be—for it will not remain unknown to the world. I shall give my opera here on commission. Then I will put notices in the papers and offer it to the directors, gaining reputation and money, and you will have an efficient husband. In any case I am sure of an engagement here from the next year on, and with such a prospect I can marry you with a clear conscience, for I have done something for our future. Only the immediate future must still be your care, for, if I can't be with you in fourteen days at the latest, I'll come on foot and beg my way to you. Then you'll have to receive and take care of me, a poor sinner, for I can stand it no longer without you, and Berlin is secured for me and shall not slip away from me. Write, write, do you hear? Write much, good things, everything, my sweet angel, and hide nothing from me. See, Minna, is it not quite terrible that I can't learn even now where you stayed here? I didn't arrive here until Wednesday morning, but if I had arrived as early as Tuesday morning, according to our agreement, you would still have been here and I would not have known where, and might not even have seen you again. Was this your intention, you terrible person [*Abscheuliche*]? Tell me! Oh, you sometimes do such strange things that I often don't know what to think of it! You ought to avoid such things; after all, you know how sensitive I am. Come, you terrible, lovable, good, sweet girl! But write soon and don't leave me here in trembling uncertainty!

"The 27th. Today a letter should come. O my God how agonizing! Yesterday I read in the *Königsberger Zeitung* of the 21st: 'To theatergoers we bring the good news that Fräulein Planer, the charming actress who has been engaged for our stage from Magdeburg, arrived in this town.' Alas, this news has filled me with many misgivings. I see you far, far away from me, owned by strange, crude people. You appear to me as no longer *my* Minna at all. I see how all of them enjoy you and I begrudge them this enjoyment, I want to enjoy you all by myself. It won't be easy for you with me now, Minna. Perhaps even with the best intentions you will not be able for the moment to put through my Königsberg engagement, but I shall become suspicious and believe that you don't *want* to have me with you. In the long run you may like your life as it is now, then will you forget me and no longer think of me? No, Minna, has it not become impossible that we could forget each other? What am I thinking of? Of course such a thing could never be. It is true, it is true, that you love me, you have at the very least a warm feeling for me, and for this I shall thank you as long as I live, my angel.

"After lunch: Today at noon your letter came. The impression it made on me was too strong; it left me speechless for some time. Even now I still feel too much shaken and moved to answer everything and express all that I feel; I will do it when I am calmer. To love a human so, nay, to *adore* her, as I love and adore you, to know how warmly she responds to my love, and still to have to face a still longer separation, this is more than hard, this is *terrible*. O my sweet blissful wife, my all, my all. You are more to me than you can conceive or imagine; a letter like yours which I can hold in my hands means more to me than a world; oh, I could rave to you of my love! My Minna, our love *must* be rewarded, and, believe me, a devotion like ours is rare in these days. So let us have confidence in Heaven, in the heaven which we bear in our hearts, it must make us happy, happy. Steadfastness, firm courage, firm unshakable trust one in the other, and 'A curse and a shame forever on the first who breaks the faith!'[4] Hold on, my child, have only *one* thought—your Richard with all his grief, his pain, and his love, and remember the oath we exchanged with hot tears, when we swore never to separate in life, to bear everything with courage, never to waver in fidelity and faith. So, God helping, trust and faith, firm trust, firm faith; let this be our motto—and bravely to bear trials, even though it robs me of my night's sleep, every waking moment I'll cling to your sweet image, and then I'll not need to sleep; to think of you is more restoring. I will remain in Berlin until you release me from my exile with the happy news that I may hasten to you. I am certain, as I have already written you, that Schuberth is to return to Riga in the autumn. (But write me at once if you should learn anything to the contrary.) If I can't come to you any earlier, I'll wait here until Gläser begins his leave of absence, then I'll take his place in the meantime and perform my opera. But then you must release me, for I'll never find the strength to endure our separation. But if there is a *single possibility* for me to come still earlier to Königsberg, never hesitate to call me *quickly, quickly* to you. How I shall get along here until then, how manage to earn something, how satisfy the Gottschalks so early, that is more than I can tell you at this moment, but it is obvious that it has to be done. How I have roughed it so far and squeezed through, you may already have recognized by the fact that I had to send the last letter and this one to you 'collect.' But see, a firm hope makes us bear any misery. I'm not complaining of my fate on *my* account, but only on *yours*—that I have subjected you to privation and misery pains me to the depths of my soul. My poor, poor wife, what have you not suffered through me! If I can't make it up to you in the future, God remove me at once from this earth, for then I'm not worthy of you! Alas, see I am weeping again, I grow despondent, all my strength is leaving me. I implore you, I embrace your knees, *make it possible, move heaven and earth*, strain all your powers, to get me soon to Königsberg, to you, to you. I'll not bear it, I can't bear it, I am afraid of a serious mental breakdown, I can't stand it any longer, I *must* be with you. Honor, fame, gold,

[4] A cross appears before and after this sentence—perhaps inserted by Minna.

and magnificence may beckon to me here, but I'll collapse under the burden, for you must know, my dear, no one *has loved as I*, no one has been *loved as you* are loved!! The strength of my love takes always deeper root, and see, there is *no part* of my being which is not filled with a bright, clear love for you. If I had more luck, then you could be proud, for you would be the happiest being on earth—Oh, why must I say: Farewell! Why can't I kiss you until I die!—

"Your

RICHARD

"Karl, the good boy who bitterly wept when he left me, left Magdeburg one day after me."

Speaking of Wagner in these Berlin weeks, Ernest Newman, who had not seen his letters, wrote that "separation from anyone he loved or in any way needed was a torture beyond bearing." Mr. Newman's perception of the Wagner psychosis is here eloquently borne out!

Wagner's friend Heinrich Laube encountered him in Berlin and comforted him in his loneliness. Compared with his letters, this remark of Wagner in *My Life* takes on a new significance: "Laube could not fail to notice from my untidy, mediocre, and wasted appearance that something was strangely wrong with me." Laube was plainly aware of what was wrong with his friend. Again the autobiography says: "On my departure, my friend warned me, speaking in the warmest sympathy, that my desired success in a conductor's career should not involve me in the shallowness of stage life, and that after a tiring rehearsal, instead of going to my sweetheart, it would be better to take a good book in hand, in order not to neglect my greater aim for the cultivation of my powers." Of course Wagner was far too Minna-struck at the moment to heed this excellent advice.

69 *(Berlin, May 29, 1836)*

"O my Minna, I could cry out aloud in sorrow and distress. What a day yesterday, after I mailed the letter to you, and what a night that followed! I am so excited that I hardly can stay in the company of people. At the opera I was so carried away by every tone, by every moment, that I broke down crying. My whole being is seized by a sorrow which I could almost call despair. Thoughts, thoughts!

"Minna, if you should die before I could see you again! Everything around me seems like death, I detest life without you. Am I not deserted by everybody? I don't recognize family ties any longer; for your sake I have gladly renounced everything. But now I don't even possess *you* any longer! What can be equal to the state I am in! To do without you for three months more is impossible. For how could I stand it? Either you must come to me or I to you. Here all jobs are filled, and even for me a definite engagement is impossible right now; only next year. Therefore I implore you once more, spare no effort to make it possible for me to join you, that we can marry soon and bring to an end this state of torment. Use any means, disdain nothing, for see, it is not for me alone, but for both of us. I have just now a good and honorable occupation, but I'll throw away everything, I hate it all—oh, I need tell you no more, you know me and know how I would pine away without you. Yesterday the whole history of our love passed through my mind, from our first meeting in Lauchstädt until now. People say love in its first stages is more glowing and ardent, but never during the two years we have been in love have I been in such a state of burning and consuming passion. No, you will never again be loved as I love you now, and I must be away from you for *a quarter of a year longer!!* No, no, don't believe this, Minna, a miracle will happen, it *must* happen. Why should God permit this blight on my life? What have I done? I can't go on, my misery is overwhelming me; more later!

"May 30th. Oh, this eternal anxiety and excitement; I don't enjoy a single happy moment. I have to confess to you that I was distrustful of my first stroke of luck here. It was strange that right after my first appearance in Berlin things seemed to take a turn for the better. I found Cerf in the best humor; he immediately offered to let me substitute for Gläser during his absence, and he also held out the best hopes for my opera; my friends even started talking about my staying here permanently, etc. But all this made a very sad impression on me; I thought: 'Will this good luck put your love and faith to the test? Will it perhaps force you to settle into a secure position without the possibility of marrying Minna?' I had no liking for that kind of luck and would have preferred making no use of it at all. Ah, if you would write to me in your next letter, 'Richard, come,' I would knock down houses with joy. You will see what a good husband I will make. And now the point is to secure Berlin for next year, when my reputation as a composer will have grown so much that I hope then to take you away from the theater. Don't you agree, Minna? Will you not also be content to leave the stage? O let the future be *my* care, for united with you I am confident of finding my highest powers. But *now*, right *now*, it still rests with you. Don't bother about my limited prospects here, summon me quickly to your side! Kill Schuberth, O God, do anything, anything; I can't bear it any longer, I can't go on this way. If you could only see what a dreary figure I am here!

"31st of May. Is there no end to this misery? What a terrible month this has been, Minna! It was my birth month; is there any human feeling that hasn't filled my heart this month? I lie under torture in the true sense of the word, I look pale and miserable. I have not been able to get rid of the vivid impression of your letter, contrasting so sharply our love and our separation. Only the last passage gave me some hope that perhaps I may come to you soon, and see, this is my nature; from this single ray of light I am still hoping you may write to me in your next letter: 'Richard, you may come.' What is more, I'm hoping so strongly that I haven't yet arranged to leave the hotel and to move into a private lodging, because I keep thinking your next letter may call me to you. Alas, Minna, this last weak hope is all my comfort, to keep me going at all. Yes, I hope, I hope! You may perhaps wonder, my dear child, that I don't write anything about Berlin, its life, etc., but all this doesn't exist for me at all; I live, God knows, merely for you and in the thought of you. The only acquaintance whom I see during the day is often Schwabe, because he dines with us at the Kronprinz and is often there in the evenings too— Since your letter came I almost never go to see any one; the best I can do is to associate with those who know my grief and respect it. You know how subject I am to my single thought, how it never, never leaves me. My heart is always oppressed, I feel always that it is going to break; if somebody tries to make me laugh I begin to cry; and the night's restlessness; every morning I am roused from sleep as if with a contraction of the heart; thoughts, hundreds of images are whirring through my brain as if I had already been awake a whole day. Thus, Minna, we are consuming our youth! An end, an end to this condition, I have already suffered too much!

"*The 1st of June:* I remember one evening, Minna my soul, in Rudolstadt I had missed you when the play was over; it was already dark; I had gone all the way back to your house without having found you. Believing you would still come, I sat on the stone bench in front of the house—I *had* to see you again and to speak to you, for you had just been harsh with me. The sky was black and clouded, not a star was to be seen; I stared into the dark night, my eyes filled with tears. Then already I felt so lonely and abandoned without you! I started at every footstep. Is it she? I sat for a long while like this; it grew darker and colder; my whole body became numb from the cold stone on which I sat; it had become very late. Certainly you had come home earlier; you were already in bed. I couldn't even see your room, only a cold wall stared at me. O Minna, I now feel as if I were still sitting on that bench, in the dark gloomy night, crying, unable to see you. If only my heart doesn't break, I will gladly be brave, I will do my best, will no longer be so pliant; but what if I don't succeed even so?

"Minna, Fate is more than cruel, it treats us outrageously, when all we wish is to forget everything around us, and to belong to each other. Does it not seem to deride our love? And what is equal to our love! Now, now to have you beside me, to feel your presence, to be lost in your glance, to be wedded to your darling body, then all my sufferings would be dissolved in a wonderful, sweet embrace. Minna, what prevents me? I will join you, come what may. Perhaps it will be good if I am with you; everything may speed up, take another turn. O God in Heaven, do you feel as ardently as I? Tell me, may I, may I come? Are you hopeful? How unhappy I am!! These lines must be quickly sent, they are burning in my hands. Tell me, may I come? Quickly, answer quickly—

"Your

RICHARD"

70 *(Berlin, June 3, 1836)*

"I didn't really intend to write you again so soon, until I'd received a letter from you to answer. I almost feared to tire you, my good Minna: with all my suffering I am too soft. You have a new sphere of action, a new public. You act on the stage and spend many an hour with no time to think of your Richard; with me it is different, I have no other interest than *you, you* alone, no other thought can rise in my mind than the thought of you. I have become a pitiful specimen for any social purposes. Among people I fall into deep musing and ponder how to remove the distance between you and me; I tell you it has come to the point where I will decide to stop mingling with people entirely. I will shut myself off from everyone to whom I am burdensome, flee them, and wait until you bring me release, my angel! Ah, my Minna, soon everything may be over with me. You also write that nobody must know anything about our relationship until the time comes. This was not your wish before. But how can you hasten my release except by using our relationship as a threat, on the basis that you will leave if we cannot be soon united in Königsberg? Was this not also your opinion before? See, I have so much idle time for brooding. So, you want to conceal our relation? You are afraid of losing the attraction that you have as an unattached person for the public and even for the director. Do you believe that you still need that attraction? Do you feel the need of making yourself interesting in this way to hold people in suspense? I know well enough that you will continue to be pestered by young people and troublesome gallants; I know those cursed attentions an actress has to encounter; people wouldn't refrain from molesting you even if you should declare yourself to be my betrothed; it is all the worse now when you conceal it and each holds some hope. Will you not tell them that you love me? If the director remains in doubt will he not strive to the utmost to prevent our union while you remain vague and fail to declare: 'Either I am leaving your theater in two months or you offer me the chance of being united here with my fiancé'? Minna, why do you still hesitate *now*, when at last you can put a stop to our suffering? Write to me *often* and *much*, that I may breathe again; my heart chokes me, I must perish, for I love you too much to be able to breathe and live except in *you*, who are the *breath* of my *life!*

"The 4th of June—I have your letter, my sweet child, it was the only thing left for me to hope for in this dreary moment, and I read every bit of it a hundred times. Well, it is not to be; I am to remain separated from you. I was indeed prepared for it; when I was in Leipzig I resolutely gave up everything which could separate us, so that without you I stood quite alone. I believed that I had secured this way the good fortune never to be parted from you again, and this was the comfort of my isolation. If I had even suspected that I might have to live a whole summer without you! Minna, I am *inexpressibly unhappy*; our love is under an evil star--it is a blessing for you that you don't sense our misfortune as much as I. This is no indictment against you, my child; you could never have based everything on me, all the hopes of your life, all the happiness of your youth, as I have based mine on you. It is unthinkable that you could love me as *much* as I love you. And this is not even a reproach, it is the conviction only, impressed upon me by my overwhelming feeling for you, that I can't believe that such a feeling could never be reciprocated. You always appear to me *lovely, noble,* and *kind,* but how often have you seen *me* in the most disagreeable light—with my whims, my unhappiness, my excessive susceptibility [*Weichheit*], and all the hardships. No, no, you can't possibly love me so much! But I make no complaint about this; if you could feel for me half as much as I feel for you, I would be richly, richly rewarded. I must confess to you, my angel, that I had hoped until the last moment that it could be arranged for me to come soon; I hoped for it as the poor sinner taken to the scaffold hopes for pardon until the death blow; and may I confess my weakness to you? I am *now still,* now still, hoping, quite secretly in my heart, that perhaps something will suddenly happen to release me. What am I to do with myself until Gläser leaves? He doesn't leave before the end of July, and only then will my work begin. If it weren't so terribly far away, I would take the coach, visit you, see to my affairs myself, sign a contract from September on; then I would go back to Berlin, finish my affairs here and return to you in the fall. Perhaps, perhaps! I knew well enough that Königsberg offers no great opportunity. However, it is there that we must join, and if it can be done no other way I entreat you to arrange for a contract from September. Schuberth is to go to Riga, that is certain, so there is no reason why you couldn't make a definite move; but I believe you are afraid of betraying our relationship. This is painful to me and I'd rather have everything else break down than have you disown me. We won't make a contract for more than a year, this is sure, my child, for I plan to return to Berlin with my dear young wife in the Easter season of 1837—until then Königsberg must suffice! When this unfortunate period is once over you won't have a bad time with me, and I will try to repay all your love a thousandfold. I don't doubt that Cerf will engage me with a good salary, for he wants to have two first conductors as in the largest theaters, where they counterbalance each other. He declared not only to me but to others that he wouldn't ask for Gläser's consent; he could even engage five more conductors without Gläser's right to object. It's true I am on very good terms with him, for I judge not only by what he tells me to my face, but by what he says behind my back, and both statements always agree. When the new opera personnel assembles, I am supposed to conduct the first performance. Well, I shall do my job. I'll conclude the contract with him from next Easter on in any case, and he must give me 1,000 to 1,200 thaler. If he wishes to engage you along with me, well, I would leave it to you, but I don't like the idea, not at all! For I would be better off through my compositions, which I could perform in Berlin for the first time, and if you are not engaged in the theater we won't need so much. I will do what I can now, but you must secure my September engagement at Königsberg. Then the future is cared for. In October, at the latest, we must have our wedding. Minna, my angel, my God, my delight and joy. The wedding—we shall be husband and wife, and no bad luck can part us after that moment. But—until then—the present!! All my limbs become lifeless when I measure the eternity until then! I ought to have pity on you, my poor girl. How can I believe that you can be happy now if you love me too? O Minna, let's always live together in spirit, let's write each other every day; do as I do. You certainly can find an idle quarter of an hour each day to devote to your poor Richard. Always keep a diary, and when one of us receives a letter we'll mail our diaries to each other; the postage costs will be managed. So, listen, my good sweet girl, every day each will write a few lines and on receiving a letter, mail them. Swear it to me. This way we will overcome the distance by our faithfulness and give an example of loving trust, even in separation. Minna, you surely do not doubt my fidelity for a moment? Come, come, you are lying, you never thought of such a thing, even in your dreams you couldn't think of your Richard as faithless. Now look, I don't doubt you in the least, either, and when two love each other as we do, it is ridiculous even to think of infidelity. But all the same, be on your guard! Where you are there are said to be some handsome men. Be careful, *Minnachen*, do you hear? Don't look at them! Do you hear? It's silly, how can we think of such a thing! Can you conceive the slightest possibility that we could—become unfaithful! Pfui, Pfui, that horrible word—how bad it already looks in a letter. We'll never mention it again, never think of it again, do you hear?

"My poor traveling child, what will you not have to endure and suffer! It's too hard, it's terrible. Why should we spoil our fair youth like this? I will be very industrious now, it is my only means of somehow subduing my grief. But see, from each note, each syllable I write or read, your image is looking at me, your dear sparkling eyes kindling me with a longing which only he who suffers as I do may know. In such moments tears are my only comfort, my only relief, and my only delight is to know also that you are weeping for me. Well—*with those beautiful tears* we are bound to become happy.

"Your

RICHARD

"P.S. I have written to the Gottschalks and asked for an extension; if those people have a trace of heart in their breasts, they won't bother you with anything, I made this my *main* point." [5]

The next letter, covering sixteen days with only three days skipped, is crowded upon two folded sheets, one large, one smaller. It is closely spaced, and each margin of the eight written pages is vertically filled. Wagner, apparently ashamed to send another collect letter to his sweetheart, as he had before,[6] must

[5] Gottschalk and his wife, Jewish moneylenders in Magdeburg, had helped Wagner out of his difficulties, and evidently lived to regret it.

[6] See 68.

indeed have been short of pfennigs when he crowded more than five thousand words on two sheets of paper!

71 *(Berlin, June 5, 1836)*

"Ah, my dear sweet girl, my Minna, my angel, my own—What a terrible situation! Believe me, I am never going to be happy, I shall never have a single happy moment, until I can hold you fervently in my arms. See, I am looking for anything that will quiet my pain; I keep working—but it won't do, my strength always fails, my heart melts into a thousand tears, and sometimes I despair of living to see the next morning. For I always feel as if everything would fall to pieces within me suddenly, so that I could exist no longer. I still don't believe that everything will end as I last wrote you; some miracle is going to call me to you soon—it can't be otherwise. Everywhere, everywhere I miss you; even on the street, among the motley crowd, I miss you on my arm where you nested warmly and sweetly. See—everything around me is cold and heartless, I have no affection left even to give to a friend, for every fiber, every spark of love has been taken by you; all my love has gone to you only, you cruel one! I'm too unhappy; I can't control myself even in the company of those with whom I usually dine. I have nothing to say; I am dumb and introspective; and the unfortunate people, like Herr Schwabe, who think they can cheer me by teasing, succeed only in paining me. Opposite me as I sit at table, hangs a map of Germany, and I keep looking at it and just imagine—the map doesn't even reach to Königsberg. So tears often come to my eyes. You seem out of the world altogether, so that we can never meet again. Tell me, my dear, what have you against Schwabe? You spoke of his envy. Tell me frankly, did he ever let you see that he is *envious* of me? I suppose you understand me: Did he ever show an equivocal attitude? Was he ever inclined to court you? I'm ready to believe anything. Why not this too? Who would have believed, during our last days in Magdeburg, that we would have to endure so long a separation? If I had realized this, I would at least have asked you for your picture; you would perhaps have left it with me if you hadn't already promised it to your friend. I made a last call on him before my departure; I wanted to make up for what, in your opinion, I had neglected to do in your apartment after you had gone. Your picture hung in his room; Minna, I have to confess to you: my impression from this was not of the sort to make me bid your friend a more friendly farewell. First, I realized that you had deceived me by repeatedly pretending something quite different about this picture; secondly, I became painfully aware how little I still meant to you in certain respects, since you let the picture of my fiancée hang in the room of your friend, although we had before agreed—when you had done the same thing for a short while—that this means a betrayal of me and that nothing could give me more pain. But *now* you have done the same thing again, you have given—consider this!—*your* picture to a third person, and,

Minna, this was not kind of you. It was even worse than that, for you could still have taken it back when I strongly urged you, since at that time it was not yet in your friend's hands—but you failed to do it; you kept it a secret from me, made it even *impossible* for me to get it—and *this*, Minna, I *can't* forgive you, for you lowered me in my own esteem and showed me my own insignificance. I assure you, my dear, if you had wanted to punish me for anything, you might at least have chosen a less wounding method! This lucky man, though he is separated from you—has your picture after all, and with it the fairest token of your faith before his eyes, and before the eyes of others—I—am not so lucky. Well, it is your work and was your will. Let this be my last word on the subject. I would have spared you this, if in my present state my longing for a picture of you were not so great. So forgive me, and rest assured this is the last reproach you will hear from me.

"The 6th of June: You may well imagine, my dear wife, what a simple and retired life I lead here; you know me and know too that since I have been in love with you I have cared little enough for noisy activity, even if it had come my way; and so I'll tell you my simple daily schedule, and you may know what I do hour by hour. As soon as I wake up early in the morning from my dreams of you, I write to you first of all; it is my morning prayer and you are my God whom I implore to hear me; then, strengthened, I tackle my work and usually keep at it until two o'clock. Then I go to my dinner, and after that I usually walk to the Friedrichstadt [district], where I meet Laube, Glasbrenner, and some others with whom I go on to Charlottenburg; there I usually see Cerf, drive back to town, and attend one of the theaters,[7] from there to supper and at ten o'clock to bed. The only exception to this way of life is not to drive to Charlottenburg at all, but either to go back again to my room or pay a visit to Schwabe or some other indifferent person. I am always taciturn and sad. O my God, how I miss you! Be sure to write me, my angel Minna; whatever happens to you, your life is much more colorful, anyhow, than mine; tell me everything that happens to you and let me share it. Last night something unpleasant turned up. A gentleman from Altenburg sat at our table, who hadn't been there for a long while; in the course of the conversation Dedal inquired whether he had known you and praised you quite a lot; the man answered: 'Oh, yes, the Planer; some one went off [*entführt hatte*] with her, and in a hotel, once, in Meissen, I learned that she had arrived; when I went to my room in the night, I made a

---

[7] Wagner's mere phrase "attend one of the theaters" is an example of his inability to confide any artistic experience to Minna. In his misery he found time to absorb himself in the special talents of Spontini, who was then conducting his *Ferdinand Cortez* at the Hoftheater, and to receive from Spontini stimulation toward an opera of equally magnificent proportions, an impulse which was to culminate in the composition of *Rienzi*. It is worth noting that Wagner also sent an article to Robert Schumann's *Zeitung*, but found no occasion to write a single word about a subject so alien to Minna as his new operatic impressions and thoughts in Berlin.

mistake and got into hers instead. There I had a highly interesting time; it lasted three quarters of an hour.' Of course every one was taken aback, and it was my duty and my interest to ask for a more exact account, for I was concerned about you. 'Fräulein Planer?' he said. 'Well, it may be that I have the wrong name; yes, yes, of course, it was Mlle. Wünsch, or Christiany; excuse me, etc.'—I retorted that how he may have carried on with Mad. Christiany was the least of my worries; what I strongly requested of him was never again to try any name switching of this sort and about such matters. He did his best, then, to reassure me and to apologize; but you see, my dearest, what people are like. With no intention to harm you personally, but only out of indifference about one name or another, this man—had I not been present—would have helped you to a doubtful reputation. A girl or wife in the theater is really too much exposed, and I consider it my holiest duty to do everything to take you away from the theater as soon as possible. In no case would I permit you to come with me to Berlin as an actress; it is much better for me to have you, my good wife, for myself alone, and not for the theater gaper; that way you are much more sacred to me. O my Minna, my delight! With what rapture I think of the future, when *I* will be able to advise and help you—Who is to advise and help as things are now; this terrible, evil state of affairs! A death shudder seizes my whole body when I think: *three months* still! Do you know any way? Will no miracle happen? Minna, my Minna— Is there no comfort?

"7th of June—If I wrote you books and volumes, I could never write enough about my love, my longing. O my sweet, delightful life, must I then be so far from you in order to tell you what powerful feelings gather in my breast, feelings for you alone! Minna, believe me, my Minna, would you have thought it possible that my love for you could *still* grow? Didn't I find everything, all my expectations for mankind, realized in you alone? Wasn't your dear, good heart the only one where, with all my troubles and joys, I found deep consolation? But now is not each day spent in pain and agony another bond which ties me to you anew and forever? My God, Minna, there is agony, a terrible agony in each day as it comes and goes; in order not to succumb to it I have but one protection—my love for you.

"I see that we still have to find happiness, great happiness; and it is my aim and hope to secure that happiness, to return your love which I have so little deserved, and to deserve it. It is this alone that keeps me going when pain crushes my heart. Minna, why must this weary condition of living take our strength from us? Why must we be separated by such a miserable situation? If I knew you to be in danger, in serious distress, how I would rush to you, tear away and sweep aside all obstacles to save you, to free you with the power of my love! Oh, tell me, Minna, my adored wife, can I do nothing, can I make no sacrifice for you? O Minna, my blood and life, to leave everything for you— how splendid, how beautiful this seems to me! Oh, tell me that you must have me, that I am necessary to you; tell me this and I'll override all the barriers in the world and stand before you, even if you are still farther away from me than our cruel fate has hurled you. Tell me what you demand from me? O God, O God, perhaps you are happy without me? Demand my life, my soul, but not that I give you up to make you happy, for see, this is the only happiness I would begrudge you.—Forgive me, Minna, but I am out of my mind, and what is to become of me? Don't believe that I will calmly bear this separation; *something* must happen to end it soon or *I* shall finish it with a bold stroke! I feel in the mood to smash everything, respecting no traditions, no fetters; if you are not *given* to me—well, then, I will win you. Minna, would you sacrifice your life for me gladly as I would mine for you? It wouldn't be worth a pin to me any longer, if I had to lose you; anyway, my life has lost so much of its value for me—it is dear to me only if it can bring *you* happiness. Tell me. Will I really bring you *happiness* by giving myself forever to you? Oh, take me, with every drop of my blood, with every fiber of my heart, with every tear of woe and longing, the only comfort I have for my sorrows, take them all—and—be happy! O my Minna, my ardently loved, adored wife, my sweet, dear angel—Will you be happy?

"The 8th of June—Yesterday I took a long walk for half the day, trying to benumb my excitement by bodily exhaustion; my nights are dreadful—you know that excited state, my Minna, which deprived us both of sleep at night: it was then on account of my opera, the restlessness, the dream visions, the terrible perspiring. Now all my nights are that way, and absorbed as I was by my opera at that time, now I am all the more absorbed in the thought of you and our separation! Yesterday I roamed through all of the suburbs of Berlin until I was exhausted—I was quite alone, it was a beautiful clear day; ah, Minna —as I wandered around so aimlessly, a certain holy inward calm came over me, a sweet hope filled my yearning; it was the conviction that one day we shall become very happy; it is my single thought now to make you happy, completely happy in your love for me—some light carriages drove past, in one a betrothed or married couple were seated. How I envied them! Dwelling on my hopes of settling in Berlin later, I thought: 'Then you must drive around like this with your young wife; how fine that will look, how you will be envied! And so for the future—Minna shall have everything she wants, and when you bring happiness into our home, how splendidly we shall enjoy it after such a long struggle!' Minna, with fancies like these I gradually begin to cherish again the life which I had held as so little; the thought had often come to me that it would be very easy to throw it away. My dear wife, don't dismiss that as absurd; consider my position; to be yours, yours with every breath, to be never, nevermore separated from you, I forsook all my family ties, all relationships; in short, everything that had bound me before; I did it of my own will and gladly, for I believed I had so won the delight of not being separated any more from you, but of sharing with you my whole life. Who would have guessed that we would have to part at once and for a long time? How terribly alone I am here during this separation! Besides you I have nothing to cling to with ardent love. I am *entirely alone*—I am much too sensitive; I cling to you with too many thousand bonds to be able to stand my misfortune with calm and firmness. I am unable to look up a friend; I even avoid those I already know; I don't want to be diverted or disturbed by *anything* from the image of Minna; any other thought seems unholy and hateful to me. See, Minna, if the storms of life could seize and hurl me wherever they wished, nothing could bring me back into my former circumstances; nothing could take from me the hope of possessing *you*. But, my dear, this separation— How can I stand it? I wonder whether the pain is going to crush me entirely—whether— Minna, my Minna, will no miracle happen? Is no hope yet in sight? No comfort? I am beginning to doubt whether there will be anything for me to do here; the new opera company is to assemble very late; there may be little work for me until September, and it is a very great question whether I could produce my opera then. On the other hand, it would be an easy thing to get a contract from next year on—my angel, release me; call me soon to you or I shall go to pieces— Do you not want me?

"The 9th of June: Tell me, my dear adored creature, am I not growing bothersome to you with my endless writing? I can't write to you of anything but my feelings, my pains and miseries, for I know nothing else. Even for you it may not be pleasant—now you may feel in your heart anxious and annoyed, and then the feeling that I am suffering too may be a consolation to you, but what a consolation! Minna, my dear wife, it is hard, very hard seeing you in that severe climate exposed to many discomforts; and if I knew that something might happen to you it would release me from my exile and you would be pleased to see how quickly I would be at your side. My only remaining thought is to secure your happiness—and yet if you should write to me now, 'I am happy,' I would be out of my mind, for any happiness that *I* didn't bring to you would become my greatest unhappiness. You would never believe, my sweet child, with what a true, heartfelt blessedness am I now thinking of our wedding —quite new sweet images of it are always going through my head. How we will hasten it, dear Minna, as soon as we are together. I see you now, looking sweet in simple white satin, with the small wreath in your hair—my fantasy pictures everything, even the smallest detail—ah, my dear child, when we rise from our bed in the morning for the first time we shall not need to be bashful; and then the sweet calm in our poor hearts, which have suffered and bled so much! We must live quite simply to begin with; we will find our first happiness merely by having each other quite, quite inseparably—then we may look forward with calm assurance to our new life, which will grow ever more beautiful and happy. For see, dear angel, *I* cherish the hope that I can only advance each year; I am not like many others who profit only by their youth and its gifts, and then, reaching a greater age, lose out and keep sinking lower; that is the time when I hope to rise, for my gifts and talents will never age. Therefore, don't despond; even if the start is not so alluring and pleasant, it will *always, always* improve, and the more the charms of youth fade, the more worthy will our outer life become. O my Minna, you can now venture life with me. I have again collected here many fine hopes for my future, and I am a good faithful fellow too, as God knows; no evil is in my soul, believe me; I am honest and true. You are the same, and now may God protect us!

"The 10th of June. God knows, my splendid girl, whether I pass a single hour without a thousand thoughts of you! It is both joy and torment; for thinking of you is joy, and seeing you vividly before me but knowing you so far away is torment! Only one thought, as I said, still sustains me; it is that *your happiness* will be mine too! We must free ourselves of these grubby theater surroundings; as a married couple we must rather mingle with a bourgeois society; and see, my sweet child, I have a firm hope and belief that happiness will enter our home when we are married, for your calm and sure intelligence will make the most of what my talent and earnings bring in. So, listen! On leaving Königsberg, we must also take our farewell of the regular theater world; you must leave the stage for good. You know, I hope to be employed in Berlin again for 1,000 thaler; to be able to count on 1,000 thaler here is certainly [page torn] . . . as having perhaps 1,500 thalers [page torn] . . . in Magdeburg. Further, my sweet child, we should not forget the advantage for my compositions which a Berlin appointment offers: I can give the first performances of my operas, etc., right here in Berlin, and if they are successful their fortune is assured for the whole of Germany; and so I have every right to expect that my standing will become very profitable. So it will be our greatest triumph, Minna, if after our marriage we reach a secure, happy, and honorable position— Then even our relatives will approve. Oh, those relatives— Why should we care about them? Tell me, don't you also long to get away from these disturbing and doubtful theater affairs? O Minna, if I could only make you really happy! See, it's my only desire, my only thought, and to accomplish it is the entire goal of my life. See, it may happen that my greatest wish, to come to you right now, will be fulfilled; but one thing is quite certain: Cerf is about to give my opera.

"The 11th of June. Minna, dear Minna, why do I have no letter from you? See, I'm already filling the last empty space on this sheet and there is no letter yet to be answered. This alarms me. Minna, if you should meet with an accident and if I weren't near you—this would be terrible— O my angel, things are so bad now, how much more wonderful will the future be? Minna, I picture it to myself in such fair colors—when we live in Berlin and I make a whole lot of money with an opera, I'll get a horse and a two-wheeled carriage, a *Gigue* it's called, and I'll drive you around in it every day; it is not so expensive—this I'm sure about. Oh, see, it's my only amusement to build castles in our future, and the bright colors must make up for a drab present. I have a real prospect now of paying my debts regularly, without taking too much from our marriage fund; if Heaven wills that I can't come to you earlier, I would start my position here on the first of July, but only for the two months of July and August; Cerf ought to give me a decent fee for my opera, and so I think I shall be able to pay Gottschalk's as well as some other debts; but they must wait; it can't be helped; and if by chance they should write to you, make this clear to them; I on my part am doing the same. I see the time coming when gradually our ill luck will take a turn for the better; but I won't take the slightest notice of my relatives. What would you say if I should settle in Leipzig again? You may be sure that no misfortune could bring me so low; only when *we* are very happy will I show them how we can put them to shame. Our happiness and prosperity are going to be the best triumph over our enemies. Isn't this so, my dear wife?

"The 12th of June—Dear Minna, see, now the whole sheet is filled up and I have no letter from you yet, and nothing to answer, and the worst part of it is, I believe there will be no more mail today, but only tomorrow I will be able to get a letter— What is the matter? Don't you love me any longer? I just got up from my bed and actually awakened myself by stretching my arms and clasping them together—for I clearly imagined I could actually embrace you, so vividly did you walk through my soul and stand before my eyes. Tell me, my charming sweet angel, what will it all lead to? Did I ever think it possible that my love could still grow, become still more violent and ardent? Shall I not go mad when finally I can really hold you in my arms again? I can't imagine yet that excess of joy; it is still far enough off! O God, I was prepared for anything in the world but such a separation; suffering, need, cares, sorrow, and pain, these were familiar enough. I knew them and didn't fear them, but a separation from you! Doesn't it seem as if an evil demon is haunting me, to inflict on me this additional torment after so much suffering? But perhaps this evil power has been for the best after all, for it has made me see that all the grief in the world is nothing compared to a separation from you; I know now that everything I once called suffering will be as nothing when we are united forever. Yes, my sweet wife, at your side I will know no more pain and suffering, for possession of you will atone for all; and when this last and greatest trouble is over, we shall know only good fortune and joy, for our trials will be ended, and none worse could exist to torment us. We shall be rewarded for overcoming everything so courageously and well; and see, this hope, this conviction is now so firmly and surely engraved in my heart that it fills me with a divine and inspiring faith: *we must become very happy*— O Minna, when I look ahead into this happy time my heart beats so proudly and joyously that I could also burst with grief at not being able to press you to this happy and confident heart. Perhaps you are hopeful too, and are preparing for the beginning of our happiness by calling me soon to you. Do this, dear child, and don't shrink from it because the circumstances there may not be very pleasant either. At least, it was so described to me yesterday by a man from Königsberg. But when I explained to him that I would go there for about eight months only, from about September to May, he said that in such a case I could well stand it, for around that season the theater company always stays in Königsberg and I had nothing to fear in winter about my salary, either. So if it must be like this, dear Minna, we will put up with Königsberg this winter, for as a young couple we can live for the first half-year wherever we want; we surely will be happy and we'll not care whether we are living in Königsberg or Paris if only we earn a decent living; and then in May, 1837, we'll go to Berlin; and when I have closed my contract here I will rent at once for Easter a nice apartment which Schw. [Schwabe] will fix up suitably, as we agreed. We'll surely get away from Königsberg. Arrange it, my dear, that I may soon count on coming to Königsberg; overcome all bashfulness and warn your director that you will leave in the autumn in case he doesn't engage me; so much is clear in any case: if I can't come to Königsberg we must go somewhere else, for we can remain separated no longer. Well —courage and steadfastness, we must conquer!

"The 13th of June—Today a letter must come— O you dear, wicked girl, do you know what grief you cause me? I have no peace any longer, my heart beats so violently! Minna, my Minna, how does it go with you now? Perhaps you are quite unhappy and avoid writing about it? My good, dear sweetheart, my wife, my lovely wife, how long is this to last? God knows I can't stand it— O you have *no* idea, how I suffer—the conditions now are too terrible; there is not a *single* suffering, not *one* sorrow that doesn't oppress me and clutch convulsively at my breast. Minna, my God, I am too unhappy! God deliver me from this misery in which all my thinking and feeling languishes. My Minna, I can write no more now; God grant that I may still have a dear letter from you today, that I may have some comfort!

"The 15th of June: Minna, I am in despair. I have been mistaking the date all along by one day— Today is the 15th already, and I have no letter from you. God, this is real anguish, and it will soon be fourteen days since I have had a letter from you. O God, Minna, if something has happened to you! How wrong you are not to write sooner; a thousand alarming thoughts are haunting me. Minna I have heard that you won't return to Königsberg now, but will go on to Tilsit and then to Memel. Oh, this is fearful! It is terrible! Is all the misery of heaven to descend at last on the two of us? Minna, I am inconsolable that you have joined such a traveling company; Minna, Minna, let's rather pinch and adapt ourselves for the time being, but you must get away from the theater altogether; it is an ever burning reproach, burdening my conscience: my poor, good girl wandering around with a theater troupe. I am beside myself; if I don't get a letter from you *today* I don't know what I shall do.

"The 16th of June. Minna, I'm *beside myself;* I have no letter yet from you. My senses are leaving me; I am quite out of my mind. Good God, if it is only negligence on your part this time, Heaven prevent you from doing it again, for I am more dead than alive. What, for heaven's sake, am I to do, if I get no letter today? All my thoughts are scattered. Minna, Minna how terribly you are torturing me! The misgivings and anxieties that keep running through my poor head! God help me, I can't go on like this. I'll quickly read your last letter and will try to imagine that I just got it—so I'll deceive myself—

"The 18th of June: No, Minna, this is more than I can stand!! I didn't leave my room from early in the morning yesterday until five o'clock in the evening, expecting a letter from you any minute. None came. I went to Sch. [Schwabe] He tried to console me; the dusk came; we took a walk to the Tiergarten. How my feelings for you overwhelmed me; how the past, the present, and the future filled my heart! Minna, I could never describe to you the feelings that rule my whole being. It is impossible to find words depicting the state of my soul. Only let me hope that *you* will understand what I can't put into words. You must divine this, you must feel it. Even if the distance between us were *still* greater, your spirit, your heart must sense those holy pangs filling my whole existence— O my child, I am crying hard while I am writing this! Perhaps everything is a bad dream, my life is a bad dream, or are my beautiful dreams my real life? My mind is so distraught that I can't discern any longer between waking and dreaming. Oh, what a delightful dream I had this morning. Unfortunately, it woke me up. You lay, yes, you lay at my side; I felt the dear warmth of your body; your head rested on my arm; I kissed you so tenderly and warmly on the mouth, but quite softly, for I didn't want to wake you up, since you seemed to be sleeping. And yet, no, your good wonderful eyes had opened and looked upon me so sweetly and lovingly; for a long time you had felt my kiss, and reproached *me* for having slept and having done all this while sleeping. Then I pulled myself together, too, to open my eyes and prove to you how much awake I was! I looked around me and saw that everything was empty, desolate, dead, and deserted. Indeed I was awake and am still awake. It was a dream. I have no letter yet from you. I am awake and am reading a book in which every passage, every sentiment like the one tearing at my heart, makes me shed the hottest tears. There must be some change soon, that is certain, it must happen soon; dearest, if you would see clearly how immensely I am indebted to you, you might realize how yearning and pain, tormenting pain, are simultaneously crushing me. God in heaven is my witness that I think of nothing but making it up to you for having sent you a hundred miles away, poor child, only to leave you in pain and suffering! Or—is this not so? If not, it would be terrible —no *you could never forget me, not you, not you,* for you are my guardian spirit, my angel, my God.

"The 20th—Well, it is true. You have abandoned me. And *you* too, Minna! You too! Oh, this is hard, very hard—my pain has been strangling me all yesterday and all last night. Now it dissolves in a stream of hot, bitter tears, and only now I find words! You have abandoned me, Minna, abandoned; do you know what it means to me, a poor unhappy man, who has been left by everybody, who has devoted his entire life only to the possession of you, who had nothing but you, and now you desert him too!! Well, so it must be. I am most at fault, I *love* you *too much,* I have to go through this misery, too, in order to realize the ridiculousness of everything I have suffered so far. So you have forgotten me, and given me up—and, indeed, who am I that you should not be able to forget *me*? Could I ever be to you what you are to me? I know only this: if you could have seen me in these days, you wouldn't have left me. You would have felt the same compassion for me which has always been the main source of your love for me, for you have a kind heart; but the evil, evil hundred miles, they chill your sympathy do they not? It was the 31st of May when you wrote me your last letter. Today it is the 20th of June, and that letter still is your *last one.* O God, what a wretched, miserable life! Nothing lives in me any longer except you; if the image of you should die then I too would live no longer. But that you should desert me just now, at the moment when our star of hope is rising, when we are on the verge of happiness! So it was only amusement, after all. Or was it serious? Tell me! Was it serious? Have we really been happy and unhappy together? O my God, how I suffer! Was that your *last* letter? Maybe I have been wrong—I hope to God that I have! O my Minna, forgive me—you have no idea what I suffer, this loneliness, this whole situation; maybe people less sensitive might bear it, trusting to attain their goal in this way. But, God knows, *I* can't, even if I had this certainty. My soul is mortally sick, and so cold, so icily cold is everything around me. These people who are not attached to me by any spark of affection, these circumstances, *this* life was never meant for me; I need a *heart* to which I can yield completely, with all my love, with all my sensitive soul, in the same unquestioning and exclusive way that you possess me. Therefore it happens, Minna, that I appear cold and repellent, gruff and un-friendly to anybody else. Only the one can possess me who offers a *heart* in exchange. And these people are rare, very rare. Minna, it was you who offered me this heart; and it was the more precious to me because it was seldom effusive, but held aloof from every first encounter with seeming coldness and reserve. Minna, I opened this heart; it accepted me warmly and lovingly, with all my weaknesses, faults, and peculiarities, and so now I am yours with all my heart and soul, forever and ever. If you abandon me Minna, and turn coldly away, then you would be killing me; for if I were to go on living, you still would hold my heart and love forever in your possession, and never would they return into me. I would wander through life as a cold and heartless man and scornfully I would push that life from me. I am bound to you with numberless ties; if you cut them they will rebound, bleeding, and you will see a man fading away wretchedly, whom you have killed and bereaved of his best. My God, my God, no, you will also kill his body. For every vein of blood in me flows for you— each nerve, each sinew of my body belongs to you, Minna; we are *of one blood;* consider that our mutual blood flows mixed in our veins; consider also the murder which you would inflict on me—and then try to forget me, desert me!

"The 21st: Just now I got a letter from you. God, how my heart beats. I haven't opened it yet!

"I have read it! Is there anything that could bind our love more firmly? See, my angel, the sweet hope that had left me entirely yesterday has returned into my heart. For you stood before my eyes again, in all your dignity and purity, I saw you could not abandon me. Reading in the Prussian Law Codes, I found to my great joy that there is no obstacle to our marriage, since we have already lived more than a year in Prussia. Only today I was thinking about a letter which I intend to write to my mother before our wedding. It should take a conciliatory tone, not to ask her consent, but peacefully to open my heart to her about you. For I want peace, in case of her refusal, to sever all bonds, and indeed justly! Then your letter arrived. I can't yet describe its impression on me, I'm still too much moved in my heart; it was like an angel of light gliding down across my gloomy despair. O my wife, where are the words to express how I worship and adore you? It's a religious, holy sentiment to think of you. Each part of your being is a God to me to whom I am fervently praying. So much for today; let me read your letter another hundred times, then I'll continue—Minna my delightful wife, goodbye.

"Your deeply touched

RICHARD"

Reading Wagner's reproaches to the "silent" Minna, one should remember that Wagner too was silent, so far as she was concerned. When he remarked forlornly on June 20 that she had not written him since May 31, he may not have stopped to think that she had not heard from him since his letter of June 4, sixteen days before, on which day he had mentioned just having heard from her. His accumulation of reproaches and urgings simply did not reach her until the need for them had passed. The obvious explanation of this extraordinary "diary" letter is of course found in the installment of June 15, which shows that Minna was on tour, and presumably out of postal reach. Yet it is hard to believe that Wagner could have found no way to get word to his silent sweetheart. His pride may have held him back. The faintheartedness, the renewed reluctance of Minna's last two letters may have filled Wagner with caution as well as alarm, for he had tried to cajole her (on June 4) into keeping up her end of the correspondence, as if fearing that, in writing his diary letter to come, he might be pouring out his heart to a stone image. If he had not heard from her again, if he had found himself really abandoned, as he plainly feared, he would probably never have sent his abject effusions.

72 (*Berlin, June 22, 1836*)

"I have a letter, I have a letter; now I can breathe again, [now at last I am] [8] happy, for you are still mine, you are not lost to me. I feel new energy, the [faintness] of my spirit is gone. You are *mine,* you *love* me, now we have to act, now [something must] happen. Forward, forward! O Minna, what a power you have over me. Every [detail of] your features and appearance is an important event to me. Accompany and strengthen me in [all that I] do. God give me power to bear everything and let [me realize] my aspirations.

"The 23d of June. Yesterday I was with Wolf, following your advice which will always be [held as] sacred by me. I spoke with him on many subjects. He said that he had recently received [a letter] from Hübsch in which he stated that you were a great success and he is very much pleased with your [standing]. He strongly defended Hübsch, saying he is dependable and fair-dealing, but often too [inclined to be] thoughtless. I told him my attitude toward him; in any case he was ready [to agree] to it, so that if he should hear about something for me—for leading actresses [*Liebhaberinnen*] are also often needed—[he would] immediately let me know. This would be good only in case Schuberth should not go to *Riga* and I thus couldn't come to Königsberg, so we could still arrange to come together in the fall. I would call for you in Königsberg, where we could perhaps marry right away. Try to find out, anyway, whether this might meet with difficulties there. In any case the best course would always be for me to be engaged and so come to K., which would be the most likely and certain solution. Isn't it so, my Minna? At Easter next year, we will quit the theater and go to Berlin. For, as I have already written to you, I hope to get 1,000 thaler anyway, since even Kugler has 800 th. Besides, I have already inquired of Cerf himself what kind of extra work is in store for me, for whatever else I do, together with extra rehearsals, etc., will be separately paid. This should bring the amount to 1,200 thal.— And now it seems that my compositions should gradually earn me something. Don't you think so? For that reason I see no need for you to remain any longer at the theater, although Schwabe argues that we may not make ends meet with 1,200 thaler. What is your opinion? In the beginning of July, Gläser is at last to leave. O God, I really must have some occupation again soon, for I have lived here under the most depressing circumstances, as you know; but I'm too proud to appeal to my family, and I'll persevere as I started. I have written to Gottschalk again and presented everything to him in an emphatic and orderly way, so don't worry too much, dear child, they can't do us any harm; they will have to wait, and if they become insolent it is only *intimidation,* for they can't force me. By the way, Schwabe claims to have just heard the news that Mad. Gottschalk has died.[9] What do

[8] The right-hand corner of the page is torn away, leaving the ends of thirteen lines missing. The words in brackets are conjectural.

[9] See postscript to 70.

you think of that? She always looked miserable and she also was a wicked person, but at the same time she made a strange impression on me. O God, my Angel, I have experienced a bitter youth, God knows, my manhood must compensate for that. And where but in your arms, and on your heart? Oh, my delight, this is my surest and sweetest hope; since you have been entirely mine I have known so much tranquillity, in spite of all troubles, that, having won you entirely, I hope to gain completely the firmness and poise I shall need to live successfully for my art with free and unhampered courage. Oh, see how you are everything, everything, to me, how I hope to achieve everything through you, my sweet life, my blissful heart!

"The 26th of June. Only today I'm writing you, for only today have I found clear vision and regained my composure. I have let three days pass without writing. During those three days I have found out what my fortune is and what I am to expect from fate. Minna, you may leave me too, for I'm an unlucky man. I have decided to leave here in a week, for after that I have nothing more to do here. Cerf is a rash, light-minded man who certainly had the best intentions in offering to me continually during my stay here Gläser's position whenever the latter is on leave. You know how conveniently this would have supported me here until I could come to Königsb. I conferred about this first with Gläser, and nothing seemed more certain. The reason it can't be done after all is not that Cerf has changed his attitude, but because the opera will have to close down completely, which he didn't surmise before. Yesterday, the Gerhardt sang for the last time, Greiner left long ago, and Holzmüller and Fischer, who were supposed to stay until the end of August, are to leave as early as the first of July, owing to a lawsuit. The matter is quite simple and obvious—I have become the superfluous one here, in spite of all my hopes. So I must leave Berlin now. The only advantage I will get, and it is of the first importance to me as an artist, is that Cerf will buy my opera from me, and in the opinion of Gläser and Genen [?] he should pay me generously in order to compensate me for my stay here. Gläser behaved quite splendidly toward me; he assured me in a most cordial manner that he will study my opera with the greatest care and attention as soon as he has the available means, and this reassured me.[10] Now I can be more content at leaving Berlin, for I know that my opera is in good hands and

[10] Needless to say, these promises of Cerf and Gläser were of the easy, verbal, cushioning variety—the kind which are forgotten as soon as uttered. Wagner's rather mild treatment of Cerf here is not in accord with the tone of ironic contempt with which he dismisses him in *My Life* at this point. He must have been very painfully aware that he had been needlessly dangled and suddenly dropped, with utter disregard—else he would not have ended his paragraph on the subject in *My Life* with this characteristic remark: "This wretched experience has been an ominous and painful memory to me through my whole life." It is plain that he is here trying to save face before Minna by minimizing his humiliation, a humiliation the more complete after his various boasting remarks to her of his "good standing" with Cerf. For the rest, he can only piece together the sorry remains of his hopes in Berlin.

the best interests of my future career are cared for. When I asked Wolf yesterday, among other things, the best way to get my opera accepted on other stages, he said that the best road to acceptance by all the stages of Germany would be a success here in Berlin. And in this he is quite right. I think my opera should be successful here. I have changed much in it and it will be well performed. Besides, all the outstanding writers here are my friends, who will do their best to give it special attention in outside papers. Laube has already written a great deal about me and the opera in a Stuttgart paper. So I think I have attained an objective after all and I consider it as a guarantee for our future, which should bring about our eventual return to South Germany. Besides, I will use my time here to induce Cerf to make a contract with me for next year, for our relations are not strained at all and we are still the best of friends. It would be best, however, if it should happen only after the opera's performance. Wolf told me that Haake [?] is about to engage, through him, a quite new and extraordinarily fine company for Breslau; and now I called his attention to *my* great interest in Breslau too, and reminded him that the conductor there is said to be no good at all, whereupon he offered at once to write to Breslau. He could recommend me with the best conscience, for he had heard high praise of me from Magdeburg. I shall send my opera book to Breslau today. Wolf is also to procure for you Corona by Salzgo [?]; Herr Hübsch would have to pay for it, he said. I am also going to write to Braunschweig, and you see, my dearest, that I have nothing to reproach myself for, because I am giving the most careful attention to my prospects. But what to do next? I pondered on that all of yesterday; I thought over everything well and decided that two ways only are open to me. Either I'll go to—*Leipzig*—or I'll go to—Königsberg. Don't be alarmed, Minna, but that's how it is. My decision is: to Leipzig I *won't* go. Now listen: I hope about 60 thaler will be left to me here.[11] With this money I must either attain my goal or sacrifice it. I'll go from here to Königsberg; everything will be decided more quickly if I am there in person. *You,* my Angel, cannot speak and act for me as well as I could myself; this is in no sense a reproach to you, dear girl. I see the reasons for it very clearly, and your last letter confirms my opinion. You would expose yourself too much and would compromise your own position. I am convinced of this. I will do it myself and this is how I have thought it out: it is certain that Schuberth is to go to *Riga* in September. Now I will talk to this man, whom I have already known, in this way: 'You expect to stay here (in K.) two more months. Then you are to return to Riga. You have your family in Riga. Doubtless you would love to see them soon. I have no work for those two months and I would prefer to spend them with my betrothed than anywhere else. But I don't want to spend this time without occupation. Please, then, leave me in your position from now on; go to *Riga* to your family, draw your salary for the next month, and make it up in this way; I'll use my own means until

[11] This must have been the sum which Laube raised for him among friends, to pay for his journey.

then.' [12] I hope, my child, that I come to an agreement with him, and I will use the 30 thaler left to me after the journey to live on for a month, trying to make ends meet without bothering anybody. The second possibility is that Schuberth will not wish to return to *Riga*; in that case I would start negotiations immediately with *Riga,* for I once knew well in Leipzig both the director and the Stadtmusikdirektor Dorn, so that we may be together there. If the worst should happen, and even that should fail, I'd use my last funds to travel back to Leipzig, and—shoot myself. What do you think, my child? Are you *for* or *against* this plan? It is the only way left to me, and it is not chatter; I am in sober earnest. Something has to happen now; this I have felt for a long time, and I have even written it to you. It is my utmost, my most serious effort; if it doesn't lead to our happiness—then there is to be no happiness for us! Besides this, I have obtained the means to dispose Herr Hübsch in my favor. First of all, Herr Wolf, who is an intimate friend of Herr Hübsch, will give me a letter which should work to my best advantage. Secondly, I have found out through him that Hübsch is in serious need of a tenor—Wolf has in view Schmitt in Leipzig, whom he deems the best and indeed the only one. But Schmitt is also negotiating with Breslau and surely would prefer Breslau. It lies quite in my power to persuade Schmitt to decide on Königsberg, and thus I could render a great service to Herr Hübsch. Tell him this. You certainly will be surprised, my Minna, at my decision and plan; at first you may be inclined to call it foolhardy and headlong. Consider it calmly, my angel, it is the only path I can see which will lead to our happiness. Now it must be either the one thing or the other, and I have reached my decision in a solemn hour of dark and serious thought. I expect news from you by *return mail* if you agree with me, and I hope *you will!* I HOPE!

"Before leaving, I am going to write to Magdeburg to my *Justizkommissar* that he may postpone my dates of payment, and if Herr Gottschalk proves to be *obstinate* I will give the matter over to him and will make the situation clear to him so that he will compel that man's indulgence. My dear wife, misfortune is now gradually giving me fortitude, and you may perhaps find me much changed. Don't imagine that I am in the least excited at this moment. I am in a serious, solemn, and determined mood. My decision is firm, and you won't be able to divert me from it by anything, unless you should write or intimate to me that my presence now would be disagreeable or bothersome to you. Only this would keep me from carrying out my resolution. I have to see you now, Minna, and together with you decide our fate. God will give us courage and strength and at last happiness, too. If not, well, then everything may break down and

---

[12] Wagner had known Schuberth as first cellist in the Magdeburg Orchestra. This remarkable solution of restoring Schuberth to his family—and Wagner incidentally to his sweetheart—was presumably dropped when Wagner arrived in Königsberg and learned how matters really stood. Schuberth, instead of pining for his "family," was more than content to linger in the favors of Henriette Grosser, the first singer of the Königsberg Theater. Schuberth was to meet his former colleague with hate and active enmity.

fate may rid you of a lover, of a betrothed who was born to bring you *misfortune,* grief, pain, and anguish. Write by *return mail,* for in a week, at the most, I shall expect your answer. See what you can tell me in this short time; probe Schuberth and Hübsch a little, and God be with you! I can go no further! Think of me as kindly as you can, my Minna, for I have a terrible suspicion about myself, that I am a disturber of the peace, a tormenter, a troublesome fellow, who will bore you in the end, etc. Indeed I am a disgusting man, a gray and black leaf in your book of life, an unlucky chap, ha, ha, and on top of it a hypochondriac; it's bad. But things will be better, better, much better! Good luck—or— See, here I am dropping again into my favorite mood. You may catch me often now in these amiable monologues. I become a melancholy, dismal fool. Ha, ha, Minna; life, luck! Have pity on me, pity, my angel; you will restore my health, then either my heart will break into a thousand fragments or luck—luck —Minna! Alas, I begin to despair of luck on this earth; love me, keep loving me, but never abuse me; have pity on an unlucky one, for after all, he is

"Your
Richard"

This letter straightens out some long-standing misconceptions. The catalogue of the Burrell Collection describes it as Wagner's "supreme effort to make her marry him"! [13]

Wagner left Berlin, on July 7, to traverse the hundred miles which had seemed such a formidable barrier between him and Minna. He found Königsberg, the musical outpost, the "Prussian Siberia," as he called it, as bleak as he had expected, Minna's lodgings as gloomy as his own prospects, and the whole relieved only by the radiant presence of Minna herself. He endured a cold and miserable winter, taking an insignificant place as a sort of reserve assistant conductor to the grudging Louis Schuberth.

Wagner was acutely aware that he was frittering away his life by tying it to the fortunes of an itinerant actress. Minna was equally aware that Wagner was unreasonably proprietary, stormily jealous, subject to depression, and down on his luck. Physical attraction, which held him so strongly, must have been felt by her too, or she would hardly have yielded to the little man who left trails of debts, talked of prospects unfulfilled, and had nothing to commend him but his own voluble insistence. The natures of the two, in the quaint language of W. Ashton Ellis, were "immiscible." They quarreled interminably. Even just before their wedding, as they were waiting for necessary papers, the entrance of the minister

[13] Unfortunately, the brief résumés of the letters, until now relied upon by writers and even quoted, are sometimes complete misapprehensions. Turning further back to what passed for years as recorded history, one rubs one's eyes at the statement in the Glasenapp-Ellis biography that Minna "induced her fiancé to leave Berlin. . . . As there were no enterprising theatrical agencies in those days, it was *she* who had acquainted him with the approaching vacancy at Königsberg—what more natural than that he should obey her call?"

interrupted a sharp spat between them. They were married, before a company exclusively of theatrical folk, on November 24, 1836. Even as he stood beside Minna, in his "new dark blue frock-coat and brass buttons," he was hardly aware of the words being spoken, and acutely conscious that their vow was a "twofold enormity" against all reason, while an "extraordinary recklessness" [*unerhörte Leichtsinn*] compelled his step. "At that moment I saw clearly, as if in a vision, my whole being divided into two cross-currents that dragged me in completely different directions: the upper one, that faced the sun, swept me on like a man in a dream, while the lower one held my nature captive in a great and incomprehensible fear."

❧ VIII ❦

THE FIRST YEAR OF MARRIAGE

(December, 1836, to September, 1837)

We have a brief but characteristic glimpse into the life of the newly married couple in a story told by Natalie to Mrs. Burrell and written down by her (98). Natalie, than a child of ten, was the third member of the Wagner household:

"One evening she [Minna] was to play Fenella in *The Dumb Girl of Portici* —somewhere in town there was a fire and the performance did not take place. They had to walk across the square. It was covered with snow and full of soldiers; a small path only had been swept clear. Minna walked ahead in a red and black checked cloak with a long collar, as long as the coat, which was the fashion at the time. Richard followed, and I tripped along in the rear. A soldier said: 'There goes a pretty girl: she could be my sweetheart.' Now Richard attacked him and Minna had to pull him away and drag him home, still raging. I said: 'Minna, your Richard is naughty, you must unmarry him' (*abtrauen*). I was a little girl and didn't yet know the word 'divorce.' At that point, he gave me some sweets to pacify me."

The first months of their married life together were anything but auspicious. Wagner was extravagant about fitting up the new household, overriding the anxiety of the practical Minna and the continual demands from his creditors in distant Magdeburg. This was her first grim experience of what it was like to make ends meet with Richard Wagner for a husband. Natalie was able to give a clear picture of her mother's predicament to Mrs. Burrell (99):

"Early in the morning (at Königsberg) she got up to attend to her household, then at eight or half past eight she hastened to the rehearsal in the theater, and returning, not before twelve or one o'clock, from the ice-cold, unheated, cavernous theater, she had to hurry to prepare the dinner. For the winter that year was very severe. Right after dinner she sat down to sew and make ready her wardrobe for the evening performance, always memorizing at the same time a new part. Often her hands trembled in her anxiety to have her wardrobe ready in time, while I did what little I could to help. She did everything tastefully and even with assiduity, and as the sewing machine was not yet known at that time every stitch had to be done by hand. She did not dare sit near the window because of Richard's mad jealousy. Then she had to bundle her repaired

73

wardrobe together and hurry for the evening performance; I always accompanied her so as to be able to help her dress and make her quick changes without delay. The dressing rooms were very far from the stage. Then she came home, quivering with cold, for the big theater was not and could not be heated; she had to appear in white satin shoes and with bare neck and arms for a summer scene, while the audience sat in the pit and galleries wrapped in thick furs and bulging muffs. Even on her way home, if she had been applauded and called back many times, Richard would make a scene in senseless jealousy, rave all night long, and treat Minna in the most brutal way. When at last he got tired of raging and fuming, Minna, crying bitterly, would sit down to memorize a new role for the next morning's rehearsal; but it often happened that she lay for hours shaken by convulsions on account of Richard's outrageous treatment . . . as she lay there, he would fall on his knees before her, crying and begging for pardon like a baby. But the peace lasted only a few hours at the most, for he would soon start again to torment Minna with his degrading rough treatment."

In short, the married status proved no guarantee to Wagner of the exclusive rights over Minna that he had hoped for. He kept discovering evidence of her "condescensions," for so he named them, past and present. How far these infidelities went will never be known: Wagner's account of them is a catalogue of suspicions. But that she persisted in them, harmless or otherwise, and was secretive about them was enough to drive him frantic. She would be angered by his outrageous abuse, and as one tempest followed another he found that the tranquillity he had prized above all in Minna was giving way to "passionate resentment." Sometimes she would retire into injured silence, and the ominous pall hanging over the Mankenstrasse apartment was hardest of all to bear. The penitent husband would humbly beg her forgiveness. Wagner had few friends at Königsberg and met no congenial artists. His attempts at composition were negligible. When in early April, Schuberth left at last, Wagner found his task as full conductor worse than his long-forced idleness. Hübsch's company was tottering, facing collapse, and its ranks had been poisoned against their new conductor by his predecessor. He threw himself into the breach and in his usual energetic way strove to save what was past saving.

Returning home on May 31 from an exhausting day of rehearsal, he found the drawers and closets bare, Minna gone, together with Natalie. "Horror-struck," Wagner learned on anxious inquiry that an ostentatious theater patron named Dietrich, who had been the subject of many disputes between him and Minna, had taken a coach that morning for Berlin. Drawing conclusions, Wagner at once took the express coach, in pursuit. But the fare exhausted what money he had, which was enough to take him only as far as Elbing. He sold two pieces of the wedding silver which he had had the foresight to bring along, and so paid for his disconsolate journey back to Königsberg. It took him two days to raise enough money to rid himself of this depressing town for once and all, and to effect an undercover departure so as to avoid restraints by his Magdeburg and Königsberg creditors. He soon assured himself that Minna had carried out her oft-repeated threat to return to her parents in Dresden, Dietrich having no more than escorted her part way. Overcome with penitence, so he tells us, he headed for Dresden, where he arrived, after a visit to Leipzig, in the second week of June. There he found Minna with her family and implored her to return to him. We now have a firsthand account of this dramatic moment. Mrs. Burrell, remembering that Natalie had accompanied her mother in her flight, wrote to Natalie in 1892, asking her where Minna had stayed in the months of July and August, 1837.[1] This was a searching question, for it was in those two months that Wagner, deserted by Minna, knew little or nothing of her whereabouts and accused her of living with Dietrich in Dresden. This question Natalie could have answered only if she had stayed with Minna; since she answered it wrongly, she probably did not. But she had much to say about June. The reader should bear in mind that the following account was written fifty-five years after the events described and that the young child could have realized their true significance only in later years, and then only from prejudiced conversation. Natalie writes from Leisnig on November 24, 1892 (89). After discussing other subjects relative to her mother, she ends the letter in this way:

"You want to know where Minna stayed in August and July, 1837. This is certainly possible. As you know, Minna had married Richard on the 24th of November, 1836, in the Church at Tropheim, the name of a district in Königsberg. There he made her life a very hell by his unjust, boundless, frantic jealousy; and often enough I cried aloud with anxiety and wept bitterly over his brutal and rough treatment of Minna, for I was still a child when I was taken to Königsberg. Poor Minna, however, after such hideous jealous scenes had crying fits and often lay unconscious. Then, when his rage was over, he was filled with remorse, and with tender words implored her pardon, but the next day the brawl started again, lasting all night. How often did she tearfully entreat Richard not to mortify her with such undignified suspicions and jealousy, and he promised in deep emotion and with tears, but never kept his word. This dreadful and shameful treatment went on and on. She told him: Richard, I can stand this no longer. If you don't change I will leave you and go back to my parents. You can see with your own eyes that I am serious, for my trunks are packed. But Richard did not change in his rude, brutal dealing with her; rather he grew worse, so that Minna really couldn't stand it any longer. So one afternoon, with thousands of bitter tears, either on the last of May or the first of June, 1837, she actually left with me, from Königsberg without stop, by express coach directly for Dresden, to our parents. They were quite upset and alarmed by Minna's sick, careworn, and tearful appearance. But in a few days Richard

[1] Mrs. Burrell has written this query on a slip of paper: "Have you letters of W. to Minna in *July* and *August*, 1837? Or any *proof* that he knew where she was?"

came hurrying after her with all speed, and early one morning—Minna was still lying in bed—he burst in, threw himself on his knees by Minna's bed, and kissed her and nearly strangled her with his embraces. I know all this happened, for I was still in my bed too, in the same room. My mother [2] who was already up, and who was highly indignant at this rough treatment of Minna, had denied him admission to the apartment, and especially to Minna's bedroom. But he had pushed her aside and had forced his way to Minna. Luckily for Richard, my father, according to his habit, was still taking his morning walk. He would have thrown Richard down the staircase in his first wrath, so terribly angry was he that Richard had treated Minna so brutally and rudely. Well, my father, on his return, was none too friendly toward Richard; he ordered him plainly and concisely to leave the house. But my good, softhearted, dear mother was sorry at last for poor Richard in his despair, his entreaties and tears, and tried to appease and to pacify my heavily irritated father. So he finally was allowed to stay and to become reconciled anew with Minna. After complete reconciliation, the two, Richard and Minna, took lodgings in Blasewitz, situated on the Elbe, for the whole summer." [3]

There is nothing surprising in Natalie's misstatements that Minna stayed at Blasewitz through the summer (through "August and July"), and that Wagner, on leaving Königsberg, "hastily and hurriedly followed her to Dresden, within a few days." What matters is her vivid description of what happened in the Planer household. Even allowing for exaggeration and possible faults of memory, it challenges the theory (based on remarks in two letters) that Wagner coldly contemplated divorce, and almost at the very moment of breaking in upon Minna, filed divorce proceedings. What we know about Wagner's actions is this: He went from Königsberg to Leipzig, where, on June 7, he wrote to his colleague Schindelmeisser asking his help in getting an engagement at Riga with Holtei, adding that the plan did not include his wife; he went to Dresden and stayed with his sister Ottilie Brockhaus and her husband, from there making his tempestuous call on the Planers. But although he wrote again to Schindelmeisser on June 12, mentioning divorce, he refrained from discussing his crisis with Ottilie and Brockhaus. Obviously too proud of inform gossip within the profession that he was chasing a fleeing wife, he had every reason to assume an air of indifference toward her. That he does not mention any inten-

[2] It should be borne in mind that Natalie still assumes that her grandparents were her parents.

[3] In 99, Natalie gives a similar untruthful answer to Mrs. Burrell: "After a final reconciliation, Minna and Richard moved to a small summer lodging in Blasewitz for several months, until Richard had to go to Riga." Whereupon she hastily switches to the perfidy of Cosima, revealing that she is aware of the charge: "It may well be that Cosima's blindly devoted friends are magnifying Minna's visit to her parents into a crime of the blackest sort."

tion of divorce in *My Life* at this point is only added evidence that he had no such real intention.

Wagner again applied his persuasive powers. He had equipped himself with a prospect for the theater at Riga in the autumn, where, he no doubt assured Minna, a secure and debtless future lay ahead for them both. He went to Berlin and closed this engagement, and on the eve of his return to Dresden (June 20) wrote her this letter:

84 *(Dresden [Postmarked Berlin, June 20, 1837])*

"My good, dear, dear Minna!

"It is a year now since I sat in a Berlin hotel in my lonely back room and thought of you in pain and longing. How much things have changed since then; you have become my wife and you flee me again! Minna, another serious word before I return to you. You became my wife when I was in the greatest distress of my life; you bore misfortune and painful privation with me, and that was splendid and beautiful of you. Now you blame me for harsh and cruel behavior toward you and unfortunately you are right, since I have to confess that under these circumstances I ought to have treated you not only not harshly, but even in a particularly tender way. You are right, my wife, and God knows that I heartily repent it. But you punished me cruelly for this, and consider whether your behavior has not offset a great part of my guilt. Stop now, my dear wife, and work no longer toward destruction of my love; consider how great this love must be that with all your exertions you have not yet succeeded in extinguishing it. If you charge me to "Be a man," I answer, "Be a wife." See, my Minna, you ask for a temporary separation; what a disastrous thought! How little do you know the true nature of an honest love, if you expect it to subsist on a separation. We must either separate completely, or not at all. Minna, do you realize what is implied in those words? This agonizing state of affairs of which your last farewell was one more proof must be brought to an end. Minna, I saw Holtei; all is arranged, we are agreed, and tomorrow we shall make a contract. Riga is described to me as the most pleasant place in the world, especially for earning money; Dorn has sent me word that he could leave to me many lessons in first-class families, since he has no more time for them. I may expect there an income of 1,000 R.S.[4] So at last I shall be in a position to offer you a pleasant and carefree life, which will be good for you after so much worry and distress. Do you still condemn me? Do you really believe me so mean as to abuse my independence by anything less than the most reasonable behavior? Minna, if so, then you never have loved me. Our recent troubles are the sort that one goes through only once in life. Minna, become my wife again, cast away all your evil thoughts, be entirely mine once more! But not halfway, my Minna! If you don't feel the power within yourself to banish all

[4] Silver rubles.

memories of the past, to grant me your fullest confidence, your heartfelt love again, and to give yourself to me again body and soul, this would be bad indeed. How then could I treat you with the tenderness and love which is due you, and which is the only thing to make a marriage happy? You have already seen how it is. Could I, or anyone, have remained undisturbed by your continued hard and repellent behavior in Dresden, to meet it only with tenderness and never with bitterness? You sought to trample down my love—you failed, but would you not have succeeded in the end? Dear wife, conquer yourself once more; become a wife again. Tear all your gloomy grief out of your heart; devote it to me again; conceal nothing from me, for this has been the source of much trouble between us. See, Minna, this is my only way to make you happy again. By continuing in your old way you make it quite impossible for me, and rather than this I would say: Better a separation forever. We must choose between them. My sweet wife, when you receive this letter, consider quietly what I have said, and ask your heart whether you can trust me and love me completely again. If you cannot, then close the door upon me on the morning that I come to see you. Then I do not wish to become your misfortune, but I will part with you for ever and always! But if God makes your heart kind and fills it once more with love for me, then rise early, put on your wedding ring again, and when I arrive let me know by your eyes alone whether we are to be joined again, and this time for ever and always. Then let there be no more words about what has happened, no reproach, no blame; we shall belong to each other again [*neu und frisch*]. Goodbye, God be with you, my dear wife—

"Your
RICHARD W.

"On Friday morning I shall be back."

Back in Dresden, Wagner prevailed upon Minna, still hesitant and unconvinced, to attempt a reconciliation. Unable to ingratiate himself with her parents, he took her to an inn on the banks of the Elbe, in near-by Blasewitz. There he tried to prove himself a reformed husband by being solicitous and conciliatory and by avoiding dangerous subjects. But Minna remained reserved and uneasy in spite of his blandishments; he was "surprised to find the situation growing worse without any apparent reason." At length she announced her intention of taking a "pleasure trip," and from this he was unable to stop her. He sadly saw her off on her mysterious journey and promised to wait quietly for her at Blasewitz. But he must have known that this was her answer to the two alternatives set forth in his letter from Berlin—to live together in full love, or to part forever.

When he heard that she had asked for a passport, he went in alarm to her parents, but they coldly refused to give him her address. He made inquiries and convinced himself that she was, or had been, living with Dietrich in Dresden. And now Wagner seems definitely to have hardened his heart to the inevitable. He found peace and sympathetic understanding with his sister Ottilie and her husband Hermann Brockhaus. Creative thoughts began to stir and expand within him, and plans for an opera on Bulwer-Lytton's *Rienzi* took rapid shape. Wagner may have told himself at last that he would put Minna out of his life. But his longing for her was not dead. In Berlin he encountered her sister Amalie, who had been for a short time with the Magdeburg troupe, and who had developed a fine alto voice.[5] The two became firm friends and wept together over his lost Minna. But later Wagner heard that Minna had dwelt with Dietrich in Hamburg as well as Dresden, that she had encouraged insulting talk about the shipwreck of their marriage. Now he remained indifferent when Amalie wrote interceding for her sister, and he authorized his friend Möller in Königsberg to take the necessary steps toward a divorce.

At the end of August he journeyed to Riga to begin his new duties. Learning that the theater had suddenly found itself without a leading singer, he persuaded Holtei to engage Amalie. And unexpectedly there arrived a letter from Minna, a "positively heartrending" letter, so Wagner describes it. She admitted her errors, presumably including the affair with Dietrich, which had left her stranded, sick, and forlorn. "She craved my forgiveness, and assured me that she had now become fully aware of her love for me." [6] Needless to say, Wagner, even after telling his friends—and himself—that he was through with Minna, melted at once. He was more than ready to forgive, to wipe out the past, and to receive her in Riga with open arms. He arranged at once that she and Amalie should make the long and difficult journey together. His first letter to her, his letter of forgiveness, is lost,[7] but two have survived, written just before the departure of the two sisters, addressed one to each. There are no thoughts of divorce here! One can only marvel at the strength and resilience of his love for Minna. He writes in a characteristic state of elation:

87 *(Riga, undated)*

"My Minna!

"I have just read your letter; both my last ones you may have already received; perhaps you are now on your journey with Amalie, which would be the best, although this letter would miss you; or perhaps you are still in Dresden; I

[5] Natalie refers to her as an *Altsängerin*, who sang Romeo, which would probably have been the contralto part in Bellini's opera. But Wagner, according to Dorn, designed the mezzo part of Adriano in *Rienzi* with her in mind.

[6] Surely Wagner would have tended to exaggerate her contrition, for the sake of his pride. Once more one regrets the loss of every letter from Minna in these years.

[7] Ernest Newman astutely remarks that the absence of this letter, and this letter only, among Wagner's love letters in the Burrell Collection, indicates that either Minna or Natalie destroyed it as evidence of Minna's infidelity, yet by the act of its destruction admitted to posterity that the guilt was there. That this is not the *only* missing letter will be seen in Wagner's, which here follows. But Mr. Newman's point still holds: the absence of so important a letter is suspicious.

hope that you are at least getting ready to start; if you are still hesitating, my wife, may God give strength to my lines to spur you quickly on your way and prevent every hour of delay. Forget everything, my poor wife, I take no heed of the past, no heed of the present, nothing—nothing any more—only *one* burning desire, one longing is still alive in my heart; I count every minute until I can hold you in my arms. How am I to wait until then? I am sick again, with no one to take care of me! Keep warm, both of you, only love me, hurry, and come soon! That long, miserable trip! Just see what silly stuff I am turning out in my emotion and joy, nice, silly stuff, and I am weeping all the time. You found me worthy of your limitless good faith, you smoothed out every wrinkle of care, which hid so much misery and pain, and do I deserve it? No: in return I can give you limitless faithfulness, nothing more. See what you can do with it! But to do this you must come here—how often have I had to say this! You are not listening to me, you are supposing that I haven't given much thought to how we can live here? When I rented my lodgings (for a year) I first took note of both large rooms, the kitchen so that you may sometimes prepare for me something in the evening, a Bratwurst or a bit of pancake, or a cheesecake, and now I have rented an apartment for Amalie right by the staircase of our home. So she will be close by if we ever want to stuff ourselves [*schlampampen*]. But a year from now we'll be sure to rent a large apartment where we may all squat [*hocken*] together, and if Amalie tries any nonsense she'll catch it, won't she? So, wrap her up well so that she doesn't leave her voice somewhere on the road, for here you don't get anything forwarded; that's also why you must bring our things with you from Königsberg. So, obey all my instructions, even if you can't stand old Möller.[8] This is the only way to get our things here. You can also give a piece of your mind to old Karl. Have the carriage come right to the door here on the broad Schmiede Strasse at the house of the wine dealer, Zau (don't begin to think that I tipple!!). There you inquire after the bad and incompetent *Kapellmeister*. Bring along the beds too, for they are devilishly expensive here. We will cut them apart; yes, that's what we'll do. What else shall I write about—my Minna, I'd better stop, for nothing comes out but nonsense. I am quite crazy; Minna's coming back, Minna's coming back! And what a wonderful letter she wrote to me! How true, frank, just, and, my God, how unhappy! You poor, poor Minna—don't cry, good Gnaugust;[9] I also bought two black poodles with white muzzles, since we have no children yet, but when children come the two black poodles must leave, mustn't they? For wouldn't that make too many poodles? I suppose you will have enough money

---

[8] Abraham Möller, an elderly devotee of the theater, had befriended Wagner and Minna from the first at Königsberg, and played handy man in such matters as contracts, marriage technicalities, or passports. The fact that he had been acting as informer to Wagner on Minna's recent conduct wo..ld account for her dislike of him at this time.

[9] The nickname may be a contraction of "Gnau-August," which might imply a habitual complainer.

for the trip? I will call the two black poodles *Dreck* and *Speck*, don't you agree?
Wrap yourselves up warmly. And now, in heaven's name, let me stop, I can't
sit still on the sofa any longer; I must do a bit of dancing around the room.

"My God, come, come! Pay good tips, or I shall go crazy. Forgive all this
nonsense, it's your fault, your fault, just wait till I—no, no, come and don't
wait, come, come, my dear own wife, to your

Richard W. W. W. W. W. W.[10]

"Don't worry about *my* debts—we'll come to an understanding with them—
how, you will learn!

"A day later: The mail doesn't leave until today, so I am adding a few
words. Excuse my unworthy manner of answering your letter yesterday, your
letter which I read so many times, which bears so much pain. My Minna, what
experiences we went through, what trials of our love! Think of the last three
years of our life, and what obstacles we met, and see, now our love is revived
again, new and youthful. Oh, Love is of godlike descent after all! Come to me,
my wife, let me heal your wounds; let this be the task of my love. My heart is
so full of you, my poor angel, I bear you so firmly and warmly in my bosom
so *you* must come into my arms too, let us each protect and care for the other,
and we shall never die, we shall live united—forever. O Minna, a man capable
of such a love as mine could never be a bad man. Don't listen to strange people
any longer. See, my child, you have experienced many things and I understood
every part of your letter; you ask for forgiveness and ask me to forget completely. So you see, you look upon me as a good man. Oh, how honored I feel
by this confidence, how I thank you for it! I can thank you only for your love,
your confidence; let's each forgive the other, as we both deserve. Ah, my Minna,
I could never be unfaithful to you!

"Now, let us see how much we can make up for the happiness we have
missed. We should have learned by now that we need it. Care well for Amalie,
she has been our Angel. If we are happy again, we owe it to her alone. All
honor to her, she has finely fulfilled her pledge. God bless you both and grant
you a good journey. Farewell, my dear, dear wife, soon in the faithful arms
of your

Richard"

85 (*Riga, September 9–21, 1837*)

"My good Amalie,

"In great haste I add a few lines to the money; they shall be about your
journey. If Minna joins you, as I wish and hope, be good enough to advance
100 rubles for her traveling expenses. I hope you will carry out the plan in my
last letter for your journey through Königsberg. Therefore I will write today
to Herr Möller in Königsberg, who may go as far as Frauenberg to meet you,

[10] W, pronounced *Weh*, would also mean "Woe."—Tr.

deliver our things to Minna, and accompany you two stations beyond Königsberg. This is the safest and best way for Minna to get her things, since there is no way of sending them. But in order to be sure to meet, it's essential that you leave on time. Probably you will get this letter on a Friday or Saturday, the 1st or 2nd of October. On the following Tuesday the mail coach leaves Dresden, and I rely on you to leave on this day and to continue by the next coach from Berlin, to book only as far as Frauenberg so that you may go on from there with Herr Möller.

"Now, children, keep yourselves nice and warm, make no blunders, don't run away with the money, arrive nicely on time; have courage, and everything will turn out all right.

"In a great hurry your
RICHARD W.

"In case Minna should have any trouble about her passport, I enclose some more lines giving my permission.

"Madame Günther writes here some additional nonsense which she asked me to enclose. Give it as much attention as you wish. I should hope that lodgings, etc., are my affair—

"10th of Sept. I had to open the letter again because it was overweight—so I'll take out the letter of Madame Günther and briefly render the short meaning of her long discourse: You may bring her two dozen ——— [?] of very pretty make-up, 18 els of black lace as they wear it around mantillas, 12 els of white lace one finger wide, and a pair of pretty, modern gold earrings and half a dozen short gloves. You will be reimbursed right away, of course. I leave it to you to do what you like about all this nonsense. Pretend you have her letter— you may still see it when you get here.

"Now one more thing, dear children, if you travel together, take the route through Tilsit; the postmaster there is ——— [?], Holtei's friend, and he will write to the postmaster to provide you with a driver and a good, big carriage which will bring you here easily in one journey, and also take care of the many trunks Minna will get from Möller; for by the express coach you would not have a vehicle of your own, and Russian coaches have the most abominable wooden seats in existence. Besides, the postmaster will receive you in his home until your luggage has been inspected, you could also stay overnight in his house for rest and sleep. This will do you good. So follow all my directions! God keep you—

"Your
RICHARD"

How Wagner, pressed by a fresh pack of creditors, made his spectacular flight from Riga in 1839, made a perilous sea voyage to London, and then reached Paris, penniless and unknown, is circumstantially related in *My Life*. But Natalie wrote her own version of it for Mrs. Burrell (95 b). Natalie tells how

Minna agreed with Wagner on his plan to escape from Riga and go by sailboat to London, bravely committing herself to a wild and precarious adventure, and how she used her resourcefulness to raise the necessary funds. "Resolute and practical as always, Minna decided to star a few more times in Riga, where she, the talented, amiable artist, was rewarded by enormous, unmistakable, and most flattering applause. Nor did the expected good receipts fail to come. After this she sold her large, beautiful, and complete theater wardrobe and anything else she could dispense with in order not to face with quite empty hands the insecurity of their future, at least at the beginning."

Natalie's description of Wagner's secret flight from Mitau, in order to escape his Riga creditors, agrees in the main with the story as Wagner has related it, and so does the dash of Wagner and Minna across the Russian border, almost under the eyes of the sentinels and at the risk of being shot in the back.

"Wagner evidently was not fully aware of the danger of such a flight. But Frau Minna, against whom there was no charge and who therefore might have crossed the Russian border freely, unhindered, and in safety, had learned at the very last moment through the fiancé of her sister Amalie, a higher Russian officer, about the great danger threatening Wagner."

But when Natalie relates the incident of the overturned carriage en route to the seaport, there is a significant piece of information, upon which Wagner is conveniently unspecific, and which, true or not, Natalie must certainly have heard from Minna's lips:

"Before they attained their goal, they met with a bad accident on the next morning, when the driver, unacquainted with the road and in complete darkness, got into a narrow farmyard and upset the carriage turning it around. The old friend [Natalie, apparently not remembering Möller's name, always calls him this] was injured, Wagner was thrown into a manure heap, but Minna was caught beneath the vehicle in such a way that she, severely injured, was deprived of an incipient motherhood, the greatest happiness of a young wife."

All that Wagner has to say on this point is: "The clumsy conveyance upset in a farmyard, and Minna was so severely injured in the accident by an internal shock, that I had to drag her—with the greatest difficulty—as she was quite helpless—to a farmhouse."

But Natalie tells it differently:

"After the carriage had been righted again with the help of some farm hands and Minna had been lifted in, a goodhearted farmer, on being well tipped, agreed to take her with a lantern to the nearest *Krug,* as the inns are called there. Luckily the distance was not too far for both men to walk along beside them. When they arrived there, Richard was not permitted to stay even long enough to wash and change his clothes. For the perfume adhering to him was too bad, although this miserable *Krug* was itself as dirty as anything could be. It was only by promising to leave them all his discarded garments that he was allowed to stay. The next day they had to rest on account of Minna's very sick condition, but then they had to continue so as to reach the boat in time. Arrived there in the evening, they had to take hiding in a rather remote inn, and to leave it shortly after midnight. The whole long way to the boat they had to creep on the ground, through high wet grass, so that none of the watching beach guards would notice them. Arrived at the boat at last, they were quickly concealed by the captain, who had waited for them. They were hidden in the very lowest hold, behind barrels, crates, and bales of goods, so as not to be found when the ship was inspected. In this terrible position they had to remain for many agonizing hours, until they reached the open sea and the captain could free them."

There is a small discrepancy. The Newfoundland dog, "Robber" (the English word), who accompanied them and so made the whole venture thoroughly impractical, is named by Wagner as "originally the property of a Riga merchant," and adopted by the Wagners out of sheer affection. Natalie describes Robber as the gift of the Russian officer von Meck, soon to become the husband of Minna's sister Amalie.

Of the voyage itself, she has nothing new to tell except that the storm which washed the figurehead from its place in the bow of the *Thetis* also "swept a trunk of Minna's containing silver as well as clothing, from the deck into the sea."

⤝ IX ⤜

THE PARIS ORDEAL

(1839–1842)

"At first in Paris they called him 'Monsieur Vagner,' to rhyme with *gagner*."

—Natalie to Mrs. Burrell (106)

Wagner's vivid picture in *My Life* of his first sojourn in Paris is here amplified by notes to his young artist friend Ernst Benedikt Kietz and by various scraps of memoranda. These documents entirely support Wagner's tale of the near starvation, the cold and raggedness and humiliation he and Minna experienced in that time. He never felt at home in Paris. He never readily accepted the language of the French, their ways, or their ideas of what music ought to be. The Parisians no doubt looked upon him as an outlandish object; in their turn the Wagners associated almost exclusively with Germans,[1] and most of their friends seem to have found it about as hard as they did to earn a living in a strange country. Wagner's pride may have taken comfort in the fact that Kietz was better off only in that he had no wife to support, and never learned to earn when, in later years, Wagner's fortunes rose. At any rate, Wagner liked to patronize Kietz, and Minna to mother him, then and later. His cheering presence was always welcome in the Wagner lodgings, especially when, with other friends, they were able to find a loaf or a bottle to share.

Wagner describes Kietz in *My Life*:

"He was an exceptionally kind-hearted and unaffected young man, whose talent for portrait painting (in a sort of a colored pastel style) had made him such a favorite in his own town that he had been induced by his financial successes to come to Paris for a time to finish his art studies. He had now been working in Delaroche's studio for about a year. He had a curious and almost childlike disposition, and his lack of all serious education, combined with a certain weakness of character, had made him choose a career in which he was destined, in spite of all his talent, to fail hopelessly. I had every opportunity of recognizing this, as I saw a great deal of him. At the time, however, the simple-

---

[1] Or other émigrés who were anything but French. Wagner mentions as friends in his letters, in addition to Anders, Lehrs, Heine, and Pecht: Monzen, Glöckner, Rochow, Heinze, Jebens, Merzberg, Maack, Vieweg, Venedei, Januskewits ("only the devil knows how it is spelled," adds Wagner about this last).

85

hearted devotion and kindness of this young man were very welcome both to myself and to my wife, who often felt lonely, and his friendship was a real source of help in our darkest hours of adversity. He became almost a member of the family, and joined our home circle every night, providing a strange contrast to the nervous old Anders and the grave-faced Lehrs. His good nature and his quaint remarks soon made him indispensable to us; he amused us tremendously with his French, into which he would launch with the greatest confidence, although he could not put together two consecutive sentences properly, in spite of having lived in Paris for twenty years. With Delaroche he studied oil-painting, and had obviously considerable talent in this direction, although it was the very rock on which he stranded. The mixing of the colors on his palette, and especially the cleaning of his brushes, took up so much of his time that he rarely came to the actual painting. As the days were very short in midwinter, he never had time to do any work after he had finished washing his palette and brushes, and, so far as I can remember, he never completed a single portrait. Strangers to whom he had been introduced, and who had given him orders to paint their portraits, were obliged to leave Paris without seeing them half done, and at last he even complained because some of his sitters died before their portraits were completed. His landlord, to whom he was always in debt for rent, was the only creature who succeeded in getting a portrait of his ugly person from the painter, and, so far as I know, this is the only finished portrait in existence by Kietz. On the other hand, he was very clever at making little sketches of any subject suggested by our conversation during the evening, and in these he displayed both originality and delicacy of execution. During the winter of that year he completed a good pencil portrait of me, which he touched up two years afterwards when he knew me more intimately, finishing it off as it now stands. It pleased him to sketch me in the attitude I often assumed during our evening chats when I was in a cheerful mood. No evening ever passed during which I did not succeed in shaking off the depression caused by my vain endeavors, and by the many worries I had gone through during the day, and in regaining my natural cheerfulness." [2]

The letters to Kietz were acquired by Mrs. Burrell in 1891 from Gustav Kietz, surviving brother of Ernst, who guaranteed that they were a "complete collection" and had "never . . . been in any other hands" (9). The Paris letters show the prodigious joint ingenuity of the two men in the problem of negotiating bills without means:

100 A *(In Paris, to E. B. Kietz, 29 Quai des Augustins, Paris, June 3*
[Kietz has added "1840"])

"In case we shouldn't meet today, good Kietz, two words in writing! I received the news, and I am sure now that I won't get any money before four-
[2] P. 218.

teen days—three weeks; why, I shall tell you. Now, pray, don't deny a favor to a harassed friend, and—when you get your money—for heaven's sake let your tailor wait two or three weeks more and help me instead; by that time you will get it back. God bless you. In great anxiety, your

RICHARD WAGNER"

The next three notes Wagner must have written under the impending threat of the debtors prison, to which he was sent a few days later, presumably October 28.[3] (To the first of these notes Kietz has added the year, 1840, no doubt in vivid memory of what it referred to; the other two notes are postmarked.)

101 *(Paris, October 19, 1840)*

"It's getting warm at the Wagner's! [*Bei Wagner's wird's warm!*]
"3 sous"

100 B *(Paris, October 23, 1840)*

"If you will favor us with a call today, try to persuade your uncle[4] to come along. I don't know his address, otherwise I'd take the liberty of writing to him.
"*Santo Spirito Cavaliere*[5]
"Friday morning, 7:30.
"P.S. Please ask Pecht in our name too to visit us tonight, for we're really going to have a good time!

R. W."

100 C *(Paris, October 25, 1840)*

"DEAR KIETZ!
"Be sure to come tonight, it is important.

WAGNER"

An item in this Collection (112) is a draft, in Wagner's hand, of a letter to his boyhood friend Theodor Apel, to be copied by Minna and sent as her own. It is valuable for the light it throws upon one of the few events in Wagner's life which remain enveloped in mystery. This is his imprisonment for debt in October and November, 1840. Wagner makes no mention of a debtors prison in his autobiography, or in any letter save this one. Natalie, who shared the poverty of the Wagners in Paris, has only this to say in her talks

---

[3] See 112 (p. 88).
[4] Kietz's uncle Edward Fechner was drawn upon as far as possible by both Kietz and Wagner.
[5] Quotation from *Rienzi*, Act III, upon which Wagner was then working.

with Mrs. Burrell: "I know too much about the misery of this time—it is an agony to think of it." (106) [6] Unless the whole story was an elaborate hoax (and Wagner was never that kind of liar), we can only infer that the three who underwent the searing humiliation of this experience wanted nothing more than to forget it. The ring of genuine despair in Wagner's words is just as unmistakable in a second letter from Minna, this one the unprompted plea of one who did not take easily to begging. Evidence of Wagner's imprisonment is his statement in the copied draft that a projected performance of his newly completed *Rienzi* Overture had been canceled for want of its composer's presence. There is also his plain hint to Laube in a letter of December 3 [7] that he is in danger of a second imprisonment.

Wagner's desperate need in the autumn of 1840 was real enough. He had turned repeatedly to every possible source for loans, until his sister Cäcilie and her newly acquired husband Eduard Avenarius stated quite flatly that they could do no more. He had left nothing untried and had undertaken the most miserable kind of hack jobs for Schlesinger. When one of his creditors descended upon him, he was quite helpless.

He wrote to Apel on September 20. Receiving no answer, he decided to make a fresh approach as if from Minna herself, in behalf of her imprisoned husband.

The beginning of the letter is missing in Wagner's draft. But the whole letter as received by Apel has been published by his heirs. It is as follows:

(Paris, October 28, 1840)

"Esteemed Herr Apel:

"I hope you will not be surprised at receiving a letter from me, and a letter such as this. God knows that I would have preferred to begin with words of sympathy for your own misfortune [8] instead of disturbing you with a plea on my own behalf. But my misfortune is that I cannot control my own fate, and I am forced either to turn to you or give way to despair. I shall state the purpose of my letter in a few words.

"This morning Richard had to leave me and go to a debtors' prison [*Schuldgefängnis*]. I am still so terribly agitated that my senses are in a whirl. The one thing that has enabled me to calm my thoughts a little is a letter from Herr Laube [9] which has just arrived, and which I have opened in Richard's absence.

[6] Mrs. Burrell's notation continues: "Natalie slept on the sofa in the salon. The salon could not be warmed in winter—large fireplace that took too much wood, so Richard had to put his writing table into the bedroom, where they all huddled together during the day to keep warm."

[7] *Richard Wagner an Freunde und Zeitgenossen,* p. 20.

[8] Theodor Apel had been stricken with blindness.

[9] Apel had referred Wagner's first appeal to Laube.

"On the one hand it takes away all hope of assistance, in our distress, but on the other it gives me strength to take my ultimate step—a desperate one, I admit."

The surviving portion of Wagner's draft begins at this point (112).

"But along with it Herr Laube says that you expressed yourself as friendly and sympathetic; if you could know, worthy Herr Apel, how much we are inured to the unfriendliness and indifference of those whom we are compelled to approach for help, you would understand how this report revived my hopes to some extent. What would there be left for poor me, if I couldn't even attach my hopes to an expression of sympathy. In this you may find what gives me courage to approach you. My poor husband, who as a foreigner doesn't even enjoy the advantages open to a native under such circumstances, is in the hands of a German residing here, who behaves toward him with such stubbornness that I can't count on any softening or release from him.[10] I am quite bewildered at what to do next. Even if I myself had the means to get away from Paris, I would under no circumstances leave Richard in such a position; for I know he didn't get into it by recklessness, but by following the noblest and most natural striving of an artist, as would have happened to anyone else without special help. It was only after much opposition that I had agreed with his plan to go to Paris; but the more closely I understand his projects here, the more I realize that if he perishes without reaching his goal, which would otherwise be possible, it will be due solely to the lack of support. He has by now really got so far that he soon may expect the fruits of his efforts, and it is only the sacrifices he has made until now which stand in his way. He had work and was earning almost enough so that with care I could myself manage our small household; but what has happened today brings it all to nothing. And now it has come to the point where a work of his was to be performed at a big concert. In two weeks there was to be performed the overture of his *Rienzi,* which he has just finished and of which there was every prospect of a great success. But without his personal presence at the rehearsal this will not be possible. Is this not enough to throw us into despair? What can I do? Poor and alone, of what use is it for me to weep? Could this really be the end for us? Can it be that you, who for so long have held friendship for Richard in your heart, would allow him to be lost to us because a greater sacrifice than usual is required? God forgive me, I can't bring myself to believe that this is to be the end for us. It is on account of my indescribable predicament, if I am overstepping the borders of propriety in making

[10] It has been conjectured, on the strength of an angry letter from Wagner to Fechner, that Kietz's uncle was none other than the relentless creditor. Wagner's letter to Kietz of May 12, 1842 (119), in which he sends Fechner "to the devil," would bear this out. But his letter to Kietz of January 5, 1843 (128), definitely exonerates Fechner. There Wagner pays him off, forgives him, and declares that after all there has been nothing worse between them than "silly trifles."

a plea to you which is prompted by despair. To my horror I learned some time ago how much Richard already owes you. You used to get money for him by your credit; but what was his situation then compared to ours now? Wouldn't this sacrifice be much more adequate now, since there is a sure prospect of paying off such a debt in the course of one, or at the most two years? Believe me, I usually fail to share Richard's exalted hopes, but now I know from what his own acquaintances say that he is within a single step of attaining his goal. My God, what more can I say? I haven't the composure to express clearly to you all that I could say, but I will make up for it later—all I can say is: Help! Help! If you can make this great sacrifice for Richard, and make it as quickly as possible, God will reward you, if Richard's grateful heart and my prayers should be not enough; I can add nothing more; Heaven grant that my prayers be heard and our thanks shall be boundless. Hearty wishes for your welfare from your

FAITHFUL FRIEND . . ."

Wagner's draft of this letter, in the Collection, may now be compared with Minna's copy, as received and published. The catalogue states that "whole passages from this draft occur in the letter." Let us examine the manuscript draft.

It is written in ink, in Wagner's cramped hand on both sides of three small scraps of paper (2½ by 5 inches in size). The scraps are numbered II, III, IIII, and the opening of the letter, which was evidently on a scrap numbered I, is missing. The text in the three surviving bits of paper is identical with the text as published. If the absence of scrap No. I means anything, it means that either Minna or Natalie found there, and there only, a reference to a debtors prison, and destroyed it accordingly. It is another case where the would-be destroyer of evidence has so proved what she was trying to hide. That Wagner wrote his draft on these awkward bits of paper might mean that he did it in prison on his first day there, using what paper he could find, and somehow conveyed it to Minna. (The authorities would not have prevented the attempt of a prisoner to discharge his debt.)

According to Natalie, who evidently talked to Mrs. Burrell about her memories of Paris while that lady made a brief of her remarks (96), the relations between the families Wagner and Avenarius were more than strained at this time. Natalie, according to her own statement, joined Minna at their lodgings in the rue du Helder in November, 1840, which would have been just at the time of Wagner's imprisonment. Natalie found that the two families were then not on speaking terms. Cäcilie had evidently met the Wagners at some public demonstration on the Champs Elysées. His sister had protested to Minna that Richard must stop borrowing money from her husband. Whereupon

Richard dragged her away with the furious remark that they would "have nothing more to do with such relatives." Mrs. Burrell also writes: "Richard met Avenarius' errand boy in the street and he said 'Monsieur Wagner, a little son has arrived at the Avenarius house.' Richard and Minna sent their congratulations in the New Year of 1841, Natalie met Cäcilie for the first time then, she never reciprocated the visit."

Wagner, insensitive about borrowing, was always piqued at persistent refusals. His principal memory of Cäcilie and her husband at this period, as he wrote his autobiography, was that they came to pay a visit at the very moment when Wagner, having come into a windfall, had proudly heaped a mound of silver pieces on the table. The visitors were plainly astonished at this affluence, much to Wagner's inward gratification. But Wagner soon forgave Cäcilie and her husband and wrote of them from Dresden in affectionate and grateful memory of what they had done (119, *et seq.*). He knew well enough that as a hopeful composer who had achieved a single dubious operatic performance (*Das Liebesverbot*) years before, he could not count on perennial faith in his future from friends and relatives. They could not have known, nor did he know, that the turn in his fortunes was about to come, that the *Rienzi* he was then completing would shortly be accepted in Dresden.

Natalie draws this picture of Minna in the worst stage of their adversity (107): "She well knew how to make the small household cozily neat and clean, by meticulous order and tidiness. . . . Calmly and quietly she worked like a maidservant, sweeping, washing, cooking, cleaning his suits and shoes, since they had no money to leave those chores to hired people. She always looked rosy, fresh, neat, and exceedingly clean, so that nobody would guess that she did all his menial work. How she enjoyed buying a few cigars or a screw of snuff for her beloved Richard when marketing at a distance, since it was cheaper to buy the needed victuals there, enabling her to save money and so surprise and please him. Richard always welcomed this love offering like a child, and couldn't thank Minna enough with kisses for what she had done."

The following domestic incident is described by Natalie (107 C) as having happened one "dull autumn day," which would have been in 1841, when Wagner was cultivating a beard, "much to Minna's annoyance," says Natalie. After a day's work on a commission for Schlesinger, Wagner lifted his chair, which Minna had placed by the window for him, to put it back where it belonged. But he stumbled against a mirror and almost broke it, bringing a sharp remonstrance from his wife. He answered in kind and stamped out of the house. But when he returned, Kietz, Lehrs, and Anders had joined him, and the three laughed at the incident. The following morning Wagner rose quietly, wrote the following little poem, and put it on Minna's bed as a peace offering (107 A):

"Verzeihung, liebes Mienel,
Ich flöhe [11] dich darum,
Du bist mein gutes Bienel,
Nun aber nicht mehr brumm!
Du weisst jedoch auch selber,
Der Stuhl ging nicht hinein;
Ich wurde immer gelber
Und fluchte wie ein Schwein.
Bist du noch länger böse
So geb ich mir den Tod;
Dann ess' ich nicht mehr Klösse
Dann kau' ich Blei und Schrot!
Verzeihung, liebes Mienel
    "—Vom Anfang, da capo."

(Forgive me, dear Mienel
I implore you—
You are my good little bee,
But please, no more buzzing!
You know how it was, but still—
The chair was balky.
I turned yellow
And cursed like a swine.
If you are still cross
I'll kill myself.
Then I'll eat no more dumplings,
But chew lead bullets!
Forgive me, dear Mienel)
    —From the beginning, da capo.)

Beneath this, Wagner sketched himself with a beard. And Kietz contributed a sketch of a frantic mother holding a baby (Wagner) who is tearing out its own hair.

104 A *(January, 1841)* [12]

"Listen, Kietz: if you get these lines in time, be sure not to forget to come to see me today *in any event,* and as soon as possible. It's important and concerns
"Your
RICHARD WAGNER
"Twelve o'clock"

104 B [*March 28, 1841*]

"DEAREST KIETZ!

"Your news, which I received only last night, took me by surprise; it came too quickly, my wife hadn't bought anything yet, and even if I had had money Minna would have had no time for shopping, or rather for getting things tidied up. But if I had had 8 francs to spare yesterday, I would have given them to Glöckner anyhow. But Lehrs thinks he'll get me a chance again, then it won't fail,
"Your
RICHARD WAGNER"

104 C *(April 5, 1841)*

"Kind regards to his amiable charge—*Benedictum* Kietz—from Reissiger
R. WAGNER"

104 D *(April 7, 1841)*

"If you want to learn what I have written about Vieuxtemps, come to see me today. Tomorrow morning the essay is to be sent off.[13]

"Wednesday."   R. W.

On April 29, 1841, Wagner moved to Meudon, near Paris, and sent Kietz directions as to how he could be reached:

104 E *(Bellevue, May 1, 1841)*

"DEAR KIETZCHEN!

"If you come to see me, you must not take the railway ticket to Meudon but to Bellevue; I was mistaken in my first directions. There are, as I have now learned, two stations, Bellevue and Meudon, at the same price, but the one at

[12] Letters C, E, G, H, I of 104 are postmarked; A, B, D, F are dated by Kietz.
[13] ". . . Vieuxtemps, an old school fellow of Kietz. We had the great pleasure of hearing the young virtuoso, who was then greatly fêted in Paris, play to us charmingly for a whole evening—a performance which lent my little 'salon' an unusual touch of fashion. Kietz rewarded him for his kindness by carrying him on his shoulders to his hotel close by."—*My Life.*

Bellevue is quite near us. Goodbye, don't despond, come on Sunday and tell Lehrs what I have just told you in this letter.

"Your
RICHARD WAGNER"

104 F *(Meudon, July 5, 1841)*

"GOOD KIETZ!

"Berlioz didn't get me a ticket, so I'm not staying in town and won't sleep at your house. I have put my case in the hands of God and Meyerbeer. Here are 50 fr. for the time being. I was able to get hold of them. How? You'll find out soon enough. God be with you. Don't do too much pederasty!

"Your
RICHARD WAGNER"

104 G *(Meudon, July 8, 1841)*

"His Excellency Herr Hofmarschall von Lüttichau has officially communicated to me the definite acceptance of my opera *Rienzi* for the Court Theater in Dresden.[14]

"Recommended for sympathy
RICHARD WAGNER"

111 *(Autograph poem, September 5, 1841, to Minna on her birthday)*

Under the heading "Hurrah for September 5, 1841!!" Wagner wishes Minna many happy returns of her birthday, and tells her the following story in verse:

The month of September had arrived, and again Wagner was poor as a church mouse. Yet this would not have made him desperate if only *The Flying Dutchman* [15] were getting along. However, Minna's birthday, the 5th of September, was approaching. On this day, when all the friends would gather in order to praise her, he did not want to be without money, but no money could be found in his pockets. What use was the "flying" Dutchman at this moment? He would prefer a "creeping" lobster or something else he could give to Minna. So he was furious, cursing Europe and the World which had left him without money. But suddenly there was a scent of lilac. A cloud came down from which a servant emerged asking for Richard Wagner's house. Then God himself shook hands with Wagner. God said he certainly had caused Wagner a lot of trouble; this time, however, he wanted to help him; he was so much pleased with Wagner's wife, that there should be no worrying next Sunday; Wagner could look forward with pleasure to his wife's birthday. He, God, was the man to arrange this. Then God reentered his cloudy chariot and departed. Wagner cried: "That

---

[14] It was in June that the committee of the Hoftheater in Dresden had decided to produce *Rienzi*.

[15] Wagner was just composing *The Flying Dutchman*.

is good news for me. For the time being may God reward you." [16] Just after God had left, Wagner found at his feet some charming, beautiful things for Minna.

Wagner concludes:

"These things are for you—take them and enjoy them! God remembered you: In His opinion, you are a good wife—therefore give up worrying! One who has such a good reputation with God can expect many good things in the future, as a reward for faithfulness and confidence. Just keep *this confidence*— Everything will be all right!

RICHARD"

104 H (October 13, 1841)

<table>
<tr>
<td>

"GOOD KIETZ!
BEST ERNEST!
BELOVED BENEDIKT!
DEAR FRIEND!
DEAREST BROTHER!
   etc.
     etc.
       etc.

</td>
<td>

"We got a bottle of rum as a present; next Sunday we will prepare some punch. You will come, I hope?

</td>
</tr>
</table>

"Take once more the trusted sword and slash through the knot of my misfortune! The enclosed letters are of great importance to me, as you may well imagine; they have to be dispatched by the next mail. But I can't manage the postage these days. Reach into your magic pocket and lay it out; do me this one more favor! At the end of the month will come the explanation and money too, for you; you may rely on it, never worry! You will do what I ask; I count on you.

"Besides—

"An errand for me—

"I have locked myself up in a country house to put the last touches on the *Holländer*; the town won't see me again until he *flies*. Meanwhile, there is an urgent business for you. Look at this pawn ticket. On the 15th of last month the date for redemption or renewal actually expired. But when I went to see about it, they granted me without any trouble the four additional weeks I asked. So, until the 15th of this month the pawn is safe; and I know now that they certainly will grant me another postponement too, until the end of this month or the beginning of next. I know it from this last time. All you'll need to do is talk to them. Now, since you have a real passion for spouting French eloquence, do me the favor of going to the address on the ticket, rue Saint-Honoré, and talking to the people or, rather, asking what is the very furthest extension they will give? Do you understand? If you are afraid of getting stuck with your eloquence, then ask Lehrs, who won't be able to talk anyway on account of

---

[16] *Nimm Gottes Lohn*, meaning that the person himself cannot pay back the gift.

hoarseness; but the two of you together should get somewhere. Be kind enough to notify me quickly about everything. Do you hear? The country air is gorgeous, fresh and brisk. Our teeth are chattering. If I had 100 fr. to pay Jadin, I would move to town right away; you know where I live: 14 rue Jacob. The whole story next time we meet. When will that be? Do you have trouble moving out? I hope you haven't already left? etc., etc., etc. Hearty greetings from me and Minna. God preserve you and your hair.[17]

"Your

RICHARD WAGNER

"Meudon, October 13, 1841"

104 I *(October 19, 1841)*

"MY GOOD KIETZ!

"I believe Tichatschek [18] must be in Paris now; so it seems to me. Be good enough to find out! Inquire from Anders among others at Schlesinger's. If you discover him, I hardly need tell you how important it is to me to be notified at once. On Sunday I hope to see you?

"Your

RICHARD W."

On April 7, 1842, the Wagners turned their backs to Paris and set forth for Dresden and the promised *Rienzi* production. "Our emotion at parting from our dear friends," so Wagner writes,[19] "was great, almost overwhelming . . . Kietz . . . touched our hearts once more by his countless and almost childlike good-nature. Fancying, for instance, that I might not have enough money for the journey, he forced me, in spite of all resistance, to accept another five-franc piece, which was about all that remained of his own fortune at the moment; he also stuffed a packet of good French snuff for me into the pocket of the coach, in which we at last rumbled through the boulevards into the barriers, which we passed but were unable to see this time, because our eyes were blinded with tears."

[17] Wagner liked to joke about his friend's tendency toward baldness.

[18] Wagner writes in *My Life* (p. 230) that his first choice for *Rienzi* was Dresden "because I knew that there I should have in Tichatschek the most suitable tenor for the leading part."

[19] *My Life*, p. 264.

❧ X ❦

RIENZI PROBLEMS

At the lowest ebb of his misfortunes in Paris, Wagner completed *Rienzi*—he may even have put the last touches on his score while he was imprisoned for debt in November, 1840. He turned his hopes toward Dresden and sent the score, together with a letter to the King of Saxony, on December 1. He followed this three days later with a letter to Baron von Lüttichau, intendant of the Dresden Hoftheater. Official action and even official communications being deliberate in such matters, it was not until June, 1841, that he was notified of the acceptance of *Rienzi*. But Wagner had not been simply sitting in the darkness of doubt for seven months. He had made unofficial inquiries and kept himself and his opera before the favorable attention of every influential acquaintance at the Dresden Opera. Ferdinand Heine, the costume designer at the Hoftheater, had been an actor at Leipzig, a colleague of Ludwig Geyer, and a friend of the Wagner family in Wagner's youth. Wilhelm Fischer, the stage manager and choral director of Dresden, he had also known in a similar capacity at Leipzig. "Fischer," writes Wagner, "sent me reliable and reassuring reports as to the state of my affairs." Hofrat Winkler, another old family friend of the Wagners, was secretary to the theater, and so was in an even better position to keep him posted. Winkler was also editor of the Dresden *Abendzeitung,* and Wagner sent him articles for his paper, expecting no fee, so he tells us, but personal efforts in behalf of *Rienzi*. There was the conductor, Karl Gottlieb Reissiger, who had to be treated carefully, for he was a rival composer, with an opera of his own. Wagner approached Tichatschek, the principal *Heldentenor* at Dresden, whose voice was ideal for the title part, and who was a certain advocate of the opera's acceptance. Mme. Schroeder-Devrient, the prima donna, was already favorably disposed toward Wagner. The part of Adriano was less suited to her and was secondary in importance to the tenor part. But Schroeder-Devrient was "magnanimous" enough to push *Rienzi*.

Wagner found a cool aloofness in the intendant von Lüttichau, Reissiger, and Winkler, but in Heine and "old" Fischer genuine cordiality. "It has been my constant experience," he wrote in reference to these, "that help and encouragement have always come to me from the most humble, and never from the more exalted ranks of life." Wagner wrote at his ease when he addressed a number of letters to Fischer and Heine from Paris on the burning question of how *Rienzi* was to be staged. But before this, when he had no more than gotten wind of

97

the favorable consideration of *Rienzi,* we find him at that vital moment when the door of opportunity seemed to be opening to him for the first time. The impatient composer pushed his cause with might and main.

105 *(Paris, March 27, 1841, to Herr Hofschauspieler*
    Ferdinand Heine in Dresden)

". . . Permit me a word about the special project of my own which to my great delight has, so I am told, your continuing sympathy. A few days ago I received a letter from Winkler wherein he conveys to me the resolution of the Dresden General Management in regard to my opera with the following words: 'The resolution of the General Management was that at the moment they look forward to receiving the libretto.' Since they had awaited this in vain, he would advise me to send the libretto from Paris as soon as possible.

"After recovering from the first shock, I made a copy of my book, adding to it the modifications which would be necessary for the performance in Dresden. This book has been dispatched and will shortly arrive, but I am left with some additional doubts and worries. Having had no detailed news about my opera, I am still uncertain whether Mad. Schroeder-Devrient has seen to the matter as I wished. Has my letter been delivered to the King? Has the score officially been submitted to Hr. von Lüttichau? Did it come into Reissiger's hands? All this of necessity is important for me to learn; I am especially worried by uncertainty about the last point. I mean the judgment of Reissiger. Without being immodest, I believe I have reason to consider myself no longer a beginner. Unfortunately, I have failed so far, or rather I haven't yet succeeded in acquiring fame. For this reason I and my work have first to undergo an examination, and I am deprived of the advantage of those who may have their poorest work accepted only because it carries the name of a composer who is already known and applauded. What a variety of reasons can cloud such a judgment, even if it is merely a matter of opinion, and though we know that every German has a different opinion about the same thing. For the only reason that my works have not yet won a reputation (they have been nowhere yet produced) is that my own practical experience is not allowed to have any weight. Certainly I can justly claim that I did not submit an immature work. It's my third opera and I am insisting on its performance quite as conscientiously as I have until now kept back my first two operas. I have given an extravagant form and expansiveness to this last composition; it was not in my power to reduce it. The concept of this opera caught hold of me and fascinated me to such an extent that it is impossible for me to think of anything else but to complete it as I had conceived it and as it had to be planned. By the same urgency I have also felt obliged to declare to Herr Léon Pillet, the director of the Académie Royale, that I cannot possibly extend the subject I have submitted to him to a three-act opera as he demands, but can give it only *one,* or at the most two acts.[1] These are innermost compulsions which have always guided me. If I had conceived my opera project three years ago, I probably would have sent a one- or two-act opera to Dresden instead of a five-act opera as now. A serious cause for objection will be the difficulties of the performance and doubts about the effect on the public. In this matter I shall have to rely entirely upon the unconditional good will of those who must decide these matters in advance, for they concern questions about which each one may express doubts or confidence according to his individual view. Fortunately, I was compelled to earn my living by the baton for six years, and this at first in theaters whose insufficient means compelled me—often to my greatest discontent at the time—to get experience and practice which perhaps others of my profession do not get. I may flatter myself that I have acquired in this way a knowledge of the effect on the public, and especially on a particular occasion: there came into my hands for the first time a score of *La Juive.* Being accustomed to read the most complicated scores with a good deal of facility, I couldn't help foreseeing a lack of success for that opera, when I ran through the aphoristic mazes of this score which seemed to lack all the elements for popular understanding. But I must confess that when it came to the rehearsals and to the performance, I entirely changed my opinion, the more so as it was generally confirmed by the public. The difficulties of a performance are always only relative and are of consequence only in so far as they involve willingness, time, and toil. May I therefore be so fortunate as to count on good will in my case. Everything depends on this, and on the basis of my own experience I may appeal to the benevolence of those who have to vote on my work, and whose opinions may differ as to its success, asking them to pass a definite judgment *after* the performance only. You see, my dear Herr Heine, what worried stuff is running through my head, while I am tempted to bother you with such boring discussions. You must excuse me for pondering here day by day what may be happening in Dresden. But perhaps you in your friendly sympathy will be able to use to my advantage this or that point which I have mentioned. For, unfortunately, people don't know me in your city and they will naturally judge me in one way or another differently from what I really am. . . .

"Finally, one more thing! Kietz told me last night you had reported to him, among other things, that Herr Fischer is warmly and genuinely interested in my opera. You will easily understand how pleased I was with this news. If there is anyone I have cause to esteem for his practical ability and common sense, it is Herr Fischer, whose accomplishments as a director of the Leipzig Chorus I could never forget. It is, of course, of the greatest importance to me to have found the cooperation of such a man in my Dresden plan, and it would

[1] Wagner had sold his plot for *Der fliegende Holländer* to Léon Pillet, who composed it as *Le Vaisseau fantôme.* Wagner had just completed his own *Der fliegende Holländer.* The first two operas referred to above would have been *Die Feen* and *Das Liebesverbot.*

have been my duty to write at once to Herr Fischer to ask for his friendship and so atone for what I should have done at once on receiving the news. Unfortunately, the Paris post office is terribly particular about the weight of letters, and since I am enclosing friend Kietz's letter too, I'm afraid of a heavy conflict with that institution which has already drawn a proper toll from me. May I therefore urgently ask you to recommend me warmly to your friend and to convey to him my heartfelt thanks for his sympathy? In his hands rests a large part of my fate; may he make it as favorable as possible, and above all may he help to bring about the performance. For this is always the main thing, and from this alone, in my opinion, can grow the esteem which more than anything else I hope to win from people like you and Herr Fischer. If you too, dear Herr Heine, would deign to give me some direct news, you would make me very happy. Kindly commend me to our great Devrient and to Herr Reissiger, who may perhaps have found my last letter a bit strange, according to what Herr Winkler has told me. But more especially may *you* continue to give me your sympathy and your confidence. I will try never to show myself unworthy of it. With heartfelt esteem

"Your most faithful
RICH. WAGNER
25 *rue du Helder*

"P.S. In the book recently sent to Herr von Lüttichau the directions for the pantomime are missing. Do you perhaps know a way of supplying this?"

Another letter to Heine (116) is undated, but the text implies January, 1842. It shows that Wagner had grown dependent upon Heine to repair his errors in tact in Dresden, as well as to keep him posted on the progress of his case.

"I consider it as a lucky coincidence that you happen to live in Dresden (where I am destined to be), also that Herr Fischer is the stage manager of the Dresden Opera (for of course you can't call it coincidence that he is a decent, honest man!). Besides, I held it a happy coincidence that Hofrath Winkler is editing an evening paper and still employs correspondents from Paris; and so I came to look upon it as a lucky turn of Fate that Mad. Devrient was sympathetic with my aims. Never, even in my orgies of conceit, could I reach the point of imagining that Mad. Devrient favored my work out of true, firmly based conviction and liking. I always preferred to attribute it to a favorable mood of hers. But I well know how important whims are in an artist, and even in such a great one. It seemed quite natural to me that her fancy for me would cool off, turn to someone close to her, and due to this constant anxiety *Winkler's* news was the sort to strip me of my artificially construed illusions. He wrote me in such plain, unmistakable terms that *at first* I had to believe him completely—anxious as I was. On top of that I imagined in my rage that it was about Rossini's *Armida*, and so I regarded the whim and temper of Mad. Devrient as an unholy Italian fit, and couldn't contain myself. Unfortunately, nothing wiser came to

WILHELM FISCHER (243)

my mind than to write instantly, in my first wrath, and now you will understand how it happened that I brought forth such silly stuff. I am quite filled with regret and remorse! Oh, what an apology I owe to my great protectress! May I write to her myself? With all her kindness, I am afraid she will be bored by my letters, while through the word of a dear friend everything would more quickly touch her heart. Therefore, I entreat and implore you, be my intercessor with Mad. Devrient, apologize for me, if I can be apologized for, win her pardon for me and assure her of my repentance. May God help!

"Well, *Rienzi* is being worked at—God be praised and thanked, and an eternal obligation to my dear, excellent friends. Good Heavens, what do bad experiences of the unreliability of this or that man amount to when one receives such evidence of unselfish and undeserved sacrifice by noble friends like you and Fischer? I am reconciled with a million of this globe's inhabitants, if two such fine men are my friends. It was not easy for you, I can imagine! I don't know yet what to think of Freiherr von Lüttichau's miraculous change of mind. All the same I may assume that it wasn't simply a bad influence that produced this change: it seems so natural to me that this *Freiherr* is simply having qualms of his own about my opera. Such a man can't bring himself to believe in what he can't grasp or feel. Winkler wrote me that Meyerbeer is supposed to come to Dresden—he would like to ask Meyerbeer to pester Lüttichau on my behalf. What came out of this? You don't mention a word about *Reissiger*—how is he? Do you suspect him? To put it frankly, Reissiger's position, both as an opera composer and as a conductor, must be seriously considered; he may be the best man in the world and yet succumb to the temptation to do harm to a competitor—even an imagined one. Therefore I have to use diplomacy in dealing with him. If his attitude is really a friendly one, I would be delighted to offer him in return a friendship just as genuine, and I really would be sorry if my maneuvers in the future were not in keeping with my true sentiment toward him. Herr Lewy, who is in Paris for a week, and who will probably leave today, spoke favorably and with great respect about Reissiger, about his opera, etc.; but yesterday, speaking, so I flatter myself, with a friendly impulse, he recommended great caution in regard to Reissiger: without doubting his good intentions he believed him to be a weak man with no great firmness of character. He warned me and strongly advised me to travel to Dresden soon, in order to be present and have a look at things myself. There is no doubt that I will be there for the performance of my opera, even a week earlier. I'll see then what's happening and your friendly advice alone may guide me.

"I am happy with what I learn on all sides about the beauty of the Dresden theater, the splendor of its scenery, the efficiency of the orchestra, and the excellence of the ensembles. If Herr Fischer will stand by me throughout (as I confidently expect), I have every reason to look forward with joy to the performance.

"The clever and careful way you have considered and are still considering the *mise en scène* of my opera is an amiable proof of your great kindness: on these matters I have no anxiety whatsoever—everything is in the best hands. But what about the scenery? Much will have to be renewed, and though I am not foolish enough to demand that the suitable material now on hand should not be used, considering the present good condition of the Dresden scenery—it will not be possible to do some parts of it *appropriately* without new sets.

"For instance: (1st Act) The Lateran Church in the background; (4th Act) the same in the foreground on the side; (2nd Act) the perspective of Rome through the gate; (5th Act) the Capitol itself in the background. Are these things being considered and worked out?

"My detailed communications to Herr Fischer concerning the performance have been conveyed to you, I believe—unfortunately I am afraid that my proposals won't be sufficient. According to your previous news, I had expected that Herr Fischer himself would draft an outline for an abridgement of my opera. This decidedly would have been the best, most serviceable, and expeditious way. The author himself being naturally biased, a second person can often handle this sort of thing even more satisfactorily. The cuts proposed by me will not much reduce the over-all length, and I indeed fear that they are often clumsy and harmful. So once more I ask Herr Fischer to make the cuts as he sees fit. I'll be pleased with everything. The best place for cutting is always the ballet. In case the numbers and order of the ballet should be maintained according to my recent suggestions, they should be reduced considerably in themselves, which would also facilitate their execution. Have the ballet numbers performed with less actual dancing, that is, leg-flourishing [*Beinschwenkerei*]—this is deeply contrary to everything in me—even in the perfect way it is done here in Paris. The warlike festival dance (Act II) is performed mainly by soldiers, and the grand concluding dance is more like a festive round with groupings, interspersed with small solo steps by the leading couple. This is the best way to avoid the exposure of Dresden's weak spot, the Court ballet. But I still have a great fondness for pantomime, and if the opera, as I hope, is performed in Berlin, the pantomime will have to be presented in any case; and it would then look strange if it had been omitted in Dresden, particularly as it is much easier to have the pantomime performed than the still nonexistent ballet—for three or four actors can be found anywhere, and no more are needed. The question is: Will there be 3–4 actors in Dresden who would care to undertake it? I saw Lewy about this matter: he considered the pantomime in this sense as something novel for Dresden and advised me, among other things, to go quickly to Dresden in order to acquire those needed 3–4 actors by my personal intervention. But I have strong reasons for considering my personal influence as very poor, and I am sure there are other and better ways. What is Herr Fischer's opinion about this, and what is yours?

"How are the parts cast? Have my suggestions been considered as apt and good ones? As author I am anything but happy over the casting of Mad. Marr as Irene; a laughing coloratura singer, as I visualize this lady, will play a sadly isolated part in my opera: I can't see where she could use coloratura singing, and wherever it might occur to her to introduce it, I should most strongly oppose her. Indeed, I conceived this sister of Rienzi as a quite pathetic, noble woman, and counted a great deal on her for the last act; Wüst (apart from her height) would have met my requirements completely; if Mad. Devrient would prefer her too, we might try to have the part go to Mad. Wüst. But if Mad. Devrient doesn't care and the role is already given to Mad. Marr, and if a change couldn't be managed without inviting ill feelings and perhaps bad consequences—then unfortunately things must remain as they are! Look into this and act in my name as you find best.

"I am not ready to forfeit a single detail of the musical pomp on the stage; it is absolutely necessary and can easily be managed with the help of the military and other musical bands—certainly my requirements are not usual ones—I demand an extraordinary band, not put together like an ordinary band, but even so it can be found, especially if Reissiger is willing to do it. See to it that the trumpeters and trombonists accompanying the warlike cortège of Colonna and Orsini in the first act are chosen from the cavalry and appear on horses: this (as I imagine it) will look splendid and in keeping, and it certainly can be managed on the Dresden stage: the director must not balk at the expense and difficulties, for, in operas like mine, it must be all or nothing—you understand me!

"You see how I talk! An Emperor is nothing compared to it: 'Do this! Do that!'—as if I had only to command! Well, I hope you will do just as much as you really wish, and since I am now abashed to find that you feel like doing a great deal for me, I may also count on your forgiveness."

Wagner wrote to Kietz from Dresden on September 6, 1842 (123):

"My whole efforts are devoted to my *Rienzi* at the moment, and how they are needed! If I were not here to watch my interests with the greatest attention, God knows when my opera would be performed. And it is still to my great advantage that the whole opera staff, singers, conductor, and stage manager, are tackling the work with such splendid zeal that everyone says there has never been such harmonious agreement! But those numberless confusions daily emanating from the excessive narrow-mindedness and stupidity of the director are continuously putting obstacles in my path which I must keep removing like manure from a stable. It would take too long to enumerate them here; we've had so far fourteen rehearsals with piano, and in about four weeks, in the first half of October, the performance is to take place: unless I'm mistaken it will be remarkable: about Mad. Devrient I have only to tell you that people assure me she never tackled a role with such zeal, considering that she always finds it very difficult at first to get familiar with something novel: at the very end of the opera she wants to enter galloping on horseback as a *man*. Tichatschek has given up his vacation in Salzburg: his voice is almost created for my *Rienzi,* and so he looks upon this part as the most splendid he ever sang. He is to have a suit of armor made from German silver, richly ornamented with massive genuine silver, which may cost him about 400 thaler. The rest of the cast is very well selected and I have great expectations from Mad. Wüst, since her part excellently suits her voice. Besides this, nothing is being stinted and my opera—as people here express it—is to become the strongest one they have ever had. Here and there favorable notices already appear in the papers. There you have everything I can tell you about my opera; communicate it properly to my friends! . . . Pray for *Rienzi!"*

Wagner labored to make the most of his first great opportunity, and at the opening performance of *Rienzi,* on October 20, had his first taste of popular success. Along with it came his first experience of critical hostility; but with popular acclaim squarely behind him, he could afford to despise the critics. Wagner boasts, writing of this time, that he recoiled, then and always, from "showing any special deference to a man because he was a critic," that he carried this point "almost to systematic rudeness." It is no doubt true that Wagner would never have bribed a critic, which was then common practice, even if he had had the ready money to do so. But he could not help encouraging favorable attention, nor would his eternal passion to elucidate and justify Wagner the artist allow him to leave false charges unanswered. It is possible that, having relieved his thoughts in the following draft, he may have refrained from copying and sending his protest. His mention of the division of *Rienzi* into two evenings would date the draft at about the end of 1842 when this was done:

130   *"Allgemeine Wiener Musik-Zeitung* [2]
                 "Nos. 16 and 17

"Note: Wagner is no longer a novice; one should read his biography in the *Zeitung für die elegante Welt,* and one will see from it that *Rienzi* is not just a *first* attempt, but a more mature work.

"Text often one-sidedly and insufficiently explained. Musical critique: Chief mistake of the composer: originally to have expected the public to hear two operas in one evening: The division into two parts has restored the correct proportion.

"'There is no question of lyric passages in the entire opera.'—In the following remarks we shall call attention to the lyric passages which escaped the critic after five hearings, despite the fact that they always brought the *singer* loud applause. There is no fast march in the overture."

"No. 1. There is no 'uproar in the orchestra' in Rienzi's recitative, but simple quartet accompaniment in short chords.—The end of these numbers, which is

[2] Article by Schindelmeisser (See 133).

absolutely appropriate to their character, is omitted by the critic. After the confused, anarchistic conditions in Rome under the nobles were described in the first part of the introduction, the second part points the way, in quiet, noble dignity, to the hope for, and the enthusiastic confidence in, the elevation which Rienzi is to effect, up to the *buono stato*. The lyric theme to the words which the critic mentions earlier could have been easily brought out; but, to be sure, it would have directly contradicted his accusation of general confusion.—It seems to me that the whole ideal of the opera is expressed in this number.

"No. 2. The critic betrays his meager musical knowledge by citing the following theme:

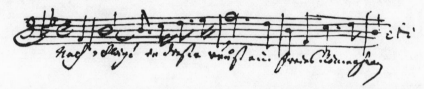

"Text: 'A free Roman heart still beats in this breast.' Although after five hearings the critic is still not more familiar with the musical peculiarities of this opera, we submit that already after the first performance the public began to improvise by *ear* on themes from *Rienzi* which were always correctly taken.

"No. 3. Duet. The critic complains of too much confusion and bewilderment, and yet he criticizes the correct time in which the composer interwove lyric passages, such as this duet, which, by the way, are always conditioned by the situation and the Spanish [?] economy, etc.

"No. 4. Shouldn't the chorus in the Lateran, 'Awaken ye sleepers near and far,' have been mentioned? Why does he omit the cantabile of Rienzi, 'Let Rome's liberty be the law,' which, at first accompanied by the cellos in B flat major, then taken up by the violins in D major to the accompaniment of the chorus, is so effective that the audience often could not refrain from breaking out into loud applause while the music was going on? The theme is as follows:

"Why is the chorus 'We swear to you, so great and free' unsatisfying at the end? Merely a way of saying things!! (These are the 'troubles [*Leiden*] of the first act.')

"Act II. No. 5. The song of the messenger of peace is not at all instrumented, but a small arioso of the first message of peace is, and the critic could have mentioned this specially.

"No. 6. Why far-fetched and unclear? The aim of the composer to give his ideas melodic contours comes out to good advantage just here. This number has, by the way, never failed to make its impression on the audience.

"No. 7. Weren't there several things to be mentioned in the finale? Isn't the adagio-sextet with chorus before the finale a song in the true sense of the word? The theme:

("Text: 'O let mercy's heavenly light enter my heart once more! Whoever promises to be loyal to you after you are pardoned, also feels the bitter pangs of remorse.'
"If it is capable of being performed as beautifully as Tichatschek does, isn't it a lyric theme?)

"Act III. No. 8. The effect of this act can be gauged only when one hears it as the first act of Part II. The vigorous scene with chorus which opens it always brings loud applause through the enthusiastic final theme, 'Romans! To arms!'
—The critic does not mention the whole number.

"No. 9. Neither does he mention Adriano's aria, even though it is one of the gratifying quiet spots which the critic claims to look for in vain. This aria alone makes the part of Adriano a very grateful one.

"—Always the eternal hollow phrases 'vagueness of ideas,' etc. If every singer is so absorbed in what he has to sing and so eager about it, as is the case with this opera, there can be no question of vagueness. How did it happen that singers were able to make an impression with vague music?—Dear Heine, see what you can do about this 'vagueness' clamor! It makes me terribly mad.

"No. 10. A critic who has to add to every one of his criticisms 'if I'm not mistaken'—should keep quiet until he knows that he makes no more mistakes. In the battle hymn which, incidentally, he praises, he also makes a mistake in citing the theme. It is as follows:

("Text: 'Santo spirito cavaliere,' etc., not:)

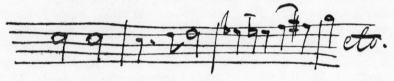

One easily senses how important the difference is.

"With the division into two parts, some other material which was originally omitted has been included to the *advantage* of the finale, as the success has shown; the number as such is therefore not 'boring and drawn out.' Here is the turning point of the drama which was to be significant. Why were passages such as Rienzi's 'Maidens, weep,' etc., omitted in the criticism? This finale is important for Adriano, and is magnificently performed by Madame Devrient.

Act IV. After the critic has heard the opera five times, has he still missed a musical climax; namely, the music to the procession in which Rienzi goes to Church, with its melodious themes?

("Text: 'Rely firmly on me, the tribune! Stay loyally at my side,' etc.)

Rienzi's arioso [see above] did not strike him either, even though the audience always greeted it with the warmest applause—that means: *to have bad will.*

" 'The *Te Deum* resounding from the church mingles with the rage of the excited populace'? ? !! after hearing it *five* times!!

"Act V. The theme of Rienzi's prayer is neither in G nor in A major, but in B flat major.—Fine pitch!!

"No. 14. Duet between Rienzi and Irene—again *obscure! [unklar]* This can drive one crazy! What the devil *is* actually clear.—Rienzi's cavatina 'Ardently did I love my exalted bride' is again not mentioned at all. Characteristic touches such as the suggestion of the theme of the Roman oath from the first act also escaped him in the last finale. He hears nothing but 'noise and confusion.'— The composer will, by the way, remain in Saxony for a while, if not as tribune of the people, then as conductor; and his operas will be performed despite the open malice of the critics. *Flying Dutchman* not to be forgotten.—To hell with it! By God, I'm happy to get some honest criticism, but I must fight maliciousness, for I'm still too young and not secure enough for that."

Wagner found the Berlin critics generally hostile and their leader, Rellstab, a hopeless reactionary. The only one who supported him, "stoutly but uselessly through thick and thin," was Karl Gaillard. "Uselessly," because Gaillard carried little influence. Gaillard had praised *Der fliegende Holländer* in spite of its semifailure in Berlin (January 7 and 9, 1844). Here as always, Wagner was ready to encourage favorable publicity on the part of well disposed critics.

142 *(Dresden, January 30, 1844, to Karl Gaillard in Berlin)* [3]

"DEAR SIR!

"While expressing my special thanks for your gratifying comprehension, I would like to add that I am very much aware of the way in which the mediating press conceives and presents so strange a phenomenon as I appear to the public. Your intention to assume part of the burden in your paper of acquainting the public with me and my artistic point of view would certainly do me a signal service. In order to comply with your wish, however, I would have preferred to find somebody around who would have communicated to you all that was necessary; but since I know no one suitable for such a purpose, I myself have made a beginning toward helping you with notes you want. Luckily this is much facilitated by the account in my own biography which Herr Laube drew up after my own draft, and which is to be found in the *Zeitung für die elegante Welt* in last year's numbers 5 and 6, if I am not mistaken. From that you may easily put together all you need; it goes as far as my return from France to

---

[3] The third and fourth paragraphs of this letter are printed in *The Letters of Richard Wagner,* ed. Wilhelm Altmann.

Germany, and as additional dates you may briefly state that the first perform-ance of my *Rienzi* in Dresden finally took place on November [October!] 20, 1842; and this had such an unusual success that two months later, on the demand of the Dresden Court Theater management, my *Flying Dutchman* was also performed, and, having until then been quite unknown, I was promptly appointed a royal *Kapellmeister*. This was a distinction no one else has received, not even C. M. v. Weber, since everyone petitioning for such a position has had to prove his ability for a year. The rumors about the extraordinary diffi-culties of the *Rienzi* performance—by the way greatly exaggerated—have so far delayed a performance of that opera by other theaters, but it will shortly be given in Hamburg, and in Leipzig this fall; as for Berlin, a heroic tenor for this opera is still to be found.

"The presentation of my *Flying Dutchman* has so far appeared to be easier for the theater managements; in addition to Dresden it has been given in Cassel, Riga, and Berlin, and Prague plans to do it very soon. It seems peculiar to me that this difficult music, not quickly or easily understandable, and which I really ought to offer to an enlightened audience only, has become most popular so far. Those who first come to know *this* opera of mine may easily be misled about me, and could believe that what is exceptional in the character of the book as well as the music is my regular way. But this is not so; and I certainly can't prove it with anything better than by pointing to my opera *Rienzi*, where both the plot and the music should demonstrate to the public that I have no prefer-ence whatever for the gloomy atmosphere which persistently prevails in the *Flying Dutchman*. I believe I can meanwhile no better prove it to you yourself, dear Sir, than by presenting to you both books for your friendly consideration. I presume that you will find that the man who invented the plot of *Rienzi*, with its abundant action, didn't equip the *Flying Dutchman* with a quite different and apparently poorer and scantier book out of mere clumsiness and lack of knowledge, but that he followed a conviction which conditioned that particular treatment of the plot. On this point I refer you to a letter written to a friend of mine last summer, which is reprinted in an article of the *Illustrierte Zeitung* dealing especially with the aforesaid opera; it should be in the October issue of last year.

"Those, therefore, who know me only by my *Flying Dutchman* usually hold it against me that I write the texts of my operas, inferring from the diffi-culties I have encountered in this plot that I am not equal to the subject. Those who know my *Rienzi* judge differently, and claim on the contrary I could not have found a more grateful book than this which I made myself. I really do not pride myself on my abilities as a poet, and I confess that it is only out of necessity, and because no good books have been offered to me, that I have set out to invent them myself. But I couldn't possibly compose a text alien to me for the following reason: My way is not to select any plot I like, put it into verse, and then ponder about how to add suitable music; if I should proceed in this way I would subject myself to the inconvenience of having to inspire myself twice, which is impossible. The way I produce is different: the only subject which can appeal to me is one which presents practical as well as musical possibilities. Before starting to write a verse, or even to outline a scene, I must first feel intoxicated by the musical aroma [*Duft*] of my subject, all the tones, all the characteristic motives are in my head, so that when the verses are finished and the scenes ordered, the opera proper is also finished for me and the musical treatment in detail is rather a calm and considered afterwork which the moment of real creation has preceded. Furthermore, only subjects should be chosen which are suited only for musical treatment: I would never choose a plot which could just as well be used by a good playwright for a spoken drama. As a musician I am free to choose subjects, to invent situations and contrasts, which are quite outside of the province of the poet-dramatist. Here we arrive at the point where opera and drama part completely and where each can quietly pursue its own course. While nowadays it is the task of the dramatist to purify and to spiritualize the material interests of our time, it falls to the poet and composer of opera to conjure up the holy spirit of poetry which has come down to us from the legends and sagas of past ages. For music offers the means for synthesis which the poet alone, especially in the drama, cannot command. This is the way to raise the opera to a higher level from a debasement which has come about because we have expected composers to treat commonplaces, intrigues, etc., subjects which spoken drama and modern comedy are far more successful in presenting.

"I have chosen for my next opera the beautiful and characteristic saga of the knight Tannhäuser, who dwelt in the Venusberg and then went to Rome on a pilgrimage to seek absolution! I linked that saga with the singers' contest at the Wartburg where Tannhäuser takes the place of Heinrich von Ofterdingen—by this combination I achieve a richer dramatic life. It will be obvious that only a musician could treat such a subject.

"But I am afraid to have imposed too long on your sympathy; if you continue in it in the future and prove it by your actions, I believe I shall have helped you enough to deserve our closer acquaintance. I repeat the assurances of my greatest gratitude for your kindness and look forward to speak to you of this in person on my next visit to Berlin.

> "Most faithfully yours,
> RICHARD WAGNER"

153 *(Dresden, June 5, 1845, to Karl Gaillard)* [4]

"MY ESTEEMED FRIEND!

"I could have no worse punishment for my negligence toward you than your gentle vengeance in persistently helping me and my young reputation

[4] Published in part by Wilhelm Altmann.

whenever occasion has offered. You have often caused me to wonder at your consistent wish to help me, and I must accuse myself of not having answered in kind. But if you had beheld me during the winter you might have understood that not all negligence is to be put down as a sin. Annoyingly subjected to an abdominal ailment, exceedingly busy in my duty (sometimes the most tasteless in the world), passionately absorbed in finishing my opera, I became so much of an egotist that I used each of my few remaining idle moments in lonely walks, that is, in consulting with myself. To be sure, I am in a crisis now from which I am not able to rise and extricate myself! After a single lucky stroke by which I quickly got a reputation and a position so important and necessary for Germany—my lucky star all of a sudden failed me. I have not been able to make another decisive step forward since my first appearance in Dresden. What I need is a great—even the greatest—city of Germany to support my Dresden success. But Berlin's function seems to be to weaken it. To appear before such a large public with a work like my *Flying Dutchman* was in itself alone a bold venture, especially since they were not yet ready to befriend me. Thus my introduction to Berlin ought absolutely to have happened with my *Rienzi*. But since the *Dutchman* was quite effectively presented after all, in spite of the unmusical playhouse, so unfavorable to my music, the Berlin manager had to offset the advantage gained by presently dropping the opera from the repertory, merely to make way for the accustomed routine. In this way my labors were entirely discounted, and any further expression of them is for the moment quite out of the question. How I worked to make my *Rienzi* a possibility in Berlin! Meierbeer [*sic*], who had attended its twentieth performance last summer and had the chance of making sure of its effect, witnessed the calling out of the singers by thunderous applause, after each of the five acts, even the recall of the author after the fourth act—and accordingly promised to do everything in his power to produce that opera for the Berliners as soon as possible. I don't yet doubt the honesty of his disposition toward me, but the persisting reason which makes a production impossible—the lack of a heroic tenor—is enough to drive me mad. Now the difficulty of popularizing my works is doubled for me by the attitude of the Dresden critics. Dresden is a place which a century of dull routine has sunk into complete insignificance: *Weber* found here a flowering Italian opera as a foreign cultural product; he had to establish a German opera under the most irritating circumstances in the world, since above everything else the Court was all against it.

"The artistic means at his disposal were at that time not yet truly significant, and he preferred to introduce his work elsewhere. Since Weber's death the artistic means have greatly increased, especially by the abandonment of the Italian opera; but meanwhile the spirit of the management has succumbed to the crassest philistinism, and deplorably undermined the work of Weber to raise Dresden to musical importance. Inspired by the resources I found there I made a point of continuing Weber's work, that is, advancing Dresden's musical emancipation, smashing philistinism, educating the public's taste for what is best, and so raising its level. And what was the first thing I encountered: *Envy!!* So long as I was the poor unknown musician who had suddenly won a great success with an opera, everything was all right; but when this success extended as far as to getting a life position at 1,500 thr., the milk of sympathy turned sour. The hostile effects of this envy I have fortunately overcome where it was an obstacle to my actual work; but in that province where for honor's sake I can't interfere—in the realm of criticism, it continues to be rampant. But what does *criticism* amount to in a city like Dresden? They have *one* paper only, and for foreign journals we have only *one* correspondent. Your old friend *Schladebach* may have his merits, but in his attitude toward me he succumbs unconditionally to the effects of a deadly envy; and so it happens that he either strongly disfigures my activity when reporting it abroad, or, which is still worse, he kills its good success by complete silence. For instance, when I began my work here I found Marschner's *Hans Heiling,* the score of which had been accepted for performance ten years ago, but which now quietly slept in the library: I unearthed that opera and performed it. Learning that Marschner had finished a new opera, *Adolf von Nassau,* I insisted upon its being given here for the first time and so not slightly surprised the composer, who would sooner have expected the Dresden Theater to collapse than to make any such decision. A great festival was to be given by a men's chorus; my predecessors had nobly withdrawn from similar activities. I put myself at the head and achieved one of the most magnificent performances in the Frauenkirche. The orchestra itself suffered from manifold defects. After considerable struggles I received the neces-sary increase in funds, a better arrangement of the orchestra, reinforcement of the strings, etc. In spite of the decisive repugnance of the Court and the general manager, I effected the moving of *Weber's* remains to Dresden; the funeral, the dignified ceremony is *my* work. Did you read anything about it in the Dresden reports? Did you ever find a mention of the fact that my *Rienzi* since its first appearance here is still—even under the most unfavorable circumstances—the only opera which attracts a capacity audience? That the twenty-fifth performance was attended by the King of Prussia, who displayed a striking interest in it? Certainly not, and this is the sort of information which one would expect to be reported. You may find it petty to be put out by such trifles, but consider how much all this concerns me as long as my activities are still restricted to Dresden, since after the happenings in Berlin I had virtually no way of making myself known abroad. I know quite well that newspaper reports can't make a good work into a bad one, or a bad one into a good one—but the papers can prejudice a good thing by hindering and retarding its dissemination; they can be discouraging. Actually, I must confess that this special difficulty of the making known of my operas, though it did not discourage me, gradually undermined my plan, which might have been of no slight value. For after the fine success I achieved in Dresden, I had proposed to cut all the threads that had connected me with Paris, and this I did in fair hopes of the moment when a dramatic composer could make an impress upon Germany through German channels. I still now consider it important for the whole future of our dramatic music that a personality appearing in the very heart of Germany should be made known across Germany; and I confess to being painfully aware that this thought turns involuntarily toward Paris, where the mud hampers my every step: Must my road to Germany go by way of Paris? I cling to this thought of Paris. I am as unhappy and ill at ease as if I were about to sell my good mother. Is it good to entertain such perfidious thoughts? Help me to wipe them out entirely! Along with this I am sending you my *Tannhäuser,* for he is a German fellow from top to toe; accept this as a present offered in friendship. May it win the hearts of my German compatriots more completely than my former works could once do. This work *must* be good; if not, I can never accomplish anything good. It worked a true magic on me; I would no sooner touch the music than I would quiver with warmth and glow: in spite of all the great interruptions in my work, I was always freshly suffused with that peculiar fragrance which had intoxicated me at the very first conception. I am sending you the score for no other reason than to get you acquainted with it, and I ask you to show it only to the closest of your friends; after the first performance of the opera in Dresden this September, the score will be sent about as a novelty by the book trade; until then it is to be withheld. Right now I beg you not to look in these lines for any journalistic discussion or commendation. Nowadays there is so much *artificial promotion* and I myself—aside from what *you* did for me—am completely convinced that almost all newspaper articles spring from the personal interest of those concerned. That is why I fight shy of everything which smacks of favoritism. I have told you all this because you have repeatedly shown a rare sympathy for me and because I found it necessary to get rid of these annoyances for once and all by discussing them. If my disclosures have any other purpose, it is to warn you to be specially cautious, if such a case should arise. I have delivered the opera itself to the Berlin management with the request for a production, if *Rienzi* cannot be done by the end of the year on account of the lack of a heroic tenor. God knows what the great Küstner is going to do.

"I have done some touching up of the book, following your advice; among other things, the *schwärzliche Gefieder* in Wolfram's song, p. 40, has disappeared. But I have left the end rhyme *Gott* and *Spott,* because I find *Spott* not a forced rhyme but a poetic word suggesting the distortion of God's mercy at the hands of a callous priesthood. God help me!

"At the end of this month I want to go to Marienbad to cure my disgusting stomach trouble; in August I am to return to Dresden for the studying of *Tannhäuser*; the piano scores, etc., everything has been worked out, and on the day after the first performance I shall be free and on my own.

"Then I intend to idle away a whole year, that is, to put my library to use without producing anything, although even now, unfortunately, I feel the urge to work again, being absorbed in a new subject; but I shall force myself to hold off, first, because there are many things I still wish to learn; secondly, because I am convinced that a dramatic work which is to have concentrated significance and originality must come from traversing a higher sphere of life [*Eines höheren Lebensschrittes*], a certain period in the cultural education of an artist; but such an advance, such a period can't be achieved every half-year: several years are required to create this concentrated ripeness [*gedrängte Reife*]. A single unimportant product is enough to satisfy *money-makers,* but *I* shall *never* earn any money; I have resigned myself to it.

"In this lazy period I want to shelve my special interests a bit and I ask *you* especially to look out for me and to tell me in detail how I can reciprocate your friendly services. It would be best of all if you could visit me in Dresden in September: I would take better care of you than the last time.

"In order to wind up this long letter (I think I haven't written such a long one in six years), I repeat my heartiest thanks for your many evidences of sympathy and friendship. Wishing you the best of health and an early success in your productive career.

"Farewell and hold in affection your most devoted
RICHARD WAGNER"

The first impresario to attempt *Rienzi* outside of Dresden was Cornet in Hamburg, on March 21, 1844. Wagner journeyed there, and wrote his wife after sizing up the production from the rehearsals. As usual in his accounts to Minna of his operatic prowess, he tends to put a good face on the matter. His description in *My Life* is far less favorable. He there finds that Cornet is intent only on a quick spectacular success, resorts to tawdry scenery and stock costumes.[5] The "one ray of light" in the whole production is the Adriano, Mme. Fehringer (who later sang Ortrud for Liszt at Weimar). But here we have a different story:

146 (*Hamburg, March 17, 1844*)

"GOOD WIFE OF MY HEART!

"Today is Sunday and there is no rehearsal; before dressing to make my visits, I am sitting down to give myself the pleasure of a little chat with you; I mean by writing, for I often hold conversations with you and sometimes hear your answers quite distinctly. But first I'm going to tell you what you may be most anxious to hear: how things stand with my opera. After Friday had passed with various necessary conferences and arrangements, we held the first stage rehearsal on Saturday, that is, of the first two acts only. It lasted from ten to

[5] Herr Cornet presented Wagner with a gray parrot, the parrot whom Wagner named "Papo" (from *Papagei?*), and who was to delight the hearts of Wagner and Minna for seven years. But this was lefthanded generosity on Cornet's part. He skimped the composer's fee and paid it in small installments.

three o'clock, and everyone worked hard. I was greatly pleased with the singers and chorus; the chorus was augmented for the first time in Hamburg by soldier singers and was splendidly prepared; they are giving their utmost; the greater part have good voices and are often so strong that the orchestra is completely covered. The solo singers are truly remarkable, and I frankly confess that I could wish for none better in Dresden—except our Tichatschek, of course: Wurda certainly can't even remotely be compared to Tichatschek in regard to voice and energy in singing; well, I need not tell you what we possess in Tichatschek, we all know that well enough. However, this I hadn't expected at all, and I had nothing to be disappointed about. Wurda is doing his best, and with this I have to be content, especially because I recognize that he will finally come through with his part quite well; singers of his sort sing differently, and there is never the danger that they may overdo; besides, he is in good standing here and the public is used to him. Of course when I hear him at the rehearsals, I must not think of Tichatschek: that I must never do! So, there is no call for comparison, and those points which are beyond all comparing should not be thought about. But while I still include Tichatschek in my thought, I am obliged to say that as long as I live I never expect to have better singers for this opera. Adriano stands first. This woman Fehringer, powerful as she is, is worth her weight in gold! It is a voice, I tell you, such as I have never heard! Strength, freshness, resonance—in high, middle, low register—however you choose—quite remarkable! This woman has fire like no one else: she sings with energy, with ardor— wildly! On top of that she is well rehearsed—nothing uncertain about her! We need such a one—you know my troubles! If Rienzi's part should prove at last to be less striking, then I almost fear that Adriano will outshine Rienzi to the point where the opera on the playbill would need to be called ADRIANO. Irene, Mlle. Jazedé, is very good and takes her place well in the ensembles. You ought to hear the two women do the duet in the first act, the one that never pleased you! I will wager that duet will cause a furore here. But now for the other parts! Colonna, Orsini, then especially Cecco, Baroncello, and the Cardinal are excellent: all of them strong, fresh voices full of life and fire in the acting; Lord, when I think of our Riesse, Vestri, etc.!!! In a word, my good Mienel, everything is in hand; and when you add to this Tichatschek for the summer, I believe the opera will arouse the public here to a real furore.[6] Meanwhile, it's just as well that they've not seen the part of Rienzi better done.

"I've been less satisfied with the orchestra so far, and right now I'd prefer to have my own orchestra here with me! I have let Krebs conduct that rehearsal, and shall myself take over the last two. Krebs is really an excellent conductor; he has prepared the singers well, everything sure and precise, and in the future when I am away I could have no better conductor for my opera. But naturally, in the matter of interpretation there is much that only the composer can indicate, and therefore the last two rehearsals will have to throw the right light upon

[6] Tichatschek did sing Rienzi as guest in the following summer.

the whole work. But there is good will on every side, and the musicians are enthusiastic about the work. One thing is certain, that everybody without exception predicts the greatest possible success; and Cornet's only worry is what opera he can give afterward, for he says: 'Rienzi kills everything else, what other could come up to it?' . . ."

The Vienna Court Opera, having approached Wagner in May, 1843, for a production of one of his operas, on the strength of his fame in Dresden through *Rienzi* and *The Flying Dutchman,* received the composer's suggestion that *Rienzi* would be suitable. However *Rienzi,* which showed a papal legate on the stage, hung fire on account of the strict Austrian religious censorship. Liszt, having heard *Rienzi* in Dresden, in 1844, became its enthusiastic advocate, and Wagner naturally looked to help from him when he was visiting Vienna. The reference to Pakorny shows that Wagner looked for a possible production at the Theater-an-der-Wien, of which Pakorny was the director.

159 *(Dresden, May 20, 1846, to Franz Liszt)* [7]

"HIGHLY HONORED FRIEND!

"I still owe you my best thanks for the friendly letter which you wrote me from Prague! May you succeed in your very friendly endeavors to make me favorably known to the Viennese! Herr Pakorny has not given me any news; if the main obstacle to the production of my *Rienzi* in Vienna really lies in the censorship there, I would be unendingly grateful to you if you would exert your influence on Count Sedlitzki in my favor. If a renewed request may be permitted, which might strengthen you in your friendly attitude toward me, then I shall not neglect to sue for your continued protection—if possible until the goal is attained.

"Herr Löffler has written me that he would still like to examine the score of my *Flying Dutchman*; so I am now sending him this opera, instructing him to deliver it to you, my generous friend, as soon as he has sufficiently read it; please do with the score what you please.

"Excuse me for bothering you with these lines, but I shall treasure the hope that they may revive a little your friendly recollection of me. God knows I need friends, and in you, with your continuous good intentions, I see a powerful one, hence my boldness. In the highest and most grateful devotion, I remain

"Your

RICHARD WAGNER"

[7] The letter is addressed simply to Dr. Franz Liszt, Vienna, and postmarked May 29. Only three letters earlier than this one appear in the published Wagner-Liszt correspondence.

310 *(In Wagner's hand: authorization for cuts in* Rienzi, *signed
Richard Wagner, Zürich, July 17, 1858)*

"In order to shorten the time length of the performance of my opera *Rienzi,*
I herewith indicate the following cuts as the least disfiguring.

"*1st Act.* In the finale a cut *can* be made from p. 144 to p. 156. I do not,
however, like to suggest this cut.

"*2nd Act.* P. 68 (after the 5th measure) to p. 72 (6th measure). Very advisable. Then: Instead of p. 80, go right to p. 99. Likewise very advisable, since the
remaining ballet music already has completely lost its true character through the
omission of the originally intended pantomime. The gymnastic divertissements
which were arranged for Dresden could only appear unsuitable and unworthy
to every cultivated listener, much as they pleased the gallery, and I for my part
wish that they may definitely be omitted. In their place only (E)—festive dance,
by the entire company of dancers and extras, shall be performed as a characteristic, serious, festive round dance. In any case, that shortens it and sacrifices
nothing important.

"*3rd Act.* For the very considerable cutting of the finale, the arrangement
which I made expressly for *Hamburg* is to be used. I therefore request that the
score of the theater there be examined and the finale of this act arranged accordingly. The great war march is completely omitted, and the martial procession
strides forward as if to battle, to the first verse of the battle hymn; then the
scene between Rienzi and Adriano, as in the score, and the second verse of the
hymn; the act then closes with the departure for the battle. A special conclusion
is to be found in that Hamburg score.

"*4th Act.* No cut.

"*5th Act.* It is left to the singer's discretion to omit the arioso in A major,
'*Wohl liebt' ich glühend meine hohe Braut,*' and the final address to the people
in the finale.

RICHARD WAGNER

"Zürich, July 17, 1858"

❧ XI ❧

THE DRESDEN YEARS

(Reminiscences of Marie Schmole)

Hunting in Dresden for data about Wagner half a century previous, Mrs. Burrell could hardly have hoped to obtain much firsthand information. But she actually did in one case. She found the daughter of Ferdinand Heine, Wagner's intimate friend, once the costume designer of the Hoftheater, and his colleague in the first production of *Rienzi, The Flying Dutchman,* and *Tannhäuser*.

Marie Heine had been a little girl when *Rienzi* was in production, attracting the amused attention of the composer when he visited the Heines; *Tannhäuser* she remembered as a *Backfisch* of seventeen, just old enough to thrill to the idealistic fervor then first manifesting itself around the works of Wagner. In 1895, about fifty years after this, she was Frau Schmole, still living in Dresden. Mrs. Burrell supplied her with notebooks, which were returned between July and February of the following year, filled with tales of the Wagner she knew and, still more, she had heard him discussed in the household where his talents and his exploits were a constant topic.

126 A *(Dresden, July 12, 1895)*

"Richard Wagner in Dresden [1]

"Although I was then a child of ten, I distinctly remember the first visit of Wagner and his wife Minna to my parents' home. It was in the summer of 1842. On coming home from school and looking for my parents in the garden, I found with them a gentleman with a fine face and—what most impressed me— with *bright kid gloves*. But later on I noticed that they had been washed repeatedly and were worn out on the inner side. Although in pretty straitened circumstances, he always attached great value to an elegant and neat appearance. The Wagner couple had experienced need and privations of all kinds and in full measure during their stay in Paris. Often Richard had slipped out in the evening, a music manuscript in hand, perhaps wishing to sell some of his work [*Geschaffene*]. When the two lived in Meudon, they had sometimes passed by gardens in the evening and knocked down some walnuts from branches of trees hanging over the walls, because they were starving.

"His wife, then a very beautiful lady, conquered my heart, as he had, by

[1] This and later titles are Frau Schmole's.

118

her friendly ways. When I was introduced to them, he saluted me as the *Mariechen* who had come through bad sicknesses while he was still in Paris. From that time on, the Wagners came several times each week in the evening to have supper with us in the garden, where Richard especially liked the full vines. Only later did I understand why his glance would dwell so fondly on the simple dishes which were laid on the table. I once heard that Minna Wagner told my mother that on some days this had been their first substantial meal since breakfast! Standing in front of the spread table, he would often say to his wife: 'Minel, now we will stock up' [*pampen*] (in purer German, *satt-essen*).

"His greatest delight before the first course of cold meat was new potatoes in the skin with herrings in a piquant sauce. He called it *'Lake'* [pickle].[2] When my mother once jokingly remarked that he consumed too much butter, he handed over to her the next evening a large lump of butter. On those evenings he was harmlessly merry, like a child. When fall approached, I often heard lively discussions about the opening rehearsals of *Rienzi*.

"Schroeder-Devrient often put him into a state of despair. As almost always when she was studying a new part, she was often quite intractable at rehearsals and in many places couldn't grasp the meaning. At a stage rehearsal it came to the point of a vehement outburst from that highly talented but passionate nature. Wagner had repeatedly objected to her presentation of the duet between Adriano (Schroeder-Devrient) and Irene (Henriette Wüst). It had not been performed by Devrient as he wanted it. Thereupon she threw the music at his feet, exclaiming, 'Let him sing the trash himself.' This greatly perplexed poor Richard and he had misgivings about the performance. But it is known how splendidly Devrient made up for her vehemence and how marvelously she acted and sang Adriano.

"Frequently Fischer also took his meals with us and told us about the enthusiasm of the chorus members, with whom he had been working some time before. Later on, when the question came up of the probable duration of the opera, the old gentleman often ran his hands through his hair in comic despair and uttered many a 'Hm, Hm'; but Richard, being used to the Paris Opéra, did not consider it extraordinary to spend five hours in the theater. On the day of the opening (20th October, 1842) the Wagner couple had their dinner with my parents—but they didn't each much at noon. Frau Minna frequently pressed her hands to her heart, anxiously sighing. Richard kept shifting to and fro on his chair, as he always did when uneasy and restless, or he would jump up, run around the room, and every five minutes pull his watch from his pocket. At last, between four and five o'clock he couldn't stand it any longer; neither, however, could my father. Both gentlemen decided to go for a walk.

[2] This dish seems to have made a special impression on Wagner, who wrote in *My Life* many years later (p. 270): "We generally spent our evenings with old Fischer at Heine's, where, amid hopeful conversation, we regaled ourselves on potatoes and herrings, of which the meals chiefly consisted."

"After a short time they came near to the theater. Around five o'clock the theater square began to show life. Richard stood at a distance and began to count: 'Look, Ferdinand, there come three. Are they going into the theater? They are. And there come some more.' It went on this way while the public came flocking from all sides. *'Heinemännel,* I believe the theater will be full! Don't you think so?' Finally the two friends could not contain themselves any longer. They entered the theater and went first to the stage, but Richard didn't stay there long. Before the beginning of the performance he stole into an orchestra box, where he kept in the back. As the volume of applause increased, his courage swelled too, but he also became aware of the superabundance of wealth with which he had equipped his opera. During the performance my father hunted up Richard in his dark corner of the box, and the further the opera progressed the more restless the composer grew. He fidgeted on his chair and reproached himself: 'Such an ox—oh, what an ass! What nonsense!' Those were the honorary titles which he murmured to himself. His neighbors, to whom the restless fellow was unknown, began to frown at him—for when he was stormily called forth after the first act, the public had seen only the tip of his nose despite the powerful push administered by my father from the wings. Fearing further outbursts, my father dragged him out to the corridor. 'Isn't it stupid of me? I could have written ten operas from all those melodies. Nobody will endure it to the end!' When the clock, mounted above the stage, approached ten, Wagner couldn't refrain any longer. He climbed up the stairs and stopped the clock 'so that people at least wouldn't see how late it was.' But it is well known that except for a very old gentleman in the parquet, not a *single spectator* left the theater before the end of the opera. So Wagner had obtained his longed-for goal. His opera had its first performance with a strong cast and splendid scenery on one of the most important stages. He had made his first step toward his later fame.

"There was an amusing sequel to Wagner's splendid debut, due to a joke of his wife. Frau Minna had laid some laurel leaves beneath his bed sheet and asked him next morning how he had rested upon his laurels. On his complaint that his bed must have become somewhat disarranged, Minna drew forth the laurels and handed them to him. 'Oh, this was what tickled me whenever I moved!' he said laughing over the innocent joke.

"Cuts were made to shorten the opera at the second and later performances, but nobody, not even the chorus members, wanted a single number cut. Only the ballet was cut, and later on the third act was deprived of some of its finest pearls, so that in its present shape the loud marches and choruses dominate.

"The *Meister* had great anxiety about Tichatschek in this same third act. When the troops march out, Rienzi appears on horseback and incites the citizens of Rome to defend their rights. The chorus repeats the battle song 'Santo spirito Cavaliere,' and only then is Rienzi supposed to join in. Tichatschek could not refrain from blaring forth the battle song with his glorious metallic voice

FRAU MARIE SCHMOLE-HEINE (188)

during the preceding choruses. Since the fourth act contains Rienzi's extended cantilena *'Baut fest auf mich, den Tribunen,'* and the fifth act the prayer, Wagner was always worried lest Tichatschek overexert himself in the third act. So he worked out different plots with Fischer and my father to render Tichatschek silent until that moment. Fischer told him it would look better if he should gallop forth from the wings immediately before his address to his fellow Romans. Tichatschek also found this very effective, and stayed within the wings with his horse; but when the chorus began the 'Santo spirito' out on the stage, Rienzi behind the wings blared forth too! Wagner, at his conductor's desk, almost dropped the baton with terror.

"Before the next performance another plot was hatched. The horse stamping behind the wings had a disturbing effect on the music, so Tichatschek was told, and there was no help for it but to place Rienzi with the horse at the furthest end of the stage until he had to appear. There an apparatus with a big doorway served to introduce the horses and trappings. Tichatschek agreed also to this. Now Richard could proceed in peace. The chorus begins and from a distance there sounds brilliantly above all other voices the unconquerable heroic tenor voice of Rienzi. Now Wagner knew no further way out, and said to Fischer, 'He may wait with his horse on the prompter's box for all I care, but he mustn't sing.' Fischer smiled, adjusting his spectacles, and from then on everything remained as it was.

"Another amusing thing happened in my parents' house at that time. Wagner was supposed to conduct *Rienzi* in person but had not yet been appointed *Kapellmeister*. At that time only a royal *Kapellmeister* or music director was allowed to use the conductor's baton. Others had to give the beat with the bow of the violin. On that day the Wagners again had dinner with my parents. With his peculiar, rather nasal voice, Wagner lisped between his fine lips: 'Well, how is it to be tonight? I can hardly be expected to conduct tonight with a yardstick of a fiddlebow!' My brother, a youngster of seventeen and a great worshiper of Wagner, disappeared from the dinner table. After some time he reappeared with a small white conductor's baton. 'Well, Herr Wagner, will this do?' he asked. 'Yes, of course, Wilhelm! But where did you get it so quickly?' Now my brother laughingly turned to my mother. 'You see, Mother, this will cost you the handle of your best mixing stick, which I sawed off, and a spoon of flour for paste to cover it with white paper.'[3] My mother only smiled at the despoiling of her kitchen. With this stick Wagner conducted that evening. After his appointment as *Kapellmeister* father asked for the white baton again. He put the music and words of the battle song and the date on it and kept it as a precious relic. After father's death the historic baton came into the possession of my brother, General Heine. When on my brother's death it was my sad duty to attend his property, the baton could nowhere be found. Later on I learned that it was in the Dresden Civic Museum. Who knows how it got there? In any

[3] The conductor's baton was then customarily covered with white paper.

case we must be satisfied with the thought that this family keepsake does not lie in an unworthy place."

126 B

"From *Rienzi* to *The Flying Dutchman*

"For a considerable period the wave of enthusiasm about the new star in the heavens of the German opera kept rising. But the material circumstances of the celebrity continued meager for a long time to come. Old debts and the necessity for keeping up outward appearances often oppressed Minna and Richard, and the unassuming hospitality and faithful friendship of my parents for both of them, now as always, remained their most cherished resort. The Wagners moved from the first small apartment in Waisenhausstrasse to Marienstrasse, of course also in a very modest neighborhood, but at least so situated as to receive an increasing number of visitors. I remember one evening in that period with special vividness. Frau Minna had been told confidentially that the *Liedertafel,* even at that time the most important men's choral society, intended to pay homage to Wagner in the form of a serenade. So far as I know, relatives of Richard were present in Dresden at the time. Earlier than this, mention had been made of a great tragedy which Richard had written as a boy and read out to his family as it progressed.[4] He himself described it as a work of Shakespearean spirit, full of hatred, vengeance, and murders. But having disposed of most of his characters in the first three acts, he was asked who would appear on the stage in the last two acts. The play *had* to have *five* acts. The young poet answered that he would bring on the ghosts of the slain ones, for he could not be disturbed by such trifles. This boyhood work gave Minna a pretext to invite Richard's relatives, the indispensable Fischer and my parents, my brother Wilhelm, and myself to tea as a supplement to the occasion. Richard had dug up this youthful work and recited it in humorously tragic tones, not without laughter and interspersed remarks from the listeners. I can't quite remember the actual plot of this drama, but much intrigue, noble-mindedness, bravery, hatred, and love were thrown into it. Several persons had been duly done away with and we were looking forward to further ghostly apparitions, when there came an interruption to Richard's recitation from the small front garden on Marienstrasse. The singing of fresh, male voices was heard and Wagner listened with delight—his guests no less. On finishing the songs, the committee appeared to cheer the celebrated Master—and the ghosts remained in their weird realm.

"Soon after this the preparations for *The Flying Dutchman* began: I heard many doubts expressed concerning the difficulties presented by the two ships in

[4] Sixteen years after these notes were written, the details about Wagner's first dramatic attempt, *Leubald,* written at fifteen, were made known in *My Life.* Wagner there spoke from memory, supposing his tragedy to have been long since lost. But Minna had kept the neat manuscript, left it to Natalie, and Natalie sold it to Mrs. Burrell (23).

the first and last acts. Mechanical contrivances at that time were still far short of their present standard. The sea waves were produced in a quite primitive way and the ships made a pretty crude appearance and disappearance, but people then expected less of scenic equipment than they do now. Even so, the Dresden Court Theater was considerably ahead of other German stages. Good 'Father Fischer' took great delight with the coaching of the choruses, but the soloists still made dubious faces over many passages. Wilhelmine Schroeder-Devrient sang the part of Senta and was especially anxious about the ballad. On Minna's intercession I was admitted to the full rehearsal. When Schroeder-Devrient was about to begin her ballad in the second act, she stopped at the very first 'Jo-ho-ho,' shook her head, stamped her foot, and said to Wagner, 'I cannot, cannot handle that stuff.' Wagner became discouraged and made the orchestra begin again, and now it went better; but this gifted woman as usual caught the true spirit of it only on the evening of the first performance. A very amusing incident happened in the same rehearsal during the spinning chorus. Although it had already been sung in the previous orchestra rehearsal, it was not until this general rehearsal that the girls really caught the idea. The musical laughter closing their merry song sounded so natural that Frau Sch.-D., resting in her easy chair as Senta and gazing at the Dutchman's picture, turned her head with startling suddenness and cried out to them: 'Well, you geese, what is there to laugh about?' Of course *real* and general laughter met this exclamation of Wilhelmine, deep in her own problems. On the opening night different places in the first act brought vivid applause, especially the charming sailors' chorus. Compared to later performances of the opera, the first casting of the main role was not a quite satisfactory one. Wachter was an able singer with a beautiful voice, but he lacked the poetry needed for the uncanny figure of the Dutchman. Only later, when Anton Mitterwurzer took over the part, did the great air in the first act have its perfect presentation, as well as the duet with Daland, sung by the clever but somewhat dry Risse. The public became generally enthusiastic during the second act, which is so abundant in dramatic and musical beauty. The spinning chorus got endless applause as well as the air of the hunter and the scene between Senta, the Dutchman, and Daland. At the end of the act Wagner was enthusiastically called forth. As usual he struggled violently against appearing on the stage until, as usual, Fischer and my good father actually pushed him out from the wings. Richard was so bewildered that he didn't know where to put his feet, and while trying to bow his way out, he backed into the spinning wheels of the women's chorus and with difficulty forced his way back into the shelter of the wings, to the great delight of those who knew the easily flustered Wagner. In the third act also a roar of applause broke loose several times, especially at the always exciting sailors' chorus and the women's choruses, singing merrily about the ghostly ships. Richard's despair was the transfiguration of Senta and the Dutchman, which at that time may have been presented with a good deal of literalness. Compared to the heaven-storming *Rienzi,* the success of the *Dutchman* showed a certain contrast, but Wagner's friends and worshipers may well have first divined in this the unusual trend which his great genius was to take in its further development.

"I hold many friendly and interesting recollections of Wagner's brightest period in Dresden as a royal *Kapellmeister* and we often spent cozy hours there. My horror was his beloved Peps, a white and brown speckled little monster who tyrannized over the household and probably imagined that his master could not accomplish anything without his presence. It is known that there stood next to the piano an upholstered stool, on which Peps had to lie when his master wanted to compose. If the dog was not there, the whole household was set into motion to look for him, and many a time Minna herself had to go out and fetch him from the park near the Ostra-Allee. I often made a timid and anxious detour when I had to pass Wagner's apartment, for as soon as Peps got sight of me he circled around me with such a pitiful howling that we attracted the gaze of all the passers-by: hardly a desirable prominence for the schoolgirl I then was! When later I complained to his master, Wagner, highly delighted, burst into laughter and said: 'Well, my dear Mariechen, he well knows the friends of the house and wants to salute them too!'

"That was also the time of the first appearance of his niece Johanna [5] in the Dresden Court Theater, which led to her ensuing engagement. I can't write the name of this dearest idol of my youth without visualizing her standing before me as she was then. Above the usual size, slender, with very rich blond hair and infinitely dear blue eyes: thus I see her before me—'Our Hanns,' as Richard preferred to call her. Although not a regular beauty, she won all hearts. In her first part, the Greek Irma in Auber's *Maurer und Schlosser,* the public sympathy went out to her right away, for it was known that a niece of Wagner would appear on the stage. As her ardent admirer I was allowed to attend the performance in a small box installed on the stage and put at the disposal of 'Father' Fischer for opera performances. From the same place I later on listened to *Tannhäuser.* Johanna did not have to appear until the second act, and stood behind the curtain while her uncle Richard took his place in the wings to encourage her. 'Oh, uncle, I am so anxious,' she whispered to him when the curtain was about to rise. 'You are a dumb *Liese,'* he laughingly retorted and disappeared in order to follow the further course from the front. Frequently now the brothers and their families came together, my family and Fischer joining them. During a few summer months Richard and Minna lived in 'Lord Findlater's' vineyard, on the approximate spot where the castle on the bank of the Elbe now stands, as built by Prince Albrecht of Prussia. There Richard liked to gather all of us; the coffee table was laid on the large terrace with the glorious view across Dresden, whose dignified Frauenkirche was a special delight to Wagner, and a view over the wide Elbe Valley. In those hours Richard was specially amiable and merry, and was amused by the most harmless jokes of

[5] The daughter of Wagner's brother Albert.

his friends. His real favorite was my brother Wilhelm, who on his part clung with great enthusiasm to the gifted man. Both 'long ones,' as he would call Wilhelm and Johanna, had always to be near him. About *Tannhäuser* and everything in connection with it, I will report in the next notebook."

Frau Schmole, sending more of her reminiscences, writes to Mrs. Burrell's daughter (126 C, Dresden, May 18, 1895):

"As for Frau Cosima's enterprise, you may feel sure that I will keep aloof from it in *any event*. So far I have neither seen nor heard anything of Herr Schwarz, but if they should knock on my door, they would get nothing for their pains. After becoming acquainted with your dear mother and her noble aspirations, I would never make common cause with Wagner's widow. *How different* have the *once so noble festivals* of Bayreuth become through her, so different from what Richard would ever have guessed. Meanwhile, I have again written down some of my recollections and have about finished *Tannhäuser*. What follows will include the period of his conducting, his life, and the beginnings of his plans for the future until the first rehearsals of *Lohengrin* under the Master's leadership were frustrated and his hopes also defeated."

141 A   "Wagner as a Royal *Kapellmeister*

"The next chapter in my memoir of our Master refers to the preparation and the scenery of *Tannhäuser*. As to the latter, everything had been mustered to render it magnificent. The stage decoration was painted by the Parisian artists Desplechin and Ditterle, renowned as the foremost in their line. The Valley of the Wartburg was very similar to the present set, only Wagner's strong desire to have the scene for the third act painted in autumn colors could not be carried out at that time. The Hall of Song, on the other hand, was intrinsically different from the present historically truer one—without impairing in any way the magnificent entrance of the guests and singers as well as the staging of the singers' contest. The costumes perhaps were designed more idealistically than the present ones, suiting the idealistic parts taken by the artists, who at that time fullheartedly strove for the solution of the task given them. Venus: Schröder-Devrient, though no longer in the prime of her life, captivated by the classicism of her movements.

"Before the real coaching of the opera began, lively discussions often arose between Schröder-Devrient and Richard. The irritable woman seriously or jokingly raised objections against this or that 'unsingable' passage. Annoyed, W. said: 'If she doesn't like the part, somebody else can sing it.' 'Then you don't find me young and beautiful enough?' was the laughing retort of the wanton Wilhelmine, looking enchanting with her beautiful blue eyes. 'Yes, when you wish to be.' 'Of course, I do!' Peace continued until next time, while Venus naturally remained in Wilhelmine's hands. She avoided the often Megaera-like, impetuous spirit to which nowadays impersonators of Venus often feel tempted, especially in arias subsequently composed, and so forth. One could imagine that *that* Venus, with her animated countenance, made Tannhäuser forget time and space.

"The Landgraf was a splendid presentation by the old, much celebrated Dettmer, who with his bass, which was both powerful and gentle, brought to the part its fullest value.[6] Tannhäuser—Tichatschek. How magnificently he trumpeted forth his praise of Venus in the first act! Oh, and how deeply felt was his awakening in the outer world! His duet with Elisabeth, his singing in the contest, how subtly graduated in its ascent; and the most splendid of his achievements—the pilgrimage to Rome!

"Tichatschek was nervous by nature and susceptible to passion, a faulty actor in many spots, but Wagner taught him to grow both as singer and actor. How nobly he sang the passage: 'The eyes closed, not looking at their wonders, I blindly wandered through Italy's delightful fields,' and so forth. I never could listen to this without being moved to tears.

"Wolfram—Mitterwurzer. This noble figure remains unforgettable to me! Beautiful and chivalric in his appearance, noble in his movements, and entirely engrossed in Wolfram's noble character, I have never since heard a baritone voice of such a soft euphony matched with manly beauty. Also the other singers were the equal of the two heroic singers. And now the only womanly part in the opera: Elisabeth—Johanna!

"Tears come to my eyes as I write, at the recollection of that youthful, pure, beautiful girl! Slender, with the most marvelous fair hair. I see her hastening into the brilliantly lighted Hall of Song. In her close-fitting, white silk dress with a flowing bright blue cape and a wreath of white roses. Delighted applause after the entrance air and the duet with Tannhäuser.

"She was quite like a princess at the reception of the guests, and a noble maiden in her astonishment at the increasing wildness in Tannhäuser's song. Warmth without straining after effect at the disclosure of Tannhäuser's misdeed. And, oh, how heartfelt her intercession with the indignant knights. Perhaps others would conceive this figure more tragically, but would this be in accord with Wagner's spirit? Johanna *was* at that time what she represented; the pure virgin, hardly conscious of her love in the beginning, whose heart was *bound* to be broken by the pain of deceived hope. Touchingly she sang and played the scene in the last act, and one understood that *only* her hope for the expiation of the lover had preserved her virginal soul for so long in her tender body, until it now had to escape: 'There to become a holy Angel!'

"Oh, my poor unforgettable Johanna!

"In spite of the frequent and often stormy applause and the most splendid

[6] "D. later on followed a call to Frankfurt-am-Main, where he stayed until the end of his career."

accomplishments of *all* the participants under Wagner's masterful conducting, he himself and his friends after the opening night didn't yet carry home the feeling of a really *full* success.

"That evening the Wagners had assembled the most intimate friends in their home; among them were his warmest and most faithful worshiper, Dr. Pusinelli,[7] 'Father' Fischer, and my parents. I gathered later on, from the talk of the last-named, that the small party may have taken a somewhat quiet course. A cake bearing the legend *Vivat Tannhäuser,* dedicated to him by his friends, was set aside unnoticed, and they left rather early, especially since Wagner, after all that excitement, must have been quite exhausted. During the next performance the public's understanding of the opera's enchanting beauty grew more and more and rose to enthusiasm. A complete triumph was the finale of the first act:

> " 'We greet you, brave singer,
> Missing among us, alas, for so long!'

"The great ensemble with Wolfram's decisive call, 'Stay with Elisabeth!' And Tichatschek's unforgettably beautiful tenor: 'Elisabeth! Power of heaven, do *you* utter that sweet name?' And how nobly Wolfram (Mitterwurzer) made the listeners divine his deep love for Elisabeth in the following arioso: 'When by brave singing you contested . . .' In the second act only Wolfram confesses to himself:

> " 'Thus every glow of hope
> Fades from this life!'

How few artists nowadays understand how to produce all this as it was under the spell of Wagner's conducting! Like a magnetic ray it flowed from him to all the participants.

"A striking issue was Wagner's change, some time later, of the end of the opera. While the men's chorus sings, 'The soul's salvation, fled from the pious martyr's body,' and so forth, he had a funeral procession come down the hill and Tannhäuser die at the side of Elisabeth's body, crying, 'Holy Elisabeth, pray for me.' This close may have been perhaps more effective; but a more practical close than the first conception can hardly be imagined, where, mingled with the sound of the men's chorus, the chimes of the funeral bell are heard above, while the Wartburg's windows are lighted. Tannhäuser, his failing eyes directed heavenward, sees his good angel soaring away and sinks dying into Wolfram's arms!

[7] "P. had supplied the means to Richard to furnish his apartment in the Ostra-Allee suitable to his position. Even later on he proved a generous rescuer of Richard from many of the predicaments so numerous in his life. P. was an entirely noble and high-minded man who remained a faithful friend to Richard until his last breath and who probably never divulged to his family *how much* he had sacrificed to this friendship. Does not such a spirit of sacrifice and devotion speak undeniably in favor of the man to whom it was offered?"

"Who and what may have induced the otherwise so clear-sighted Wagner to shelve and change so much in this opera and even in later years—who can tell?

"Anyhow, *Tannhäuser* could gain nothing by the multifarious changes; and at the time of the first ferment, there were many debates between Wagner, old Fischer, and my parents. My good father, especially, couldn't conceive that Elisabeth would have been put on the bier at her last breath and brought right away to Eisenach. The friends, otherwise so intimate, never agreed on this point. Whether it was performed with the original close or with the changed one, the opera always had capacity attendance and in the long run was unanimously applauded. How often could we hear the Overture to *Tannhäuser* in our even then mostly excellent garden concerts, the so-called 'Singers' March,' or rather the ceremonial 'Entrance of the Guests' from Act II, and—as a French horn solo —the 'Song to the Evening Star,' with orchestral accompaniment. Two evenings will remain unforgettable to me, when I heard that song—both times on the water—long after W.'s departure from Dresden. The first time [was] at an evening's gondola trip on the Elbe, when many members of the Hofoper and Kapelle had gathered. Four French horns played the accompaniment and Mitterwurzer sang, with tears in his eyes, '*O du mein holder Abendstern*' almost more beautifully than ever before!

"Ten years later I was with my dear father and Hermann Müller—a lieutenant of the Red Guard,[8] once Wagner's ardent admirer in his homeland, later his and Minna's faithful friend in Switzerland—on the Zürich lake in the moonlight when a small band sounded the 'Evening Star' on the beach. In tearful melancholy we listened then. And Richard was far away."

141 B
"Wagner's Activity as *Kapellmeister*

"With *Tannhäuser* my communications on Wagner's activities as a composer are really closed. He had won recognition and enthusiasm; now part of his restless aspirations turned to his position as *Kapellmeister*, and what he accomplished in this position assures for him until the present day the most grateful memory of Dresden's artists and friends of art.

"By the consummate performance of musical works which he put on the programs of the so-called Palm Sunday concerts,[9] he probably laid the foundation of the Subscription Concerts of the Dresden Court Theater Orchestra which in our time are enjoying an attendance and fame not surpassed by any other town in Germany. *He* knew how to draw together outstanding artists as well as the less important members of the Court Orchestra into an entity which re-

---

[8] See p. 186.
[9] "These concerts were given in the *old* opera house, which was destroyed by fire in the year 1849."

sponded to the slightest indication of his baton, to his every glance, arousing the audience to enthusiasm. But that success was not *made easy* for him. A large number of the artists with years of experience could not resign themselves to a young conductor who threw overboard so many customary ways when his broader purpose demanded it. So he put the magnificent Ninth Symphony on the program. Never before had there been so many rehearsals for a single work as for the Ninth—and especially the separate rehearsals for the cellos and basses which were held in the rehearsal room of the Hoftheater behind *closed doors.* 'No,' they said with meaningful shakings of the head, 'no, there has never been anything like this before! As if our cello and bass players haven't learned long since what to do.' But those involved soon found out what Wagner was working toward. They had their rehearsals and only smiled when the other colleagues grumbled, for they were looking forward to the first rehearsal with the whole orchestra. There *they* and *Wagner* with them enjoyed their great triumph. Cellos and basses started the recitativelike passage which introduces the theme of the 'Ode to Joy'; they played the theme first with an evenness and tone volume giving the effect of human voices; the theme itself murmured like an ideal inspiration, surging and fading until at last it joined the full orchestra with violins and violas. Then all of them forgot to continue rehearsing and burst out into an enthusiastic cheer. That was a happy moment for Wagner and probably meant more to him than the public enthusiasm later. He had conquered the whole orchestra!

"Wagner accomplished another great deed when he restudied and recast Gluck's *Iphigenia in Aulis.*

"In this Wagner put through an equally difficult and courageous undertaking. Many a discussion arose between him, old Fischer, my father, and, as a fourth in the group, his own brother Albert, who was often like an old powder barrel. Really lively scenes were enacted during the family walks, which we often all took together, for we lived in the same part of town, through the shady alleys of the so called *Grosses Gehege.*[10] Far ahead strode the four men, absorbed in their conversation; bringing up the rear were Minna, Albert's wife, my mother, and, finally, we young folks, Johanna often included. Usually peace did not last long between the gentlemen. The two brothers gesticulated right and left, with ever increasing emphasis. Albert grew red in the face, for he couldn't stand contradiction; and when one of the brothers got ahead by himself, father Fischer would sound his hearty laughter and my father would shake his head. 'Will they come to blows?' the two sisters-in-law would often ask. 'They won't hurt each other,' said my mother, reassuring them, and soon you could see the opponents come to terms and continue quietly walking together again. Those

[10] "This *Gehege* [park] had rows of mighty linden and chestnut trees and flowering meadows. It reached from the bank of the Weisseritz as far as the village Übigan on the Elbe and was the choice gathering place of children and adults. Soon this part of Dresden won't be recognizable any longer owing to railway and harbor installations."

days were harmless and full of content, and our walks usually ended in the so-called *Schusterhäuschen,* a small village inn with a country garden. We all sat together over a cup of coffee or simple supper, and Richard was often in his high spirits. We would walk home on a moonlit night, and I was happy when I could be beside my worshiped and beloved Johanna. During those walks the plans for the staging and the whole mounting of *Iphigenia* were discussed, for the opera was to have a brilliant production. Wagner undertook to connect the single numbers and choruses, which, according to the ancient style, had each its own short close; besides, he arranged an orchestra accompaniment for the recitatives, instead of the accompaniment on the orchestra *Klavier,* and adapted the instrumentation to the developments of a later day. Of course he found opponents here. Changes prompted by an inspired devotion to the old master Gluck were interpreted as a lack of reverence on the part of the young conductor. But Wagner worked undisturbed at his task. Score and parts were written out; Fischer studied the choruses with the same devotion which he brought to any undertaking by Wagner. The cast for the principal parts brought into the fray the first talents of the Dresden Opera: Agamemnon, Mitterwurzer; Klytemnestra, Schröder-Devrient; Iphigenia, Johanna; Diana, Frau Kriete-Wüst.

"According to all conversation in musical circles pro and contra Wagner's courageous enterprise, people were looking forward to the opera's first night with most tense interest. But Richard was confident in his task, and so were all those who had understanding for his genius. And how splendidly Wagner had known how to adapt himself to the great Master. There was no showing off on *his* part; it only mattered to him to show off *Gluck* in his whole greatness.

"Everybody played and sang with enthusiasm; the performers, the theater chorus included, in acting and gestures expressed the ancient epoch. The tonal beauty of the chorus of young warriors sung by women will remain unforgettable to me, and the effect of the orchestra! Mitterwurzer and Devrient came through magnificently, and how lovely the slender Johanna appeared as the Greek princess. The opera was a perfect and complete success, and still nowadays it remains a sublime delight for a distinguished musical audience.

"What more splendid refutation could be given to the frequently uttered indictment that Wagner was interested only in his own compositions than those two magnificent proofs of his reverence for the inspired creations of those two heroes?

"Soon, however, a new work absorbed him. The book of *Lohengrin* occupied his mind. But for new creation he needed a temporary retirement, which he sought in the village of Gross-Graupe near Pillnitz. There he settled with Minna and his beloved Peps. As well as I can remember, he took a mineral-water cure there. My good father responded to the repeated invitations to spend some time with him and may have lived in the simple farmhouse, there enjoying nice cozy days with the couple.

"An ardent admirer of Wagner and well known as a friend of Devrient, Hermann Müller, a first lieutenant of the royal guard and called 'the red miller' on account of his uniform, frequently came, when on duty as a commander of the Pillnitz castle guard, to Gross-Graupe to visit his friends. This also happened during my father's presence there. The men, followed by Peps, took one of their customary walks through the shadowy wooded paths. The conversation turned to *Rienzi* and its most outstanding numbers. Müller, though he had no voice, could not refrain in his enthusiasm from humming this or that motive. At length, in his excitement, he was moved to blare out more or less wrongly, '*Baut fest auf mich, den Tribunen.*' After a few minutes Peps, accustomed to better music, sat down on the path and burst into a pitiful howling. Richard hurried to his distressed darling and comforted him: 'Never mind, Peps, I wasn't singing.' Only the peals of laughter made Wagner realize the ludicrous side of the incident, and he heartily joined in. Often afterward if the friends disliked something, they exclaimed, 'Never mind, Peps!' Those lighthearted days were soon followed by grave days of trial for my poor father, days in which Richard and Minna proved to be true friends. As previously mentioned, the splendid scene painting by the Parisian artists Desplechin and Ditterle had inspired my brother [11] in this realm of art, and the youth, scarcely twenty years old, effected his purpose of being allowed to study with them. He owed that permission largely to the recommendation of Wagner, who greatly liked the idea of having the scenery for his operas painted by the son of his best friend. One day my father heard the news that his son had had the misfortune to slip from the uppermost platform of the high painting scaffold and to tumble down about four stories. Striking against three scaffoldings broke the force of the fall, but he was carried to the Hôtel Dieu, then the principal hospital. It was expected that the end of the third day would decide what were to be the consequences of that horrible fall, whether life and reason were to be preserved. The accident was to be kept secret from my mother, who worshiped her son like an idol, until some decisive news would come; this was done on the urgent advice of Fischer and Wagner. Now both as true friends helped the poor man to bear his burden. Both on long walks tried to reassure him by their comforting reasons and to divert his thoughts by inspiring talks. Richard put aside his music manuscripts and sacrificed all his free time to his friend. For the evening, when the decisive news was expected to come, he invited us and Fischer to tea. Fischer, then our housemate, undertook to wait for the letter's arrival. Wagner and his wife shared the hard task of diverting my mother's attention from the father's mortal dread and agony and to entertain her by forced cheerfulness. At last Fischer violently rang the anteroom bell and high above his head he waved the letter on the back of which was inscribed, '*Bonne nouvelle.*' It would be beside my purpose to describe the scene that followed; suffice it to say that Richard showed striking proof of his ability to feel warm, true friend-

[11] Wilhelm Heine.

ship, for usually sparing in outbursts of emotion, he swallowed his tears and said the most crazy things to quiet the excited hearts.[12]

"The overwhelming excitement caused my dear father to have a long sickness, confining him to house and bed for nearly two years. Of course, during that agonizing time his connection with friends was restricted to visits only, at which exciting conversation had to be avoided.

"The costumes for *Lohengrin* had been outlined earlier in sketches; and when my brother had returned from Paris after two years of study and had proved his ability by his first stage scenery for *Joseph* by Méhul (1848), Wagner had started negotiations with him about the scenery for *Lohengrin*, meanwhile finished. After detailed discussions about the scenery, conditioned by the plot, my brother designed the sketches for the first act which were completely approved by Wagner. Since an operation had improved the health of my father, intercourse with his friends became more frequent again. Together with Fischer the casting of the main parts was discussed. The performers of them probably were vividly present in Wagner's mind when he created the opera: Lohengrin, Tichatschek; Elsa, Johanna; Telramund, Mitterwurzer; Ortrud, Schröder-Devrient!

"Though the opera was not submitted, there was a continuing prospect of a performance.[13] On the strength of it my brother made the sketch of the first scene for a small model theater and put it up in the workshop of the Court Theater. This model was used by my brother's successor when, many years later, the ban on Wagner's work had been lifted. Also, the costumes were made exactly according to the outlined designs, since my father had conveyed them to the theater board when he was pensioned.

"Meanwhile storm clouds threateningly arose on the political horizon. The general unrest also affected those who usually kept aloof from political activity. In Wagner's case those impulses for changed conditions were of course at first connected with his musical activity. The coercion imposed upon him by submission to the theater intendant and his views was more and more felt and resented by him. This increased his irritability, which was a part of his nature anyhow, and frequently led to exasperation. From his apartment in the Ostra-Allee he moved to Marcolini's Palace, situated in the Friedrichstrasse. The much greater distance (considering the period) hindered more frequent social gatherings. Ill humor caused by the procrastination over his *Lohengrin* drove him more and more into politics. He outlined plans for ideal theater conditions in the future which seemed impractical to his friends. How often the waves beat high in friendly talks! At that time there emerged ideas which Wagner tried

[12] "Although this episode has no relation to Wagner's *musical* work, I felt urged to include it here since it casts a warm light on his feelings for friends."

[13] "An obligation survived from old custom for the Court conductor to submit a new opera of his own composition at certain intervals of time. On this fact Wagner based his hope for having *Lohengrin* studied in the near future."

to achieve much later, with the difference that only the upper strata of 'the nation' got the full enjoyment of it.

"As in the times of the Greeks, the theater ought to be dedicated to the people. The structure should stand on a mountain visible far and wide, like a temple of art. Then from all parts of the country people would have to flock together to be edified by the proffered beauty. Only truly great and sublime art would be brought to performance and offered in a suitable manner. Thus festivals would be arranged for the nation. If friends objected that those people for whom he wanted to create such beautiful art might be prevented by distance from coming, that the artists' financial demands might be too high, the idealistic Wagner brushed all those things aside, for to him there was no obstacle too great to be surmounted. The artists and all those contributing to the success of the enterprise wouldn't demand any fee. The nation ought to prove its gratitude, and so forth. Poor Wagner—money all his life was a source of disappointment and distress! The existence of the Court Theater appeared to him more and more as an absurdity. From the regimentation of the theater he turned to the question of government in general; he also wanted ideal conditions here. The foundering of his hopes of having *Lohengrin* performed was made certain to him by the cancellation of the order for scenery mentioned before, and this was the last impulse needed to bring Wagner into the hotbed of political writing. His 'Letter to the King' weakened his position and was a mighty weapon for his adversaries. But still he scarcely realized the implications of his action. When my father and Fischer remonstrated, he naïvely retorted: 'The King can't really be angry about it! In my letter I put him high above all the others. How could a King be shown greater than by relinquishing his throne and living among his people as the first nobleman of the liberated nation? His leanings are not those of a ruler but of a man who would like to indulge at his leisure in natural science. By his resignation so many calamities would be done away with. The theater ought to be ruled only by those who really have a call for it, true art only should be fostered . . .' and so forth. But of what use were all those ideas? The King *was* angry, the intendant still more so and—*Lohengrin* was shelved.

"Wagner's most intimate friends quite correctly claimed that he would never have been involved in the political troubles to such a degree if his energetic mind had been occupied with the studying of *Lohengrin*. Embitterment about the Court Theater's regimentation and the consequent disappointment made him accessible to the agitations of a man who by egotistic motives was driven to join the revolution: *Röckel!* The way this man understood how to take material advantage of Wagner's friendship, only a few have learned. To elaborate on this subject and to describe the events in May of the disastrous year of 1849 would lead too far from the point. They put an end to Wagner's activity as a Court conductor. But all the same, his works were accepted with ardent enthusiasm at the very place where fate had driven him, and nowadays they remain the principal attraction of the Dresden Opera!"

Frau Schmole's last installment is entitled "Wagner as a Politician (Revolutionary!)." Her main thesis is to decry August Röckel as Wagner's "evil spirit," who fomented his discontent with the conditions in the Hoftheater and was responsible for Wagner's plunge into the political maelstrom. Röckel, and later Bakunin, "made him believe that the overthrow of the existing government" would bring to pass his ideal plans for a popularly supported administration of the arts. Röckel deliberately planned the outbreak of the revolution, according to her account. He had nothing to lose by his drastic program, having already lost his position at the theater and involved himself deeply in debt. Against this indebtedness, he got Wagner to pledge his own household belongings, whereby Minna, after Wagner's flight, found herself stripped of her furniture. Only the generous help of friends saved her.

Since Frau Schmole was a girl of seventeen at the time, this denunciation of Röckel can only be a reflection of the opinion of her father and other friends. She tells how old Fischer taunted Röckel angrily on the street and how Minna looked upon him as Wagner's seducer. It is hard to realize through the perspective of years and subsequent revelations that Wagner could have been looked upon by his friends as a sort of innocent, deliberately led astray by designing men for their own ends. In a later day this seems a curious incomprehension of the basic Wagner who, while susceptible to every thought about him, invariably formed his own opinion and went his own way. That way, in a moment of storm tension, was to the very center of the trouble. Röckel we now know as an idealist of reckless courage, who had everything to lose by his actions, including his life, which he nearly forfeited. Wagner appears throughout as excitable, expostulatory, brimming with theories (of which there was already a superfluity on all sides), unfit to handle arms or organize revolt. That he could have been anything but in the way at such a time seems an equally naïve point of view.

It was natural that Frau Schmole, like Wagner's friends and Wagner himself, would have tried to minimize his actual participation in a revolt officially looked upon as treasonable. She protests that he could not have made "pitch rings" for the barricades, lacking dexterity. He may have carried a rifle, she continues, as almost everyone did at the time, but he could not have known how to use it. "When Wagner came to our house during the days of the Revolution, he certainly had *no* rifle. He appeared in greatest excitement and asked my father:

" 'Ferdinand, do me the favor of going with me. I know how we can get through to Neustadt. You are more closely acquainted with many officers; we can look them up and you can remind them how wrong it is to shoot their compatriots! When *they* stop it, the others will leave them alone too!'

"Of course my father explained to him the impracticability of this plan. Now Wagner proposed that they climb the Kreuzthurm, which would give them a splendid view of everything: the street-fighting, the various reinforcements coming from the country to the city, and so forth. Does not all this distinctly indicate that the fantastically excitable Wagner was inspired mainly by the romantic features of that Revolution?" Frau Schmole denies that Wagner rang the tocsin on the Kreuzthurm, or that he was there at all. She had this from Fischer's daughter, who told her that she had accompanied Minna to the tower with provisions for Wagner, only to find that he had not been there. But in *My Life* Wagner was later to describe his experiences on the tower in detail. Such is the reliability of even eyewitnesses of the revolt. Frau Schmole reproaches Ferdinand Praeger for stating in *Wagner as I knew him* that Wagner, in spite of his efforts later in life to disclaim any direct part in the revolutionary uprising, was definitely implicated on several points. Later investigation has borne out Praeger on this. If Wagner was a spectator in effect, he was a very close one, constantly in the company of the revolutionary leaders Bakunin, Röckel, and Hübner. He must have known their every plan and put in his word. If he was an amateur revolutionist, he was active enough as watcher and messenger. He may have been ineffectual in these respects, but there are many indications that as a writer and orator he was a firebrand.

❧ XII ✵

TANNHÄUSER PROBLEMS

Several letters in this Collection touch upon *Tannhäuser*, its composition, and its varied stage career in Wagner's time.

The composer writes to Kietz on September 6, 1842, in a letter anticipating the first *Rienzi* performance of October 20 (123):

"The only thing I accomplished this summer is the complete scenic sketch for the *Venusberg* [1]—I regard it as a complete success, and I am convinced that this opera will become my most original creation. When I find time to work out the verse (and I'll try to do it as well as possible), I'll send you a copy. I started the sketch on a small walking tour, which I undertook from Teplitz to the mountains and Aussig, etc.; I stayed overnight on the Schreckenstein (if you know it) and began the job. My children, it is marvelous there! Anders, Lehrs, and all of you, pray for *Rienzi,* and so we shall celebrate a festival next year on the Schreckenstein!

"In the village church of Aussig I asked to see the Madonna of Carlo Dolci: the picture gave me an unusual thrill, and if Tannhäuser had seen it, I might quite well account for his turning away from Venus to Mary, without being carried away too much by piety. Anyhow, the *holy Elisabeth* has now been decided upon."

Wagner writes to Kietz on December 18, 1844, about the progress of *Tannhäuser* (149):

"Unfortunately I have been hampered in my work until now, owing to my continuous occupation. After a long interruption, caused by the publication of both my operas, it was only last autumn that I got around to working again on my new opera. Now I have had to lay it down again and hardly expect to finish it before the beginning of next year. Since the scenery for it is being painted in *Paris* by Desplechin, who did not promise it before Easter, my opera can't be produced before, let us say, August or September of next year. But I expect to make a real revolution with it; for I feel that I have approached my ideal with giant steps. This between ourselves!"

[1] 121 in this Collection.

136

Between the introduction of *Tannhäuser* in Dresden in 1845 and its misadventure in Paris in 1861, the opera was taken up with alacrity by a number of Central European theaters. Wagner, believing that the unaccustomed poetic concept to be intelligible to the audiences should in the first place be made intelligible to the performers, wrote and circulated among the managers an explanatory brochure to serve in his enforced absence. The fortunes of the piece, and of the overture, making its way into concert programs, were sometimes strange.

François Seghers, the Belgian violinist, was the director of the Société Sainte Cécile in Paris, which he had founded in 1848. His promise to Wagner to conduct the *Tannhäuser* Overture failed to materialize because of the non-arrival of parts. In the following letter Wagner appeals to Liszt to obtain and send them. This Liszt did by early March, but the society's season being then nearly over the performance did not take place until the following season, on November 24, 1850.

198 *(Wagner in Paris, February 9, 1850, to Franz Liszt in Weimar)*

"Dearest Friend!

"Seghers is leaving at this moment—I wasn't able to speak to him earlier. To my surprise I learned from him that he would really like to perform my overtures, but for the present he balks at the copying of the orchestra parts, a matter which the Society has been too poor to carry out. Belloni had written to me previously that the Society would meet the expenses, so I had done nothing more about it. Now, the parts for the *Tannhäuser* Overture, at least, must be prepared as quickly as possible; I myself can't possibly pay the expenses for the copying here.

"So I urgently beseech you, dear Liszt, to have the *engraved* parts of the *Tannhäuser* Overture sent here as quickly as possible by Meser in Dresden, where they are published. This must be done by rail as soon as possible so as to minimize the loss of time. Meser should add the duplicate parts, thus:

"8 copies of the 1st violin
"8   "   "   " 2nd "
"6   "   "   " viola
"11 doublebasses and cellos

"I'm not writing directly to Meser, since I don't know whether he would send the needed copies on my request alone; for I no longer have any rights of ownership in my published music, as you know. That is why I turn to you as my intercessor, mediator, or whatever else you may be. Only be kind enough to push the thing through, for time here is very precious to me—needless to say— and I confess that what I have just found out has rather upset me, for it leaves me in the position of not being needed.

"Will you forgive me for bothering you again? Whenever I am in need, and something really important comes up, each time I instinctively apply to you. And that's how it is today.

"A thousand warm greetings from your faithful and grateful

RICHARD WAGNER"

218 *(Zürich, December 13, 1850, to E. B. Kietz in Paris)*

"MOST EXCELLENT FRIEND KIETZ!

"I thank you 7,500 times for your two overture letters, which in any case made more enemies for me than the overture affair itself. I was only wondering why, after you had written me so conscientiously about the rehearsals, I had to wait so long after the performance to get further news from you. Before receiving the latter I had already read, to my greatest satisfaction, the following witty remark about my overture in the bulletin of the *National:*

" 'This composition' (I translate faithfully) 'contained the noisy accompaniment of a nonexistent melody. Wagner certainly understands a great deal about harmony and instrumentation, but unfortunately Heaven has stubbornly denied him the gift of melody. No laws prohibit writing; certain laws in various countries prohibit only certain ideas: well, the laws of no country could have any objection to the performance of Wagner's works, since they contain no ideas whatever.'

"Herr Blanchard writes in the *Gazette Musicale* on the subject of Tannhäuser that the latter is a dissolute knight of the Middle Ages who subsisted on robbery and theft: without the description of the subject which he gives one cannot understand the overture, and that is bad, etc. My dearest friend Ernst Benedikt! When will you ever wake up? I can't really hold it against you for taking pleasure in the rehearsals, but your many worries and troubles with the performance were your just punishment. Let me assure you on my part that the news of Seghers' intention only put me in a bad humor, and that this bad humor disappeared only after I had made up my mind that fundamentally it didn't matter at all whether Paris liked the overture or not.[2] Also I'm afraid that you have an exaggeratedly strong ear for the applause that took place and drew the wrong conclusion from it. But the most delightful part of it all is your description of the whole thing and the adventures you had in connection with it: I've told them to my friends here with great effect."

On the strength of the growing success of *Tannhäuser* in Dresden, after a discouraging start on October 19, 1845, Wagner journeyed hopefully to Berlin with his score in December of that year. But Theodor von Küstner, intendant of the Royal Prussian Theater, considered it "too epic," while Graf Wilhelm

[2] Wagner's efforts to obtain this performance were in part due to the goading of Minna, who was as ambitious for tangible results from his Paris visit as he was skeptical about them.

von Redern, general intendant and closer to the throne, was suspected by Wagner of being too friendly with Meyerbeer to be of any real use to him. His Majesty, as it turned out, would be quite content with nothing more than band arrangements from *Kapellmeister* Wagner.

It was not until 1852 that the smaller theaters followed the lead of Liszt in Weimar in 1849, and found that they could produce *Tannhäuser* with profit. Wiesbaden was the first, and before long Wagner was approached on the subject by the Berlin Opera manager Mantius. Berlin offered the opportunity of continuing fees (not merely the initial payment as in the smaller towns). Wagner considered his stipulation of 1,000 thaler down payment as an assurance that the opera would not be too quickly shelved and as a test of the good will of Hülsen (Küstner's successor).

Hülsen, who had a greater liking for *Tannhäuser* than for its composer, was willing to make an effort in its behalf: it will be seen that there was a limit to how far he could go in meeting Wagner's conditions. Wagner was reluctant to entrust his opera to either *Kapellmeister* at Berlin: Taubert, uninstructed, would maul it; Dorn he bitterly remembered from Riga days. A blundering performance in so important a capital would brand both *Tannhäuser* and its composer with the mark of failure. Wagner, being himself debarred from Germany, turned to Liszt as the only one he could trust to conduct *Tannhäuser* in Berlin. But at this suggestion the resident conductors felt directly insulted, and on Wagner's insistence a tense situation ensued. On writing the following letters to Heine, Wagner hoped to save the situation, with the valuable help of Heine on scenic matters. But the Berlin *Tannhäuser* was to fall through.

230 A *(Zürich, August 11, 1852, to Ferdinand Heine in Dresden)*

"Dear old Friend:

". . . I am not in the best of health: I now have to suffer for the passion and violence with which I have always spurred on and made use of my nervous system. My nervous ailments have lately centered in the brain, and I must seriously consider rest and relaxation if I am to avoid very alarming conditions: recently I have again overexerted myself very much with writing the text of the *Walküre* (the first of the three Nibelung dramas) by finishing the whole thing in four weeks without the slightest pause. Difficult as it will be for me to restrain my passionate love of work, this last experience will have made me see the light after all, and I plan in the future to accustom myself systematically to restful interruptions from work. This will not, of course, remove the cause of my ailment, which is that, through the peculiarity of my nature and the artistic and living conditions of today, I am drawn into the realm of fantasy, where real, actual life can never have a refreshing and diverting effect on me, and this especially in my art. This observation brings me to a point which is certain to cause me new pain: the intended production of my *Tannhäuser* in Berlin. This production is quite against my wishes just now because I know that it cannot turn out well, at least that it will not correspond to my wishes and the requirements of a proper understanding. In Berlin everything affects me as so cold and heartless that there is not a single person to whom I can turn with confidence. Through your messages to Uhlig, for which I am very grateful to you, you yourself have done much to increase my misgivings about the undertaking. The male personnel of the Berlin Opera is certainly unqualified for my work: you have made me suspicious, and very justly so, of falseness in Mantius, whom *Formes* has recommended to me here in Zürich; on the other hand, I know Pfister too well as an industrious but completely ungifted and uninteresting singer to entrust my *Tannhäuser* to him. It is also an important fact that I have already come to know Dorn in Riga as perfidious and treacherous toward me. On whom then can I depend? On first considering the situation in Berlin, I was inclined to withhold altogether my permission for the planned production, but then I found a way out which should at least favorably dispose the manager toward my work: I have asked for a royalty of 1,000 thaler, to be paid immediately, and I have carefully motivated my demand so that it should not appear as merely presumptuous. (The royalties for the fifteen passable performances on which I must at least count would certainly bring me the sum I asked for.) If Hülsen does not accept this demand, it will be perfectly all right with me; in that case I'll *wait,* as I have waited so far, until the time when a better male cast gives me better reassurance for the production. If Berlin *now* comes along with a feeble performance and a lukewarm success, the harm to me will be irreparable; I should prefer to let *Tannhäuser* be performed at all other good theaters, and when a general success is established let Berlin have its chance too; then they can hurt only *themselves,* but no longer do me any harm.

"It is quite another matter if Hülsen accepts my demand (from which, incidentally, I don't retract one iota); in this case, if I could be sure of Hülsen's energetic cooperation, something could be risked, and then, dear friend, I would count on your most active assistance. Uhlig has already reported to me that you at once remembered on your own initiative the needs for scenery and costumes; I thank you warmly and only ask you to permit me, in case Hülsen accedes, simply to transfer to you all my authority to deal with him in the above-mentioned matter, as I have already appointed *Liszt* to be my 'alter ego' in all musical affairs.

"In the main you will probably use the Dresden scenery as a basis but with more appropriate modifications, especially for the first scene (Venusberg) where the greater depth of the Berlin theater is to be used. But concentrate especially on the *last act*: I absolutely insist on the modified, that is more completely realized, close of this act; don't ask my reasons here, they are well considered and remain unshakable. In Dresden the difficulty with this new close was, apart from the unsatisfying and almost always unpleasant performer of the part of Venus, the lack of special scenery, since we had to content ourselves with whatever was available. In Berlin, however, special scenery would have to be prepared, scenery which would present the reappearance of the Venusberg *completely differently* than in the first act; namely, *much farther in the background,* in confused uncertain contours, so that Venus especially appears far back, not so unfortunately far forward and not so concrete as in Dresden. *For me this is the most important point.* Since—as you correctly thought—I want also to include the final pilgrims' chorus, a nice sunrise effect (morning glow) might be taken into consideration, which can be satisfactorily achieved only if the valley in this act—with a slight change perhaps (then spring, now fall)—is freshly and specially designed. This, my dear, I leave in your hands, and—if the matter materializes at all—I'll give you, as I said before, the fullest authority to act on my behalf.

"Goodbye for today. I hope I may count on early news from you; then more from me! Greetings to your family from both of us, and give old Fischer an affectionate kiss from me.

"Your

RW

"I have just spent four weeks on a vacation trip on which I visited the high Alps and finally Italy (Lago Maggiore), then also Chamonix and Mont Blanc. Minna is still limping from a Chamonix expedition, where she had a fall." [3]

230 B *(September 11, 1852, to Ferdinand Heine)*

"Oh! Oh! Oh! You wonderful man! How shall I praise, prize, and extol you? How well you've taken care of my *Tannhäuser!* What more can I bring myself to say than a hundred thousand thanks! What's the idea, in heaven's name, of letting yourself be put upon like that, as if your possible objections would make me angry, etc.? Certainly you've misunderstood Uhlig, for *that* he cannot have meant! Nor do I see what I could find objectionable in your (excellent!!) settings? What I indicated in that 'message' is a generalization for the lesser theaters; a more detailed analysis for those theaters with greater accommodations at their disposal was taken for granted. I made only the roughest outline. Well, Ferdinand Heine! You are a deserving man, very deserving! You are a devil of a fellow who will fry in the very hottest of hells for your efforts on behalf of a heretic like me—a fate which since you can stand heat so cheerfully will not be at all unpleasant for you! I thank you from head to toe, and with everything that lies, stands, hangs, and dangles in between.

"Only for one thing do I not find forgiveness in your eyes, and that's my conduct toward the Berlin management: I should regret it if you failed to understand that in no way did stubbornness or presumptuousness motivate me, but solely the most legitimate concern for the welfare of my *Tannhäuser,* in which

[3] See *My Life,* p. 588.

connection I don't in any way mistrust the honorable and noble sentiment of Herr v. Hülsen, but I do doubt his exact knowledge of my extremely difficult position with this opera in Berlin. I immediately withdrew my royalty demand when Albert gave me to understand that Hülsen saw in it a vote of no confidence against himself; I therefore asked only for a written assurance from Hülsen that he *recognizes* the difficulty of my position and intends to overcome it. What happened after that and what I in turn *had* to do you will gather from the content of my last letter to Albert, which you should presently receive from *Uhlig*. Be smart, my little Heine, and understand *what* is at stake here.

"Hülsen is still too inexperienced and is duped by Meyerbeer and Meyerbeer's agent with the King, Count Redern: the sudden change according to which they all at once believe that *Tannhäuser* cannot be given either on the birthday of the King or on that of the Queen (Hülsen has explained this to Albert) does not come out of the clear blue sky; this is the work of Meyerbeer, and toward him Hülsen must act with a high hand, otherwise we're both lost with *Tannhäuser*. For Prague I should like to have new scenery prepared after all: I'll write to them (for only out of ignorance did Stöger not ask for it), and you keep some ready!"

The project of a Berlin *Tannhäuser* persisted, and reached a new activity of negotiations in 1854. Wagner held to it principally because he needed the money it would bring. Hülsen wanted it because the opera had been prospering in one theater after another.

The following letter is undated, but Wagner's reference to his demand for 1,000 thaler from Berlin in advance royalties as having been made "two years ago" would place it in 1854. The intimate *du* indicates Ferdinand Heine (254 A):

"DEAREST FRIEND!

"I'll have to write to you once more about the matter, although—God knows—I am at a loss to make the main point any clearer than I believed I had already done in my last letter.

"I *repeat*: I *don't* really distrust *Dorn*, and misgivings about his *ability* as conductor and even about his *good intentions* are *not* the reason for my way of acting; furthermore, I state *more clearly* that I *don't* at all base the guarantee of a bigger success in Berlin on Liszt's greater *ability as conductor*, but (if not) at least for the most part on definite abilities which are inherent in Liszt's nature and his past as well as in his position and which enable him and *him alone* to paralyze very definite influences in Berlin which are extremely hostile and harmful to me. I KNOW what tremendous influence *Meyerbeer* has in Berlin, and I KNOW how very much this influence has already harmed me there and that he is now intent on making it completely impossible for *Tannhäuser* to have a big success. Just believe me when I assure you that I KNOW that. I found out, for example, that, despite inadequate performance and despite the fact that the press did not in any way conduct itself favorably beforehand, my *Rienzi* made a completely *favorable* impression on the still UNINFLUENCED audience at the first performance in Berlin, so that I was certain of success. But I also found out that the press (which in its chief publications was already completely subservient to Meyerbeer) immediately slandered *Rienzi*; and I then confirmed what already is common knowledge—namely, that the public allowed itself to be taken in by this attitude of the press to such an extent that the second performance was already badly attended. I found out further that Meyerbeer (through his friend Redern) knew how to keep the King from attending one of the three performances conducted by me, as well as from receiving me in audience: I have *proof* of this. These and similar experiences have made me determined not to permit anything more to be performed in Berlin without extraordinary guarantees against the above-mentioned influences; and I repeat *again* that it is not the Berlin *acclaim* (this can indeed be won) which matters to me, but the Berlin *receipts,* which, after all, I can use. The guarantee through Liszt's influence occurred to me only as a last resort, after I had been refused all other guarantees. At first, two years ago, I asked—simply keeping the main point in mind—for an advance payment of 1,000 thaler on the royalties. Since this was refused, but since, on the other hand, my niece *Johanna*[4] assured me that she would use *all* means at her disposal to serve me, and since Hülsen himself also agreed to certain promises in the matter of the repetitions, I was satisfied. But my confidence in Johanna's influence and enthusiasm, as well as in Hülsen's determined good will toward me, were forfeited when, at the time *Tannhäuser* was scheduled to be produced, Auber's *Lac des Fées* and Flotow's *Indra* were (all of a sudden) brought out. I gathered from that how serious Johanna and Hülsen were, withdrew my score, and turned the whole matter over to *Liszt*. After these last experiences I see *in him* alone the guarantee for the determined effort which is needed, but which I have been unable to find anywhere else. But Liszt can counteract those harmful influences only in an *official* capacity: he himself states that it does not matter to him whether he actually takes his place at the conductor's desk; but it does matter that, as representative in Berlin, he exert his influence on the conduct of the management as well as on the party which is harmful to me—an influence which, with his many different connections and associations, he is especially capable of exerting.

"Can I be more explicit than this?

"But one more word about *Dorn*. He did not inform you correctly about Riga. If I had become impossible for Riga, how then could Holtei's successor,

[4] Wagner's brother Albert attempted, by letters, to bring Liszt and Hülsen to terms. He no doubt hoped to gain for his daughter Johanna the boon of a Berlin Elisabeth. But his attempts were clumsy. He had little patience with Richard's ways; when Richard tried to touch his niece for a substantial loan, Albert wrote tartly and communications between the two families ceased for the time being.

Hoffmann, who was obliged to engage Dorn for *one* year only, offer to keep me in Riga for that year by getting me lessons in return for which he at once offered me a new contract *after* that year? But *Dorn* was my intimate friend, and when Holtei told him about this arrangement it was up to him—before settling the matter with him—to inform me (as his friend) of Holtei's intention; he could then still have accepted the position. But Dorn settled with him, secretly in the face of all the world and myself, continued his intimate friendship with me, and only later did I discover this—*treachery*.

"But these are old stories: I don't even hold them against Dorn—if my confidence in him is not excessive there are good reasons for that. Here they do not count: I would be quite satisfied with Dorn's direction of *Tannhäuser* (under *different external circumstances*).

"Forgive me for making excessive demands on your friendship with such explanations; but let me assure you that this time I have no other intention than to justify my way of acting only to *you* as my trusted friend.

"Accept once more a thousand thanks for all the goodness and kindness which I owe to you!

"Your

RW."

As interchanges of correspondence over a Berlin *Tannhäuser* dragged on, Wagner would have been ready to let Hülsen do pretty much what he pleased with it, if only he could be relieved of the bother and collect his fee. But the figure of Liszt now rose up as the only obstacle. Having made an issue of his presence and assistance, Liszt found it impossible to withdraw with honor. But Hülsen could not permit the insult to either of his two *Kapellmeister* of allowing Liszt's interference in their duties even in an advisory capacity. Wagner would plainly have been willing to dispense with Liszt for the sake of breaking the deadlock, but he was too loyal, too tactful in his letters to Liszt to so much as hint at a capitulation. Liszt budged not an inch, while the issue became a *cause célèbre* in Berlin.[5]

In 1855, Wagner resorted to a desperate plan. He sent Minna, in October, on a journey to Weimar and on to Berlin, where she consorted with Alwine Frommann, as a zealot near the Prussian throne, and with Hülsen himself. There was still a way to solve the problem while saving Liszt's face: if Wagner himself could somehow get permission to go to Berlin, Liszt could remain in Weimar in all honor. Minna made the lone journey to Germany, probably coached by her husband to try to obtain this permission. But her expedition

[5] When the production at last took place, on Jan. 7, 1856, the public curiosity had reached such a point that mail orders would have filled the house ten times. A cartoon (254 B) which appeared in the *Kladderadatsch* on Jan. 13, 1856, shows Wagner with a score of *Tannhäuser* and a harp, applying for admission to the "Berlin Wartburg." He is riding Liszt, who is on all fours. Hülsen, as tournament master, is saying: "All right, honored minstrel! On foot, with pleasure, but the steed must be left outside!"

took an unexpected turn. Without Wagner's knowledge she went from Weimar, at the Grand Duke's advice, to Dresden, where she presented a petition to the King of Saxony for her husband's pardon (192). She was given some verbal encouragement. On her return to Zürich she wrote a hopeful letter to Hülsen on November 4, 1854. Woldemar Lippert (*Wagner in Exile*) believes that Wagner even then knew nothing of her suit nor of this letter. But a draft for the letter, complete, in Wagner's handwriting is in the Collection, and so proves the contrary (266, undated):

"Esteemed Herr General Intendant!

"Bearing in mind your kind reassurances, I take the liberty today of informing you of the state of affairs about which I recently had the honor of talking with you personally. During my visit to Weimar, and no less after my return to Zürich, I convinced myself that now the only problem is how to withdraw the previously stated condition of the official collaboration of Herr Liszt at the performance of *Tannhäuser* in Berlin without exposing to *any harm* the much-tried friend of my husband. Therefore it would seem most suitable to me if it were made possible for my husband to come to Berlin himself, for this way the former condition would be automatically obviated. Therefore I decided to leave from Weimar for Dresden directly, in order to obtain in the highest quarters the authorization for my husband to return to Germany. Supported by a letter from the Grand Duke of Weimar to the King of Saxony, I was fortunate enough to meet with a favorable reception of my application; however, it was intimated to me that no political action, such as an amnesty, could take place before three months. In case, honored sir, you are really interested in having *Tannhäuser* performed this winter, you might be in a position to make this possible by being so very kind as to have the appropriate authorities inquire in Dresden whether they would object to Wagner coming to Berlin for a few weeks now, just for the performance of his work. Judging from the atmosphere I encountered in Dresden, I think that I am justified in presuming that such an inquiry, which would reflect honorably upon my husband, might well serve to speed up the amnesty of Wagner, which I so much desire, whereby also any obstacle to the performance of his opera in Berlin would be removed immediately. Incidentally, Wagner would in no way insist upon an official summons to Berlin, neither does he intend to conduct his opera himself; what really matters to him is the permission to be in Berlin at the time of the rehearsals of his work, so that he may serve the spirit of the intended performance by personal contact with the performers, without making any further claims.

"Since according to my experience I consider this the only way to get out of the situation regarding Herr Liszt, and since at the same time I could not long more ardently for anything than to see *Tannhäuser* performed as soon as possible on the brilliant stage which is under your direction, I dare submit this request, encouraged by your great kindness, and assure you that by granting it you would bestow great happiness upon a wife who is deeply worried about the fate of her husband.

"Looking forward to a favorable reply I remain with the greatest respect your most devoted

M. W."

Hülsen was quite unable to do anything about these suggestions. Not only was Minna's petition to Johann, the new King of Saxony, to meet with a downright refusal, but Johann, as a later communication shows, looked upon Wagner as a dangerous enemy of the state.

Tannhäuser was not produced in Berlin until January 7, 1856. Liszt's presence at a few piano rehearsals was no more than a placating gesture by von Hülsen. The production, under Dorn, was elaborate but, according to the initiated, far from faultless.[6] Thus *Tannhäuser*, established as a money-maker in many a small town, had at last made its way into the Prussian capital, while the other large centers, Vienna and Munich, yet made no move. But the name of Wagner, even in Paris, was one to excite curiosity and stir controversy.

The letters following will convey something of the enthusiasm which *Tannhäuser*, as a new apparition in Europe, aroused on every side.

279 *(Elise, Gräfin Schlik, Honorary Sister* [Ehrenstiftsdame], *in Prague, January 2, 1855, to Wagner)*

"DEAR SIR!

"I wish to thank you myself for the page which Liszt sent me from you for my music album. It has given me indescribable joy, and I am much envied for it. At the same time I beg to express the genuine admiration which, after having heard *Tannhäuser* six times, I felt for this colossal work! At first it seemed to me as if I saw a building before me, of such dazzling height, of such gigantic proportions, of such strange style, that I could marvel at it in astonishment, but could neither quite grasp it nor understand it. Only later did it grow clear to me how wonderfully poetry and music are interwoven here, erecting a fairylike palace, full of the loveliest, the most overwhelming apparitions! What a treasure of poesy and melody you bear in your breast, dear Sir! What can misfortune, what can the hate of mankind do to you? The source of purest joy lies deep in you, and nobody can deprive you of it. But is it possible that the earnest and noble path you tread *could* ever find imitators? I am afraid, no—only a person

---

[6] Wagner received this description of the Berlin critics from his sister Cäcilie (301) on Jan. 7, 1858: "How furious I was about that crowd of Berlin critics who tore the music to pieces when *Tannhäuser* was performed here. As for that Rellstab—I could have scratched his eyes out! I realize that such stupid people with their reviews are nothing but dogs barking at your genius, but nevertheless I could hardly contain myself with fury. How frequently and how badly this marvelous work has been performed here, and how crowded the house is each time, as you may have learned from your receipts."

as talented as you could climb to such heights! And where to find such a person —somebody whom nature has endowed as lavishly as you with two rare gifts? And so I believe that your works will in time exist for posterity—great, lofty, powerful, and solitary as, for instance, one of the highest Alps! The first performance of *Tannhäuser* was awaited here with feverish impatience—the rehearsals were as crowded as a regular theater performance, and everybody was grateful to Director Kittl, who by the participation of the Conservatory had made the performance possible. The Bohemian, I should like to say, is a born musician, and even the people hold in affection their old, generally serious, and simply constructed songs. The usual sugar water of Italian operas does not meet with approval here! And so I can say with sincere joy that I have even heard people of the lower classes utter the wish: 'If only I could hear *Tannhäuser.*' Seats are still in such demand that a great number of my acquaintances have not as yet been able to attend any performance. . . ."

283 *(Franz Lachner, in Munich, August 13, 1855, to Wagner)*

"HIGHLY RESPECTED SIR!

"I cannot deny myself the pleasure of telling you that yesterday, Sunday, the 12th of August, your *Tannhäuser* was performed with the most splendid success.

"Even the overture was enthusiastically acclaimed and the applause increased from act to act. I can also testify that our artists endeavored to solve their hard task with warm love and enthusiasm, and that Frau Quinz as Elisabeth and Herr Kindermann as Eschenbach were especially successful. Intendant Dingelstedt will report to you more fully about the performance and its success, but meanwhile permit me to express to you my warmest sympathy with your splendid success and to assure you that it will give me the greatest pleasure soon again to undertake one of your works.

"With distinguished respect,

Yours most faithfully,

FRANZ LACHNER"

302 A *(Strassburg, January 15, 1858, to Minna in Zürich)* [7]

"DEAR MUZIUS!

"I call this an adventure! I have just heard the *Tannhäuser* Overture and experienced a stirring homage. What do you say to that! Listen, and you will hear about a real magic of Fate.

"Last night I was not able to close my eyes until Basel, and I arrived there quite exhausted at four o'clock in the morning, spending one and a half hours in the restaurant room until the departure of the omnibus for the train. Finally

[7] Wagner writes over the letter "nine o'clock in the evening," which would mean that he wrote it immediately after the incident described (cf. *My Life,* pp. 672–673).

I was overwhelmed by a deathlike sleep and I stretched out on the bench. When I awoke, the omnibus and express train had already left a good half-hour before. Nobody had noticed me or called me, and now there was nothing left to me but to take a final nap in 'The Stork' and leave next morning around ten o'clock by another train, by which I was to arrive in Strassburg about three o'clock in the afternoon, thus giving up, of course, the continuation of my trip to Paris.

"While pondering about my fate and musing about the consequences of not arriving in Paris on Friday, I started out to take a good look at the cathedral again and to make straight for the theater after having no more than read the title of some presumably silly French play on the large poster. I liked the very pretty theater, got a floor ticket in a front row near the orchestra; there the enclosed program was handed to me and almost in a daze I read *'Tannhäuser.'* Good heavens, what is this? Looking closer, I saw that it was the overture which was to be offered to the public as a special item. I felt very queer. Meanwhile some of the musicians who know me from Zürich had discovered me, especially the good Dresden tympanist Hahnemann, your former admirer. Like wildfire, of course, it spread through the orchestra that I was there; the conductor, a clever young Frenchman, quickly had himself introduced to me at my seat before he started. Beaming with delight, the whole orchestra was looking at me. Now they began playing and, to my greatest surprise, I heard a full-sized orchestra excellently prepared, the tempi quite correct in the main, everything clearly and well executed.

"My God, how mightily I was carried away by hearing something performed of my works, actually without my doing and without any consideration of me. And nothing else than the *Tannhäuser* Overture! I sat there in an indescribable inner excitement. Unfortunately I was strongly observed by the public, which had learned about my being present, but I didn't realize it and burst into a grateful flood of tears. There I sat and amidst the turmoil of the instruments the grave expiating Pilgrims' Chorus met my ear. At the end, during the mighty applause of the audience, which didn't realize how it happened, the conductor and the whole orchestra turned around to me and clapping their hands cried out to me to rise and express thanks, whereupon I left the theater immediately. Outside in the corridor several gentlemen from the audience welcomed me right away, among them an architect Weiher, whose name you should remember. My music director was in a condition of delight, and revelled in his experience of this evening.

"Well, I went home and here I am writing you this story which is nice enough to be related to the neighbors. I don't deny that that strange incident has deeply stirred me. With hot tears I felt that laurels were destined for me. Well, I hadn't looked for them!

"Tomorrow at eleven o'clock I am to continue to Paris, when I shall probably be in a state of anger and annoyance only, as a counterbalance to that nice freak of destiny. . . ."

❧ XIII ᕽ

TICHATSCHEK: THE FIRST TANNHÄUSER

Joseph Aloys Tichatschek (1807–1886) was the principal tenor in Dresden when Wagner went there in 1842. He remained there during the years that Wagner was neither performed nor mentioned at the Hofoper, and in those years sang elsewhere as guest the *Rienzi* and *Tannhäuser* he had brought to performance under Wagner's industrious supervision. Although Wagner was well aware of his limited intelligence and anxious to preserve their friendship in expectation of his possible usefulness, there is no denying a genuine warmth in the letters here revealed. This tenor was singularly free from the self-interest and insufferable airs that so often go with his breed. He was unfailingly good-natured, even in those difficult moments which always come up in a rehearsal, because he deeply revered the *Meister,* and put before every other consideration his eagerness to satisfy him. Wagner had good reason to keep up his friendly relations with Tichatschek even in their years of separation, for *Heldentenören* equal to his tremendous vocal exactions were scarce, and as a rule his operas relied most heavily upon them.[1] He kept a weather eye open, as he composed his scores, for a tenor to give them life. His first thought for Lohengrin was naturally Tichatschek, although he was barred from coaching him. He would have welcomed him as the first Tristan, had he been available. For Siegfried he first visualized Albert Niemann, because of that singer's youth and splendid stature. But Wagner, after *Rienzi,* was unfortunate in his tenors. Niemann, singing the Paris *Tannhäuser,* brought down his hopes by proving to be of the brainless variety. Ander's fear of the part of Tristan kept Vienna from first producing that opera. Schnorr von Carolsfeld, a Tristan after his fondest dreams, was suddenly cut off by premature death.

Tichatschek would not have been equal to Tristan, for, as Wagner was compelled to admit, he was not equal to Tannhäuser. He had a splendid, vibrant voice and the willingness to obey directions, but he did not possess the understanding to feel the anguish of a tragic scene nor the ability to moderate and color his voice to what the composer desired. Rienzi was his outstanding part. Wagner, then first on trial before the public, readily forgave him the "childish limitations" and "superficiality" of his talents because of the "lighthearted enthu-

[1] Note that the tenor part commanded the title of *Rienzi, Tannhäuser, Lohengrin, Siegfried, Tristan und Isolde,* and *Parsifal.*

siasm with which he flung himself into his congenial role and the irresistible effect of his brilliant voice." Indeed, Wagner counted on Tichatschek, resplendent in silver armor, exhorting the Roman populace in ringing tones, to carry *Rienzi* to a popular success. It was a triumph for both men, and the memory always bound them in affection.

The following letter is undated, but the context shows that Tichatschek had hastened to send a message of loyalty to the outcast Wagner, just settled in Zürich:

189 (*[Zürich, 1849]*)

"My dear Tichatschek!

"You may rest assured that your dear letter has given me extraordinary joy: you are still the old Tichatschek and with the best will I could ask no more, for with that the utmost has been said! Even before you wrote I repeatedly heard how kindly you were thinking of me and how often you remembered the time we lived and worked together. It was always a joy to me to hear this, for my recollections of you and of our life together are really the only pleasant ones of my seven years in Dresden: you were the only really cheerful and enthusiastic man in that general environment of leather, old-fogies and philistines. The evenings we spent in your home after my operas were really my only recompense for the thankless drudgery and toil we endured together. It is almost with a shudder of disgust that I look back on Dresden, where every step forward cost me the trouble of a hundred steps, ninety-nine of which were in reverse. You were really the single ray of light to illumine that night.

"Uhlig will report to you everything you may wish to know about me and my retired life here. I am quite pleased on the whole with my personal status; the future troubles me not in the least, for if I can't live a free and independent life I should prefer not to live at all. At least I no longer pursue an occupation which doesn't appeal to me. Never again will I be assigned to rehearsals of *Martha,* etc. As you know, Liszt [2] takes endless pains to perform my operas with his entirely insufficient personnel. I am pleased about it, for even when my works are being performed on the most limited stage, I know at least that they are led by a highly gifted conductor who penetrates my spirit.

"Now I am going to write an opera especially for Weimar,[3] and should be quite satisfied with this plan only if I knew *you* were to be with me. Also I should like to have Johanna [4] there; but she is wandering about the great world,

[2] When Liszt had mounted *Tannhäuser* at Weimar, Feb. 16, 1849, he had engaged Tichatschek on Wagner's urging.

[3] *Siegfrieds Tod.*

[4] Wagner's niece, the daughter of Albert, had sung opposite Tichatschek as the first Elisabeth.

and her parents won't allow her time to devote herself to my works. But it was pleasant to hear from you that she thinks kindly of me. About half a year ago I once wrote her in Hamburg apologizing for not having yet answered her very friendly letter. She has not answered so far. I can almost believe that her parents are a bit uneasy about me; they may even be thinking, now that they are so well off on account of Johanna's success, that it would be human decency to offer me something in my stranded position. May they overcome that worry! I count only on those who love me because I am what I am, but never on those who want me to be something else!

"Dear friend, you mention your hope of seeing *Lohengrin* performed in Dresden soon; Fischer also writes to me that Lüttichau has told him of his decision to give that opera in the winter and that he wishes to get the King's permission.[5] I ask you now in all seriousness to notify Lüttichau in good time and before he takes the necessary steps, that I sincerely thank him for his friendly attitude toward my opera, but if I am to have any say in the matter, I would *in no case* give my consent to a performance of *Lohengrin* in Dresden. You, dear friend, are the only one whom I had in mind for the principal part, and who could perform it to my satisfaction. Nothing will be more painful to me than to give you up. I would not entrust my work to *any of the present conductors in Dresden* to be studied and performed: it is quite out of the question for Reissiger or Krebs to perform my *Lohengrin*. I declare it quite impossible and refrain from saying more. With Liszt it is quite different: he is a man of genius and an artist, and enthusiastically devoted to me. I could trust him with anything, as I could trust no other conductor, for no one knows better than I the sort of conductor needed to perform this opera with understanding and effect. I urge you to explain to Lüttichau before he commits himself to this, that for his own sake I wish he would not! I'm in no position to write to him myself, nor would he expect it. It is only you I am sorry for: not only shall I lose you as the interpreter of Lohengrin, but I must also deprive you of a pleasure, for you surely took every conceivable trouble to bring Lüttichau to his decision. From the bottom of my heart I thank you and beg you to forgive me if my decision ends your hopes of seeing your endeavors crowned with success.

"But now let me hear from you soon; if so, you will give me the greatest joy, and if you could visit me some time that would be the best of all. Just ask Uhlig, he will tell you how glorious it is here in Switzerland! Above all, stay well. Greet your wife and child for me and keep loving me as much as you can.

"Your old friend and brother

RICHARD WAGNER

"You may write to me without fear, my residence now is Enge near Zürich."

[5] This intention on the part of Lüttichau is not mentioned in *My Life,* where the intendant is presented as having turned sharply upon Wagner at the crisis and as having remained hostile.

In 1852, when the German theaters on every side were beginning to show an interest in *Tannhäuser,* its composer wrote a brochure, *On the Performing of Tannhäuser,* and sent a copy to each theater contemplating a performance. Portions of his treatise were published in the *Neue Zeitschrift,* December 3, 1852, to January 14, 1853. In his efforts to demonstrate clearly how the part of Tannhäuser should be interpreted, he was constrained to remark that Tichatschek, although its first interpreter, was not its model. That Tichatschek did not take this in good part is shown by the following letter:

253 *(Zürich, December 17, 1853)*

"TSCHEKEL!

"You are a crazy, good, dear fellow! Don't let any envious asses talk you into anything. It is true that they would only be too glad to sow dissension between us. I readily confess that I hadn't thought out what kind of misconception might arise from those printed remarks, if they unexpectedly got around to persons for whom they were not intended: but only malicious busybodies without the intelligence to understand what I really wanted to say could conceive that I had meant to criticize you. *What* I urgently wanted to make known at the time when *Tannhäuser* was about to be rehearsed at theaters entirely unfamiliar to me was the experience I had had with it in Dresden. I am of the opinion that at that time I yielded too fearfully and too quickly to individual demands of singers who likewise had become fearful, and that in this way certain tasks remained unfulfilled which—so I believe—can be fulfilled nevertheless, and by nobody better than you, if we can find the courage which we lacked at that time.

"However, let us drop that subject! Above all, no arguing! I shall be only too glad to be in the wrong with a good friend!

"Thus, many thanks for your unfaltering love for me and particularly for giving me the opportunity of finally saying this to you again!

"Kindest regards to you and your family from me and my wife, who charges me to give you a marital kiss!

"Farewell and always think well of your devoted

(though sometimes peculiar)
RICHARD W"

269 *(Joseph Tichatschek, Dresden, February 5, 1855, to Wagner [by hand])*

"MY DEAR RICHARD,

"You should and must have the firmest conviction that, though I rarely take up a pen, my thoughts are with you every day, and that you have in my heart, which is so empty of joy, a very dear, comfortable, and spacious place. Though some gloomy cloud may have arisen to darken my interest in you as friend and artist, my attitude has not changed, I am full of enthusiasm about your genius, as well as your inspired works and the products of your spirit. With your departure the spark of life has left our artistic horizon; and the farther the time recedes when you were *one of us,* furthering the spirit of art in our midst, the more the conviction prevails that that time was the 'golden age' of our opera. Operas by Gluck are now *pia desideria.* Our singer Ney (three days ago become Mad. Bürde) likes to sing *Norma, Lucia, The Merry Wives of Windsor,* Rosina —Isabella (in *Robert*), wherein a certain unmentionable part must perform its *moving* function. Too bad, too bad for this really marvelous, fine-sounding voice.

"But what does it matter? Certain quarters favor this kind of *music,* or rather 'musical whining' [*Tonwinseley*]—how stupid of me to get on this subject—you know it just as well as I do and better. But in a little circle dedicated to everything beautiful and lofty, you are celebrated, dear old fellow [*lieber alter Schwede*]; and this was especially the case on December 12 of last year, when on the founders' day of the *Zehner* (Society to which I have the honor of belonging, and consisting of ten persons) I had musical director Hünerfürst perform two numbers and the overture from *Rienzi,* two numbers from *The Flying Dutchman,* and instrumental excerpts from *Lohengrin.* We reveled—I was more enthusiastic than ever—I sang with a voice of rare inner feeling. There was no end to '*Vivat* Richard'—we parted at four o'clock in the morning. The festival was given in the hall of the Kaufmann Verein, which had put it at my disposal as a member of long standing. We were about sixty persons; all adherents of art, of true and serious art. Many a tear was shed for our Richard—'Oh, if only we had him back,' was the general sigh. —Dear, good Richard, don't get impatient if I bore you here, but you will forgive this effusion of an old friend, who is faithfully attached to you.

"I have almost mastered your *Lohengrin,* and shall sing it for the first time in Danzig in April, as well as *Tannhäuser.* In May both operas in Darmstadt as well as in Frankfort—and finally *Tannhäuser* in Würzburg. I am urgently asked to go to Prague, but I cannot go, for I have been refused *extra* leave. How much I am looking forward to *Lohengrin!* If only you were with me!!!

"For sixteen days now we have been busy with rehearsals for *Nordstern* for five to six hours a day—first performance on the 9th— You know my profession of faith—dealers in fancy goods must do business too— You are going to London? I hope to be there in June too. Would it be possible to have fragments of your operas performed, or could they have a hearing at a concert? The Peace March and Cantilena from *Rienzi (Prayer, Act V)*—the Sailors' Chorus from the *Dutchman*? On this last let me know soon, very soon. Kindest regards to your wife, and remain fond

of your
TSCHEKEL"

The letter is surrounded by the following marginal remarks:

"Won't you entrust me with a copy of the *Ring of the Nibelung*? Please! Please!

"Half past seven in the evening: I have just received a letter from Johanna.

"As for Hl. Eberle whom you have recommended, I shall be pleased to give him all support if an opportunity comes to give him something to do.

"My dear *Josephine* and Fränzchen are now my only happiness."

The suggestion of Tichatschek for London was goodhearted rather than self-seeking: he did not languish for engagements. But he did not figure in the plans of the London Philharmonic Society, and his customary fee was high.

Tichatschek saw Wagner for the first time since the Dresden days when he visited him in May, 1856, and made an Alpine excursion with him to Brunnen, on Lake Lucerne. Wagner was pleased to hear that his friend had been agitating for the restoration of his works in the Dresden repertory; he was also pleased to find, when he sang portions of *Lohengrin,* that after seven years, and having turned fifty, his voice was still a resplendent organ.

295 (*Mornex, near Geneva, June 27, 1856*)

"DEAREST OLD FRIEND!

"I expected to have some news from you, but all of a sudden you have disappeared entirely, so that I no longer have any idea where you have gone.

"Certainly if anything has troubled me lately, it is that during your dear and friendly visit I couldn't feel quite as happy as I should have been at other times. You know how constantly I was held in fear of a new eruption of my awful ailment, and you even saw for yourself how justified that anxiety was. But after the enormous pleasure of your visit, I should have liked, with your help, to drive out the calf. God knows I was completely depressed and downcast that that was impossible! As soon as you had left my sickbed and I had somewhat recovered, I also started out and came here, where with the gorgeous air, the view of Mont Blanc, and under excellent medical supervision, I am undertaking a thorough cure which will delay me longer from work but promises to heal me *completely* from my ailment. I already feel much better and I don't contemplate any relapse into erysipelas. I hope it may never come back again!

"While I am lazing about like this, half awake, I become more and more conscious of the great pleasure you gave me. My most pleasant recollections in the pursuance of my art are certainly only those in which you were so much involved; I can't think of them without thoughts of you too. Your visit has so vividly revived these recollections, that new hopes were almost reawakened which I hardly believed I still held. That you were still so vigorous, in every respect as of old, played no small part in this, and so I want to enjoy the pleasant prospect of realizing that seven years ago in Dresden we were not united for the last time in glowing enthusiasm for our art. Well, let's hope for a beautiful *Wiedersehen!*

"Give my best greetings to Frau Pauline and to everybody who still remembers me in friendship!

"And now farewell! A thousand thanks! And answer my request soon to give me news of yourself.

"Your old friend
RICHARD WAGNER

"Minna is on the Seelisberg."

297 *(Joseph Tichatschek, Dresden, December 20, 1856, to Wagner)*

"DEAR RICHARD!

"I have something more to add that I left out of my last letter of the 18th of this month. While thanking you cordially for the piano score of the *Walküre,* I must nevertheless ask you please to send me the conclusion as well, since, as you can see from the return package, I have only two acts.

"Will you make me happy by also sending me the piano score of the *Rheingold?* There's really nothing which gives me more pleasure than to be able to occupy myself with the products of your spirit.

"Have you completely gotten rid of erysipelas? How much I wish that you are enjoying the best of health. If no special accidents occur, I shall see you again next summer, though I should not want to be afraid of keeping you from your work. I should not want to do this for anything in the world, and I shall probably visit the Bernese Oberland.

"When you have the opportunity, give my regards to Herr Andermauer.

"—Farewell and remain faithful to your

TICHATSCHEK"

Another visit by Tichatschek to Switzerland came at an unfortunate moment. He was installed at the Asyl while Minna was at Brestenberg, under treatment for her heart ailment, but even in her absence relations between Wagner and the Wesendoncks near by were strained and embarrassing to a guest.

312 *(Zürich, August 9, 1858)*

"MY DEAR GOOD FRIEND!

"You have much moved and touched me by your understanding and deeply felt expression of sympathy for my situation! You know what has depressed me, for you were with me, and you will therefore pardon me for not treating you in the gay and carefree manner your friendly visit deserved.

"At the end of this week I am to leave Zürich. In upper Italy, probably Venice, I'll try to arrange a study to work in. Heaven grant that I soon find again the quiet for work. This alone can help me over my life of suffering.

"My wife intends to leave our little house at the end of the month: some of our goods she will sell; the best things will be stored away. It is my wish that she soon settle in Germany again with our furniture. I can't say yet what my fate is to be. I look for one thing only: peace; and I hope for one thing only: the return of my desire to work.

"Friedrich has had an offer of a position here, but he wishes to return to Germany and will be especially content to begin serving you. So he gratefully accepts your conditions and is ready to serve you from the 1st of September on. But I have a favor to ask of you. My wife just now badly needs Friedrich for packing and moving. She hopes to have everything ready by the end of the month, and Friedrich should then accompany her to Saxony. If this should be delayed a few days longer, I ask you not to be angry with the servant, and to manage as well as you can without him those few days (in case of delay); I should feel much better about it. You don't mention the money for traveling and I am almost afraid that it may seem to you too much. It is getting difficult for me, too, since only nine months ago I had to pay Friedrich's way from Dresden to Zürich; nor was he able to save any money during that short time, so I take the friendly suggestion of sharing the expenses for the servant with my wife whom he is to accompany. As you may imagine, it will be hard for me now. Having just disentangled myself from the debts for furniture bought last year, I have to give it all up now and take upon myself almost twice as many responsibilities. In this matter too, so it seems, any considerable success is denied to me forever!

"It's terrible that you haven't received your trunk yet. Would you send the baggage check? It might be easier to attend to it here, and Friedrich could take it along. I have marked again the cuts in *Rienzi,* as you asked. For the third finale I refer you to the Hamburg score. The wish of Krebs to add a number for his wife I consider insolence. You could well have had trouble with a conductor of such mentality. It was lucky that you took the matter in your own hands. Nobody else would have had the energy and authority for it. Well, inform me of the success of your noble, genuinely friendly, and artistic endeavors, for which I can't be thankful enough. A telegram would still reach me in Zürich, but a letter should be sent to Geneva (*poste restante*). You'll be kept informed *where* I am living, and for the rest of our lives under all circumstances I hope for and count on the continuation of our well tested friendship! Farewell, greet Fischer, Heine, Mitterwurzer, and my faithful *Kapellmeister!*

"A thousand cordial regards from your

RICHARD W.

"Perhaps Fischer will be kind enough to have some scores prepared according to the recent cuts and the Hamburg alterations."

330 *(Venice, February 15, 1859)*

"My dearest Friend!

"At last I have an opportunity once more to express my thanks to you for the continued selfless proof of your friendship for me. Don't be angry with me that this comes so late! You had every right to expect to hear from me sooner, for I've often heard so many nice things about you, especially the way you always champion my interests and my works with so rare an energy and endurance and defend them against every attack. Don't hold this against me. So rarely do I get a chance any more to do something which gives me pleasure; often and much have I been kept from my work, even for long periods of time, by the most disagreeable letter writing [*Briefschreibereien*] even if still longer illnesses don't happen to interrupt it entirely. I really don't lead an enviable life; all that I think about gives me grief and worry; I hardly have any hope left, and joy I no longer know.

"That my wife comes among these worries you can well imagine; the state of her health affects me deeply, and it is my serious concern to make her life and suffering bearable in any way I can. I was quite grieved to hear that she was not received by you in Dresden, dear friend, in the way I and she had come to expect. She never actually complained about it to me, but I could tell from her simple report about her life there that you asked her to your house conspicuously little, and that otherwise you practically avoided her. Whenever I asked about you in my letters or gave her short friendly messages, she had nothing more to say about you than that she was not seeing anything of you and that she was almost never asked to your house. Now I must almost suspect that you maintain an attitude toward her—out of sympathy for me, I realize—which causes her pain. In this respect I ask you, friend, not to go too far. Look at the poor woman and tell me if she is not above all only a pitiful object? Ever since her health has been so terribly affected, and every doctor who treats her can give me only small hope for the ailing woman, I see her only as in need of help, and I release her from all responsibility. I therefore ask those who are truly my friends to help me in my good intentions to ease the remainder of her very tormented and troubled life. And you, too, would therefore oblige me very much if you would be quite friendly toward her and treat her as your hostess during your first visit to Zürich. Don't hold any grudge against her, even—as I know—in my interest, or out of sympathy for me. I have forgiven her everything; she has atoned for many things, and in some things one must be prepared to be just toward her.

"But, my dear, no more words between us about this matter!

"What will become of me, God only knows. I'm using all my energy only to complete *Tristan*. What my end will be then is immaterial to me. I have to endure a life which can no longer really attract me. To subject myself to an examination in Dresden [6]—now after ten years—no one who knows my extremely irritable mental and physical condition can seriously expect that of me, even if it should bring me the greatest relief. I'm firmly decided never to agree to that. If this hard-hearted pedant whom you call your very revered King cannot follow the example of Baden, Austria, or even Russia, Germany will never see me again.

"Therefore I shall henceforth watch you only from afar, but nevertheless I shall always find pleasure in your never-aging youthful freshness, your faithful friendship for me!

"Farewell, my good old faithful friend! Cordial regards from your

RICHARD WAGNER"

The Dresden opera did without Wagner's music from 1849 until 1858, except for a few performances of *Tannhäuser,* quickly dropped, in 1852. In 1858 *Rienzi* and *Tannhäuser* were restored to the repertory, and in 1859 *Lohengrin* was added.

337 A *(Lucerne, September 3, 1859)* [7]

"YOU POOR, POOR, TSCHEKEL!

"How could I have suspected you so falsely! You saw that I could scarcely believe it myself, and could only assume that for the moment you were downright insane. I was even almost sure that I had been wrong. For my wife sent me the text again (from Dresden) and that passage was marked with pencil: so I believed it had been omitted at the performance. Now—without having yet asked my wife about it—I account for it by supposing that she marked the passage because she especially liked it. In this case it might have been a queer *Qui pro quo* [*sic*] and the mark might have meant the very opposite. My suspicion was strengthened because a cut would have been so easily possible here. But enough of this strange mistake, and accept my best thanks for your prompt explanation. If you want to do me a favor, I implore you: insist upon the restoration of the omitted passages at the end of the first finale and in the third act duet (omitted by Ney). This wouldn't add much to the length. But in the finale-allegro the whole effect of the increasingly rising musical structure gets lost and such a thing is mortifying to me; the cut, however, in the duet is so silly and pitiful that I make this declaration: If I were pardoned and came to a *Lohengrin* performance, I certainly couldn't bring myself to go to the theater and take such a box on the ear as that cut. Tell this from me to Frau Ney-Bürde, and if she wants to answer for this later it shall be *her* affair. In spite of her various disturbing features, I had become reconciled to the idea of her for my

[6] Wagner never submitted to this indignity as the price for his pardon by the King of Saxony.

[7] A few sentences from this letter, much altered, were published by Altmann (in German).

parts, considering the great rarity of good singers and her extraordinary voice—and saw in her a good future prospect for my operas. I counted on her good will and the influence which her respect for so serious a task might exert on her. But now the real test has come. If she can't bring herself to restore that disturbing and damaging cut I will recognize that she is not to be taken seriously, and she won't exist any longer for me.

"When I also insist on the restoration of the cut in the finale, don't take this, dear one, as stubbornness. Think of it, rather, in this way: for the sake of the receipts I have to hand over my operas to any theater, as when, having the worst misgivings about the expected performance, I became quite callous about Berlin, which is to bring me in the most; but if people for whose judgment I care ask me where they should hear my operas, I strongly advise them against Berlin and let it go at that. On the other hand, my only concern is to have a theater once more of which I can say: *There* you are! There you get the best notion of my work. This I always do now with Dresden as long as *Rienzi* or *Tannhäuser* is concerned. Ought I to say now as to *Lohengrin*: Go rather to Vienna? Merely because I know that there such nonsensical and silly cuts wouldn't occur, while for the rest I know that the whole performance would get an otherwise unattainable splendor and nobility by your glorious performance? At the same time, if those shameful spots were not corrected I should forever hate the Dresden production.

"It seems silly that the present Dresden chorus can't manage the cut passage in the first finale. The devil, let them try again; in other places they managed well enough.

"This now brings me to your conductor question. Even last fall, Conductor Schlick in Venice told me he knew that the management was looking around for a good conductor, but where to get him? Recently I was told Rietz is under consideration. I am grieved that the selection is always made without any sense and reason and that the people who understand the job are never considered. Rietz I know positively to be a very good leader, who is capable of conducting and keeping an orchestra together, but he is entirely unable to penetrate a dramatic work which demands something far more than a good orchestra leader, the only qualification which kept him in Leipzig. What would you get from such a man, stubbornly hostile to my operas, musically an orthodox 'Mendelssohnian'? Evidently not what the Dresden opera needs. If asked for a recommendation, I would first of all confess that any recommendation here would be very difficult, since generally recognized clever and talented conductors are not just now functioning in any important German theater. I would then recommend with the best conscience a young man whose enormous abilities for the task are known to me and whose eligibility I would back with my full authority. It is Herr *Karl Klindworth,* established in London at present as a music teacher. He is from Hanover, and as early as his sixteenth year was employed at a little theater as musical director. Having acquired the most perfect routine in that difficult assignment (especially difficult in a small theater) after five years, he heard Liszt playing the piano and was so carried away that he decided to give up the ungratifying . . ."

[Incomplete]

337 B *(Paris, October 19, 1859)*

"MY DEAREST FRIEND!

"I am in an awkward position. You could have no idea what the past year, since we met for the last time, has cost me. On top of it the unheard-of increase in expenses for my move to Paris and just *now*—no receipts at all. I'm not telling my wife anything about it, and I'm trying my best to get through the bad situation. Next year *Tristan* should bring me in a lot and *Tannhäuser* in Paris should yield a profit too. But just *now* I don't know where to turn. There is a sure fee of more than 5,000 francs in prospect for about next spring, and I should like to receive it in advance now: it is the fee for *Tristan* from Vienna.[8] They are very anxious there to get the opera soon, but I can't give it to them now before having it performed myself. They have already paid more than 5,000 fr. to me for *Lohengrin* (that is, 2,000 fr. payable in old currency). As business is transacted, it was impossible for me to get that money in advance. So I see I have to resort to the help of friends. I keep getting news over and over again about how I, poor devil, am loved and highly esteemed in Dresden. Now let us try, dearest friend, how this can be put to good use. Do you know anybody who would be able to advance me those 5,000 fr.? I am sure there *is* somebody, only I don't know him. So don't be angry that I burden you with this care. Should it be really impossible to procure right away what is, after all, a reasonable sum on the time-tested strength of such a certain income? Since I am greatly and increasingly in debt (I neither can nor will let anyone know of this) I herewith enclose an IOU, which will perhaps serve at first. For heaven's sake prove to me that friendship's trust is not in vain. You would rid me of a terribly painful situation if you could help me. If the loan in its *entirety* could not be realized at once, half of it would suffice for an emergency provided that I could count on the remainder before the end of the year: but I wouldn't be really contented unless I could have the whole sum right away. But it must be handled decently; that is to say, they must trust my word and not compromise me prematurely in Vienna. In any case I would pay interest. If a simple draft for Easter of next year were preferred, I would be ready to issue it. Now see to it!

"But above all *my wife* must learn nothing about it; she would be terribly upset if she knew I were in such a predicament. Therefore *your wife* must not know anything about it, either.

"That L. [*Lump?*] Lüttichau has been airing his views about you; he even didn't refrain from abusing you: he preserves a silence toward me after unex-

[8] But *Tristan* was not to be performed until 1865, and then in Munich.

pectedly having made my mouth water with news of you! I think *Tannhäuser* can be produced here by the middle of January. Then—I will at last get something from it. Pfui! You German! My head feels quite dizzy: my things have arrived from Zürich. What a trouble and expense! I have to make my last two rent payments in advance to secure my flat; but . . .

"Now let's see what kind of fellows you are in my dear homeland!

"Goodbye, a thousand greetings from your

Much harassed friend

RICHARD WAGNER"

Die Meistersinger, having been first produced in Munich, on June 21, 1868, was planned by several theaters for the following year. The first of these was Dresden, where the new opera was performed on January 21. Wagner had no faith in the ability of the average *Kapellmeister,* Rietz in particular, to realize *Die Meistersinger.* He insisted that his young disciple Hans Richter step in and take control, thus stirring the same kind of official resentment he had once caused by insisting that Liszt direct the first *Tannhäuser* in Berlin and von Bülow the Munich *Tristan.* Tichatschek, to whom he was evidently glad to turn for the role of Walther, was then sixty-one!

461 A *(Lucerne, October 16, 1868)*

"DEAR OLD FRIEND!

"Don't be angry at me for not answering earlier. I was away, then not well, out of sorts, and God knows what! Many thanks for your usual friendly help: the newspaper announcements which you took care of have satisfied me very much; that was very nice and good of you. Otherwise, too, everything is in good order: many thanks! Only—I'm not happy about the whole thing! *You* will sing your part magnificently and carry everybody away: that is certain. But otherwise, the spirit of the performance, etc., there I can and will not look! All the shallow *Kapellmeisters* from A to Z cannot conduct my operas because they are at best only routine music makers and know and understand nothing about the theater, nothing at all except, perhaps, the bad habits of opera singing. Yes, someone else would have to do it, but I should hardly know whom to recommend; your Jew Schloss will know devilish little about how to prepare a thing like this. Away with them!!

"Altogether, I'm sick of it now in every respect and I've decided not to move a finger for any theater. The way everything is administered is too stupid: people like us can have nothing to do with that! Well, you'll always be in good form as long as you live—and that will probably be another hundred years— and you'll be the only one who is any good. But then you are something special!

"My dear fellow! It's not so easy to get an autograph from the King of Bavaria. I don't have any unimportant papers from him, only confidential letters: you understand that under no circumstances can I let any of them out of my hands. But I'll look, and perhaps I'll find something appropriate after all: then you shall surely get it!

"Now farewell! Regards to your family and remain faithful to your old

RICHARD WAGNER"

461 B *(Lucerne, December 22, 1868)*

"DEAR OLD FRIEND!

"You wish a few lines 'for reassurance'?

"Best friend! *I* long ago became reassured about the fate of my works and all that is connected with them. When I was forced to give in to your own explanations and admonitions about the mutilation which was deemed necessary for my *Meistersinger,* I told you clearly enough that I'll have nothing more to do with all this at the expense of my work. But from that time on I also decided not to worry any longer about anything of this sort. I now consider the matter as if it no longer concerned me at all. If you now have reason to complain about the 'time-beater,' Rietz, I've had the same reason for a long time, ever since this musician, who is a complete stranger to the opera, was called to Dresden through your own recommendation and against my warning! Moreover, I'm completely unclear about this matter and cannot see the actual motivating reasons. That Mitterwurzer was cast as H. Sachs confuses me: to be sure, some years ago, when I was planning the whole thing, I had thought with pleasure of a man as peculiarly talented as Mitterwurzer; more recently I heard that he was losing very much ground and could no longer be trusted with anything. I therefore would have thought of using him elsewhere in the opera. Now so much the better if his voice is still sufficient: for—he does have talent. (Pardon the sow!—Have you seen my h-hog yet?) [9]

"Now, old fellow! Nothing more remains to be said except: think of what you've accomplished for so many years to the astonishment of the world! Besides—take me as an example! Where should *I* have to begin if I wanted to ask for justice? Also, I shall always have this to tell you, that you were the only one who defended the *Meistersinger* in Dresden! Farewell and stay faithful to your old friend

RICH. WAGNER"

In 1871, long after the usefulness of Tichatschek to Wagner had passed, the composer still thought of his first *Heldentenor,* now sixty-three, and wrote (478, Triebschen, July 20): "The whole world must now be lenient with me; I don't write to anybody—for I am composing and so all else stops. When you study *Siegfried,* consider how disgraceful it is that I finished it too late for you. Only you could have managed the stuff: I always heard only your voice in my imagination. And now who can take your place?"

[9] There is an ink blot *(Sau)* at this point.

ॐ XIV ॐ

ERNST BENEDIKT KIETZ

(1842–1870)

"We sometimes think of adopting a child; I feel that this would be a good thing, especially for my wife. Now it occurs to me that we could adopt *you*: for you are and remain a real child. In spite of your advanced age, you would be the best fulfillment of our wish; and I'm suggesting to you in all seriousness, if it should at some time suit you, to make your home with us for *good*; be our house and family companion and so remain. . . . Think it over! If you accept, you can start *immediately*: you are always welcome."
—Wagner to Kietz, May 8, 1858 (303 E)

It seems often to be the case (it was certainly so with Beethoven) that a superior artist enjoys the company of a small one; finds relaxation and amusement in him, uses him for a convenience and as a butt for his exuberance. The victim of all this knows that a genuine affection goes with it, and this eases the sting of contempt; he takes what comes and allows the right of genius to overlord and even to insult. Kietz accepted heavy humor at his own expense; he received the Master's dissertations on art or politics and refrained from replying with "muddled" thoughts of his own. Sermons, no doubt delivered directly in the Paris days, continue in the letters on page after page of Wagner's fine script, and through the years Wagner never ceases to play the parent and treat his old friend as a lazy and irresponsible but always lovable child. Minna, on her part, mothers Kietz, but this relationship is always kind and gentle. At last, when Wagner has left Minna and become too absorbed in his career to give much attention to this relic of his youth, Kietz turns with renewed affection and sympathy to the "mother" who once faced dreary days in Paris as cheerfully as himself.

The wonder is that the correspondence between Wagner and Kietz kept up as long as it did. The two did not see each other after 1841 except when Wagner made his various brief visits to Paris, or when Kietz may have responded to one of his many invitations from Dresden or Zürich. Wagner's lingering correspondence, which kept up intermittently until 1870, shows what a bond misery can be, even in recollection! Friendship is tried when one ascends to the top of the ladder while the other remains in the same old place. The famous one finds it hard to explain that though wealth now pours upon him it still drains away more rapidly than it comes in.

In Paris the two were partners in adversity. The main difference, as Wagner saw it, was that he was as surely destined for greater things as Kietz was not. But he had as yet neither demonstrated his claims nor found the way to turn them into cash. From the time that Wagner left Paris and poverty with Kietz for Dresden and fame with *Rienzi,* the paths of the two diverged increasingly.

119 *(Dresden, May 12, 1842, to E. B. Kietz)*

"My good Boy!

"God and Minna are my witnesses that today I finally sat down for the second time to write to you and my Paris friends, and this time at length. Your letter and Anders's arrived, so now I am answering simultaneously two letters which gave me great joy—and pain. I am not yet settled and have had to lead a frightful, unsteady life so far: from Paris to Dresden, from Dresden to Leipzig, from Leipzig to Berlin, from Berlin to Leipzig, from Leipzig to Dresden, then to Leipzig again, and now once more back to Dresden; in ten days I have to go again to Berlin, so you'll see how rest is impossible, especially since I've had to stay several days in each place. I have not yet had the necessary conference, not even got around yet to the conferences with Fischer and Heine for detailed discussion of the mounting of my opera, and we'll begin that tomorrow. On top of that I am very sluggish, nothing arouses me to the proper zeal; I have paid only the most necessary calls. With things as they are, you, my dear friends, have to be a bit lenient and forgive me for being so late in keeping the promise I made in Berlin. I couldn't bring myself to dash off this letter so quickly—the time and the mood have escaped me until now.

"First of all, I suppose you'll want the news about myself and how I am. Therefore, I will begin with myself and reserve the discussion of all that concerns you, especially you personally, dear Kietz, for the second part of my letter. You like your news full and detailed: this I gather from your letter—to my *great* delight, so I'll not hold back, but get to work point by point.

"You know that the first time I stayed only one day in Dresden. I rented lodgings to give my completely exhausted Minna some rest, hastily greeted Heine and Fischer (the latter receiving me with hearty kisses), and at once continued to Leipzig, where I found my relatives well and in full health, I would almost say, changed to their *advantage.* After a few days' stay I went on to Berlin, where I haven't yet met Intendant Küstner, but could promote my plans by conferences with Meyerbeer, Mendelssohn, Redern, Rellstab, etc. Gr. Redern was very affable, and I found out that my opera not only has been accepted out of consideration for Meyerbeer but has finally passed the judgment of the Royal

ERNST BENEDIKT KIETZ IN HIS OLD AGE (466)

Prussian Court Opera critics. This is very important to me in my relation to Küstner: the affair also cost me four expensive days at the hotel. I stayed in Leipzig a few days more for financial reasons. My needs have been arranged for and this in a way that was the most agreeable to me after all. My sisters Luise and Ottilie and my brother-in-law, Hermann Brockhaus, had conferred and arranged among themselves to give to me from their income 30 thlr. a month for half a year. This was by far the best, since third persons were left out of the question and the money will quite suffice to meet the most urgent needs of life. Besides, I'd have been *compelled* to accept the offer anyhow, since no other way was open to me to get a sizable loan. You would not believe how much changed I found everything: a hundred friends I once knew now no longer exist, or have become so strange to me that I can't count on them at all in such a matter. I haven't met Laube yet; he is on tour; so you may see for yourself how my money matters stand and whether I can manage with a single thaler less. But enough for the moment about money!

"Now let's go on. At Dresden all my time was taken by State visits. Everywhere I was received as a man of importance. Lüttichau saw to it at once that whenever I appear at the box office with my wife there will be excellent seats for us. Reissiger received me with great cordiality and hearty kisses and immediately played his new Mass for me; I was assured on all sides that he had never yet spoken so well about a new opera as mine. As for Winkler, that goes without saying. *Tichatschek* (by the way, just the singer I need—excellent) was most enthusiastic and especially wished me luck, and that I would be here myself for the coaching, for Reissiger, in spite of his excellent attitude toward me, is *too* lazy. . . . I found in Heine just what I hoped to find—a good sympathetic fellow, and well educated at that. He was the only one I could visit with my wife. We both liked Mad. Heine very much and look forward to a pleasant friendship. My opera will be taken up at the beginning of July and performed at the end of August; Heine himself assures me that the month of August is favorable to the extent that guests from all the health resorts flock through Dresden at that time and will spread the reputation of my opera through half the world. Nevertheless, I rather think it will be postponed until the end of September. With all this running around, another week passed by. At last I sat down to write letters and began with my good Cäcilie and Avenarius, when I got the news from Leipzig that Küstner was to pass through there. So I had to postpone again my letters to you and go to Leipzig for four days more. I was pleased to tell Küstner before his arrival in Berlin how things stand with my opera; and of course I got no definite promise from him, so that I shall have to go to *Berlin* again before the end of this month. I had no sooner returned from Leipzig and sat down to write to you, than the letters from you and Anders arrived.

"So you have a short outline of my recent life's history; and now let us discuss you and your letter. Your letter to Heine was quickly disposed of; he was very angry with you about this because, so he told me, he couldn't possibly answer it—he didn't know the answer. You may well imagine that we spoke much and at length about you. No particularly good things could be said, of course, for there is little gain from being an excellent man with much talent if you do nothing whatsoever about it. He reported a thousand foolish things about you; we had a good laugh over it. The main thing is, that you come back soon again. 'That's soon said,' you may think, but I answer: 'It must also be soon done.' So listen and be sensible. In your letter I detect again your own (perhaps involuntary) confession—that generally speaking you are no longer of any use in Paris. Any illusions you still hold are bound in the course of time to be injurious to a man of your character: all that will come of it in the end will be wearing out one pair of shoes after another dancing after an occasional franc for subsistence. Rest assured that nothing more than that will come of it— your material progress in art will come to nothing at all; you yourself admit this to be a proven fact. But if you can return to Germany and get substantial orders, as I confidently believe, your Paris experiences will help your development and progress, for they would inspire you here to produce, while there you would succumb to them. This is my firm conviction: you are sufficiently inspired and have arrived at a point where distraction is harmful to you. Your three years' life in Paris has been nothing but a continually inspiring distraction: now you'll have to pull yourself together, and you'll do that in no other place better than here, where your active studies can also become a source of earning. You are not able to do this in Paris. I tell you this in all seriousness to bring you *to the decision to leave Paris* even before I propose a means to carry out the decision. You ought to give up all your damned drifting as soon as possible, ought to sit down on your behind, get those half-finished oil portraits done, start a couple of new ones, and get them done too. If you are short of models, I shall get you two excellent ones—*Anders* and *Lehrs*: they surely will like to sit for you for the time being. Paint these portraits for *yourself*; as soon as I have money I'll buy them from you. It certainly won't take more than two months to accomplish this task, when once you've dropped your deuced tedious works; and when you are through, you will notice that you have gained a good bit of routine. Then pack up your oil paintings, come here, and you'll not fail to get along nicely. You can do all this if you are a bit reasonable and if you can get out of your head your Eulenspiegel holiday plans and other so-called 'necessities'—all you need is 1,000 francs, and these you will have within four weeks. You understand that I have no money myself; but anyhow I will procure some for you, be assured.

"I haven't yet seen Mad. Devrient: she happened not to be in Berlin when I was there, nor in the other places. As I told you, I am to go to Berlin again before the end of this month, and I will surely meet her there this time. I mean not to leave her alone until she gives me those 1,000 fr.; and I don't think this will be too hard, because I'll find her just at the moment when money is coming in. If she refuses me on account of some whim or stinginess, I'll certainly get the money from Schletter.[1] You must know that this man is your warmest admirer; he got to know me at Luise's, etc., when he had only seen you once, and he made a solemn oath—but I won't tell you this so as not to turn your head! To be brief, I am sure to get the money from him when I first mention it. The one of us two—you or I—who first comes into cash will pay back the 1,000 fr.—so that's agreed; of course I'll have to borrow it in your name for there's no chance of borrowing any in my own right now. So you will find out by the end of this month from whom you are going to get the money— Good. . . . You are a poodle-foolish chap [*Pudel-närrischer Kerl*]. I may feel heavy-hearted about you but I have to laugh at you after all: we were doubled up with laughter when we read your remarkable letter. Cäcilie even wrote me you have been running around early in the morning, crying like a baby for the mother's breast.

"By the way, especially after your letter, my regret at having left Paris is dwindling a bit: my friends—this is something different; otherwise, I am only sorry that my friends didn't leave Paris along with me; for, with all its advantages, Paris for us as we are is nothing but a brilliant grave in which our best powers fade away unused. To the devil with it! This, however, I would hardly have admitted a week ago. One's first impression on coming back from Paris, even to our largest cities, is horrible. It's hard to find the reason, but I suppose a fish who happened to get from the ocean into a small river must feel like this. He still breathes water, but the waves, the vast motion, the majesty of the element, all have been changed to something puny and pitiful—it's the same water all the time, and only our imagination shows us the depths and expanse which have really nothing to do with our course. Here—I feel—is my *home*; I belong here, and the only yearning that lingers in me here is for my friends, you; everything close to my heart belongs to my home. What do you have there? Hunger, yes, and—inspiration, but it is in Germany that you must develop the fruits of your inspiration. Whenever I find myself getting attached to Paris, I only have to pick up the latest number of the *Gazette Musicale*—and my attachment is gone— To the devil with it!

"I'm not writing to Lehrs and I'll write to Anders on our special matter only: you may read to them from this letter what should be read, as if it were addressed to them too. If Lehrs will write a few lines too, my next letter will be addressed to him as today's letter is to you. The story of renting the summer lodgings is very nice. Oh, Kietz!—I am very glad that good Lehrs likes his country house so much. That his material circumstances seem to improve more and more is priceless luck: may all this help his badly shattered health!

"O my God, when I think back to those terrible times at the beginning of

[1] Wagner refers to Schletter in his autobiography as a "wealthy art patron of Leipzig" who in December, 1841, sent him a 500-franc note through the intervention of his brother-in-law Avenarius.

last winter! Lehrs *without firewood*—it will be unforgettable to me forever— and I not able to help! [2] This *could* never happen in our homeland. Damned Paris, I hate thee!!

"*Lehrs* must come to Germany too: his reputation is good. In Leipzig I saw a book dealer, Rutthardt from Breslau, who very much praised Lehrs's last book: he surely would do a good business here. Meanwhile may his country life do him good! I hope so! Does he feel vigorous and is he able to work efficiently? Doesn't he have some orders for Leipzig?

"I'm enclosing a little letter for your uncle Fechner; you may mail it by city post. I'll have to risk the contempt of this man by admitting that I can't pay him before fall: I CAN'T—I can't play the part of the borrower who snatches a rag every now and then, as in Paris. If your uncle doesn't sue me for not paying HIM only, I'll have to run the risk of his contempt, which I don't mind at all. The suffering I have gone through is greater than the conventional expectations of people like your uncle. But all the same it annoys me to say this. Let him go to the devil!

"I visited Mlle. Leplay; she came later to Dresden and honored my wife with a friendly visit. I see that my letter has grown longer than I intended; since I want to add a few notes, I'll have to mail it tomorrow. Besides, your brother didn't come. This afternoon I am going to have a long opera conference with Fischer and Heine; if there is time left I'll look up your brother. I'll soon be going to the Freemasons Institute, if you send me another nice long letter, with drawings, etc., you'll hear much from me too—dumb fellow! [*Tumber Mann.*]

"Meanwhile do as I have advised you: wash the brushes, I implore you; don't dabble in anything else any longer, no drawings, nothing! Brush and oil. You lazy boy. [*Du fauler Junge.*]

"Money surely won't fail to come. Work hard so that you may come by the end of August at the latest. Here you certainly will fare well. Schletter will arrange that 1,000 thaler right away. Follow this up.

"Now Minna's calling me to the table. Poor dear, she's still always worrying.

"There will probably still be a few postscripts. Goodbye for the moment, good dear friend! Regards to everybody and tell Max that I like him and that his beautiful handkerchief has made a sensation here. May God protect you! To the devil with everything.

"Forever your RICHARD WG.

"My things have not yet arrived, nor have our portraits. I am sorry about it! Luise spoke enthusiastically about your letter, but at the same time she pitied you. ANDERS must always keep me posted about how matters stand with the Parisian *Flying Dutchman*, if it is to be performed shortly, etc. It's of great im-

---

[2] Wagner tells in *My Life* how Lehrs, wasting away with tuberculosis, suffered acutely from the cold. He would often find him "in his icy cold room, huddled up at his writing table," unable to complete the work for which his employer was pressing him.

portance to me to know this. Your brother hasn't come yet, nor was I able to look him up. Soon! (I beg you to seal the enclosed with wafers before mailing them.)"

120 (*Teplitz, June 13 to July 1, 1842, to Kietz at 18 rue Jacob,*[3] *Paris*)

"BEST KIETZ!

"This time I have written in detail to Lehrs about general matters concerning me; I hadn't much else to tell. The Berlin question about the date of the first performance of *The Flying Dutchman* is still hanging fire. I was not in Berlin but in Leipzig and Halle only (where I saw my brother Albert), and on the 9th of this month I arrived in Teplitz. At the end of August or the first days of September, *Rienzi* is to be put on absolutely *Punktum!* I haven't yet run into Mad. *Devrient*: Your intimations about her in connection with your money affairs, your misgivings, etc., had induced me to consider her as the last source of help rather than the first, so I just approached *Schletter*, warmly and fully explained to him your position, and found a sympathetic listener in him. He felt touched by the matter, and it certainly was no empty excuse when he asked me for a short respite to consult himself and his condition. Schletter is not the millionaire people consider him, and his inclination to be a benefactor is handicapped by the fact that people are overwhelming him with money demands from all sides and expect sacrifices far beyond his means.

"This is true: Every day he gets an average of two to five letters claiming his help, so that he had to stick to the principle of making small loans or donations only in order to satisfy several people. . . .

"July 1st. I have been looking forward in painful expectation *to a letter* from *Schletter* only to learn that my steps were futile for the time being. In vain I waited for ten days after having started this letter to get news from Schletter, and pained at not being able to write you I wrote him again in Leipzig to remind him of his promise. At last I got a letter explaining at length and in a deferential tone that the demanded sum, even if considered as a loan, would be too large for him, that he couldn't withdraw it from those who are really in need, etc. I was really not prepared for it for these reasons: Schletter himself aroused the idea in my mind of approaching him when I met him repeatedly at Luise's in Leipzig. Then after the highest praise of your talent, your 'genius,' he declared that if he ever wanted to have himself or anybody else painted he would choose only *you* to do it. And so I approached him to describe your precarious position as an artist and to ask him for help. Even when he declared that he could grant only small money aids, I explicitly showed him that this was quite a different situation; for it was not a question of paying a needed sum

---

[3] Kietz had taken his quarters here when Wagner lived next door, at No. 18 rue Jacob, an inexpensive neighborhood. Natalie, who had then lived with the Wagners, told Mrs. Burrell that the two men could hail each other from their respective windows.

from that part of his income which he had set aside for the support of poor people, but he was to grant you an *advance* of money as a part of the sizable sum he spends yearly procuring works of art. He doubtless would have a fund for *this purpose* and would help an artist of whom he himself thought highly, and who according to his own utterances would certainly be given sizable orders. Punctual repayment, even if he demanded it in ready cash, would be sure for him since it was not unknown to him how easily you had saved *bigger* sums in Germany before this. This is how I had to deal with him in order not to give you away, and I based my hopes on this kind of presentation. But unfortunately I had to learn that I was dealing with a *businessman* who is used to considering as lost all sums spent this way, and not to *counting* on their repayment, and in this sense I may imagine that the demanded sum (1,000 fr.) was too big for him. To hell with him! [*Scheiss auf ihn!*] Let's not talk of it any more! Every word is too much! The *only* reassurance I can give you is that nobody in Leipzig knows of it. Schletter won't speak of it either.— (At last I have new ink.)

"And now further: The trouble is that here I am sitting in Teplitz where I can't do a single thing about your affair. Minna still has to take the cure until the end of this month, and I can't return to Dresden earlier than this for the simple reason that I can't pay two lodgings. I won't arouse new hopes in you again after this silly experience by which my firm confidence has been abominably deceived. I can only give you my most holy promise to proceed with all possible care and policy when I see Mad. Devrient after my return to Dresden, so as to get a better result from her than from that lousy businessman. If I fail with *her too*, I can only feed you with hopes for myself, that is, for a good success for *Rienzi*—you understand me! . . .

"Alas, there is nothing left for me to do at this moment but cry out to you: 'Try to get back!' I am barred from doing anything now! You may believe that I am depressed about it! Well, if you were a different fellow you would spare me much worry. May God bestow his blessing on Laforgue! I can't tell you more. As soon as I am in Saxony I'll act on it again. You may have learned from my last letters to my sister and to Lehrs how *I* am. Since then, of course, nothing important has happened: I still feel terribly burdened by my obligations in Paris. Here, where I would feel in the best mood to tackle a new work, I have to repress everything within myself—in order to arrange music. Of course it won't remain like this. So last week I sent finished arrangements directly to Schlesinger in Paris. Tomorrow I am going to start work for Troupenas; when you find it necessary, call on *Heinse* again and tell him that he will shortly get an arrangement from me. I enclose a few lines for the good Loizeau; [4] it's quite out of the question for me to pay the draft due at the end of this month. I already prepared Loizeau for this eventuality while I was in Paris, and so he made the following arrangement with me. I signed two notes, each for

[4] Wagner's long-suffering tailor (see Ernest Newman's *Life*, Vol. II, pp. 134–135).

200 fr., one payable on the last of July, the other at the end of September. In order to negotiate these notes easily I had to give my Paris address, and I chose No. 69 *rue Richelieu, chez M. Avenarius.* If I should be unable to pay the note when it falls due in July, Loizeau himself would discharge it and I would repay him the amount of both at the end of September. Of course this has been done only to facilitate the purchase of his own materials by Loizeau. I'm carefully reporting this to you so that you may read this passage to our friend Avenarius and he may understand when he is presented with a note in my name at the end of July that all he will have to do is to say I am not there and didn't leave any instructions; then the note will go back to Loizeau and *he* will pay it as arranged between us. I really don't know whether or not I communicated this matter to Avenarius, and I wouldn't like him to be surprised by not being prepared. A splendid business!

"Be good enough to go to Draese, No. 4 rue d'Assas.[5] They behaved so kindly toward me recently that I'd hate leaving them without any comfort, at least for the time being. Tell them how I am and that I haven't been able to earn more so far than barely enough to live on, but I hope to earn more in the autumn and they may rely then on my not forgetting them. Tell them everything you know and give them my regards. They are *poor* after all! . . .

"Don't take it amiss that my wife doesn't write to you; but she is really writing along with me each line of this letter. With her heart she is quick, but with her pen a bit slow. Besides, she has to abide her time too. Goodbye, you old Hans. God grant that better times may come! We both will need it. Be sure to write soon to reassure me about yourself, although your letters really can't reassure very much! At the end of July I'll go to Dresden again; so write here meanwhile. Greet everybody ten thousand times and remain faithful to me.

"Your

Richard W."

The spectacle of Wagner deep in debt is as familiar to us as it is unfamiliar to behold him applying his elaborate ingenuities to raising money for someone else. We may only guess how far the following letters and the efforts described were prompted by his own indebtedness to Kietz and how far by genuine commiseration with a fellow pauper. That he was distressingly poor at this time, shabby and underfed, is attested by Marie Schmole in Chapter XI.

123 *(Dresden, September 6–20, 1842)*

"Dearest,

"Yesterday, on my wife's birthday, I got your last letter of the 18th of August. That was a bad day for us, and in fact the worst birthday I have ever experienced with Minna. Our whole fortune consisted of one thaler (3 fr. 50 ct.).

[5] Wagner mentions Draese again in 149.

When I think of the 5th of September last year!! Your letter was the first and only event that cheered us up, and even brought a smile from us. I had carried it around unopened more than three hours, for I was terribly afraid of learning its contents: with all those misgivings we were truly surprised to find what you had written. But though you seem to have regained all your composure, all your lightheartedness, don't believe that the stone has been lifted from my heart. Actually, I didn't want to write you yet because another possible way was still open of doing something for you: perhaps I should find a clear answer a week from now, and it would be more advisable to hold my news until then: but I am moved to give some news about myself to all of you, and at the risk of having to write a second letter very shortly I won't hesitate any longer. You will see from what I have to tell you what an awful disappointment I spared you by not writing to you too hastily. So, first of all about you!

"As early as the 18th of July I left Teplitz, where my wife remained for two weeks longer. Your last letter addressed there was forwarded to me in Dresden by Minna. What I would have had to answer no longer applies as things stand now. I went right away to Mad. Devrient, whom I found in the theater at the rehearsal: as briefly as possible I explained to her that your case is serious, and she immediately gave me an appointment for noon at Heine's. There I put before her what she would have to do for you; and Heine, although he is a little timid about money matters with Mad. Devrient, backed me up. She didn't seem disinclined to help you and asked me for a respite of a few days only, to order her financial affairs. On leaving, I asked her if I could write to you that she is 'graciously minded' toward you, whereupon she jokingly replied, 'Notify him of my Grace!' I believed the matter as well as settled and certainly felt very much like relieving you right away with a report of my good success. But why not wait those 'few days' so that I could write that the matter was concluded? So I waited. But just at that time I had to write to my sister and so I couldn't refrain from telling her about Mad. Devrient's 'generous' attitude toward you. Now I happened by chance not to get into any considerable conversation with Mad. Devrient for a full two weeks, but finally I was greatly astonished to find her completely changed toward you: in vain I squandered more than a full hour's eloquence on her, she steadily stuck to such phrases as 'she can't,' 'it would be useless to help you,' 'you wouldn't come anyhow,' she had 'lost too much money before in a similar way,' 'why wouldn't Brockhaus help you,' 'why,' etc., etc. Finally she persisted that she had no ready money at the moment, and I retorted that this was a small matter, I could procure credit for her; she earnestly asked me not to press her any longer. I found out from Heine what probably caused her change of front: For about two weeks she has had a 'serious' liaison with a Lieutenant Müller whom she absolutely wants to marry. She has entrusted her business affairs to this man, since she has been cheated very often, and she had waited to consult him about your matter. He definitely advised against it—or rather forbade her to send you money since he didn't know you at all. Now I was convinced that nothing was to be done. Was this so interesting that I should write to you immediately? I found it very tedious. However, I made new plans for getting you money. Reissiger moaned about his need for a good opera book. I read aloud to him my sketch for *Die hohe Braut*; he grew enthusiastic about it, and offered to me half of all the profits resulting from the opera, etc., if I would write the book for him. Of course I declined. But then it occurred to me that on delivering the completed book to Reissiger I could perhaps make the most of the occasion by telling him: 'You consider my book good and you would gladly pay a nice fee for a *good* book; you need not do this, instead you may lend Kietz 200 thaler for two years at 5 per cent and thereby the matter would be settled.' [6] With this prospect in view I sat down and started my verses. The book is finished and Reissiger has it already; he will want to get more thoroughly acquainted with it, hear this or that opinion about it; but when he is ready for a final settlement, you know the conditions I am to present to him. Meanwhile I have become skeptical and don't expect a great deal from it; of course I spoke about you to Reissiger, and each time he shrugged his shoulders: 'Well, if one could do all that one wants to do! O dear God!' etc. I believe that if it comes to a showdown, he will rather renounce a hopeful opera than reach into his pocket for money. We certainly know how incredibly stupid people are! All the same—this is the only hope I see ahead of me and I have no reason yet to give it up. The decision must come within a week. Now I shall go to a rehearsal of *Rienzi*—I will continue in the afternoon.

"The 7th of Sept.—Another day has passed, and how does the land lie? The kind of thing I have to report to you is always timely enough. I told Reissiger you had written again to me and given him your best regards. Answer: 'The poor chap! Yes, how can he be helped!' He says that he is still pondering over my book. Keep pondering, you philistine! Oh, what a damned philistine country this is! We are pining to death with boredom. The 5th of September last year taught us that it is not so much money as *friends* that are needed to celebrate overflowing, happy days.[7] God forbid that I should remind Minna or myself of all that again. All the same, yesterday the old magic spell was re-invoked by an amiable letter from Cäcilie congratulating Minna on her birthday. But today we didn't refer to it even once.

"Heine's family is the only one with whom we associate. Heine is really an excellent, amiable man, who gives me his unfailing sympathy. We have spent our only pleasant evenings in his garden.

"But I want also to tell you a word about my opera affairs. I can't do anything about the *Dutchman* just now; for one reason because the Berlin Stadt-theater for the present is in such a disorganized state that Küstner, try as he may, can't have anything new studied yet; the second reason is that Meyerbeer, before leaving for Paris, gave me his word that he wants to rehearse

[6] *My Life*, p. 277.
[7] See 111.

[*einstudieren*] my opera himself, and this is the first one under his direction, and it is to happen right after his return from Paris in November. So I can't do anything about it but wait, since it would be impolite to Meyerbeer to insist that the *Dutchman* had to be given before his return. By the way, I believe that the Parisian performance will do me no harm; actually it would be the first opera of *this* kind to reach Germany; in any case, it's not progressing so rapidly; it will be a year anyhow before it is given in Germany, and until then, with good luck, my opera may have been performed at several theaters. . . .

"Now for my personal situation. It is not of the best. We imagined life here to be cheaper than it really is. Returning from Teplitz, I had to take a better apartment than the former one because I could no longer avoid receiving visitors to whom my real condition must remain unknown; finally I had to rent a piano, which I had been doing without for four months. Lodgings and piano cost 16 thaler a month—I am making 30 thaler—so I have left 14 thaler for living expenses, shoes, etc., so you may figure how we have to eke it out considering the high prices, and what embarrassments I have to face at times when borrowing is quite out of the question. My three shirts are literally falling to pieces. The worst thing about the procrastination over my opera is the impossibility of getting rid of my obligations to Loizeau within the legal term. I had to ask the poor man either to extend the notes until the end of October or to advance me the amount for a month—it is absolutely impossible to manage it otherwise. My pawn tickets have not yet expired: one of them is due on the 8th of November, the other on the 9th of January. *My thanks to you for your pains, if you are able to redeem them!*

"The 9th of Sept.: How miserably long it takes to get through with this letter! I didn't see Reissiger again and may have to dispatch this letter before settling the matter with him; how could I have believed three months ago that I should face such difficulties, nay, nearly impossibilities, to procure money for you! My experience on this subject has taught me the following: Friendships based entirely on sociable intercourse are not worth two pennies, least of all 200 thaler. If your dealings with Mad. Devrient were more serious than that, how could that woman have made the answer she did? When I reminded her that she had already offered you money at one time: 'Yes, but that was three years ago—what I once offer to such a "Hans Taps," I don't always offer to him.' But if I go on this way I'll be writing a whole chapter of reproaches, and to heap reproach on you would be my last desire in the world, now that I can't help you; for I have seen *how* you can defend yourself, how you even use illegitimate weapons and try to inflict injury, even if you don't succeed in defending yourself. If only you would apply more evenly in your whole character the bitter earnestness which you display on such occasions. Then you wouldn't be so much of a clown on the one hand, and on the other not so much like the nephew of your Parisian uncle Fechner. To Mad. Devrient, as I noticed to my annoyance, you are unfortunately only the former—you tried hard to appear as the latter in your letter of July. Don't be a fool, and learn somewhat better how to despise men, while putting implicit confidence in your friends. If it were possible to become altogether a frivolous clown, what a happy state that would be! One would start like you, but carry it on differently! You must permit me such remarks, for along with it I am judging myself too. I don't lay claim to any headstart on you in knowledge of the world, but your faults hit me in the eye when I see all the 100,000 friends you have, what lavish care you devote to each of those 100,000, and on the other hand what a time I had trying to get a bit of money from them for you. That is why I count myself fortunate knowing that I have only a *few* friends. If you don't get any money from Reissiger, pray for *Rienzi*—I can't tell you more—but meanwhile you will have to pay the postage on this letter, for my emetics of yesterday were not included in my household budget—Apropos! Do you still care for people like the Chandons? If you don't start a new life by thoroughly scorning such rabble and by showing your contempt for them, you will never get along in life, for you will never gain real respect for yourself. I still had several things to tell you and especially to ask of you, but I forget everything with the anger I feel about your 100,000 friends. So it is. . . .

[The following is written on the margins:]

"Your letter, dear boy, that is, the last letter, gave me much joy. It's just as well that you look upon your situation as hopeless; just as you were ready to help me when I wanted to leave Bellevue, someone else may be found who will help you to leave Paris: the more unexpected, the more delightful! Meanwhile, increase in strength and in three months add five years or so to your life— without giving yourself gray hairs. As matters stand now, ambition, that is, true *diligence in art*, is the best thing, for you *shall* leave Paris and you must. Don't draw any more Chandons for 40 fr. Paint for yourself and live on Mar . . . [?], Glöckner, Avenarius, etc. *Money* to see you through shall and will come. Be an *artist*, really an artist, and not just an ass with 100,000 friends. When you are truly absorbed by your art, you will be happy even in the greatest distress, if you are aware of having a friend who is obliged to you until death. O God, what would have become of me if I hadn't thrown myself with ever growing faith into the arms of Art! To escape sinking into the mire of suffering I might as well have turned charlatan as artist. But in those hours, when art became my only comfort, it began to bloom for me in full purity and chastity. I know now who I am, even if everybody should mock and slander me! Be with me, friend!

"Although you don't tell me anything directly about Lehrs's state of health in your last letter, I am somewhat reassured about him by what you write. Did he return to Paris again? That his baron disappeared is to be expected: for people like us seem destined for poverty. Pray for *Rienzi*. About four weeks from today you may cluster together—I think about that time the devil will be loose. My best regards to our Schuster [cobbler?] on the boulevard and tell him much about *Rienzi*. Anders may at last send his letters; my address follows. It's nice for me to know that you are sitting together: keep looking around and you will see me joining you in some corner. Has Anders begun to compose verses? The good soul! Greetings to Mar . . . if he hasn't fallen asleep yet, Glöckner (whose knife I will buy and send you), the Demagogues and Patriots, and anyone else who remembers me. Minna sends sisterly greeting to the members of the old league! It pains me to recall the old miseries. I'm no better. Farewell. Hope for better news soon and don't be afraid of the great heat. Paint and God will help you.

"Your RICHARD W.

"Address: Waisenhaus-Strasse, No. 5, Dresden

"The 20th of September. I really wanted to add another letter to Cäcilie and Avenarius, and for this reason I struggled to crowd everything on *one* sheet, which I had to write to you, so that the whole letter would not become too bulky. But the trouble is, I am afraid it would take another day at least to achieve that purpose, since *Minna* wants to write along with me, and this is going to take time. For she had gotten entirely out of the way of writing letters. Therefore I will dispatch *this* letter by mail at all events today, because in my hands it is getting out of date: if I had some positive hope of soon being able to send you a favorable report, I would still hold back these lines; but I frankly confess to you I don't see any favorable prospect. Reissiger seems to divine something of my scheme, for I often mention your helpless position, and when I ask afterward: 'How is my text? Have you made up your mind about it?' he answers: 'Oh, my awful cold! I have no thoughts at all,' etc. Be prepared to learn before long how he has at last freed himself of the whole business in the most shabby manner, renouncing opera texts and everything else. He is evidently afraid of his wife, whom I regard. as more or less of a shrew. I paid a visit to her with Minna, which she returned politely: for the rest we are keeping away from each other. Well, this only by the way! . . .

"Since I am not writing this time, that is, today—to Eduard and Cäcilie, I give them all my best regards and thanks; tomorrow or the day after I shall send letters to them through the office so that they will receive the letters destined for them a few days only after you get *this* one. But it is too painful to keep this letter here any longer, so—away with it! And you—continue to paint and goodbye!

"Your RICHARD W.

"I'm not writing separately to Loizeau, writing in French gives me too much difficulty now: Tell him simply how my opera affair stands and that I can't help it! They *must* wait until the end of October: I really am very sorry— but what can I do? He is a reasonable man after all, who will have understanding and confidence. Mail the enclosed letter to Jules Heine and put it in the city post right away!"

128 *(Dresden, January 5, 1843)*

"Well, you dumb [*tumber*] man, Devrient lent me 1,000 thaler. From this I'll pay as many debts as possible, and above all help you. I'm no longer sure how much I owe you; but I am forwarding 600 fr. herewith, through Avenarius: you will notify me if this is sufficient. I don't know what you plan to do with the money, nor will I undertake to advise you, first of all because I know that you don't want any advice and would take it as an *order*, and secondly, because I'm sure you wouldn't follow any advice. Besides, on account of your long silence I have no idea of your present position: all that I have learned is that you have made no progress in your art. This was the approximate opinion of those who saw the portrait sketches of Heinrich Brockhaus and his wife. You may answer: This is 'work for money!' and I retort, it is 'money for "work"!!' However, enough of that. It leads to nothing and is no help. You are as you are and so you wish to be! The only thing is that you deprive me of the chance to deserve well of you! For I would so much like to show myself thankful to you.

"Your joy at my success brings me no pleasure; I would rather be rejoicing at your success. Enough of it!! As soon as you want to return to Germany, write to me. 200 Fr.—that is, the absolutely essential traveling expense—will be kept always ready for you. If I can do more to this end, more will be done. But now tell me, How is Lehrs? I hear nothing, and the last lines I got from him depressed me so much that I can think of him only with keenest sorrow. What is the matter with him? Write me about this at once and in detail!

"Our good Anders is hard at it, as I gather from his activity in the *Gazette Musicale*, where he is working with all his strength for my glory. I only wish I could reciprocate, and soon. Go together to my sister and get her to read from my letter to her what I report about myself and my affairs: may it give you enjoyment and hope for yourselves! If God will only give Anders the proper good health, I can doubtless procure him an agreeable old age at my side: but he will have to work. Give my affectionate greetings to the dear good friend, and tell him that my *Dutchman* is admired here as a genuine sea-wonder.

"Is Glöckner still in Paris? If so, greet him heartily. How is friend Hanfstängl? I now often see his brother, the *Hofrath*—friendly greetings to him too.

"Will you give your uncle M. Fechner as hearty regards as he will absorb? The 100 fr. I owe him you may also get from Avenarius. If you think he would accept a small compensation as interest, offer it to him and lay it out for me. Thank him in my name and tell him that what I did was wholehearted: all those things which happened between him and me are, after all, silly trifles, which annoyed me only so long as I was not able to get rid of my obligations; now that I am able to, I think only of his readiness to try to help me out of my trouble—I cannot and will never forget it! Give our shoemaker also the 40 fr. which he still has the right to claim from me. Avenarius will send that to you too. Farewell and write not only soon but promptly how matters stand with Lehrs! You have no idea how I pity him! Greet him most warmly from your

RICHARD WAGNER"

132 *(Dresden, February 26, 1843)*

"I can't write 'Dear Kietz' to such a barbarian. After my urgent inquiry about Lehrs, after my strong pleas to be notified at once about him, his health, and other matters, you keep me waiting two months for an answer? And this after having written in your last letter: 'I'm not telling you anything about Lehrs; it is too sad.' I insist upon full information.[8]

"You may know that I have become a *Kapellmeister* with 1,500 thr. for the present—in the next few years I am to get more. I am paying more and more debts now: when I get to the debts of honor at last, there'll be no end to it.

"Laube published my biography in the elegant *Zeitung*[9] and included a small lithograph which you drew of me. We shall keep a large reproduction of it. Hanfstängl is to execute it. Write me how you want it done.

"Have 100 copies of my 'Two Grenadiers' struck off after all: show these lines as authorization to Herr Schlesinger (to whom I send best regards).[10] Have the copies sent here quickly by Avenarius.

"Ask Cäcilie to greet the Kühnes from me and Minna: how does it stand about the beds? If they are not yet sold, we should like to take them back on repayment of the money they lent us for them. Greet everyone! Write instantly! I don't want to know anything about you, only about Lehrs. How is Anders?

"God be with you, you rascal!

"Your

RICHARD WAGNER

"The costs for the 100 copies can be paid out by Avenarius; he will get the sum repaid, when and how he wants it."

133 *(Dresden, April 8, 1843)*

". . . I heartily thank you for your news about Lehrs and Anders. I am going to write to each of them too. If you only knew how much we miss you here! Whenever something pleasant comes along, Minna and I curse the fate which lets you share with us only the worries and none of the good times. We still lack any substitute for your society, not to speak of the friendship, which never can be substituted. Even with Heine we haven't reached any true relation-

---

[8] Wagner's letter of Dec. 18, 1844 (149), shows that by that time Lehrs had died.
[9] *Zeitung für die elegante Welt.*
[10] *My Life*, p. 226.

ship; a person who is always believing himself slighted and passed over is an awkward candidate for friendship; with his wife the situation is still worse; nobody can put up with that; they have been on and off at least ten times with Devrient this winter. I mention this to show you that Heine doesn't lend himself to agreeable friendly intercourse, without in the least denying that he possesses all the more basic virtues of a friend. He remains the closest of all to me, only it is too bad that his frequent theatrical hippochondria [*sic*] makes him anything but agreeable. Tichatschek would give his blood and life for me, and rarely have I found such a devotion as his—but he is a bad fellow [*Schwudderer*] and a bewildered man [*Wüster*] with whom I get nowhere. The whole opera company here is really fond of me, and wherever I want one, I could have a friend; but none suits me. I have had some remarkable experiences with Devrient in this half-year; she was going through a crisis of her life; there was the question of marriage, etc. She chose me as her confidant and counselor, and so I have been initiated into some astonishing secrets of this extraordinary female—such an abundance and power of passion, such an impetuous violence of the inner demon beside such genuine womanliness, amiability, and goodness of heart our Creator will not soon again produce. I share with Minna the deepest sympathy with her fate: she is a friend to us in the true sense of the word. Our artistic collaboration has been quite remarkable. I could write a whole volume on her study of Senta in *The Flying Dutchman*. Recently she confessed she is consumed by my music, and yet—she thinks—I have still to write the real part for her. A few days ago she left us after we had celebrated the twentieth jubilee of her Dresden engagement. Her contract had expired—but she is going to return in the autumn: a new contract for five years has been practically signed. One can't tell yet when her youthfulness will fade. My other associations here still consist of several families of the aristocracy. The wives of von Lüttichau, Könneritz, Serre, etc., are my great admirers. Sometimes I receive invitations from them; that is all. But even when the most trifling thing is undertaken here, I have to be on hand. I have had to become the conductor of the Choral Society, etc.

"Lüttichau treats me like a jewel; he is always asking me whether I will be good enough to take over this or that. Friend Reissiger fits in as well as he can, only his wife can't control her venom. Before it was decided that I should be *Kapellmeister*, Reissiger, with all his friendship, did his best to intrigue against me: thus he had a Kapellmeister Schindelmeisser summoned from Pesth and did everything to put him in Rastrelli's place. But it was of no avail, and all that came of it was that Schindelmeisser tore my *Rienzi* apart in the Vienna *Musikzeitung*—so that article is accounted for! Now, Reissiger is behaving quite well, and is working to his own advantage, for otherwise he might have lost still more. . . .

"You would like to know something about my arrangements and way of life? It is very simple. I still live with Minna in a furnished apartment in Marienstrasse, consisting of a living room and bedroom. We fetch our food from the restaurant. Only in the autumn shall I get furniture and move to a larger apartment in Ostra-Allee, next to the Loge. For Minna is to go to Teplitz again in May, and this time she is to stay for three whole months.

"I shall enclose a few lines to Schlesinger. That scoundrel! He has already reduced the costs for the 'Two Grenadiers' by almost 50 fr. Apart from this I owe him nothing for any arrangement: his brother wrote to me last fall, and, in case I have no time to make the four-hand arrangement, he inquires whether or not he may have it made by somebody else. At the moment I agreed with the stipulation that I am to repay him 200 thr., which I had got for that arrangement by Moritz Schl., either in cash or in manuscripts, and he agreed. Shortly I will send a few songs to the Berlin Schlesinger and so the matter will be settled. Why is this Parisian twaddling about damages? He ought to be glad, I think, if no arrangement were made of Halévy's opera, for he would gain nothing from it.

"But now I must begin to write to Cäcilie and our friends; if I wrote it all to you, nothing would be left for the others—so you must learn from them what I have not told about myself.

"And so farewell to the person who gives me so much worry, and whom I so heartily wish were here at my side. I'm forever missing you, and perhaps you miss me too. . . . You know that in me you may always count on a true and grateful friend! Adieu, your

RICHARD WAGNER"

[In Minna's writing, on the margin]

"Dear, good Kietz, warm thanks for your friendly greetings. I heartily reciprocate them. The pots and kitchenware won't be provided until you give us the pleasant promise that you will delight us here with your dear friendly presence. Without Kietz we can't enjoy a home-cooked dinner, not even potatoes. You need no longer bring along sausages. Hasten into the arms of your true friends and be assured that you will ever be a welcome guest.

"Your,

M. W."

149 *(Dresden, December 18, 1844)* [11]

"DEAR ERNST!

"Pardon me for sending your money so late as this. I have to reproach you that you did not get me an accounting when I sent you the 800 fr. I never had made a reckoning of it and didn't really know how much I really owed you. You ought to have made it clear to me right away. Now that you have done it, I must frankly confess that I was not able for the moment to send you the money. I am now confined to my salary, which considerably restricts my

[11] Beginning with this letter, the Paris address of Kietz is 30 rue des Petits Augustins.

financial condition, all the more because—as I may be permitted to assume—my expectations of greater and prompter extra returns were not unwarranted. . . . But I have had the experience with my works here in Germany that the more sensation they make, and the more they have added to my name, the more slowly do they spread. What the reason is only God knows. As for *Rienzi*, the reason for its limited popularity is clearly the lack of powerful heroic tenors who could undertake it. But those who attended the performances we gave last summer here in the presence of Spontini and Meyerbeer may wonder how slowly the work became known, for those performances always took place before a capacity audience, the enthusiasm of the public increasing so remarkably that after each of the five acts the singers, and at last I too, were called out. To this it must be added that I have sold my operas to the publisher on terms which in the future may result in some disproportionately greater returns than would come from the customary dealings but which at present bring me nothing at all. Only from 1846 on may I count on considerable profits and this only from each *Easter-fair*. But at this moment I am compelled to restrict myself and I am now going to tell you the candid truth: I could not have sent you your reckoning of 159 fr. until today; besides, I was not able until today to pay Loizeau even a part of my debt to him, as I am now doing. Loizeau, who has been sending me many dunning letters lately, demands 278 fr. from me as a debt contracted for Brix; so I send you as much as I can today: a bill for 300 fr. in all. Be good enough to convey in my name to Loizeau the balance after the 159 fr. belonging to you, that is, 141 fr., which is the greater part of my debt to him. Tell him that I couldn't manage more for him at the moment, that he may find in it an evidence of my good will at least, and may safely count on getting the rest of the debt, that is, 137 fr. by next Easter at the latest. I hope you will take on this small commission for me. Perhaps you could also see Draese and assure him that I am thinking of him and that I shall take care of him by Easter at the latest. If I had my success in Paris instead of here, they would surely have had their money back with plenty of interest—long ago. Here profits are very slow, unfortunately! Cäcilie and Avenarius have returned again to Germany, but I have not had a chance to see them so far. For the time being I have not been able to get away from Dresden for a single day. I was detained there by the return of Weber's ashes, which I have brought about and which has been duly carried through. Weber rests in our cemetery now; we got his remains on the 14th inst., and buried them on the 15th. The celebration was beautiful and dignified and by my speech at the grave I succeeded in giving it a due and most stirring significance. But it is truly distressing how this and similar occasions bring envy against me and often much embitter my fine position.

". . . One thing I can admonish you about even now: you are lost and deservedly so if you persist in that empty shallowness which entirely surrounds you now. You can only be saved, become worthy of salvation, if you receive into your soul that highest manly virtue, seriousness. All the externals count for nought: bad attire, need, frost, hunger; these are felt only by the man who fails to pursue with *enthusiasm* [*Begeisterung*] the serious task of his life: for the shallow man they mean everything, even life itself; for the inspired man they mean nothing! When you sit down, don't look at your coat; don't ponder *how* you want to *appear* but what you want to *be*; tackle the most serious task of your art, undisturbed and disregarding everything around you, which means your life; solve it with seriousness and inspiration and you will find that miracles will happen. The one who can't give you 100 fr. today will find ways and means of giving you thousands. This *I* will do. Farewell, honest old fellow, whom I dearly, dearly love.

"Your

RICHARD W."

158 *(Dresden, February 1, 1846)* [12]

"DEAREST KIETZ!

"This is my brother Albert, with his daughter Johanna, who now wants to perfect herself in Paris in higher singing. Have you forgiven me for obstructing your higher career as an artist, as you wrote lately? Besides, can you forgive me for not sending you any money just now, for the reason that I can decently hold my own only with the utmost trouble and difficulty, facing the gossip of a city like Dresden, a truth you would hardly believe and which you can believe only if you take my simple assurance of it, and trust that I'm not lying when I tell you that I would often call myself happy if I knew how to raise 20 thaler without stirring up a sensation? So if you can forgive me all this, I beg you sometimes to extend your friendship to my brother and his daughter.

"You may learn a good deal of news about me from my brother; I have tried to hide from him or minimize my oppressive worries. Once I am relieved of them, you too will hear all about them and probably you will have to excuse me—Bendemann, Hübner, and Rietschel [13] were delighted about your charge.

"Minna sends her hearty greetings.

"Farewell, and believe: All is not gold that glitters.

"Your

RICHARD WAGNER"

Mrs. Burrell remarks in her book on Wagner a "suspicious silence" in the Kietz correspondence between February 1, 1846, and February 13, 1850. "It is inconceivable," she wrote, "that no letters were written during that time, as Ernst Benedikt Kietz remained in Paris, and Richard was at Dresden." She suspected that these, like other letters of the revolutionary period of 1848 and 1849, were somehow "kept back." The faithful Kietz "died in poverty, made no

[12] Published in the *Münchner Nachrichten,* February 13, 1908.
[13] Rietschel was a sculptor, the other two, painters, in Dresden.

legal will. . . . The literary world must regret that the poor man's sentimental affection for the letters prevented his relieving his poverty by selling the correspondence intact during his lifetime."

Since Wagner was inclined to forget Kietz when his own interests were centered elsewhere, except when he needed something of him, Mrs. Burrell's assumption would seem to be unsupported. When Wagner returned to Paris after ten years, he at once looked up his old friend, and was shocked at what those ten years had done to his appearance (Chapter XVI, 178).

The next letters in this Collection date from Wagner's sojourn in Paris from early February, 1850. Kietz is again called into useful service, culminating in the thankless one of helping Wagner to elude Minna, in his pursuit of Jessie Laussot (Chapter XVIII, 203 D, E):

203 A *(Paris, February 13, 1850)*

"Du v—— fl—— Sch—— h——! [14] Why do you never show up? Can't you do anything but go and a—— l——? Don't dare to miss Truffaut today! [15] I warn you. I need the book of *Lohengrin* back. Have it with you! L—— j——!

R. W.

(gentleman [in English])"

203 B *(Paris, April 9, 1850)*

"Dear Brother Kietz:

"If I can't call on you or meet you earlier, be at Truffaut's tonight at six o'clock!

"Kindest regards from your

Richard W

"Paris, Tuesday morning"

203 C *(Hotel Valois, Paris, April 14, 1850)*

"Dearest Benedikt:

"Please hand over the three scores to the bearer of this letter. The rest I should not like to lug about with me.

"Today we shall see each other at Truffaut's, six o'clock at the latest?

"Yours,

Richard Wagner"

[14] The "unprintable" words are here given exactly as Wagner wrote them.
[15] Evidently a meeting place where Anders was living: mentioned in Kietz's letter to Minna of May 27, 1850 (210). Cf. also published letter of Feb. 9, 1850.

221 A *(Zürich, May 2, 1851)*

"DEAREST KIETZ!

"Treat the bearer of these lines well. He is a young Pole, Heimberger (from Lemberg), whom I like very much and who is in a bad situation now. You would prove yourself a true friend if you would allow him to live with you: also you will very soon grow fond of him.

"If you can otherwise help him by word and deed, don't fail to do it. Perhaps your landlord could procure a passport to London for him.

"You may soon learn from him what you most desire to know. You owe me a letter: write me soon.

"Farewell! Greetings to Anders, and keep me in your affection!

"Your

RICHARD WAGNER"

221 B *(Zürich, July 2, 1851)*

"DEAR KIETZ!

"Many thanks for your last letter: I rejoiced in its contents no less than in the friendly spirit behind them. I enclosed the note to Seghers which you requested. Will you please be kind enough to take care of it?

"I am answering so late because I have only just come around to the letters I owe. Until now I have been deeply absorbed in work from which I don't allow myself any digression. I have just written a *Young Siegfried* which I want to set to music for Weimar in response to an order: it is supposed to precede *Siegfried's Death* and is more light-hearted [*heiterer*] in character. I now make people talk and write a lot about me in Germany: Härtels are to edit the piano score of *Lohengrin* and even want to engrave the orchestra score. Can you get hold of the Leipzig *Illustrierte Zeitung*? The copy of the 12th of April contained a fine article on *Lohengrin* by Liszt.

"My book *Opera and Drama* is to appear in about two months.

"For the rest things are going along well enough: Tomorrow I am to go as far as Bodensee to meet a Dresden admirer who has saved the money to visit me: we are to return by way of the Appenzell Alps.

"You have given out of ink again? God, I wouldn't really care whether I had ink or not! What we are now doing with ink is nothing more than onanism! If I were single—I wouldn't mind any privation: that might give me some incentive in my miserable state.

"I long passionately for Revolution, and only the hope of experiencing it and partaking in it is what gives me the courage to live.

"Well, it's natural that Paris would be the starting place! Meanwhile we beguile ourselves as best we can into our real-life denial. It is always art that alone lends itself to this delusion.

"On the whole you afford me a great deal of fun! With all your poverty and miserable existence you are always to me an amusing and jolly fellow: your troubles have something so enormously comic about them, even those caused by your friends, and under certain circumstances even a certain friend! Well, water yourself adequately, so that you'll be wet and fresh on your feet when the Devil himself is let loose. By the way, have a natural wig made by Lindemann,[16] since he produces new intestines and, if I'm not mistaken, new hearts too!

"By the way, I completely acknowledge the science of water cures. I am taking on a bit of water too—you may not believe that the object of life is absolute health, but the real question is: What does one do with that health? And at this point we recognize that if we were concerned with nothing but water cures, life itself would go to the devil. So it is not water which must cure us, but fire, if we go through fire we'll need no more water—except to refresh ourselves. We can effect now what cures we want by water, but as soon as we become involved in life at the moment, the old mess starts over again. But are you *able* to live outside our life as it unfortunately is now?

"Enough for the present with that water-philosophy! I can write you only damned little from here—of course I lead a very retired life in my villa: the only alternative is the beer parlor. Herwegh now lives here and makes agreeable company. My wife is taking a cure now—drinking and bathing. By the way, she is well and actually very good-humored. She gives you cordial greetings. With 'you' I especially include *Anders* too. Give him my best! Farewell, old fellow! Write much and soon to your

R. W."

221 C *(Hausen am Albisbrunn, October 24, 1851)*

". . . Many thanks for your long letter: but I can't make out why you saw fit to fill it with political hash [*Kohl*]. The things you expatiate about are for the most part unknown to me. I fully share your enthusiasm for the London Exhibition: I am firmly convinced that mankind will continue to find comfort in the things exhibited there, in manufactured products— The hair which modern science has been fortunate enough to regenerate on your scalp ought to be exhibited there, too, in order to demonstrate to the world *ad oculos* what happiness industry is able to produce.

"You are quite right in saying that you can't stand the Fire: it burns too brightly, and so all the pretty manufactured articles go to the devil. But why

[16] One of several allusions to Kietz's baldness. Dr. Karl Lindemann was a friend of Kietz, who regarded him, so writes Wagner, as a "quack." Wagner shows in the letters here following that even though he was in the midst of his eternal "water cures" in Switzerland he was ready enough to listen to Lindemann's panaceas. These included laudanum or, "in default of that poison," valerian as an "antitoxin" against Wagner's new troubles.

were they manufactured if they alone can make men happy? Very well! We should leave all the pretty things undisturbed!

"We were surprised and delighted to hear that you are all of a sudden doing well again. Minna and I had a hearty laugh when we read that you have actually earned money. We enjoyed it from the bottom of our hearts and would like you to continue that way!

"We are doing well enough—what I need for my bare living I receive from the Ritter family, who will probably soon settle for good in Switzerland. Then you should really visit us some time.

"Your
RICHARD W."

221 D *(Zeltweg, Zürich, December 5, 1851)*

"MOST EXCELLENT KIETZ!

"The bearer of this letter is Hermann Müller,[17] former Guard Officer of the Saxon Army, of whom you probably have already heard. Take good care of him —this is his first time in Paris. We have both become water patients: find him a good water cure, which may not be so easy where you are!

"He is bringing Anders my finished book *Opera and Drama*—if you want to read it through first, do so. For you I am saving my three opera poems with the long preface:[18] unfortunately the publication of this book will be delayed until the New Year. But you will promptly get it then—in one way or another. Müller can tell you much about me and Minna. We both heartily greet you and are looking forward to a letter soon from you.

"Farewell and be cheerful!

"Your
RICHARD WAGNER"

221 E *(Zeltweg, Zürich, December 17, 1851)*

"Tell me, dear Kietz, wouldn't it be reasonable, just, and in order, if you were to write me how you are doing? You ought to have answered long since my letter from the Water-Cure Institute.

"I sent you greetings through Hermann Müller and ordered a copy of *Opera and Drama* sent to Anders. Has this been done and did you see Müller?

"A copy of the *Three Opera Poems* is ordered for you; it will be sent to you directly by the bookseller.

"Now write! And soon! Do you hear?
"Adieu.

"Your
R. W."

[17] Once the lover of Mme. Schroeder-Devrient, later a fellow revolutionist with Wagner, and now a fellow *"Wassermann."*   [18] Nibelungen trilogy.

300 B *(Zürich, December 30 [1851])* [19]

"DEAR KIETZ!

"I thank you very much for your letter, but not for sending my old clothes, which cost me 6 frs. . . . But I found no letter with the clothes!! You didn't understand my reminder to write me: When hell breaks loose in your home, I certainly want some sign of life from you, do you understand? Your great and unctuous litany pleased me very much and amused me in many ways: especially good was the musical composition which the magic of events conjured from your fantasy. For the rest, permit me to refrain from chattering about politics and other things of the kind. My entire politics consists of nothing but the bloodiest hatred for our whole civilization, contempt for all things deriving from it, and a longing for nature. This, of course, can't be understood by a man who felt so enchanted with the industrial exhibition. Well, now you have that exhibition, an exhibition on the pillory, with all your industrial workers. I must now atone for thinking so highly of workers as workers. With all their clamor about labor, they are the most miserable of slaves whom anybody may pocket who promises them a lot of 'work' at the moment. It all stems from our servile attitude; no one in all France knows that we are *human*, except perhaps Proudhon, and even he not quite clearly! But in all of Europe I prefer dogs to those doglike men. Yet I don't despair of a better future, only the most terrific and destructive Revolution could make our civilized beasts 'human' again.

"I am now giving much thought to America! Not because I would expect to find the right things there, but because there it is easier to plant them.

"Have you received the *Three Opera Poems* with the preface by Härtel?

"Soon now I mean to begin my great Nibelungen trilogy, and I shall *perform* it first on the banks of the Mississippi.

"Otherwise, things are going well enough. If you would come and visit us! I would surely provide the traveling money. Here you'd have to paint my ugly face in oils for my friends. But first you must do Johanna, blessed by heaven, who is so kind as not even to reply when I write to her. Farewell, old chap! Warm greetings from Minna. If you like the preface, tell me. *Adieu!*

"Your

R. W."

228 A *(Zürich, February 24, 1852)*

"DEAR KIETZ!

"Give the enclosed letter to your friend *Lindemann* at once. It contains a consultation which he has granted me through Müller.

[19] This letter is dated in the catalogue 1857 (the original MS is indistinct). From the contents it obviously follows 221 C, D, and E., of December, 1851.

"Write to me the same time he does! You owe me an answer especially as regards my books!

"Books I shall write no longer but—if Lindemann helps me—soon—the complete *Siegfried!*

"Goodbye, my dear fellow!

"Your

RICHARD"

228 B *(Zürich, March 8, 1852)*

"BAD FELLOW!

"Surely it is your fault only that I have not yet received any answer from Lindemann; either you have not given him my letter or you are now putting off his answer, for you are a dawdler!

"But I consider Lindemann's answer *very important,* and therefore I ask you urgently to see that he does answer quickly; or—if he does not want to answer me at all—that he so inform me.

"I am sending herewith an explanation of the *Tannhäuser* Overture. Even if you don't want to perform it, see that it is translated.

"Farewell!

"Your

RW"

228 C *(Zürich, March 20, 1852)*

"HONORED FRIEND!

"I urgently ask you to let me know by return mail whether my letter to Lindemann has been taken care of and whether I can hope for an answer.

"Lindemann's answer is so important to me that I am hoping you still consider me worth the sacrifice of a *single* line.

RICHARD WAGNER"

228 D *(Zürich, April 3, 1852)*

"MOST WONDERFUL FELLOW!

"Alas! How can I ever flatter you enough to make up for my recent boorish and ill natured treatment of you! I did you the shameful injustice of considering you a dawdler, and now I find out that the whole blame should go to bad postal service, that it mistook medical advice for seditious literature—oh, forgive me! And tell me of your forgiveness in a letter, for I have been awaiting one for a long while. Do you hear?

"I am so-so. Now I'd be happy to have Lindemann, if he were only here or I there with him! But to go to Paris for a *water cure*—that is a little too absurd.

"And now, won't you listen to my *Flying Dutchman?* They're giving it here on the 20th of April. My objections were no longer of any avail: all necessary material is being assembled from all sides, and so I have not been able to dissuade my friends any longer.

"Well, I'll at least expect a letter from you. My wife sends her best regards: so does Müller. What is Anders doing?

"Goodbye!

"Your

RW"

228 E *(Zürich, May 2, 1852)*

"Dear Benedikt:

"Härtels want to publish a good portrait of me. A bungler recently tortured himself with my physiognomy here, but he did so badly that—despite all likeness in the portrait—he managed to do only a caricature. Therefore I turn to you, for—you know me, which is the main thing. Listen, then! Could you make a new lithographic portrait of me by using as model the daguerreotype of your last portrait of me which is in your possession? Or would it be good if I were to be daguerreotyped from life and a copy were sent to you? What do you think? Answer me at once with two lines; I'll see to it that Härtels will pay a good price. I'd be pleased if you would do it: no one here can make a good picture of me, and they want one in Germany.

"We've just presented *The Flying Dutchman* here, four times in a week, with a sharp increase in the price of admission and always with a full house. The performance was passable: I've thought of you, Anders, and Lehrs. It is now eleven years since I wrote this opera in Meudon!

"Minna sends her kindest regards. I'm exhausted from my recent exertions. I haven't even been able to give the treatment a thought. But from this week on I'll rest: then I'll start on Lindemann's regimen. Give Lindemann my best regards.

"Write soon—or rather at once to

"Your

RW"

228 F *(Zürich, May 28, 1852)*

"Dear Kietz!

"I'm writing you about the portrait. In the winter of '50–'51 a local art dealer asked me for permission to have a copy made of the lithograph of my portrait; the lithograph appeared at the time in the fashionable newspaper.[20] The artist also has your old drawing of 1840–41 and asked me for permission to

[20] *Zeitung für die elegante Welt?*

use it. I told him I don't look like that any more; I've gotten older. He then made the face look a little older, and he did this from memory, without my sitting for him, and that's how it appeared here.

"Recently a poor devil of a Swabian bothered me to sit for him, so that he could establish himself that way. I gave in and in return for my good nature—I was horrified to see what a specter he made of me and how displeased everyone was. Before this barbarian of a painter began I had, at his request, already written to Breitkopf & Härtel about his preference for a publisher. Since the portrait has been finished I have had to withdraw my good offices, and Härtels answered me that they would postpone their project to add my portrait to their collection until a more opportune occasion. But in Germany—and here also— they want a good picture of me, and I turn to you as the one who can certainly do it best, even if I don't sit for you. Therefore I've written to Härtels today and told them if they still want to publish my portrait to get in touch with you directly and to come to terms with you, for you told me that you'd like to do it. I hope they'll agree to it, and that you will be good enough to tell me occasionally how the matter stands.

"Now you mention an 'engraving'—do you mean copperplate engraving? At the moment we're only speaking of a lithograph. If it would amuse you to see the thing the Swabian here made of me I'll send it to you: it has a certain portrait likeness, to be sure, only the man is completely incapable of knowing me, and above all he is a bungler.

"I've been in the country for two weeks and have begun my cure according to Lindemann's directions: I hope it will do me good, but I expect to find really good signs only very gradually. As soon as the first month of the cure has passed (middle of June), I'll write Lindemann my report as he asked me to do: tell him this and give him my best regards! As a matter of fact, I always feel considerably better as soon as I'm in the country and my work is also proceeding quite nicely.

"In my wife I have a stubborn enemy of water, who considers the water cure, like almost everything I undertake, an exaggeration and a stupidity: I don't get anywhere with common sense; even success won't convince her, for she'll attribute that to something entirely different! Minna is well, by the way, and in fine spirits. She wants to be remembered to you and to Anders too. Do you see *him* any more at all?

"How would it be if you'd tell me some more about yourself for a change? If I ever get any money I'll come to Paris after all, in order to meet Lindemann and to sit for an oil portrait by you! Until then—let us wait!

"Farewell, slovenly fellow!

"Your

RW

"You need no other address for me than *Richard Wagner* in *Zürich*. That is sufficient."

228 G *(Zürich, September 7, 1852)* [21]

"MOST WONDERFUL FELLOW!

"Many thanks for your sympathy and friendship! But what's the idea of thinking that I've taken offense at you? My silence I can best explain by telling you briefly my recent life history. Your next-to-last letter reached me while I was completing the *Walküre,* No. 1 of the Nibelung dramas: I should have taken eight weeks for this work; instead I did it in four weeks, without any interruptions, in bad weather, and in general under depressing circumstances. But it is to the uninterrupted work especially that I ascribe the fact that I felt so badly afterward. When our friend Lindemann looks for the present main source of my illness in the *cerebral nerves,* he thereby proves to me again how correctly he diagnoses my condition; up there I now feel so strongly affected that I could no longer have room for any doubt. My illness then is of transcendental nature, and all other medical measures can have no decisive effect if I'm not cured up there. From my brain the affection spread to my entire nervous system and manifested itself in complete exhaustion with fever symptoms. Here I felt that only the greatest quiet could help me: but I found in my surroundings only a fresh stimulus to agitation and excitability; barely had I begun to recover when—toward mid-July—I went on a trip. Strange what endurance I showed here; in fourteen days I roamed through the Bernese Oberland, climbed two high peaks, crossed a glacier down into Italy, and matched every Alpine guide in energy. Only my brain would not recover; I always remained excited and restless; lack of company became particularly unbearable for me. Herwegh did not meet me; after I had visited Lago Maggiore and arrived in Lugano I finally had my wife join me just to have a human being with me. With Minna I then went to Wallis and Chammony [*sic*] (Mont Blanc) by way of the Simplon and finally back through Geneva: I had to admit to myself, after all, that the impact of this trip had not reached the main source of my illness. Every mental occupation was so difficult for me that as far as possible I even had to refrain from writing letters: I had taken your letter along on the trip in order to answer it from there; but this was impossible for me. Back in Zürich I found the wonderful news about *Tannhäuser*; a considerable number of theaters asked for this opera, and I was especially surprised about the King in Berlin. After I decided to let them have the opera, I became concerned about doing something which could take the place of my personal presence at the performances; I wrote a guide to the performance of *Tannhäuser,* had it printed, and am now sending it to the theaters. (You, too, will receive a copy.) The haste and speed with which all this had to be done, but above all the torture of this entire eternal 'mental' communication by pen and ink, again affected my cerebral nerves so strongly

[21] This and the letter following are addressed to 22 rue Bonaparte, Faubourg Saint-Germain, Paris.

that I lapsed into a condition similar to the one after the *Walküre,* and I still am in this condition as I write to you today. Feverish excitement and exhaustion, sickeningly uneasy numbness of the brain, melancholy, fear of all work; I am often so tired that I can walk only very slowly; then again a little better, but with the tendency toward excitability. That I cannot get well again, in the sense that you imagine it, is as clear as day: I'm mentally ill—and mental illness is incurable. The particular life I lead condemns me to eternal 'theory,' even though I fully realize the necessity for a strong *sensual* [*sinnliche*] existence. The world has escaped my heart; I loathe it; I cannot love it: this way it is no longer an object of sentiment for me, but only of fantasy; only through the activity of my brain can I communicate with it. I'm too genuine to be able to lie to myself; too experienced to be ignorant. Thus, extremely sensitive as I am, I can only feel sadness: my theoretical contacts with the world cannot bring me any happy emotions. Under 'theory' I also include here all my artistic creativeness, because I cannot produce a real work of art with only artistic means at my disposal. It would not help matters at all if, for example, I were now in Berlin myself: the torture of the incompleteness and inadequacy of the practical experiment would be at least as great as the torture of abstaining from all experiments. I'm bound to go to pieces in this present-day world of ours. I know this and have already completely reconciled myself to it: therefore it is for me no longer a question of *recovering,* but only of making the period of my existence bearable, and I can do this only through artistic creation, since this is the only illusion which is effective with me. I therefore desire from our Lindemann not *cure,* but merely palliatives to make my existence as artist possible as long as this existence can be maintained at all. The *six months' walking tour* I cannot consider: I'm too old and not light-hearted enough to divert myself with the trivial exterior of our country and city sights; I can no longer be purposeless and have no other purpose than my abstract health. On the other hand, I'm thinking of making it possible to buy a small piece of land with garden and livestock on Lake Zürich; if it works out I expect a great deal from the care of a small property, especially of animals. Now and then excursions, mountain climbing—even a trip to Paris. Otherwise the prescribed treatment agrees quite well with me: especially the night bath at 22 degrees, which usually gives me a restful night. I cannot take the morning bath below 18 degrees; but if I feel ill as I do now, I take the night bath at 24 degrees and the morning bath at 21-22, because if it is any colder it increases the feverish excitability of the nerves. Above all, I will now remember always to interrupt myself during my work when I notice that it affects me too strongly: then I'll immediately go into the Alps for a few days. What does Lindemann think of that? Shall I make changes in the baths? You see, I've lost myself completely in a letter to Lindemann: report this to him, and tell him I apologize for not having made a special copy of this letter for him!

"I'll have to come to the end, for I've already written more than I can stand. The matter of the portrait is a real mess! Härtels are ridiculously cautious: they're publishing a series of portraits of 'famous Germans' in quite excellent copperplate prints; they only want to accept something really good, and so they first would like to see with their own eyes what you can do before they arrange a definite commission. I did not even want to tell you this. But if you are not sensitive, I'd advise you to make the drawing of my mug [*Fratze*] and to send it to them for inspection: if they like the portrait you can be sure that they'll pay you well for it, for these people are really not stingy. But should they still have objections, I'd advise to have it lithographed at my expense and then give it to an art dealer to be sold: the success would be good in any case and profitable for you; for—and this is the reason which brings me to the matter of the portrait—even now I cannot prevent miserable stuff (third- and fourth-hand imitations of your old portrait of me) from being sold in great quantity. My 'fame' is growing, and especially my absence ('banishment') from Germany makes me interesting to many people: speculators will presumably have all copies copied again and will sell my *Fratze* for my face; in order to prevent that, I should like you to proceed quickly with what I have told you.

"*If I can possibly do it* I'll come to Paris with my wife next winter, especially also to meet Lindemann. Then you'd have to 'paint' me and then we'd have to have a good copperplate print done from it. I can now appreciate how valuable a good portrait can become to others, for example, in a fine picture of Schiller (after Müller) which now hangs in my room.

"Unfortunately, I can add nothing more about you, except that I'm making plans for you: if I come to Paris you can be sure that I'll take you away from there—namely, to Switzerland—and I'll hold you here in my house as long as you like it. But even if I don't come to Paris this winter, I'll still manage to have my way and to have you accompany me on a real tour of the Alps, as far as Italy, next summer. What I can and will earn is as yet very uncertain: in view of my debts I should actually not earn anything; but I'll manage to get enough to have you here once; you'll also find a chance to earn money here.

"Goodbye for today! Assume that what I have left unanswered is impossible for me to answer today. But spare me any theory: it frightens me when you, too, start that, because I'll then have no one who talks plainly. Minna sends you her kindest regards; she pricks up her ears when Paris is mentioned. Goodbye, many thanks for your letters, write soon again, remember me to Lindemann, and give him my apologies.

"Your

RW

"Don't think that *Fétis père*, etc., offended me; I wanted to read his stuff, but my patience soon gave out. Who in Paris—where no one knows me—could be expected to read stuff like that! How impractical of Meyerbeer!!"

240 A *(Zürich, April 2, 1853)*

"DEAR FRIEND!

". . . You have recently read a lot about my successes in Germany; you suspect that I'm getting large financial returns; you assume—because I do not write to you for a while—that I'm sitting pretty and therefore no longer care about you who are in the dumps. On this assumption you then write to me of your pitiful, undeserved misery, that you had to dissipate your talent for lack of money, and you take this as ground for reproaches and insults—even if indirect —of the most objectionable kind against me! It is fortunate that I know you and your temperament and thus don't lose the courage to be frank with you. The notion you have of your friends seems, however, to be very unfortunate. Enough: you are mistaken. If my operas can be of a profitable nature, I still have to wait for the actual receipts. None of the larger theaters has as yet given or ordered my operas: the largest were Frankfurt, Leipzig, and Breslau, of which each paid me 100 thaler. *Berlin,* with its royalties, could have—under very favorable circumstances—earned a lot for me, to be sure; but to make certain of just these favorable circumstances I had to be careful and withdraw my opera for the time being, since it would have been badly performed. Neither *Vienna,* nor *Munich, Hanover, Stuttgart,* nor similar more distinguished and well paying theaters have applied up to this time. If you'll now recall that for four years I have depended only on the good will of my friends; that besides my wife and Natalie I alone also had to support Minna's parents, then you'll be able to understand that the thought could not yet have occurred to me that it is my duty to support you also, since only last summer you wrote to me of your prosperity and your many good prospects. As soon as I get into the situation in which you assume I find myself already, don't doubt that I'll also think of you, you old rascal. But the matter of cash will always have its great difficulty. You know that I cannot save, and that I always spend more than I earn will remain my permanent failing; if I get money it is certain that I've always already spent three times as much and am in debt. My normal living requirements cost me so terribly much that I always feel intensely pressed to use artificial substitutes. Thus I have the irrepressible desire to take a nice, long trip to southern Europe: without contracting new debts I cannot consider such a thing. Furthermore, my future earnings are so indefinite, and it is possible that from today on I shan't sell a single score, since I myself don't advertise them, but have to let everything come to me, in which case I then have to rent them out often on a part-payment basis—as recently with Berlin. All that I have left to offer you definitely is therefore the following: come to see me when you feel like it and stay as long as you like, even if it should be for the rest of your life: I shall give you a nice room for yourself and everything you need to live on; I shall certainly provide you an opportunity for earning necessary money, and in any emergency I stand as a brother with ready cash at your disposal. This I offer you because I see—I *can* do it, the *living together* makes it possible. But any considerable cash payment will always remain impossible for me. I hope at least that you are not so foolish as to take this as a 'good sermon.' But enough!

"I couldn't go to Paris—as I first wanted to do—this winter: I never had the money available, and without that I couldn't have done it. *In January* my health broke down completely; I believed in my imminent death. After suggestions from all sides I finally went to a doctor to whose extraordinary solicitude and watchfulness I have now permanently entrusted myself. Lindemann's genius will not be able to overcome the difficulty of my absence from him: all that helps here is constant daily supervision with minute directions for treatment according to my quickly changing condition, and this not only for several weeks, but, really, *always*. So I'll have to write to Lindemann to thank him cordially for his friendly solicitude and his advice. It shall soon be done.

"I have completed my poem; it is called *The Ring of the Nibelung*, a stage-festival play for three days preceded by an evening. Evening, *The Rhinegold*; first day, *The Valkyrie*; second day, *The Young Siegfried*; third day, *Siegfried's Death*. If I'm well, I'll begin the musical composition this summer.

"I could send you a copy of it at this time: only I'm afraid it will not get there by mail; I have already had the worst experience in this way: I cannot send it *sous bande*. If I don't even find a good opportunity, I'll bring it to you personally in the autumn, when I really do hope to come to Paris.

"I am at this moment completely unable to send you any money since we are about to move into a larger apartment and have to be so much more careful with our cash, which already consists of borrowed money. But don't let this stop you from writing to me again: I think we also have things other than money matters to tell each other. If you see Devrient, give her my best regards: I look forward very eagerly to seeing her again; it would be very nice of her if she would let me know the time of her arrival so that I'll be in Zürich. Liszt is coming to see me at the end of May or the beginning of June. At the end of May I also perform one of my works. Goodbye! Regards to my friends, and be a little more reasonable with me.

"Your

RW"

240 B *(Zürich, June 6, 1853)*

"OH, *Du Mensch!*

"Here is my poem which I promised you and which you now receive because I have a safe way of sending it.

"If you still have a good word for me, write to me soon again: if not, write to me anyway!

"Greetings to Anders and Lindemann! Goodbye, you wicked animal!

"Your

RICHARD WAGNER"

240 C *(Zürich, November 7, 1853)*

"O! O! O!
"Kietz! Kietz! Kietz!
"What a ——— you are [*sic*].
"So you are offended again!

"You dig up a lot of unholy nonsense about me in your letter: I am a poor, public-coddled, applause-seeking man, and on top of this, I have the mania of fancying that I am misunderstood by you, whereas you judge so correctly that I, puffed up by my successes, am contemptuous of your fewer successes. And then one shouldn't say—shame on you for again taking offense! Kietz, what kind of fleas have you got in your head!!

"If I have often been running you down, it has always been almost entirely due to your unreliability in the matter of favors, your dawdling, etc., with which you have really spoiled our days together. Shouldn't one then be sorry to see that this dilly-dallying [*Temperei*] is the *only* cause of your deterioration? Am I conceited when I say that?

"Otherwise you are completely agreeable and lovable to me as you are, as long as you don't want to be something entirely *different*. But unfortunately, you hear wrong every time: that stuff I'm supposed to have said about your charge against me you've completely misunderstood. God, what a rumor monger you are!!

"Admit this one thing—that you are simply proving to me again how one must have great patience with you! If I lose it at times, you really must not be offended.

"Now stop this nonsense, you old hypochondriac! As proof of how immaterial you are to me, I assure you that I shall make every effort to have you here with me next summer: Liszt and his women are also coming for a longer time!

"Listen—for God's sake finish that picture for the Wesendoncks and send it here as soon as possible: otherwise you'll see me getting rough!

"As soon as I can I'll send money: right now I'm hard pressed.

"Hurry up!

"Your over-eager public figure [*übermüthiger Publikumsmench*]

R. W."

240 E *(Undated)*

"Dear Friend!

"You are terribly prompt—that must be admitted! I cannot be so prompt. That I can't make sense of your letter will probably be all right with you, for you laid it out in such a way that one wouldn't make sense of it—which you accordingly succeeded in doing. But I've already explained in my last letters that I'm now in a tight place financially; it shouldn't make any difference that I myself have no money, so long as others—who usually help me out—have some. But I have now completely exploited these, and if opera money doesn't soon arrive from Germany, and I mean in large amounts, my prospects are for a more unpleasant situation than ever.

"Let us be frank! To send you the lump sum of 100 francs by the 20th of this month is quite impossible, for I know no one from whom I could borrow it: Minna already has no more household money.

"You must set different date limits: you are asking me at the worst time of the whole year.

"My difficulty is temporary, however, and in a short time I'll be out of it: my prospects are otherwise good, and my successes are growing steadily—much to your dismay, for you are going to worry about my conceit.

"Well, to make it short: as soon as I have money you shall have some too. In any case this will be *before the end of January*. With this you must content yourself—as far as help from me is concerned.

"As for your oriental trip, I'll first have to hear some more about it before I seriously believe it. If you are actually leaving before I can send money, find out where I can forward it to you so that you'll get it.

"What nonsense this is! I feel as if I'll have to suffer terribly for my recent Parisian excesses!

"Well, I hope to get a more detailed report from you—and also from *Lindemann*. It will certainly be difficult for him always to have to worry about us: What does he get out of it, after all? But I live in the firm hope of getting him to come to Zürich for a while.

"Give him my best! *Adieu* from both of us! The child is pretty.

"Your
RW"

265 A (*Zürich, June 3, 1854*)

"O KIETZ!

"I am sorry for you, for I am *badly* off; I cannot help you now. For a sensible man of your experience that should be enough. But if you want more, know hereby that my last Paris extravagances have had this aftermath for me, that with the exception of yourself I have already looted all my friends, if only to be able to get along until fall; then and *only* then may I hope to recover somewhat through new returns from the theater. I have tried many ways to get larger advances on these expected returns. Relying on this hope, I promised Lindemann 100 frs. in May. Nothing worked out. I am and remain extremely hard pressed.

"It made a very sad impression on us that on your return from Turkey you had absolutely nothing to tell us from Rome except complaints, misery, and distress: not the slightest word about your impressions, which would have made us glad for your sake. Therefore you still owe us the account of your trip to the Orient.

"The *Wesendoncks* send their greetings to you: the order for copying the Raphael still stands; they do not withdraw it. If you came to Zürich, they would like to have their portraits painted by you. There might be some further orders. You *must* write to them some time. Within a few days they are going to the summer resort of *Schwalbach:* by the middle of July they plan to be back again. If you want to come, my house, kitchen, and cellar are open to you whenever and as long as you like. I have a small room with a north light which at present is occupied by Natalie, who, however, could be put up somewhere else.

"I *keep up my spirits* merely by intensive *work*. My *Rhinegold* has been completely finished in these last few days. This work has had a good influence on my health: personally, I really feel pretty much as I should like to, even though there is not a day without bad hours. I often take some of Lindemann's powders. Give my best regards to the good one: how sorry I should be for him for being such a wretched composer!

"Minna is supposed to take a drinking cure of whey on a mountain near Lake Lucerne. Lindemann will probably not object, as these cures are said to have an excellent effect on digestive troubles. She is always ailing a little: but less since she no longer follows the medical prescriptions for the imaginary gout.

"Unfortunately Liszt too is very badly off at present: some time ago I had hoped to get some help from him.

"Now write me soon whether we may expect you? Don't forget the Wesendoncks either! Otherwise there is nothing more that is new about myself. Avenarius was here for a few days recently: he asked me to send you his greetings.

"Farewell, and if possible give me a treat with some good news.

"Kindest regards from Minna and also to Lindemann!

"*Adieu!*

"Your

RW"

265 B *(Zürich, December 7, 1854)*

"O KIETZ!!

"You are crazy— What will become of you next? Come here in the spring; you can count on six portraits—for the rest we shall see later. We can find good use for a crazy fellow like you here.

"I couldn't answer your letters from Rome: I really didn't know what to say. Should I give as further reasons for my silence the thousand worries and torments which have been consuming me all this time? Upon my word, things have been going very badly with me, and my only consolation is that it probably won't happen again, because I hope I shan't soon again be as crazy as I was last year, when some devil's urge made me want to live well for once. By this I got myself into incredible debts; however, I thought I could save myself if I could drag it out until this fall, when I expected *considerable* revenues from the German theaters. In my anguish and need (which, moreover, I had to hide from my wife) this longed-for time approached, and lo and behold! none of our expectations materialized. God knows what the reason may be: in short, orders dropped off almost entirely. Everything that was to materialize, like Berlin, Munich, etc., came to nothing, and I was completely bankrupt: now a friend [22] helped me in extreme need: however, until the repayment of my very large debt I signed over all my current revenues to him and restricted myself to a very limited budget for my household which barely enables us to exist. You can imagine that all this would bring with it heavy and *disgusting* worries, troubles, and annoyances of all kinds. These conditions took away my desire to do anything, least of all to answer your puny letters [*Flohbriefe*].

"But now all this must come to an end. *Minna* was in Germany for nine weeks visiting her parents and acquaintances, and also saw my operas. My situation there remains unchanged. The *Presse* of Nov. 30, which I read on your suggestion, knows more about it than I do: probably a false rumor! I won't go to the Prussian Court, don't worry about that: I can manage in Switzerland for the time being, and probably for always, even if one day I should be pardoned. So you will be sure to find me in Zürich in the Zeltweg.

"Kindest regards and thanks to Lindemann: I am happy that he cured you from cholera, though not for your sake. We are now in pretty good shape: the trip did Minna a lot of good, and I am the dog that has become accustomed to beatings. The Wesendoncks also advise you to come. You are sure to find work; come the sooner the better, a rich family *Jochmiss* [?] wants also to be painted by you. Farewell, keep loving me, and always think the best of your old friend

R W"

303 A *(Zürich, January 12, 1858)* [23]

"MOST FAITHFUL OF ALL FRIENDS!

"So I have to change my plans after all! It was my intention, in the face of your stubborn disbelief in me, not to write to you again until I could send you at least 100 francs at the same time. Not even your remorseful letters could shake me in this, because I hoped to hasten the fulfillment of my wish through the compulsion put on me. Well, it has not yet been possible for me to do so: I must continue to live from hand to mouth, and for the last four weeks I've been in no position to finance my intended trip to Paris, because I haven't yet

---

[22] Otto Wesendonck.
[23] Addressed care Mr. le Vte Chandon de Briaille, Epernay, France.

got the money for it. But I'm telling you now that I hope to be able to reach Paris *by the end of this week*; if not, I'll come sometime next week in any case. I would be very happy if you could meet me. You'll accordingly get another letter from me on the morning before my arrival in Paris. And so—farewell! Best regards,

"Your

RW"

303 B (*Zürich, January 14, 1858*)

"DEAR KIETZ!

"I'm arriving *Saturday* by the last train—between ten and eleven o'clock— at the Strassburg station. Meet me if you can and get me a room, comfortable and well heated, in the Hôtel de Lyon (rue Richelieu, rue Filles St. Thomas)!

"Your

RICHARD WAGNER"

303 C (*Grand Hôtel du Louvre, Paris, January 22, 1858*)
"KIETZ!

"Please send me your *text* of *Rienzi* quickly! I'm staying till the end of next week! More next time! I'm in a hurry!

"Your

RW"

303 D (*Paris, February 1, 1858*)

"O KIETZ!

"If your gracious host [24] wants to put me up for one night with all that that involves, I'll arrive in Epernay on Wednesday at 4:30 and hope to be met by you.

"Please give my kindest compliments to your dear friends and apologize for me in advance for the trouble I'm going to cause them.

"Farewell!

"Your

RW"

[24] "After I left Paris, on the 2nd of February . . . I looked up my old friend Kietz in Epernay, where M. Paul Chandon, who had known Kietz since boyhood, had interested himself in the ruined painter by taking him into his house, and giving him a number of commissions for portraits."—*My Life*, p. 677.

303 E *(Brestenberg,*[25] *May 8, 1858)*

"My good Kietz!

"I was much troubled by your birthday congratulations on the anniversary of Napoleon's death (May 5), when (even if somewhat ironically) you didn't do it last year until the 22nd. It would be all right with me if you had congratulated me on the anniversary of *my* death, then things would be just as I want them.

"Since my last return things have become increasingly gloomy with us: despair and desolation on all sides. The worst was that during the second half of the winter my wife had an aggravated and sustained relapse of an old ailment which finally became unbearable for her and those around her. It turns out to be a seriously aggravated heart ailment against which decisive steps finally had to be taken. For the last three weeks she has been under the care of an excellent hydropath a few hours from Zürich who has already treated similar cases successfully. We're hoping for an improvement and are seeking to check the progress of the disease. I visit her frequently and am in Brestenberg today for a visit. While she is taking a sitzbath, I'm writing to you so that you'll hear something from me again.

"Things have gone badly with my work so far: the sufferings, tortures, and cares were always great and robbed my spirit of any freedom. Now I'm all alone in my little cottage: even my neighbors—the Wesendoncks—are away. But a week ago I welcomed a dear guest into the house, the magnificent grand piano which Madame Erard gave me. I play a lot on it and am now able to work again. This shall—if it succeeds—enable me to forget everything: I must rely on my art alone.

"I'm thinking of sending my wife to Germany for diversion in the fall; then I'll presumably go to Paris, to stay there for the winter, so we'll have a long time to see much of each other. But I'm not counting on successes in Paris at all; I'm not looking for anything, and they won't look for me either. So it is— as usual!

"We sometimes think of adopting a child; I feel that this would be a good thing, especially for my wife. Now it occurs to me that we could adopt *you:* for you are and remain a real child. In spite of your advanced age, you would be the best fulfillment of our wish; and I'm suggesting to you in all seriousness, if it should at some time suit you, to make your home with us for *good;* be our house and family companion and so remain. . . . Think it over! If you accept, you can start *immediately:* you are always welcome. All the rest is easy to arrange: you count as a regular member of the family.

[25] Minna went to Brestenberg, on the Halwyler Lake, a few days after she had intercepted a letter from Wagner to their hostess, Mathilde Wesendonck, and brought on a crisis between the two families (see Chapter XXIII). Wagner was about to begin composing the second act of *Tristan und Isolde.*

"Goodbye for today! Take what I told you seriously. I have to decide one way or the other now; your acceptance would result in something better and more bearable.

"My wife sends you her very best regards from her sitzbath! Give my regards to Lindemann, to whom I sincerely apologize for my disagreeable behavior when I left.

"Let me hear some good news from you soon!

"Your

RW"

303 F *(Venice, October 18, 1858)*

"O KIETZ!

"You see, at last I'm thinking of you too! I've had much to endure recently. Now there is some peace and quiet. I left Zürich in August: we've given up our household there. My wife's terrible disease, a very advanced heart ailment, against which we applied a three-month water cure, very sensibly directed, has caused her and those about her much distress. Now she has gone to Germany to look for diversion and quiet. At the beginning of November she will settle in Dresden. I'm living in Venice for the present, in the greatest seclusion so that I too can recover and collect myself—I'm already succeeding. I had my grand piano sent here and am working again. I'm living very nicely on the Grand Canal and am altogether charmed by the place. Having no plans, I'll wait to see how things will shape up. There you have everything I can tell you about myself without going into impossible details.

"You could do me a big favor if you would get me some snuff. Can you afford to lay out the money for 3 pounds (1½ kilograms)? I can't send money to France in a letter, and no one will give me a draft for 12 to 14 francs. If you find it possible, please buy me 2 pounds of the regular and 1 pound of the special kind *à la divette*. Send them via Marseille, *par mer*. Since one can bring in only very little for personal use, I'll ask you please to send it in two packages. One to me: Canal Grande, Palazzo Giustiniani, Campiello Squillini, No. 3228; the other one to Herr *Karl Ritter*, Sottoportico die S. Zaccaria, No. 4691.

"And now, behave yourself. I'll soon come to Paris again. Let me hear from you before then and remain faithful to your

R. W."

331 *(Paris, April 2, 1859)* [26]

"MY DEAR SIR.

"As a result of my absence from Paris on some family matters, which lasted until today, I received your letter only this morning, and hasten to answer it:

[26] This and the letters following are addressed to E. B. Kietz at 10 rue des Mariniers, Epernay, France.

The prose translations of the operas of Richard Wagner are all finished, but they have to be completed in verse: a task which I shall conscientiously pursue now that I am back in Paris. It will be finished before long. As soon as it is printed, I shall send you several copies; be good enough to let me keep the German libretti some time longer, I still need them.

"Please accept the assurance of my high consideration and my friendliest greetings.

S. DE CHARNAL"[27]

339 A *(4 avenue de Matignon, Champs Elysées, Paris, October 10, 1859)*

"Tell me, unworthy man and libertine, when will you ever sever yourself from the arms of your mattress[28]? (My wife claims to know that you are keeping one now.)

"I have rented an apartment for three years, 16 rue Newton, avenue des Champs Elysées, and shall move there on the 15th inst. I expect my wife to come here around the middle of next month. If you can make up your mind to come to Paris, you now know where to find me, which you can best do any forenoon until two o'clock.

"God bless you!

"Your

RICHARD WAGNER"

339 B *(Paris, October 12, 1859)*

"DEAR KIETZ!

"The costs of moving and the furniture, contrary to expectation, have increased to such a degree that I had to write to Germany for more advances in order to keep going. If it arrives in time, I promise to pay you your two installments. In any case give me the exact address of Mr. Cliche so that I may find out, if worst comes to worst, whether he can be satisfied with a pledge, or a note.

"Owing to the possibility of a performance of one of my operas here this winter, I believe I can undertake such a promise. Even if things turn out well so that I can hold on and stand firmly behind you, I still have doubts, since you seem to cling to the opinion that the fate of man depends only on external circumstances.

"Write me what I must do—affectionate greetings.

"Your

R. W.

"Until the 15th inst., 4 avenue de Matignon, Champs Elysées."

[27] Wagner entrusted the *Rienzi* text to De Charnal for translation into French and later that of *Tannhäuser* for its Paris production in 1861. But later he discovered that "this charming young man" was utterly incapable. Wagner dismisses him as "an obscure journalist on a theatrical newspaper."

[28] A pun on *Matratze* and *Mätresse*.

339 C *(16 rue Newton, Paris, October 20, 1859)*

"Here, dear Kietz, are the receipts of Herr Cliche for your reassurance. I can't tell you more because I am much fatigued. I have just moved into my new apartment.

"I hope you won't really have it on your mind to pay me back. So don't hurry. As soon as I can manage it, I'll send you a little money.

"Goodbye!

"Your

R. W."

339 D *(16 rue Newton, Paris, December 31, 1859)*

"DEAREST KIETZ!

"I really intended to write you one of these days; I am glad you forestalled me.

"I was very much put out to learn that you are to be had only for money. I should have liked to have you here; but I have no money to send you now. If you can't afford even the trip from Epernay to Paris so as to visit us, I really don't know what to say about it and what value to put on your assurances of friendship.

"All that I can tell you is: start out, come to see us as soon as possible; you will be reimbursed at once for the expenses of your visit, this you may be sure of. I can't write you much; I really shouldn't know where to begin. I have already much to write. If I am not worth the small sacrifice of a visit, I really have no time to chat with you either.

"Enough of this! Come tomorrow if possible! You will be heartily welcomed: for that will prove that we really still mean something to you.

"Then you shall learn all kinds of news from us. If you were in Paris, as I certainly assumed would be the case when I came here, we could help you in many ways and you could stay with me from morning until night. But I am almost in despair. God knows what is keeping you in Epernay! I really can't understand it. Well, no offense.

"Hearty greetings from me and Minna, and in return for your good wishes our wish is to have you here soon.

"Your

R. W."

367 *(E. B. Kietz, 10 Rue des Mariniers, Epernay, January 18, 1861, to Wagner)*

"MY OLD FRIEND!

"You see, here as well as in Paris my address has been the same and will remain so for some time to come—unfortunately! You have known my flat in Paris for a long time, indeed you even have a claim to it since you recently advanced me the money for a payment which I am not as yet able to repay you— In time one picks roses—until now I have not harvested anything but thorns—those I neither can nor will send you, so I keep silent.

"By the end of last year I had hoped to give up this apartment and my Parisian one; but I could not manage it and so still I have this burden on my shoulders, but also the advantage that letters addressed there are forwarded to me here. I herewith recall my present local address as well as myself to your memory. By the way, letters without detailed specification of my address reach me too. I've become a true *Epernacien*. Your new address has been forwarded to me. You are everywhere and nowhere! Nowhere at least for me.

"Since we saw each other you have been in London, in Belgium, in Germany, and in many other countries, even in Epernay! For I don't doubt that the railway has carried you through here at least four times. Probably it only occurred to you later that I live here, otherwise you would probably have notified me in advance of your trip through here, so that I might have met you at the station as in former times, or, since I live just opposite the station and since the train stops here for a considerable time, you might have sent for me or might have skipped across yourself—you did not make this skip because I could not make the greater one to Paris, which at that time was impossible for me. You misjudge my situation, and therefore you want to misjudge me: *tu cherche querelle allemande!*

"For a long time I have been preparing myself for this letter as if for a trial sermon that shall grant me the readmittance to the temple of friendship. An awful fear or shyness kept me from finding a beginning or end. I really don't know how and what to write to you under such circumstances as mine. I had hoped to get the theme from you. For days and years you have owed me a reply. That you don't give me any, seems to be proof for me that you are offended, and that—oblivious of our old friendship and my faithful love—you do not care for any news from me, you want to break off.

"With these lines I am making one more desperate effort—if there is no answer soon, your silence will have confirmed my sad suppositions.

"I have been struck by fate so hard that I am becoming almost insensitive to new blows. This one, though, would still hurt me deeply, though I have known already for a long time what a low opinion you hold of me. In fact, I succumbed to all misfortune whereas you gained strength in your resistance against it. To fight and to create, these are vital necessities for you. However, whereas my body was stronger than my spirit—yours succumbed, for as I have been told, you have even been very ill, my poor friend. But fortunately I learned about your complete recovery at the same time, and I am glad to see you well and steering towards a goal that will crown your efforts and will embellish your good wife's housekeeping.

"Forgive and forget! Think of me as you knew me in former times and herewith receive with good will my "Happy New Year" and my congratulations for this Year so decisive for you, of course also the best wishes for your good wife.

"It is just three years ago that I embraced you here and saw you for the last time.[29] You made many beautiful promises at that time, both orally and written. Now I am facing contempt and indifference. However I am not angry with you at all, you are not the only one, I get well enough accustomed to it. The only evil is that one generally thinks of those good intentions and promises as if they had become reality, and one does not understand at all why I continue to remain in misery. But still worse is the good advice which is being dealt out to me as cash payment from all sides and in the most contradictory ways. If it is not complied with, the most bitter reproaches follow, again in lieu of cash payment, and that's the end. However, for a long time I haven't been considered worthy of either. 'There is nothing to repair in a complete ruin,' that is what the dear and faithful friends whisper to one another, and they console their consciences by convincing themselves that they have done what they could.

"Well, it is all the same to me, all the same! As far as a place to sleep and a feeding trough are concerned, they are provided for me here. So I am vegetating like a plant growing among ruins. Memories alone still live fresh in me, and the dearest ones are those of our former friendship. Do not destroy them for me.

"Since that time I have had one more happy period in my life, and that is here in the house of Paul Chandon.[30] You too appeared there at that time as if the former happiness were to be joined with the new one.[31] Unfortunately both of us were not in our *Elysé* that day! You even regretted this one day's stay as inconsistent, and did not show any gratitude to the Chandons, though I had requested you for my sake to do so, in written form at least. All sorts of petty quarrels like this have expelled me from this paradise. And however much I, grateful soul, would like to show myself grateful to them, they bar me from every opportunity to do so. Until today the abyss between us has grown more and more insurmountable, at least as regards the wife and her obstinacy—her blank stare struck you already at that time. By the way, Paul is an enthusiastic adherent of you and your works, and he defends your works and tendencies with zeal and *bon sens*.

"But I am chattering a lot of useless stuff in order to fill my letter, which is not meant to say anything more than: have pity upon me, give me as a New Year's gift your old friendship again, and I also ask Frau Minna for hers; and do not let me wait for this reassurance.

"In faithful love your most faithful friend

E. B. KIETZ."

[29] Cf. Wagner's published letter to Minna of January 17, 1858; "Kietz met me at Epernay, at the station; he can't come to Paris at present, which is a pity for me and seemed to cause him great regret."

[30] Cf. published letters of R. W. to Minna of January 17 and February 1, 1858.

[31] Published letter of R. W. to Minna of May 31, 1859, vol. 2, p. 516

Wagner's answer was at least prompt. His excuse for a curt reply—*"Meine Beschäftigung ist unsäglich"*—is legitimate:

370 *(3 Rue d'Aumale, Paris, January 22, 1861)*

"DEAR KIETZ!

"I travelled back and forth by way of Cologne, to call for my wife at the spa, and therefore I didn't pass Epernay.

"I have been unspeakably busy; I have to neglect my most important duties. I can't write and have no spare time for anything. And this has been so for a long time.

"Write me how much money you'll need to get here for the first performance of *Tannhäuser* (in three or four weeks). If I can manage it, it will be done.

"Goodbye— My wife greets you as well as I,

"Your

R. W."

Three letters from Minna to Kietz (376) about the Paris performance of *Tannhäuser* are quoted in Chapter XXIV.

393 *(Minna, Bürgerwiesen Strasse 8, Dresden, December 14, 1861, to E. B. Kietz)*

"DEAREST FRIEND!

"Although I was the first one to propose, when we were saying goodbye to each other in Paris, that neither of us write to the other until we were both better off, since this has still not happened, since I at least belong to the race of unlucky people, I am once more the first one, despite all the misery which seems to pursue us forever on this treacherous earth, to reopen our correspondence and to ask you for news about yourself very soon! How are you? Are you well? Do you have much work? Do you ever think of the Preisenwienen? Are they married? You must answer me all questions; please don't forget any. I talk and tell a lot about you here, especially to the family Heine, who send you their best regards! I also had to tell a pretty but not very young widow Pfotenhauer about you; but I dug out all the bad things, as you can imagine, since I am considered a bad gossip.

"I've been away from Paris since July 10 and for the last four weeks I've been in Dresden, which has grown big and beautiful and where business and the arts are flourishing. Last month I spent my so-called silver-wedding anniversary *(fato)* here: that was a fine day! I would not have spent it so sadly if I could have struck the twenty-five fateful years from my life. Well, they are past, and in the end one must always be glad to have come out of it whole.

"Since our separation I have seen my husband for only one day in the resort town of Soden, when he hurriedly passed through there on his trip to Weimar, where I also spent six weeks in September by myself and where I got to know many kind families who made it very hard for me to leave. If Richard had not objected, I should have gladly settled down there for good. I am thoroughly tired of chasing around homeless from place to place in my old age, and unfortunately do not see any chance for a permanent home.

"On the 24th of last month I received *congé* for one year from my dear husband in Vienna; he wanted me to settle here during that year. After that year we may possibly meet on the Rhine, where I shall perhaps await his further disposition of my insignificant self. It will be difficult for me, as the wife of such a democratic criminal of '49 as R., to get permission to settle here; they still have not even given me the permit to stay here for an indefinite time. Meanwhile, I am staying here till the end of March despite all the authorities; they cannot have me expelled by the police since I am not well enough to continue my trip in the winter, as my doctor will confirm. That, my dear friend, is how I get along in a strange place, a homeless person in her former home.

"You have probably heard or read about Richard's failure with the performance of *Tristan* in Vienna; the trouble was the lack of a suitable tenor for the main part, because Ander, the only one, had lost his voice through a cold. It is possible that Richard will go to Vienna again later on; there he takes advantage of the hospitality of an acquaintance. He writes to me often that he longs for his former home life, which he gave up too quickly, but unfortunately too late. Now you know everything that has happened to me since our farewell. But no, not yet everything. Shortly before I left Paris, my cherished, dear friend and companion, my dear, good little dog, met with an accident. He lies buried in Hf. Stürmers. [32]

"I often get letters from Frau von Szemere; she recently had two successful eye operations. She urged me to ask you to keep your promise and to return the 100 francs to her. If I were not myself in the most dreadful financial embarrassment, you may rest assured that I would have already taken care of the matter without mentioning a word about it to you; as it is, however, I must *urgently* ask you, best friend, to send them to her, petty as she is, or, if you cannot do so yet, at least to write to her at ONCE and to set a time *when* you can or wish to return the 100 francs to her, so that *I* may get out of this embarrassing situation. I expect this small proof of friendship from you most definitely.

"I also spoke with your brother Gustav; he sends you his best regards. Last summer, in August, he visited me when he passed through Soden.

"Farewell! Fulfill my request; write to Frau v. Szemere and to me *very soon*. I greet you in old friendship.

"Yours,

M. Wagner.

"The address is: Frau Leopoldine von Szemere, 9 rue Chateaubriand, Paris."

[32] The dog Fips had died in June.

395 *(E. B. Kietz, in Epernay, January 26, 1862, to Minna in Dresden)*

"My dear, good Frau Wagner.

"How could I better begin this letter and renew my correspondence than with a cordial New Year's wish? May this year be happier for you than the last ones and many earlier ones. The wish is so much the more fervent since your letter of December 14th has affected me deeply and has paralyzed all my strength to answer you quickly. It is truly a cry of pain from a tortured, good soul. I can only suffer with you, but not help you and console you; I made the last unsuccessful attempt in Paris. I had to remember that 'What isn't my business doesn't concern me!' the more so because I could recognize my powerlessness; the more so because I had to realize, to my sorrow, that I have one friend less; that I've even lost my last one in Wagner. (Lindemann hasn't written to me at all. Paul M. tells me that his experiments and discoveries have become quite lucrative to him.) It would be nice if we were both wrong, but . . . he hasn't written to me so far. Until he does, I won't bother him with a letter. As if I haven't already been a personal burden to him too long in Paris—necessity forces one to do many things!

"At the same time I've had strange experiences with him, and my shyness, which I already had at the concerts, has increased, because for the third time now he is partly the cause (innocent and best intentioned) of my distress. To recover from this last trip which he suggested will probably take me more than one and one-half years; perhaps I'll not recover at all, for I'm getting worse and worse.

"I have already written this to you in a letter of October 10, 1861, which I sent to Karlsruhe under the impression that you had settled there, as was your intention. You see, therefore, that it was not you but I that first broke the silence—though with a broken heart!

"When I saw from your letter that mine had not reached you, I at once wrote to the postmaster there and told him to send the letter to your address in Dresden if it should still be there. Perhaps it got into Wagner's hands, for it was really more intended for him than for you, dear friend. Still, it is written in a mood which is not unlike yours! For that reason it would perhaps be better if neither you nor he should receive it. But it also contained the sincerest thanks for all the good deeds which both of you have done for me. My new situation is faithfully described in it; and thus, such as it is, there is no hope for me of happiness through marriage. By the way, please don't reveal to any one what I told you about my dreams and castles in the air in Paris; it would only make me look ridiculous!

"I thank you for the messages from Pfotenhauer, Heine, and Gustav. I wonder why Heine sends regards to me; he may not have meant it so seriously, since he hasn't bothered with me for about fifteen years: that's the fault of his dear son! At that time he did not deign to answer my last letters. Friends who are not reliable when things are bad are as good as none; often they even develop into great enemies, as I found out about Heine, who did not say the most friendly things about me, so that people who saw me again personally were quite surprised to find me completely different and better than the picture he had given of me. Politeness demands that I return his regards. This does not prevent me from remembering with affection the beautiful time when we were intimate friends. But if he were to write me himself, I would certainly forget all insults. I imagine, by the way, that, since his position is—and I'm glad of it!—a good one, he is afraid that I'll borrow money from him. This, to be sure, could have happened, or can happen, in my needy state. Therefore just tell him he'd better not get in touch with me again until my position is better too.

"That you lost your Peps [sic] grieves me sincerely for your sake. Since we outlive animals, I don't like to become attached to them; if it were not for that, I would very much like to have something alive around me, since they are, for the most part, more faithful and grateful than human beings.

"Give my best regards to Tichatschek, if he should still remember me. Also give my regards to the King and tell him he should forgive Wagner and myself and help his faithful subjects out of a dilemma.

"You still owe me your and Wagner's photographs. Shan't I be able to enjoy them soon? Above all, write to me soon; you see I'm a faithful Peps. I'd like to have two working texts of *Rienzi*. One for me, one I have owed Paul Chandon for a long time.[33] And since I'm not on very good terms with him, I should be so much the more grateful to you. Recently he gave a great ball and invited me! Therefore I believed myself obligated to entertain at a ball the following month. She [Madame Chandon] rejected the idea, and thus we are on friendlier terms than before. There are many balls here now, and the R. W. tails and vest really shine there. In their reflection I always see your dear image next to mine. Keep your motherly friendship for me.

"Your faithful

E. B. KIETZ."

437 (*E. B. Kietz, in Epernay, April 4, 1865, to Minna*)

"BEST MOTHER-FRIEND!

"Thanks to your dear letter, the past with all its joys and sufferings has come back to my memory most vividly. In my terrible loneliness this letter was a real blessing to me and, as a proof of a most faithful friendship, it would have filled me with still greater joy, had it not at the same time contained so much that saddens me deeply. He who suffers himself has a sympathetic and open heart for the sufferings of others; and it is for this reason that I give you some

[33] Wagner tells us that Chandon was a great admirer of *Rienzi*, which he had heard in Dresden.

news, though for ages I have not answered anyone, not even my beloved brothers and sisters. Could there be anything enjoyable in my reports? It is this situation and mood that has always prevented me from writing to you too; and today I am really forcing myself, as I surely know that my letter will grieve you, all the more because you have remained my friend. Yes, I am getting worse and worse: I flee from all human beings so as not to infect them with my bad mood; I don't want to approach anybody, not even in writing; and by writing to nobody, I am not unjust to anybody. Therefore I do not wish my relatives to know anything of this letter. But your letter is too dear not to be rewarded by my most affectionate gratitude, even though it may be confused and obscured, for my poor head is full of troubles and distress. What have deranged it most are the beautiful hopes which my well-meaning friends have always implanted in it and which, never ripening, have made me sink still deeper into misery. From all hopes that approach me now, I flee as though they were the seeds of weeds which threaten to stifle me. That is what has become of your formerly sociable and merry old friend Kietz. The world has become absolutely strange and joyless for me; soon I shall be thrown out of it. Formerly it appeared to me like a well filled orchard; now it is empty like the beautiful purse you gave me as a farewell present.

"Moreover, if I look at myself in your mirror, I have to realize what an ill turn the years and suffering have done to me. But close to my Kietzenface [*Kietzengeschicte*] the face of a guardian angel is reflected, yours, dear motherly friend! It looks at me faithfully and cordially, and so I feel that I am not altogether forsaken, that despite all sorts of misfortune I still am very lucky, for to me also faithful friendship is the best source of support.

"If I look into my own heart, I find that basically it has remained the same and that, just as no tempest can shake the bottom of the sea, all the stress of life has not shaken it. Also, friend Richard Wagner has his permanent place in this heart—just as his wife has her permanent seat in the Dresden theater—though he takes little advantage of it. I still love Wagner as I always did. Even our last reunion on the occasion of the unfortunate *Tannhäuser* performance has not narrowed this place occupied by him. As to his whims, I pardon them as only touching the surface of his personality, as alien to his basic character, which is so lovable to me. His cordial welcome echoes more vividly within me than his later indignant exclamation, uttered at the time when everything harassed him: 'Now finally you had to come too!!' Was it my fault? Had I not resisted? Did he not consider just this refusal as a lack of sympathy and friendship? And when after that fateful fiasco I wished to relieve you of my hungry presence, you too, my dear benefactress, forced me to stay, thinking that I wanted to forsake you in your misfortune. On the contrary, this bound me all the more to you. The *unhappy* Wagner was again closer to me than if he had functioned as my helpful adopted father. The *happier* Wagner of today, the favorite of the King, is no less close to my heart; I take the greatest interest in his good fortune. After all, it was I that always prophesied his good fortune and desired it for him at a time when all the world still refused to recognize his success and his talent. However, I do not wish to be personally with him, as I must have become a stranger and a disturber to him. Our external situation and our reputation separate us widely, and such as I have become; my feelings toward him are depression and shame. You must have noticed this right away on my arrival in Paris. But what further suppresses my desire to be with him is his behavior toward you! Already in Paris, when the gulf between you and him was not so big, I did not know what attitude I should have to take toward each of you, whom I loved equally; and once I faced the wrath of you both, when my only intention was to reconcile you.

"Nor can I follow his most recent artistic flight; it is too far beyond my understanding. Nevertheless, not a day passes without my thinking with affection of him and his work.

"How could I console or advise you? I can only suffer and endure with you, for Wagner, as it seemed and seems to me, has pushed me aside too. I see Pecht [34] is his friend again, Pecht who once scoffed at me for getting into debt in the interest of Wagner, debts from which I have never recovered since that time; today together *they* may sing a duet of contempt about me as a failure. Fortune offers its abundance only to him who has brought a bundle of egotism into this world. That I lacked this quality now proves to be my fault and disgrace! Also, as an artist I no longer create with the same facility as formerly, and now you talk to me of a civic-merit medal. I have no doubt about your influential connections with authoritative personalities of Saxony, but by what arguments could you support your request for a medal? Perhaps by referring to my ability to keep up a moratorium of my debts for so many years?

"The money which I earned here and there was enough to keep me afloat. Actually, once I got a small sum I always worried about it, unable to decide who should be paid first. For every creditor had the same right. You will probably know that my debt toward Madame de Szemere is now entirely repaid. Two years ago, when I was in Paris for a week, I paid *him* a visit—to my regret I could not see *her* on account of illness. I left my card with Mlle. Everty (the cousin of Meyerbeer), who unfortunately was in the country. To her as well as to Fräulein von Meisenbug I have not been able to repay my debts; apart from that I had no idea of the latter's address. What will these good people think of me!! I am sorry to say that by acting in this way I have brought discredit upon you. How could you even think of adopting such an insolvent son? Please write me how the Szemeres are. Are you still corresponding with them? By chance I read in the paper—for unfortunately I see a paper very rarely—that Szemere shed tears of joy on passing the Hungarian frontier, whereupon he was immediately taken to a hospital in Pest. What does that mean? If you write to

[34] The painter, then in Munich, remembered from the early Paris days, whom Wagner apparently admired more, and loved less, than Kietz (see *My Life*, p. 225).

Madame de Szemere, I beg you to submit my respects to her. For at that painful time, through your kind mediation, she rendered me a great service, which, on her account and yours, I shall never forget.

"Much has happened and changed since that time, and I hope to hear some details from you. I have not heard anything from Liszt; I know that his daughter, Madame Olivier, has died. Neither have I heard anything from the Wesendoncks. I regret to say that on mentioning this name I become conscious of all my sins, for to him, too, I owe money. I should like so much to show myself grateful to this good man. But the most painful debts are always those which urgently ask for immediate payment, like the debts to a landlord, shoe-maker, tailor, baker, grocer! Already in Paris this is awful, but in a small town like Epernay it would be enough to make me tear my hair out—if I had any left. There remains nothing for me to do but to go mad. My only benefactress, old Madame Chandon, died a year ago. I no longer see her son Paul, who at the end of the year lost his little daughter, the oldest one. I haven't seen him even once since then. In short I live quite isolated, alone in a small house without bird, dog, or cat. I had my furniture brought here two years ago: everything arrived either broken or rotten. Only in the summer do I take care of a few flowers; these alone are my silent company; therefore you can imagine what joy you will give me by writing again soon, and as I have spilled my entire box of sorrows today, I promise you a more cheerful letter next time.

"Determined to bother nobody with my complaints, I don't want to be remembered nor do I send greetings to any one of my Dresden friends.

"We, however, who have suffered much together, understand each other, and complaints are half the relief of sufferings.

"Your old faithful

E. B. KIETZ

"Here I almost forget how to walk, as I go to the near-by inn only to take my meals, from there directly home—occasionally to give a lesson. These lessons to my amiable pupil have also been interrupted by the death of her grandmother. Everything goes wrong with me.

"About Wagner I have not read nor heard anything since our separation, as I do not see any papers, as he himself does not write to me, and as I do not correspond with anyone at all."

459 (*Wagner, in Triebschen, Lucerne, February 22, 1868, to E. B. Kietz*)

"Dearest Kietz! It is not so easy to answer your letter. To do it right, where should one begin, and where end—

"During the winter of last year I dictated my biography; my first stay in Paris afforded many agreeable details about you.

"And now how am I to begin to set you straight about me, you who have nothing in mind but 'success' and similar pleasant things and who—as it seems—judge my life as it appears according to the newspapers!

"Perhaps it might be best to give you short and dry answers on several points. Well, then!

"Nobody has gossiped with me about you: I know absolutely nothing about P. Chandon, and have no champagne of his either.[35] Further: whether they will give *Lohengrin* (not *green!*) in Paris or not has absolutely nothing to do with my change of residence. Even *if* they perform *Lohengrin* there (which I do not even yet believe), I will not go there in any case, and you will have to wait patiently for a long time for me to come through Epernay.

"All in all, what you manage to say about me is all wrong. You see it is quite different from what you think. *How* things are—well! That is not so easy to say, and if I wanted to tell you about that, I would only confuse you more. In any case I live a strange, difficult-difficult life; battling against it and only by applying with the utmost energy have I now created after many years a new opus which is called *Die Meistersinger von Nürnberg*. It will be performed for the first time in Munich about the end of April;[36] it will probably have much success and will spread very quickly in Germany.

"And now I am looking for the enjoyment of a real retreat in complete retirement from all society: it is situated here among the mountains, and I owe it to the great and romantic though rather agitating [*aufregend*] love of the young King of Bavaria for me. If I am permitted the good fortune of undisturbed rest, which is all I look for, then, always working hard—I could hope to finish the works I have planned.

"I have nothing at all against you, my dear fellow, except what you have against yourself. Our last time together in Paris[37] was—in spite of all the excitement—time lost, a lazy time in which nothing was created and in which nothing gave me pleasure, not even—you. Forgive me!

"I shall soon go to Munich for rehearsals. In the summer I shall be here again, where—at half an hour's distance from the city—I live in a solitary house with various cattle and some servants. Should you care to visit me one day, then come! You will always be well received.

"I cannot tell you any more. Now try to explain the rest to yourself and—remain fond of your

old ami

RICHARD W

"Tomorrow Herm. Müller will come to visit me from Zürich. I shall see him again for the first time in nine years. From that you may conclude my sociable inclinations!

[35] See Chapter XXIV.
[36] The first performance took place on June 21, 1868.
[37] In 1861.

465 *(Lucerne, March 29, 1869)*

"DEAR OLD FRIEND!

"What is all this that you are repeatedly telling me? If I were quietly going to pieces, you wouldn't know anything about me: now that I'm so often a public topic, you mistake this notorious person for the friend who was once close and well known to you for several years. Do you by any chance think that all this is just a comedy for the sake of getting ahead and that basically everything is still the way it was in the rue de la Tournerie or in Meudon?

"If you complain about a lack of replies to your letters, it may console you if I assure you that—notwithstanding all my fame, etc.—I have 'friends' who never, never answer me as soon as I ask a favor of them, but that on the other hand I receive letters every day asking me to use my 'tremendous influence' for this and the other thing.

"So far as I know, you are always in a situation resembling actual ruin: As often as I've seen you since those days, you always had to be 'rescued' [*zu retten*], to use your expression. Whoever knows you and esteems you as I do regrets this much, much more than you probably believe. I have learned that in such situations I was protected from bitterness on your part only when I was able to prove to you quite plainly that I myself was no less desperate. How gladly I should now invite you to come here, to be a friend of the house, to do what you like, to earn what you can, and otherwise to take advantage of what I can offer you as friend of the house! But I know you have a very definite standard which you think you have to live up to; also that you always need this or that sum to rescue you, etc. There I simply *cannot* help you; I *cannot* make any rescue payments, etc., available to you, simply because I am not *able* to do so. If *Rienzi* is now successful in Paris,[38] the receipts for a *long* time first belong to Herr v. Erlanger, whose loans supported me in Paris at that time. If I have accomplished anything at all, it is only and solely the pension which the magnanimity of the King of Bavaria has granted me. My whole strength in the outside world lies in the fact that I *don't* speculate on success and the like, and it is due only to that person that I don't have to do so; it has no other significance, nor does it mean that I can give myself false airs as a wealthy man.

"Perhaps this seems very hard to you, and you could answer that you did not give me any immediate cause for such statements in your various letters to me, all of which I admit I have received. But you must excuse me: I like to jest, but I'm not making fun of anybody, least of all of an old, faithful friend: if I see he is miserable, I believe I should help him; merely groping around with jokes I consider unworthy treatment of such a friend. But how could I help you? It grieves me to know that some one who was once as close to me as you

---

[38] *Rienzi* was produced by Pasdeloup at the Théâtre-Lyrique on April 6, 1869. It was well received.

is in the miserable situation into which, by all indications, you seem to have sunk in that silly Epernay. But how can I help you?? I have told you above what I *can* do. But what good does that do *you*?? That is my question! And this is a serious, well meant question.

"And now something to cheer you up!

"Your assumption that I'm seriously concerned about making a great success in Paris, and that this is actually the main thing in life, is especially amusing because on the other hand you think you have sufficiently familiarized yourself with my writings and my 'tendencies' [*Richtung*]. So I shall horrify you with my pamphlet *Judaism in Music*: you'll be able to gather from this what a terrible uproar it has created among the now most active part of the European public. Just imagine what kind of man it must be who does a thing like that, and how much he resembles the one to whom you think you must give repeated advice about his appearance in Paris! This just for fun. Moreover, it is possible that *Rienzi* will make the grade: well, then you'll have to come to Paris after all! Just paint hard: Pecht can do it better! Now, old fellow, light up your lamp! Good night! All in all you must see that I mean well by you, and that consoles me!

"Your old

RW."

469 *(Triebschen, Lucerne, May 21, 1870)*

"MY DEAR ERNST BENEDICT!

"I'll be able to pay for your trip from Zürich to Lucerne and return. What kind of dawdling is this, anyway! So, we'll see you at Triebschen: you can stay here.

"I didn't get your letter to Berlin. That I sent you the pamphlet twice was pure coincidence.

"God! What will happen to me next!!

"O Kietz—is simply an exclamation! You don't seem to understand this any more either, do you? Things will really be fine! But just come!

"Cordially,

Your RW."

471 *(Lucerne, June 10, 1870. Addressed to Züricher Hof 26, in Zürich)*

"Dear Kietz! I hesitated to answer your superb letters because I didn't want to address the answer to Zürich—always believing that you would leave there the next day. But I see now that your genius is remaining faithful to you and that you'll stay around in Zürich for a while. What can I possibly say to the news of the many incidents which happened to you? I understand that you don't want to return to Epernay. In the end—I imagine—would you like to stay in Zürich? Possibly the change would be profitable to you. I know of no popular portrait painter there. I'm eager to hear what other experiences you had (also in M.). In any case—don't hold it against me—I'm very much surprised that you are still in *Zürich*. In the final analysis you must have your reasons. If you don't have any, I have nothing to say about it either. But I hope I'll soon get some explanation. Your letter today was very explicit, but it contained nothing at all about your traveling plans, whereas I thought—as a result of one of your earlier letters—that you had already come through Lucerne.

"Well, let's hear! Be assured that we think of you, and—since you are still young—become a fine *man!*

"In old friendship
Your R. W."

474 (*Lucerne, September 6, 1870. Addressed to Zürich*)

"DEAR HERR KIETZ!

"Richard, overloaded with work, requests me to tell you that he immensely regrets the calamity in which you are involved. He hopes that the soon-to-be-expected end of the war will restore you to where you live and that you will find employment in Zürich in the meantime. We have not asked you to see him in Triebschen because our guest room is occupied by Conductor Richter, and after the completion of a pressing work my husband and I will start off for a little trip.

"With best thanks for your friendly congratulations, and cordial regards
C. WAGNER"

≫ XV ≪

THE REVOLUTIONARY *KAPELLMEISTER*

As *Kapellmeister* in Dresden, Wagner retained a certain veneration for the aging Spontini, whose influence is marked in *Rienzi*. When Spontini's *La Vestale* was about to be produced at the Court Theater, Wagner conceived the idea of inviting the composer, then in Berlin, to conduct. He accordingly wrote a letter, in French, and received a gracious acceptance which, however, stipulated, concerning the orchestra, his requirement of "twelve good double basses" *(le tout garni de douze bonnes contrebasses)*. This according to *My Life,* and Wagner goes on to say that these exalted expectations, as compared with the very limited resources of the Dresden Opera, threw all concerned into embarrassment, that he tried in vain to put Spontini off altogether. Wagner's description of Spontini, whom he revered but found impossibly pompous and ridiculous, is one of his most delightful bits of writing.

If Spontini's letter is the one in this Collection, Wagner has quoted his French phrase from memory and indulged in the familiar practice of exaggerating freely to improve his story. The letter is in French:[1]

"MONSIEUR

"I am infinitely grateful to you and satisfied with the artistic points you have been good enough to give me in your kind letter of last October on the projected staging of my opera *La Vestale* at the new Dresden theater.

"I can give myself the pleasure of answering in no more than a few lines, since I am indisposed, and suffering from a chill brought on by the three or four degrees of frost around here, suddenly and prematurely. I note then, purely and simply, without being exacting, that:

"1. Twelve first violins, twelve seconds, directly backed up by ten violas, the whole surrounded by eight or ten violoncellos in close rank and six or seven [2] excellent contrabasses [*excellentes contrebasses*]—that is the least that the size and height of your auditorium permits, in grand opera! Nor do I remember precisely whether the conductor has the first violins at his left and the seconds at his right, not separated from the wind instruments as in the Royal Academy of Music in Paris and the State Theater in Berlin, where the effect is quite vicious and ridiculous; for the ensemble of a good orchestra the complete separa-

[1] 147, Nov. 2, 1844.
[2] Four were listed in the roster of the Court Theater, 1844.

tion of the strings on one side and the wind instruments and brass on the other results in two distinct orchestras!!

"2. As for the choruses, I find that in every full chorus the men are well trained and, having voices which are passable but well placed, can well support the women's voices, except when the Vestals are alone on the stage, such as the morning hour, the evening, and the prayer in the third act. I hope that my precedent will be respected, and that in all the choruses of *La Vestale* and *Cortez,* the high and contralto parts written in this clef [the alto clef is indicated] be taken by the first tenors in unison with the male contraltos; otherwise all the effect and the force of the choruses would be entirely lost!!

"As soon as I can, I shall give you the parts for your theater here (for the text); and I shall bring the full score with me to conduct from, if my health and the horrible cold permit me, when I have received your second letter, which you tell me about, before fixing the day of my departure from Berlin. I beg you, Monsieur, to present my respects to M. the Count Lüttichau, and my sentiments of esteem and friendship to all the artists of both sexes, together with a good share for yourself, and believe me, with the best and highest sentiments,

"Yours sincerely and devotedly,

SPONTINI

"My writing is terrible!!"

In the spring of 1848, having completed the score of *Lohengrin,* Wagner turned his thoughts briefly to matters of reform, and wrote his *Plan for the Organization of a German National Theater for the Kingdom of Saxony.* His scheme, which would put the Dresden Theater under primary state control, was intended to lift it out of Court routine. It would have offset and eventually dispensed with an intendant accountable only to a king's nod; it would have reconstituted the orchestra in the interest of economy and efficiency, the repertory in the direction of a higher and more enlightened standard. This plan, so Wagner tells us, he submitted forthwith to the State Ministry of the Interior and the Ministry of Education, thereby incurring the displeasure of Court Intendant Lüttichau, whose very office was made out to be useless, and those members of the orchestra who already resented the unsettling influence of the reforming *Kapellmeister.* They accused him of agitating to eliminate those he considered undesirable and to put himself in sole control. Neither ministry was ready to endorse this scheme of high aims and damaging individual consequences; the Revolution of 1849 put it out of mind altogether. In 1850 Theodor Uhlig persuaded Wagner to let him publish parts of it for its abstract or historical interest. It was published in 1871 in the *Collected Writings* (German edition).

Mrs. Burrell, who was loath to accept so controversial a document on its face value, as officially published, induced Dr. Otto Richter, of the Dresden Court Council, to search the royal archives, and accordingly located the manuscript copy which had been read and passed on. Comparing this to the printed text, she found an important passage omitted which referred to the explosive subject of the proposed powers of the intendant (who was Lüttichau) as against the *Kapellmeister* (who was Richard Wagner). After the following lines: [3] "Wherefore the task to put the new organization into operation, gradually, but as far as possible at once, might be intrusted to one of the present *Kapellmeister*"— the following was suppressed (169):

—"who in this way would replace the present general manager. As, however, every kind of double rule is extremely disadvantageous and disturbing, and paralyzes necessary enterprise, it would be now suitable to combine the managing council, as described above, with this one *Kapellmeister* only; whereas the second *Kapellmeister*, though not eliminated entirely, would be kept away from active service to the extent that he would be exclusively entrusted with the care of the church music according to its present condition; this would also serve the purpose of preventing the man who prepares the intended new organization from becoming overburdened, so that he would be able to pursue his important task with all the greater clarity. After the second *Kapellmeister* leaves, he should have no successor."

This consignment of the second *Kapellmeister* into the background could hardly have helped Wagner's none too cordial relationship with Reissiger. For, contrary to the impression given in *My Life* that Wagner simply went over the heads of his colleagues of the theater, it now appears that this very manuscript was submitted to the *General Direktion*. So says Dr. Richter, and he adds that the judgments which were made by "Reissiger, Ed. Devrient, Ferdinand Heine, and others" are to be found in the archives of the Hoftheater and that these gentlemen have added to the document some marginal notes in pencil. Opposite the passage quoted above, Richter found the remark, presumably by Reissiger: *"Das ist des Pudels Kern!"* [4] (Here the poodle shows his colors!)

This taunt brought from Wagner the following marginal reply, in ink:

"The author of the essay cannot refrain from pointing out to the honored reader who wrote the marginal note the baselessness of the suspicion implied. How could I have intended a mere personal advantage in drawing up that voluminous outline for reorganization of one of the most important institutes of art? What advantage would come to me if the sole leadership were conferred upon me? In my salary increase? Besides 1,800 r. [*Reichsthaler*], guaranteed, a yearly gratuity of 300 r. has been granted to me under certain conditions: on entering the aforesaid position my yearly income would be reduced by 100 r., since the salary of 2,000 r. would be without the royal gratuity. Or would I look for an increase of my absolute power? I am even now in the possession of absolute power, but under restrictions. Thus anyone who reads my essay can hardly

[3] English ed., Vol. VII, p. 358.   [4] Goethe's *Faust*, Part 1, Sc. 3.

suspect me of writing my elaborate treatise out of mere egotism, he must recognize that I wished to be useful to the institution in question and not to favor myself, since my income would rather have decreased and not increased in spite of my enlarged activity and responsibility. Therefore I feel greatly offended that the whole outline as presented appeared to the honored reader as nothing more than a poodle's trick, bespeaking only my selfish interest.

RICHARD WAGNER"

"In order to give myself some diversion" [*um mich zu zerstreuen*], writes Wagner in *My Life*,[5] "I decided (it was early in July) to make use of a short leave of absence by a visit to Vienna." He wrote to Lüttichau for the necessary permission on July 2 and also to Reissiger on July 3, 1848, asking him to take over his duties. (Both letters are published, in German, in the Kapp and Kastner Collection.) He may have persuaded himself that he was mentally weary and in need of a change. Lüttichau, who was certainly forbearing with his troublesome *Kapellmeister* at this point (his activities had split the orchestra into factions for and against his dismissal and put him under suspicion of wanting to take Lüttichau's position), granted his request at an interview on the following day. Wagner's "vacation" consisted of busily furthering his cause in Vienna, proposing a coalition of the theaters there, and observing the not inconsiderable revolutionary agitation.

166 (Dresden, July 3, 1848, to Karl Reissiger)

"MOST HONORED FRIEND:

"I find it difficult to ask you for an extreme proof of your friendliness toward me since I know that it is not through lack of consideration but through the pressure of your work that you have been unable to grant my request. Nevertheless, I must ask you urgently not to oppose the request which I addressed to the general manager and in which I asked for an extension of my leave of absence. The granting of this request is a matter of life and death for me; I *cannot* now return to my duties, it is *quite impossible* for me to do so. Should I have to take the consequences—well and good; I am willing to take them whatever they may be, dismissal or anything else; I am prepared for everything except a return to my duties. Let me not go into the reasons for my determined frame of mind, which is perhaps partly attributable to the state of my health. I must take a trip now in the hope that the change of atmosphere and surroundings will restore my peace of mind and make possible my continued duties in Dresden. In view of these urgent reasons our general manager will surely refrain from disciplining me as soon as he realizes that the work itself won't suffer; only you can help me by reassuring him in this matter. I

[5] P. 444.

fully realize the great sacrifice I am asking of you; if you could determine by some suitable agreement with Röckel how the work can be carried on without me for a while, and if you would give our general manager a reassuring explanation of the matter, I would be indebted to you for an extraordinary service. When I return to my duties in good health, I shall be at your disposal as you see fit, and I shall also be prepared to discuss with you a new distribution of all duties in order to give you less exhausting ones. But all I ask of you now is: consider me incurably ill and unavailable!

"His Excellency has asked me to come to his office tomorrow morning at ten o'clock to discuss the leave of absence with him. I wish I could speak to our kind director after I have become calmer about many things: no one but you would be better qualified to explain my absence since you alone can make a definite and unselfish decision in the matter at hand. May you find it possible to do this great service for me!

"Let me hear a kind word from you.

"Always your

RICHARD WAGNER"

The following letter (161), addressed from Vienna, was delivered to Minna in Dresden by the hand of an unnamed friend. The date, "Wien, 18 Juli, 46," can only be Wagner's error. He was at the resort of Gross-Graupe in mid-July, 1846, and indeed did not visit Vienna between then and 1861, except in the summer of 1848, with his plan for a national theater and his hopes for a permanent position. A published letter to Minna from Vienna, July 15, 1848, describes the political restlessness but gives no hint of marital dissension. Not having heard from her, he gives her his address and hopes for a letter. This letter may have come by July 18; it may have been filled with distress at Wagner's insistence upon meddling with reform and jeopardizing his career.[6]

[6] Ernest Newman, who has kindly examined this letter, persuasively refutes the thought that Dr. Pusinelli, neighbor and friend of the Wagners since 1843, could have been the bearer, the "noble and excellent" man described: "I can't see any reason for assuming that the bearer of the letter was Pusinelli. I think it more likely that it was Liszt. Just about that time (really mid-April 1848) the Princess [Karolyne Wittgenstein] left Russia and joined him at Lichnowsky's place in Krzyzenwitz. They stayed at Schloss Grätz for a little while, then went to Vienna, whence they were driven by the Revolution. About July they went to Weimar via Prague, Vienna and Dresden. No doubt Liszt was in Vienna more than once during these weeks, and Wagner would be pretty certain to get on to him, for he was coming then to regard him as the heaven-sent friend who would help him out of his financial and other difficulties: he had already tried to interest Liszt in his affairs. I don't think Wagner would have been talking like this about Pusinelli in 1848: he and Minna had known him for years already. The person referred to in the letter is manifestly someone comparatively new to Wagner and quite new to Minna, and someone whom Wagner regards as of great power in his own (Wagner's) world. Why shouldn't it have been Liszt who took the letter, for safety's sake, to Minna in Dresden? What would Pusinelli, a busy Dresden doctor, be doing in revolutionary Vienna in July 1848?"

RICHARD WAGNER—PHOTOGRAPH TAKEN IN VIENNA;
DATED BY MRS. BURRELL AS OF 1848 (162)

"MY POOR DEAR WIFE!

"Your sufferings touch me more deeply than I can express! A single thought, ever repeated, goes from me daily: Is poor Minna crying or is she jolly? Your letter tells me that you are crying!!!

"I can't comfort you by words, for you as well as I have to be *helped*. We two are *one*, even though, according to my nature, I too often follow my impulses, and think of you only when something goes wrong. I can answer your tears; it would take a mighty doctor to cure us!

"Regard with courage and confidence the noble and excellent man who brings you these lines; God tells me he is my true friend. He will help you and me with his best advice, perhaps something more. Pour out your whole heart to him, shed freely your tears: reveal everything to him without restraint, concerning our position and your misgivings: a *friend* should know about this. I trust all our life to him and to his advice, and you too must confide in him your sorrows, my faults: he is prepared through me to learn *everything* from you. We will both follow his advice. I pledge my loyalty to you and my fullest trust in your decisions. May God lighten your heart and restore hope to you, my poor harassed wife!

"Your

RICHARD W."

171 *Poem, "Die noth,"* [7] *unsigned but in Wagner's hand, and dated March 30, 1849 (a fair copy, without corrections)*

Wagner could hardly have intended to publish this poem, for its earthy expressions are unknown from him except in private letters (of which there are several in this Collection). After the excitement which engendered it had passed, he surely would not have wished to acknowledge it. He may have read, or intended to read it. It is in the vein of his anonymous article "The Revolution," published in the *Volksblätter* of April 8, and the poem "To a State

---

[7] The word, signifying "want" or "need," has a broader meaning than any English equivalent. In his money-seeking letters it is what stands between Wagner and his creative work. *Nothung* is the sword without which Siegfried is helpless.

"Die noth" (the nouns are not capitalized) was published in the *Gesammelte Schriften*, Vol. 12, in German only, when the following verse was omitted (the date—a significant point—is omitted):

"Die dorten in den städten sitzen auf tauben weisheits ei, die kopf und hintern sich zerschwitzen ob nichts gebrütet sei— die tugendhaften sabbathchristen, die niemals stinken wenn sie pfisten sie seh'n die zehn gebot— doch dich nicht, hehre noth!"	(Those in the cities who brood on addled eggs of wisdom, their heads and bottoms sweating, hoping that something might be hatched; those virtuous sabbath-Christians, who never stink when they fart; they behold the ten commandments,— but not thee, sublime Want!)

Attorney" of March 22. Want, like the Revolution of the later article, is an avenging goddess, advancing with her firebrand, destroying the old order of privilege, parasitism, and ineffectuality. But if "The Revolution" is a poem in prose, a high-minded anticipation of release, "Die noth," for all its neat rhyme and meter, is a vicious and scornful attack upon those who are doomed in the miracle which is about to happen. The writer is not merely the frustrated artist, bent solely upon theatrical reform, as his later apologists would have us believe: he is in politics to his neck, swept on the full current of socialistic anticipation of a dawning new order. A synopsis follows:

Want

From now I recognize *one* God only—Want! He alone can free us from fraud and greed and idle pleasures. The self-righteous ones in cities, who brood on the addled eggs of wisdom, do not know thee, sublime Want! They love the state because, living idly, they subsist on it. By book philosophy and intellectual tricks they hold themselves superior and aloof from earthly contacts. But Want they never meet! They revile God, man, and all about them, and teach the poor to submit, for nothing must be changed. But now Want, grown from man's suffering, steps powerfully to the fore. They despise one another, but consider themselves alone as able to control, for Want they do not see! But thy fearsome aspect will expose and silence them. The fire of men's age-long sufferings will kindle thy torch, which shall destroy all sham and greed.

Thy torch shall sever our bonds, it shall consume the robbery wrought by paper and parchment! Brightly the firebrand burns, cities become skeletons, and the power which enslaved us is gone! Those who lived on the toil of others are now without wealth—they must learn to find their daily bread, and Want shall be their teacher! Empty, boasting knowledge is sterile; only from life can you reap fruits—only from the vital accomplishment of universal work. For though all be ruin, life will spring anew; humanity is freed of chains, nature and man are restored—as one! What separated them is destroyed! The dawn of liberty has been kindled by—Want!

❧ XVI ❦

THE FLIGHT FROM DRESDEN

(May–August, 1849)

On May 9, 1849, Wagner decided that the time had come to get away from Dresden. The revolt which had begun five days before, which had been stronger in optimism and fervor than any intelligent direction, had fallen into confusion with the arrival of Prussian troops. The remnants of rebellion were scattering, retiring from the town itself. Röckel was in custody; Bakunin and Hübner had been taken a few hours after Wagner, by a miraculous stroke of luck, had left them.

Wagner, who had followed every development with intense excitement, must suddenly have wakened to the disturbing reality that the existing order of state control, instead of dissolving before the threat of righteous determination, had every prospect of continuing. Those who had opposed the monarchy by force of arms would be looked upon as traitors rather than heroes. The royal *Kapellmeister*, having constantly associated with the leaders and aided them in every way he could, having made inflammatory speeches, printed propaganda of revolt, let himself be seen on the barricades, and on ʰhe Kreuzkirche tower, the watching post of the rebellion, had put himself in a more dangerous position than he would admit to Minna—or even to himself.

Wagner's brother-in-law, Heinrich Wolfram, and his sister Cläre were then harboring Minna in the suburb of Chemnitz. Wolfram smuggled Wagner out of danger in his own carriage to Altenburg under cover of darkness, and from there Wagner made his way to the one friend on whom he had come to depend in time of need, the one friend who could help him. He arrived at Weimar on the 13th and went at once to the Erbprinz, the hotel of Franz Liszt.

Liszt and Wagner must have had a long and serious conference on that day over Wagner's present and future, and for once Liszt must have done most of the talking. Wagner could have had little to say for himself: a strange and nightmarish jumble of events had carried him on its fateful, downward course and landed him, in a state of mingled elation and dismay, a fugitive from justice, jobless and penniless, on his friend's hospitable doorstep. The courtier Liszt, to whom monarchism was a *sine qua non*, could have had little sympathy with the mad and self-destructive path he had taken. Wagner was not anxious ʰo discuss politics: probably Liszt made him promise to keep out of them in the future.[1] In *My Life* he tells us that he was not inclined to go into the subject of how far he had involved himself in trouble. This is borne out by the expressed opinion of the Minister von Watzdorf, who, if he had been told of what Wagner had been up to, would hardly have advised him to go quietly back to Dresden and face the consequences of his deeds. Wagner himself had as yet no idea of the position he had allowed himself to be drawn into. He still hoped to retain his post as *Kapellmeister*; to be given by his gracious monarch a leave of absence until things had quieted down. Since this was by no means to be counted on, Liszt speculated about opportunities elsewhere. The Court at Weimar might grant him a yearly sum in exchange for the performing rights of his future operas; a pleasant house might be found for Minna; meanwhile, two important and wealthy capitals lay open to him: the still unperformed *Lohengrin* might be translated into English and put on in London; Wagner might write an opera suitable for the Paris stage.

Wagner, under the tranquil, protective spell of Weimar and Liszt, was not moved to carp at these suggestions or to examine them too closely. They also offered persuasive arguments for the winning back of Minna, who had remained behind in a state of furious disapproval of her wayward husband.

Liszt led Wagner to the Princess Karolyne von Wittgenstein, and revolution was waved aside for the more engrossing topic of music. They spoke of *Tannhäuser*, which was to be performed at Weimar within the week. Wagner outlined a plan for an opera on Jesus of Nazareth which may have made them doubt whether he had any judgment left whatsoever.

Wagner's immediate concern was to see Minna. She had watched him deliberately ruin the position, official and social, which the two had built up for themselves in her beloved Dresden. He knew that it would not be easy to persuade her to join him in a flight even more mad than the flight from Riga, with consequences perhaps as wretched as before. A letter from Minna, which has not survived, was brought to him on the night of his arrival at Weimar. She must have shown some tenderness in her alarm for his safety, for this was his reply, sent under cover to Wolfram, and mailed special delivery:

173 (*Postmarked Weimar, May 14* [*1849*]. *Addressed to Heinrich Wolfram in Chemnitz, "by special messenger"*)

"MY BELOVED WIFE!

"I received your letter last night when I had gone to bed late: I have gotten up early to answer you. All that your letter contains counts almost nothing as compared with the one fact which I read in every line: the evidence of your pure and warm love which this time you expressed to me without any

---

[1] "I promise you to leave politics alone as much as possible, and therefore will not compromise you or anyone else."—Wagner to Liszt, June 5, 1849.

torturing reproaches. Ah! In this you have done me immense good! Thank you, and preserve for me yourself and your loving heart.

"The ways of fate with men are incomprehensible! The terrible catastrophe, I have just experienced and the events of yesterday in Weimar have made a different person out of me and have shown me a new path. Imagine, my dear wife, how for years in my Dresden position I have nursed the deepest dejection: a new path which I entered with my art opened up for me thornily enough indeed; wherever I trod, I was hurt; with an inward fury I finally turned my back to my art which yielded me nothing but suffering; you know that I almost begrudged the ink and the paper which I needed to write a new opera. Thus, in a state of extreme discontent with my position and almost with my art, groaning under a burden which, unfortunately, you were not really willing to understand, deep in debts, so much so that my usual earnings would have satisfied my creditors only in the course of many years and under shameful deprivations, I was at variance with this world, I ceased to be an artist, I frittered away my creative powers, and became a mere revolutionary (if not in deeds, at least in conviction); that is, I was seeking in a wholly transformed world the ground for some new art creations of my spirit. Now the Dresden revolution and its whole result have taught me that I am not a real revolutionary by any means, and I have seen from the evil outcome of the revolt that a real and victorious revolutionary must proceed completely without scruple—he must not think of his wife and children, nor of his house and home—his only goal is: destruction; and if the noble-minded Hübner had been willing to proceed in this manner in Freiburg or Chemnitz even now, then the revolution would have remained victorious. But men of our type are not destined for this horrible task: we are revolutionaries only in order to be able to *construct* something on fresh ground; it is not *destruction* which attracts us, but the *formation of something new,* and that is why we are not the kind of men whom Destiny needs—these will arise from the lowest dregs of the people; we and our hearts cannot have anything in common with them. You see! *Thus* I AM PARTING *with the revolution. . . .*

"I already came to terms with myself about this on my way to Weimar; and in view of a worthless future for Germany for perhaps a considerable number of years, I was pondering only about how I could settle down with you somewhere, in quiet seclusion in the country, when suddenly a new way was pointed out to me in Weimar. Liszt and his friend the Princess Wittgenstein are in this respect in a certain agreement with the Grand Duchess of Weimar —an agreement which has existed for some time—and they have decided together to lead me and my talent out of the miserable situation in Germany and into the world's broader path. They say that here in Germany I would perish and that my art in the end would disgust even myself; that, they said, they must not allow: they must keep my creative powers fresh and joyous for the world. They are directing me to London and Paris: to London, in order to have translated there my most recent opera *Lohengrin* and to have it first performed by the English theater—*not* in Germany! That would bring me fame and especially *money*. To Paris, in order that I may write another opera for that city in the meantime. Liszt takes it upon himself to arrange everything; as he knows the present conditions, he does not doubt in the least that he will bring about the Paris commission and the London enterprise in short order. How seriously he and my friends are interested in the matter you can best see by the 2,000 francs I have been offered by him for this purpose; and in general he has bound himself to provide me fully with the money for these under-takings—and as long as I may need it.

"Ah! Dear, good wife! This has given strength to my heart, and at one stroke I have become an entire *artist* again, I *love* my art again, and I *hope* by means of it some day to make my poor much tried wife happy. I also hope by this remarkable means to be able soon to satisfy *all* of my creditors. Good God! How is it possible that even the worst has turned into the best?

"I have not yet had a chance to tell Liszt about the worrisome contents of your letter; I shall see him in an hour, and I shall come to an understanding with him about the next steps; you will then hear about it immediately. And now, only a few requests, before I forget them. (1) My *Lohengrin* score is with the *Kammermusikus Uhlig* in Poliergasse; you must get it from him. (2) The young *Ritter,* in Waisenhausstrasse next to *Semper's* house, has my text of *Siegfried* and another sketch—*Die Gibelinen*—which I should also like to have. These things, together with a score of *Rienzi,* one of *Holländer,* and one of *Tannhäuser,* you must also send along with the other things. I also should like the portfolio which you had with you, and its contents; on the big shelf at the left-hand side of the desk there is a folder containing some compositions which I also want to have. I also should like to have sent some copies of the texts of *Rienzi, Holländer,* and *Tannhäuser* (at Meyer's house). The copies of the texts of *Rienzi* and *Holländer* are in one of the inside compartments at the right-hand side of the desk.

"I have just consulted Liszt and Professor Wolf [Wolff]. They think that I am completely safe here for the time being and that a sudden legal action against me is in any case impossible; the most anyone could do would be to apply to the ministry here to arrest me; in such a case, I could depend on the protection of the Minister Watzdorf. He is a very liberal-minded man and a sympathizer with the German party; in the worst case he would provide me with a passport and send me on. I am surely safe against a surprise attack. Now I shall tell you, my good wife, what is most on my mind: I must see *you* once again before I go to London or Paris. Listen! This coming Sunday there will be a new produc-tion of *Tannhäuser;* and my birthday is coming at about the same time; you *must* be here for that. Meanwhile, I might ramble around on foot a little in the beautiful country of Thuringia, Wartburg, etc. I also might visit Professor *Wolf* in *Jena,* who has invited me to live on a farm near Jena in complete safety and as long as I may want to, in case things should become very bad. I should then come back so as to be in Weimar and meet you there on Sunday, in order to go *with you to Tannhäuser* (which Got . . [?] is supposed to sing very well). Perhaps we might then stay together for a few more days until my birthday, and console each other quite freely about the future. Then I should go to Paris and London; and as soon as I have signed a definite contract there, you could follow me in order that—God willing—we may never be separated again. You see! This is how it stands. Help to carry it out, and be in Weimar on Sunday!

"Everything for me is to be sent to Liszt's address.

"I must close now; at ten o'clock there will be a rehearsal of *Tannhäuser*; the Grand Duchess wants to see me today—I shall get a dress coat from Liszt.

"Now, give my most heartfelt greetings to the dear darling Wolframs! And you, my poor suffering wife! Let the ray of light, which is now revealed to me, enter your tortured heart too! Everything will yet turn out better than we thought. May God save you! Faithful, good Minna! Farewell! Farewell!

"Your

R W"

Wagner did not go to Jena in that week, as he expected, but in the week following. Nor did Minna answer his call to go to Weimar and attend the performance of *Tannhäuser*. He did make a three days' excursion to Eisenach (May 15–17), whence he wrote Minna with repeated urging.

172 (Eisenach, Wednesday morning [May 16])

"MY DEAR GOOD WIFE!

"Writing these few lines and thinking of you will relieve my mind, and at the same time will give you briefly the news about myself.

"As I wrote you the day before yesterday—I came here yesterday in order to wander a bit through this delightful country on foot: Liszt, who was starting for Frankfort for two days, accompanied me by railway to this point. By coincidence also, the Grand Duchess had taken the same train to Eisenach in order to visit the Duchess of Orléans. At the station she learned that I was here and at once sent word to me that I might visit her in Eisenach tonight. I excused myself because of my traveling clothes, but it was of no avail; I had to promise to come anyway. When I came from the Wartburg (which you must see with me whatever happens), I walked to the castle in my jacket and gray trousers and my cap (which I bought here), through the rows of all the nobility to the Grand Duchess, who received me with extraordinary friendliness and started a long conversation with me: I had to promise to see more of her in Weimar. I am made much of here by everybody, but I have only *one* desire—to have my dear wife here to witness all this and to recover from her recent troubles by an agreeable visit. Won't you listen to my entreaties and come to

Weimar on Sunday to hear *Tannhäuser* with me? I have already attended an orchestra rehearsal of it which was so wonderfully striking that I was often moved to tears—tears which did me good.

"Here, my dear wife, I am certainly safe. Besides, I seem to be looked upon rather more leniently in Dresden than at first. Surely, if the reactionaries would bring vengeance on all who participated in any way in the upheaval, they would have to prosecute half the state of Saxony!

"Tomorrow I plan to return to Weimar again, and I shall use the first quiet hours to write at length to Devrient [2] and Heine: I shall offer my help to make the breach with Dresden no longer irreconcilable and perhaps I'll succeed in getting an agreement soon for a half-year's leave for London and Paris. Everything depends on whether and how much I have been denounced in Dresden: if I have been heavily compromised, a matter about which, naturally, I cannot judge, any agreement would certainly be difficult, and I should have to carry out my plans for Paris and London without any consideration of Dresden; but this very plan may reconcile my adversaries, who have to consider that the more of fame and honor I acquire abroad, the more disadvantageous it would be for Dresden to exclude me entirely. So I am hoping for the best.

"About the King of Saxony and the whole situation there only *one* opinion prevails abroad, an opinion which you will surely not hear just now in Dresden and Chemnitz. God knows how everything may turn out! It's certainly not over yet!

"Oh, my Minna, if I only could know that you are not sick! You will now have much to attend to, and I feel ashamed at having left everything on your shoulders alone. But your cleverness and care will bring everything into the best of order. Well, dear wife, I now recognize that you are my good angel! If it had not been for you, and if the thought of you had not restrained me, who knows into what I might not have plunged myself!

"Now remain faithful to me! In any case come to Weimar; I certainly will *not* leave before I have seen you for a few days.

"A thousand kisses and greetings from your

R. W.

"Heine has my text of *Lohengrin*; get it from him so that I may have it here!"

But Minna was anything but reassured by this letter. The day before it was written, the police had rapped on the door of their Dresden lodgings and made it clear to her that her husband's offense was grave. A warrant for his arrest would be declared in four days. He was subject to the charge of treason, and

---

[2] The letter to Eduard Devrient has survived (Altmann, Vol. I, p. 147). In it Wagner tells the story of his part in the revolution at considerable length, showing his motives to be in the cause of art rather than destructive or criminal. What he tells Minna shows his deliberate purpose of so bringing his case to favorable attention in high official quarters.

treason was punishable by death. While he argued calmly that he was only one among countless offenders too numerous to make prosecution possible, the law had singled him out as one of the first that were "wanted," and even while his picture was about to be posted far and wide as identification of a criminal at large, her crack-brained husband was "wandering a bit" through the "delightful country," the *Tannhäuser* territory of Eisenach!

Minna apparently wrote to him in alarm, urging him to flee Germany and Weimar at once. But Wagner did not receive her letter promptly. (It was probably sent under cover to Liszt, who had not returned.) He began to worry, not about himself, but about her, and he wrote anxiously to Wolfram:

174 (*Weimar, May 18, 1849*)

"My best Brother-in-law!

"I haven't yet had any news at all from Minna since my letters and I am upset about it. I can't get rid of the terrible thought that she may be seriously ill and that you may be concealing it from me in order to prevent me from a sudden and perhaps dangerous return. If I don't get news soon, or have her here by Sunday, I shall certainly go back to make sure—whatever the consequences. O God, if only *she* could get over that fear and anxiety and regain her composure, then everything would be all right and the position of both of us would be not nearly so bad as it may appear. The suspicion that might be directed upon me from Dresden can't possibly be so strong that I would be actively searched for—but even if it were, I am safer here than in Abraham's bosom, because every precaution has been taken so that even in the case of a warrant of arrest I would be warned in time by the official authorities and could stay incognito near Weimar as long as I wished. But it must at last become evident in Dresden too that I can't be considered as really guilty, and a general amnesty for Saxony seems to be inevitable.

"As for my special plans, I intend to stay in Weimar or near by until my future is safely settled. Yesterday I wrote to Eduard Devrient in detail: I offered an agreement by which I might later return to my position in Dresden again. If I succeed, I should have a half-year's leave in order to effect in London and Paris the acceptance and performance of my operas. If such an agreement were possible (and nobody could arrange it better than Devrient), everything would be fine and better than ever. Minna could safely stay in our apartment in Dresden and could expect me back before very long. But if no agreement is possible, if the hatred and envy should turn out to be so great that I had to lose my position in Dresden, well, then nothing could be done, but even so it wouldn't be too bad. Equipped with everything necessary, I would go to London and Paris, establish my connections there for the future and make contracts. At the same time my friends here would see to it that the Grand Duchess of Weimar would put at my disposal a little house with all necessities on one of her splendidly situated estates, where Minna with father, mother, and sisters could safely settle, perhaps have a small farm to supply themselves, and in any case, well cared for, they could await the development of my fate to come. As soon as I have attended to my affairs in London and Paris, and closed the necessary contracts, I would come to her myself in order to compose, quiet and undisturbed, the new opera which will be in consideration. Then she herself would go to Paris with me and we would never separate again. Our old people could quietly remain on the little farm for the rest of their lives. So this is the plan, toward which everybody here is giving a helpful hand, and the Grand Duchess would be proud to restore Weimar's old glory, that is, to be the protector and promoter of the arts: for you would hardly believe how much I am loved here.

"Thus fate is more friendly to me than appears on the surface: I am revived by the hope of being able to exercise again my artistic creative powers. So be reassured and persuade my poor wife to come here as soon as possible to await developments together with me, and then reach a decision on her own account. Is she in Dresden? I suppose so! Mail this letter to her quickly! It is no good for her to stay there now—here she will breathe more healthful air with me.

"Again my most heartfelt thanks, my dear faithful brother-in-law, for your devotion and friendship, which I have never so closely realized as in the hour of danger. May Heaven grant that I can reward you for it! Greetings to my dear good sister Cläre; thank her for her great love for me and for my Minna. Comfort her too, for things are better, perhaps, than could ever be expected. Adieu, my beloved ones! Send news! Farewell and be happy!

"Your

R. W.

"*Tannhäuser* is to be given here Sunday."

Meanwhile, he received Minna's letter with her news about the police, for he answered on the next day. (The letter is an enclosure, inscribed on the outside: "Please deliver immediately to Minna Wagner—R. W.")

175 (*Weimar, Saturday, May 19, at seven o'clock in the morning*)

"MY DEAR MINNA!

"You are right in worrying about me and insisting that I continue and hasten my flight; but I am correspondingly confident about my situation, and you must believe me when I assure you that even if the worst happens I am in no danger here. Everything has been foreseen and taken care of by my numerous friends. Even if I am prosecuted with a warrant of arrest, the first person who is informed of it, twelve hours before it is published, will be the police director here, who is ready to notify me immediately, so that I may have plenty of time to leave quietly, or to move somewhere near by under a changed name. Why I don't want to make full arrangements for a precipitate flight to France I'll have to explain to you at length, for, you bad woman, you don't seem to understand me at all.

"First: *I must first see you again and be with you for a few days.* This is the main thing and everything else is unimportant compared to it. I will not be separated from you this way. First I must come to an understanding with you about everything and about our future, and give you thousands of passionate kisses. Our meeting will strengthen us both, and everything which we will then begin will be more blissful than if we were now roughly torn apart. This is the most important of all.

"Second: I first have to await the result of a statement I have made about my whole participation in the late Dresden catastrophe, and which I sent to Devrient; you yourself still seem to be uncertain whether I am not more deeply involved in the affair. What you heard everywhere in Dresden on your last inquiry may best reveal to you what silly and exaggerated stories and distortions concerning my person are going about, and all that disgusting stuff must in the long run turn out to be unfounded. Now God knows what kind of suspicion has been caused by one circumstance or another; and since Bakunin appears to be the most compromised, and since they have probably found out that I was associated with him, I imagine that they are making every effort to find evidence of a plot about which, they suspect, I could perhaps give some information. If it were not for my disgust with everything which is called questioning, arrest, trial, etc., as well as other considerations, I would straightway go to Dresden and confidently present my case; for my participation was a quite general one and my acquaintance with Bakunin has only a purely human and artistic interest. I certainly heard about his plans for a united action of the Slavs and Magyars against Russia, whose liberation from despotism was his aim; but of course these matters were of the most remote significance, particularly to me; I was mainly interested in him as a most witty and wonderful man, and he himself knew that I could have no other part in it. It is therefore of great importance to me to wait for the news from Devrient about this; and if the affair turns out better than it looks now, I may keep my Dresden position in the future after a rather long leave of absence.

"Third: I must know exactly what will happen to you, my good wife, and to your poor relatives— How can you believe that after all the sacrifices you made for me I would not be concerned to know, if we must be separated for some time, that you are in an adequate and independent position? If I should lose my Dresden post, and if my salary is already being withheld, I should be to blame for not doing everything to find a quiet and worthy place for you. I hope you have already read what I wrote yesterday to Wolfram about this: You with your whole family must stay here securely and pleasantly on one of the splendid grand-ducal country estates. The details about this and a full assurance of your future are things which must now be arranged in detail by Liszt with the

Grand Duchess. Unfortunately Liszt has gone away for four days; today he is to return; after a conference with him I shall tell you the particulars. Until then only these general points: Germany, my dear wife, is now going to become a morass in which Art, having until now brought only trouble to the German artists, will be entirely bogged down. In Germany we could either live only a retired life or not at all. It probably is of the greatest importance for my whole creative work of the future that a thorough change in my life should now begin: Think how, in my Dresden position, my art continuously disintegrated [*zerfiel*]! Believe me, only the most mediocre, philistine artist is able to reconcile himself with those sterile conditions and to feel at home in them; he who has higher aspirations must perish in them: I came near to it!

"Sunday Morning: Last night, when I was in Liszt's room in company with others, your last letter arrived, poor Minna! So it is really true, the long-nurtured hatred for me of many worthless people, the outward circumstances and the mean, vengeful feelings of the reactionaries have combined to produce a warrant for my arrest? Good, then! So be it! The measure of the torment of my soul is full: at last—I feel *free* once more. I know only *one* care now; it is the care for my beloved wife! Everything has been arranged for you; your position is to be worthy of you and secure at all times against the need for charity and against the worst eventualities; only one thing is not in my power: to keep you from defeat by new strength, pride, and vigorous health. Minna, my one and only, have courage! Don't forget that such a warrant of arrest can only *honor* me and that a faint heart before such baseness would only mean a triumph of the enemy. Be brave and steadfast, and so we have now already defeated them! For your sake, I won't yet reject every means of reconciliation; but I would almost prefer to part with Dresden at once and completely. You know my intention of going to Paris and London; I am to receive the means to attain my goal there entirely from Liszt or through him. But hear me further: you must depend on no relative, no friend. I am secretly negotiating the following arrangement with the Court here: I am to pledge to deliver all my operas, finished and to come, to the Court without fee; to make every necessary rearrangement for the Weimar stage, also to prepare them where needed. For this I am to get a yearly salary of 300 thaler (I didn't demand more) and free lodging for a whole family in a special house on one of the Grand Duchess's estates. So you, my Minna, are now going to move to this charming countryside, together with your parents and sisters, and will take over the house and with the 300 th. you will have sufficient means for you and your family to live on; at first I shall turn this over entirely to you, while I create a new future for us both in London or Paris. When I have once concluded my contracts in those cities, I need never stay there long, but for the greater part of the year I shall return to you; and thus our often and dearly cherished wish will come true: to own a pleasant country house for our whole life. I shall send exact reports to my creditors: according to my present plans they have a better chance to collect soon than would otherwise have been the case.

"In an hour, beloved wife! I am to leave Weimar, because I am too well known here in public; I shall stay for a while on an estate two hours from Weimar, under the name of one Professor Werder from Berlin; I could live there safely for years if I cared to. There, my Minna, I shall eagerly await you; you will, you must, come to me there for a few days. Take the train to Weimar, apply to Liszt at the Erbprinz, and he will surely take you safely to Professor Werder from Berlin; for the *Kapellmeister* Wagner from Dresden has already left today for Paris via Frankfurt, and you certainly wouldn't meet him there, nor would any one be able to tell you where else he might be. In case you are not able to come in the next few days, I urge you to oblige Liszt by immediately sending to him in advance to Weimar the score of *Lohengrin* (get it from Uhlig), likewise the libretto (from Heine), the poem of *Siegfried's Death* (from Ritter); you might also send on a score and the libretto of *The Flying Dutchman*. Don't pay postage. But be good enough to let me know exactly when you are coming—address your letters for me to Edouard Dewen (at the Erbprinz, Weimar). He is really Liszt's valet; or send it to Professor Wolf in Jena. From both places I receive letters promptly.

"Yes, dear Minna, here I realize what it means to have friends! Liszt is a fine person; of this I am getting more and more convinced.

"You, my poor, dearly loved wife, be brave! Despise the baseness now let loose against your husband, who pursues only the noble and the great. This thought should give you the strength you need to go on and to be happy with me *after all*— Yes, yes, farewell, farewell! My old, true love!

"Your
R. W.

"I have had no money from Leipzig."

So it turned out that Minna was not present at the performance of *Tannhäuser* in Weimar on the 20th. Nor was Wagner present. For precautionary reasons, indicating that for all his reassuring words to Minna he was at last aware of his danger, he not only avoided showing himself in public, but left Weimar that same Sunday morning, went to Magdala, not far distant, and took shelter in the house of a Herr Wernsdorf, assuming the name of Professor Werder. Minna, according to arrangement, arrived there on Tuesday, which was Wagner's birthday. The meeting brought no understanding between them. "She persisted in regarding me," writes Wagner, "as an ill advised, inconsiderate person who had plunged both of us into the most terrible situation." He persuaded her to linger with him and not go on at once to Leipzig, as will be seen by the following note to his sister there, written from Magdala on the 22nd and postmarked Weimar, the 23rd:

176 *(Magdala, May 22, 1849. Addressed to Frau Cäcilie Avenarius, Marienstrasse 2, Leipzig)*

"DEAREST CÄCILIE:

"Two lines in haste! Minna is staying on at my request for two days more. Only then will she come to you. Will you be so kind as to inform Natalie in Dresden (in our apartment), so that she won't worry about Minna's delay. Soon you will hear more about me. Goodbye—and all my thanks for your love. A thousand greetings from

"Your

R. W.

"For the rest, don't be anxious. Minna herself has become convinced that I am perfectly safe."

Wagner walked to Jena (in six hours) and rejoined Minna there, according to agreement, at the house of a Professor Wolff. After a distressed parting, Wagner made his way to France, but went for safety's sake by way of Switzerland. Using the passport of an obliging Professor Widmann, he traveled through Coburg, Rudolstadt (which revived memories of his first meeting with Minna), Lichtenfels, Lindau. Thence he crossed Lake Constance and found himself, "on a lovely spring morning," in Rorschach and safe at last in Swiss territory. "I employed the first moments in writing a few lines home to tell of my safe arrival in Switzerland, and my deliverance from all danger," he says in *My Life*. Here is the letter:

177 *(Rorschach, "In the morning, 7:30." May 28,[3] 1849)*

"MY DEAR TRUE WIFE:

"I have safely arrived in Swiss territory! I hoped to be able to write you from here a day sooner, but unfortunately the journey progressed very slowly,

[3] The date on this letter has been changed to May 31. This is strange, because Wagner in *My Life* also states that he arrived in Rorschach on "the last day of May." The date of May 28 is absolutely established in his own careful itinerary in the letter following (180). From this and other letters here made known, compared with available data, the following itinerary of Wagner's flight from Dresden to Paris is derived:

Wednesday, May 9	Final departure from Dresden	(after midnight)
Sunday, May 13	Arrives in Weimar (morning)	
Monday, May 14		(letter to Minna, 173)
Tuesday, May 15	Goes to Eisenach	
Wednesday, May 16		(letter to Minna, 172)
Thursday, May 17	Returns to Weimar	(letter to Devrient)
Friday, May 18		(letter to Wolfram, 174)
Saturday, May 19		(letter to Minna, 175)

many stops, etc. The passport only was demanded in Lindau, and the visa for Switzerland was granted without any fuss.

"This morning I came here from Lindau, across the Bodensee, and in half an hour I am to go on to St. Gallen and Zürich. In Zürich I am to treat myself to a little rest so as to write you at length.

"I am in safety!

"May God keep you cheerful! I have grieved for your sake, but my spirits have returned. Goodbye, my dear best wife! More tomorrow from Zürich.

"Your

R. W."

[On the envelope in Wagner's hand:]
"Dearest Eduard:
"Convey this to Minna quickly!"

[In Cäcilie's hand:]
"Sweet Minnerl, he is in safety! God be thanked and praised! But now be calm too and give us the joy of a visit. Also tell me what to do so that I may know that my young ones are in good hands during my absence.

"Your

CÄCILIE"

In Zürich, Wagner renewed his acquaintance with Baumgartner and Alexander Müller and met Sulzer, his destined friends for years to come. His enchantment with the place is obvious in the letter following.[4]

Sunday, May 20	Goes to Magdala (morning)	(Tannhäuser performed at Weimar)
Tuesday, May 22	Joined by Minna at Magdala	(letter to Cäcilie Avenarius, 176)
Wednesday, May 23	Walks to Jena	
Thursday, May 24	Leaves Jena (evening)	
Friday, May 25	Arrives in Coburg (evening)	
Sunday, May 27	Arrives in Lindau on Bodensee (evening)	
Monday, May 28	Arrives at Rorschach; goes to Zürich	(letter to Minna from Rorschach, 177)
Tuesday, May 29		(letter to Minna, 180, and O. L. B. Wolff)
Wednesday, May 30	Leaves Zürich (evening)	
Thursday, May 31	Arrives in Basel (morning), Strassburg (evening)	
Saturday, June 2	Arrives in Paris (morning)	

Wagner went to Reuil on the evening of June 8 and returned to Zürich shortly after June 19.

[4] 180, Zurich, May 29, 1849. The date on this letter, in Wagner's hand, appears to be *Dienstag,* 26 June, but the month and numeral are an alteration, and unclear, as if 20 had been changed to 26, which would have been Tuesday. The correction is wrong. The contents make Tuesday, May 29, the only possible date.

"MY DEAR, PRECIOUS WIFE!

"At last I have a peaceful moment for conversing with you in writing, just as I almost always do alone with my thoughts, in spoken but unheard words. My four days of traveling to this point, in great heat and after the highest excitement, with only one night's sleep (in Coburg), have fatigued me greatly; my blood is terribly agitated, as if about to rush out of my ears; if I had gone on traveling another day without a break, I fear I might have had a stroke. So I am treating myself to a little rest here in Zürich, with the relief which comes from the feeling of reassurance. Besides this, my stay here may facilitate my further journey: for Alexander Müller from Würzburg, an old friend of my youth, has been settled here for many years; he is still in the country today but tomorrow he is to return, and I hope that he will be able to procure me a passport for France just as readily as Wolf's friend in Geneva could. If my hope is realized, which I have hardly any reason to doubt, I would save myself the great detour by Geneva and could go directly to Paris by way of Basel. This would be desirable in every respect, for I am especially afraid of the great fatigue I should have to undergo in that longer trip via Geneva. So I'll not close this letter until tomorrow, when I can tell you definitely about my shortened itinerary.

"My journey until now has been without adventure, but was much delayed by between stops. You know I left Jena on Thursday night, but unfortunately there was no direct express coach; and in Rudolstadt and Saalfeldt I had to wait so long for mail coaches coming from somewhere else that I didn't arrive until Friday night in Coburg, and from there the coach to Bavaria didn't go on until Saturday morning. Sunday night to Monday brought me to Lindau on the Bodensee, the last German town, where the passports were demanded at the gate. I gave mine up and went to the inn, where I wanted to sleep until four o'clock in the morning, but I couldn't, owing partly to my overwrought state and partly to anxiety that some bad calamity might still arise from the passport affair. I felt just as you did during the second night in Magdala. I imagined that at any moment I would hear the inspector of police coming to cross-examine me. It was foolish, but I even practiced speaking in Swabian dialect in order to pass as a Stuttgarter.[5] I was at last released from those painfully comic attempts when at daybreak the police clerk arrived and handed me back my passport with visa for Switzerland—without any trouble. When he had left, I thanked God and cried aloud repeatedly, "My dear Mienel, now I am safe." So I boarded the steamer in a pretty good mood; how refreshed I felt by the glorious trip across the Bodensee, with the view of the snow-white Alpine glaciers!

"From Rorschach, the first Swiss town, the express coach took me straight

---

[5] Wagner was traveling under the passport of Prof. Widmann of Stuttgart. "I spent the whole night in feverish unrest," he writes in *My Life*, "trying to perfect myself in the Swabian dialect, but, as I was amused to find, without the smallest success."

on to Zürich, and things I had to attend to left hardly enough time to write the few lines you will get through Avenarius [177]. I arrived here last night, after a charming trip through St. Gallen and Winterthur, and put up in an inn on Lake Zürich. O my good Minna, I hardly dare tell you how heavenly it is here: it would be like a bitter mockery of your harassed situation if I should tell you about the unimaginable beauties of this glorious country. The greatest prosperity [*Wohlstand*] and the sublime beauty of nature suddenly lie here before me as if by magic: each time I yielded to my delight I had to exclaim your name as if asking you to share it, but then I remembered your serious look and the dreary cares with which I left you, my poor wife. So, while I am here enjoying my newly won freedom, you are involved in the adverse conditions my wildness has brought about. The whole painful pressure of a disastrous situation is weighing on your martyred soul, while I am already renewing my strength to step courageously into the future. May God strengthen you in the last (I hope last) miserable job which you undertook in order to take care of me. But all I implore from you now is this: shorten your disagreeable job as much as possible; what cannot be solved must be severed, only to escape from that unhappy Dresden as soon as possible and to breathe a different and more wholesome air. Go next to Leipzig, then immediately to Teplitz, or better still go now at once to Teplitz. Clärchen surely will accompany you, perhaps Cäcilie too. Only when I know that you are in Teplitz shall I be able to sigh with relief, for every additional day you spend in Dresden weighs heavily on my conscience.

"Yes, dear wife, the trip by way of Geneva through the whole of Switzerland is very enticing: but for that very reason I will try *not* to go that way, because I don't want to have any occasion for enjoyment while I know of your distress. I will do it like my Tannhäuser: '*Verschloss'nen Aug's, ihr Wunder nicht zu schauen, durchzog ich blind Italiens holde Auen.*' I have before me only *one* goal: Paris, and no other desire lives in me than to let not a single day pass by without incessant energy and work toward the realization of your future and mine. I must open for myself a free, independent career and so bring my talents, without any further hindrance, to the utmost effectiveness. If I succeed, you will be pleased with me too, for always: liberty makes me fresh and vigorous, but when I am confined, or even in public service, I shall always be to you an unbearable fellow who would bore and pester you and himself as well.

"Wednesday morning [May 30]: Yesterday my friend Müller came back to town: we met again for the first time in sixteen years and enjoyed each other's company. We began by discussing my passport situation, and he assured me that if he and his friends don't succeed in getting for me the wanted passport nobody else in Switzerland will. For I find that here in Zürich the whole musical world and the public hold me in the highest esteem: *Rienzi* and the *Dutchman* have been played almost complete in concerts, and with the most extraordinary success. Now the public is about to be initiated to *Tannhäuser* in the same way, for the quality of the theater is inadequate. At Müller's I found all the piano scores of my operas; in the evening I met a number of my most enthusiastic admirers; first, the two town clerks [6] who will take care of my passport have both sung in *Rienzi* and the *Dutchman*. I sincerely appreciated this clear proof of the popularity of my works and the great interest shown in them even in most distant places: only the German theaters . . . ! ! Oh, let's speak of something else! Well, today I hope to get a passport, and tomorrow I start out again on my journey, to go straight on without stop, via Basel to Paris.

"For Paris I have already made a plan for an opera which one day shall be given in all languages and which—so I believe—shall put the theater in quite a new position. Whatever battles and conquests it may involve, I have something in my mind which must succeed and can succeed from Paris only—my strength is exerted to the utmost and I am almost grateful to the fate that it is driving me anew into the great arena [*Laufbahn*], for now I feel strong and fully matured to accomplish the most decisive work of my life. I can't go further into the subject now, but I have already arranged my plan in detail and considered every means to put it through into performance—it must succeed, and—it will succeed, for now I have help on all sides, whereas formerly I was alone and unknown. And now? Do you believe that I could so take courage and build up this hope unless a sincere thought of love led me on? You know that, although I love freedom from restraint above all else, I am not in the least inclined merely to roam around the wide world; I must always know a home of my own, and this home for me, my dear wife, is you alone. Where my love is, there is my home, and in the last days of our painful parting one thing became convincingly clear to us again—that we really and truly love each other! Indeed, my Minna, when all our arguments are over, you too must feel after all that you wouldn't quarrel with me unless you tenderly cared for me. The only difference I can discern between now and the past is that now I know more surely that I love you. So receive with courage every new test of our love: it can only become ever more pure and deep. Hold the philistines and lackeys ever resolutely at a distance, and don't accept their pity. The weak ones and those who are dead deserve pity, not the strong and those who live! Above all, keep your health! As long as you are well, my home blooms and prospers, and all my efforts strive toward the goal of being permitted to return to this home as a successful artist—this will not be Dresden, not Saxony—but the little house where you will dwell with parents, sister, bird, and dog, and to which my fondest longing and my most restless striving will always seek to return.

[The remainder of the letter is written on three margins.]

"O God, how much I could write you! I am with you every hour and keep talking to you! All my plans may still seem vague and indefinite to you; I shall not be able to report on them in more detail until I am in the course of

[6] *Erster Stadtschreiber* is a high administrative office in Swiss cities.

carrying them out. I hate to speak to you about Dresden: why should I spoil my conversation with you by bringing in those annoying and deeply distressing subjects? My world is not the past but the future, and my whole endeavor is to enjoy the future with you as much as possible in the present. Another favor, dear wife, while you are still in Dresden! Wrap up a score and a libretto of *Tannhäuser* and send it to Herr Mühling, Director of the National Theater in Frankfort am Main—I'll write to him; you won't need to write anything more. Did you send the package to Liszt? But my more urgent request is that you write me a letter to Paris, so that I'll find it when I get there. My address is to be: To Monsieur Belloni,[7] 36 rue des Martyrs, Paris. My first visit will be to him: Oh, if I could find a letter from you there! It occurred to me in Coburg to write a letter to Tichatschek in Berlin: I asked him, in case *Rienzi* had been performed there, to draw the royalties for me and to send them on, because (as you know) a few necessary purchases must be made, and I don't want to become too heavy a burden to Liszt at once. I should also very much like to know exactly how you, my poor wife, are getting along with your money: be sure to write me when you are afraid it may run short, so that *you* at least will not be compelled to borrow from anybody. I confidently hope that my Weimar contract will soon be concluded, and then you will be supported honorably by your husband's earnings; but if you run short before that, I'll send you at once what you need. Be sure not to forget about sending the score and the book to Frankfort. Now a couple of hasty parting words. My passport for France, valid for a year, with a full description of me, has just been visaed. I have quickly made a number of friends here who are keenly solicitous about me: I had to promise them to come here with my wife for a longer time, and that is the only way I could make them let me go today. I am to leave tonight at seven o'clock and with God's help, in a few days I'll be in Paris, from which you will promptly get another letter from me. Well, my dear beloved, good wife! A thousand kisses go with these lines! Be confident! Have courage and pride! Think of me only as being noble! Now I am on the right track, and it will soon lead me to you again! Greet all the faithful ones cordially from me. Farewell, farewell!

"Your
RICHARD"

As the following letter confirms, Wagner left Zürich on Wednesday night, May 30, having spent two nights there. He traveled with all speed by way of Basel and Strassburg, and arrived in Paris early on Saturday morning, June 2. He waited until Monday, hoping for a letter, which did not arrive, and then wrote Minna, now in Leipzig, for the first time by open post:[8]

[7] Secretary to Liszt, who was to help Wagner.
[8] 178 (Paris, Monday, June 4, 1849. Addressed, care of Bookdealer E. Avenarius, Marienstrasse 2, Leipzig).

"MY DEAR MINNA!

"Here I am once more, sitting in that Paris where we arrived as long as ten years ago and eked out a joyless life in heavy worries day by day. My feelings are indescribable. The long trip, the fearful heat, past memories, the present and the future—everything oppresses me. Already hating all cities, how could I be impressed by Paris in any favorable way? I expected to be undisturbed in the comparatively quiet quarter, but I find it as noisy here as in the most crowded districts. And the heat, the agitation and restlessness make my head spin, for I have not had any news from you for such a long time! My courage regained in Switzerland is almost gone, and I have no other longing than to be united again with you, and the familiar remains of our old belongings, in a small quiet place. I want to work and create, write poetry, compose, whatever the world may demand from me—but to have to run and rush about this way, to plunge into that turmoil—why must it be? I would have preferred to leave it to others who like noise and knocking around! You see, my dear wife, Paris is no place of joy and desire for me. In Switzerland with its magnificent, invigorating landscape, in a friendly small town with the company of a number of friends, there I could better hold to the thought of being happy with you! But there is still one great task which lies before me: When this is done, I shall have gained something for the rest of my life, for then people will come to *me* and I shall no longer need to seek *them*; this is the advantage of an established success. So, courage! Courage! It can't be helped! Forward!

"The only thing that could now refresh my soul would be some good news from you! It was stupid of me to write you from Zürich that you ought to write quickly to Paris so that I could find a letter here on my arrival. I did not consider the fact that I would be here so much sooner! All the same, I am hoping every day for a letter: God grant that you write me in good spirits and health. Nothing else bothers me. Before sending this letter I'll wait for the expected one from you so that I may answer it along with this. Until then I shall only tell you what has happened to me from Zürich until now. Well, on Wednesday night—as I wrote—I left Zürich. There my friends warmly urged that if things should not go in every way according to my wish, I should be sure to return to Zürich with my wife; board and lodging and everything else would be provided, and no one would expect anything of me except to work to my heart's content. These were not empty words—that I know! So I left and arrived in Basel on Thursday morning; in order to go directly to Paris I would have had to wait there another day, so I preferred to go by train to Strassburg. From Strassburg I left for Paris by mail coach [*Mallepost*] at five o'clock in the evening—although I had to pay 83 frs.; but I was ready to pay any price, after so long a journey, to get quickly and without delay to my intended goal. In thirty-six hours I was in Paris—I got there Saturday morning at five o'clock. Right away I began to run around in search of an apartment in the quarter where I would feel at home beyond the boulevards. I believed they would be cheaper by now, but God knows what the reason is! I ran from one apartment hotel [*hôtel garni*] to another, and 100 or 80 francs was the least they wanted; until after a frightful perspiring and climbing of stairs I found one on rue Notredame de Lorette No. 11, second floor, a room with a small bedchamber at 60 francs a month, where I decided to stay. At any rate I shall soon have to go to London; and on my return, later, I'll find something more suitable and possibly cheap too. Next I looked up Belloni, Liszt's secretary: he was informed about everything, and since he is well acquainted with all the conditions here I shall follow his guidance entirely, as Liszt also wanted it. But what is to be done here can be only preliminary. My goal probably can not be attained until the autumn, at the beginning of the Paris season. My next concern is to make myself well known through the papers and journals and to take a firm stand against the numberless intrigues to which I shall be exposed, the threads of which are in Meyerbeer's hands. After Liszt's article on *Tannhäuser* appeared here, Meyerbeer must have marked its intent. When I dropped into Schlesinger's music shop and was received in very friendly fashion, Meyerbeer was also there but by chance hidden behind an office screen; he remained there when he heard me talking, as if he were startled at my presence, and as if a bad conscience because of his Berlin intrigues kept him there. When I finally learned that he was there, I stepped behind the screen in a very casual and friendly manner and led him forth: he was embarrassed and dull [*fade*], and I know enough to be wary of him.

"The most important thing now is that I myself come out with a big article, giving my views on the theater in general and its future, and also on my own position as an artist, in the most striking and convincing way possible: as for those who can't work among such people by bribery, they must rely on their talent to make themselves respected. I think that my intelligence will set things right, and if I tackle the thing from the right angle I shall be able to accomplish something great here. I already feel strength in myself for this. It is only that I must take the first disgusting steps which don't suit my nature at all. Today I have already made many visits with Belloni. In a week—I think— my great article should appear in one of the leading papers. I can't tell you much yet about conditions here; in any event I must soon leave for London, where I can now more quickly achieve my goal, since it is the season there at present and there is even a German opera company. The principal concerts are also in full swing. It was with a pang that I saw Kietz and Anders again: they have both stayed still just where they were; they made an almost specterlike impression on me, and I felt as if I myself were just where I was ten years ago. I can't tell you much about them. When I saw Kietz I asked him about the young Heine; he knew nothing about him. Then the bell rang and Wilhelm came in.[9] He is working hard here. Otherwise I didn't get to see anybody from

[9] The son of Ferdinand Heine.

Dresden, except in Zürich, where I met Klepperbein (but only for a moment). I no longer know anything about conditions in Germany. To be frank, I don't much care. All I care about is you and seeing you again *soon*. If I only could get some news from you!!

"*Tuesday, 5th of June.* No news! Perhaps you will wait to answer my Zürich letter, in which case there will be no letter for me for at least a few days. Oh, what torment! I can't bear letting a letter which I have started to you lie so long in my desk; I must at least mail it, for then I feel as if I had spoken aloud to you, and even this makes me content. Well, a few more words to wind up, and then to the post office.

"Yesterday I lived through another very dismal hot day. After having run about a good deal with Belloni in the morning and having written you, I went to see Franck and Vieweg in the store which formerly belonged to my brother-in-law. Franck delighted me by his alertness. Then I dined alone, went home again, and took a promenade in the evening after ten o'clock out to the Barrière with the young Heine to cool off. You can't take a walk before ten or twelve o'clock at night: earlier the heat wouldn't permit it. Alas, my dear, dear wife! These are bleak, dreary days. God, if they were only passed, and if I could only get started in my proper activity! Only the greatest activity can give me comfort, while I am still without good news from you. Oh, write to me much and often! Without knowing anything about you, it seems ridiculous to keep asking about one thing or another; at least I shall refrain in view of the awful burdens about to be loaded on you.

"Across the street there is a parrot in the window which is very like our Papo; besides, he makes similar tones and whistlings: you may imagine how this makes me feel! There is nothing else in my head but the thought of suddenly coming to you again. But all this is like babbling into thin air, for, alas, I know nothing about how this or that is going with you. At one moment I try to reassure myself; in the next I begin to worry, especially about your health. Oh, comfort me, if only for the sake of doing me some good. No sooner do I close my eyes, than my hot blood conjures up pictures and dreams which make sleep a torture.

"There is only one memory I rejoice in: that we have seen each other again. In spite of all the pain and argumentations, I have, after all, renewed my firm conviction that you love me dearly, even though your love is evident mainly when you worry about me. I do bring you worries: that is true! But forgive me, be kind to me and friendly; in this you can give me happiness even from a distance.

"Farewell my old faithful heart! Have compassion on me, but be proud toward strangers. Greetings to Cäcilie and Eduard, with whom I hope you will be now. Thank them for their sympathy with me! Farewell and give early good news to your

RICHARD"

Wagner's eloquence on the subject of London and Paris as written in his destiny sounds more like eagerness to placate Minna and to accede to Liszt in the warmth of his gratitude to him as benefactor than any honest or thorough conviction. Bewildered by the tide of events, he was not yet ready to consult his own infallible instincts and so go against both Minna and Liszt. The spectacle of Paris, to him a city of bondage, in gloomy contrast to the free and spacious Zürich, awakened him to full realization of what he must do. His disgust with his surroundings and all that they implied are expressed far more guardedly in a letter to Liszt on the following day, where, no doubt as a result of their stressful meeting in May, Wagner uses the intimate *du* for the first time. It took only two more days in Paris to convince Wagner, if he was not already convinced, that he was wasting his time there, would waste time and money in going to London, and that his obvious course was to join Minna in the one spot in his recent travels where he felt he could compose in peace and live in congenial surroundings: [10]

"God be praised, my dear wife! I am given new life by a decision I finally made after three of the most agonizing days! I have found myself again and now I know what will be best for me. Listen, my own dear wife: We may hope to see each other in fourteen days at the latest, and it will be a long time before we are separated again. Does that startle you? Well, think it over, and you will find that there is nothing hasty in it, but that my plan is the most natural thing I could hit upon, when I thoroughly consider every angle and look calmly and without exaggeration into the future. I beg you to listen and help me with all the love for me you are capable of.

"I can't stay here in Paris any longer—for the present I can get nowhere at all. Some necessary connections have been made, especially with a poet with whom I could collaborate—even from a distance—in my opera text for Paris. Just now everything else lies in the future, and until the winter nothing can be done here. Everyone has left Paris, principally on account of the cholera. I need only refer to my strong disgust with Parisian mismanagement to make you understand that only a very definite purpose could induce me to remain in this great, atrocious, noisy, and expensive prison. That purpose has been attained for the present; for at least a half-year nothing further is to be done about it: therefore—away from Paris where the atmosphere oppresses me. Shall I go to London? I have made thorough inquiries, and if I don't mind spending a lot of money—perhaps to no purpose—I certainly may go to London, though I have nothing to expect there. Their season is already half over; all the musicians of Europe have congregated there and are offering themselves like sour beer without avail—but there is no English opera there at all right now, only a bad German one which would be of no use to me whatsoever. I am convinced that

[10] 179 (Paris, June 8, 1849. Addressed care of Bookdealer E. Avenarius, Marienstrasse 2, Leipzig).

I should not go to London without long advance preparation. I can do this just as well from a distance, and my plan cannot be realized before the summer of next year: Should I now throw away 100 thaler for this without result? No, I shall see to everything that is needed *without* going to London; that is the sensible thing. What shall I do now? My dearest thought and wish in all the world is to join my dear wife for good, to set up house with her in one of the most splendid spots on earth! Listen now: I can't yet return to Weimar, which we once considered, but I offer you now a place where body and soul may recover—splendid Zürich in Switzerland, a highly appealing, wealthy, and friendly city, whose situation is hardly rivaled by any other. We'll live there in a simple house quite near the city, on Lake Zürich, with a view over the snow-covered Alps. Teplitz will not help you, but the lake baths at Zürich, the most healthful in the world, will strengthen and refresh you, giving you power and a new zest for life. There in German Switzerland we will feel at home: a dear friend together with his family and his companions are quite devoted to me; they will do everything they can, and gladly, just to keep me there and have me do my writing *there*. For see, dear Minna, if you are with me, and Nette, Peps, and Papo too, I'll be able at last to follow my true calling—and write an opera. Everything urges me to a new creation; but I must have tranquillity of spirit, and that is possible only when I am near you!

"See, dear wife, in Zürich I am in every respect—mark it well—in *every* respect, assured, calm, and free. Nobody can bother me there in the least. There we shall draw the small income from the Grand Duchess of Weimar, and I am taking the steps necessary to double this income through the cooperation of some other art patrons. You will receive 50 thaler from me every month, and so we can lead there a most pleasant and independent life. For the present, dear Minna, let's assume that we are to stay there at least a year. In the autumn the railway from Paris to Switzerland will be ready; and the only real interruption would be if I should have to go to Paris sometime for a week to conclude my affairs there, if they should reach that point. In any case I would keep writing new works with joy and love, and those works would at last some day come forth and would bring me success in the future; but if success should fail to come, I would still be happy in the process of writing them, having you always at my side. There we could also calmly wait and see how things would develop; and what we don't know now, we would find out later. But anyhow we are united, and this is for me not only the greatest happiness but the first need for my life and creative work. This I feel *with the strongest emotion!*

"If I had to stay like this in Paris a week longer, I would die; that is certain! You can't imagine my nostalgia: whenever I am alone, I sit weeping and can't take hold of anything. Nothing in the world can arouse me but your nearness. Oh, this Paris! Even today I shall escape into the country five miles from here,[11] where Liszt's secretary Belloni has his summer place: there, my

[11] Reuil.

dear wife, I shall await your decision. May God fill your heart with love for me sufficient to bring you to it. So listen again to what I shall propose. What furniture you still possess you could store somewhere safely. Father and Mother will have to make out at Riedel's for the present, or somewhere else, until it has been decided about the house in Weimar: we'll provide for them what money we can. With all your movable things, and accompanied by Natalie (who must take care of Papo, while you look after Peps), you will board the train at Leipzig for Nürnberg and go on directly by way of Donauwörth, Augsburg, Kaufbeuren, to Lindau, which will take you two days and one night; from Lindau you go by boat across the Bodensee to Rorschach in two hours, and there in Rorschach I would meet you and go on with you to Zürich. There everything will be modest but cozy, ready to receive you. O Minna, my eyes are dimmed with tears when I think of it; when I imagine the happiness of holding you—you, my old true, dear wife in my arms, never again to be separated from you for more than the shortest time! My good Minna, never before have I implored you so urgently for anything; never has my happiness, my health, my existence so depended on the granting of an entreaty such as I make to you now: say Yes! And come! Come as quickly as possible, Minna, I beg you, for the sake of all you hold dear; say Yes! And come. You shall fare well here; you shall, you shall! I have friends; of that I am now sure! Come and stay with me! You and Natalie won't need more than 50 thaler, at the most, until you reach Rorschach, where I shall meet you with money. Scrape together all you can, or borrow it; I'll return it right away. Or if you can't possibly raise the money, write by return mail and I'll try to send it from here, for I'm expecting to get some money any day. I'm arranging to get some, and some more should be coming from Frankfort: it was offered to me too. In short, I'm not worrying about anything if only I can have my dear Minna again; in that case *all, all* is well! and never again will our heaven be clouded, for now we have come through everything, even the hardest experiences.

"Tonight I'm going into the country to escape Paris and—the cholera. This disease is raging here horribly! Yesterday 1,300 people died of it. It's awful! Oh, for purer air! Minna, Minna, give me good news; say that you will come. Then I'll write you everything in detail and in Switzerland, on the Bodensee, we shall meet! Farewell! Oh, be kind to me! Farewell and forgive all the evil deeds of your ever devoted

RICHARD W."

But Minna was unmoved by this rosy prospect. She not only did not want to live with him in Zürich—she suggested that their correspondence cease. According to her lights, this was not unreasonable, for their ways only continued to diverge. Wagner saw in Zürich a break from official ties and political predicaments. He saw there stimulating friendships which would respond with understanding to his deeper searchings; he saw natural grandeur as an inspiring background for his creative imaginings. If music and musicians there were unimportant, they would at least not bother him, involve him in the bureaucratic strait jacket of a Dresden or the sordid market place of a Paris. Minna saw Zürich as a hinterland of music and civic life where the former *Frau Kapellmeister* of the Dresden Court would be buried in a petty provincialism. Deeper than this was her absolute noncomprehension of the fundamental needs of the composer Wagner. Wagner has much to say at this point in his autobiography about the "fundamental incompatibility" of his life with Minna. "Although her manner of taking leave of me," he concludes, "had been both harsh and wounding, I could not bring myself to believe that I had finally parted with her. In a letter I wrote to one of her relatives, and which I presumed they would forward, I made sympathetic inquiries about her, while I had already done everything in my power, through repeated appeals to Liszt, to insure her being well cared for."

The Burrell Collection contains this letter. The "relative" mentioned is Natalie, and the "sympathetic inquiries" turn out to be something far warmer than that—a humble plea for her return: [12]

"DEAR NATALIE:

"I am turning to you to learn something about Minna, for I know nothing about her, not even where she is staying just now. I hardly know what I ought to write her myself. I don't want to reproach her with coldness toward me; nor would she understand my defense, for the person who is not able to defend me on her own account would not concur with my plea, nor would she be ready to understand it. So nothing more is left for me than to express my deep yearning for her: but this I could do in no other way than by inducing her to come to me so as not to aggravate still further our miserable situation by the greatest of evils—separation. But she especially asked me, in consideration of her health, not to pester or urge her about this. What am I to write her now? Should I write about myself? How could she, taking such an attitude, be genuinely sympathetic about news coming from me? If I write her that I am discontented about my enterprises or affairs, she might be scornful and exclaim: 'Don't you see that you brought it on yourself?' But if I write about my successes, prospects, and hopes, she would be skeptical and call it a delusion. She might be entirely cautious and prudent in this, but I find no trace of love in it, only lack of affection and stubbornness. Yet in my present situation I can't turn to Minna unless I feel sure of her love: only love can overcome all that must now be overcome; only love can justify, excuse, understand, and reconcile. But the first admission of this love in our case should be made by the wife, who should go to her husband since he cannot go to her. If Minna is incapable in any case of making this decision, she frankly and clearly proves that she has no love for her husband; that a place, a flat, tables, chairs, and things—about which

[12] 181 (Zürich, July 10, 1849. Addressed care of Mad. Wagner, Friedrichstr. 20, second floor, Dresden).

she is now mourning and complaining—are dearer to her than the living person called her husband; that she prefers listening to slander, narrow-minded judg-ments, condescensions, et cetera, rather than finding out the truth by joining him. Once more, in a word, she proves that she has no love for him. Under this very rational supposition what am I to write now? Only useless and annoying stuff, and I don't want to add to all her troubles about her affairs, vexation over my lost position, and the evil reports, not of my own making. If she has lost her love for me, it can't be revived from without; it can arise only spontane-ously from her own heart: so I can do nothing but leave her to her own char-acter and cherish at a distance the most ardent desire that she may soon become mine again.

"You, my dear Natalie, are near Minna most of the time—so I hope, at least: therefore I turn to you to observe her closely and to find out how it is with her heart and what she says about the possibility of an early reunion with me. Therefore I am going to notify you as often as possible about how things are going with me and how my affairs are standing, so you yourself may be able to give Minna information and encouragement when there is need or oppor-tunity. Above all, be sure to let me know exactly how Minna is managing: she absolutely refused to accept borrowed money from me, so I hoped to send her some earned money one of these days, especially a fee from Frankfurt for my *Tannhäuser,* although unfortunately I got a negative reply yesterday. But if Minna is really in need, write immediately and I'll find ways and means to get money to her secretly through you—even if it should have to be borrowed from a friend.

"As for myself, I first want you to know the following, so that you can give information to Minna should the case arise: After receiving, in the country near Paris, Minna's very depressing letter, I wrote right away to Liszt; he is to stop all pending negotiations about a salary and not inquire of Minna as I had asked him to do. After I had waited for some answer to my letters—they take much time at this distance—I returned to Paris to come to a formal arrange-ment with my librettist. Since I had then nothing more to do than to work, for which purpose I wouldn't stay in Paris at any price, I left for Zürich. I had been warmly invited to go there by my friend Alexander Müller, Professor of Music, who has his own home in which I occupy two nice large rooms. In one of them two beds were ready for me and my wife: one of these remains still empty and unused. I can't gaze at the glorious view from the window of the other room without thinking: How this view would hearten Minna at the side of her husband, if she could love him! Müller has two young daughters and a very nice, friendly, and sympathetic wife. Both have no greater desire than to keep me and my wife in their home and to have us as their guests, in the fullest sense of the word, as long as we should wish. First of all, they are excellent, kind people whose greatest pleasure is to be able to help others—such as me and my wife; besides, they are flattered to think that I may live with them and in their house bring my future works to the light of day. I declared to them that their friendship would make me truly happy only if my wife, too, could share in it: without her I find no peace of soul and mind and so cannot yet work. I well understand now that Minna would have to have much love for me if she were willing to join me in accepting the offer of my friend. By helping Müller's wife in the household and working in sympathy with her, she would offset any obligation: I would stay in Müller's home, if Minna should come, only until my other affairs were settled. For I hope to strike a bargain with a very wealthy art patron here to the effect that I will sell him all my *German* operas to come for a fixed yearly salary in advance, which would enable me to lead a carefree existence with my wife in Zürich, which is a very inexpensive city. Here I would make my home once for all: my Parisian affairs would take me to Paris for a few months only, each year. Even now I could sell my finished opera *Lohengrin* outright. If Minna only would declare that she is willing to come, everything would be easily and quickly in order: but now while she stays far away, cold and unloving, I don't take an interest in anything and can't go ahead with any enthusiasm. If Minna would only come, she would receive the necessary money from me at once. The furniture and household goods which she has kept would all have to be sent afterward, for such things are expensive here: for the present she still could live here in the Müllers' home with me, so that we could get ready a small apartment for ourselves later, after the transaction of the business I have mentioned. You, dear Natalie, would have to come along in any event, first because you belong to us, and right now you would find some very useful occupation in Müller's home: but if it comes to the *worst*, I could easily procure for you a position here right now, if you weren't too much needed by Minna. All this has already been carefully considered here and talked about.

"I could feel quite well and cheerful here on account of the most amiable care of my friends— Oh God, if only Minna were here with me! This way I languish in loneliness, while Minna worries and grieves in loneliness too; together we would have the same troubles, but now they are further aggravated by our separation. Oh, if only the good spirit, the spirit of love, would soon come to Minna again. If she is not soon overtaken again by the purest and noblest feeling for me, I am afraid she will *never* again be capable of loving me: then she may tell me that she will never see me any more, that she can't love me any longer, and then farewell to art and everything essential to my life! Then I am going to take my walking stick and wander out into the wide world where no one will find a trace of me!

"The Müllers intended to write Minna: I prevented them; for nothing will affect Minna from without if she hasn't it inside her heart; if she is moved by love she will come, and come under any circumstances; if she doesn't love me, not even the most pleasant conditions in the world could entice her out of her gloomy, resentful, bad humor.

"That's how things stand, dear Natalie! Perform well your task! Write soon and often so that I at least shall always know how you are doing, and arrange that we can also see each other again soon. Greet the poor old parents! If they will have courage, they may come along with you to Switzerland; here there is room for all!

> "Farewell and keep loving
>> Your
>>> RICHARD WAGNER

"Zurich, Care Herr Alexander Müller
   Professor of Music"

This letter brought an answer a week later—not from Natalie, but from Minna herself. It brought Wagner the news he wanted, even though a good deal of reluctance went with it: [13]

"MY DEAR RICHARD!

"Yesterday I received from Natalie the letter which you had written to her; she thinks I had better answer it, since it concerns myself only. I am sorry that you didn't get my letter of the 28th addressed to Belloni in Reul [Reuil]; I assume you left your present address, for I don't want it to get into the hands of strangers; so you will receive it, even if you haven't already.

"I wrote you that I would come to you in Zürich, but you should not press me; those things can't be arranged so quickly as one imagines from afar, for taking one's final leave of a place involves settling many disagreeable matters. I hope you will understand, my dear Richard, that in coming to you I make *no slight sacrifice*. What sort of future do I face? What have you to offer me? Almost two years may elapse before you, by a stroke of luck, may count on some income, and depending on the good will of one's friends only is a dreary existence for a wife. When we once lived under the most wretched conditions, we at least had a prospect of better times. But the present restless state of the world leaves art in a very precarious position, since art can thrive only on peace and prosperity. I have no wish to dampen your courage; but to venture once again into the unknown, to court worries and misery in a foreign country, for this *my* courage is not enough. I have lost my faith in your beautiful promises, and there is no longer any happiness for me on this earth! What you wrote in your last letter about refusing the fixed stipend from Liszt seems to me almost ridiculous when I think it over; as if you didn't need the money for yourself. Besides, I had not refused at all to accept from you money that you had earned, and for this purpose you wanted to do your best; don't take this amiss, but I now believe that it was Liszt himself who called it off, or the whole thing from the beginning was only a fairy tale. In your letter to Natalie you reproach me repeatedly for my lack of affection toward you. I really do not understand you; to be sure, I never showed you any unkindness, but what proof of love have *I*

[13] 182 A (Chemnitz, July 18, 1849).

had from you? You ought to have set me a good example, but you have not done so; otherwise you would have listened to my entreaties and for once also made a sacrifice for me; now it is over and this shall not be a reproach, but you will admit that you have done me a *great* injustice, and in the end yourself too, by exchanging a carefree life for a highly insecure one. I wish that you may *never* have cause to regret this.

"Dresden cannot be my future place of residence; I would play a sad role as your abandoned wife. You don't want me to accept a position such as has already been offered me, assuring me a carefree existence, and this would bring with it a long separation which I myself could hardly stand, for I still love you in spite of all you have done to me. You may judge, my dear Richard, how strong this love must have been; but if you don't believe it and if you deny having done me any wrong, I will know how to control myself and I would die rather than go to you.

"You write that I should bring along to Zürich the remaining furniture. You had forgotten that you have sold all that has any value and that my Hamburg furniture is entirely old-fashioned and worn out, is badly cracked and not worth transportation. The freight to Zürich is very expensive; only mattresses, curtains, and a few easily transportable things would be worth sending, and I haven't anything else. As for the hospitality of your friend Müller, you could hardly take advantage of it for both of us for more than two or four weeks—certainly no longer, for this would cause your wife the greatest embarrassment and prove awkward on both sides.[14] We need two rooms, a small kitchen, no more; whatever furniture we may need we can decide when I am with you. It can't be very expensive. By the way I am told that a small apartment of this sort is certainly not to be found at a *cheap price*. On my part I won't be of much use to our hostess; it is always a doubtful matter to help in a strange household, and I no longer feel like serving as a goodhearted bootblack. Anyway, you are wrong in pressing me too much to come to you; don't attribute it again to a lack of affection, for it is natural that my health has suffered a great deal from the terrible excitements and hardships. I am very irritable, even bitter. I tell you this in advance to avoid reproaches in case I should long for my home; alas, I forget that I have no longer a home. In short, I do not yearn for other conditions. We must try now to make life as easy as possible for ourselves; if only God gives us health we should be content now. If you have a *sure* position for Natalie, I shall bring her along; otherwise, *certainly not*; we ourselves shall have to manage very carefully. I have recently been doing without luxuries, but I shudder at this prospect. I had little, but could count on it, and the reassuring prospect that we might make our way again was happiness enough for me.

---

[14] Müller had insufficient room for Wagner alone, even before his wife arrived, and Wagner was soon to perceive the embarrassment of his host at the too ready acceptance of his offered hospitality. On Sept. 3, Wagner and Minna moved to "small lodgings" in the Zeltweg.

Some time you will be wistfully reaching back for that honorable sphere of action where you reaped so much joy and honor. I can't imagine you will ever find conditions which are pleasant in every respect; however, in Dresden the advantages outweighed the drawbacks of your position. I received [the notification of] your dismissal only last Monday, shortly before I left. You may have read it in the Leipzig paper too. You must write me what I am to bring along of your work; the rest of the music I will put away for safe keeping. You can have it sent to you when your address is again definite. It has become very voluminous and very heavy, and expensive for shipping. Forgive my writing for not being very distinct or fine enough, but I can hardly see any more. This comes from much crying; how many tears did I shed in those disastrous days. The good Frommann sends you her cordial greetings. She wrote from Berlin full of concern for us; you could write to her too sometimes: she still lives behind the Catholic Church No. 2. I wrote her that you would get a commission for the grand opera. I am to stay here for two more weeks and am feeling quite well. Write me again whether you got my letter of the 28th of last month, how you are doing, etc. Farewell, give my greetings to the Müller family, whom I have not met. The Wolframs all send you their best love; they are happy people after all. You ought not to be so sparing with your letters—you may send them unpaid to Wolfram, who will convey them to me unopened. Goodbye, be happier than your wife,

"Always your

MINNA"

183 *(Zürich, July 23, 1849. Addressed to Heinrich Wolfram in Chemnitz)*

"MY GOOD MINNA!

"Although you are likely to receive my last letter today or at the latest tomorrow, I can't let today pass, having received your letter from Chemnitz, without sending you a few more lines, because I want you to know something about myself and the shape of the future as often as possible during our—let us hope—short separation.

"You may easily imagine that I now have nothing in my mind any longer but your coming here: everything depends on that. I can't speak to you about anything else today because I know that—once we are united again—everything will be brought to a peaceful and trusting agreement between us. You are ready in spite of all that lies heavily on your spirit to come to me and to share my lot: Good! Now you will surely learn that it won't be so bad and so difficult as you imagine and expect it to be. Really, I am living in the firm and well founded hope that soon, perhaps very soon, everything will turn out according to my wishes.

"In the first place, I repeat again, dear wife, that Liszt's endeavors to bring about an annual salary for me have been interrupted for the present only, according to my wish, but they have by no means been abandoned. The time was very unfavorable to me so soon after the Dresden catastrophe. I have been painted much too black, as I have also seen from your own reports; but even now I gather from many signs that the general feeling is beginning to turn in my favor; I perceive it clearly in articles about me in the *Augsburger Allgemeine* and the *Deutsche Zeitung* which I have just seen here. I see, after all, that I am treated with respect, justice, and sympathy. Let only a few more months pass by, and then perhaps the general opinion about me will have changed in a way which may lighten Liszt's task and permit him to go warmly into my case without compromising me. If I had no other prospect whatsoever than this (and I do have other ones), it would be only a matter of gaining time and meanwhile making life as bearable as possible. But that we can really do only if we are together. It is already arranged so that we can do this. You will get as much money from Liszt one of these days, I believe, as you will need to get away from Dresden and to come here. I have borrowed from friend Müller 300 Swiss gulden (that is, 5 kreuzer less than an Austrian gulden and 5 kreuzer more than the Rhenish gulden), this on the strength of the future receipts from my opera, *Lohengrin*. In case Liszt doesn't send a little more than you actually need, so that you don't bring any money along with you, those 300 gulden would be quite enough so that we could live here for three months comfortably and free of care, while we wait for our expectations to be fulfilled.

"Since you, my dear wife, don't deem it advisable to have the remainder of the furniture transported here, let's agree that you sell all you can beyond what you need: if you ship the beds, mattresses, etc., perhaps also the two mirrors I mentioned recently, then Müller, whom I have consulted, thinks that we could procure the necessary furniture here for 60 gulden. See what you can do to get 60 gulden from this sale. As soon as you write me, dear Minna, exactly when you expect to arrive here, I will rent a small furnished lodging by the week for us both—Müller protests that you too may put up at his house—but I think we should be alone when we are first together again; besides, it is not expensive here, the usual charge is 8 gulden a week for room, dinner, and supper for two people. So we would wait for the beds, etc., and meanwhile we could rent a permanent apartment of our own, buy furniture, and you could take part in procuring our little household needs as you wish and as far as you are able. The heavenly beauties of nature and the clear air should be the best support for my endeavors to make your lot at my side as easy and happy as possible. You will also make some female acquaintances, which should appeal to you. People are inquiring after you with warm friendliness. You will watch me then doing my work for Paris—and be convinced. Before three months are over, you will breathe freely and without worry about our future, for then we will have gained time and, I hope, put it to good use. Be reassured, dear Minna! The past shall not be repeated. Although a storm now has taken much from me, I have become another person from what I was ten years ago, for I have proved to people what I am able to do. The clouds will disappear, and the calm, friendly sun will at last rise for us for good. Be reassured!

"Well, dear wife! Bear in mind that even if our present unsettled state lasts a little while longer—we are on our way: our journey may be rather variegated at times; things may not always be just right and what we are accustomed to, but that is what journeys are like. Finally one does settle down; and we shall find a home everywhere that we are together; at least, I have no other home than *you*; and where I have you, there is my home.

"So write immediately, as soon as you get the necessary amount from Liszt, and let me know the exact day of your departure; find out so that you can tell me definitely when you are to arrive in Rorschach, your first stop in Switzerland on the Bodensee, because I want to meet you there. Well, I'll close for today. I may have forgotten many things, for I have nothing else in my head than your trip. Ah, dear good wife! My soul can be at peace only when I know that you are coming to me! God knows what otherwise would have happened!

"Greet the Wolframs very heartily for me: may they win in the lottery so as to spend some of it on us! At least they should always keep a sympathetic heart for us. So, a thousand greetings and a thousand kisses! Dear Minna, be of good cheer; the sun is shining again! Be fond of me, then everything will go well! Farewell and write soon again!

"Your
RICHARD

"Last time I forgot to answer your inquiry on the alleged financial sacrifice which Röckel made on my behalf: Will you feel appeased if I authorize you to call that allegation a shameless invention, from whomever it may come?"

Wagner had written Liszt on July 19, asking him to send Minna traveling money, and Minna accordingly received a remittance from him, with this note (184) sent from *"Weymar, Juli 27, 1849"*:

"HONORED MADAME!

"In compliance with the express wish of W., permit me to send directly to you the enclosed sum (100 thaler).

"A fair and auspicious journey; bring comfort and content to Zürich—and remember, both of you, in friendship, your devoted

F. LISZT"

Minna wrote her husband twice before she at last started forth for Zürich: [15]

"DEAR RICHARD!

"I duly received both your letters, and was pleased about the good prospects mentioned in the first. But your last one almost brought my hopes down again.

[15] 182 B (Aug. 3, 1849 [Draft?]).

God grant that you get results now, when you may quietly count on a certain assured earning, otherwise I am greatly concerned about the livelihood of us both, especially in these present times. It is fine and good that your friend, on the strength of your new opera *Lohengrin,* has advanced you 300 fl. on which you believe you can live with your wife for a quarter of a year; but this can't be any reassurance to me, dear Richard—for it is very depressing that my husband is not able to provide for his wife out of his own means and must live only on the kindness or charity of his friends, who every now and then lend him 100–300 fl. on the strength of his receipts to come. Although—don't take this amiss— it is very doubtful whether you will ever be able to pay it back, since you never adapt yourself to the world as it really is but demand that the whole world adapt and form itself according to your ideas. If a man lives alone and depends upon his friends to support him, it is not nearly so conspicuous, in my opinion, as if they are supposed to take care of his wife along with him. You know, dear husband, what little claim, if any, I made on you for my wardrobe and that I am not at all the spoiled wife, fond of dress; but it comes to the point where one hardly dares to put on an untorn dress without being pointed out as a luxury-loving and extravagant woman, as happened in Dresden in spite of my simple clothing. I learned this to my great regret from a letter of Pusinelli. In such a case it is always very obvious and convenient for people to say, if the man has made a bad speculation and contracted debts so that he does not know which way to turn: 'It's the fault of the wife; she has been lavish with the money!' See, dear Richard, this is too sensitive a point for a woman like me, who rather avoids everything for her husband's sake so that he may remain a man of honor in people's eyes. I am a woman of such petty views, which with the best will I can't argue away, so you must excuse me. So far I have received no money or letter from our friend Liszt; [16] probably he hasn't got it; after all, he needs much himself, so I don't resent it. Also, you mustn't expect too much of him; I'm sorry for him. I can't be certain when I shall be able to come; at all events I hope it will be this month. The cholera is raging now in Dresden, and many deaths have occurred so far. Dr. Baumgarten also died of it. Natalie and Friedericke wrote me too not to go there just yet. The Wolframs won't let me leave either as things are now, so my arrival in your town may still be delayed for a week; certainly you will agree with this too. To everyone's astonishment here I made a remarkable recovery. Clärchen's everyday life offers much pleasure and amusement; she would never be content with the kind of life I have led: this she frankly admits; it would drive her crazy, she says, or into melancholia; they didn't change their daily routine on account of my presence here; this is reassuring to me considering the expense it would involve.

"Only today I got to the point of finishing my letter to you; don't resent it. Next Sunday I plan certainly to leave here, although the cholera in Dresden is still steadily increasing. I read in the paper that eight to twelve deaths occur

[16] Liszt had evidently sent his letter to Dresden instead of Chemnitz.

daily, which is enough to scare one to death; all the same, I feel pressed to arrange everything completely in order to leave my beautiful Dresden for good. I must honestly confess to you that *this* time I am parting from my home with a heavy heart. Shall I ever see it again? God knows! And then my poor parents! I can't even think of leaving them behind in their helplessness without shedding bitter tears. May God grant them an early and peaceful end and pardon my sin for wishing it. But one thing I must ask you to tell me truthfully: do you believe that Natalie will soon find a position there, if I bring her along? I should prefer to keep her for myself, for I know how it was in Paris, where I found her very useful as a helper. I am not willing to do everything alone, for if you go to Paris I shall again be quite alone among strange people. I find it very hard to feel at home among strangers. You are more fortunate than I in this respect—anything new appeals to you more; I believe that is why you are much loved and honored, but it is hardly possible that you will be more worshiped and idolized in Zürich than was the case in Dresden at the beginning. You *know how to be very charming if you want to.* Your comparison of the thoroughbred horse and the rider is very beautiful and exalted, but there could be many objections to it. First of all, you do me too much honor by putting me above the everyday philistines. It is true I once had some courage; but when the rider has been repeatedly thrown by his mettlesome horse, and without quite breaking his neck, but so painfully injured that his courage is gone, he is afraid to mount that unruly horse again and prefers to mount a less highly bred one which will reach its goal a bit later, but with more safety and without neck-breaking danger.[17] The owner won't turn it over for slaughter (as you put it) because, after all, he loves it too much for that; but he won't feel any pity for it when they try to curb it to humdrum work and scanty fodder. What the thoroughbred horse hasn't learned by fine training in earliest youth, even coaxing will not teach it later. This I have often experienced, and that is why it's too bad that even the best thoroughbred horses lose much of their value.

"I have still a favor to ask of you: Don't write to your friends in Dresden that you want to settle in Switzerland; it has a bad reputation now on account of the insurgents who have fled there by thousands, and people say that the unruly, idle revolutionaries will continue to be a nuisance there. Well, now I know that you are not a revolutionary; you wrote that to me, and I couldn't be the wife of such a man, but all the same they all are expecting the worst from you here. So, I should like to deprive those people of their triumph by telling them that you are still living near Paris and will get a commission for a new opera in October or November. It has already been announced in the Dresden *Journal.* Would God it were true! I read that the Grand Opera House is now entirely closed; this means a bad prospect. Write me whether the Swiss aren't afraid of being attacked by the Austrians and Germans; they want to

[17] Wagner had evidently compared himself to a thoroughbred horse, not to be tamed by its rider (Minna) to a jogtrot.

recover the fugitives from them again, so one reads in the Leipzig *Zeitung*. If this is true, I hardly know where you could find a refuge except in England. France in particular, as a republican state, is behaving miserably. If in any case you are already very industrious and have freed your mind of several ideas which had been swarming there, I shall be surprised when I come to you. Have any students of advanced composition applied to you? I would wish it for you. In Dresden you sent them to Schumann.[18] Mad. Ritter has expressed her regret that you didn't teach her son. If I had stayed in Dresden, I would have seen a great deal of the Ritter family: they often visited me and I them; she is a very honorable, refined woman in whom I could have much confidence. The three daughters are simple and good girls; the second son is the opposite of the one we know.

"Tell me also in your next letter all that you want me to bring along in the way of music and other papers, of course not too much or it would become too heavy. I don't know whether one can go by train as far as Nürnberg. If I have to shut up Pepsel in a dog crate, I would prefer to travel in a hired carriage by way of Zwickau, etc.; they are said to ride easily and to be much cheaper than mail coaches. I would arrive two days later, which wouldn't matter, in order to make it a little easier for the poor animals. Papo's stand would have to be taken apart and brought along. The poor fellow couldn't stand being cooped up so long in his little box. This will make some trouble, but I am much too fond of them to entrust them to strange people. You really seem to have forgotten them entirely, since you no longer mention them in any of your letters. Don't start getting any furniture, and be sure not to get into debt. Later on we can get it together. I am not so eager to establish a little home for me, since it has no permanence; no sooner is it furnished than it is torn away again without mercy, and one must start from the beginning if one has any desire left, which I haven't, for one never prospers that way. You might write a few words to Wolfram sometime about your debt of 25 thlr.—it is very embarrassing to me; they seem to need it badly, since business is at a standstill; also, Clärchen is wondering why you haven't mentioned it. Don't expect me to borrow from Avenarius; he himself has nothing, since Cäcilie is in far too great need of money to indulge in her vanity and strengthen her health. I was present when she received 70 thlr. from her husband for her trip to a bathing resort. At that they complain and lament so much that one hardly dares to eat one's fill. I should rather be carried off by the cholera than live on the bread of charity where they always make you feel under obligation to them. A letter has just come from Natalie, announcing that the 100 thlr. from Liszt has arrived. Now it is all the more certain that I shall leave here next Saturday. Letters are slow; they usually take four to five days, so you will have to address your next letter to Dresden. If you have any more commissions for people, let me know at once. . . . The beds and a few trifles will be shipped according to your wishes. Beau-

18 Minna writes "Schuhmann."

tiful landscapes no longer impress me as they would under different circumstances; one becomes indifferent to all beauties of nature. Excuse my bad scribbling. . . .[19] Farewell for today, dear man of my heart! I shall write again, telling the exact day of my departure. I would to God I could be really happy about it! The Wolframs send their warm regards. *Adieu!*

"As ever
Your
MINNA"

182 C *(Dresden, August 11, 1849 [Draft?])*

"DEAR RICHARD!

"Today I believe I can tell you with certainty the day of my departure from here. Of course you will say again: At last! What a long time it is all taking! But I wanted to sell everything that was left, for the sake of the precious money, without which we precious humans can't get along—so as not to arrive with entirely empty hands, and this can't be settled in a moment. People have no money, so don't grumble any more about my delay. On Saturday the 25th of this month I'll *surely* leave *here* for *Leipzig*; on Monday the 27th of August I'll go direct to Nürnberg by train, from there by the good and quick accommodations which go daily from Nürnberg to Augsburg; so Wolfram assures me, for he has made this trip often and cheaply. Natalie will be a cheerful standby for the pets and in the future helpful to have around. I am glad that you saw it this way and agreed to have her come along with me. Perhaps I shall send you some more lines from Nürnberg to tell you the exact day of my arrival. I would certainly have liked to have you meet us in Rorschach, but you forgot to send me the exact traveling route, and now it's too late. Your letter wouldn't reach me here on account of the slowness of the post from Zürich; and I think, since I'm not traveling alone for the first time, I'll reach my destination without any detour by Australia. If I shouldn't find you and you get no further news from me, I shall send a message to your friend Müller, where it will find you, so that we may come together under one roof. I am going to bring along what you requested. The reproach in your last letter about my longing for a lifelong employment, and my clinging to externals like dead furniture, etc., doesn't touch me at all. You have proofs to the contrary. I don't know what egotism is; my personal needs are too slight for that. You shouldn't misinterpret my concern about our livelihood; I don't want to live over again what I went through with you before. The thought of the petty cares which went with the struggle for existence, when I sometimes didn't know what to put into the boiling water because I had nothing: this certainly makes me shudder to contemplate a future when similar things might happen; I have never concealed from you that I have become discouraged.

[19] The end of the letter is crowded and scarcely legible.

"My Richard, you are planning to give a concert there this coming winter, as in Riga. That is good, and I have no doubt of its success. But a lecture? [20] And for money, by a *Kapellmeister*—that struck me as a little strange when I read your letter, and the thought of it humiliated me very much. My greatest pride and pleasure was seeing you as the head of the greatest orchestra in Germany.

"You may remember that I missed almost no performance which you con-ducted, I saw only *you* and was happy. I believed that what I was hearing emanated from you only. *Don Juan* was your last opera here; it will long remain to me as a sorrowful memory. But the Ninth Symphony will be *forever unforgettable* to me on account of you. You appeared to me like a God governing all the powerful elements and working enchantments upon men. Don't deny that it gave you much joy to be able to integrate such resources, such strength, and to merge them into a great entity. See, dear Richard, you own the power, the glorious gift of creating something great even as a conductor, and you deviate so much from the true course of art that you now want to bring about a concert in Z., but with what forces? How do you feel about it? I feel very sad about it—but no more of this; by word of mouth I shall have much to tell you if my thoughts, which often slip quickly from me, will not have left me altogether. Fischer came to see me. The good old man beamed with joy that you had thought of him. Uhlig was here too and wondered at your cheerful letter; he is going to write you and leave it with me. Both friends shared the opinion we should tell no one that you are in *Zürich*. So I told them that you won't stay there, so that they may feel reassured.

"I have nothing else to write now; keep in good health, that is the main thing. Rent two rooms, not more, for that would be too expensive. Some of the small things I will give to Seebe, it usually takes twenty-two days to Zürich. Farewell now! Please don't take any sudden mountain trip at the time of our arrival. Recommend me to the Müller family. The cholera here is diminishing; you needn't be afraid. Papo calls. Peps barks his greetings to you.

"Affectionate greetings from your

MINNA"

The reunion, at last effected, hardly offered great promise for the ten years of these two in Zürich, the years of exile—years which were not to be without altercations, interruptions, and separations.

[20] "I thought it over, and decided to give public lectures in Zürich during the coming winter—hoping to keep body and soul together for a little while." *My Life,* p. 516.

⇘ XVII ⇙

WAGNER TO FERDINAND HEINE

(1849)

"If I am left undisturbed from without, I shall create work after work, for I am brimming with subjects and art plans. . . . My soul is eager to write at last the music for my *Siegfried*. . . . What matters most to me is *to gain time,* and that means *to win life.*"—Wagner to Ferdinand Heine, November 19, 1849 (186).

Wagner's basic problem through most of his career, but more than ever at this time, was to find a living in a "philistine" world only half inclined to bother with him, in order to fulfill his creative destiny and so conquer that world. It was a self-assignment that would have appalled anyone else, because it meant getting money without burying himself in routine to do it, writing scores prodigious in concept and complexity, following them through endless practical detail in production by performers whom he had to train, in a theater which he had to build, before audiences which had a totally different idea of what an opera should be. How protracted, how intense this struggle was can never be properly realized except by viewing his daily life at close range. The close view does not always present a likable person. It unfailingly presents an artist of incredible conviction and courage.

In the autumn of 1849, an exile in Zürich, he was balked at every point in this basic aim. He was barred from those theaters which could have performed his operas, but only under his direct eye, while the Court theaters, for political reasons, let them alone. *Lohengrin* had never been performed. He was constrained to listen to Liszt, whom he loved and respected, and who alone offered him the prospect of money, but who could not understand that his nature was incapable of a pot-boiling opera, trimmed to a French pattern. His heart was in the poem of *Siegfrieds Tod,* written in Dresden. But he could not find the money, which meant the freedom, to go ahead with it. Nor were his musical powers yet ready —and this he may not have admitted even to himself—to create his mighty Norse domain in tones. He was planted in a musical byway, with a reluctant and uncomprehending wife. But he saw one obstacle, and one only before him —the need of funds. Wagner expressed his needs in the following letter—which is as remarkable for its prelude, the laying forth of his situation, as for his limitless readiness to receive money sacrifice from his friends, which is the conclusion:[1]

"DEAR OLD FRIEND!

"I wanted to include your letter with the package which I am to send by mail coach one of these days and which is to contain a number of letters besides the new manuscript for Wigand. I am beginning the day with letter writing, and I figure that I may well need three additional days for the rest of the letters and the continued study of my very voluminous manuscript.[2] This would delay too much the dispatch of the letter, part of which I have much pondered during the last two weeks and which, once put on paper, I could not possibly keep. For that reason I am going to write to you separately and send the letter right away, by itself.

"For the moment I shall refrain from expressing my joy in your last letter, in order to keep to my main subject, and that main subject just now is *myself* alone. For some time I have been looking for the one to turn to about the matter in question; as soon as I thought of you my search had ended. My choice is very definitely made. So listen, old true friend of my heart!

"On my flight from Dresden and Saxony I arrived in Weimar; and the real catastrophe, so far as it concerned me alone, happened there—actually in Liszt's home. Liszt, who has always pointed out Paris to me, seized the moment to manage things in such a way that I had to go to Paris and make use of his numerous connections for the purpose of an opera commission, while he was to provide me with the necessary funds. So he offered me a credit up to 2,000 frc. I had little chance to ponder or choose, but accepted the plan, received the necessary traveling expenses from Liszt, and proceeded through Switzerland—for passport reasons—and so to France. Before this, I had arranged with Liszt the following on behalf of my wife: He was to use his influence with the Grand Duchess of Weimar, who was especially fond of me, to make me a year's allowance of 300 thlr., in return for which I was to agree to deliver all my finished and future dramatic works to the Weimar Theater without further honorarium, and to take charge of all corrections and alterations, and when circumstances permitted to take over the coaching gratis. At first, this income should be conveyed to my wife [in Dresden]. Only the haste of the moment induced me to adopt the Paris plan as my own: a week in Paris was enough to make clear to me the great mistake [*den gewaltsamen Irrthum*] I had been pushed into. Spare me from expatiating here in more detail on the revolting baseness of Parisian art tendencies, especially in opera. In recent decades, under the mercenary influence

[1] 186 (Zürich, Nov. 19, 1849. Addressed to the "Royal Court-Actor," Herr Ferdinand Heine, in Dresden).

[2] His essay, *The Art Work of the Future*. Wigand published it in the following year.

FERDINAND HEINE (188)

of Meyerbeer, the condition of opera in Paris has become so ruinously horrible that it is useless for an honest man to devote himself to it. Liszt's secretary, Belloni, a very smart, locally experienced, and at the same time a very good-hearted man, has taken charge of the situation most successfully. He put me in touch with a poet, Gustave Vaez (now president of the *Commission d'auteurs*), who awaits from me the plan of an opera poem, so as to deliver to me at once the book which he will make acceptable to the management of the Grand Opera. But all the same I am firmly convinced that I shall never succeed in having an opera really performed at the Academy, at least not under present conditions, with its new ruling spirit and under the present regime. As things stand now, Meyerbeer holds everything in his hand, that is, in his moneybag; and the morass of intrigue to be traversed is so big that fellows far more cunning than myself have long since given up the idea of waging a battle in which only money is decisive.

"Quite apart from this practical view, anyone who knows the nature of my soul as an artist may estimate how I feel when I consider composing to a modern French text. The present public of the Paris Grand Opera and a French opera book—these together are enough to ruin me, to whom music is everything, completely. *It won't do*, and I have no further words to waste on him who fails to understand this. Enough! Just now these and other disheartening impressions are sufficient to drive me away from Paris altogether. Glad to have freed myself of these scruples through my robust nature and refreshed by glorious Switzerland and a few sympathizing Zürich friends, I have taken new courage to live in my own way, according to my nature! I wrote to Liszt and only cautiously expressed my disgust with Paris, knowing his very biased point of view on this subject; I told him he should first see to it that I can exist at all; I certainly wouldn't let my works lapse, but I should want those who loved my works to leave to me and my good judgment the choice of *what* I am going to work at. I knew that besides the Grand Duchess of Weimar there is also the Duke of Coburg and especially the Princess of Prussia who are sympathetic to my art. Therefore I wrote to Liszt that if this is true, and if these people would prove that they are real princely humans (not only so-called human princes), they ought together to offer me a moderate salary sufficient to make me independent of the need for speculation. Well, there I was mistaken again; we enthusiastic commoners think much too generously of those in power; they are much better known to people who revere them unreservedly. Liszt is such a one, and he made no secret about it to me that as things stand now he doesn't consider it at all advisable to put in a bid for interest in me on the part of these same notables. It goes without saying that nobody was more ready to discourage such an attempt than *myself* as soon as I got the hint. Liszt alone—as I have also found out—is incapable of supporting me—he himself is in a perpetual pinch for money, increased by the fact that he must provide entirely for his beloved, Princess Wittgenstein. He is a truly admirable man with excellent qualities and he holds me in lively affection, but my real intrinsic nature as artist is unknown to him and must always remain alien to him; that lies in the nature of things. Well, for more than three months I have had to live on a few hundred gulden, which a friend here has had to do his utmost to advance. At the end of this month I shall not know where to turn for my existence, which would not be so fatal for me alone, but it is a terrible prospect for my wife, to whom I remain in many ways an unintelligible puzzle.

"Let me pause here for the question: What are my real intentions? If my bare existence were assured, it would lie before me to do what I have to do—I have poured out my heart to the world, that is to say, to my friends, with my latest essay, *The Art Work of the Future*. From now on I shall be no longer a writer, but only an artist. If I am left undisturbed from without, I shall create work after work, for I am brimming with subjects and art plans [*ich bin übervoll von Stoff und künstlerischen Vorhaben*]. So long as the outward form of the world remains as it is now, these works can be only mute ones addressed to my friends; but when it changes its form, as it must, they will speak out and take their rightful stride. My *Lohengrin* is long since finished. My whole soul is eager to write at last the music for my *Siegfried*. Subjects for five operas are alive in my head: to bring them to light, one after another, is a necessity to me. I shall even keep an eye on Paris, but I can't line myself up with the conditions prevailing there now: only with what is bound to come, and in a not too distant future. I am working right now on a plan for Paris; it is *Jesus of Nazareth*. First I shall try to win over my French poet to the subject, in the hope that we may agree on it and be ready with it when the time comes. Only by looking at things this way can I remain an artist and work as one; otherwise, I should have to stop. What matters most to me is *to gain time,* and that means *to win life*. Unhappily, I am no artisan to earn my daily bread; it must be offered to me as things stand now, so that I may remain an artist. Who is to do this? Only those who love me—me, my works, my strivings and aims as an artist, and love them sufficiently so that it matters to them to perserve me for my art and for my artistic endeavors. There are not many of them, but those few in this case have the peculiar feature of loving me *energetically*. I have had some fine and comforting experiences of this in the course of time. There are not many of them and they are scattered, but they are friends of my true self. The most natural thing in my position would be to turn to these friends openly and before the whole world; to lay my case and my aims before them without reserve, and to call upon them to join in helping me as much as they can in order to bridge over this period of my life. In my present circumstances I am unable to help myself. They should see in me not a person in need of help, but an artist and an art trend which they want to preserve for the future and not allow to perish. The works which I am eager to create will be their property until they can be handed over to the *people* for whom they have been preserved. Even if I were mocked and ridiculed for this by all the people in the world, I wouldn't mind if I only knew that my friends at least understood me. If I were entirely alone, I would take this step quite publicly; but I can't do it on account of my wife, for she wouldn't understand me and would listen only to the baying of the pack. So I must look for someone who—without publicity—will stand up for me here and will undertake to achieve quietly, in a roundabout way, what I might have done publicly with a single stroke. To find this someone was the point. I believed I had to select the most *influential* one of my friends, and I rejoice in having surely succeeded in choosing the one who I know has done more for me than any other.

"And so I ask you now, my dear friend, to take care of me and my art! Without wishing to encroach, I want to tell you *how* I consider you should act according to these circumstances. You might perhaps begin by inviting one or two who are friendly toward me to join you in a kind of committee—you will know best whom to choose; perhaps Löwe would be quite unfit. (By the way, I would like to mention the Ritter family about whom Uhlig will tell you more, perhaps also introducing you, for they have behaved well toward my lonely wife—quite of their own accord and without even knowing her; perhaps this family could give you some hints where you could find friends of my art, not yet known to you.) You would have to initiate the greatest possible number of intimate and congenial people into your plan, which of course will have been officially started by you alone, and to induce them to collaborate; perhaps some discreet circular could be issued for that purpose. For the sake of appearance, Liszt in Weimar would have to be invited, as well as Frommann in Berlin (behind the Catholic Church No. 2), to be helpful in a discreet way, in your enterprise. The aim would be quite simple—to collect as large a sum as possible, which would be given to my wife so that she can attend without worry to what is needed for our life, so that I may be left to my work! How you would then want to dispose of my work would be up to you. Enough! In making all these suggestions I am guided only by consideration for *my wife*: she should not and must not know that I brought up the subject—even though only in a confidential communication to you; she does not understand what is the essential point for me in this affair, and would only yield to a feeling of shame which in this matter I cannot feel. But it would be entirely different if she were told that an association of friends had come together spontaneously, which would help me as long as possible, and according to their ability, over the present reverses of my life, would endeavor to keep me in undisturbed activity for my art—that should have a quite different effect on her. Since I have to avoid publicity also for this reason, you would have to help by interesting only favorably inclined people and furthering the project by spreading it from one friend to another. The first one you approach may already have heard that the undertaking originated with you, and I really believe that it is only the loquacity of this letter which has given you a different role; for I know that the first part, the detailed description of my circumstances, need only have been told you, and you would have been able to write the second part quite alone and out of your sympathetic and solicitous heart.

"So forgive me! I am afraid I have spoken more than enough about myself. But even as I begin to speak of you and Wilhelm,[3] I'm still in the picture. The day after I sent you my last letter, I received one from Wilm in New York containing among other things, an invitation to send him my operas as soon as possible so that he can best arouse interest in them and in me. America now and at all times can have only a money interest for me. If the conditions here continue until I no longer have the air to breathe, I would certainly look to America, but only for job work—with a baton in my hand—a profession which at least would yield better earnings there than here. *I have no children.* This is the difference between you and me. As the father of a family, you will start a new and endlessly long life in the New World. Mine would be completely extinguished there at my death; so you have a future there, *I* none; my art alone must be to me what your family is to you. You with your family are an entity wherever you are; I without my art would be a miserable egotist who would have only his stomach left to care for, not a future. So now I beg you to send my operas to Wilhelm. The scores are in the attic of my old flat in Friedrichstadt—Professor Hähnel's wife will let you take them if you ask in my name. The piano scores would have to be got from Meser. I am no longer in touch with him, nor have I the rights over a single note in my operas. Therefore go to see him. He could even send them to New York as a music seller if this is only made known to Wilm so that he may have them bought there by God knows whom. You would probably have to prepay the postage as far as Havre. If this bothers you as much as I think it will, leave it until you go over yourself and take it with you. I don't know any other way.

"Much as I enjoyed Wilm's letter, what really enchanted me was the news I had of him through you. This really goes beyond all wishes! But I was almost less delighted about Wilhelm than I was about you old people, and to hear that you have lived to see such joy! To go on living into the future through your real flesh and blood is something very different from living on by script and notes: all hopes which tend toward a long life in art are actually based on the unproductive sterility of mankind. If men were as they ought to be, a work of art would bloom today and die tomorrow, while a new one would meanwhile appear in full and fresh bloom. But real bodily perpetuation is indeed something more beautiful. Its existence depends upon the fullest love; our loveless culture has had to manage with all sorts of immortalities which are of little worth, and this also applies to what is called Art. I would give up a hundred thousand years of art-immortality for a single year of true, actual, human living. You happy man!

[3] It will be remembered that Wagner had found Heine's son in Paris in the previous June (178). Wilhelm was to become an American citizen, serve in the Civil War, return to Europe as consul, and at length to Dresden, where he died in 1886.

"I am writing Wilm this week; if you hear from him meanwhile, let me know. I can't get used to the idea that you want to go to America so soon. I simply can't grasp it; my heart refuses to believe it! The Heines are going to America!! Perhaps the autumn mists here are the reason that I no longer see things so clearly; perhaps, too, I am overworked. I am very low in spirits and many times bad thoughts overtake me—bad or good—but those thoughts point to an early death, which often doesn't seem too terrible to me. I feel so useless, so boundlessly superfluous—as lonely people do—and I often feel very lonesome, especially when I think that the Heines will soon go to America!

"Many thanks, too, for your fine letter! You have no idea how delighted I am to see your handwriting, and I am happy also that you seem to like writing me. Write soon again and don't be angry if I close now. I would like to say much more about you, but now I can't do it. Farewell, farewell, my good, old true friend! Kind greetings to your wife and child, also from Minna, who on the whole is not doing so well.

"Soon more from your

RICHARD W.

"I am providing for you an opportunity to read my new essay before it is sent to Wigand: it has grown voluminous. It's the latest I have to say *about* the subject which I myself plan to tackle again as soon as it ripens within me.

"What more have I to tell you? Much, but I don't quite have it in my head yet! Greetings to Fischer, whom I shall write tomorrow or the day after tomorrow."

Nowhere else in his known writings has Wagner so clearly and explicitly stated his point of view about expecting as his due from those who believed in his unborn music the means to live in order to compose. There could be no argument with the logic of this point of view by a posterity which beholds the value and the ultimate paying power of his works. It must have been this long view that made him such an extraordinary borrower—a borrower ready to expend (without squeamishness) an incredible amount of mental energy in the business of raising money. His friends, with all the good will in the world, could not have had quite his assurance about the future, nor were their own resources equal to his expectations. Wagner did not always take refusal in good part, but in this instance he was contrite at having embarrassed his friend with a charge he could not undertake. But, as the following letter to Heine shows, the "need" remained uppermost in his mind: [4]

"DEAR FRIEND!

"I wonder which of us was more startled, you when you received my last letter, or I when I opened yours! What a great evil is distance after all! Your letters until now have taken such a cheerful tone that I, deceived by

[4] 187 (Zürich, Dec. 4, 1849).

distance, always imagined you in an aspect quite different from what I would have assumed. I forgot that you, poor devil, must be thoroughly punctured by now, and that at the lightest touch you would shed streams of tears, and blood would flow from your wounds. I have been thoughtless and inconsiderate, and I am at a loss what to do to stop the open wound. For the sake of your love for me, forgive the painful and agonizing trouble I have caused to you; I can't blame myself enough for it! I am not to be blamed for having been deceived about many other things, especially about the attitude and behavior of my Dresden friends, that is, the friends of my art, and for having largely overlooked the effect of the May events on their bourgeois minds; but it was inexcusable of me to forget for a long time what you have had to suffer in recent years and times, and how wrong it was suddenly to inflict on you new and unexpected sufferings. I could easily say now: act as if you hadn't received this letter at all; but this wouldn't help the sting of worries about me, worries which are the main cause of your suffering, and which would remain with you. So let me try to undo my big mistake by picturing in somewhat brighter colors the dark contents of that letter. I can see clearly now how the letter reflected the very wish of my heart, and no doubt became so explicit that it bobbed up in the form of a decision. Dear friend, no one, not even you yourself, will take amiss my supreme wish for a lucky turn of circumstances which will allow me to withstand miseries of these times and to yield to my special artistic creative trend; at a time of utmost inward inspiration—as when I worked on my last essay—I felt that wish so intensely that I could believe in the possibility of its fulfillment. This will be understood by anyone who can imagine the impression made by news like that about the collection for Todt [5] by his friends, which resulted in relieving him for some time of the cares of livelihood. What Todt was to his political friends I hoped to be to my friends in art. Only now do I recall the evidence of a most passionate sympathy with my art, which came from near and far places at different times, and even today I could believe that a *public* appeal in the papers would be likely to bear fruits for me. But I am also ready to confess that I may be mistaken in this; I know with absolute certainty that a *secret* campaign, and especially one in Dresden, would be of almost no avail; and I can't forgive myself for having just demanded from you that fruitless endeavor, from you, poor, honest grief-laden friend. Besides this, I believe I have already told you quite plainly in that upsetting letter that I'll by no means fail to keep an eye on Paris. I only presented to you the difficulty of finding a suitable subject and especially—because I have no illusions about it—I have pointed out to you that between an agreement with my poet and an actual performance of my opera in Paris there lies a wide gap in which Meyerbeer (and rest assured this is true!) provides a deep hole, and that one or two years at least would be needed to bridge that gap. I have such a practical view of this that my judgment

[5] Bürgermeister Karl Todt took part in the provisional government in Dresden, fled, like Wagner, to Zürich, and died there in 1852.

may appear to you as an exaggeration. When I look around in clear, unbiased appraisal of all natural and real obstacles in regard to Paris, I ask myself two questions: 1. How can I manage to make a living until there are receipts from an opera performance in Paris? and 2. How will things be in Paris at the time when I plan to perform an opera there? This now is directly connected with political issues. If one examines the conditions in France, or watches what is generally admitted to be an irresistible progress of Socialism among the population, facing which the royalist factions [*dynastischen Parteien* [6]] are in disagreement, lacking sap and vigor [*Saft und Kraft*]; it is not fantastic to predict for France no more than a year of calm—but rather to recognize a tremendous social upheaval as a very immediate probability. Quite apart from whether I may hope for this or fear it, I must take it into my reckoning when my enterprise even at best will require a few years. As to the finding of a suitable subject—you mustn't think it absurd that I keep returning to my *Jesus of Nazareth,* which today appears to you as a mere chimera but may appear no more so half a year from now. But putting aside the question of a subject, what I must now take up is my problem No. 1, adding that you are mistaken if you believe I already have a commission from the management of the Opera; my progress so far only extends to an understanding with a poet, Gustave Vaez, who has declared himself ready to work out a plan outlined by me. He shall assure the acceptance of the opera and the recommendation to the management by the (truly powerful) *Commission d'auteurs,* as well as the agreement of the management to assign the composition of the subject to me. To make this possible I should perform some of my works in Paris this winter; my *Tannhäuser* Overture has been chosen for a Conservatory concert, and so I am thinking of going to Paris next month. I thought I had written you about this. The question now is not whether I *want* to write an opera for Paris, as you seem to think, but how I can manage to *live* until the opera is ready and performed. Liszt, as I gathered from his last letter at the beginning of November, has the *best will* to maintain me for this period, but he won't be able to. He had to ask me (surely with regret) to manage for the present without his help, although he hoped to be able to send me some money at New Year's. So I hit upon the idea of a collection for me to which *Liszt also was supposed to contribute,* since it isn't possible for *him* alone to support me permanently. This accumulated assistance should serve to support me *for the present,* or better still until the time when I can rely on receipts from Paris. When I expressed myself in my letter to you as if I wanted an annuity in order to drop Paris completely and to follow only my own inclination as artist, either I didn't make myself clear or else my innermost inclination—very pardonably— became too apparent. If you look at the matter exactly as I am presenting it here, you will see that it is not really my *will* but difficult external conditions that contradict your opinion of me and your wishes for me; and considering this you might have spared me many of the reproaches your mistaken view led

[6] Wagner has not capitalized the nouns in this letter.

you to make. You must realize clearly enough that I feel a disgust for Paris; but I don't have to reproach myself with having rejected an offer or a possible one on account of that disgust. On the contrary, I can write to you today more optimistically, because just recently—yesterday in fact—there came to me a fortunate idea (as I believe) for a subject—possible for Paris under all circumstances; I intend to work it out immediately and send it to my poet. (About the subject itself next time!) [7] Thus, my dear good Heinemännel, we need no longer differ over what my intentions are, but only on the means of realizing them: it is plain enough under present conditions that money will also be needed; but if I did wrong in dragging *you* into my troubles, let me make up for this by seriously urging you to bother about them no longer from this moment. At least don't worry yourself to death over them as you did in your last letter. Wigand has offered either to wait for the *success* of my brochures, or to settle at once for 10 louis d'or for both published ones: I wrote him to send the 10 louis d'or, and if he can, the same amount for my new manuscript. With regard to this offer I have already borrowed some money here. From Liszt I expect something around New Year. I should like to get enough to provide for my wife for a few months, so that I may go to Paris in January, and from there, if possible, to London. For London I am planning to have my *Lohengrin* translated into English and to have it performed there. Since you, poor man, now have to go through hell for my sake (which I deeply regret), at least get hold of what has been so far offered you for me: if you have collected something, even if not much, it will serve well the plan I told you about, and my heartfelt thanks go to you for your great trouble. But—don't worry any longer, be reassured about me, think only about yourself and your family again. Unfortunately you have enough sorrows of your own anyhow! The devil won't carry me off bodily. All I am worrying about is my wife and her inner peace. The worries about her, the autumn fogs, overwork, misfortunes of many sorts, and whatever else can burden one's mind was the cause of the dull mood of my last letter—which I might have spared you. Don't be cross with me any longer, and accept my thanks for the new proof of deep, sincere sympathy which your answer showed.

"Now I have yet to philosophize a bit with you. You expound general theories I can't approve of, apart from their special reference to my decisions about which you were largely mistaken. Only one thing I mention as concerning myself: you say that I *rashly burned my bridges behind me.* In this you are wrong. It is not *I* who have burned my bridges, but they that have collapsed of themselves behind me with a fearful crash, because they were badly and shakily built and connected me with a shore where, if I still lived there, I should find no air to breathe. I didn't want to push things so far, but they did it of their own accord, out of inevitable necessity. As for the subject of necessity I hit upon in the bridge discussion, we don't see eye to eye; my God who moves me and through whom I act is the *inner* necessity; the God to whom you humbly sur-

[7] *Wieland der Schmied.*

render is the *outer* necessity. The individual must indeed finally surrender to the whole, but in doing this he will be able to preserve his noble human pride only when he recognizes in that whole something corresponding to the general human character born from true human nature; in this case he should be humble because as one of the collective whole of humanity, with their common views and emotions, he becomes aware of something infinitely higher than himself, the individual. At all times men have recognized God as the highest being, the strongest emotion they have in common, the mightiest conception which we all share—and since we are capable of imagining things only from our point of view as humans, we personify God. If men recognize—not because they are taught, but by feeling it in their inner being—the good, noble, true, beautiful as the highest principle, then this becomes their God; and what denies this in the egotistic nature of a single man rightly passes as damnable, *godless*. We have really found in our life this God, that is, this conception of the community of men, if we have derived it from its genuine, its essential being; indeed, from life itself; if only this God rules us, He whom we identify with ourselves, with united humanity, then we feel happy and blessed. But the power which nowadays rules life—occupying all our thoughts, all our aspirations, our wishing, worrying and striving—which we at any day and hour feel and recognize as the most vigorous, most decisive and all-pervasive—this power—note it well—is nothing but Money, that is, abstracted and idealized *selfishness*. So the individual, in this modern sense, is really God, and every wealthy man gives evidence of it, for he even commands *God*; namely, money. *I* certainly don't feel a God in this sense, nor probably do you. But just ask Kaskel [8] what he believes in. At the same time we feel that we are living in a godless time, for the real God can't be the individual, but all together: On behalf of all, we therefore revolt against the God in the individual, against egotism; but to surrender humbly to this God is the utmost disgrace; he who is strong enough revolts against him, that is, he who in his inmost nature feels such a compulsory urge that he must still it; this natural inward urge of the individual, however, is common to all people, for, being invincibly strong, it does not originate in a single man, but in humanity in general. The suppression of this impulse (so-called self-control) fundamentally therefore means nothing else than becoming an absolute egotist, that is, denying one's true nature in favor of one's *external well-being* in connection with the general selfishness. Thus when we push personal selfishness to extremes, as we do nowadays, we demand self-control by the individual only for his own profit; that is, we encourage him to become selfish too, since nowadays no one considers himself happy unless he need not care about anyone else. Well, in order not to perish completely, but somehow to meet inner needs, one commands one's inner self, only in so far as it seems outwardly necessary, considering the general depravity, in order, through mere living, to save at least a part of one's nature. Raising this merely shrewd, fundamentally egotistic self-command to a religious duty means to recognize the exist-

[8] A banker and art patron in Dresden.

ing general egotism as the highest necessity, but to consider the inner necessity of human nature as something bad and subordinate, and this is the whole politics and philosophy of our time. The Future, on the contrary, is going to raise the inner, that is, true human nature, to a general necessity and will put the bad, false egotism of the individual, now perverted from nature, in that place in which humanity in general must now content itself. When you now call to me: Obey necessity! what are you really saying but this: Think of your own person and give up God? For my God is my art and the principle of beauty, nobility, and truth as such. At this point you admit that people in general are bad, ignoble, and false, and that you have to yield to that general depravity. Here your thinking is godly only in Kaskel's sense, but godless in the sense of a true God. On the other hand I have this to say: people will not always be as they are now; they are like this only so long as they cling to their evil God; some day they will chase this God to the devil, and then the right one will prevail all by himself. I am also one of those 'chasers,' even now I am hunting with all my might; but a good gun, powder, and shot are needed for that—in this you are right; well, I shall procure them too; and, since there is no other way, in Paris and London. To this extent I shall control myself in order to go on living and be a hunter too. But do not consider this self-control as a virtue, but rather the *power* of inner need which makes me a hunter—this power I have not derived from myself but from God, and that God is nothing but the genuine and originally common human nature.

"Now we agree—and if we don't the fault is with my confused chatter, not with the subject itself, about which all people must agree as soon as they understand it. You are a dear, splendid fellow, while I am an ass for having tormented you so much by my last letter. Forgive me! I won't do it again as long as I live. Fischer also should recover from his shock! But now don't make a blunder with my manuscript by considering it also as some sort of bridge which I am about to burn. Let it be burned; what must be, must be—for Gutzkow says, 'And still it moves!' From the shore I have left there is no fresh breeze to fill my sails, only the farts of Lüttichau and Winkler: but I'll sail no further with such winds.

"One thing more: Write me, all of you, with greatest care, and separately if possible, about the last affair; it's *on account of my wife*: she is not so impervious to this subject as I am.

"Now God protect you! (Which doesn't mean *Kaskel* protect you!) Don't worry, and do what you can when occasion offers, without too much trouble! Forgive me, and love me as dearly as I do you.

"Your
RICHARD W."

As his first winter in Zürich ran its course, Wagner's situation had not improved. Liszt still urged him to compromise with Paris, and Minna gave him no peace on the subject. He agreed to compose an opera on a French text, and

Wieland der Schmied was his choice. But the more he thought about it, the more he realized that *Wieland* could not conceivably be transformed into a French commodity, nor himself into a purveyor of music *à la* Meyerbeer, which was the formula for success at the Opéra just then. He made his third visit to Paris on January 29, 1850, and the capital had never seemed more alien to him. He attended a performance of *Le Prophète,* which was bringing its composer a fortune, and came away with the disheartening realization that the noisy pretensions and simpering roulades of Meyerbeer stood for a theatrical point of view which he had outgrown and left behind far back in Magdeburg and Riga.

A letter to Liszt at this time is interesting as showing his discontented state of mind, while he is careful to minimize before his friend his disgust with Paris, where he had recently arrived. His truer feelings on the subject are to be found in letters in the same month to others with whom he is more candid. He tells Sulzer that he is "heartily sick" of Paris, which to him means nothing but "constraint and burden"; to Uhlig he calls it a place of "art wallowings"; and to Minna, a "hell from which all I wish for is deliverance."

But he writes to Liszt from Paris, February 6, 1850 (197): [9]

"MY EXCELLENT FRIEND!

"The strong excitements and emotional agitation of the past year and the consequences of rheumatic sufferings, to which I am exposed in the winter, for some time put me in a state of utmost exhaustion of the nerves, making me unable to work and imposing absolute rest as a duty upon me. In that state I received your last letter. You may judge its indescribably refreshing effect upon me when I simply tell you that in spite of my indisposition I couldn't hold out in Zürich any longer but hastily set out forthwith for Paris a week ago, even without waiting for word from Belloni.[10] At the moment when you wrote to me you must have felt healthy and well, in order to convey to a friend such a refreshing and amiably encouraging inspiration. Judge once more its influence on me, the poor feeble devil whom you gave such a quick lift forward! A thousand thanks!

"Certainly the journey inflicted a new exhaustion on me: Paris itself is not exactly the place for rest, and on top of this it was very hard to find a lodging as peaceable as possible, and so I feel worn out after all the running around, etc.; but I hope gradually to recover, now that everything is well settled: the first fruit of my hopes is this letter to you. I expected to find Belloni back here already, on account of a letter of December in which he makes known his intended return to Paris by the 15th of January. As I have now found out, at this time he went to Weimar—luckily, however, I can put up with his temporary absence more

[9] This letter has appeared in a German magazine, and in a French translation by Marcel Herwegh ("*Au Banquet des Dieux*").

[10] Belloni, Liszt's former secretary, who was supposed to further Wagner's cause in Paris, did not put in an appearance until March. This was no deprivation to Wagner, who was content to follow up opportunities—or avoid them—in his own way.

easily now, because before tackling our business I have to finish a little work which I hadn't been able to complete before. The somewhat detailed plan of the opera plot which G. Vaez is to work out for me is in my possession, but first I have to get it translated into French; by the time Belloni has returned I believe the work will be ready. The subject of the poem is *Wieland the Smith*. Remember me cordially to our dear friend Wolff and get from him the German hero's tale of the same name—worked over as an epic by Simrock. By reading this you certainly won't get the right notion of my dramatization of that subject, but all the same you will learn the general character of the topic. Wieland, the free artist, magic blacksmith with cut foot tendons, invents and forges wings for himself on which he flies away from his misery. The exact nature of my intentions I shall meanwhile outline as follows: There is nothing I can promise and nothing that stands within my power but to write texts and compose music. Since I know that this doesn't suffice for a success in Paris, I would drop my aspirations for such, unless someone should be there who would achieve for me what I can't do myself. Thanks to your thoughtful care I found that someone through you in Belloni. We two will form a team and steer together toward a success from which I shall gladly allot to him any share he wishes. This, quite simply, is how the matter stands, and I believe you will say 'Yes' to it.

"I never would stay in Paris any longer than is absolutely necessary for my purposes; so I made my residence in Zürich. The delights of my stay there and some excellent friends I made induced me to do this. I left my wife there with her sister, dog, and parrot in our little household. As soon as everything has advanced so far that I can compose the opera sketch, I shall do it in the fresh Alpine air."

It is hard to believe that Wagner really had any such intention. There is a great deal more of his repeated reference at just this point to his state of "nervous exhaustion." This condition is not hard to account for. He was moved to plunge into his Norse epic, but a net of petty circumstances, bills, commissions, obligations, kept him from doing so. He was headed in a wrong direction not of his own choosing, and he had reached an impasse. His progress had once before been impeded, when the offender was the deadening bureaucracy of the Dresden Court Theater. He had reacted by throwing caution to the winds and, in a headlong impulse, breaking free in the first way that offered. Now he had a similar impulse to burst all fetters of obligation and flee to a fresh world where his creative life would be quite unimpeded.

❧ XVIII ❦

THE INVOLVEMENT WITH
JESSIE LAUSSOT

(1850)

It was in the spring of 1850 that Wagner was moved to break the bonds of an environment which seemed to restrict his creative development at every hand, and to take flight eastward to strange parts and freedom. A friendship with a young English lady at this moment ripened by way of artistic sympathy into passionate interest. She planned to join him in his flight, and might have done so had not her husband and her mother intervened at the last moment.

This episode remained for many years unknown to the world at large. Mrs. Burrell evidently got wind of it by 1887, and located in Florence the lady involved. Her name, by a subsequent marriage, was Hillebrand. A letter brought this reply (in English):

219
> "The Honble
> "Mrs. Burrell
> "Hotel Bellevue
> "Munich
> "Bavière

> "From: 30 Lung' Arno Nuovo
> "Florence
> "7 January 1888

"MADAM,

"I have duly received your letter, and although I am quite at a loss to understand what interest it can have for you, as a stranger to the persons concerned, to know the names of those to whom allusion is made in the passage you quote, I do not like to commit so gross a breach of courtesy towards one of my own sex and country as to leave your note unanswered.

"As you will, no doubt, have yourself observed, it is not to *one* person alone, but to *several* to whom Wagner thus expressed his recognition of their friendship at a time when he stood greatly in need of it. As the great German composer moreover did not think fit at the time to allude more pointedly to those to whom he addressed the passage, and as he never did so afterwards, as moreover some of them are still alive, you will, I trust, excuse me, if I do not divulge the names which are well known to me as well as the persons to whom they belonged and still belong.

"I remain, Madam, with sincere sympathy with your admiration for the works of the great genius,

"Yrs. truly,

JESSIE HILLEBRAND"

We cannot know what clue had led Mrs. Burrell in 1888 to the lady who still held (and kept to herself) recollections of her near elopement with Wagner, thirty-eight years before, as Jessie Laussot. The "passage" referred to, which alone could have been the excuse for Mrs. Burrell's approach, was evidently Wagner's reference to this crisis in his *Communication to My Friends* of 1851. Having there spoken of his "illness, racking all my nerves," in Paris in 1850, which forced him to contemplate an escape into "God knows what wild unknown world," he adds: "But in this extremity, my truest friends took hold of me; with a hand of infinitely tender love, they led my footsteps back. Thanks be to those who alone know of whom I speak!" Wagner was plainly referring to Frau Julie Ritter and Franz Liszt. But Mrs. Burrell had reason to suppose that Mrs. Hillebrand, once Frau Laussot, was another of those who alone knew of whom he spoke.

Few people could have known in 1888 of any intimacy between Jessie Laussot and Wagner. The first real public disclosure was to come four years later in 1892, when Ferdinand Praeger gave out a completely jumbled version. He claimed to have had the "Bordeaux story," as he called it, from Wagner: "the wife of a friend, Mrs. H————, having followed Wagner to the south, called on him at his hotel, and throwing herself at his feet passionately told of her affection. Wagner's action in the matter was to telegraph to the husband to come and take his wife home" (*Wagner as I knew him*, p. 196). The truth, of course, was that he did not meet the husband first, that Jessie did not follow Wagner south, but lived there with her family and invited him there. Wagner did not telegraph, but wrote to the husband from Paris, announcing his own journey south. The irony of Praeger's story that Wagner quietly put the wife back where she belonged will be apparent.

The leakage from that point was for many years a trickle. Glasenapp, in the first edition of his biography (1876) had merely mentioned Bordeaux as a place visited by Wagner at the time. In his expanded edition of 1896 (Vol. III, p. 40), he spoke of a lady admirer (unnamed) of his works, a friend of Julie Ritter, who had wished to join her in a contribution, who invited him to visit her in Bordeaux, where an understanding for continuing payments might have been reached had not "an unexpected obstacle on which it is not for us to dwell" spoiled the plan. Houston Stewart Chamberlain, in his life of Wagner which appeared in the same year, made no mention of Bordeaux, but listed among Wagner's benefactors a "Madame Laussot, personally unknown to the *Meister.*" If this phrase was a herring, it was certainly a clumsy one. Ellis, preparing his English translation of Glasenapp in 1900, chafed under censorship and surmised that "perhaps the veil of this mystery can never be completely lifted, in the absence of letters so private that they are never likely to be given to the world." The veil was lifted by the publication of *My Life* in 1911. But even after Wagner had laid forth his story, the ludicrous phrase appeared in the English translation of Chamberlain's book in 1915: Jessie Laussot, whose husband had threatened to shoot Wagner, was "personally unknown" to him.

Mrs. Burrell, not discouraged by the uncommunicativeness of Mrs. Hillebrand, was to acquire, even before Praeger's bit of twisted gossip, not only *My Life,* with its revelations, but a very considerable store of documents on this very subject from Natalie.

Evidence appearing since *My Life,* Wagner's letters to Julie Ritter (1920), and now the Burrell Collection, differs from the account in *My Life* principally in emphasis: in his autobiography Wagner tends to minimize the whole affair by offhand treatment. It was Jessie, he writes, who first suggested going with him to the Orient—an idea which he at first received with doubts on her account. This we cannot disprove: all we know is that Wagner very definitely included her at an early point in his plans. That he was infatuated beyond sober reason is shown by his letters (published in 1920) to Frau Julie Ritter on the subject, written in the moment of his sharp disappointment and wounded pride when Jessie turned away from him.

The Burrell Collection does not fundamentally change this picture. It fills gaps in the sequence of events, reveals for the first time letters of Jessie and her mother, and shows Wagner going through the difficult ordeal of breaking with his wife with something short of candor as to his real intentions, utilizing the ever good-natured Kietz to help him elude the pursuing Minna, and trying to justify the unjustifiable.

The letter from Wagner to Liszt from which quotation was made in the last chapter (197: Paris, February 6, 1850) brings up the first mention of Jessie Laussot:

"Now I have to report to you about a beautiful occurrence which has recently delighted me: In Dresden, at the time of the performance of my operas, there lived a young Englishwoman, who is now married to a merchant in Bordeaux. I hardly knew her at that time. Recently I was notified by a third person in a delicate fashion that Frau Laussot in Bordeaux is setting aside for me a not inconsiderable sum of money, which is to be delivered to me in five months and serves the purpose of securing me against any contingencies, against any hazards, provided I am content with a modest way of life.

"You know, dear Liszt, I have a few friends only; you also know, on the other hand, that each of those *few friends* is devoted and energetic. Recognize this lady as your sister and as your own kind [*Gleichgesinnte*].

"From a friendly Dresden family [1] I have also received so much money that I can take care of my house and provide my wife with necessities until the time when I may expect sizable sums from Bordeaux."

Jessie Laussot (at that time still Jessie Taylor) had moved into Wagner's orbit as one of his many female adorers, a friend of Frau Julie Ritter and her son Karl in Dresden, where she had attended the first performance of *Tannhäuser*. She had since married Eugène Laussot, a Bordeaux dealer in wines, unhappily according to Wagner, and called upon the composer together with Karl in 1848, when she would have been nineteen. After Wagner's political troubles, during which time she had settled in Bordeaux, Jessie heard that Wagner was hampered in his creative plans by the lack of money and delicately offered to join Frau Ritter in providing him with a yearly 3,000 francs. She accordingly wrote to Wagner at the end of 1849, and to his wife at Zürich (as 213 reveals). The prospect of a living income, intended to free him from the bonds of Paris promises and make possible his higher aims, was of course immensely welcome to Wagner, who always favored the combination of spiritual and financial support. Perhaps in response to Jessie's request, he had Kietz do a portrait (200) which he sent to her in Bordeaux, where she lived with her husband and her mother. This gift brought the following acknowledgment to the artist: [2]

"MOST HONORED SIR!

"Through our friend I received the portrait which you so kindly sent me. Through him, honored sir, you will receive these lines which are intended to give you an idea, even if it is a very weak one, of the happiness which I felt when this picture was brought to me. Wagner himself will tell you best how very happy you have made me with this courtesy, with this kind proof of your friendship.

"That the joy of owning a picture so beautifully conceived and executed cannot be greater than the happiness of knowing that he has so sincere a friend in you—this I need hardly tell you. But what today I write so unsatisfactorily I hope to be able to express to you somewhat better after this summer, when, as is my intention, I shall go to Paris and meet there a friend of Wagner about whom I've already heard much and who, I know, is also interested in me.

"In this hope and with high esteem for you, honored sir, I remain,
"Yours,
JESSIE LAUSSOT"

[1] Frau Julie Ritter.
[2] 201 (Bordeaux, March 6, 1850).

The Laussots invited Wagner to visit them at Bordeaux; and Wagner, on the eve of leaving Paris, wrote to Minna in Zürich (March 13), and told her of his visit, taking a cajoling tone. He knew this news would not be welcome. He had pictured Jessie to her as a godsend and benefactress. Minna had bitterly resented accepting charity from a strange Englishwoman and her rich mother. She may well have scented a romantic attachment, for Jessie had every possible advantage over her. She had youth and beauty. She gave Wagner the support he most craved—unquestioning sympathy and encouragement for "impractical" musical plans. Minna, on the other hand, had, since his flight from Dresden the year before, shown resentment over everything he did. She had reproached him for throwing away his post as *Kapellmeister,* for pamphleteering when he should have stuck to his music, and she had hurried him off to Paris to become once more a money-earning musician. These attitudes meant a lack of faith in his higher aims, and such a lack of faith was always to Wagner the last unpardonable breach. Wagner had contemplated returning to Zürich and his beloved Alps to compose his *Siegfried.* But Minna's baneful and disapproving presence would have encroached upon his mood.

In Bordeaux, Wagner found a new and delightful environment where recriminations did not exist and where his dreams for the future were eagerly devoured. Jessie was well educated and mentally eager. She spoke German fluently, so we are told in *My Life,* and was an excellent musician—when she didn't try to sing. At the piano she had the skill and good taste to choose Beethoven's *Hammerklavier* Sonata, if not the comprehension to play it as it should be played. When she was not playing for him, she was listening with rapt attention to his creative plans. She preferred *Wieland* to *Siegfried* because she visualized herself as Wieland's bride, Swanhilde, who was far more appealing than the ill fated Gutrune. But all this was the sort of thing Wagner's self-confidence subsisted on. It was enough that she had the intelligence to follow and the romantic impulse to believe in him. When Wagner, after a visit of eighteen days, left Bordeaux, Jessie wrote to Minna in Zürich: [3]

"HONORED LADY!

"Together with the dear letter which you wrote me in answer to mine, I have also received the news, so welcome to us, that your husband intended to grant our request and pay us a visit, and it was my intention to wait for his arrival in Bordeaux in order to write to you and give you news about him at the same time! But during his visit I did not get a chance to write four coherent lines and finally had to give it up with the intention of writing to you about us as soon as he had left and of thanking you for your dear letter and for the sincerity with which you approached me. Yes, dear lady, we admirers of your husband are especially concerned that he should live and write in complete accord with the inspiration of his soul and that he should seek to work toward

[3] 202 (Bordeaux, April 7, 1850).

his great goal unhampered by any outside considerations. We are prepared to do everything in order to attain this goal; let me assure you of this with all my heart, dear lady.

"The fact that your husband cannot at this unfavorable time attain the success which all of us would have wished for him is a sad truth which we must recognize more clearly every day and which is for us as distressing a realization as it could possibly be. May we only become convinced that our love and admiration can offer him some consolation, a small compensation for everything—then we shall be happy and content in this conviction. We wish to console you too, dear lady, and may you try to forget the suffering which you have so far borne so steadfastly—God grant it.

"Herr Wagner has brought us the greatest happiness with his visit; I also think that his stay here was not a disadvantage to him; we have always had the best weather, and he will I hope retain a happy remembrance of his visit.

"I would have gladly had you, honored lady, here with me also, I would have liked so much to meet you; but I hope that we shall become acquainted at some later date. I hear from the Ritter family that Karl went to Zürich in the expectation of meeting Herr Wagner there; should he already have arrived, as I suspect, I ask you, honored lady, please to give him the enclosed letter. Your husband will probably have to spend a few days in Paris, but you'll soon see him again and hear from him how things are with us in Bordeaux. May you, distant though you are, sometimes think kindly

of your sincere friend

JESSIE LAUSSOT"

Across the bottom of this letter Minna has scrawled in pencil, perhaps at some later date, "False, treacherous creature." [4] The envelope, which bears no postmark and was evidently an enclosure, has been roughly torn open.

Wagner divulged to Jessie a plan to make a clear break with the routine, the discouragements, the endless entanglements of Europe, and take a ship for Greece, or farther east—a new world and freedom. Jessie hinted her willingness (if *My Life* tells the truth) to throw in her fate with his, but they parted with no definite understanding. Back in Paris, he pondered in solitude whether to take the rash and possibly ruinous step, or to go on in the familiar hated treadmill. The evidence is plain enough that he was only too ready to ride on the more alluring prospect.

His first step was the disagreeable one of breaking with Minna, which he did in a letter of April 16, here published for the first time (204). The letter was preceded by one to Uhlig, on April 15 (not in the published Uhlig collection), in which he rehearsed his arguments for the benefit of his friend. He followed the letter to Minna with another on the following day, in which he reproached

---

[4] "*O falsches, verrätherisches Geschöpf.*" The cataloguers' mistranslation of *verrätherisches* as "devastating" has been widely quoted.

her for addressing him by the formal *Sie,* himself using the intimate *du* to heap coals of fire on her head. This letter is published in the collected letters "to Minna," without explanation of Wagner's sudden about-face from loving solicitude to resigned aloofness. The letter in the Burrell Collection, like the one the day following, is inscribed "Paris"; but this was a piece of deception, as Wagner betrays in *My Life,* where he writes that he had just found himself a "modest hiding place in the suburb of Montmorency."

Wagner refers to this letter in his autobiography: "I . . . wrote her a long and detailed letter in which I kindly, but at the same time frankly, retraced the whole of our life together, and explained that I was fully determined to set her free from any immediate participation in my fate, as I felt quite incapable of so arranging it as to meet with her approval. I promised her the half of whatever means I should have at my disposal now or in the future, and told her she must accept this arrangement with a good grace, because the occasion had now arisen to take that step of parting from me which, on our first meeting again in Switzerland, she had declared herself ready to do. I ended my letter without bidding her a final farewell [!]."

Wagner proceeded with devastating logic to prove, by her own words of past reproach, that they were unsuited and should part: [5]

"If I can no longer be anything but unhappy in our life together, then I ask you, are you happy in it? No! Certainly not! And perhaps you are much more unhappy even than I am, for with all my suffering, with all my self-consuming, I have within myself a great, transcending faith, the faith in the truth and splendor of the cause for which I suffer and fight. You, poor woman, share no such faith. I am completely strange to you; you see only angles and deformities in me; you see in me only that which is inexplicable to you, and nowhere do you find compensation for the suffering I cause you. You cling to the peacefulness and permanence of existing conditions—I must break them to satisfy my inner being; you are capable of sacrificing everything in order to 'have a respected position in the community [']'', which I despise and with which I don't want to have anything to do; you cling with all your heart to property, to home, household, hearth—I leave all that so that I can be an individual [*Mensch*]. You think only of the past, with nostalgia and yearning—I give that up and think only of the future. All your wishes are directed toward conformity with the old, toward giving in and submitting, toward reestablishing—I have broken with everything old and fight it with all my strength. You cling to people, I to causes; you to certain human beings, I to humanity. Thus there is only disagreement between us, irreconcilable disagreement; thus we can only irritate each other without bringing each other any happiness; and perhaps you are the more unhappy—for I understand you well enough, but you don't understand me! Could it satisfy you if I were willing to force myself to a life together in which I would

[5] 204 (Paris [*sic*], April 16, 1850).

always conceal myself from you, deceive you about my true nature, in short, in which I would seek to lie to you about myself? Certainly not! For you are above all an *honorable* woman, a woman who wants to belong to her husband completely, just as she wants her husband to belong to her completely! Do you believe that I had wanted to reproach you with all I've said in this letter? Oh, no! I merely wanted to defend myself against reproaches. Everything, what and how you act and think, is completely correct and consistent with your whole nature: you are a real woman, a woman whom I advise every one fully to respect, a woman who would have made thousands happy, who even today would make every one who thinks like her happy, but who must be correspondingly unhappy with me since her way of thinking is completely different from mine. With me you are unhappy, you consume yourself, you see yourself perpetually exposed to suffering the cause of which lies in a temperament which is alien to you—namely, mine; thus you are and will remain unsatisfied, and if I were to keep a last remnant of happiness before you by deceit, that would sap my strength more every day. Here there is only one cure:

"*To live apart!*

"Just because we were united and have lived together so long and under such varied vicissitudes, should we also see our later years waste away as we have seen our youth fade? Now that after fifteen years we understand each other *less* than ever and are, according to our innermost being, strangers to each other, should we let the misunderstanding continue to rankle to our dying day, to our mutual, increasing misery? I know—unfortunately! unfortunately!—that I *cannot* make you happy by living with you! More than ever I feel the need to be able to devote myself undisturbed to my views and my beliefs in order, if need be, to take *action* accordingly: I can thrive only in the company of kindred souls. How terribly harsh would I seem to you, you—whom I don't even want to condemn for being what you are? I recognize your virtues, your splendid qualities in the fullest measure and can therefore only hope not to have to torture and torment you any longer. You have often said to me, 'When you are this way or that, or do thus or so, I hate you!' Dear Minna! Why hate me? If we remember each other in the spirit in which we understood and loved each other, we'll be able to love each other even after the separation. For the sake of the love which still remains between us I say: *Let us remain separated!*

"Thus I actually merely confirm that with which you have often threatened me, which you often frankly longed for, half carried out even, and recently have again had in mind. Thus I am determined that I for my part shall make no further attempt to hold you by deceptions—deceptions which only aggravate our life together. I now say to you: 'Do what you have already wanted to do repeatedly, and have threatened me with doing at every opportunity'—only just recently when you wrote me: 'If I must move again by the end of summer, I would rather leave today.' I could *not* possibly spend next winter in Zürich; the climate is definitely harmful to my nervous system: I would have had to ask you to leave Zürich with me. This way I merely say to you—Carry out your threat—it will be better for you and me! Let us sever our fate—forget me the way I *now* am and be happy without me! For *with* me you cannot possibly be happy any more!

"But while I say this quietly and as a sensible human being, I feel at the same time the tremendous grief that is involved when I take leave of all my old, familiar world! What you have often and violently spoken of, separation, I now confirm after a long and terrible inward struggle: I do not say it thoughtlessly, but in the final and firm conviction *that it must be so* and that it *can no longer be anything else!* When I say to you: 'Yes! Let us separate!' I mean that we will not see each other again, that I part with everything I have owned and all that habit has made dear and precious to me: neither dog nor bird do I want to see again, no keepsake do I want preserved. Whatever else has belonged to us does not belong to me: it is yours; dispose of it as you see fit: I don't even want to see anything of my writings. Leave Zürich or stay! Alas, I even have to give up my Zürich friends. Where I am going I do not know! Don't inquire about me! But I shall always do everything to find out whether you are well.

"So then I have only *one* last request to make of you. It is the most important one I can make in these difficult circumstances. Minna! Minna! Dear Minna! Grant me this request or you will make me boundlessly unhappy! Whatever you choose to do, wherever you go, just do this one thing! I beg you, I entreat you fervently to do it, as a token that you still love me a little tiny bit: *Of the yearly allowance allotted to me take half in support of your pitiful existence!* It is *earned,* believe me; it is *earned*; you don't have to be ashamed of it! I could prove to you that the half which would go to you will be the equivalent of an obligation I have assumed. I know your great pride, your strong feeling of independence! Oh, don't use it against me! Overcome your resistance just this one more time! Just see! You will drive me crazy and surely hasten my death if you refuse me this last request, if you leave me with the terrible idea that the poor woman who has sacrificed her youth, everything to me—in vain—is destitute or serves strange people! I implore you, by all that is holy to you, grant me this request! Permit me for the time being to send your poor good mother in Dresden 100 thaler quarterly: it shall start with the 1st of July! Some day, when your parents die, I shall always send it to you directly or any other way you wish! With the other half I shall, in the greatest seclusion, get along so much the better since I can easily earn something here and there. I can almost assume, dear Minna, that you'll grant me this last, most sacred request! I assume it, as the last token of love you have to send me. Baumgartner, to whom I am turning in this matter, will get you what you need till the 1st of July! The grand piano is yours! Ten—earned—louis d'or also will be sent you by Wigand from Leipzig.

"After this last request, just a final piece of advice, although you might no longer be inclined to accept advice from me. If you want to avoid sensation, conceal from our more superficial acquaintances in Zürich what has happened between us, tell them, when you leave, that your departure from Zürich is because of a message from me according to which I was to remain in Paris and you were to follow me. In this way you will best avoid all sensation. If you go to Dresden, you will merely have to hold to your old story when speaking to your friends; since I no longer have an established home and don't want to write an opera for Paris either, you are carrying out your intention and are for the moment living—by your own choice—in the enjoyment of your friendships there which you actually do desire—separated from me.

"And if you should say: *Divorce?* Why that? Why get a divorce? Even though we can no longer *live* together, we can still belong to each other before the world. Before the world you will always remain my wife, as long as you wish. Only when you should not want it this way any more, when our complete divorce could be of use to you—when you perhaps may find a man who would be more capable than I of making you happy—only then would our divorce make any sense; only then would I find even this last awful and painful resort necessary.

"O Minna! Minna! Separated from you I am separated from a whole world! From a world in which I suffered, in which I received hardly any consideration and appreciation for my suffering, but which had become familiar, dear, and cherished to me. Yes, I feel it! He who wants to follow his inner call completely must be endowed with iron courage, for he must make terrible sacrifices: whether I have this courage I do not yet know, I only know that I must no longer hesitate to break off a relationship openly and honestly in which both of us fellow sufferers have long ceased to belong to each other, in which we were bound one to the other artificially, to our mutual consuming torture. May my courage not forsake me! But may you also gain the courage, without scolding me, without hating me, to turn toward a new life in which you can still enjoy many a happy hour, if you only have the courage! Farewell! Farewell! My wife! My old, dear companion in misfortune! Oh, if you could only have shared the joys which I draw from *my great faith,* how happy you would have been with me despite all privation! It was not granted to me to reward you in this way! May I now succeed in this way—through the separation—in reconciling you to your life, in bringing you peace and comfort! Farewell! Farewell! For two weeks I have wept a thousand bitter tears over this distressing separation! But it must be! Every hesitation would be fatal weakness! Fatal for you and me! Farewell! Farewell! My good Minna! Farewell! Think only of the happiest hours we spent together; then you will be happy in remembering me, just as I will think of you only with nostalgia and love after this separation! Farewell! Farewell! [6] For the last time I kiss you fervently.

"Your

RICHARD W."

Minna was thoroughly alarmed by this letter. She was distressingly aware of the possibility that Wagner himself had broached: she might be reduced to going into domestic service. At forty, any resumption of her career as *erste Liebhaberin* on the stage was more than doubtful. Her suspicions of Jessie as a rival must now have grown into a virtual certainty. Yet Wagner, "frank" about her past shortcomings, was anything but frank about his immediate intentions. We cannot know whether he told the Ritters that Jessie was included in his plan to flee Europe; but he kept Minna, Uhlig, and Kietz dark on this point. Minna may have scented a woman behind his devastating letter of "farewell." In desperation she turned to Jakob Sulzer and Wilhelm Baumgartner, Wagner's cronies and intellectual companions in Zürich, and obtained their written plea for his return to Zürich and his old life there; armed with this letter, she hurried to Paris. Since Minna retained the letter (why Natalie made a copy of it for Mrs. Burrell is a puzzle), the supposition is that, not finding Wagner, Minna never delivered it to him.[7]

"DEAR FRIEND:

"You can easily imagine what sad hours your last message has caused your wife and us. When you read these lines, you will already know that nothing could have prevented your heroic wife from hearing the confirmation of your fateful decision from your own mouth. Nobody except your wife and we have learned about your intention which—only remember all your preceding letters —seems to be *without* psychological motivation, and to have been caused by an unfortunate misunderstanding. For this very reason, and only for the sake of you and your own future, we beseech you: examine yourself again without any prejudice, examine the reasons of your recent decision before establishing them irrevocably. A third person, though influenced by the warmest sympathy, could only cause new trouble by interfering in such circumstances. Therefore we will not venture to influence your final decision by arguing with you, much as we are moved to do so. However, you will certainly consider one request of proven friends: you should take the manly resolution not to oppose the arguments of your wife by an unalterable decision, and therefore to listen to her favorably. Of course we were looking forward to your coming to your new home at Zürich which we have already christened 'Villa Rienzi' and which certainly would satisfy all your wishes. There, we hoped, you would again grant us many eve-

[6] But note Wagner's curious remark in *My Life*: "I ended my letter without bidding her a final farewell."

[7] 205 A (Zürich, April 21, 1850).

nings similar to those which, though spent under less favorable conditions, count among the most beautiful of our lives. However, this hope is not the motive of our request but solely the ardent desire that you yourself may not be at enmity with your own destiny, already laid down in letters of fire, nor obstruct your own well-being. In any case, whatsoever your decision may be, never forget that you have friends in Zürich, the most faithful you could ever find.

WILH BAUMGARTNER
J. SULZER"

Natalie has added at the end: "It was with this letter that Minna's friends sent her to Paris, where Richard was supposed to be. Unfortunately she did not find him, despite all her searching with the help of Kietz, and she returned to Zürich sad and inconsolable."

Minna's state of mind at this point is described by Natalie in a communication to Mrs. Burrell (206: April 24, 1893). As usual, her version must be somewhat discounted, for she uses all the emotional stops: "Minna, frightened to death, went at once to Paris to find Richard. On one hand she feared that Richard had fallen seriously ill and had written this fateful letter to her in a delirious state of mind. On the other hand, if by some chance this were not the case, she wanted to hear this terrible decision from his own mouth, in order to learn from himself his bitterly painful intentions. I remember still as though it were today what Minna suffered after having read these unhappy lines, how she broke down and fainted, overcome by her all too great grief and heartbreak. In her unspeakable misery and heartbreak, in her persistent fear that Richard might be seized by a sudden mortal fever, she could not grasp the terrible horror. She was hardly able to walk to the coach station and travel to Paris."

When Wagner got wind of her journey he returned to Paris, as a safer hiding place, and turned to the long-suffering Kietz to protect him from being found. There are two notes, similar in content. One was posted and seemingly went astray. The other was delivered by messenger.

203 D *(Paris, April 25, 1850)*

"DEAR FRIEND:

"If letters *addressed to me* should be delivered to you, please be so kind as to keep them for the time being. Later on I will write and tell you where to forward them. For good reasons let it right now be my secret where I am going. I am retiring into solitude!

"Farewell!   "Your

RICHARD WAGNER"

The letter, addressed to Kietz in the Faubourg Saint-Germain, is post-marked and on the envelope is written "Delivered by mistake 12 . . . R. 8,"

203 E *(Paris, April 25, 1850)*

"DEAR FRIEND:

"If in the meantime letters addressed to me should be delivered to you, be so kind as to receive and keep them for the time being. Later on I will write and tell you where they should be forwarded.

"Where I am going must still remain a secret for you as well as for every one of my friends. I am retiring into solitude in order quietly to get comfort and healing for my serious wounds. Let me be alone—this is my request to all of you. Soon you will know about the serious crisis of my life which of necessity I have to face now.

"Farewell! Don't be angry with me for my deception!

"Your

RICHARD WAGNER

"The messenger is paid."

[In the handwriting of Mrs. Burrell:]

"E. B. Kietz must have sent this to Minna. I bought it from Natalie."

Wagner writes in *My Life*: "I summoned Kietz to my hotel and instructed him to tell my wife, who had already been trying to gain admittance to him, that he knew nothing of me except that I had left Paris. The poor fellow, who felt as much pity for Minna as for me, was so utterly bewildered on this occasion that he declared he felt as though he were the axis upon which all the misery in the world turned." That night Wagner left Paris, took a train to Geneva, and "retired" to Villeneuve, at the other end of the lake. He decided to take a boat for Malta, which was to sail from Marseilles on May 7. On May 4 he wrote similar letters of farewell to his wife and to Kietz, telling of his trip, but not mentioning Jessie. He explains to each that means have been placed at his disposal from London—from "an eminent English lawyer," he tells Minna. Of course the lawyer is a fiction. It would be interesting to know how he expected to receive funds from the mother of the married daughter with whom he was about to depart. The letter to Minna is published in the correspondence as translated by W. Ashton Ellis. The bewildered translator, not knowing what was afoot, can make nothing of the letters, and detects (in true Ellisonian lingo) "transitory signs of slight mental unhingement." The letter to Kietz, of which Kietz belatedly sent Minna a faithful copy (210) on May 27, is in the Burrell Collection.[8]

"DEAR FRIEND!

"You must have been surprised to see me suddenly disappear from Montmorency and Paris. This was connected with the most decisive catastrophe of

---

[8] 207 A (Geneva, May 4, 1850).

my life. Know then that I'm leaving modern Europe for some time to visit Greece and the Orient. This is a desire I've cherished for a long time: the means with which to realize this desire have now been put at my disposal from London in a surprisingly gratifying manner. The only distressing thing for me was that it involved a temporary separation from my wife and a personal leave-taking from her. I therefore wrote to her in Zürich some time ago to let me leave without saying goodbye. It would also have been painful for me to discuss this matter with all of you, for reasons which I must prefer to keep from you even now. It will probably be very difficult for my wife—to whom I'm going to write to Zürich about it again today—to approve my decision: that's why I carried it out as soon as I had made it.

"It will be hard for you to understand my innermost reluctance to continue in our modern artistic life; still less will you understand why I'm completely withdrawing from Germany and France for the time being. So I must go my way alone.

"I'm in a hurry because I've just found out that the boat on which I want to go first to Malta—in order to continue my trip to Greece from there—leaves Marseilles early next week, so I'm going there today. Perhaps I would have written you more fully later on, but now I felt pressed to ask you to forward the letters which might come for me at your address to *general delivery in Marseilles* at once. I suppose I'll hardly be able to wait for them there, for the boat is scheduled to sail on the 7th—but in this case I'll leave word with the post office as to how they should be forwarded to me: anyhow, I don't expect much of importance.

"Farewell, then, old friend! Give my best regards to Anders and my other friends. I *had* to undertake something special in order to cure myself in every respect. I hope that when I return I'll find you healthy and well, and that things will be better in our homeland. I'll see that you hear from me now and then! Farewell! and remain faithful to

"Your

RICHARD W."

In the usual course of things, Minna's answer to Wagner's farewell would have been lost. It has been preserved in the form of her own rough draft, acquired by Mrs. Burrell through Natalie. It is unquestionably a draft—full of corrections and often scarcely legible. Whether she sent the letter according to her draft, we cannot know. The letter as it stands is the more pitiable in that Minna spoils her case by harping once more upon the very points in which she has failed to understand and support Wagner. This letter prompts the reflection that Wagner was wise in avoiding her in Paris and so forestalling a bitter and fruitless scene: [9]

[9] 208 (Zürich, May 8, 1850).

"Dear Richard!

"Even though your lines of the 16th of last month really did not deserve an answer, I feel induced, through your letter of the 4th of this month, which I received yesterday on my return from Paris, to wish you with all my heart on your coming birthday lasting *health* for your great and dangerous journey as well as the *best of good fortune* in all your *future undertakings*. After I had read your letter in which you definitely come out for a permanent separation, I was most deeply shocked and affected, and I could find some degree of composure, for the moment, only in the decision to see you *personally* in *Paris,* to hear those terrible words from your own lips. Experience has taught me that one says, *even writes,* something in a bad humor (and what haven't you said to me in the course of your life which would have been *impossible* for me to carry out); no one, therefore, could dissuade me from my plan. On Sunday the 21st I went to the mail-coach station accompanied by our most faithful friends Baumgartner and Sulzer, who were deeply grieved about your decision. I arrived in Paris on Wednesday afternoon; the first thing I did was, of course, to go to Frank[10] to find out your address, but I learned unfortunately that you had already been away several days, where they did not know; evidently you shrewdly kept your new whereabouts from your friends. I missed Kietz several times; finally I rode to Montmorenzi [*sic*] with him; there I heard once more that you had already left *Thursday.* If you have any trace of human feeling, through lengthy days I've wandered around in this fateful Paris . . . [illegible] you can imagine how I must have felt. I had made the long trip under the most terrible emotional stress and could not reach you. Richard, *now* I am more firmly than ever convinced that there is a Providence; otherwise I would have *this time* lost my mind through this hard blow which you gave me. I implore you, what is happening to you again *this* year? Nothing is holy to you; nothing more remained for you to destroy but our *marital happiness*; that's why you drag in the pettiest, most unjust, most contemptible accusations to guard yourself against reproaches; you talk yourself into things which *never* existed between us; finally you lie to yourself to gloss over the abominable way you are treating me again. I don't want to reproach you with this, but I must be granted the opportunity of defending myself from those insulting accusations against which every fiber in me revolts. Naturally I am not a good fighter, and in your *present* mood I face a *very dangerous opponent,* but I dare it anyhow, exerting my last remnant of strength and courage, and Heaven grant that you may recognize that I draw the courage (the truth) from the very depth of my oppressed soul. First you speak of the complete difference between our temperaments; I confess that I never even heard you say a single word about the fact that we did not suit each other until *now,* after we've already been married *for fourteen years.* You speak of the earliest scenes between us, frequent and ugly; you credit me with a good memory for things like that, and

[10] Albert Franck? See p. 304.

for that very reason I remember those which you repeatedly brought on when driven by a terrible jealousy; after these were overcome, *both* of us got along so well and lived together more happily than is often the case with married people. Only during the last *two years,* ever since you turned to miserable politics, which have destroyed many a happy relationship, have I been unwise enough not to avoid violent scenes with you; I just simply could not understand you *in this matter,* but one thing was clear in my simple mind—that nothing good would come to you from revolutionary activity. For that reason I was also against the association with Bakunin and Röckel, because I saw what a destructive influence they exercised on you, even on your health; for that I can be excused; only for *your sake* did I expose myself to the most violent scenes. But at least we have had no more in Zürich *itself.* Now you unjustly spread these over our entire past. I only wanted to preserve you for your art, which I admire and idolize; I wanted you to let the genius within you have free rein, not to oppose yourself by force; eventually the time would surely have come again when you could see your wishes fulfilled, but you should not have lost your patience right away. I saw with unspeakable anguish how you tore yourself away from the path of art, from Germany for which I so much wanted to preserve you, and I always had the painful feeling that you were also tearing yourself away from *me.* Never was I ashamed to say that I was following you to *Zürich,* I promised myself to say to *every one,* so as not to give your enemies any cause for new slanders, that I was going to join you in Paris. Just as little did it occur to me to *boast* that I suffered with you; I only mentioned that Paris misery in order to emphasize *your* accomplishment rather than my *duty,* to assist you to the best of my ability; and only he who never knew or did his duty could consider it a crime, as you do in your letter to me; still, *duty* only develops from *love,* especially with a *woman,* and I have always borne the *worst* with *love, courage,* even with a *smile.* How else would it have been possible? I never had any personal interest; I look back with righteousness on my behavior toward you. Finally you humiliate me to such a degree that you don't even shrink from writing that I made the mistake of *coming* to *Wagner in Zürich,* expecting to find there *the Wagner who was commissioned to write an opera for Paris;* I ask you now: What were you, after all, when I married you? I'm sorry to have to tell you: you were a poor neglected, unknown, *unemployed musical conductor*; and what prospects did I have to look forward to at that time?—O Richard, you are in a bad state of mind; you are hurting me terribly again!! The reason I did not keep you here was because I was actually not permitted to on the advice of the doctor; you grew more irritable, more violent every day, so that it became clear to me that a change of air, of occupation, would divert you from your moods. The date of the performance of your overture was approaching; Liszt sent the money; you yourself became restless; and now it is my fault that I drove you away for *lack of love.* Just remember how you found me in tears with Sulzer two weeks before your departure, and for so many days before that I swallowed nothing but tears during meals whenever I thought of your going away. I was miserable with longing for you every time; after the departure I was always embittered and angry with the restless Richard Wagner, for it was always *he* who would tear my husband from my side. Oh, my God, what else shall I tell you? Whenever I could find a little surprise which made you happy, how happy I was too! Everything that kept me busy and active in our home was intended only to please you, and from the earliest times I did *everything* out of *love*; even my *independence,* which I valued so highly, I gave up gladly to be *able* to *belong* to you *completely.* As for your spiritual development, I was happy in the knowledge that you were close to me while you created *all* the *beautiful* things, and *that* shows that I understood you *completely*; you always made me so happy, sang and played almost every new scene for me. But since *two years* ago, when you wanted to read me that essay in which you *slander* whole *races* which have been fundamentally helpful to you, I could not force myself to listen; and ever since that time you have borne a grudge against me, and punished me so severely for it that you never again let me hear anything from your works.

"In spite of all our petty frictions and political squabbles, you have not felt so unhappy nor so *lonely* in my company as you harshly claimed in your letter. Just remember all your earlier letters, especially the one you wrote to me four weeks ago from Bordeaux in which you still said *that you knew of no greater happiness than to live with me peacefully and undisturbed in the magnificent Alpine world.*[11] You withdrew from all company so that you could be at home; and no man does this if the grief, the sorrow which his wife causes him has eaten into him as you like to say. Just remember how once, when you could not avoid going out, you called to me as soon as you got back: Oh, my good Mienel, how glad I am to be back with you. Your verbal statements to your Zürich friends prove you a liar a hundred times. Why do you tell me, why do you write me *all* this when you've felt so boundlessly unhappy with me ever since our marriage? This seems unnatural to me. One single letter arouses you about our past, a letter which I wrote in the most humble and submissive mood. Your letter from Paris in which you told me that you did not want to write another opera reached me when I was sick: the apartment hunting, the approaching move had excited me so much that I could not sleep for many weeks and had to take medicine for four weeks. I considered your aversion to Paris as merely a momentary mood; I did not know how strongly I should urge you, and I freely admit that I hurt you, for which I ask forgiveness. As far as the untimely joke with the *Du* is concerned, you shouldn't even have mentioned it; and you should have realized from the expression *Hänschen* that it was nothing more than a stupid bit of foolishness on my part; but I likewise ask for forgiveness. If you want to fulfill my *last* request, then look back once more on our whole life peacefully and without bitterness, and you will find

[11] See published letter of March 17.

that I was right and that *both* of us were happy and content with each other.

"Now that I've summoned up enough strength to write you all this, seek what happiness you can in a *permanent separation* from me; I would have to reproach myself forever if I should interfere with your decision and press for a reconciliation with you. I gladly yielded to the desire of our friends to remain in Zürich a while longer, the more so since I would find it very difficult not to leave them, for their sympathy and love comforts me and cheers me in my sad position. But how long my stay here will be I cannot definitely say; just as little can I say *where* I'll then go to close my sorrowful life. If I go to Germany, I have no reason to keep our separation a secret from the world; I have done nothing for which it could condemn me. In Dresden I cannot live, I cannot see your relatives again! I don't want to share anything; I want to go into service or on the stage. Oh, it is terrible!

"Only the last reproach in your letter is justified—that I cling to certain human beings and things; but I cling only to *living* ones; I cannot, like you, leave my bird and my little dog without breaking my heart for grief; they shall accompany me everywhere as long as I live. I should like to send you many affectionate greetings, but I'm no longer able to write; the pen slips from my hand.

"Farewell! Farewell, dear Richard. Many kisses from

"Your
Minna"

[A postscript has been cut off at the end.]

If Minna believed rumors of an affair between Wagner and Jessie, which in a letter to be quoted shortly (211) she told Kietz she had heard, she could not have been sure enough of her information to confront Wagner with it in the foregoing letter. Nor did Jessie's mother know that anything of the sort was contemplated, or even that Wagner was estranged from Minna, as will be seen by the following letter to her, written in French: [12]

"Madam,

"I hope you will pardon me for addressing these lines to you, but since the subject I'm going to deal with interests you and me almost exclusively, I thought that it was preferable to talk to you directly about it. My daughter, Madame Laussot, has already expressed to you the keen sympathy which we felt for you, and our earnest desire to provide for your livelihood until the time when your husband can reach his goal without having to sacrifice his talent to making a living.

"Grieved because they were unable to accomplish in any way what they wanted to do, my children have turned to me, convinced that, being in a more favorable position than they, I could have this pleasure. Even though I don't

[12] 209 (Bordeaux, May 8, 1850).

pretend to be able to appreciate the works of your husband as much as they deserve, I was so infected with the enthusiasm of my daughter's description of them and so enchanted with the hope that his genius might be able to have free rein when no longer in fear of financial difficulties, that I was only too happy to see you accept my offer, that is to say, to have you receive the yearly sum of 2,500 francs quarterly and for two years, to start on the 1st of August of this year. My purpose today, then, is to ask you how you wish these payments made to you in the future, and whether it would be agreeable to you if I should deposit them to your credit every three months with a banker in your town who would make quarterly payments against a receipt from you. When, at the time of his departure, Mr. Wagner announced his intention of joining you promptly, I entrusted him with the amount for the first quarter, that is to say 625 francs, to be remitted to you.

"I don't know whether Mr. Wagner is already with you, but you would oblige me very much by telling me whether the delay in his return to Zürich leaves you in need of this sum, for in that case I'll have the money for the second quarter sent to you at once for your use while you await the arrival of the first sum.

"I hope, Madam, soon to receive a reply at the address below, and I shall be only too happy if the excellent companion of a man whose talent I admire would favor me with the agreeable name for which I hope—that of your friend

ANN TAYLOR

"26 Cours du 30 Juillet, Bordeaux"

Presumably as he was about to start for Marseilles, a thunderbolt fell upon the head of Wagner. In a letter from Bordeaux, Jessie informed him that she had told her mother of their plan.[13] Jessie's husband, learning of it, threatened to shoot Wagner at the first opportunity. As for Jessie, she refused to join him. Wagner was disappointed, annoyed at those who had blocked his plan. But his overmastering emotion was his grievance with Jessie herself. She had committed the unpardonable crime in failing to believe in him strongly enough to cast all caution to the winds and pledge her lot with his. And equally characteristic of him was his next step. He wrote to Eugène and hurried to Bordeaux to see him alone, and to point out with his usual unanswerable logic the husband's "error" in standing in the way of a wife who did not love him.[14] But Eugène's retort, according to My Life, was to carry the family away from Bordeaux before he arrived and to leave instructions for the police to warn the visitor away

[13] That this must have happened at the very last moment before Wagner's intended departure is proved by 209 (above), clearly dated and clearly postmarked "May 8," and showing the mother to be in complete ignorance of the plan.

[14] Wagner made a great point of not having informed Jessie of this second Bordeaux journey. When he related the story to Liszt "years afterwards" (he could not have brought himself to confide in him in anything less than years afterwards), Liszt remarked whimsically that his friend's great mistake was not to have told the lady herself.

from the town. Jessie later informed him through Karl Ritter that she had learned enough about him to be ready to drop his acquaintance entirely. Having thus lost the lady and forfeited the money, Wagner had no choice but to forget his venture into the unknown.

Able to speak freely at last, and hoping to cheer Minna out of her distress, Kietz wrote to her as follows: [15]

"DEAR AND KIND MADAME WAGNER:

"Really, it seems like a dream to me that we have once again strolled around Paris together. I remember this dream with great pleasure, and I wish I could dream it again as soon as possible. This, of course, is quite apart from the purpose of your trip and its failure. What left me such a fond memory is the joy I felt in myself; as for you, dear friend, you had not changed at all, however much you might protest against that, and as our dear good friend Anders had changed—by 'changed' [anders] I mean had become younger—and had been transformed in your endearing presence into a young and gay man; it did not seem to be as if seven bad years had raced over my slippery head since we had given up our communists' life here. What a juive errand [sic] Richard has become! There he storms forward into the world, and will perhaps hurry back as a Turk with three horsetails and a turban as high as a tower,[16] for when the Oriental insects will have pinched and sucked him enough, he will surely be longing for home. Perhaps he has a position in view as a drum major in the Great Mogul's Army, to carry the Dschinnerädädä up in front, and to turn somersaults instead of beating time, until he finally tumbles back to us.

"My laziness in writing is known to you, since I myself admit it to everybody; long ago I should have written to you in accordance with my promise, and even without it; but as you were informed earlier than I about Wagner's enterprise, and probably in greater detail too, I did not think it urgent; I must even admit that I expected a few lines from you about all this, as I certainly take no small interest in everything that concerns you and my friend. There is a letter of his, of which only the Devil could make head or tail, as is the case with his latest tendencies. In any event, you will be able to give me some explanations of it.

"Here is the letter, given to you word for word:
[Wagner's letter 207 A, is quoted verbatim],

"Unfortunately I received this letter too late, for the date for forwarding letters to him was already past; and I was right in not sending them, for I wrote to him (to write me sensibly) so that I might know where in the world to forward letters—but I have not received any reply to that. At first I kept silent about it to our friends (except to Anders, whom I have not seen

[15] 210 (Paris, May 27, 1850).
[16] Turkish symbols of authority and marital subjection.

face to face so far, but whom I informed through Truffaut), because I first wanted to have other news from him or from *you*; now they are all quite astonished and do not know what to think of it. The news was confirmed by German newspapers. It arrived yesterday through Lindemann, and I send you my very best thanks for your greetings. Von Zychlinski sends you cordial greetings—who, with the good fortune to know you, would not do so, my dear Mad. Wagner. Richard is a blind Hessian.[17] Let him wear out his feet in the sands of the Orient; after that he can't run away a second time. Yesterday I was with Semper and Kill and other fellow countrymen; they all send their kindest regards. Please write to me soon. As soon as I learn anything, you will get news at once. With love and esteem, your old

E. B. Kietz"

[Marginal postscripts by Kietz:]

"One cannot get hold of Anders. He is also a *juive errand*. I do envy you the flat in Zürich, which you described so beautifully; here among our vast and hazy cold walls one does not notice anything at all about spring— I am in good health and am working hard— Up to now Paris is quite calm; however, as I feared at that time, it was close to behaving differently, and one walks on a seething volcano. Please give my kindest regards to your sister, *Fräulein* Nathalie."

Minna's answer to this letter tells us when and in what garbled fashion the information came to her of Jessie's part in Wagner's plot: [18]

"My dear Friend Kietz!

"Now it is my turn to apologize for my tardiness, and I don't want to convince you by words but by deeds. You know yourself that with long apologies one uses too much time, paper, etc. Therefore forgive me! After returning from Paris, I too received a letter from Wagner in which he informed me about his sudden decision concerning his prodigious, I might almost say crazy, journey. His letter to me which I gave you to read in Paris [204], informs you more closely than his hypocritical lines to you [207 A]. Since I have been away from my faithful friends, you and Anders, my dismal thoughts have by no means become brighter; on the contrary I feel even more weighed down by the troubles my husband has caused me— Just think of it, my dear Kietz: immediately upon my return I was told that Wagner had struck up an acquaintance [*Bekanntschaft*] with a married woman in Bordeaux whom he leads around with him. Now, you know people talk foolish stuff everywhere; I did not believe it; but two days ago I received an anonymous letter from Bordeaux by which I was informed in exact detail how W. was secretly in B. a second time from the 10th to the 18th of May, in order to elope from France with that

[17] *Ein blinder Hesse,* a jocular expression, meaning "a foolish person."—Translator,
[18] 211 (Zürich, June 12, 1850).

woman; but she herself had had doubts. At last, police measures foiled the plan, so he went to Lyons. I was also told that W. would demand a divorce from me, and that I should find means to put an end to those lamentable activitise of W. which could finally become a disaster to me, that family, and himself. This too I would not believe were not that letter written by a person who intimately knows my situation as well as my correspondence with a certain lady in B. [Mrs. Taylor?]. Now I also have my doubts about the journey to the Orient. Yesterday I even got a hint that he was staying at Lausanne. Did I not feel too much scorn, I would go there to convince myself; however, I will make inquiries through some acquaintances here as to the truth of the matter. *This,* then, would be the loneliness about which he wrote so much! Oh, what a stupid, silly, faithful wife I always was! It is possible that next fall or winter I shall come to Paris to learn the French language; perhaps you could put me up with Mad. Haenele: I need only a small corner to live in. I hope that all is well with you, my dear Kietz; that is to say, that you are in good health: that is always the main thing, for which I pray to God. It would really be no wonder if I broke down after the excitement I have had to undergo recently. I marvel at how I can stand all this. The warm sympathy which you and my other friends have for me is the only thing that keeps up my spirits. Do not deprive me of this, my dear friend, and prove it by giving me news about yourself very *soon* and always inform me about all that might concern me too. Give my kindest regards to all the German fellow countrymen who are well disposed toward me. Perhaps when I am once there, being an industrious woman, I could be of some use to them. Give my special best greetings to Herr von Zuhlinsky [Zychlinsky]. To you both I owe the gayest hours of my stay in that disastrous Paris.

"Farewell, my dear friend, write to me soon to comfort
"Your
Most faithful friend,
MINNA WAGNER"

"Natalie wants to be remembered to you too.

"If you have not yet called for the letters which Natalie wrote to me and which are still at the Paris post office, let them be buried there; their contents are not worth the trouble.

"N.B. After having closed this letter, I notice that I still have a whole empty page, it is a matter of course that this page shall not remain blank, even though it is nothing much that I am writing. Unfortunately my thoughts are now so faint that often they disappear completely. I would not care—I would even prefer to be dead right now, for *this* life is miserable! How happy I was at the time of our poverty in Paris, when starvation was cook [*wo Schmalhans Küchenmeister war*]; but we had at least some peace of mind and a future to look to—now everything lies empty and dead before me, only that I have become ten years older. Oh, this Richard! If there only existed a God, a justice, it would be a great comfort for me. Should W. come to Paris sooner than I, let me know, but *secretly*. Just this moment I received a letter from the intendant of the theater in Weimar, in which he informs me that Wagner's newest opera, *Lohengrin,* is to be performed on August 28. He asks me for the text, which I am about to send. What pleasant news that would be for the blind Hessian.[19] Now this page has been filled, after all, with foolish chatting. Write to me. Your little letter, for which I thank you belatedly, has given me so much joy. *Adieu!* As always

"Your

Old friend

MINNA"

"One more request, and I thank you in advance for the favor. I hope you will post the enclosed small letter by city mail and will not keep it in your pocket for an eternity. I know that this used to happen sometimes—"

In a letter to Mrs. Burrell (212 A, undated) Natalie writes that Minna had rashly confided the information of her husband's Bordeaux adventure to an "old maid" in Dresden, and that this old maid had promptly spread it all over that city. One result was a proposal of marriage to Minna which Natalie encloses.[20] The signature and address are carefully blacked out:

"MOST HIGHLY ESTEEMED MADAM:

"Though I only twice had the pleasure of seeing you and speaking to you in society, though probably I am hardly fortunate enough to be remembered by you, I nevertheless venture to approach you with regard to a matter on which the whole happiness of my life will depend.

"It is not unknown to me that your husband has left you, and I am not entitled to discuss the question as to which of you will be the most to be pitied.

"Will you permit me to assure you that generally speaking he is severely blamed here, as people know very well how to appreciate your altogether excellent qualities, so rarely found in women. Of course I can fully understand that owing to the bitter experiences you have had to undergo you will hardly be willing to enter into a second marriage. Nevertheless, as an honest man I feel encouraged to offer you heart and hand.

"It is true, I do not own much property; however, what I already possess and a good flourishing business are entirely sufficient to provide you with some comfort and might recompense you for many a privation.

"If you fulfill the desire of my heart which I, as I freely confess, have secretly nourished for a long time, I shall consider myself as the happiest of all men, and my ardent endeavor will be to earn your love and esteem, which at present I cannot yet claim.

[19] See 210.

[20] 212 B (Dresden, June 12, 1850).

"If you are not disinclined to fulfill my ardent wish, oh, delight me very soon with a letter from your dear hand. Then I will not hesitate to do everything in order to dissolve the bonds which now still bind you to Wagner, as quickly as possible, so as to lead you back soon into a *lasting* home where I will be yours in most faithful love and devotion during all my lifetime.

"Longing for a very early and favorable answer, I remain in deepest admiration,

"Yours

Most respectful

E——

——"

Wagner tells in *My Life* of an unfortunate incident. He once made an "innocent remark" to Jessie in a joking way, saying that his marriage to Minna had been "solemnized by a hypocrite," and therefore, from a sectarian point of view was questionable. Mrs. Taylor, according to Wagner, picked this up and retailed to Minna that she was not "legally married." There is no documentary evidence of this bit of malice save a letter from Wagner to his friend Baumgartner in Zürich: [21]

"DEAR BROTHER:

"An event of most disgusting significance makes me turn to you quickly for information. Though I had to grieve my poor wife, I did not want to offend her by my attitude nor by any of my actions. Nevertheless I fear that she has been brutally subjected to an intentional and infamous deception about myself and the reasons of my separation from her.

"In order to obtain full certainty about the matter and consequently—not so much for my own justification as to be able to take the necessary steps for the consolation of my sorely tried wife—I have asked Karl Ritter to go to Zürich immediately to see you. He will inform you about all the incidents of my recent past: may you on the other hand take the opportunity to tell him faithfully and in detail what in the meantime has happened to my wife. I have reason to believe that she has been hurt, and I consider it my holiest duty—as soon as I know everything—to enlighten her for the purpose of reestablishing her honor!

"This in haste! Farewell and always believe me honorable!

"Your brother

RICHARD W——"

Alwine Frommann, the sister of a Jena bookseller, met Wagner when *The Flying Dutchman* was first produced in Berlin in 1844. "She was already past her first youth," writes Wagner (p. 374) in the first of numerous warm refer-

[21] 205 B (without date or postmark).

ences to her in *My Life,* "and had no beauty of feature except remarkably penetrating and expressive eyes that showed the greatness of soul with which she was gifted." He valued her human understanding and her artistic sympathy. Her intercession for him at the Court in Berlin, where she was reader to the Princess Augusta of Prussia, was one of many ways in which she used her influence in his cause.

This letter, written on the verge of Wagner's return to Minna, but without knowledge of it, surely oversteps obligation and bespeaks a genuine affectionate impulse:

194 (*Alwine Frommann in Coblenz, July 3, 1850, to Minna in Zürich*)

"Your letter of yesterday, dearest Minna, expresses a thought which came to me as I pondered over your situation—I don't want to enter any further into your grief. Your trouble must be so deep that it can't be adequately expressed by words—I too have kept thinking about the theater for you, but I hardly know whether that could be possible for you. Anything you undertake will be a great mental exertion, and you must know what steps you can take—only a desperate exertion will enable you to hold on to life; even if the aforesaid thought has much to be said against it, it has also much in its favor, for such an unusual situation in any case demands the most unusual means. If you should make up your mind to return to the theater, have you any idea where? May I write to Detig,[22] your relative, and tell her what is much more difficult for you to tell her: only that Richard is now unable to care for you since he has not yet found a position? Couldn't she give you advice, since she so often appears in guest roles on small stages and her recommendation certainly is of value in Austria? Or may I attempt it with the new little theater in Berlin (Friedrich Wilhelmstadt)? This stage, which has acquired Lortzing as *Kapellmeister,* is beginning to develop, and there is a character part of yours not yet well cast. The Königstadt is somewhat shaky. You see, though I have thoroughly pondered this subject, I can only in a general way urge you to do *something,* nor can I dismiss the idea in my heart of hearts that R. will later on come back to you; and for that reason do not despair; how often has he told me that you have been his support, his better self, his help. If you are to bear your fate you must remain firm and courageous; in this you must believe me!

"Don't imagine that *he feels happy*—he may be *intoxicated* but *never truly happy;* he is not bad enough for that. One bewilderment has drawn him into another, and his character is not firm enough to resist; but even when he is wrong he will have his better moments, and he will think with repentance and longing of the wife who was his good angel. I entreat you as strongly as I can to make up your mind to something; I in your place would choose the theater,

---

[22] Although the name is not clear, it should refer to Minna's younger sister Amalie von Meck, who, as an operatic alto, was conversant with the theater.

since the normal course of your life is *now* broken for you. It is for *you* alone to decide; and you must know whether you can make that tremendous decision, because you have a different kind of character and because whatever you do you must do as well as possible, even with an agonizing pain in your heart. I don't know whether you will have a hard time on account of your situation, but since as an actress you can use another name, I don't think so, unless people object to any kind of relationship with Richard.

"Oh, my dear, I'm not sparing you, but I can't help it; all I can do is to beg you again and again quickly to reach a decision; it will be best for you. *Work, activity,* are the only relief when circumstances upset our usual way of life; I can appreciate your misfortune in some degree—if not the depths of your sorrow, at least enough to understand.

"I am still here, nor is it quite certain when I shall leave; probably in 5-8 days, when I have to see to the property left by a friend in Bonn, which may take 3-4 days. It is not yet certain whether or not I'll be able to go to Berlin right after this or via Weimar to see the Goethes again.[23] But write to me here under the address: Frl. Fr., Coblenz, c/o Herr Friedr. *Bohn,*[24] Rheinstr. He will forward it if I am not far away. I'll soon write you again and I keep to my promise about my room in Berlin. The whole world is upset now and so is the fate of us all.

"Yours,

ALWINE

"Pondering about your misery is of no avail; either you must create new conditions for yourself or if you have relatives where you would *like* to live in *concealment* you can go to *them,* perhaps for a long time. For a short time you can always stay with me."

Written about this time (although undated) is the most remarkable letter which the whole affair brought forth. Wagner, at last ready to return to Minna, undertakes to explain everything, with his usual air of having done the only thing that a reasonable man could do under the circumstances. Natalie at first withheld the original of this letter from Mrs. Burrell and wrote a copy for her (214), faithful except for the omission of Minna's running commentary, written in the margins.[25] Later she sent the letter itself (213):

"MY POOR, DEAR WIFE!

"Karl arrived here only last night and brought me your letter. After reading it I need not tell you that I'm coming back to you *in any case* and within the

[23] Alwine's brother had been an intimate friend of Goethe.

[24] The cataloguer mistook this name for the signature of the letter!

[25] Messrs. Hurn and Root, in *The Truth About Wagner,* quote the bulk of this letter. Evidently they were shown Natalie's copy, for the remarks by Minna, excepting the last one, are missing. Instead they have peppered the translation with gratuitous expletives of their own.

next few days. I only add the assurance that in the beginning of May, when I learned in Geneva of your trip to Paris and your efforts to locate me, I would have come out of hiding and given you the chance to talk to me, if *just at that time—and just at that particular time—*I did not have to consider another person, which made it absolutely impossible for me to act as openly and as much in accord with the dictates of my deeply grieving heart as I myself would have wished. Since I now had to assume definitely from various indications that you had received an extremely distorted report about what recently happened, there was nothing I wanted more to do than to enlighten you about the true course of events, less for the sake of my own personal justification than to remove the deep insult and affront which that dreadfully false report must have caused you.[26] In order to get exact information about this, I sent Karl to Zürich. I now see from your letter that my fears were well founded, that you absolutely believe the most stupid distortions of the truth on the part of a mother who is only concerned about outward appearances, and by a vengeful and cowardly husband; that you therefore condemn me summarily as guilty—and nevertheless you want nothing more ardently than my return to you, because—separated from me—you think you would have only death to look forward to. But even though I realize that you are greatly in error, not only about this, but also about me in general, I also see that your love for me is stronger and more powerful than all your errors—and this single fact is sufficient to remove all doubts about what I have to do now. I *never* said that I no longer love you—and now I know that I have only to come back to you. But, my dear Minna, you are too greatly mistaken about everything that happened as well as about our mutual relationship in general for me to wait for a word-of-mouth discussion to enlighten you about it. Such discussions could only be of the most repulsive kind, and would probably so involve all sorts of passions that I feel obliged to do everything in my power to obviate them. That's why I'm writing you once more in advance and asking you to consider calmly what I am going to tell you. First of all, you are wrong when you link my decisive last letter from Paris to happenings in that family which did not actually influence my actions until after this letter. I hear that you base your mistake on a disparity between the contents of my last letter from Bordeaux and this last Paris letter, a disparity which seems very great to you. You don't understand this clearly. Listen, once more. After I did everything to make you understand my views on life and art, especially with my disgust for Paris; after I persuaded that young woman—purely to calm you —to write to you as she did; after you expressed yourself as pleased with this letter, and after you had actually copied the answer which I had drawn up for you—according to your point of view, as I thought—and sent it to her, I believed the deep disharmony of life between us had been resolved, and I looked forward to a happier future at your side and expressed this feeling and this hope to you in my first letter from Bordeaux. My shock and pain were in-

[26] See 205 A.

describable when I received your first letter to Bordeaux and had to realize that you were standing on *absolutely* the same old ground; that the messages of that woman had made no lasting impression on you whatsoever; that you had copied that reply but had not really felt it; that you persisted more than ever in your error about me—about my aspirations in life and art. Then the hope of converting you failed me. I wrote you my next reply immediately upon receiving your letter, in the first excitement. You will find in it no decision as yet, but only my desperation about you. Read it once more attentively, and my state of mind must become clear to you. This day my good humor, which I had only just recaptured, had vanished; my nervous ailment has come back again. People like the mother and the husband, who, as I soon found out, understood me only very superficially, failed, of course, to notice my increasingly deep melancholy: such philistines only see the fantastic, the half-crazy, or perhaps only high-strung, artist in a person like me: but my mood did not escape my young friend who understood me and even realized that *I was unhappy*—as I indeed was. No declarations and understanding took place between us; she knew and learned from me that I really loved you, and for that reason was just as unhappy that *we have not been able to understand each other*.[27] I now insisted on going away, I couldn't stand it any longer. I left with the intention of staying in Paris one or two days only in order to go right to Zürich. I arrived in Paris in bad shape; the old nervous condition had taken hold of me again. I began to be increasingly afraid of the journey to Zürich. I continued to expect each day a letter from you in Paris—if only for the sake of the commissions—I hoped that it would put me at rest about your attitude after that letter from me! In vain— no letter came, and I was compelled to believe that you were stubbornly persisting in your attitude. If I were now to return to Zürich, I foresaw that we should soon have the most disagreeable scenes: the mere thought that you would receive me as you have unfortunately done so often before,[28] coldly and reproachfully, was terrible to me! I foresaw that—in my present state of mind— I would take hat and stick after one of those scenes and never return; how often already have I gone off alone in such an awful state of mind! Influenced by these thoughts and considerations, I decided to write to you—and not to go back to Zürich at all! [29] Those who were around me at the time know how pitiful my condition was! I read your letters from Zürich once more, and among those few I found *two* in which you threatened to leave me—just as you told me as soon as you arrived in Switzerland that if ever I did not behave well you merely had to write in order to receive traveling money for your return! Really, Minna, it was your fault that I began to get used to the idea of a separation!!— Believe absolutely what I'm telling you here, then you'll under-

[27] Note by Minna: "Unknown to me until this disastrous moment, but he must give an excuse."
[28] Note by Minna: "Obvious lie."
[29] Note by Minna: "Shameful!"

stand that letter which seemed so terrible to you, and you will not have to look for any other motives. What drove me to this step was something which concerned you and me alone, and absolutely no third *person*—even though, to be truthful, I will in no way deny that my acquaintance with that third person and the knowledge that I really could be understood without inspiring horror— as I do in you—caused me to feel my unhappiness really keenly and bitterly. Up to this point, dear wife, we have had only each other to deal with! However terrible it is for you, I ask you to read that letter once more; yes, I even plead with you to take it to heart to sympathize with my unhappiness; and it would make me very happy if in the future you'd give the lie to the reproaches contained in it—for on the other hand, as to a *separation* being the only solution, I am now fully converted and convinced of the contrary.

"I revealed this decision to the only ones who took an active interest in my fate; namely, Frau Ritter and that young woman in Bordeaux. I did not hide from them the grief and the deep misery which I felt, the bleeding pain which that apparently necessary step caused me, and the feeling of the most infinite abandonment. Through the impression which this message made on the latter, it became apparent that I had kindled a violent attraction in the heart of the young woman. As a sixteen-year-old girl she had been married to a very handsome young man with whom she had fallen in love, but about whom it became clear to her, even before the marriage, that both—as she expressed it—did not have three thoughts in common. Her mother, a pleasant woman, but without any depth and merely worldly-wise, is, as I have found out recently, very rich, and had helped the son-in-law out of an impending bankruptcy with a not insignificant sum of money. As a result, husband and mother were always bound together—by a business as well as a personal interest—and the young woman, who felt more like a financial hostage, reconciled herself to the fate of living with a husband toward whom she felt indifferent, but who left her wholly undisturbed in all artistic endeavors and inclinations. From a distance she had already for years had a lively interest in me as an artist: after I got into this financial trouble, she believed herself called upon to help me substantially. I learned from her later the cause for the delay of her help: husband and mother did not understand her and could not see why my fate concerned them. Only after the Ritters had sent money, as agreed upon, was she able to persuade her family, by making them feel *ashamed,* to agree to what she offered you. Now she hoped to bring me into closer acquaintance with her family, hoping thus to make them feel even more ashamed. Indeed, the husband and mother were unusually courteous toward me after my arrival in Bordeaux, as I already wrote you. The poor young woman, who until that time had stood entirely alone in regard to her family, in that disgusting misers' nest and without any support, now took new hope. She strongly urged her family to leave this miserable Bordeaux: they had no need to keep on with business, they should get together with the families Ritter and Wagner, buy a place in Switzerland, etc. So long as her family looked upon this as a mere fantasy, they agreed gladly; when it became more serious, they grew silent and did not understand. I realized that this woman, too, was unhappy and was becoming conscious of her unhappiness. Her family was thinking of business and property administration, whereas she, on the other hand, thought of life itself. In the hour before my departure I had another terrible experience. They were talking about a hat which the husband once had brought her from Paris and which she had never put on. Then suddenly the husband broke forth with the words: 'I know it; she never liked anything that came from me: I ought to thank God that I did not give her a child, for she would not have liked it either.' [30] To my horror, I now realized that the man *knew* that his wife did not love him, and with disgust and loathing I suddenly beheld a mother who for her part knew it too and yet was completely calm about it. But what else were these experiences for me than a confirmation of my long-nurtured opinion about the miserable loveless and heartless void of our whole so-called great world! It made no other impression on me than the greatest pity for the poor victim! But the resolution somehow to breathe freely had taken root in the soul of this victim. That message from me made a decisive impression on her, and she suddenly wrote to me that she was determined to leave her family and place herself under my protection.[31] She told me this in such glowing and desperate passion that I was astounded and most deeply affected. I wrote her a wholly serious letter, described my situation to her in the most frightening terms, and emphasized the tremendously daring and fatal elements in her decision; she ought to think the matter over,[32] whether she could decide to ruin herself in cold blood, for she would have to be prepared for that. At this same time I received a letter in Montmorency from Frank, who asked me, without any further explanation, to come to Paris immediately, since he had something urgent to tell me. I supposed one of my Zürich friends had written to him and asked him to sound me out about my last decision. It was simply impossible for me to discuss this matter just at this time, even with so well meaning a friend; I evaded him and left immediately for Geneva. I was in every respect so terribly perturbed and shaken that, come what might, my only thought was to go far, far away. I suddenly made the decision to go to Greece and therefore wrote to Bordeaux for the means to do it, leaving everything else uncertain, even almost untouched; this was rather calculated to discourage her. Then I received the news from Kietz, who had taken the chance of writing to me, general delivery, to half a dozen cities, that *you yourself had been in Paris,* hoping to find me and become reconciled. If you will concede me any heart at all, then you must understand how unutterably this news moved

[30] Note by Minna: "Strange to say, this creature—I could almost call her contemptible—wrote me that she had married the man of her choice."

[31] Note by Minna: "To roam about the world as an adventuress—very honorable."

[32] Note by Minna: "Briefly and to the point—'I have already a decent wife.'"

and grieved me. As I have said, even though you were in error [*Irrthum*] about me, I still saw that your love was stronger than your error and that in any case you were differently affected by my letter than I had supposed. But, also imagine my torture, just now, and under this other desperate situation! I felt urged to write to you, but I could not possibly write you the truth; everything here was uncertain; [33] it would have been the most insane cruelty on my part to reveal to *you* what had been going on, since I did not even know what the end of it would be. [34] I only felt the urge to go forth into the wide, wide world. But I wanted to give you some consolation, however feeble! I wanted to treat you as a humane doctor would, to accustom you for the time being to a separation which then seemed more necessary than ever, even if I did not know whether it should last for a short while or forever. [35] I had to assume that the news that I was going to Greece must seem almost conciliatory to you, since you could gather from that that I was not leaving just you but rather the whole world. If I was mistaken about this, forgive me. My intention was good; I could not write you that I knew you had been in Paris, for then I should have had to follow my heart and let you know that I would no longer hide from you. Truly, I was in great trouble, and the most disagreeable part of it was that I had to lie to you. For now I finally got the news from Bordeaux that the young woman was so violently affected by the content of my serious letter, and by the news that I wanted to go to Greece, that she could not hold back any longer: she openly betrayed her state of mind and revealed herself to her family. After this discovery they assumed the mask of hypocritical pity toward her and pretended to understand her decision, but they described me as a seducer and dishonest intriguer; [36] I learned that the happy husband, in order to frighten his beloved wife, had written to me in Zürich and threatened to look for me everywhere and to take revenge on me, etc.—that was really too much! I wrote immediately, not to the young woman, but to the husband, enlightened him completely about my conduct as well as about his unfortunate relationship with his wife, and finally showed him that I would arrive in Bordeaux at the same time the letter did, but merely to defend myself in person and show him that I was not afraid. And that's what happened: honor and everything were at stake, and my position in regard to you, you poor woman, was so desperate that I did not fear death a moment more. [37] For after such slanders it must have surely seemed as if I had left you for another woman! [38] Neither the woman nor any one else had heard about my trip to Bordeaux, *only the husband,* and I pointed this out to him. I

[33] Note by Minna: "That's why!"

[34] Note by Minna: "Driven out of Bordeaux by the police—nice end."

[35] Note by Minna: "Depending upon whether that woman, with her flighty nature, did not change her mind."

[36] Note by Minna: "Not without justice."

[37] Note by Minna: "Because of a flighty woman."

[38] Note by Minna: "And so it was, according to proofs I possess."

stopped at a hotel and wrote to him that I expected him. Then he showed how cowardly and miserable he really was! He had threatened me, and above all in a letter which, I had to assume, had fallen into your hands; and when I came to give him an explanation he eluded me, packed up wife and mother, who did not know the least bit about my arrival, and took them to the country in order to wait there in safety until I had been expelled by the police *to whom he had reported me* and against whom I could, of course, not defend myself [39] since my passport had not been visaed by the ambassador. Thus ended this lamentable story; I really think not to *my* shame!

"Enough; under all sorts of threats they wrung the solemn promise from the young woman not to write to me directly or indirectly, nor to receive messages from me.[40] And they even pressed you in order to get evidence against me. That to me is the lowest thing, that they even tormented you, poor woman.[41] They did not need any more and could have been satisfied, for never —they knew that—would I have divorced you, never married another. Thus the matter resolved itself! But still one cannot blame me if I feel deeply *sorry* for the young woman in question, just as I *despise* her husband and her mother from the bottom of my heart.

"Let this suffice, dear Minna, to clarify my conduct in this affair. If you don't believe me, if you don't believe me absolutely, as I should be believed, you will only make yourself very unhappy! I'll not impose any conditions for my return to you, for—since I have learned of your state of mind—I have determined to return to you *unconditionally.* After what I have said, take counsel with yourself whether you can be completely reassured about me! If after all you can acquit me unconditionally, then try to understand also that my report to you from Paris deserves a different consideration than the one you are inclined to give it. Try to understand that I was *very unhappy* when I wrote to you as I did, and—try as much as possible to keep such unhappiness from both of us in the future. It lies in your hands! Be more unprejudiced toward me, and in general try to enter with a more friendly spirit into my whole character and thoughts! I hope we shall live together peacefully and happily till the end of our lives! Frau Ritter has asked me to look for a place for her and our family in Switzerland; only let it be near Zürich; that is my favorite place. And so, my good, sorely-tried, and steadfast wife, we have a new life to begin. Let the old one, with its recent experiences, be over with! Let us carry into our new life only the memories of pleasant things, faithful friends, and our good animals. Now we *know* definitely and clearly *what* we are to each other, and let us be sure to remain this way!

"Give my heartiest greetings to my friends; tell them that they'll see me within this week. I'm delaying my trip only until you've received this letter

[39] Note by Minna: "Honorable courage."
[40] Note by Minna: "Not the custom with honorable people, either."
[41] Note by Minna: "Only because of *real* uprightness."

and have made up your mind about it—for no other reason. May all disharmony have disappeared when we finally see each other again at last, after
our painful separation! Let us now think only of the present and quietly and
securely live for the future in the enjoyment of noble friendship. Give my
special regards to Sulzer if he's still in Zürich—his letter made me so happy, and
I thank him for it cordially!

"Farewell, then, for today, my dear good old Minna! Within a few days
I'll be with you and embrace you with all my heart,

"Your

RICHARD

"Have you a room ready for Karl? He was really happy about you and your
faithfulness and now he's happy as a god that we're going to Zürich!—Greetings to Nette!"

[Note by Minna:] "I owe the reunion not to this letter, which contains
many untrue accusations as well as insults, but solely to my great love, which
makes me forgive and forget what has happened."

The following letter (216, undated) not only reveals a previous correspondence and understanding between Ann Taylor and Minna, but suggests that
letters of Wagner to Minna may well have been used to turn Jessie against him
forever.

"MY DEAR MADAM:
"I am returning herewith the two letters and the documents which you
had the kindness to send me, and I thank you very much for the trouble you
took in this disagreeable affair; also for your very dear letter which I shall keep
as a sacred pledge of our friendship, faithfulness, and sympathy.

"From my last letter you will probably have guessed that the fear lest these
important papers fall into other hands was my only reason for not returning
them sooner, for I assure you that the responsibility of keeping them caused me
great anxiety.

"The sacrifice which you are making with regard to the return of Herr W.
inspires me with the utmost gratitude; this step seems to me the surest way to
reestablish the domestic peace of my children, and I hope, provided the Ritter
family no longer interferes with our affairs,[42] that in due time you will somehow be rewarded for your noble action.

"If I no longer send you the money I had promised, it is because your husband wrote me in his last letter: 'Owing to these changes I must request you
to take back the sum of f. 625 which you recently sent my wife. Within the next
few days I shall have arranged all that is necessary to repay this amount, to-

---

[42] This indication of an estrangement with Frau Julie Ritter is not surprising, for this
lady stood stoutly by Wagner through everything, reducing her allowance to him only
because she had no choice.

gether with my appreciation and my cordial thanks for your noble intention, now however no longer called for. With deep respect, etc. etc. . . . !' But dear Madam, if later on I could be of some use to you in one way or another, I beg you on behalf of our friendship to turn at once and directly to me. For this purpose I give you the address of a friend who will immediately forward every letter addressed to him under special cover, no matter in which country I may be.

"I rely on your kindness thus to inform me of every new event about which I should know.

"In case you may have seen a certain French letter which I wrote at that time in Bordeaux, but mailed to your husband from Paris, I must apologize, for then I had no knowledge of his return.

"Finally I beg you, if time permits it, to acknowledge the receipt of *this letter* as soon as possible, and I assure you of my true friendship.

"Respectfully,
ANN TAYLOR" [43]

Wagner returned to Zürich on July 3, and four days later wrote to Kietz (207 B):

"DEAR ERNST BENEDIKT!

"Many strange things have happened to me: when I expected to receive the money for my intended trip to Greece I received instead a message which brought the confusion around me to a head, but which above all made it impossible for me to carry out my project. Be satisfied then to hear the result of all this confusion without wanting to investigate its particulars. This result is as follows:

"To my joy I have arrived at the conviction that my wife's love for me is stronger and more definite than her error about me: that as a consequence it is not the separation but a renewed and continued life together that is capable of healing the discord which had arisen between us. I therefore consider—together with Minna—that what has happened is beneficial, in that it has shown us both what we are and can be to each other now. Four days ago I came to Zürich with Karl Ritter (without horsetail and turban!). Tell this to my friends in Paris—

"I've told my wife that I received the news of her trip to Paris as early as the beginning of May, and from none other than *you*—who, in your anxiety, had taken a chance and written letters to me general delivery in half a dozen cities, one of which did reach me in Geneva half by accident. I don't want to keep it a secret any more that I knew about her trip to Paris—for that really did move and affect me very much.

"Now see to it that you soon get chased out of Paris, so that there'll be

[43] One line cut off, evidently with the address above mentioned.

nothing left for you to do but to come to us. I wish the same thing for Anders. To Semper I'll write shortly. The whole Ritter family is coming to us next spring in order to buy a house here and start a colony with us and any one else who is ready for it.

"From Minna I hear many good things about you: accept my warm thanks for that! Farewell, greet everybody for me and write soon again!

"Your

RICHARD WAGNER"

If the flight with Jessie was planned as an escape from the Paris obligations which blocked his advance as a composer, the break with Jessie and the abandonment of the *Wieland* plan further cleared his vision. It is well to bear in mind that through the ins and outs, the implications and extrications of this affair, Wagner's imagination was increasingly absorbed by the Siegfried legend. He was going through a period where challenging musical images began to come to him. He wrote a preface to *Siegfrieds Tod* in Villeneuve in early June, probably under the stimulation of the Ritter family, who had just been with him there. In August he wrote to Liszt: "*Siegfried* vibrates all through my nerves—it depends upon a favorable mood." What it really depended upon was further musical growth. He was not ready to begin composing his *Siegfried,* but his mind suddenly leaped into the full consciousness that neither the theater in Liszt's Weimar nor any other that had ever been built could contain the drama he was about to create. A week before his famous letter to Uhlig (September 20, 1850), outlining a fantastic plan which would further expand into the realization of the *Ring* at Bayreuth twenty-six years later, he wrote to Kietz in a gay mood on September 14. Putting behind him what he calls "the blackest period" of his life, he lays out his scherzo fantasy, as reckless as Siegfried himself in its challenge to all sober caution and money prudence (207 C):

". . . Since I happen to be alive and cannot live at any other time than *now,* even with the best will, I have to do something which corresponds to my ability. I'm thinking of setting *Siegfried* to music after all, only I have no intention of letting any theater perform it: I have on the contrary the very boldest plans, for the realization of which, however, I need nothing less than 10,000 thaler. Then, according to my plan, I would have a theater built of boards right here where I happen to be; I would send for the most capable singers and have everything I need especially made for this one particular occasion, so that I could be sure of an excellent performance of the opera. Then I would send invitations to all those who are interested in my works, provide for a good attendance, and give three consecutive performances—free of charge, of course— in one week. After this the theater would be torn down, and the thing would come to an end. Only something of that sort can still stimulate me. When Karl Ritter's uncle dies, I'll get the amount!"

⚘ XIX ⚘

WAGNER TO MINNA

(The Zürich Years, 1850–1858)

> "Snow-white trousers; sky-blue tail coat with large buttons, projecting cuffs; extremely high, black top hat with narrow brim; a stick as high as himself with a huge gold knob; bright, saffron-yellow, glacé kid gloves."
>
> —Description of Wagner in Zürich, noted by Miss Lermonda Burrell, at Natalie's dictation (255)

Although Wagner and Minna were never long separated during the Zürich years, these were on the whole not happy years. Minna was even less pleased with the provincialism of Zürich than Wagner, and longed for Dresden and her lost status of *Frau Kapellmeisterin*. After the Laussot affair, in 1850, had confronted her with the prospect of being left to her own resources, this terrifying possibility was always at the back of her mind. Their life in Zürich, and indeed their life together on any enduring basis, came to an inglorious end with the Wesendonck affair in 1858. The letters from Wagner to Minna in these years are written mostly in the summer season when Wagner was taking a cure or making an Alpine excursion.

Undertaking one of his summer Alpine climbing expeditions in July, 1851, Wagner persuaded his young friend Theodor Uhlig, the theater violinist at Dresden with whom he had struck up an intimate correspondence, to accompany him. He also persuaded his other young friend Karl Ritter, then at Saint Gallen, to join them. Wagner tells in *My Life* (pp. 566 et seq.) how Uhlig, then advanced in tuberculosis, scarcely survived the effort and altitude, while Karl, neurotic and far from sturdy, dropped out altogether. The following letters inform Minna of his progress.

222 A *(Wagner, in Saint Gallen, July 5, 1851, to Minna in Enge [Zürich])*

"My very best Mietze!

"Uhlig arrived in Rorschach only this morning (Saturday). He had a slight accident. This afternoon we are to start for Appenzell. I learned, however, that the trip will cost us another day, for we want to go from Weissbad across the Säntis to Wildhaus, and this can't be done in *one* day: we'll have to stay overnight in an Alpine hut. So we can't reach Zürich until Wednesday night, by steamer. I tell you this so that you won't be anxious and so that you may meet us with a rowboat. I'm telling nobody so as to surprise them (Karl had already intended to come along). Where will you put him up at first?

"It is clearing up and the forecast announces the finest weather. I have been at the Lindemanns' several times. She and cousin *Roth* send you their best greetings. I for one am a little out of sorts and now hope the mountain climb will strengthen me.

"Uhlig's trunk will go by post and has been addressed to Zürich by us: be so kind as to keep it if it arrives ahead of us.

"Meanwhile, behave yourself—I mean, keep nice and quiet and take your cure. Peps must behave too: give him a beating from me. I hope Natalie will be less excitable. So! I have put the house in order, and we are off for the Alps. Therefore, may God in His mercy protect you and avert all evil! (Don't cry too much when the Vreneli girl leaves!) Goodbye! and as you lie in your soft bed, think of your poor husband who must get along in a poor Alpine shack. Greetings to our friends and be there to meet us on Wednesday night!

"Your

RICHARD THE FAT"

222 B (Wagner, in Engelberg, August 3, 1851, to Minna in Enge [Zürich])

"DEAR MIETZE!

"You will believe we have disappeared! So I am writing to you tonight because for the first time I can be somewhat definite, now that the weather promises to be good. We have had three whole days of continued rain on the Vierwaldstätter See. We would have been back long ago if the weather had not suddenly appeared to clear up each time we had decided to return home; so we were always tempted to go on a little farther. On Friday night we were already on the way back to Lucerne when the weather became clearer again and Uhlig proposed the advance to Stans from Beckenried: there we stayed over night Saturday and descended into the Engelberg Valley in spite of rain and mist. Here in Engelberg we have sat all Sunday long, quite rainbound since morning. Tomorrow (Monday) morning we intended to return to Lucerne; but today the weather took a definite turn for the good, and we made a fine excursion. Gorgeous Alpine glow on the Titlis. So we are going to cross the Surenen tomorrow morning at five o'clock. If weather holds out, we shall see the great glacier in the Maderan Valley on Tuesday, returning on Wednesday via Schwyz by the mail coach in the afternoon at four o'clock. I am writing you all this so that you may know how things stand. I for one am terribly depressed and quite annoyed at having been so long away from home. I have a real case of homesickness. Pep's heartrending farewell is still ringing in my ears.

"So, if the weather only makes it up to us, all will be well. It is indeed beautiful here, tonight I am regaining my good humor. The last few days I could have howled like a watchdog. But there was nothing to be done.

"Now keep healthy, bathe properly, so that I may find you well. Don't flirt too much! I am eager to return—be assured of that!

"Goodbye and behave nicely.

"Besides, be glad that you were not with us. This is the sincere wish of your very melancholy

HUSBAND"

224 A (Wagner, in Albisbrunn, to Minna in Enge [Zürich])[1]

Wagner stoutly defends the water cure: "I now have full confidence in its success. I have no idea, of course, whether it will make me a complete lamb. That's something only *you* can accomplish, and in the course of time." The money question comes up again: "Why the devil must you rave about expenses and about pawning and selling things? If you are short at the moment, it is surely your own fault for not asking me for more. If you are short of money— foolish wife—or if you ever need some more, for the theater, for example, I suggest this: Go straight to the Zug music shop. There is a draft for 3 louis d'or for me which hasn't yet been paid; with the enclosed lines I ask him to pay the money to you."

224 B (September 17, 1851)

Wagner describes the routine of his cure: "Here I am in Abraham's bosom— or at least on Abraham's back—for my bathing attendant is called Abraham, and every morning he carries me pickaback down to the bath wrapped in a woolen blanket like a mummy. I am pleased with the doctor; yesterday he put me through a dry perspiration, but that caused heart congestion, and he changed it so that I perspire now from being wrapped in wet sheets up to the chest. This did me a great deal of good today—I have perspired sulphur prodigiously. I take many walks. Otherwise it's frightfully tedious."

Wagner begins the letter in Latin script, and remarking on the fact midway, changes to German.

224 C (November 2, 1851)

Wagner chats about domestic matters. His boredom is increasing: "What else can I write about this place? O Lord, water, weather, and whist—that is everything . . . . My cure has taken on a new phase—my whole skin is fever- ish and irritable; it is as if it would break out like a rash all over me. But I must put up with it. I learn more and more that the only reasonable thing in the

[1] Undated: Wagner was at Albisbrunn from Sept. 16 to Nov. 23, 1851.

long run is to do everything for one's health . . . soon I'll be itching to work and get going again."

With the advent of "real summer weather" in 1852, Wagner undertook "a walking tour over the Alps, which I felt would be of great advantage to my health." So he writes in *My Life* (p. 583), and proceeds to describe in some detail his journey, largely on foot, from Alpnach on Lake Lucerne by way of the Bernese Oberland to Italy and Lugano. There he was joined by Minna, Herwegh, and his companion Dr. François Wille. Beside this account may be placed three letters to Minna in Zürich from Interlaken, Meiringen, and Lugano —the first and third here published, the second in the collection of *Letters from Richard to Minna Wagner* (p. 47). The two letters (229) offer an amusing contradiction to the statement in *My Life* that, bored and restless at Lugano, he suddenly decided to send for Minna: "A mysterious instinct made me telegraph my wife to come also. She obeyed my call with surprising alacrity, and arrived unexpectedly in the middle of the night, after travelling by postchaise across the St. Gotthard Pass." Actually, Wagner seems never to have ceased to long for Minna, and to urge her to join him. The telegram may have meant that he had at last succeeded in extracting 25 louis d'or from the good Sulzer in Zürich, and thus removed the only obstacle to her coming— the money to do it with.

229 A *(Interlaken, Sunday night [postmarked July 13, 1852])*

"DEAR MIENEL!

"With this heavenly pen [2] I am writing you the first love letter of my journey: it will look its part! So far the trip has gone very well. I arrived in Lucerne at three o'clock, immediately took a boat (fr.6) to Alpnacht [Alpnach], where I landed at seven o'clock, and then at once, in the cool of the evening, started on foot to get as far as possible. A returning coachman wanted to take me to Lungern for fr.3, but I proudly dismissed him. So, the same evening, at ten o'clock, always on foot, I reached Gyswyl [Giswil], three and a half hours from Alpnacht; there I roused the people from their sleep, after I had been very much frightened by a black monster that stood before the inn and shyly stepped aside when I took courage and walked straight up to it. I was tortured until morning wondering what kind of a monster the black creature had been, until I convinced myself the next day that it had been a black sheep. In Gyswyl I took neither supper nor breakfast, but had only a night's lodging (and a very good one). At half past four o'clock I left, and in the most beautiful weather I tramped across the Brünig to Brienz. In the afternoon I crossed the lake by steamboat to Interlaken and was looking forward to marching again in order to reach Lauterbrunnen, when misfortune struck me: *the new boots!!* My left foot is so chafed that I cannot go on with them; here I

[2] *himmlische Feder* is ironic. The writing is blurred throughout.

looked up a shoemaker who is putting the boots on a wide last from four o'clock in the afternoon until four o'clock in the morning, pounding and soaking them. If that does not work, I am in a bad way. Imagine my joy! Apart from this I am quite well, and must now sit in the inn to wait until the boots are softened. But I have just bought a pair of slippers which will enable me at least to walk around in the neighborhood. Otherwise it is heavenly, it was particularly marvelous yesterday evening on the lake and in the valley of Unterwalden. But I am longing now for the true Alpine air: tomorrow night I shall be on Wengern Alp (some 6,000 feet high); perhaps I shall remain there for a day.

"While I was looking out of the window, I suddenly thought of— Lauchstädt, and I remembered the time, eighteen years ago, when I first met you!! You think of it too, and tell Pepsel everything that comes into your mind! In fact, you are an immensely silly woman: Why was it that when we parted, we almost started crying? Was it perhaps because eighteen years have already gone by! Now, be well and take care of yourself; and think much of your poor husband whom you proclaim to the whole world as bow-legged, and who nevertheless is already so famous that at present he only worries where to get money for the journey, which, I note, will cost not a little. But there's nothing to do about it: not every year am I thirty-nine years old.

"Now I am through: I am *not* going to write any more with this brute of a pen! However, you must write to me nicely: if you write at once, you can send the letter to *Meiringen*: later on, wait to hear from me. Farewell; there you have a kiss, don't do anything foolish and keep loving

"Your quite good

HUSBAND"

In a letter from Meiringen, July 15 (published in *Richard to Minna Wagner*, p. 47), Wagner has waited at Meiringen an extra day in hope of having an answer to his letter from Interlaken. He urges Minna to join him "as soon as money arrives," and concludes: "I'm looking forward eagerly to being picked up by you somewhere—preferably at Lugano."

229 B (*Lugano, July 21*)

"*Carissima Minna! Vita della mia anima! come stà?*—I can hardly speak German any more, I have become such a raving Italian! But in order not to put you into a bad humor, I'll write in German, and avoid appearing again in the guise of a Vestri.[3]

"Yesterday, at the Lago Maggiore, I smoked a divine cigar given to me by Otto Wesendonk [4] which inspired me so that I wrote him at once some silly

[3] Gioachino Vestri, singer in the Dresden Opera.

[4] Although two spellings of the name are to be found, the signatures in this Collection appear as "Wesendonck."

lines, the best of which were greetings to you, and these, I hope, he forwarded to you. I did not want to write to you, my darling, until I got to Lugano, because I wanted to go into detail at the same time about our rendezvous, which I could do only after having seen Lugano and found out whether it was worth while to chase you to this place; besides, I was expecting a letter from you here. (Here I am using a mantelpiece as a standing desk.) Today at noon I arrived here and at last found letters from you; namely, the one sent to Meiringen (where I had given orders at the post office) and the other written to Lugano directly. I thank you heartily for both; they made me very happy. However, you are doing me an injustice in believing that I had given orders for my mail at the post office: I had only written to Uhlig to send his next letter to Lugano directly—and to the point! Regarding my trip and the impressions I received there, I am not telling you anything else today than that it went excellently and that I did very well on foot, almost too well, for the days' journeys were often too short for me. I sent a few words to Wesendonck about the impression that Italy made on me when I came down from the Gries Glacier through the Formazza Valley toward Domodóssola. However you shall learn 100,000 times more if you are nice and sensible, if you follow my advice and my request, and come *at once* to join me here. Now I come to the main point! My impression of Lugano again has decided it: I urgently beg you not to hesitate a moment; pack your three stockings and two chemises, take Peps and put yourself on the mail coach with him; it is too heavenly here. And rest assured that you will not regret having followed my advice this time, for I cannot enjoy, and I do not like to enjoy such things alone; and what's more, it is with you above all that I wish to share this beautiful trip. So listen to how we'll arrange it! Either money has come to you from Leipzig, Frankfurt, or Wiesbaden, or it has not. In the first case you take 20 louis d'or and come along; as for the second case, I am writing today to friend Sulzer, asking him to advance me 20 louis d'or for these few days. Don't worry about that; the way my income is now, and since I can pay back the money at once, this is only a small favor which surely nobody will grant me with greater pleasure than Sulzer. I *can* very well use the 20 louis d'or for our enjoyment, and you are certainly worth that; since I am now already on my way, and since the weather is so beautiful, it would certainly be foolish if, instead of asking the favor of a friend, I should allow a fine opportunity to slip away by waiting day after day. Is this not true? So—let us agree! If money has arrived already, all the better; however, in any case start on your way at once, for—I am longing for somebody to share with me the beauties of the trip. I am so lonely that I really can't stand it any longer! It is you and Peps that are dearest to me!

"I advise you (either as soon as the money has arrived or Sulzer can provide for the loan) to leave by the night-express post for Lucerne the evening of the same day you get this letter; from there you will cross Lake Lucerne to

Flüeln, whence a direct coach goes to Lugano. You may want to book your journey only as far as Bellinzona at the Angelo (angel). That is a good hotel. But if you delay for a day after receiving this letter, then write me quickly *when* you will have left, so that I can receive you nicely. However, don't delay anything for that reason; and if you come at once, there is no need to write ahead. I shall look out carefully, and in any case I shall leave a letter for you (Mad. M. Wagner) here at the post office and tell you in detail how to find me. Today I am staying in the Albergo di laco; I do not yet know definitely whether I shall remain there.

"Now, you may be sure that you will make me very happy if you don't hesitate but come at once; then we shall celebrate in such a way [*das Kalb austreiben*] that Peps will be astonished.

"Lord, what a lot of things I have to tell you, and how wide you will open your eyes— If you knew what kind of roast I ate in the Formazza Valley! Now guess! However, you will not guess it. Therefore, to close, I give you a big kiss and I await you longingly as your

immensely loving
RICHARD
Roast marmot devourer" [5]

"For the time being have *letters* addressed to me sent by Natalie to Lugano. Härtel wrote to me and asked me urgently by no means to approach anyone else but them about the publication of *Siegfried*. So you see how things are! Therefore come."

Natalie tells of what befell Wagner and Minna when, at the end of July, 1852,[6] they were making their way back from Lugano to Switzerland, by way of Chamonix. Arriving exhausted after a long day's walk in a "small Italian town," they found the only inn full; but when the landlord learned of Wagner's identity, he gave them his own room. Thus they had to share one bed, a custom which "Mathilde, that worthless creature," had recently refused to permit. Both were attacked by fleas; but Wagner, too tired to wake up, began to pound Minna with his fists, until she succeeded in rousing him. Deciding to drive from that point, they found themselves in a floorless carriage pulled by an aged and decrepit horse. When they came to a grade, the two Wagners were filled with concern for the poor animal, which could scarcely hold its own, and both got out and pushed.[7] Natalie, of course, was not present on this expedition.

Wagner tells us in his autobiography (p. 600), that in the late summer of 1853 he prepared to compose again, with the text of the long contemplated *Ring*

[5] *Murmeltierbratenfresser.* In *My Life* (p. 585), Wagner writes of Formazza: "Here for the first time in my life, I had to eat roast marmot."

[6] See 229.

[7] 231 (undated, Natalie Bilz-Planer, in Leisnig, to Mrs. Burrell).

before him. "I felt that before entering on such a gigantic task as the music to my drama of the *Nibelungen* I must make one final effort to see whether I could not, in some new environment, attain an existence more in harmony with my feelings than I could possibly aspire to after so many compromises." His recourse was a cure at Saint-Moritz, in the Engadine Valley, and later a journey to Italy. We know from the autobiography that he was moved by the grandeur of Mount Bernina and the Alpine scenery, that he delved into Goethe for intellectual stimulation, and in his longing for solitude found the presence of Herwegh, his companion, a burden. He undertook the Italian journey alone, in September, and, falling into a sleep of exhaustion in Spezia, after a temporary illness, so conceived the mysterious, persistent chord which was to open *Das Rheingold.*

Four letters in this Collection were written to Minna from Saint-Moritz, Geneva, and Spezia.[8] They do not speak of creative intentions, but throw a workaday light on the Wagner in whom mighty music was forming.

246 A *(Saint-Moritz, July 20, 1853)*

Wagner describes his expeditions, his cure, and the accommodations at the Hotel Fall, which are meager. He calls Minna "Minako."

246 B *(Saint-Moritz, August 2, 1853)*

Wagner, with less than two weeks to complete his cure, confesses that he would rather be alone and without the excitement of company. He hopes that Herwegh will leave. Minna had evidently intended to join him, for a letter addressed to her has come from Mathilde Wesendonck. He has opened it, knowing that both will understand. He suggests that Minna and Mathilde do not come to Saint-Moritz, a tiring trip for Minna, but go to Chur, where he will meet them on Sunday week, August 14, whence the three will make their way back to Zürich in three days, by way of Pfäfers, Wallenstadt ("or even across the lake as far as Wesen"). But Wagner does not mention Minna and Mathilde in *My Life.* He says that he returned to Zürich "about the middle of August," and was impatient to be off to Italy at once.

246 C *(Berne, August 25, 1853)*

Wagner, on his way to Genoa, by way of Turin, has just consulted the French ambassador about his passport, for his difficulty with the Saxon monarch would be unfavorably reflected in Italy. He apologizes for leaving Minna so soon again after his return to her.

[8] 246 A, B, D, and 248.

246 D *(Geneva, August 27, 1853)*

He is still apologetic. He has telegraphed her and will do so again before leaving Switzerland. He relates the usual minutiae of the traveler. He is to leave that night for Turin.

The next letter is a sequel to the four in 246. Wagner must have written it on the day the first music of *Das Rheingold* came to him at Spezia. *My Life* must be quoted again for an interesting direct comparison. After describing how he woke from his daylight sleep possessed by the opening E-flat major chord of the flowing Rhine, he continues: "I then quickly realized my own nature; the stream of life was not to flow to me from without, but from within. I decided to return to Zürich immediately and begin the composition of my great poem. I telegraphed my wife to let her know my decision, and to have my study in readiness." He started at once for Genoa, was of two minds about giving up his tour, which would lead him to the delights of Nice and the Riviera, and suddenly realized that his sudden sense of "refreshment and invigoration" was not from outward sights, but from "the resolve to take up my work again." He returned with all expedition to Zürich.

The following letter, written at the very moment when at Spezia he was moved to resume composing, reveals Wagner making a sudden about-face in his travels for a reason of the most imperious sort, which nevertheless he cannot explain to his wife without seeming absurd to her. Instead he pours out a string of petty complaints, concocts every possible reason but the real one for his vacillation, and bids, not too convincingly, for the credit of longing to be with her again:

248 *(Wagner, in Spezia, September 5 [1853], to Minna in Zürich)*

"O MY DEAR MINEL!

"If I could be with you today, I would give the whole of Italy for it! My state of mind is beyond description: You know how we once made fun of Eisner in Paris, and now I am doing the same as he; I have only one thought: how I may quickly get home to you again!

"Certainly that change in my mood has been brought about by my sickness. The main trouble is that a drink of fresh water is here out of the question; now I perhaps took too much ice and ice water; to be brief, within three days diarrhea all of a sudden appeared and consequently an increasing weakness, dizziness in the head, and feverish inclination; a very depressed melancholy mood followed. On Saturday evening, as I already wrote you, I embarked on the sea; I thought the sea air would help me. We had a strong headwind and a rough sea: nice old recollections. People succumbed to seasickness all around me; I too willingly delivered overboard my noon meal taken on land, but then I lay down in my berth and from that time on I was spared from seasickness by lying down stretched out for the whole night.

"Yesterday morning we arrived in the Gulf of Spezia. The diarrhea had subsided, but the dizziness and heavy nausea had rather increased. Thus nothing could delight or distract me. Though I soon started out to wander in the mountain region for an hour at sundown, and though everything was glorious and beautiful, the marvelous flora astonishing—nothing worked well with me. My mood became more and more sentimental, and when I thought of your birthday being tomorrow, and me a five days' journey away from you, I felt like crying aloud in my misery. My depression almost choked me. After dinner I took a carriage and let myself be taken around on the gulf for a few hours of idle driving. It was Sunday, everything trim and orderly! This also I couldn't stand, and went back to my room, swore never in my life to take a trip by myself, and finally yielded to my weariness. But before falling asleep I grew so anxious that I inquired for a physician; but then a quiet night followed. Unfortunately, my dizziness and nausea are the same as before; my mood is unbearable and the thought of being so far away from you lies upon me, pressing me with a heavy weight. Now I feel so helpless here and so pitiably alone that I am hardly able to think any longer of continuing my journey. Still, today or, at the latest, tomorrow morning I will return to Genoa; let's see then how I feel! If I still feel as I do today, nothing can help me but an immediate return. I'll then give up Nice and hurry as directly as possible to Lago Maggiore so as to return to Zürich across the Gotthard: in that case it would be wonderful if you would come to meet me at some point, perhaps as far as Flüeln, provided you feel well enough. But if my condition should improve a bit and if I should feel able to continue the journey as planned, I certainly would still go to Nice, and, if my passport matter is straightened out, even as far as Paris. But about this I can't tell you anything at all definite yet. Well—if *you* would come to Nice, this would change matters. With all my heart, and beckoning you with both hands, I invite you to come! But will your state of health permit it? I am afraid that now such a long trip can't be imposed upon you. But see Dr. Rahn, my good Minel, he may finally permit it after all.

"O God, I'd hate to think that my trip has been in vain; and whatever I can do in order not to run away à la Eisner, I should like to do it. But my present state mustn't continue any longer; otherwise I can think and plan nothing but my return. In order to reach some sort of provisional decision, we will agree to the following. You answer this letter to: Nice (Kingdom of Sardinia). If I should *not* go to Nice, but return home from Genoa, I would telegraph to you from Genoa, so that you would get the telegram before this letter. If you *don't* get any telegram, but only this letter, that will mean that I have gone on to Nice. So as soon as I telegraph you that I am coming home, you must hold all the letters from that moment; whereas you should send them to Nice if you haven't got any telegram until the arrival of this letter. (Unfortunately no telegram can be sent from here, otherwise I would certainly have congratulated you today.)

"God knows what may happen to me today: at this moment I believe I'll be coming home rather than going on. My condition is awful, and how much I yearn for a friendly soul can't be described. After all, I am a much too emotional man to find delight in alien things for any length of time. I will never again take a long trip without you, or at least without a close friend. Otherwise all of a sudden a feeling of misery arises in my soul which completely chokes me. Then introductions to strangers are of no avail. In Genoa I finally delivered Caronti's letter. I didn't meet the man; the other day *he* didn't meet me; and so I continued my trip. Well, if I were younger and if fate had not subjected me to so many fateful experiences! Now only those I know can help!

"Today it started to rain at last; it's possible that it helps a bit in my state; so far I have had bad luck, since the horizon has been never quite clear but always shrouded by a heat haze; so far I have nowhere found one of the beautiful Italian evening illuminations.

"The whole Sardinian court is now staying here in Spezia, with the exception of the King himself; even the Saxon Princess was married here; but I have not seen her yet.

"Once more: Alas, if I were only with you today! I must not seriously think of it; otherwise I'd burst with sorrow! Today as I write this miserable letter my jubilant letter from Genoa will probably arrive. What irony! Soon you will learn more about my decisions; farewell, my good Mienel! Be merrier than I! Greet Pepsel and keep in good health when we meet again. Adieu! Adieu!!

Your very melancholy
RICHARD"

267 A *(Wagner, in Seelisberg, September 12, 1854, to Minna in Zwickau)*

Wagner on a sudden decision is making an Alpine expedition with the Wesendoncks. "We went to Stachelberg, on the Sand Alp, then through the Klön Valley, over the Pragel, and to Brunnen by way of the Muota Valley; yesterday I brought them to the Seelisberg, and here I'm writing to you, my good wife, with deep emotion, to offer you a thousand greetings."

267 B *(October 15, 1854. No address given.)*

"You'll be pretty unlucky about my operas, and you won't get to hear *Lohengrin* anywhere. *Schindelmeisser* wrote me that even in this month *Lohengrin* has already been given twice; because of the small size of the audiences, a third performance is not possible so shortly afterward. On the other hand, he wants to come to see you in Frankfurt (as soon as you have promptly notified him of your arrival) and perhaps perform *Tannhäuser* for *you* in Darmstadt. *Liszt* probably doesn't have *Lohengrin* in the repertoire either. So you'll have to console yourself with the hope that I'll perform it for you some day.

"Now I only wish that you come back *healthy* and *invigorated*. I have really nothing more to tell: this contains *everything*!

"Give *Liszt* my very best regards!

"I long for you fervently.
"Your
RICH."

Wagner had written to Liszt on September 29, saying that Minna was going to Germany "primarily to visit her parents." She was to visit Berlin and Leipzig, returning by way of Frankfurt. If he could manage a performance of *Lohengrin* at Weimar, she would visit him there to hear it.

281 (*Wagner, at Saint-Moritz, July 27, 1855, to Minna*)

"Hurry and send a million Zwiebacks and several Cacoignas [?]

"One can't get anything of the sort here. It's just six o'clock in the morning, the mail coach is about to start. Then I am going to the spring. I arrived yesterday in the finest weather; unusual, beautiful country!

"Goodbye, I have to be brief
YOUR RI-RA-RICHARD"

In March, 1855, Wagner made his journey to London (Chapter XXII). In April, 1857, the Wagners took possession of the Asyl in Zürich, and in August the Wesendoncks occupied their mansion near by (Chapter XXIII). In January, 1858, Wagner's *Tristan* and his friendship with Mathilde had developed to a point where he was ill at ease and made a trip to Paris, apparently to take stock of himself. The following letter indicates that on the surface, at least, his relationship with Minna was still equable.

302 B (*Wagner, in Paris, January 29, 1858, to Minna in Zürich*)

"DEAREST MINNA!

"I think I'll come home as early as Thursday after all. Perhaps I can still settle the matter with Madame Erard by a simple visit; or if I attend the party in my honor on Tuesday night, I'll go on early Wednesday morning, reaching Basel in one day, and in the afternoon around two o'clock I'll be in Zürich. It will exhaust me a bit, but the aimless spending of money exhausts me too. So arrange your party—Herwegh, Semper, Wesendonck, Müller—for *Thursday* night. If I should stay until Saturday after all, I would announce it to you in time. The music from Dresden has not arrived yet, but (through Ollivier) everything now can be arranged without any bother to me.

"Blandine is back. Yesterday I had dinner at Ollivier's, then I went to the concert with her, where the Overture was played passably well, was *greatly* applauded, and will be played there every day. People knew that I was there. Blandine—whom I had on my arm, as it is not possible otherwise in such a locality—naturally was considered to be my wife. Tomorrow I shall go to Erard in Passy with her, and if possible, I shall try to get rid of my obligations by that visit. In the evening I will be with the Herolds.

"Min! God greet you! Be good to me and I hope we may meet again as early as Thursday evening!

"A thousand greetings from your good husband.

"Please pay 100 fr. to Müller when the Viennese money arrives. (He didn't have more.) The other 100 fr. I had borrowed from Semper—which I herewith tremblingly confess to you—Semper doesn't need so badly, but you may offer it to him too."

Frau Heim, the wife of the conductor at Zürich, had an attractive voice, and although Wagner found trouble keeping her on the beat, he was ready to have her sing Sieglinde, opposite his own Siegmund and Hunding in a reading through of the newly written first act of *Die Walküre* for Liszt.

305 (*Emilie Heim, in Zürich, March 30, 1858, to Minna in Dresden*)

"MY DEAR GOOD MADAME!

". . . As for our life and doings in Zürich, there has been no change, except that now, especially at the beginning of the winter, the gap you have left in our small circle of friends is more and more noticeable. When I look over at your little country place, I always remember with emotion and delight the many beautiful hours and wonderful evenings we spent there so pleasantly in song and sound [*Sang und Klang*], or in inspiring conversation. And how often you called for me last winter to go to the theater. Now I rarely go there since I have no one to urge me. And besides, the company is even more thoroughly bad than it was before, which is saying a great deal. Our sanguine hopes in the new management not only didn't materialize, but Schell had the satisfaction of being generally wanted again, since in the last few years he at least gave us something better than this. The opera, which, by the way, I haven't yet attended, is said to be much worse than last year, but even so the director is supposed to be planning productions of *Lohengrin* and *Tannhäuser*. What do you say to this bold idea? Let's hope that he thinks better of it. In the realm of concerts we had two quite good ones by the singer Bochkolz-Falkoni[?], who is outwardly so impossibly ugly that one can enjoy her only by listening with closed eyes. The *genre* of our other winter concerts which have started already is known to you. Alexander Müller hasn't grown more inspired in his conception and conducting. The beautiful days of Aranjuez, when Wagner conducted symphonies by Beethoven, unfortunately are over and won't return. In yesterday's concert the chorus of the peace messengers from *Rienzi* was sung, and recalled to all of your friends pleasant memories of previous days. The female voices really were less off pitch and more vigorous this time than a few years ago. The Rone [?] seems to improve after all.

"You may already know that the Wesendoncks suffered heavy loss by the death of their oldest boy. I saw the poor lady immediately after the mournful event and found her so worn-looking and suffering that she aroused all my compassion. I haven't learned anything yet about Friedrich's employment by the Wesendoncks, and I believe that that fellow may have told you a lie: knowing his character, I shouldn't be surprised.

"Give me more news of yourself soon, my dear Frau Wagner, and accept the most cordial greetings from my husband and myself, with the assurance of our unchangeable friendship and devotion,

"Affectionately yours,

EMILIE HEIM"

Between the letter previous and this one, the crisis with the Wesendoncks had taken place, and Wagner had just sent Minna to Brestenberg for her heart ailment. Hence the propitiatory tone of this letter (and those following):

302 C *(Wagner, in Zürich, April 17, 1858 [?], to Minna in Brestenberg)*

"WELL, MY POOR GOOD MUTZ!

"How are you doing in your exile? You can imagine how eager I am to get some news about your state of health and the beginning of the cure. As long as I don't know anything about you I can't tell you more, but only call out to you: Patience and again patience! It's a nasty thing, I know, to leave at one time house, dog, and husband—but all will be budding and blossoming again in the spring. There is no help! Better a great sacrifice than a growing torment! So—endure it! Be brave and resigned! And announce to me each of your treatments in detail; they interest me in every regard.

"Yesterday I was at Herwegh's and found his wife in very good health, full of hope and confidence. So not only the state of health but the state of finance seems to have improved. Herwegh promised to see me today; maybe I will go to the Wesendoncks with him. There I also learned that Rahn has gone out again, but he didn't come to us. Today I have just written him such a mightily long letter that you will have to be content with these few lines, especially since Friedrich presses me to let him go. I think Rahn will be reasonable; I wrote him in a very friendly way.

"Yesterday I arrived as late as half past eleven. I had expected it so. Fips has gobbled his food in Bremgarten, and that is my latest bit of gossip. For the rest, he is reasonable, a bit dazed, but composed. He didn't disdain dainties, and today when I rose from dinner he promptly jumped upon the chair to lick the plate. I too miss Jacquot. The lower floor seems dismal to me, but at least I'm thinking of you. You're never out of my head. May God grant that we have taken the right course. Keep up your confidence! But if you should lose it, don't conceal it from me. Then we must find out what is best to do. I remain hopeful!

"So, keep being fond of me! Put troubles out of your head! Be calm, reasonable, and above all: *have patience!* All is well with the house; Friedrich is very ambitious in the garden; everything will turn out beautifully.

"So: Send good news. Goodbye, good old Frau Minna! Warmest sympathy and greetings from your

RICHARD!"

302 D *(Wagner, in Zürich, April 29, 1858, to Minna [in Brestenberg])*

"God be praised that I can find a trace of good humor in my wife again! O Minna! Minna, I'll say—I'll say nothing more than this: if a wife keeps so melancholy, a husband has to grow gay in sheer despair! Well, everything indicates that after all the worst is over, as I had been hoping. It's fine that the wet pack is doing you good. If you get out of hand again, I'll always order the same treatment. I believe you will suddenly get much better. It is this way with nervous troubles; and when you are once calm again, you gain everything you missed!

"I won't relate much to you today by letter; besides, I have damned little to tell you: I live the still and lonely life of an abandoned cat, and this I find basically desirable; I know how to manage for myself, and rest is a fine thing.

"I don't want to make your heart heavy about the garden, but it gives great pleasure and in this splendid weather it's a real glory. Well, that has been a sacrifice you had to make this year—better this than your health!

"Well, on Sunday afternoon at five o'clock I'll be in Wildegg if the time-table is not wrong, and I expect you to be there with a fine coach; I may bring along a man (Müller or Herwegh); but perhaps you will have to be content with Fips and me only. Then we will see how red your cheeks are. Today a letter for you from Russia arrived in 'Zierig.' I'll bring it along and I hope you have enough patience, or shall I send it now? As for your worthy commissions, I will see to them in the most interesting way: it's too bad that you didn't demand a dream book too! Frau Herwegh—so far as I know—is still hopeful; perhaps she is going to give it up finally. The day before yesterday I was at the Willes' again. They and the Heines give you their best regards—what more do you want? Now keep going, and finally—whether you want to or not—you will be reasonable. Best regards to the doctor: he may wrap you up well and leave you wrapped until you promise to drop all your whims.

"Once more, God bless and protect you and very soon restore to me a healthy, merry wife of whom I can make good use.

"Goodbye—a speedy and delightful reunion.

"Your devoted

HUSBAND"

302 H *(Wagner to Minna [undated])* [9]

"You good Mutz!

"I am in the midst of preparations for packing and leaving, so only a hasty good day to you! Many thanks for the letter I have just received. It seems that you feel a bit better. What more could I wish than soon to breathe with relief again when I think of your present dreary state of health! I hope the cold showers will not excite you!

"Well, tonight, at half past nine, I shall be in Lucerne, tomorrow at the Grand Duke's. On Thursday I expect to arrive in Wildegg at one o'clock; but perhaps it is nearer to come directly from Aarau. Then I would take a carriage in Aarau. I think I'll write this to you. Now I am a little confused.

"Bülow wrote and enclosed a very politic letter from Albert to him. I'll bring it along to you. Everything goes smoothly. Nothing else has happened.

"Don't be angry with this accursed scribbling, but Tausig has just arrived for dinner (with a crooked haircut). So—God protect you! Be sure that I find you in good health. I am certainly looking forward to Thursday. I commend you to your handsome Englishmen and Frenchmen. A thousand greetings, be in a lively and good humor—then I'll be happy.

"Your

RICHEL"

302 E *(Wagner, in Zürich, May 19, 1858, to Minna in Brestenberg)*

Among routine matters, Wagner reveals to Minna that the Arnold Bookshop in Dresden had a prior claim on the books which he had forfeited to Heinrich Brockhaus for a debt to him. Arnold has put a collector on his trail, but Wagner has persuaded him to wait until his amnesty.[10] The letter continues:

". . . Yesterday I had a fine morning. Friedrich invited me to have breakfast in the garden, it was really wonderful, and I enjoyed that pleasure to the full. Afterward my work went very well. In the evening I had company: Frau

[9] The month of May, 1858, is fixed by the reference to the Grand Duke (of Weimar), who met Wagner at Lucerne in that month to assure himself that the *Nibelung* project was still destined for his theater.

[10] See 185.

Heine with her brother (since her husband is never free) did the honors; young Hinzel came too, and Herwegh; Semper—the rascal—didn't come. I played a lot for them on the Erard.

"At Sulzer's—last Sunday evening—no whist was played; the hostess had laid out a terribly lavish dinner and was annoyed when I stuck to tea, bread, and butter; she made the first cup of tea so strong that I still feel it today. We chatted about politics and Napoleon until eleven o'clock. Well, it's over now!

"Now I won't see anyone else this week. On Saturday I'll come to you early in the morning so as to have dinner *en famille* on my birthday. The train is supposed to be in Wildegg about eleven o'clock; so send the carriage, for Herr Müller can't be prevented from coming with me. Then we shall be together for about two full days, and I only hope that the doctor doesn't mind, for it is a definite interruption of your cure. Arrange it according to your state of health; if you have bad nights just before, we won't come until the seven o'clock. Well, you will soon see it all! Be patient for the time being and stick to the cure; if it should not help you, it would be too bad! Everybody says that considering your state the cure had to be very long and couldn't have been otherwise; compared to the advantage you are to get from it, whatever you may have missed is of no value. So—God protect you! Don't be despondent! Keep brave and take my blessing.

"YOUR RICHARD

OLD PARSON [*alt Pfarrer*]"

302 F (*Wagner in Zürich, July 1, 1858, to Minna* [*in Brestenberg*])

"O MY GOOD MINNA!

"How can you believe that I forgot about the money for you? Especially now that it lies around here like hay. But did you not think of my coming to you on Sunday? Well, then I will bring you what you need. Two weeks from today I'll come with an enormously big, wide, and high carriage and will call for you with all the household furniture and bring you to the deserted house which will finally know what it is to have a mistress again. Your letter to Lizette, which I read out to her with great unction, was quite extraordinarily beautiful; it touched even me to tears, not to speak of Lizette—her answer I am going to relate to you by word of mouth. Your straw hat also wandered to Arbenz today. May I not order something quite pretty for you? Well, you'll tell me! But you, you good patient, try to get through smoothly with the rest of your cure. Those cold showers must certainly stimulate you in the long run; it could not be otherwise. For goodness' sake, don't exaggerate such strenuous treatments; the damage can be very great. Think of my oversevere cold cures in Albisbrunnen and how I lost all my sleep. Well, I hope the doctor is a reasonable man and stops it in time; I only do not trust *you* to be sensible (if you'll pardon me!), for I know how careless you sometimes are about yourself.

On the whole, you should not be worried if an immediate success fails to come. Generally, every cure affects one unfavorably at first, and the good after effect usually starts only with the return to normal life. You will, I think, finally also regain good sleep in your house and bed, and so everything is regained; for in the present treatment your constitution has been altered, especially by the revived skin activity. I certainly hope for the best! When I left Mornex, I was at the last very stimulated too. In any case you did the best that could be done and certainly helped yourself. The rest will come, be sure. I'll have to tell you pleasant things about Vienna. I expect a very good performance of *Lohengrin* there. Nothing else has happened. I have been paid back a lot; but there is still an immense sum of money left, and you are to resume your regimen with a well filled purse. Today I wrote again to Bordeaux for wine—so you see—I hope for tranquillity and permanent comfort. I haven't yet paid Ochsner; if he doesn't dun me, I'll wait until you are back; but you mustn't be bothered with such unpleasant trifles either. You ought to be kept quiet.

"I'll leave the Herweghs alone in any case. They now have their D'Agoult and 300,000 Frenchmen and Italians daily in their home; and on the whole I believe it is better for you to keep away from all possible excitements. My little devil of a fellow, however, wants to join me.[11] He has taken a fancy to you. So be good enough to order the carriage for *Sunday morning at eleven o'clock*:

"In Wildegg. If we like it and there is room enough, we may stay there overnight, although I now have some respect for the Brestenberg nights.

"Well, may the good God protect you and bestow on you a tender sleep, a good awakening, and a merry mood!

"This for a greeting from your   RICHARD"

302 G *(Wagner, in Zürich, July 11, 1858, to Minna in Brestenberg)*

"WELL, DEAREST MINNA:

"Tichatschek is here and intends to spend his whole leave with me; he doesn't want to see anybody else but is glad to spend all day cozily with me. It is certainly my own fault that this man believes he is thus granting me a real favor: Why didn't I more emphatically enlighten people of his sort about the great difference between us? I now long to have the Bülows here; I might have loaded Tichatschek upon them after all. But they really don't come before the end of the month. Thus also your worries about their accommodation were superfluous! Now may God give me the strength to survive that bitter draft too, for I also am longing *for rest*! I manage best in solitude; and men give me more and more pain. I could even give up the Bülows and everything else. Even Liszt need not come; now only the little and very clever Tausig helps

---

[11] Evidently Karl Tausig, the pianist, sent by Liszt, and then sixteen.

me to get over my recent difficulty. (Incidentally his father is a very honest Bohemian, thoroughly Christian.)

"From your letter today I gather that it is almost nonsensical to leave you longer taking the cure; for according to your reports about your health it seems obvious that you have overdone the cure and are exhausted. Everything which I told you about it was of course spoken to the winds, as is always the way when I give my opinion about such a thing. I let you stay there those three days supposing that you were going to rest there in that time so as not to plunge from the exhausting cure directly into the social life here. Let's wait and see first whether that kind of life will quiet rather than excite you. If the latter is the case, I shall send everybody away, as I told you, and go on a trip with you.

"Now, enough of this! Let's hope for the best: may Heaven bestow on you quiet and rest, for—to tell the truth—I need it myself! Goodbye! If nothing happens, I'll write you a few lines only on Tuesday, to announce again my arrival on Thursday. Refuse any treatment except one rubdown and follow me!

"YOUR RICHARD"

[(From Tichatschek (as an appendix of the above letter)]
"DEAR RESPECTED FRIEND!

"What do you say to my intrusion into your home at such an unusual time? I hope you get rid of your long, lingering illness so that I may soon have the pleasure of greeting you in your charming apartment, which, in all its beauty, I have been using as a guest since yesterday. Many regards from my wife, from whom I got a letter today for my birthday.

"Affectionate greetings from your
TICHATSCHEK"

The following letter is undated, but the contents show that Wagner wrote from Geneva, where he stayed for one week late in August, 1858, anticipating Minna's birthday, September 5.

319 (Wagner [in Geneva] to Minna [in Zürich])

"MY DEAR GOOD MINNA:

"I congratulate you most heartily on your birthday. I have already quietly celebrated it in advance in Geneva by choosing some local goods here for you. In doing so, I thought above all of your bare arms, which you should cover with gold and silk; and, of course, the hands should be considered too. For the head they had those pretty little Geneva bonnets here, which are good for hard wear [strapazieren]; I thought I should send you a few of these too. So that everything would smell nicely also, some perfume had to be provided, and

I add my felicitations to the whole, so that it will make a pleasant impression.

"Be healthy, be quiet and without worries—then you will also be happy: Surely!

"On *Minna's birthday*   "Your
                                                                                     RICHARD"

320 *(Emma Herwegh,* [12] *in Zürich, September 29, 1858, to Minna in Zwickau)*

"MY BEST MINNA:

"It was a week ago yesterday that I received your dear, sad lines; and if I have hesitated with my answer, it was merely because I had to run the gantlet so frequently that I should not have been able to commit anything but my own depression to paper, and that, indeed, I did not want to do. Then I helped myself with my old philosophy, which beckons to me whenever I am in a fair way to becoming the Devil's prey. Do not complain, whatever may happen, so long as you have those around you in this world who are closest to you; take heart then; your worries are only on their account, and in order to get rid of the worries you would have to bury everything for which you care to live at all—enough!

"Your request for the two caps has been *immediately* taken care of; and if no opportunity arises until tomorrow, I shall send them by mail according to your wishes, and you may wear them on Sunday. One of them rather reminded me of you; I have seen you in it once, when I came out to you in the morning; you wore a pink dressing gown with it. I already knew the fine story about Furrer; it was Tausig who told us about it, and who left Zürich a few days after you in order to travel to Geneva with his mother (his mother met him here) and to go then to Berlin, where he intends to spend three months.

"The story about Furrer [13] is so infamous that it caused unanimous indignation, for naturally it spread through the town like wildfire, long before your message arrived. What luck that you had enough to pay with, after having exhausted your resources to such an extent. It struck me when I heard of it. I thought right away: now she may have found herself in distress, since you had already shared your resources with me. If something like that had happened to me, I either should have had to stay there, or should have had to leave the things behind. A fine state of affairs! I believe that in this respect there is no third woman in Zürich whom life has treated with so much of this kind of misery as it has us two. Good, dear Minna! There you see how right I was when I predicted to you that your Richard would not bear it without you. One cannot advise anybody in things which affect the individuality so deeply that every word from a third mouth, however dear it may be, can be at best only superfluous. . . .

[12] George and Emma Herwegh were friends of the Wagners in Zürich.
[13] Furrer had withheld Wagner's baggage for payment of debts.

"Now farewell! Liszt is supposed to be in Munich. Since you two are not here, there is little hope for us to see the dear man again. I should have liked very, very much to see the Princess too. *Eh, bien,* it can't be; but one can bear such things. Be courageous, dear, dear Minna; see that you get good care, so that bright days will shine upon a healthy face. George sends you hearty greetings; and I am in faithful love

"Your

Emma Herwegh"

✤ XX ✤

LOHENGRIN

Lohengrin, destined to become in the sixties Wagner's opera of the most obvious appeal, was first the victim of a full decade of obstructing circumstance, when it was the weak sister of the suddenly popular *Tannhäuser,* undertaken fearfully (if at all), performed gropingly, and dimly understood by its hearers.

Wagner completed his score in 1848 at Dresden, and plans were made for its production. But disturbed political conditions, in which the composer was on the wrong side, caused its cancellation before the end of the year. Fleeing Dresden in 1849, Wagner sent his score to Liszt in Weimar for safekeeping. Liszt examined it and at first felt that it was too idealistic and not likely to succeed. After closer study, he thought better of this opinion, and on Wagner's entreaty he produced and conducted *Lohengrin* on August 28, 1850. The production brought Weimar, and incidentally Liszt, prestige, increased the growing reputation of Wagner, and helped to plant the idea that his operas were actually producible by the smaller theaters. *Tannhäuser* was promptly taken up by one after another, and with profit to each theater. *Lohengrin* itself was another matter. Wagner had not had the opportunity to supervise its production and establish an intelligible pattern. His presence was barred, with the result that he never beheld *Lohengrin* on any stage for the duration of his enforced absence from Germany. He had instructed Liszt at length, and Liszt put his heart into it; but the Weimar *Lohengrin* was in many ways misconceived and grossly inadequate as to performing forces. This Wagner knew by report.[1] He was also well aware that a fumbling production in a principal opera house under a routine *Kapellmeister* would have been disastrous for both *Lohengrin* and its creator. When Lüttichau planned *Lohengrin* for Dresden in 1851, and later reported his desire, Wagner withheld permission.

It was not until July, 1853, that he allowed Schindelmeisser (whom he knew and trusted) to conduct the second production, at Wiesbaden. In the following January he allowed Leipzig, under Rietz, to undertake it, but under Liszt's direct supervision and absolute right of veto. Liszt allowed himself to be duped

---

[1] Wagner wrote to Kietz about this performance (207 C): "I sent Karl Ritter to Weimar to report to me. Karl had heard me play it—the opera—on the piano, and he did not like the performance, mainly because of the carelessness and dullness of the singers. Otherwise everything possible was supposed to have been done, and on the whole the impression was said to have been imposing. But you probably already realize that I don't expect anything from all these and similar attempts either for my work or for myself."

into missing the rehearsals altogether, with the result that the performance offered a miserable travesty of the Swan Knight. *Lohengrin* nevertheless found its way into several towns, in the wake of the popular *Tannhäuser,* and at last to Munich, on February 28, 1858 (under the direction of Lachner and the patronage of Maximilian II). The major theaters followed suit: Vienna, August 19, 1858 (the conductor, Heinrich Esser, having been carefully coached by Wagner); Berlin, January 23, 1859 (with indifferent results, according to Bülow). *Lohengrin* achieved the stage in Dresden on August 6, 1859, eleven years after its completion in that city, Tichatschek singing the part Wagner had originally planned for him.

During these years Wagner repeatedly expressed his craving to hear his *Lohengrin.* (He had heard only concert excerpts, conducted by himself, in Zürich and London.) He would no doubt have liked to test the physical experience of its many innovations after *Tannhäuser.* This experience was not indispensable: when he at last attended a performance in Vienna, on May 15, 1861, he had composed the greater part of the *Ring* and the whole of *Tristan. Lohengrin* had become to him history—an early work, long since left behind. But the sense of grievance, of the world's unfulfilled obligation to the composer, remained with him until that moment.

When Wagner wrote the letter which follows, he had just returned from a lone journey into Italy and a visit to Paris, impatient with the "external" experience of the traveler and eager to create from the inner abundance of his musical imagination. On the very next day he was to begin to compose *Das Rheingold.* As if he wished to clear up an unfinished matter, he wrote to Ferdinand Heine, the costume designer of the Dresden Opera, who had worked upon the intended production of *Lohengrin* in 1848, when his son Wilhelm had sketched the scenery. Wagner contemplated a brochure of instructions for the staging of *Lohengrin* similar to the one he had prepared for *Tannhäuser.* He had sought Heine's aid, and Heine, working on the sketches,[2] had been delayed by trouble with his eyes.

251 (From Zürich, Oct. 31, 1853, to Dresden)

"DEAR HEINEMANN:

"I have just been in Paris—only for a *rendezvous* with Liszt; when he left, I sent for my old woman and am enjoying myself this week at the scene of our former sufferings. She brought along your letter for me: I thank you very much for it. You, poor fellow, must have really slaved and toiled over that work—I can well imagine it! For that you shall be in heaven with me some day!

"I believe, without having seen it, that you've done something excellent, and I really look forward to seeing your work, since it already has attracted

[2] See 230 B. Wagner's written instructions for Weimar, together with these sketches, are in the Burrell Collection (156).

Härtels to such a degree that they want to publish it sumptuously against your will.

"Your remarks about the Weimar performance showed me that even at that time you had already completely understood me; therefore I have no doubts about that. But several times in your recent reports the influence of the old stage-costume usage asserts itself so strongly that I have really had to shake my head.

"You also think that my stage arrangement is inadequate to represent Elsa's bridal procession in the second act in conformity with the length of the music (as well as with the artistic effect I intended), and you suggest a courtly ceremony—as prelude to the actual bridal procession—with which I cannot agree at all. That is much too much ceremonial for the noble, naïve simplicity of that time: Henry the Fowler did not yet know anything about marshals as they occur later on: for him 'Marschalk' is actually the stableboy, etc. His son, Otto I, when he accepted the imperial crown first introduced the Frankish-Byzantine courtliness [Hofwirthschaft]; he appointed princes to be his Marschalk, his cupbearer, etc. The particular atmosphere [Colorit] which my Lohengrin should produce is that here we see before us an ancient German kingdom in its finest, most ideal aspect. Here no one does anything out of mere routine and court custom, but in every encounter the participants take a direct and genuinely personal part; here there is no despotic pomp which has its 'bodyguards' (oh! oh!) and orders the 'people pushed back' to form a 'lane' for the high nobility. They are simple boys who make up the escort for the young woman, and to them every one yields gladly and quite voluntarily. I beg of you, for God's sake, dearest Heinemännel, take out that awful stuff with the masters of ceremonies, marshals, bodyguards, etc.: they must have no further place here. Let my Lohengrin be beautiful, but not ostentatious and—silly. Look at my 'herald'; how the fellow sings as if everything concerned him personally: no machines!

"However, only a very large stage can readily present the architectural nuances for the bridal procession with sufficient breadth: in Paris it would take care of itself. With smaller ones we cannot—since the music must remain uncut —very well do anything else than wait a little·longer for the actual appearance of the principals of the procession. On page 130 of the piano score Elsa must—on the high ground before the palace—actually come to a stop: she is moved and affected, and can lean on a lady—as if overcome by bliss; only after 8 measures does she once more proceed very slowly toward the cathedral, sometimes, pausing, cordially and naïvely acknowledging greetings. Not only does it take shape this way, but it actually becomes what I intended it to be; namely, no marchlike procession, but the infinitely significant advance [der reiche und wichtige Gang] of Elsa to the altar: during the music she has an extremely important silent part to play which must completely hold our attention.

"I know you'll understand me now, and would have understood me right away if *I* had played over the music to you. Now do it as well as you can: but the bodyguard gentlemen, etc., must go.

"Tomorrow I begin the composition of my *Nibelungen* dramas: I'm all ready for it now. Otherwise I'm well enough: I spent some pleasant days with Liszt and his family!

"I bought *Wilhelm's* book: I'm now reading in it and feel great joy about the development of this man. Give him my best regards when you write to him. Remember us to Mama and Marie and convey my most brotherly gratitude to the royal stage manager of the Dresden Opera for his loyalty. Farewell, dear old fellow: write soon again!

"Your RW"

The first production of *Lohengrin* in Vienna, on August 19, 1858, was a high moment in Wagner's career. He had withheld the opera from the larger theaters, fearing a botched reading of it without his presence. While the Court Theater held off, Wagner had become a popular composer in Vienna, through Johann Strauss, who repeatedly conducted Wagnerian excerpts at his concerts; the Musikfreunde, who did the same; and the Thalia Theater, which profited exceedingly with *Tannhäuser*. Thus the Court Theater was compelled to overlook the fact that Wagner was still "wanted" by the Saxon Court. Indeed, this was the first adequate production of *Lohengrin,* thanks to the resources at the Kärntnerthor and the industry of Heinrich Esser, who journeyed to Zürich for detailed instructions from the composer. The success of *Lohengrin* was sufficient even to quiet Hanslick and his fellow critics for the time being. Wagner's gratification at his victory, here so effusively expressed in a letter to Esser,[3] may have been increased by an awareness that in Vienna lay a likely prospect for his unperformed *Tristan,* with the trustworthy Esser as conductor. Frau Dustmann and Ander, the first Vienna Elsa and Lohengrin, were to figure in his plans as Isolde and Tristan, respectively. The scheme was to collapse, but only after Esser had expended long and patient labors, backed by industrious efforts on Wagner's part. Wagner describes Esser in *My Life* as "thoroughly honest and serious." Not a full convert to the Wagnerian idea, he was nevertheless an able conductor and a compliant instrument of Wagner's wishes.

"My dearest Friend!

"You see where my strange fate has driven me. Peculiar circumstances have occurred since your friendly visit in Zürich which quickly materialized an earlier desire to spend a fall and winter in Italy. I chose this noiseless and yet so interesting Venice in order to get the leisure to finish my *Tristan* here in perfect solitude.

"Your delightful and kind letter has already been forwarded to me. Unfortunately, I heard about Herr Eckert's well meant telegram only through you.

[3] Appendix C 4 (from Venice, Sept. 3, 1858, to Vienna).

Give him, please, my most cordial thanks for it and for all the thoughtfulness and special attention which he so successfully devoted to my *Lohengrin*. You may easily imagine, my dear friend, that this success gave me a really gratifying pleasure. According to your assertions and comforting reassurances, I could expect an especially fine performance of this difficult work in Vienna; I could assume that all the parts would be cast and supported as nowhere else. But at the same time worries remained whether this *genre,* intrinsically alien to the present Viennese taste, could have a genuine success. Now you may gather how delighted I was by your news,[4] especially since I got it at a time when—I frankly confess—a true reassurance was needed to keep up my joy of life and hope for my work. Yes, my dear friend, this I owe to you. When I met you in Zürich, new hopes arose in my heart on account of your friendliness. Well, you have fulfilled them, and in doing so have agreeably stimulated and inspired me in a heavy period of my life. The mere fact that you found joy in *Lohengrin* means much to me. My deep and sincere thanks for this! But be kind enough also to extend a good share of these thanks to the excellent singers whom I may call my dear friends too, and this from us both. Tell Frau Maier-Dustmann [*sic*] that I am cross with her for disappointing my expectations of a visit from her in May. But her fine performance in my opera makes full amends. I trust that your splendid orchestra will allow me to extend my hearty thanks to them also. Do it please. Their friendly acceptance of it would make me happy. But now I approach you with a new burden: please notify me as soon as possible about the further fate of my *Lohengrin*. I heard nothing about it except what I could gather from your letter. Although this was the main thing, I should like to know directly from you how it goes with the Swan Knight at the Kärntnerthor. Farewell! Think of me in friendliness. I certainly shall not fail to reciprocate.

"Always your
RICHARD WAGNER"

Esser wrote, on November 22, of having received from Wagner an "extraordinarily kind letter of thanks." The letter is here quoted:[5]

"My DEAREST FRIEND!

"You are not yet rid of me, for I address you again in order to repeat my increased thanks for your beautiful performance of my *Lohengrin*. I have had more first-hand reports from ear-witnesses who can't tell me enough about the excellence, subtlety, and beauty of this performance; and all of them agree that

[4] The news was good. Esser, who had written to Schott that he had found in *Lohengrin* no "pleasure," but only "ridiculously hard labor," was compelled to report, on December 17: "It is still impossible to get a seat for love or money on a *Lohengrin* night, the public makes such a rush for it." The seventeenth performance was a pension fund benefit—a sure indication of box-office appeal.

[5] Appendix C 5 (from Venice, Nov. 11, 1858, to Vienna).

a performance with finer means, with greater zeal, and under better conducting could hardly be imagined. Nor can I resist expressing my pleasure in some special lines to Herr Ander, whose artistic performance was appreciated by everybody. Please convey my special gratitude to all of the singers, of whom I have heard only the best. The warm, heartfelt rendition of Frau Meyer-Dustmann's part was known to me for a long time. She was the first and most staunch mainstay of my opera in Vienna. But now I learn about the marvellously successful performance of the Ortrud by Fräulein Ozillag too, about the splendor and energy of Herr Beck's performance as Telramund, and of the representation of the King by Herr Schmidt, also the indescribable euphony and beauty of the choruses, and finally about the orchestra's accomplishment, which couldn't be imagined as more perfect. My dearest friend, I am overjoyed and would like to embrace you before the artists, and tell you there how all this encourages and delights me! So these lines can be nothing else than an exclamation of joy and thanks. To speak of this from the bottom of my heart is an incredible delight to me, and you, my dear, should be the first to hear it. So let's cheer the Zürich visit which led to such a beautiful end in Vienna! I hope we'll soon meet again, so that I may greet you as a deserving friend upon the battlefield of honor. And now, don't forget to express my cordial greetings and warmest thanks to Director Eckert for his great share in this noble satisfaction rendered to me. Thinking of all of you, I feel as if I were in heaven. Farewell, and be assured always of the most sincere and obliging friendship.

"Faithfully yours,

RICHARD WAGNER"

Tannhäuser was produced at the Kärntnerthor on November 11, 1859. Karl Eckert, concerning whom as its conductor Wagner seems to have had so many misgivings, was the managing director of the Vienna Opera. Wagner's hope that Eckert would send Esser to Karlsruhe to inaugurate *Tristan* is another indication of the faith Wagner held in his friend. He wrote Esser as follows:[6]

"MY WORTHY FRIEND!

"I still owe you my thanks for your last friendly letter. The explanation of the reason why your director didn't grant you leave for a visit in Lucerne made clear to me, at least, the director's intentions in this affair. I find it obvious now and understand that his noncompliance with your wish did not mean contempt for me. But it was not pleasant for me to hear that your colleague instead of yourself was entrusted with the preparation and conducting of my *Tannhäuser*. I can understand that your colleague insisted on getting this opera and it is a compliment to me that he puts a value upon directing an opera of mine. May his success be the same as if you were at the heart of the performance! It was a great fortune that we two could come to such an understanding about *Lohen-*

[6] Appendix C 6 (from Paris, Sept. 27, 1859, to Vienna).

grin that it contributed to the success of the otherwise risky first performance before a Viennese audience. Now I have reason to doubt whether *Tannhäuser* will make the same striking effect. For we must confess that much depends on the conductor, under certain circumstances even everything, when works such as these are concerned. Do try to work now, as a true friend, for the right spirit of the performance, even though you can do this only through Director Eckert. Above all, no nonsensical cuts are to be made. The singers are not to be allowed entire freedom in recitative, but all passages, even those without metrical accompaniment, must first be sung strictly in time, in order to approximate exactly my rhythmical declamation and accentuation. Only then, after having mastered them, may they be allowed to modulate with a certain dramatic liberty. This is most important in order to prevent the singers from dragging, which always happens when you leave them to themselves in the quasi-recitative style. I experienced in the first song of Wolfram in the *Sängerkrieg* [*Tannhäuser*] how terribly tiring and distorting this turns out to be. When one of the singers was coaching this song with me, I could drum my intentions into him in unaccompanied passages only by adding chords with continually running quarter-notes. Thus I managed to teach him the poise [*Ruhe*] and nondragging motion along with the correct declamation. By the way, I wish to inform Director Eckert that about the end of October the *Tannhäuser* score will be published. I urge him to order a copy from the publisher (C. F. Meser, Dresden) and to demand the completely ready parts, since in the beginning, especially in the Overture and the first scenes, corrections and detailed indications for nuance in delivery [*Nüancierung des Vortrages*] have been added. I especially want them to be incorporated by the Vienna Theater from the very start. Since this involves the net price of a single copy only, I would consider this slight sacrifice as a special token of friendship.

"But now about a greater sacrifice from you and Herr Eckert. I consent gladly to a first performance of *Tristan* in your theater in Vienna if my personal presence there can be granted. This important condition which I have had to stipulate for permission of the first performance of my newest work has been complied with by the generous promise of the Grand Duke of Baden according to which I am invited to come to Karlsruhe under his special protection. This favor is of immense importance for me, for then I get the chance to perform my new work entirely after my own intentions and thus to create a model and precedent for those theaters which are planning performances of their own. But I cannot attain this goal unless the conductors of the theaters who are to present it also attend the first performance (which alone I shall be able to attend). I cannot be assured that the spirit of the Karlsruhe performances will continue after my departure. Since the Vienna theater is my very next choice suitable for *Tristan*, I earnestly beg Director Eckert, through you, to send you, at the least, as the prospective conductor of this opera to Karlsruhe. Indeed, only after the granting of this request can I give permission for the

Tristan performance in Vienna. The time will be around the middle of November and I shall announce it still more exactly. I should like you to come to some of the rehearsals.

"Well, give me the pleasure of early news, as I am always eager to hear from Vienna. Give my friendly regards to your Eckert and keep the friendship to your faithful—

"RICHARD W

"P.S. I must keep it a close secret that I am going in person to Karlsruhe: therefore I ask you please to support me in this absolutely necessary secrecy."

The *Lohengrin* performance in Vienna on May 15, 1861, was an occasion, not for level judgment, but for overflowing sentiment. Wagner, who had not seen a first-class production of an opera of his own for many a year (unless the Paris *Tannhäuser* be called one), was highly excited to behold for the first time his *Lohengrin,* then thirteen years old and long established on the stage. The audience and performers were thrilled to know that sitting in a box, deeply moved, was the composer of the *Lohengrin* so familiar to themselves, that after being blacklisted in his own land and insulted in Paris he was the returning hero.

Malwida von Meysenbug, a friend of the Wagners in Paris, where she was acting as governess, was so pleased with a dispatch from Austria printed in *Le Siècle* that she could not refrain from copying and sending it in a letter to Minna (387, undated). Her satisfaction was increased by nightmare recollections of the Paris *Tannhäuser,* which she had witnessed. She quotes the dispatch from Vienna as follows:

" 'The opera *Lohengrin* by Wagner was performed here. It seemed that the public wanted to compensate the composer for the defeat he had suffered in Paris. The house was crowded, and after the overture such a storm of applause broke loose that Herr Wagner could appease it only by thanking the public from his stall. During the first scene the same demonstration happened again, and at the end of each act the composer had to appear three times. Evidently one wanted to defend the cause of the German compatriot who had been mistreated in Paris in such a way.' "

"I am so heartily glad," she adds, "that your husband received this well earned satisfaction that I shall forgive the Germans many of their sins for it." Wagner would have been smothered in continuing ovations and demonstrations had he submitted to them. But he was in Vienna for a definite purpose—to accomplish a production of *Tristan und Isolde*—and he soon found it necessary to keep himself unobstructed. The Akademische Gesangsverein wished to serenade him after the *Flying Dutchman* performance of May 18 (when there seems to have been more applause than music). Wagner felt compelled to dissuade them—in writing. Minna made a copy of his letter, which was published in the *Wiener Presse* of May 18. Her comment is at the end (386):

"Gentlemen,

"Please believe that it is with great reluctance that I urgently appeal to you to abstain from the ovation planned for me. The enjoyment of such an unusual honor would far exceed the measure of all that I may permit my heart to feel, however hungry it might be for recognition. I made my brief visit to Vienna with no other purpose than to witness the performance of my opera *Lohengrin*, which I had not yet heard. I have not only gained the inspiring satisfaction of having attended a profoundly beautiful presentation of this work, but in a really overwhelming way I have also become aware of the most thoroughgoing cultivation of my art which had aroused the deep and splendid sympathy of the public. It was on that evening that I enjoyed what an artist may expect to enjoy no more than once in his life, and what becomes all the more significant and exalting when he in his humility does not dare to confess it to himself. I beg you now to spare me the temptation of indulging too intensely this feeling which, like a divine apparition, should delight us only in a sacred, eternally short hour. It is indescribably beautiful to keep inviolate the delicate veil that hides this feeling from one's own consciousness. This time, let me depart from Vienna quietly and deeply entranced. While I express my deeply felt gratitude to you all who have raised the artist so high by your love, I also press the hands of all of you who were certainly not far from me during that unforgettable evening.

"Should I return to spend a longer time within the hospitable walls of Vienna for the performance of some artistic tasks, I shall also be glad to take part in your own artistic achievements, by sharing which it would be my grateful privilege to be one of you. So I may hope that my wish expressed in these lines, far from injuring in any way your valuable friendship for me, will only establish it most cordially. Only in this sense could you understand me completely. In greatest esteem and gratitude, with all my heart

"Your most devoted

R. W."

Notation by Minna:

"This is a letter by R. W. The Akademische Gesangsverein wanted to serenade R. W. tonight (Saturday). W. however refused to accept it in the foregoing letter addressed to the club. In my opinion he was not right. It would have been shorter if he had spoken to them, notwithstanding the beautiful wording of this letter."

In the glow of his first experience of *Lohengrin*, Wagner turned on the following day to his friend Stürmer, a Zürich admirer and benefactor.[7] Stürmer had more recently given him the use of his house in Paris.

[7] C 7 (May 16, 1861).

"My dear Mr. Stürmer!

"I can't possibly enjoy the heartfelt satisfaction given to me here without thinking of you who obliged me so much by your friendship. In a few words only, let me tell you that I was fortunate enough to hear my *Lohengrin* here for the first time yesterday and this in a performance that carried me away and made me happy. Along with it I was honored and fêted in a way that has never happened to any composer here, so I am told. I was deeply moved by the fact that such an enthusiasm and persistence of applause was possible. As an artist who has suffered privations and endured ill treatment in an overwhelming degree, I feel compensated and in my heart deeply reconciled. Vienna will become the starting point of my artistic undertakings in future if only on account of its artistic resources. But all the same I cling to my Karlsruhe agreement as the most suitable one, and on my return I'll be able to give you more definite news about all that concerns me. Today I felt urged to make you participate in the joy which has overwhelmed me, remembering with what generosity and kindness you have shared my recent worries. With many thanks and in cordial friendship,

"Your
RICHARD WAGNER"

❧ XXI ❦

WAGNER AS ORCHESTRAL ORGANIZER

(In Riga and Zürich)

It is well known that Wagner never worked with an orchestra or an opera company for any length of time without gradually reshaping it to his purpose. His zeal always found response from those under him who were intelligent artists, resentment from the minions of routine. Three times in his life, at Riga, Dresden, and Zürich, Wagner formulated his reconstructive plan in a written brief. Two of these, the Riga and Zürich documents, are in the Burrell Collection and are now made known.

Wagner held his post as conductor of the theater at Riga for two seasons. The musical milieu in which he found himself was at least as provincial as that of Königsberg, the performing forces at least as puny and inadequate. He was looked upon, when he was noticed at all, as a small conductor fulfilling a routine job. Few could have even suspected the creative ambition which was expanding within him: he was working upon a grand opera which nothing less than a theater of the first size and rank would be able to undertake: *Rienzi*. Characteristically, he was meanwhile throwing himself into his work as conductor, handling a considerable repertory of operas, building up something which would approach adequate presentation, trying to overcome the reluctance of the money-prudent manager, Holtei, and of those members of the troupe who failed to share his zeal for strenuous coaching. But as always there was something infectious about this zeal, and he must have found some response from the feeble orchestra of twenty-four players who were at his disposal. Otherwise he could scarcely have proposed, at the beginning of his second season, a plan for a series of subscription concerts, and done it so persuasively that every player endorsed the document with his signature (90).

"To the Esteemed Members of the Orchestra

"I assume that I am meeting the wishes of the esteemed members of the orchestra in here suggesting a series of orchestra concerts through the coming winter, to be considered as the undertaking of the orchestra and to be arranged for its benefit.

"I have obtained the permission and friendly endorsement of Director Holtei, and my proposal in brief is as follows: The number of concerts—for the

first season at least—should not exceed six, since the enterprise might not yet
have attained sufficient success; the concerts would have to follow at intervals of
about three weeks each. In regard to the day of the week, Mr. Holtei kindly
indicates Tuesday, on which day there are frequent dramatic performances in
Mitau, so that the day would be available for the orchestra here. The orchestra
should invite the public to subscribe to these 6 concerts, through several subscription lists. I suggest for the 6 performances 4 silver rubles as a subscription
price, and as the admission fee on the evening of each concert the customary
one ruble. After the subscription is closed, a finance committee of 4 of the oldest
orchestra members would at once deduct the cost of the overhead from the receipts and divide the balance equally among the members; about the expenses I
shall give you my opinion later on. In order to avoid in advance any quarrel
over the distribution, as between the leading players and the rest, I suggest
equal distribution among them all; those who sit at the first desks, or, to put it
more unmistakably, those who are eligible to be soloists, may be given the privilege of applying, and they would be paid extra from the concert receipts for each
number performed. I would include in this category duos, trios, quartets, etc.,
so as to give a full opportunity to those eligible, to appear at least once in the
course of the six concerts. The concerts should average two solo numbers in
each, and the fee should be provided for in advance, according to the subscription receipts. But since variety in the repertoire calls also for vocal numbers, a
fee should also be fixed for the singers, so that we should not be subject to the
whims of those, male and female, who would be especially invited. They should
have about the same fee as the instrumental soloists, on the basis of two vocal
numbers for each concert. The fee at each concert for four solo numbers (that
is, two instrumental and two vocal ones) would have to be added to the overhead from the very beginning; even if this (overhead) may appear quite high,
since we must also take into account the rent of the hall, the printing of programs and advertising, etc. (each item to be considered at the lowest possible
price), we may still count on substantial cash receipts at each concert, which at
the end of the season need only to be distributed equally among all the
members.

"Since the enterprise as here stated may appear as something novel, and
may not yet be fully appreciated by the public, it ought to be the duty of each
member to do his best toward increasing the subscriptions, and it would give
me the greatest pleasure if I could succeed in getting a large number of signatures by personal invitation. An audience which as a whole is not yet used to
the more serious kind of music, which we are to offer in due time, will have to
be offered inducements other than the music itself, as I have observed in the
Leipzig Gewandhaus Concerts, of which 24 are given each winter to a capacity
audience. So, not only must the prospect of uplifting musical delights be offered
to the connoisseurs, but the rest of the public should be given an opportunity
for meeting and conversing, which could take place freely in the long intermis-

sion between the first and second part of the concert. A Swiss bakery, among others, could be given charge of a buffet, whereby refreshments could be offered during the intermission; in a word, everything would have to be done to combine the concerts with pleasant evenings of entertainment for the greater part of the public, since everybody knows quite well that art alone is not what the majority of people want.

"Even if after considering all this the financial results for this winter should be slight, there is always the hope that we can make the concerts so attractive that their success will increase from year to year and in time may be comparable to the situation in many other cities of Germany. The project should be in itself an advantage to an artist through its very concept of a perfectly organized body, as we may now call our orchestra, which may display its ability for independent development. For what true musician would not be distressed to see such a fine ensemble used for nothing but routine, and never of its own accord venture on what gives deep enjoyment and inspiration? *This* before everything else has moved me to offer my suggestion, for I wish to make it clear from the start that I renounce any material profit from this enterprise and refuse any fee.[1]

"My well meant proposition (which however leaves much still to be discussed) is submitted herewith to all members of the orchestra for examination and, should they agree, for signature. When signed by all of you, it may serve as a step toward a musical artists' society which in time will surely not fail to win general recognition.

"RICHARD WAGNER
Conductor at the Theater

"Riga, 11th of Sept. 1838"
[Note: Twenty-four signatures follow, some illegible.]

This plan, so far as we know, fell through, and probably because the odds against its instigator were too strong. Holtei, who had given his "friendly endorsement," probably because the venture would not touch him one way or the other, was his enemy, stirring up trouble with Minna and effecting Wagner's dismissal in the March following.

In 1851, Wagner wrote and published a plan for the development of the theater in Zürich. In 1853, he turned his organizing thoughts upon the orchestral society, the Allgemeine Musik Gesellschaft, and at a banquet in May of that year expounded to Konrad Ott-Imhof, a responsive music patron, plans for

[1] The cataloguer describes this sane and carefully considered plan by indulging in the following bit of nonsense: "This is so like Wagner: no sooner conductor of an orchestra of 7 players in an obscure Baltic town than he harangues them as if the whole world was listening." With the 24 signatures of the orchestra before him, the cataloguer prefers to misconstrue Wagner's remark in *My Life* (p. 183) that he had to increase the orchestra, which was confined in space, from a skeleton basis of a string quartet, "two first violins, two second violins, two violas, and one bass."

establishing the orchestra on a permanent basis by increasing its size, its season, its income, and by coordinating its function of serving both theater and concert purposes. He put this into written form while on his Alpine tour of that summer, and sent to Ott-Imhof the plan of which the following is presumably· the draft.[2]

The plan is fresh proof of Wagner's practical organizing sense. It was not adopted for the same reason that his theater plan had not been adopted—because receipts were insufficient, and would continue to be, as long as the available conducting talent was too provincial and dull to inspire more from the public. When Wagner had taken over and conducted Beethoven's Third or Seventh Symphony, or excerpts from his own operas, the concerts took on new life, and money came pouring in. When Wagner organized a production of his *Flying Dutchman* in April and May, 1852, he spent freely, but each performance sold out at increased prices. The one and unmistakable answer to these problems was for Wagner to relapse into a full career of music directing. This, with the bitter experience of Dresden behind him, and creative thoughts for the *Ring* before him, he was unwilling to do.

"1. The Allgemeine Musik Gesellschaft in Zürich engages a complete orchestra with the members of which it concludes preliminary contracts for 8 months from October 1st of the present year until the end of May 1854.

"2. The Society loans this orchestra to the director of the Zürich Theater for unrestricted use in the theater's performances both of operas and plays for a remuneration (for at least 5 months) to the Society, the amount to be stipulated by common agreement, according to the price which the director has previously paid for the orchestra engaged by himself.

"3. Since he will thus have a stronger and better orchestra for the same price which his smaller orchestra has cost him, resulting in better opera performances, he should accept restrictions in the use of the orchestra necessarily resulting from its more frequent use for the concerts of the Music Society. The common use of this orchestra, therefore, should be stipulated as follows:

"4. The Music Society in the course of the winter season is to give 12 concerts (instead of 6 as before) and on those 12 evenings the director shall not have the use of the orchestra; moreover, he must leave open 3 evenings for the rehearsals for each concert and call the theater rehearsals in the morning only, and not in the afternoons. In order to avoid any disturbance in the daily routine of the theater, the concert management pledges to produce its concerts in the beginning of the winter season; two of them will usually fall into one of the winter months; besides, the days of the concerts as well as of the 3 rehearsal evenings must be announced in advance. There are to be other restrictions, however: the Music Society undertakes to engage only musicians who are not bound by other obligations than the theater and the concerts.

[2] 237 (MS. draft by Wagner, 1853).

"5. Because of the aforesaid increase in the number of concerts, the Music Society expects to raise the necessary funds for the practical purpose of supporting the orchestra on a quantitatively and qualitatively higher scale than before. But since the bare receipts from those concerts will be insufficient for our needs, the Music Society, moreover, applies by visit or written appeal to the music lovers of Zürich in order to assure the enterprise by voluntary financial help.

"6. To the subscriptions from Zürich's music lovers are added the additional receipts from 12 concerts (so far as this may be used for the orchestra itself), and the receipts from the use of the orchestra by the theater director. The first indicates the total must equal the amount required for the payment of an orchestra—for 8 months and for its traveling expenses, etc. But in any event, if the enterprise is to continue, this sum must suffice to procure an orchestra of 32 men at least; namely, 8 violinists, 2 violists, 2 cellists, 2 double bass players, 2 each of flutists, clarinetists, oboists, bassoonists, 4 French horns, 2 trumpeters, 3 trombonists, and one timpanist. This is the minimum strength of the orchestra which can be offered to the director as an improvement compared to the former status. In return for that accepted improvement he could allow the Music Society the use of an orchestra twice as large as before, without any loss to himself, since the better quality of the orchestra would in its turn increase the value of his opera performances and therefore increase the interest of the public in them. To raise the level of the concert performances, however, an orchestra of the aforesaid 32 men would not be sufficient: the strength necessary for a concert orchestra would demand an increase of the strings by 14 men; namely, 8 violinists, 3 violists, 2 cellists, and one doublebass player, so as to have 16 violins, 5 violas, 4 cellos and 3 double basses. Since neither the receipts nor the additional income would suffice for its maintenance, and since in any case such a strong string quartet would be superfluous for the usual theater performances, and likewise the space for its accommodation might be lacking, the body of the string quartet in the regularly engaged orchestra would have to be reduced to 12 violins, 4 violas, 3 cellos, and 2 double basses even in the favorable case of sufficient means! (The whole orchestra therefore would consist of 39–40 men.) In order to allow for the necessary strength in the strings, and the special brass or percussion instruments sometimes required for the fullest orchestral performance, a reserve body would have to be formed in the following way:

"7. Since the Music Society cannot demand from the director further restrictions of the orchestra's use, considering the restrictions imposed upon him by the repetition of concerts, it follows automatically that no musicians are to be employed who undertake obligations beyond those of the theater and concerts, as in the case of the Harmonie-Gesellschaft of the Bär brothers here. The body of musicians should be engaged exclusively for the new Zürich orchestra, and could get rid of other obligations, such as playing at balls on certain evenings. It is to be expected that, in view of the uncertain future of the projected orchestra plan, the members will not give up entirely their present affiliations and profitable positions. Thus they should be asked to put themselves at the disposal of the Music Society reserve group, engaged for the bulk of the concerts and only obliged not to accept any other engagements for the evenings of the concerts and rehearsals, the dates of which would be given them at the beginning of the season; they would also be used, however, for the theater for important special assistance in so-called extra music behind the stage (which is often needed) with separate payment from the director.

"8. As for the administration of the orchestra, this can be temporarily stated as follows: If the enterprise is really appreciated and the music lovers of Zürich, after paying the subsidies, still declare themselves ready, at the expiration of the provisional eight months' contract, further to support the enterprise so that the orchestra can be offered a fixed position throughout the year, the Music Society should come to a close agreement with the theater committee, to the effect that the theater will only be left to a director who can also offer further guarantees for the support of the orchestra, since he will now have to provide the house rental only. The appointment of the musical director must be made by agreement between the director of the theater and the concert committee, so that the latter may be careful lest an incapable theater conductor impair the spirit and the accomplishment of the orchestra. For next winter the personality of Director Loewe could certainly be considered dependable for this purpose.[3] For its services to the theater the orchestra is subject to the theater rules, and the director must inform the orchestra's board of the concert committee of incidental fines before pay day, in order to see to their deduction in the interest of the theater director. More details about the administration should be reserved for further conferences; the discussion about the part which the orchestra might gradually assume toward public musical education in Zürich by developing a school for playing musical instruments may especially be kept for a later time.

"9. If the new propositions meet with approval, the most necessary start toward their realization would be a thorough understanding with Director Löwe, and the above-mentioned invitation for subscriptions to the music lovers of Zürich. As regards engagements already made by musicians, an understanding should quickly be reached with Herr Löwe; engagements made by them could be at once taken over by the Music Society as soon as they were found to be good and suitable for the purpose. The undersigned declares himself ready to arrange further engagements to the best of his ability and to find good musicians elsewhere.

R. W."

Wagner drew up still another plan, in February, 1855, to coordinate the Gesellschaft concerts and the opera, for the improvement of both. He now proposed a

---

[3] Loewe was the newly appointed director of the theater, who had conducted the performances of *The Flying Dutchman* in the previous spring.

ten months' season, and thirty-six performances all told. But the new opera impresario, Ernst Walther, was not interested in pulling the concerts along, nor in taking unnecessary risks for the general good. These various documents are evidence of Wagner's prodigious organizing industry, his prudent and practical means in pursuit of ends sometimes too bold for ready accomplishment.

❧ XXII ❧

WAGNER IN LONDON

(1855)

"That night, at the beginning of the concert, was the first
time that I kept my gloves on to conduct: I did that—out of
malice—for a Mendelssohn symphony, a very bad symphony;
but I took them off for the *Euryanthe* Overture."
—Wagner, in London, to Kietz, April 27, 1855 (276 A)

In early 1855, Wagner received an invitation from the "New" Philharmonic
Society in London to conduct a season of eight concerts for a fee of £200. He
accepted for the sake of reducing his debts but later found that the cost of living
in London used up the greater part of his earnings. He spent four months there
regretting what he had done, revolting inwardly (and sometimes openly)
against the necessity of conducting interminable programs with one rehearsal
for each, wherein he must accompany soloists and include mediocre English
compositions. While doing so he reflected, not unreasonably, that since he was
not a symphony conductor but a composer, he had better have stayed home at
his work, while some qualified Britisher beat his way through these dull symphonies and overtures. He counted the diminishing weeks until he could return
to the Seelisberg, Minna, and *Die Walküre,* which had been interrupted by his
English engagement. The British critics attacked him in a fairly solid phalanx.
Probably his principal satisfaction was in awaking his audiences to the fact that
the Overture to *Tannhäuser* and excerpts from *Lohengrin* (which operas they
had, of course, never heard) were not the music of a madman, but actually
uplifting and exciting; that Beethoven's Ninth Symphony, which had always
baffled them, was in a different way uplifting and exciting too.

The cataloguer remarks that "these London letters should be compared" with
the published ones "to see how artfully Natalie kept back from Wagner and
Cosima the cream of the correspondence." Although the cataloguer might so be
accused of crying his own wares, the letters here published surely make an
interesting supplement to the twenty-six in the *Richard to Minna* volumes.

270 (From 22 Portland Terrace, Regent's Park, London, March 5, 1855,
to Minna, Zeltweg, Zürich)

"Oh, my dear good Mienel! Don't be angry with me because I can write
you only two lines today! I'm leaving the dinner table to let you know, before
the mail goes out, that I've been here since yesterday and that everything is
going all right so far. But what a city!! Präger [1] did not rest until I had first
made the necessary visits, and I rode through the city with him in all directions
so that I'm really more than exhausted; but above all I literally have not yet
found a moment's quiet to write you even a line! Today we also looked for a
lodging and were at last fortunate in finding one where I want to move in and
get settled. Tomorrow I'll use my first spare time to write you more fully! Only
I didn't want to leave you without news again today. So be content with these
very warm greetings and believe my assurance that I now long for news from
you very much; don't let me wait any longer!

"Well then, farewell for today, dear good old wife! I'm terribly excited—
but not unpleasantly so. Praeger is very kind and obliging, the directors very
pleased; I don't even know who they all were that I visited. And now to close!

"Farewell and many regards to our friends.

"Your very good
HUSBAND!"

273 A (From London, postmarked April 5, 1855, to Minna in Zürich)

"BEST OF ALL WIVES!

"I have not yet received your yellow letter: that must be something good,
what with your apologizing for it in advance. Well, now I'll read it with calmness and composure. I can well believe that my pink letter gave you such pleasure; but I must ask you to moderate this somewhat, for certainly you have too

---

[1] Ferdinand Praeger (note that Wagner writes the name both ways: *ä* and *ae* in this
letter) seems to have been in evidence throughout Wagner's London visit. One
of the many deceptions in his biography (*Wagner as I knew him*) was in presenting
Wagner as a bosom friend through many years. But Wagner never mentioned Praeger
elsewhere with any special affection. He apparently first knew him in London, by an
introduction through Eduard Röckel, brother of August, who also lived in London. He
seems to have found in him the type who hangs about genius, makes himself convenient
in such matters as difficulties of language or getting about in a strange city, is ever present
and sometimes over present. Wagner remembered him in *My Life* as "good-natured," with
an "emotionalism which outbalanced his intelligence." He dismisses him in his letter to
Kietz (276 A) as "a poor German lesson-giver," and he seems to have been just that—a
Berliner who found a better living in London pupils. He had a glib pen which he used
in defense of Wagner against the British critics, sometimes with more zeal than discretion.
After Wagner's death, he applied this facility to his notoriously inaccurate *Wagner as I
knew him.*

favorable an idea of what might be in store for me here: and for that reason I'm telling you right now that *I* don't hope for *anything*. I have to answer Uncle Wesendonck's letter one of these days—perhaps tomorrow—and I'll reserve for that further details about the artistic conditions in London. Today I don't want to bother you with such things, but shall rather write about my daily life here, something which I had actually promised you the last time and which I didn't quite get around to. On the whole there isn't really much to be said about it, for I lead a pretty monotonous, melancholy existence the purpose and necessity of which is absolutely beyond my limited intelligence. First of all, I never escape the cold: the abominable London air paralyzes mind and body. Besides, there is the unbearable coal vapor, which cannot be avoided either in the house or in the street. Every moment one has hands like a chimney sweep, and I have to wash once every hour; the laundry also gets dirty very quickly; I cannot, for decency's sake, let people see a shirt which I've worn once—except the laundress, for she sees her profit in it. Most harmful of all, the air and the vapor settle in my chest, which is never clear, so that I've already completely lost my nice little voice.[2] I find it most bearable when I'm at home. Don't think for one moment that my apartment is luxurious: the living room—salon—was too small to accommodate the grand piano, so I have had to devote the so-called *salle à manger* next to it solely to the piano and the desk; the rooms are together —the doors have been taken out, thus forming a single, moderately spacious room—and are heated by only *one* fireplace. My bedroom is on the floor above; it is in pretty good shape, and in the large bed you'd have had ample room too. The *location* of my house is by no means *elegant*: it is at the upper end of Regents' Park and attracted me only because of its seclusion and cheerfulness. But even here I'm now and then entertained by hurdy-gurdies and brass instruments. In the house I'm otherwise pretty well off, and when I'm not invited out I always eat at home; then I order in the morning what I *want* to have, beef or veal; sometimes some fish beforehand, *Kartoffeln*—which they very proudly call *potados*—or cauliflower, etc. Wine, at 3 shillings, I have in the house lately— Moselle wine, as Rahn [3] advised me through you. My bills are generally considered very reasonable: for meat, butter, bread, coffee, milk, etc., for all that they charge me the cost price, and then a few pence for wood, and eggs and butter for cooking; salt, mustard, etc., I get for nothing. I've already had Klindworth for dinner several times, and both of us had enough. The bill for everything together amounts on the average to between £3½ and £4 a week (including the rent). Small, indispensable purchases are mostly very expensive, and for less than one shilling one gets absolutely nothing. The other day I wanted to do myself a favor, and ate with Klindworth at a French restaurant, which was very expensive and confirmed me in my decision to eat at home,

---

[2] Wagner writes later that he used up his voice in drilling the chorus for the Ninth Symphony.

[3] The Wesendoncks' family doctor in Zürich.

especially since I'm often invited out, to Präger's, Sainton's, already a couple of times to Benecke's[4] (where, by the way, it is dreadfully boring, so that I've now sworn off for some time!). Usually we stay together until midnight. At last we had a fine day; I promptly went to the Zoo; it is absolutely magnificent, very gorgeous, beautiful animals, very neatly kept, pretty garden, etc. During the fair season the visit to this garden will certainly be my main pleasure. I don't like to go to town at all: their Parliament building, etc., can go to blazes [kann mir gestohlen werden]. The parks are always the best. I have not yet gone to any other amusements: no theater has so far attracted me. There are as many concerts here as sand on the seashore, but no English concert will soon find me in the audience again! How these people make music defies description. But more about that some other time.

"Do you remember the young Pole, Heimberger? He came up a few days ago to say goodbye: he's going to Australia as leader of a band of Tyrolean singers and musicians with whom he has been roaming around in England for quite a while, and he hopes that in two years he can make enough money there to come back and really to be able to study for himself. Brendel recommended a Dr. Althaus to me, who has been living here for some time: I had to accept an invitation to his house for Saturday. By the way, still no Lord or Lady. They don't come to me. Don't worry about that! We are still poor riff-raff. As for the rest, I'm holding out here like a lamb to be sacrificed: inside of me there isn't a glimmer of hope about London. I'm not made for it; it will go on this way for the remaining six concerts without the least result. Good, if I hold out (only for decency's sake); but if it depended on my judgment I'd leave tomorrow. I can't complete my work here either, and shall probably bring a good part of it up to the Seelisberg. This is no place for me. I am sorry not to be able to write to you about this more hopefully: console yourself with the thought that I'm calm and determined to finish this up as well as possible. The next concert is not until a week from Monday: I still don't know what will be played, but that makes no difference at all to me. I'll always give a few people pleasure; Publikus will clap just as much as he claps at all the other miserable concerts; the newspapers will continue their efforts to get rid of me; here and there somebody will condescend, out of shame, to find this or that not so bad; the secretary of the Philharmonic will officially praise me in the publications at his disposal— and finally—I'll have one pleasure anyway; namely, to pack my bag and return to my beloved Switzerland, which I cannot today imagine ever leaving again to come back here. So the matter will come out all right at any rate, and that puts

[4] Benecke was a businessman of German extraction to whom Wagner carried a letter of introduction from Wesendonck. Wagner visited him at Camberwell only to find himself in a hotbed of Mendelssohn idolatry. Prosper Sainton, a Frenchman from Toulouse, was the leader of the orchestra, and it was he that had proposed inviting Wagner to London. His housemate was Lüders, also a Wagner admirer. Karl Klindworth, a young German pianist, settled in London, had been a pupil of Liszt.

me in a good humor. Then at home I'll be as happy as the dog who is through with his beating: then you'll rub my back. Yes, dear Muzius! Get used to looking at the thing that way, and for God's sake don't build up any false hopes: I'll save a little money, and that's all! Take good care of the house and animals, and, above all, take good care of *yourself*, so that I'll find everything in good order, especially *you*. Then we'll chat about this London dream. Keep really well, or rather: *get* really well so that you'll continue to stick with me through sorrow, misery, the lean and good times, as you've stuck with me so far; then we'll console ourselves and think—this, then, is our lot! Farewell now, good old Mienel, and keep your love for me!

"Liszt has written to me in a very calm and friendly tone, which was very comforting to me indeed. Hülsen, so Alwine writes, wants to do everything possible to get me the advance payment: he should send the money to Sulzer; if it works out, things will be all right for the time being. I haven't read a newspaper since Zürich. Remember me to my friends: tomorrow I intend to write to Wesendonck.

273 C *(From London [undated* [5] *], to Minna)*

"DEAR MINNA!

"Today, just before the rehearsal, I got your letter and Wesendonck's. During the rehearsal Eschenburg came to see me to say goodbye. Since Wesendonck wanted to have the program of the second concert with the translations and it would cost 2 shillings, 8 pence to mail it—because it *cannot* go under wrapper [*sous bande*]—it occurred to me to give Eschenburg *two* copies of it to take along. Keep one yourself, and give the other one to Wesendonck. I cannot *write* any more now: I'm very tired after the rehearsal of the A major symphony, and then Eschenburg is also leaving tonight.

"Well then, until Tuesday *after* the concert! Many affectionate regards from

"Your good
RICHARD"

"(Of course I've received the pills.)"

275 A *(Draft for a letter by Minna, Zürich, April 25, 1855, to Wagner)*

"MY DEAR ENGLISHMAN!

"Two months ago today was the hard day for me, the poor wife you left behind, fainthearted, beyond the seas. For a wife to sit alone at home, far away and separated from her husband, that in itself is inexpressibly hard (says Clytemnestra). Only there is this difference, that she was feigning, whereas what I am

---

[5] If, as is probable, Wagner refers to Beethoven's Seventh Symphony, which he conducted on April 30, this letter must have been written just before that date.

writing here comes from the most profound depth of my heart. I could not spend this day more worthily than by talking a bit with you, though I have nothing to tell you. From next Monday onward, you will have only four more concerts to conduct, then only three, etc. Then your duties will drop off with gigantic strides, then I shall see you soon, then I shall feel quite well again, and then at last we shall go up to the divine Seelisberg, and we shall be happy to have each other again; we shall enjoy the heavenly air, and admire nature. Here the beautiful weather continues to last; an inner urge drives me forth; I should like to fly off with the birds and go to you. Oh, what a stupid poor wife I am to have let you go; well, you wait, just let another queer Englishman come [6] who wants to take you away from me. I shall slap his face so hard that he will fly back across the ocean, and sight and hearing will fail him. You poor child, now I hope that you will be all right again very soon, and not cross. . . .[7]

276 A (*From London, April 27, 1855, to E. B. Kietz, 24 rue Bonaparte, Faubourg Saint-Germain, Paris*)

"OH, KIETZ!

"If I had turned back in Paris this last time, it would have been quite sensible: now I have to pay with terrible patience for the indiscretion of having let myself be tempted again. When I first arrived in London, I felt that I would have nothing to do here. My entire activity is limited to the direction of the eight concerts of which the fourth takes place tomorrow; otherwise I haven't the least thing to occupy me. The concerts attract considerable attention, and the performances are as good as possible considering the short time for rehearsals: even my music to *Lohengrin,* of which I had to perform several excerpts [8] in the second concert, met with success. But all this could be a true success only if I wanted to exploit it with all the means necessary here, or—to be more specific —if I could have a purpose here. But of that there can be no question whatever: to accept an engagement here as symphony and oratorio conductor and composer is far from my mind, now or at any other time. Outside of that there's nothing for me to do, and even a good German opera is completely out of the question. Thus the only thing left for me is to stick to the position—actually quite unsuitable for me—of a symphony conductor to the end. Then I'll see whether I'll have a few francs left with which to pay at least a part of the debt which originally was to have been paid off with this money; but it will turn out to be very little because of the enormously high taxes here and because I need much more than I first believed. Besides, Mr. Albert Franck has located me

[6] While Wagner had pondered the invitation from London, Mr. Anderson, treasurer of the New Philharmonic Society, had arrived in Zürich to press the offer.

[7] The close of this drafted letter is crowded and undecipherable.

[8] Wagner conducted, on March 26, the Prelude, Procession to the Cathedral, Wedding March, and Bridal Chorus.

here too and has reminded me in no uncertain terms to pay my debt: that's what you get out of it! Every time I earn 1 franc I must pay 10 of them!

"My acquaintances here are the following: 1. *Praeger,* a poor German lesson-giver! 2. *Lüders,* the same. 3. *Sainton,* first violinist with the orchestra. 4. *Klind-worth,* a pupil of Liszt who is only now looking for pupils, but cannot find any yet. Otherwise I've really met no one: shall I send one of them to you to increase your fame and fortune? The press usually attacks me *à cause de* Mendelssohn and the other Jews who wish me eternal life. I'd have to do strange things in order to help you through the press here! Or through the German press? Oh, you crazy fellow! Of all people, *I* who *never* bother with the rabble of the press and have insulted every one of them! [9] Be sensible and don't take me for something which I'm not. It seems you have no idea of the *loneliness* in which I live!!!! Believe me that I'm sincerely happy about your successes, more than about my own: for yours can be useful to you—a thing which in my case can be true only in a very limited sense. I shall always be burdened with an extremely sad existence, I hope only as long as my hopeless artistic productivity keeps me clinging to life again and yet again—only to torment me.

"I found a true ray of light in your letter with the many good jokes about my appearance before the English: alas, how good it is to laugh again! I received your letter when I came home from the last concert with *Praeger* and *Lüders:* I read it to them immediately. That night, at the beginning of the concert, was the first time that I kept my gloves on to conduct: I did that—out of malice—for a Mendelssohn symphony,[10] a very bad symphony; but I took them off for the *Euryanthe* Overture. Your advice especially made a very telling impression on us. Otherwise I am so put out of humor by my unsuitable position here that I don't even have any inclination for the work I brought along, which progresses very slowly: I am deeply disgusted with everything here, and I am more lonely than ever before. Greet Lindemann for me: tell him I'm not at all well. I only regret that his kind willingness to help me will never come to anything if we cannot live together for some time. Now I'm taking pills to counteract the English diet. Many thanks for your letter! In two months I'll see you again for a short time! Farewell and remain faithful to your London

SYMPHONY CONDUCTOR"

[9] The London critics expected to be called upon by any hopeful musician about to exhibit his wares. The formal calls, flattering letters, and gifts of Meyerbeer (who was then in London) were public gossip. It was Wagner's scornful refusal to pay any such calls that was regarded as an "insult."

[10] Wagner's account here confirms a story first circulated by Praeger and doubted by Ellis on the ground that the enemy critics, led by Davison, did not fasten upon it at the time. Davison may have failed to note that Wagner, emerging in kid gloves, in deference to Philharmonic elegance, carefully neglected to remove them until after the first number, which was Mendelssohn's "Italian" Symphony. Or, noticing the neat gesture, he may have been loath to face its edge of ridicule.

275 B *(Draft [?] for a letter from Minna, in Zürich, May 4, 1855, to Wagner)*

"My poor, little Husband!

"What you wrote me is really heartrending and horrible! You are certainly right in what you say about the last and the next concert program (excepting the *Tannhäuser* Overture). For that you need not have parted from your rather good wife for four eternally long months, in order to stroll about London like a lost sheep for such a long time—terribly bored and conducting the worst music, and not confining yourself to classical and good, significant music, as it had been previously stated. I quite realize that the directors of the Philharmonic had to take their obscure local composers into consideration, that finally they had to have such trash performed in winter and at the fifth concert, only they should not have brought you over there for it—for that, Hiller and his sort would have been suitable. . . ."

273 B *(From London, May 11, 1855, to Minna)*

"Dearest Minna!

"Your letter of today has really distressed me because I could see what terrible money troubles you have gotten into again, despite my efforts to keep them away from you. First of all, Sulzer told me earlier that he was prepared, for the period of my absence, to provide you with the necessary money in an emergency; for that reason he advised me not to do anything hasty about getting some money here. Secondly, however, I was completely reassured by Hülsen's promise of the advance payment and thus hoped not to have to bother even Sulzer. I sent the receipt to Hülsen three and one half weeks ago and thus could not foresee this dreadful delay. Therefore don't be angry with me, and don't increase your bitterness by persuading yourself that I spend 50 francs a day here or even that I have so much to spend. I'll write to Hülsen today; but just to make sure I also wrote to Sulzer through whom you are receiving these lines. So as not to embarrass *him* either, I just now sent over to Anderson in order to ask for another £50: he had already left, and it is possible that I shan't get the money until tomorrow. Then I'll immediately—*tomorrow* at the latest —send the 1,000 francs for Wesendonck to Sulzer from which he can then—as soon as the money from Berlin arrives—put back with Wesendonck's money and thus send him the whole amount. Oh, how unpleasant this is for me; you'd never believe it!

"I have now also written Sulzer at length, so that today I have little time left to write to you. But then I have nothing of any importance to tell you; so I just send you my most affectionate greetings, and thank you most kindly for your letter of today, even if it had to worry me. So don't be angry with me, but keep loving me. Tomorrow I have a rehearsal for the fifth concert, after which I'll write you again. Farewell, dear, good Minna, and get over the stupid money troubles which, I hope, have now been solved!

"Your

RICHARD"

277 *(Otto Wesendonck, in Zürich, May 19, 1855 [to Wagner in London])*

"DEAREST FRIEND!

"Frau Holda does not quite yet want to come out of her mountain, and still I should like to tell you something very gratifying; of course this is always my wish, but it is especially so on the day when your eyes rest on these lines and when all of us feel the separation so keenly! I need not repeat to you the assurance of my sincere friendship and my profound interest in you—you must know that my dearest wish is to see you happy and content— The most gratifying event for you and for all of us would be first of all your early return —that you have wished for long enough! Could I but bring you its realization! I had expected quite different developments there, and now I share your burden with you! Thus I can only wish you strength, courage, endurance, confidence. Say to yourself: 'It must be so,' and scorn the vulgarities which confront you. These, too, will pass, and later you will not look back on your London stay without satisfaction when, returned to us, you discuss what depressed you and what made you happy. In the distance then, the Seelisberg beckons, and in its light the glory of *Die Walküre,* veiled by envious clouds, will rise again. Therefore, don't torture yourself there. Do just what *you* think is best about staying or leaving; for each one of us can only decide for himself what is best—but one may listen to and weigh the advice of friends. A crown will certainly be yours, even if it be a martyr's crown! You've also grown richer in London, for you've won friends there. It is really a melancholy birthday letter which I'm writing you here—but sympathy should also be welcome to you there, and you will recognize, of course, what is behind all this.

"When you return I shall greet you thus:

"You have fought, O daring minstrel,
With arms which God had given you;
You have triumphed! Even though
Vulgar minds should harry noble thought yet longer!

"My dear wife sends you a purse completely filled with our best wishes. Thanks to the complete rest she is taking, she is quite well.

"Hard work is being done on Hochwyl—but one must be patient—it will then turn out nicely.

"Let me shake your hand and bid you farewell.

"Your

OTTO WESENDONCK

"Alfred Jaetl has won great praise in Frankfurt a/M by performing his transcriptions of your works."

273 D *(From London, June 16, 1855, to an unspecified friend)*

"BEST FRIEND!

"Cordial thanks for your dear letter, to which I have nothing special to answer today, except the question about the outcome of the concert before the Queen.

"First of all, as regards the false rumors about my quarrel with the directors of the local Philharmonic Society and my consequent departure from London, these are based solely on the following incident. When I stepped into the dressing room after the fourth concert I met several friends there to whom I expressed extreme annoyance and ill humor about having agreed to conduct such concerts at all; they are simply not my sort of thing. These endless programs, with a mass of vocal and instrumental numbers, tire me out and offend my aesthetic sense: I had to admit, in face of the power of established custom, the impossibility of introducing any kind of moderation or change, and thus nursed an ill humor which was more concerned with the fact that *I* had again let myself in for anything like that; much less, however, with the local conditions, which I really knew beforehand; but least of all with my audiences, who had always received me favorably and with respect, often even with great warmth. Quite immaterial to me, on the other hand, was the abuse of the local critics who, with their hostility, only showed the whole world that I did not bribe them; on the contrary, it gave me pleasure to observe how they always kept the door still open for me, so that the least advance on my part would have changed their minds; which, of course, I would not think of doing. But on that evening I was really indignant that I had to conduct a bad vocal number and a trivial overture by Onslow after the A Major Symphony of Beethoven, and being what I am, I openly told my friends in deep resentment that I had conducted today for the last time; tomorrow I would ask for my dismissal and go home. By chance, a concert singer named Reichart—a Jew from Germany—was present; he overheard my remarks and took them right to a newspaperman. Ever since then the rumors which have confused you too have been circulating in the German papers. I guess I don't have to tell you that the arguments of my friends who accompanied me home succeeded in dissuading me from my decision which I made hastily and in ill humor.

"Since then we've had the *Tannhäuser* Overture in the fifth concert, it was very beautifully played, and favorably received by the audience, but was still not completely understood. I was the more pleased, therefore, that the Queen, who had promised (which happens only very rarely and by no means every year) to attend the seventh concert, ordered a repetition of the overture. While it was in itself very gratifying that the Queen quite overlooked my severely compromised political position (which was publicly alluded to with great malice by *The Times*), and freely attended a public performance which I conducted, her continuing attitude toward me gave me a really warm satisfaction which made up at last for all the chicanery and mean attacks I have suffered here. She and Prince Albert, who were seated in front, applauded after the *Tannhäuser* Overture which completed the first part, with an almost challenging cordiality, so that the audience broke out into the most lively sustained applause. During the intermission the Queen summoned me to the reception room and received me in the presence of her court with the cordial words: "I'm happy to make your acquaintance; your composition has delighted me." In the course of a lengthy conversation, in which Prince Albert also took part, she inquired about my other works and asked if it were not possible to translate my operas into Italian so that she could also hear them in London? Of course, I had to say No to this and altogether to tell her frankly that my stay here could be only a temporary one, since the only thing which is available for me here, the conducting of a concert orchestra, is really not in my line. At the end of the concert the Queen and the Prince again applauded very cordially.

"I write this to you because it will give you pleasure, and very gladly permit you to pass my report on, since I see how much misunderstanding and malice about me and my stay in London has to be corrected and disproved. On the 25th I have the last concert and I leave on the 26th, so that at last, in my quiet seclusion, I can once more resume my work, which has unfortunately been badly interupted. Farewell! Cordial thanks for your friendship and remember me to those who share it.

"Your

RICHARD WAGNER

"I'll deliver your greeting to *Ney*."

276 B (*From London, June 21, 1855, to E. B. Kietz, in Paris*)

"OH, KIETZ!

"Wednesday the 27th, at ten o'clock in the morning, I arrive in Paris where I intend (or hope) to sleep for two nights. So I should like a very good bed. Would you be so kind as to get a small room for me for that time in the Hôtel des Italiens (where I stayed two years ago)? You may spend up to 6 francs a night. If they have no more vacancies there, get me something else and leave the message with the doorman of that hotel: I'll ask for it.

"So we'll see each other for a few days, and I shall use them most diligently to enlighten you about the 'democratic principles' which force me to the bad 'consequences' so rightly annoying to you. In the meantime, it will be enough to tell you that the captivating principles did not prevent me from conducting our 7th concert before Queen Victoria and complying with her request for a conversation with me after the *Tannhäuser* Overture—a conversation which was so long and friendly that it aroused great envy. Of course, I did not fail to tell her at once about your portraits, whereupon she explained to me that—for the sake of economy—she herself had learned to paint and that she takes care of her portrait needs herself—which I was very sorry to hear.

"Give Lindemann my best regards and tell him that I hope to spend a couple of very cheerful evenings in your company. Come over and visit me on Wednesday soon after my arrival.

"Adieu, Oh, Kietz!

Your

RW

"London, June 21, 1855"

273 E *(From London, undated,*[11] *to Minna)*

"Tuesday morning

"DEAR MIENEL!

"They want to make leaving difficult for me. Last night the orchestra and the entire, very large audience gave me splendid satisfaction. After I had already been warmly received on my appearance, and the Beethoven symphony [12] had created a sensation, at the very end—after the *Oberon* Overture—the orchestra rose and tendered me a tremendously long-sustained, loud round of applause, and the entire hall simultaneously broke out in clapping which would not end, so that between the orchestra's ever louder clapping and the audience's increasingly furious applause I simply did not know where to turn. Finally I made gestures fairly begging the people to stop and go home.

"Finally, with great difficulty, I got through with that. But now the handshaking began: the entire orchestra, about 100 persons, had to file past me and shake my hand, and during this many moving scenes took place. But from the audience, too, people crowded around me, and I had to let them all shake my hand, men and women, everybody. In short—it affected me because at last I was made to realize that the people have come to like me very much. I certainly believe that the conduct of my little Queen contributed much toward this spontaneous outburst. There was really nothing artificial about it. It was a *tremendous demonstration* against *The Times* and the other critics. And that has *never happened* before; the audience and the orchestra have *never* acted so

[11] Obviously June 26: the final concert was on June 25, 1855.
[12] The Fourth Symphony.

independently. So I'm really leaving London as a victor after all, and very much fêted.

"The Prägers, Sainton, Lüders, Klindworth and—*Berlioz* with his wife came up to see me, and we lingered together over a bowl of champagne punch until three o'clock in the morning. I finally got to know Berlioz quite well, and I'm glad to be able to say that we've formed a cordial friendship. He is really an amiable—but a very unhappy—person.

"Today I have a violent headache, and now I have to start packing. Once more I'm going to meet my friends at Präger's for dinner; then, at eight o'clock, I leave.

"Well—good Mienel—*till we meet again*—I hope, in good humor on both sides. Farewell and share my satisfaction!

"Your

good RICHARD"

❧ XXIII ❧

MATHILDE WESENDONCK

"The family Wesendonck will be pleased to accept the kind invitation of Herr and Frau Wagner for next Sunday. But Herr and Frau Wagner would give great pleasure to the family Wesendonck by spending the evening tonight quite alone with them.

THE FAMILY WESENDONCK

"Zürich, January 19, 1855" (278)

The friendship between the two couples, the Wagners and the Wesendoncks, in Zürich is the tale of a tranquil beginning, an increasing infatuation between two of them, not unconnected with *Tristan,* a corresponding tension distressing to all four, and, together with a gradual subsidence in temperature, a peaceful resolution. The contribution of the Burrell Collection is a few items, scattered as to time, but not without significance, written by each of the four.

Men who undertake to tell everything about their past are sure to touch some points of it skimmingly. Wagner's treatment of the Wesendoncks in *My Life* is one of his worst sins of understatement. He fails to mention Otto's ready purse and makes light of that loyal friend's continuing good will in full view of Wagner's many incursions upon the wife's affections. He speaks rather coolly and primly of "Frau Wesendonck," unaware that his volubility at the time, anything but cool, might rise up in the form of his own letters to contradict him.

The Wesendoncks first settled in Zürich in 1851, and remained there, intermittently, until after Wagner's departure in 1858. Mathilde was a young matron of twenty-three when she was much moved by a performance of the *Tannhäuser* Overture under his direction, and the composer was not indifferent when this lady shyly revealed an infatuation for him. The Wesendoncks were soon zealous advocates of Wagner's cause. (We cannot know to what extent Otto's interest was an indulgence to his wife.) A warm friendship was established; visits were frequent between the families. There could have been nothing more than cordiality between the two wives, the cultivated, literary Mathilde and the "bourgeois" Minna; but that there was a free cordiality between them is shown by this letter from Mathilde:[1]

[1] 245 (Bad Ems, July 4, 1853). Those who have assumed that the reliance upon water cures was peculiar to Wagner would do well to note from many letters in this Collection the prevalence of the same craze among his friends on every side.

"Dear Lady!

"More frequently than my long silence would indicate, my thoughts have been with you. Our stay at the Residenz was too short and unsettled to allow me to write to you at leisure. The house of my parents is all come-and-go, and since I absolutely need rest we fled into the forest solitude of Ems earlier than we planned. But a resort like this is an institution for the development of egoists, in which people learn to be concerned exclusively with their own selves. Drinking, bathing, resting, and walking take up the whole day, and who knows how long I would have continued in this idleness if the arrival of the beautiful sonata [2] had not so urgently summoned me to express my thanks that I cannot do otherwise than to make you, dear lady, once more their bearer? During the last few days I now again own a piano and play the glorious work, which I acquired so undeservedly, with increasing delight. I sense clearly that I'm capable of reproducing only the slightest shadow of it, but even that gives me unending joy. Shall I ever really completely fathom the 'Wisst Ihr wie das wird'? I don't know—probably not until the Master himself brings me understanding by playing it. Only in that way will the work get its true consecration—until then I shall see if I can grasp it.

"Our stay here is quite pleasant, but I fear it will be brief, because the baths have too exhausting an effect on me, and my whole nature turns toward Schwalbach. Our house is surrounded by a beautiful garden which, being unenclosed on all sides, offers a charming view over the wooded Lahn mountains which, even if not as grand as the beautiful Alpine world we have left behind, is very agreeable to the eye. Whenever the sky permits, we have breakfast in the garden under a magnificent weeping willow, so rustic and peaceful that one could completely forget about being in a fashionable resort. The little girl [3] plays outside the whole day, rides *ih ah,* as she says, and is quite well and lively. She is everybody's plaything, and even in our retired way of living has won many friends. I believe she has changed little since I left Zürich, but she speaks better. There are groves and romantic benches in our garden which are made for writing poetry! A pity that Mother Nature wastes her treasures so vainly. We are capable only of absorbing what is beautiful, but not of reproducing it. How often and with what pleasure do I look back on hours for which we have you to thank. To few human beings has the joy of giving been granted in so rich a measure. The *Ring of the Nibelung* accompanies us on our wanderings, an inexhaustible source of inspiration and interest. I cannot tell you how much I should have liked to hear *Tannhäuser* in Wiesbaden, but I was not permitted at this time to undertake the trip there. I hope that I may be granted this pleasure from Schwalbach. Otto seemed completely satisfied with the integration of the performance; some details were even better than

---

[2] In June, Wagner had sent Mathilde a piano sonata for her album, remarking that it was the first music he had composed since *Lohengrin*. In October he was to begin upon *Das Rheingold*.

[3] Myrrha, aged twenty-three months.

expected. But now back to my breakfast so that you'll get an idea of our present doings, or rather our not-doings. Until noon in the garden, then a bath, after that several hours of rest, dressing, and at four o'clock to the dinner table, then in front of the casino with coffee, busy watching the coming and going of high society and the unfolding of its styles, a walk or a donkey ride or a carriage ride, back to our house around nine o'clock, reading or music until half past ten, and then to bed. You probably know already that I won't go along to America. As difficult as this decision was for me, I was so strongly advised against the trip, for the little girl's sake, that I did not have the courage to undertake it nevertheless. What I'm going to do during the long separation from my husband I don't yet know; in any case I'm staying with my parents. Mother keeps me company in Schw. [Schwalbach], and then I'm going with her wherever she happens to go. Possibly we shall go to Badenweiler on the edge of the Black Forest. I don't want to see Zürich again until I can move there with my lord and master. As for how things went with you during my absence, about that, you bad lady, you have kept me in complete ignorance. I hope you will now let me know in detail how you are spending the summer, whether your guests and especially Liszt have arrived, and whether your husband is at last thinking of beginning his treatment? I ask you to send my best regards to Dr. Rahn and his family, also to Frau Kummer, when you write to her. Otto is just going to the post office, and so I want to hasten a little my end, that is, the end of these lines, so that you will no longer have to wait in vain for news from me. Accept, then, my best regards and the assurance of my deep friendship.

"Your

MATHILDE WESENDONCK

"Many, many regards from me and Otto to Herrn Wagner."

Wagner's spaniel Peps died of old age in the summer of 1855. In September the Wesendoncks presented him with a successor to his pet. The following verse (285), copied by Natalie, is attributed by Mrs. Burrell to Otto:

"Peps the First is no more,
Peps the Second takes his place,
Says that it will be his care
To bring you only pleasure.
Hoping to please you,
He gladly puts himself
At your disposal." [4]

[4] (Peps der Erste ging dahin,
Peps der Zweite stellt sich in,
Sagt es wäre sein Bestreben
Ihnen Freude nur zu geben.
Gern, wenn Ihnen er gefällt
Er sich zur Verfügung stellt.)

This dog, whom Wagner named Fips, and called Fipsel, died in June, 1861. W. A. Ellis, in his edition of the Wesendonck letters, suspects that Minna poisoned the animal out of spite—this on the basis of a characteristically cryptic remark by Wagner in a letter to Mathilde that the dog's death had been "mysteriously sudden." This is a base and unwarranted slander. A great affection for their pets was one of the few points Minna and her husband had in common. She wrote to Kietz almost six months after the dog's death (393): "Shortly before I left Paris, my cherished, dear friend and companion, my dear, good little dog, met with an accident. He lies buried in Hf. Stürmers."

In the late summer of 1857, the Wesendoncks took occupation of a pillared mansion which they had built on the estate of Green Hill in Enge, a suburb of Zürich. Some fifty yards distant from this house stood a sort of summer cottage, and this the Wesendoncks purchased, renovated, and equipped to be Wagner's permanent home, at a nominal rent. When the cottage was bought in the previous year, Mathilde had hastened to write a letter to Minna as its future mistress: [5]

"I have had to postpone until now my answer to your last dear lines. Accept therefore, along with my thanks for your friendliness, the assurance of my true joy over the successful purchase of the attractive property, and be assured that this news could hardly make you more happy than it has us, for we have long cherished the desire to find a friendly and pleasant retreat for our friend! Wagner's letter was a genuine delight to our hearts and our best reward, if such is deserved from a deed which in itself gives the highest happiness. The peace which came over him when he suddenly realized that he had found his home communicated itself to us and did us unspeakable good! May this little house become a true refuge of peace and friendship, a sanctified place in the midst of a world of envy and hatred and jealousy, a safe retreat from all worries and distress on this earth! I want to bestow on the house such words of blessing that only beauty, goodness, and love may dwell in it, so that the rest and peace of those who dwell there may never be disturbed!

"Es steht das stille Haus von Stein,
Und ladet dich so freundlich ein,
Und ziehst du hinein und wird es dich freuen,
Wer möchte da nicht Schwalbe sein? [6]

"Before my departure from Zürich I should have liked to look over the property but it was not permissible, since Otto still hoped to acquire some

[5] 292 (Paris, Jan. 11, 1856).

[6] (There stands the quiet house of stone—a friendly invitation. And when you move in and enjoy it, will you not be its homing swallow?)

Wagner had described himself to Mathilde as a *Schwalbe,* in search of a nest (Wesendonck correspondence, Nos. 25 and 28).

ground bordering directly on our property before the rumor of its purchase could spread. This is now the reason why he wishes the matter to be kept secret. Otto, however, inspected the interior and was quite pleased with the pleasant impression of the rooms. Everything of course is very simple and rural inside, but when you settle there and arrange everything according to your taste, it will certainly gain much in beauty. The pretty garden and especially the flowers will give you a great pleasure, for you will have the chance to develop there your skill as gardener. Don't expect too much of the little house, for you must not be disappointed on seeing it. Swiss arrangements are always a bit strange, and so here the kitchen is placed on the second floor. Each floor has three rooms, and on the ground floor are quarters for the caretaker or gardener. I myself can hardly wait for the moment to go there with you, and in my mind I have already arranged your rooms. But unfortunately there is no immediate prospect of our leaving here. The bad and variable weather is hard for all of us, and both little children are ill. I have kept Myrrha in her little bed since yesterday because she caught an awful cough, and Guido is much bothered by an eyetooth. He has fever, is sulky and restless, which depresses me and makes me long for nothing else than to have my babies in safety again. We can't even think of leaving before the beginning of next week, because the children must first get used to the air before we expose them to it. I hope the recovery will be quicker than I expect, and then we can turn to our own future homeland with sincere, joyful anticipation. All arrangements for the house have now been made and I expect to take comfort in the fruit of much labor. Errands in Paris are really exhausting and I shouldn't have the courage to undertake such a thing a second time. . . .

"Now farewell for today! How I look forward to seeing you soon again and to finding out with my own eyes that the possession of the little house makes you happy. The name for it must be found by Wagner. He has already created many a beautiful name, and he won't fail this time. We shall celebrate the baptism together!

"Goodbye, a thousand greetings to you and Wagner, and the assurance of my warmest friendship.

"Yours

Mathilde Wesendonck

"Don't say anything about the intended purchase of more land, since all endeavors have so far been in vain. The decision must come soon."

Mathilde had expected Wagner to name his new home, but she herself had already named it in the same letter when she called it "a true refuge of peace and friendship." All peace was to be lost and friendship strained, but "refuge" (Asyl) was to be its ironic title.

The Wagners moved in at the end of April, 1857, in advance of the Wesendoncks. In the Asyl at last, Wagner looked for a retreat from an interrupting world, where he could compose at will for the rest of his days. He imagined himself in that enviable state where he need no longer waste his energies conducting, organizing, writing, marketing his creations under pressure of mounting debts. Theaters were now angling for his operas; publishers were ready to gamble with them. He expected an early amnesty.

These prospects were to prove an illusion for the time being. But he had found the surroundings to support and nurture the flowering of his genius. A circle of worshipers was now gathered about him. The idolaters had begun to appear in Dresden, when the tragic figures of Senta or Elisabeth or Tannhäuser had awakened a response in the romantic idealism of the period and drawn new believers, through the poetic concept, into the stronger musical spell. These worshipers were not yet strong enough to cry down the Wagner haters, but their number was growing. The Wesendoncks, definitely to be numbered among the devout, offered their hospitality to many visitors. Wagner was the *Meister,* the center of all interest, about whose whims the whole household revolved. Many were the Wagner evenings, at the smaller or the larger house according to the company. The elect asked nothing more than to listen as he read his texts, or intellectualized, or favored them with his conversational exuberance. This sort of thing suited Wagner perfectly. An adoring audience supported his faith in his creative schemes, which by expounding he clarified for himself.

Wagner had composed *Das Rheingold* and *Die Walküre* in Zürich, under the fond and attentive scrutiny of Mathilde. He had identified her with Sieglinde (whom indeed this gentle lady more resembled than the passionate Irish queen to follow). *Siegfried* was well under way when Wagner moved into the Asyl. But he had not been there two months before he had laid the unfinished second act regretfully aside and taken up the subject of *Tristan und Isolde.* He had first mentioned this subject to Liszt less than three years before; with the *Ring* occupying him he could not have given it much generative thought. Wagner wrote more than once that his motive in this shift was to attain a ready performance and money with a "popular" work. He also admitted that the reasons were complex, and not clear even to himself. But one cannot help feeling that, without the surrounding protection of the Wesendoncks and the opportunity it brought him to bury himself in a new world of impassioned introspection, he might not have swerved into *Tristan* when he did. On the Green Hill, Wagner was enabled to enclose himself in his *Tristan* universe, immerse himself in its all-pervading mood of lowering intensity which enthralls the hearer, even today. It is also a fair supposition that if the appealing figure of Mathilde, completely subject to his imaginative will (a "blank page," in her own words, upon which he could write), had not been there to encourage every stage of the growing drama, he might have turned his efforts elsewhere, and would certainly not have attained the incandescence of the second act.

History offers no parallel to the relationship between these two as a partnership in sustaining the *Stimmung* of *Tristan,* where ardor was intimately and freely expressed, but always finely turned into the even realm of the intellect, controlled, and so applied to the mighty project in hand. Wagner once wrote to Mathilde (April 30, 1855) apropos of *Die Walküre*: "I need total inner equilibrium to complete my great work," an equilibrium which the external distractions of his London obligations were then seriously threatening. Wagner found that equilibrium when he plunged into *Tristan.* Everything around him was conducive to the desired result. His enormous vital energy, greater than the requirements of actual composition, could overflow into talking and writing, while Mathilde was ever ready to be his mirror, his muse, his "blank page." In their affectionate interchanges there was a certain amount of play-acting (for what else was *Tristan?*). It was playing with fire too, and there is every probability that these two at one point nearly lost their heads. Mathilde was saved by the realization that she was a happily (and comfortably) married wife with two small children. Wagner must have sensed that if their extraordinary relationship had become a physical one, the "inner equilibrium" would have been lost, the Green Hill no longer a paradise in the suffering presence of Otto and Minna, and *Tristan* itself in peril. On the other hand, abstinence released the full power of erotic fruition in the music (and where is *Tristan* matched in this respect?). It was indeed *Tristan* that overshadowed and directed all concerned, including Wagner himself. To Wagner, the fate that administered the love potion was the fate that confronted him, spellbound with the tender glance of Mathilde.

And as marital complications on the Green Hill made the union of these two an impossibility, Wagner was quick to seize upon a new opportunity to apply his experience with all intensity to the Tristan concept: "renunciation" according to Schopenhauer was now his watchword with Mathilde. They must ennoble their passion in its purity—sublimate it into the peaceful bliss of a *Liebestod.* Nothing was concealed from Otto, and before there was talk of "renunciation" his understanding of the artist Wagner and his forbearance with his wife were put to an inhuman test. Minna, in whom Wagner did not confide because she could not have had the faintest conception of what was happening, intercepted a "love letter" from Wagner to Mathilde and read her own meanings into it. A passing love adventure on the part of her susceptible husband she might have overlooked; what she assumed to be the complete appropriation of him, body and soul, by this formidable seductress,[7] sent her into a frantic jealousy. She made scenes which turned the Asyl into a mockery

[7] Minna's point of view was that Wagner was the victim of Mathilde. Natalie's phrase for Mathilde (299) could well have been a remembered reflection of her mother's outbursts—"the arch she-devil" (*Oberteufelin*). And in 327 Mrs. Burrell wrote: "Natalie said to me: 'He has erred, he has been seduced, but he was a thoroughly good man; it was all her fault, she has thrown him into a completely different course, she has crucified R.'"

of its name, disrupted the idyl which was so beautifully producing *Tristan,* and shortly forced the final departure of herself and her outraged husband—in different directions.

It would be senseless to blame Minna for acting precisely as any one with her point of view and in her position would have done. It is impossible to read her letter to Wagner (315) and not sympathize with her. And her position could not have been worse. Wagner had drawn about him, according to his growth, a world which socially, intellectually, musically, was quite beyond her. In the gatherings at the Wesendoncks' she had no place whatsoever except as an outgrown wife whom it would have been impolite not to invite. She could not match the ready wits and tongues of the others with a sage observation about Schopenhauer or Calderón, who were interminably discussed. She could not have found ecstatic words for the *Ring* poem because the *Ring* seemed to her a sort of fantastic aberration of her husband, impossibly remote. Wagner's dissertations on the philosophical basis of *Tristan und Isolde* must have seemed pointless and obscure, and the work itself was far too involved with the ever present Mathilde to be acceptable. Minna decided that Wagner was being led by these people into a mistaken course of learned abstractions and complexities. *Tristan* she always looked upon as the beginning of his decline, *Tannhäuser* and *Lohengrin,* created in her dynasty, as his apex.

The Wagners had lived at the Asyl not quite a year (April 7, 1858) when the situation just referred to suddenly developed at the Green Hill. Minna had noticed morning visits of Mathilde to Wagner on the second floor (she lived on the first), and messages sent back and forth. She was unbearably jealous of this woman, nearly twenty years younger than herself, who, in spite of her virtuous air of modesty and kindly courtesy, had completely won her husband's attention. One morning in the garden Minna stopped a servant whom Wagner had charged with a roll of music. Enclosed in the music was a note in an envelope, addressed *"An Mathilde Wesendonck."* The music was the first penciled draft of the Prelude to *Tristan,* which its composer was sending to his friend at the solemn moment of having just dispatched the fair copy of Act I in full score to the engraver. The note itself never reached Mathilde.[8] Minna looked upon it as an incriminating love letter and kept it till the end of her life. Mrs. Burrell acquired it from Natalie. The world was left to speculate over the probable contents of this letter. Wagner described it in *My Life* as "a note in which I explained to her seriously and calmly the feeling that animated me at the time," all of which could have been just another of his notorious understatements. The writers of *The Truth About Wagner* obtained access to the letter in this Collection and published what they considered its more purple revelations. What they quite ignored was the main purpose and content of the letter—an elucidation of Wagner's attitude toward Goethe's *Faust,*

[8] Minna later made a copy of this letter and took it in triumph to Mathilde (307). Needless to say, Mathilde did not make it known.

engendered by a discussion of the subject the night before. Characteristically, Wagner visualizes Mathilde in Gretchen and inevitably transforms her into the vividly present Isolde. That Minna should take these Tristanesque rhapsodizings (in the typical vein of the later Venice "diaries") in a gross sense would have been acutely embarrassing to Mathilde or Otto, or anyone who understood Wagner.

The letter (306 [9]) is addressed to "Madame Mathilde Wesendonck"; dated by Minna, in pencil, "April 7, 1858":

"Just out of bed.

"Morning Confession

"Oh, no! no! It is not De Sanctis [10] that I hate, but myself, for surprising my poor heart again and again in such weakness! Shall I offer as excuse my indisposition, and my consequent sensitiveness and irritation? Let's see how it will work. The day before yesterday at noon an angel came to me who blessed and refreshed me; this made me feel so well and cheerful that in the evening I felt a sincere desire for friends in order to share with them my inward happiness; I knew I would have been very agreeable and friendly. Then I heard that no one dared deliver my letter to you in your house because De Sanctis was with you. Your husband was of the same opinion. I waited in vain, and finally had the pleasure of receiving Herr v. Marschall,[11] who stayed for the evening with us, while his every word filled me with terrible hatred against all the De Sanctises in the world. He is the fortunate one who has kept her away from me! And by any merits of his? No, only by grace of her patience. I could not blame him for being so serious with you; everybody becomes so very serious when dealing with you! See how seriously I am taking it! To the point of torturing you! But why does she cultivate these pedantic obligations? What does the Italian language mean to her? Well, this I soon came to understand. But the better I understood, the more annoyed I became with that bore; he became blurred with Marschall in my dream, and out of this a figure arose before me in which I recognized all the misery in the world as my own. Thus it went on all through the night. In the morning I was reasonable again, and from the depth of my heart could pray to my angel; and this prayer is love! Love! My soul rejoices deeply in this love, the source of my redemption! Then came the day, with its miserable weather; the joy of being in your garden was denied to me; nor could I get on with my work. Thus my whole day was a struggle between melancholy and longing for you, and every time I felt a real longing for you, our tedious pedant kept on coming between us, he who had stolen you from me, and I couldn't help admitting to myself that I hated him.

[9] Ernest Newman wrote in his *Life*: "It is a pity we cannot be given the whole letter in its German form." It is here so given in Appendix A.

[10] A guest at the Wesendoncks'.

[11] A friend, a neighbor, and former fellow revolutionary from Dresden.

Poor me! I had to tell you! I simply couldn't help it. But it really was petty
of me and I deserved a good punishment for it. What shall it be?— Next
Monday I shall come to tea after the lesson and I'll be really amicable to De
Sanctis for the whole evening, and talk French for the edification of you
all.—

"What a foolish Göthe [*sic*] dispute that was yesterday! That the concept
of Göthe has been accommodated to the philistine world is fundamentally due
to a misconception of the poet. However, that this was possible at all continues
to arouse lively doubts in me about him, and more especially about his inter-
preters and adjusters. You know, yesterday too I did not object to anything,
least of all to your great delight in *Faust*; but to be obliged to hear again and
again that Faust himself should represent the supreme type of man ever created
by a poet, this (very foolishly!) made me angry. I do not want my friends
to be mistaken about this. Faust's original despair of the world is based either
on his knowledge of the world—in this case he is despicable when after the
change he rushes into the despised world with so much ado, and he is, in
my opinion, one of those misanthropes who nevertheless throughout their
whole life do not know any other ambition than to deceive men and to enjoy
their admiration—or else, and this is how it is, Faust is nothing but a dreaming
scholar who has not yet really sensed the actual world; in that case his development has merely been retarded, and one may approve of his being sent into the
world in order to learn. But then it would be better if he really learned
what there is to learn at the first beautiful opportunity, through Gretchen's
love. But how happy is the poet when he frees Faust from this deep submersion
in love, and one fine morning makes him completely forget the whole story.
Thus, for his utmost pleasure, the actual great world, the world of ancient art,
the practical-industrial world can be *displayed* before Faust's very objective
contemplation. This Faust represents for me nothing but a missed opportunity;
and the opportunity he has missed is nothing less than salvation and redemption. In the end the gray-haired sinner feels this himself and very obviously
tries to atone for what he has missed by a final apotheosis—so entirely outside
of his life, after his death, where it no longer embarrasses him, but where it
can only be very pleasant to let the angel draw him to his breast and even
awaken him to a new life. That is all very well, and Göthe always remains
for me unfailingly great as a poet, for he always keeps on being truthful and
cannot be otherwise; people may also call it objectivity when the individual
never succeeds in absorbing the object, the world (which can be achieved only
by most active participation [*Mitleid*] in its suffering); such an individual
only presents the object to himself; his mind is absorbed only by contemplation, by perception, not by taking part in its suffering (for by this he would
become one with the world—and this absorption of the individual by the
world characterizes the saint, not the poet of the Faust who has at last become
an idol of the philistine). Finally, what I repeatedly enjoy in Göthe is that he

has always felt the precariousness of his behavior and yet found no happiness in having so deliberately avoided the great compassion—and, as a whole, Göthe is for me a gift of nature, by means of which I learn to understand the world; and in this only a few can compete with him. He did what he could, and—honor be to him for that! But how can one try to turn his miserable Faust into one of the noblest types of man? The reason for this is that the world becomes frightened if the whole great problem of existence is at stake; how happy people are when at last Faust deserts his path and, since he does not want to renounce the world, decides to take it as it is. Indeed, if you only knew that even then no other than Mephistopheles remains his guide, and you should be prepared to be unceasingly tormented by this spirit of falsehood, after the magnificent Gretchen, the gentle redeemer, risen in grief, has turned her back on you. Göthe knew this very well; but you should know it too!

"What nonsense I am talking! Is it the pleasure of speaking alone, or the joy of speaking to you? Yes, to you! But when I look into your eyes, then I simply cannot speak any more; then everything I might have to say simply becomes void! Look, then everything becomes so indisputably true to me, then I am so sure of myself, when this wonderful, holy glance rests upon me, and I submerge myself within it! Then there is no longer any object or any subject; then everything is one united, deep infinite harmony! Lo, that is peace, and in that peace the highest, the perfect life! O fool who would seek to win the world and peace from without! [12] How blind the one who would not recognize your glance and find his soul there! Only inside, within, only deep down does salvation dwell! It is only when I do not see you—when I may not see you—that I can speak and explain myself—

[12] At the end of the Faust tragedy (Part II, Act 5) we find the aged Faust's famous confession:

> "Nach drüben ist die Aussicht uns verrannt,
> Tor, wer dorthin die Augen blinzelnd richtet, . . .
> Er stehe fest und schaue hier sich um,
> Dem Tüchtigen ist diese Welt nicht stumm."

> (That further vision is barred to us,
> He is a fool who there directs his blinking eyes, . . .
> Firm let him stand and look around him here,
> To him who is capable this world is never mute.)

This pronunciamento, often considered as Goethe's own philosophy of life and interpreted as the idea of the philistine, is strongly opposed by Wagner in his letter to Mathilde. Wagner thinks quite differently about the "world around us" and the "foolishness" of man's strivng. The "fool," says Wagner, is Faust himself when he tries to find peace and salvation "from without." "Only inside, within, only deep down does salvation dwell." Wagner calls Faust blind, not on account of the physical blindness that befalls him, but because of his inability to recognize the redeeming power of love. Goethe's ex post apotheosis of Eternal Love, so "entirely outside" of Faust's earthly life, appears to Wagner as an artificial device, by no means likely to silence his passionate criticism.—Translator.

"Be good to me, and forgive my childishness of yesterday; you were quite right in calling it so!

"The weather seems to be mild. Today I shall come to the garden; as soon as I see you—I hope I may be with you undisturbed for a moment.

"Take my whole soul as a morning greeting!"

Minna, according to *My Life,* immediately burst in upon Wagner with the letter. He was surprised at himself for not retorting in anger. He only entreated her to refrain from mentioning the incident in any way at the Wesendoncks'. But Minna was not the sort to leave matters unspoken. She went to Mathilde with the letter, and later to Otto, as if to open his eyes to a deception. The Wesendoncks were pained at having what had been a delicate but tacitly accepted situation dragged into the open and put on the level of a marital brawl. There was a constraint between the two houses, and visits ceased. Matters were somewhat relieved when Minna, who was suffering from an advanced heart condition, went to Brestenberg at Wagner's urging to take a cure.[13] Gossip in Zürich was inevitable.

Wagner, not wishing to discuss the subject, avoided seeing his friends. Wagner's relatives, then and later, tended to rally to Minna's side. The Collection reveals a letter from Cläre Wolfram, written just after her sister-in-law's return from Brestenberg to the Asyl: [14]

"MY POOR GOOD MINNA!

"I hardly know how to begin my letter; I want to console and calm you, and I can't even think of your letter without being most deeply moved by it even now. You poor, sorely-tried woman; no, by God, I would never have dreamed that it would come to this with Richard's good heart; I can only believe that he has gone mad! The political disease of the times has made a completely different man of him; I don't know whether it wouldn't be better for us to weep at his grave, for he is lost to us and to himself. If I had read in the papers the course of events as you wrote of them to me, I would have considered it scandalous to slander Richard like that, for he is treating you badly and heartlessly in every respect; may the righteous God not punish him for it, may he have divine guidance on his dangerous path; if things go badly with him let him suffer, he doesn't want them any better. But now for you, you poor good little sister, I can well imagine what you endured; no, by God, I don't blame you if you are deeply indignant at him; you could write a novel and it certainly would not be uninteresting. I have sent your letter to Ottilie

---

[13] Minna's irritability at this time was undoubtedly aggravated by her sickness. Nor would she have been helped by a habit of taking laudanum, once prescribed for her insomnia. Wagner confided this information in a letter to his family doctor, Anton Pusinelli (Nov. 1, 1858).

[14] 309 (Chemnitz, June 3, 1858).

and informed Cäcilie about it; I expect to hear from the sisters any hour. I have asked them for advice for you; this much is certain: you cannot and will not want to stay in Zürich. You have a family in whose midst you could best recover. I ask you urgently, good Minna, to write me soon and quite frankly whether you can come to us after selling a few things like the piano in Zürich; when you are with us again we shall make a plan for your future. Unfortunately, we are poor people; if *I* had money I would absolutely send you some; my wealthier sisters are very stiff and unfriendly; I have already knocked at their door several times (not for myself), but talk is nothing but talk; what must be must be; just write very frankly what you have in mind to do. If I were you I would have a plan for my future existence, but it is possible that you won't agree with it at all. To go back to the theater is a very, very gloomy prospect: there is much deterioration there, you have been away from it for so many years, you would have to undertake different parts, you have no wardrobe; therefore I don't advise you to do it, but even less to take a position, no matter how honorable it may be. To be a servant and to be dependent on one person from morning to night, even if it is a countess! No, by no means, dear Minna, that would ruin you: such a thing must be begun in youth; if I were you I would start a small business. When I came to Chemnitz ten years ago, I met a young woman who started a dressmaking business; her husband had been a doctor, had died young, and she, left without any means, had to do something to make her living. This business increased; she expanded it; after a short time it became the foremost dress shop; then she remarried and sold the business at a profit of several thousand thaler. No one is more suited for a thing of that sort than *you* who have such a fine way of dealing with people; you don't need a lot of money for that. It is possible that you'll reject this idea, but strangely enough my husband also had the same thought. Of course, it would be best if you could settle in Dresden; the beginning is always very, very sad, but I firmly believe that the financial return would be considerable— Richard's debts are not your worry. You are so respected, so well liked: I am sure the aristocracy would come running to you, even if there were a hundred such shops. Your sisters could give you a hand; this way you would even be able to provide a carefree life for your family. You write that you would not divulge Richard's infidelity to anyone; I don't know what your purpose is in this; I find it quite noble on your part, but you also have yourself to think of. God knows it is hard enough for me to persuade you to harm Richard: I was so infinitely fond of Richard and even now I still have a great weakness for him despite his bad character, but did he have compassion for you? If I were you I would make a petition to the Saxon Court, frankly stating what is true: 'I was never in agreement with my husband's political activities, but I followed him into exile as a good wife under the condition that he keep away from politics and that he follow his own profession.' He would not have kept his promise for long, you would not have understood each other, and that's why he would have left you. You go back to your home and ask the assistance; I believe the Queen or some princess will then advance you a small sum, and once you have started something *for yourself without Richard,* things will be all right. Richard was always a hindrance to you, he had no patience, was always eccentric, never practical. O my God, if he comes to his senses what will happen to him! My dear good Minna, don't despair. God tries you sorely, but you'll eventually find peace again, even though Richard's fate will certainly worry you as long as you live. My husband says that it won't be too long before he comes back to you as a repentant sinner; but now he has severed the bond, and I would take it much amiss if you should forgive him. You have certainly been patient enough with him, you must not let yourself be toyed with; he has much to thank you for, and he has compensated you very poorly for it. . . .

"Farewell and don't forget that you'll always find me a faithful sister and that I sincerely ask you to come to your faithful old Cläre soon."

On Minna's return any hopes that the old tranquillity of the Green Hill might be restored were soon put to an end. Minna could not bear the company of her "rival," could not face her before friends. Wagner's attachment to this unhappy, sick, nagging woman had consisted in the comforts of domestic felicity, and without this she could be nothing to him.[15] She was completely at variance with his life as an artist, nor could she leave him in peace at his work. He told her that he must go away from the Asyl, and from her as well. He would find a secluded spot where he could finish his *Tristan* with no attendant complications whatever. When he obtained his amnesty, the time might come when he could join her in Germany.

Wagner left for Venice on August 17, by way of Geneva. Minna wrote two letters—a bitter one to the woman she considered the cause of her troubles, and a sadly reproachful one to her husband:

307 *(Undated draft of a letter)*

"Honored Lady!

"Before my departure I must tell you with a bleeding heart that you have succeeded in separating my husband from me after nearly twenty-two years of marriage. May this noble deed contribute to your peace of mind, to your happiness.

"I regret that you force me, through very nasty remarks about me, to put before you an exact copy of that fatal letter which my husband took the liberty of writing to you and the reading of which finally resulted in my decision to go to see you and talk things over in a friendly spirit.

[15] Minna had just written to a friend (Emma Herwegh?): "Richard has two hearts— one part of him is entangled, while he is still attached to me from force of habit, that is all." Wagner was drawn to her by an unfailing, kind concern for her illness. But pity, and pity alone, from a husband is poor consolation.

"Just ask yourself what you would have done in my stead. I was firmly convinced that you did not fail to recognize my noble, good intention when I saw you the last time in reference to our conversation, but, unfortunately, I had to discover only too soon that you abused my confidence and made a very ordinary piece of gossip out of it. You repeatedly incited my husband against me and even accused me unjustly and carelessly to your good husband. On my return after an absence of three months my husband told me to resume seeing you. After some scenes I gave in, wanted to put the cloak of forgetfulness on what had happened merely to forestall any disgusting gossip which was supposed to have started and, quite frankly, to maintain the Asyl, but in vain, it was too late in any case—you did not want it and you did the right thing; it is the only thing for which I can thank you.

"Now Wagner will go back to his work from which, to my great sorrow, he has long been so shamefully kept.

"As I had to learn recently, this is the sole wish of an unhappy woman.

M. Wagner"

315 (*Zürich, August 24,* [1858])

"My dear Richard!

"Just a few words today to give you a greeting!

"A week ago was the black day on which my husband left me, and I still feel the same grief. God knows if I'll see him again, or when; too much happens in one year. Your last letter did not contain even the slightest consolation for me, on the contrary. Now I have to put up with so much, perhaps I'll get used to many an unnatural thing in this world. Our little house has become a house of mourning, whereas things are quite merry not far from me, which, I would say, really offends *me,* but this too I shall no longer see. I was pleased to find in your letter that you miss the little dog; there is still a spark of feeling left in you for us poor creatures. I'm convinced that it won't be long before you'll be yearning for your comfortable, pleasant home life, perhaps, but *very* much later, even for me who may no longer be living, but that doesn't matter; but later you'll curse yourself for having broken away from everything and cast your faithful wife from you so willfully. I, and perhaps several others, cannot understand it. But I really didn't want to write you about all this at all; that will stop too, but it flows from my pen involuntarily and a feeling of revenge rises up in me; unfortunately there is no God! I'm not a noble woman at all, but better than many others, if that is any blessing; whether noble or not, I only regret that I was so for such a long time; it is shameful that it has come to this. I'll probably *never* go to Dresden, nor to any other city either; I don't know. All my dear friends and acquaintances came to see me, but I can never say anything because I have to cry; oh, if I only had gotten over all these insults, then it would be well with me. I didn't want to write you this either, but this is the third letter to you which I've started and I always come back to it. I have no time, it will have to stay this way; forgive an unhappy, offended woman. It is also possible that you'll get really cheerful letters from me some day; this, like many things, we cannot know in advance.

"Since I take care of my affairs with so much pleasure, I must tell you that I have just come from the warehouse where I was to store your furniture, etc. I haven't found any place in the whole Enge where the stairway was wide enough for your sofa and the big cases, and I would have had to pay 100 or even 120 francs rent while the warehouse charged hardly half of that. This won't hurt your furniture; I asked about that. Write me oftener, a few lines, but at least once a week, not because I wish it, as you wrote me; but I would rather have it come, as usual, of your own free will; this, too, I wish I had gotten over, not to have to beg any more; it is sad! May God protect you and enlighten my once good husband!

"Affectionate greetings from

"Your
MINNA"

"The good little Fips keeps out of Friedrich's way, only because he thinks that he'll tie him up again and even take him away from me. He clings to me with unexampled love and faithfulness. Whenever he sees a man, he jumps toward him joyfully, thinking it is you."

Minna tells the story of what happened at the Asyl in a letter to an unnamed friend in Zürich: [16]

"Perhaps you will laugh, as I did when yesterday my husband wrote to me that he was in Zürich last Sunday and Monday because Herr Wesendonck had urgently invited him to stay there, and sent his own carriage to the station. Although Herr W. had forbidden my husband to enter his home again, this time they induced him to counteract gossip by his visit. The good man! But I'm afraid that they have misjudged the whole situation. For their purpose my presence would have been necessary; I should have been obliged to resume a personal association with Mad. W., which may God eternally prevent! I am firmly convinced that Herr Wesendonck would never have consented to this feeble step if he had known that my own husband had told me, calling from his room: 'Minna, we must separate; Frau Wesendonck, with whom I am passionately in love, can't stand our remaining together; she can't stomach you, she is jealous of you,' etc. (These utterances could come only from a very coarse soul.) Besides, Mad. W. secretly visited my husband and vice versa, and when my servant opened the door, she forbade her to tell me she was upstairs; all this I calmly tolerated. For husbands so frequently have liaisons—why shouldn't I allow mine one? I didn't know jealousy. Only the mean insults, the slights

[16] 361 J (Dresden, April 23, 1862).

ought to have been spared me, and my ridiculously vain husband ought to have concealed everything from me. I won't even mention the letter, still in my possession, which discloses an open, tender love affair [306], but I must greatly regret the exceeding guilelessness of that good man. Frau Wille was the go-between during Wagner's stay in Venice, but from Lucerne the personal correspondence was resumed. In two weeks my husband plans to put up in the W.s' home, where they expect to have a big party in the until-then-deserted rooms under that pretended new relationship, and thus to stop the gossip for good. God, what am I saying in this letter; excuse me, dearest friend, and consider that you are the only one to whom I can unburden myself."

The denouement of the broken Asyl idyl was the completion of *Tristan* in solitude, the eventual return of Wagner to Minna (but not, be it noted, until *Tristan* was completed), and the gradual resumption of Wagner's friendship with the Wesendoncks, on the safer and more conventional basis of their first years together. In Venice, with the full scoring of Act II in hand, and cut off from correspondence with Mathilde, he no doubt found it helpful to pour his yearning for her into a diary, in between the creative hours. When the letters are resumed, the intimate *du*, adopted at the time of the intercepted letter, is continued for a while, but poetic rhapsody gives way to intellectualizing and prosaic news. In January the *Sie* is resumed. From Lucerne, as the third act fulfills itself, Mathilde is still his remembered Muse, and is told of its progress. But now she is again the *Freundin*, the gracious lady companion of earlier days.

❧ XXIV ❧

THE PARIS *TANNHÄUSER*

(1860–1861)

"The so-called Jockey Club . . . are the rich, frivolous
gentlemen who have their mistresses in the ballet, nearly all
employed without any salary, with whom they amuse themselves after the ballet, behind the scenes, and this in the most
indecent manner. These gentlemen were furious when they
arrived at the theater, which they usually do only during the
second act, and from then on the row started. They had bought
whistles and whistled as soon as someone applauded. I did not
go to the third performance. I suffered too much from those
waggish tricks, but it is said to have been a regular *war*. All the
ladies, the princesses and the highnesses, got up and applauded,
and pointed their fingers toward those two stalls. The whole
impartial public shouted: *'à la porte les Jockeys,'* etc. The Emperor was there all three times, but he could do nothing, they
are legitimists. Richard has withdrawn his score. . . ."
—Minna to Natalie, April [?] 5, 1861 (361 F)

France first witnessed an opera by Wagner when *Tannhäuser* was produced
at the Paris Opéra by order of Emperor Napoleon III, under the influence
of Princess Metternich, wife of the Austrian ambassador, and without stint of
economy. There were months of preparation, with more than 150 preliminary
rehearsals, eight full rehearsals, beginning February 19, 1861, three performances (after five postponements of the opening) on March 13, 18, and 24.
Tannhäuser was then withdrawn. The defilement of *Tannhäuser* by the
Jockey Club, bandits in white gloves, armed with whistles, is a story told by
several eyewitnesses, including the composer. Items in the Burrell Collection,
probably saved by Minna, give us individual points of view of the event in
anticipation and retrospect.

Wagner had installed Minna in a not inexpensive establishment on the rue
Newton. It was a sort of a *ménage de convenance,* where Minna had the second

floor to herself, and servants were hired by Wagner for all heavy work, in concern for her health.[1]

Wagner's first thoughts for Paris were less concerned with *Tannhäuser* than with *Lohengrin,* which, composed ten years before, he had never witnessed on the stage, and *Tristan und Isolde,* recently completed. These three, so he tells us in *My Life,* he planned to produce for the edification "of the Parisian public in general and myself in particular." To forestall the wearisome problem of French translations, he planned to engage a theater and collect singers from Germany (after somehow raising the money). He approached Mitterwurzer in Dresden, Albert Niemann in Hanover, Luise Meyer in Vienna. He also wrote to Tichatschek in Dresden: [2]

"BEST FELLOW AND FRIEND!

"You haven't answered me. But I have learned from others that having read my statement about the Paris Opéra enterprise you expressed the conviction that you had to take part in it. I assumed this anyway.

"So hear, friend, how far the matter has advanced.

"Everything is possible, and in two or three weeks everything can be fixed and assured, that is, as soon as all the singers whom I have approached give me favorable information on two items.

"Therefore I ask you:

"1. Will you be able to arrive here in the last week of April next year and can you promise me your participation until the 16th of June?

"2. How much do you demand for that period?

"I know, dear friend, that it is especially hard for you to make real financial sacrifices, and therefore I assume you will reduce your demands as much as you can without suffering a considerable loss.

"On the other hand you may imagine that the whole bold venture can only seem acceptable to the entrepreneur here—the guarantor of the shareholders of the Théâtre Ventadour—if the balance sheet of expenses is in a reasonable relationship to the possible receipts. The actual guarantor is a man who offers his guarantee out of enthusiastic interest in the enterprise and without the slightest expectation of any gain, which he would even refuse. Since I would tackle the matter only if I were sure of offering a presentation genuine and noble in every sense, I can face only such losses as could be met by my guarantor.

"This should suffice for you. So, if your answer and those of the other

[1] When the Wagners were at last settled on the rue Newton, they were forced to leave, their landlord, while binding them to a lease, having neglected to inform them that the construction of a highway would render their street impassable. Minna wrote to Natalie (361 C, June 26, 1860): "We must move next fall; the street is going to be dug out in front of our garden gate, so that no carriage can drive up any longer, a necessity on account of the long distance from the city, for most of the people come to R. by carriage."

[2] 337 D (Paris, Dec. 24, 1859).

singers are favorable, all the rest can easily be arranged. The lesser requirements are always easy to procure. Then I shall also approach you with many requests for artists. I shall need twelve excellent choral singers: I think we may draw them in couples on leave from different theaters.

"A few second and third singers can be easily found.

"As for the soprano, I shall have to keep Ney (in spite of everything), for I need—especially for Isolde—voice, voice, voice! I can't use any insignificant or worn-out organ. I believe I shall have to give up Johanna. For a long time I haven't had anything from her which could be called a sacrifice for me: she has done as much for any other composer and even more than for me. Besides, I no longer know how her voice is. Some say one thing, some say another. On the whole it turns out that her range has enormously decreased. Otherwise—well, I would surely prefer her! But how could I rely upon her?

"As for the alternating singer, I think of Meyer-Dustmann in Vienna, although even she is not really what I need, but where may I find such a one? She at least is devoted to me, has fire, a good voice, and—will gladly make any sacrifice for me. As for Ortrud, Venus, Brangäne—Can you recommend Fischer-Nimbs? Or whom else?

"Since you cannot possibly sing such parts as mine twenty times within six weeks, and since at any moment a sudden indisposition must be considered, which would terribly embarrass us, I plan to engage Niemann together with you. Or whom would you suggest? I don't know anybody else.

"In each discussion I count on unreserved artistically cordial agreement: this is my firm condition. Everybody must help where he can, in order that we may offer something unprecedented, ideal, to the world. But I suggest the following arrangement: Each of you takes over *one* part, and each substitutes in a second part in case of sickness. You both are to study the Tristan, but *you* are to sing it first. What do you think? Everything can be well arranged, presupposing really artistic good will, especially if you can do it to favor an extraordinarily harassed author like me.

"One thing more: I badly need the *Tannhäuser* scenery and costume sketches and scenario. Try to get these for me. As for *Lohengrin,* I should rather apply to Berlin, shouldn't I?

"Help me a little, Tschekel! *You* have much experience; *I* don't know anything at all. And so God protect us for today! Let me hear from you soon, and be assured that I am looking forward to seeing you.

"Your most faithful

RICHARD WAGNER"

337 E *(Paris, December 26, 1859)*

"DEAREST TSCHEK!

"Two words in haste.

"What are you thinking of? *Me* in what is called a German opera enter-

JOHANNA WAGNER AS "PHÈDRE" (154)

prise, with all kinds of repertory, etc.? My boy, this is not in my line! Now listen attentively:

"I want to produce my *Tristan,* and in order to bring it about, I plan while we rehearse that opera—to have *Tannhäuser* and *Lohengrin* performed. Nothing more! I'll be lucky enough if those three operas turn out well; more would be downright unthinkable or everything would go wrong. *Rienzi??* And where to find the time, the enormous costs, the ballet, etc.? Especially here in Paris, where they are used to seeing everything only in a perfect presentation? Let us try to give these three operas well; that will be more than enough. There is public enough in Paris for twenty performances of *one* of the operas. So this time you have to relinquish the legitimate ambition of a singer to appear in many different parts, if you want to go on *with me!*

"Besides, dearest, you have already seen from my recent letter that I am most careful not to demand any great financial sacrifice from you. You surely are to get a margin above your expenses. Now listen! Make a computation how much you could earn in those 6–7 weeks as guest on German stages; and if you want to be kind, deduct something from it on my behalf, which you will be good enough to sacrifice. Thus we will find the way and you will not come off too badly.

"Arrange your time off and guest appearances: the last week of April until the 16th of June, that is my time. Now God protect us! Excuse my haste. A thousand greetings from

"Your

RICHARD WAGNER

"Well, Ignaz Lachner??
"Not bad! Lüttichau seems to want to get rid of me. All right!
"Goodbye."

Wagner would have indeed been "lucky" if three operas had "turned out well." He organized three concerts of his music to introduce himself to the Parisian public. They brought good applause and a wide circle of friends, but the press was hostile and the expenses were great. He consulted various influential people, receiving much advice but little money. He even set up Wednesday evening salons in his none too splendid house on the Champs Elysées. His high-geared combination of energy, conviction, persuasion, and personal magnetism at last had effect—but not the one originally intended. The Emperor, at the urging of Princess Metternich, commanded a production of *Tannhäuser* at the Opéra, in French.

The following letter to Tichatschek would indicate that eight months before the Paris *Tannhäuser* performance, Wagner's heart and hopes were not in it:[3]

[3] 347 B (Paris, July 21, 1860).

". . . Unfortunately, the best theater still remains closed to me: I cannot go to Dresden, where I know there are the best singers for my works! Thus I am actually still quite undecided what advantage I may get out of my present position, and for the moment I'm staying in Paris, where I'm held back by the imminent performance of the old *Tannhäuser*.

"I'm happy that you believe you can reconcile me with *Rietz* under these circumstances. How an open and malicious enemy of my music can go at the production of my operas with devotion [*Pietät*], must remain inconceivable to me: it is probably the devotion with which he fixed up my *Lohengrin* so magnificently in Leipzig! My dear friend, here it is a matter of the *soul*: the apparent care and scrupulousness are nothing, so long as the full warmth and understanding are not present: What good does all that orchestral conducting do me then! Many of them can do that! But this way it stays: the theater dearest to me, where I know the best singers to be, does not exist for me after all! —that is the doing of the high dignitaries who act against me!

"Well, *farewell!* Give my best regards to Frau Pauline, and accept my very best thanks for your always great interest.

"Your

R. W."

Minna wrote to Natalie in Zwickau, giving bits of news about the progress of *Tannhäuser*. On May 8, 1860 (361 A): "The translation of *Tannhäuser* is getting along very slowly. Niemann from Hanover is probably going to be engaged for the part of Tannhäuser at the Grand Opéra. God, if this opera will only be a success—let's hope so." And on May 23 (361 B): "Next winter he [Wagner] must be here to lead the rehearsals of his *Tannhäuser,* which will be performed in December; otherwise the French people might only make a lot of nonsense out of it, as they did with *Freischütz* and more recently with *Fidelio.*"

Wagner's friend Ludwig Schindelmeisser, then *Kapellmeister* at Darmstadt, wrote on October 18, 1860, about a planned production there of *The Flying Dutchman,* and remarked (352):

"My thoughts go often to Paris now! That musical Paris is to be delivered of a *Tannhäuser* is of the greatest interest to a conductor. Anyone who has been in touch with events for years and has been reading in the papers what expenditure of time and energy is required to rehearse *Meyerbeer's* operas, which surely cause no great headaches either to the one who is rehearsing or the one who is leading the rehearsals—such a one looks forward to the developments of this undertaking, so completely new and tremendous for Paris, with anxious expectation. We read in the papers that only a Wolfram is lacking at the moment; that is wonderful news, seeing that the part of Wolfram, being of a purely lyrical nature, should to our way of thinking be easiest of all to cast.[4] . . . If Darmstadt were as near Paris as Heidelberg, ten horses wouldn't stop me from going there every week to hear how things are coming along, and now the performance itself! I couldn't tell you what I would give to be there!"

And Schindelmeisser throws in this remark, showing that he well knows what is to be expected from the engaged Tannhäuser: "How is Niemann behaving? Hasn't there been a row yet?"

371 (*Princess Metternich, in Paris, January 30, 1861, to Wagner*)

"DEAR WAGNER!

"It's a *very, very* long time since I have heard from you! What are you doing and how are the *Tannhäuser* rehearsals going? When shall we be able to hear anything of it? I beg you to reserve for me two more orchestra seats.

"Accept the renewed assurance of my entire devotion.

PRINCESS METTERNICH"

Kietz, apparently with the inclination but not the price for a trip to Paris, wrote to Wagner (367) and received a short and vague reply (370). But there came a long and specific one from Minna:[5]

"MY DEAR ADOPTED SON!

"In the absence of an answer from Richard, who is really incredibly busy, please be content with a letter from me alone. Let us then get right down to the essentials without any further ado.

"The performance of *Tannhäuser* takes place here *positively* and *at the latest* on the 20th of this month. If you still want to attend the two final dress rehearsals, you must be here by the 15th at the latest, certainly no later; earlier would be better. Two tickets for the performance will be held for you, in case your friend should accompany you.

"I should also say that your traveling money will be refunded to you by us.

"And now *I* furthermore say to you, my dear, best friend, that I'll be *unspeakably* happy to see you again at last, and that we can really have a good talk together. Unfortunately, we cannot offer you a place to sleep because of our limited space, but on the other hand you will *always* find a place at our modest table, even early for breakfast, but will I be able to call you, as I used to, when you finally replied with a muffled Yes from your feather bed, for I cannot say

---

[4] Wagner finally engaged Morelli, "an Italian baritone whose sonorous tones, as contrasted with the sickly French singers of this class, had greatly pleased me during my visits to the Opéra."—*My Life*, p. 743.

[5] 376 A (Paris, Feb. 1, 1861).

that you uttered a real sound. We shall have a wonderful time, and now it is up to you alone to make it come true as soon as possible.

"Last night I went along to the rehearsal, which satisfied me very much. If you had sat next to me, I should have enjoyed it twice as much, and how gladly I would have called your attention to all the beauties of the music. It is a great, noble, original work! I can't imagine anything else than that the superficial Frenchmen will like it, that is, the impartial, uninfluenced audience. The press is another matter, it makes me shudder—we have no money to bribe this riffraff à la Meyerbeer, and it would be somewhat unworthy of Richard. This much is certain—that the performers involved will gradually come to realize what it's all about, the orchestra members are already enthusiastic over it and applauded wildly last night and played quite nicely.[6] The singers are quite good, in part unsurpassable, and they love the work.

"But I'm hoping you will find out for yourself *very* soon, so I won't add anything further today. Pardon my hurry, a friend with whom I'm supposed to go shopping is waiting for me. I'll have more to tell you soon when I see you. Richard sends his best regards, and so do I.

                              "Your old mother-by-adoption,
                                                M. WAGNER

"Don't get among the rascals [*Spitzbuben*], as they say!"

As the time for the first full rehearsal drew near, Minna wrote to Natalie (361 E, February 10, 1861): "The performance of *Tannhäuser* will take place positively on the 22nd of this month. Richard has rejected all at once many things which have been customary here from time immemorial: first the *claque*, about which you have already heard, then the ballet; both these decisions might be all right, but he also cut out the beautiful overture to his *Tannhäuser* and wrote instead a hocus-pocus of Venus apparitions. May God grant the opera is a success anyway; but he is wrong, the electric spark [7] which he hurled into the public with his overture has vanished, so that I myself am beginning to have my doubts as to a great success. All the better if I should be wrong."

But Minna spared Kietz these misgivings: [8]

[6] Wagner conducted the preparatory orchestra rehearsals.

[7] Wagner could hardly have intended to "cut out" the Overture, but his statement indicates that at this stage of the rehearsals he contemplated doing what he was to do for the Vienna production of 1875—lead the overture directly into the Venusberg scene, without the final peroration of the pilgrims' chorus motive. Minna no doubt remembered how the "electric spark" of the Overture's close had excited Paris concert audiences in January and February, 1860. Her contempt for the "*Venusspukereien*," as she called them, is not surprising. The new Venusberg music in the advanced *Tristan* manner bewildered many others at the time.

[8] 376 B (Paris, Feb. 13, 1861).

"MY DEAR GOOD SON!

"Forgive me for not writing you immediately, but I first wanted to be able to tell you with the *greatest* certainty about the seats and the day of the performance, which I couldn't do until today. As it stands now, the first performance of *Tannhäuser* will take place on the 22nd. The first dress rehearsal is next Sunday.[9] How nice it would be if you could be here for that; please try to do it. I could sit next to you during this rehearsal to call your attention to all the beauties of the work, if you'll permit me. With the exception of several parterre tickets there are no more available, that is, for the *first* performance. If your friends and acquaintances are coming here for the *second* or third performance, have them tell you what they want.

"Liszt, together with his son-in-law H. von Bülow, is coming here also. You will find the former a most gracious man; about the latter I prefer to be silent—

"Well, just come, my dear friend, if possible, *at once*. Then we'll discuss the rest. A thousand cordial greetings from

"Your *much* aged mother-by-adoption,

M. WAGNER

"Richard sends you his best."

The following letter was written on a Tuesday, the day of the first full rehearsal. The schedule, as it then stood, according to Minna, would have permitted five rehearsals (through Saturday) and brought the first performance on the Monday following, within a week of the first rehearsal. As it turned out, there were eight full rehearsals, and the first performance was sixteen days after February 25, the date intended at the time of this letter: [10]

"MY GOOD SON!

"In accordance with your wish I'm writing you at once when the final dress rehearsal of *Tannhäuser* takes place, that is, as it stands at the moment, which is not quite definite yet. Next Saturday night at seven o'clock is the final dress rehearsal; the performance is positively supposed to take place on Monday night the 25th. You know how difficult it is to get such a large cast to sing together, especially in a work like *Tannhäuser,* which has the most difficult ensembles. If I may give you advice and renew my request, I suggest that you be here next Friday or Saturday noon *at the latest* and that you come right over to your faithful parents, as it behooves a good son. You'll stay for dinner, and I'll carry you to the rehearsal, as a good mother takes her little son. That's settled now, we expect you DEFINITELY *next Saturday.*

[9] This would have been February 17. The first full rehearsal actually took place on Tuesday, February 19.

[10] 376 C (Paris, Feb. 19, 1861).

"The scenery for *Tannhäuser* was not burned; this is a false rumor. The performance would be postponed for only two days in case of other accidents, that is, until the 27th of this month. Just come, the arms of your parents-by-adoption are wide open to embrace their dear son. With the most cordial regards from

> "Your faithful mother
>
> MINNA

"We have tickets for you and a friend."

The Collection contains two notes of special interest, received by Wagner in the throes of the last rehearsals—one from Albert Niemann, the Paris Tannhäuser, and one from Niemann's wife. Wagner had known Niemann by reputation as one of the foremost heroic tenors in Germany, a mainstay of the Opera at Hanover, and a successful Tannhäuser, Rienzi, and Lohengrin. Niemann had called upon Wagner at the Asyl in 1858. Tichatschek was also there at the time, but this was one tenor too many—neither would sing in the presence of the other. Unable to hear Niemann, Wagner was delighted with his fine physique and his youth (he was then twenty-seven, Tichatschek fifty-three) and at once visualized him for *Siegfried.* He also had him in mind for *Tristan,* and when *Tannhäuser* was put on in Zürich, would have insisted upon his engagement if the budget of the company had permitted. When *Tannhäuser* was cast for Paris, Wagner would have none other for the title part. Niemann was imported to France at 54,000 francs for nine months, with *Tannhäuser* as his sole obligation—such were the earnings of a popular tenor, even in those days, as compared to a mere composer. Niemann was a tenor of the arrogant type who tended to lord it over Wagner. But he must have listened to Wagner's suggestions about how Tannhäuser should and should not be sung, for Wagner was at first pleased with him. Wagner wrote to Mathilde Wesendonck, as late as February 12, 1861, only a week before the first full rehearsal: "Niemann is altogether sublime. He is a great artist of the rarest quality." Wagner's sudden loss of confidence in him, as shown in his letter of remonstrance (February 20), can mean only that Niemann had suddenly gotten wind of an industrious plot to ruin the production and make a public scandal of it. When he believed that the *Tannhäuser* production was a scuttled ship, he suddenly turned on both the composer and his opera, giving them no more care, attention, or pains than the letter of his contract required. Von Bülow found him a "toneless baritone" in quality, but this was at the last rehearsals, when he was cynically saving himself, voice included, from the wreckage. He seems to have given not a thought to what Wagner stood to lose, nor to have shown a spark of sympathy for the harassed composer.

His favorite complaint was exhaustion:[11]

[11] 374 (January 2, 1861).

"Dear honored Herr Wagner!

"My poor husband came back so exhausted again from the evening rehearsal that I foresaw his present indisposition which prevents him from coming to see you this morning, since he will have to stay in bed till this afternoon.
I join him in sending you and your dear wife my best regards.

"Sincerely yours,

Marie Niemann"

After the first full rehearsal, Wagner made a desperate attempt to pull together some of the loose ends of a foundering title role, sat down and wrote
Niemann a letter of many pages explaining what should be done. "In the third
act," he wrote, "you are too vigorous for my liking, too sensuously strong—
everything you do is too material— Everything is calculated here in terms of a
ghostlike tonelessness, with a gradual rise to no more than an expression of
affecting softness." [12] And he pictured the weary, the hopeless tragedy of this
scene, which completely loses its meaning if a *Heldentenor* must let loose his
utmost upon it. But this *Heldentenor* was not concerned about dramatic verity.
He thought only of extricating himself without loss of prestige. Smarting under
"indignities" suffered at the first full rehearsal, he wrote this letter on the day
following: [13]

"Honored Sir!

"Although I have repeatedly and most urgently asked you to let me omit
the phrase *venant en aide au miserable,* which no singer has so far been able to
negotiate after the fatigue of the first two acts of *Tannhäuser,* and although
you must have noticed that this phrase was beyond my powers, you nevertheless
insisted that it be retained, and it was only because of my foolish reticence
[*dumme Bescheidenheit*] that I did not take a more determined stand against
you. Since this phrase yesterday caused me great embarrassment before a large
audience *improperly* admitted by you, an embarrassment about which people
are already talking everywhere and which will have a most harmful effect on
my success, you can, I hope, be induced to cut this phrase.— If, however, I
should be mistaken in this assumption, there remains no other way out for you
than to look for another Tannhäuser.—

"Renouncing any personal success for myself, I shall be very happy indeed
if I escape from this whole affair with my voice intact.

"Sincerely yours,

A. Niemann"

[12] The passages from Wagner's letters to Niemann are taken from *Richard Wagner
and Albert Niemann,* 1924 (Ernest Newman's translation).
[13] 377 (Paris, Feb. 20, 1861).

This piece of callous hostility, arriving just as Wagner had written his long and painstaking attempt to save the day, must have come as a shock. He read the lines and sadly added the following postscript to his own letter: "I had got thus far when your letter reached me. I see where you have now got to: you employ toward me a manner of speech which I find myself able to understand only by casting my mind back to the very first period of my painful career! Permit me to say that you are mistaken when you speak of having laid yourself open to ridicule, and I can only wonder who has been repeating the chatter of the boulevards to you. I ask myself doubtfully whether this letter of mine can still serve any good purpose with you, or whether it will only make matters worse. However, I will not all at once give up the last hope concerning my art. From this letter you can see how very high my opinion is of you, and the sure consciousness of this must preserve you from a superficial misunderstanding of the spirit in which I have addressed myself to you. But on one point I withdraw what I have said in this letter of mine: I am prepared to cut the passage in question.[14] May you find peace! Take care of yourself, and—should it be possible —form an opinion of me that in the future will ensure for me rather more regard on your part than is evident in the tone of your letter today."

Even if Niemann had been capable of being moved by this quiet, sensible, and conciliatory plea from a much beset composer, it would have availed little. Even those most eager to hear *Tannhäuser* had no opportunity to listen to it with quiet attention, the third act especially; at each of the three performances, the hullabaloo then reached its height, at the last interrupting the performers for fifteen minutes at a time. Niemann, taking it as a personal insult, strode to the front of the stage and hurled his property hat at the Jockeys. He was no doubt jeered at for his pains.

When the first performance finally took place on March 13, Wesendonck and Praeger, discouraged, had left. Liszt did not come, but his son-in-law, Hans von Bülow, stuck fast through each postponement, forfeiting concert engagements. He was despondent at the rehearsals, and his frayed nerves could not stand the first performance. He broke down and wept. Kietz loyally stayed through it all. Paul Chandon, a believer as ever in Wagner, followed him from Epernay with a hamper of the finest champagne in his cellar—"Fleur du jardin." But alas, it was never opened!

A note from the stage director, on the stationery of the Théâtre Impérial de l'Opéra, is dated only "Thursday." This would be March 14, the eve of the announced second performance which had been scheduled for March 15, but was postponed on account of Niemann until the 18th: [15]

---

[14] *Zum Heil den Sündigen zu führen,* Tannhäuser's opening line in the climactic ensemble following Elisabeth's intercession in Act II (373). It would not have been especially taxing for Niemann, who merely wished to save his voice for solo purposes.

[15] 369 (Paris, Thursday, seven o'clock—in French).

"Mon cher maître:

"Niemann is indisposed, which compels us to change tomorrow's performance; it will thus be impossible for us to leave the theater. Mr. Boyer wants me to tell you that Mr. Vauthrot and Mr. Dietsch [16] will be in his office at two-thirty with the score, and he requests that you be kind enough to come there. I shall be there myself, and if there are any changes to be made we shall all be there to listen to you and no time will be lost.

"I remain your devoted

E. CORMON"

A note from Cormon's wife to Madame Szemere, wife of a "revolutionary Hungarian minister" and a friend of Wagner, shows that Monsieur Cormon still hoped to salvage something from the tottering *Tannhäuser* at the third performance. Since this final performance took place on Sunday, March 24, and the letter, which is in French, is marked "Friday evening," its date would be March 22 (378):

"The third performance given before an *impartial* audience will decide the fate of *Tannhäuser*. That, at least, is the opinion of my husband, who is interested in the work of Mr. Wagner as in a *work of art*. It doubtless contains parts incompatible with our French customs; it is unfortunate that Mr. Wagner did not understand this earlier; but such as it is, his score is the product of a *man of genius,* and this evaluation, which I have personally heard expressed by persons of superior merit, will, I hope, be shared in a few years by the majority of the public. Perhaps *Tannhäuser* will never be restored to the *theater*; but the unquestionable beauties which it contains will, I have no doubt, some day delight the frequenters of the Conservatory. If Mr. Wagner is not discouraged, if he is not afraid to make another attempt at another work, let him make some concessions to our *French* taste, and all those who admire his fine talent promise him a brilliant return."

After his tribulations with the insufferable Niemann, Wagner's thoughts went back to the faithful Tichatschek, the original Tannhäuser, and he wrote to his friend on the eve of the third performance: [17]

"God, how much I've thought of you lately, dearest Tschekel! How often have I already told people the story about you, how after the first performance of *Rienzi* you had forbidden the copyists to make the cuts I indicated and how,

---

[16] P. L. P. Dietsch, who conducted *Tannhäuser* as the official conductor of the Opéra, took the baton from Wagner at the first full rehearsal and proceeded to undo much of his arduous preparation. Von Bülow referred to him as an "imbecile fumbler" and Wagner described him as a *"Schöps d'orchestre."*

[17] 347 A (March 23, 1861).

when I called you to account, you answered: 'No! I won't allow any cuts! It's too heavenly!' How the hot tears ran down my cheeks.

"This was all brought back to me as I was dealing with a miserable coward who runs around howling that he ruins his voice with my *Tannhäuser*. You can well imagine how I feel!"

Minna must have written her version of the brawl to several of her friends and relatives in Germany, for letters of "condolence" from five of them are in the Collection. The only surviving account by Minna herself is contained in a letter to Natalie (361 F [18]):

"In reference to *Tannhäuser* here, I can assure you that it has not failed, but that it is again the fault of Richard's stubbornness that it has not been performed more than three times. You know that at the Grand Opera no opera is given without a ballet, and if Richard could have decided to compose one, perhaps in the second act before the contest of the minstrels, this opera would have become a source of genuine fame and money.[19] In the first performance it was a German *clique* [20] which, linked with the unbribed critics, organized the opposition. In the second and third performance it was the so-called Jockey Club. . . . Richard has withdrawn his score, and *Tannhäuser* will perhaps be performed in another theater after some years.[21] I am very ill from all this excitement."

Natalie's reply is contained in a letter to her mother from Zwickau, April 23, 1861 (357 B); it may well reflect a general current of opinion in Germany about the Paris fiasco:

"Richard deserved the most splendid success for his glorious masterpiece and a different and more dignified reception by the frivolous, superficial Frenchmen; he could have had just as much gratification from it as Meyerbeer; with this reception of his glorious opera, which will always exercise its wonderfully powerful magic at all the better theaters in Germany, the Parisians have

[18] Minna's date on this letter, March 5, 1861, is obviously wrong. She may have written "March" for "April."

[19] That Minna, who had had direct experience in high tragedy and had witnessed the birth of *Tannhäuser* in Dresden and knew its problems as expounded by its creator, could have taken up the opponents' point of view is a lamentable betrayal of her complete noncomprehension of Wagner's dearest aims.

[20] What Minna means by the "German *clique*" is not clear. Wagner's Paris opponents were anything but German, except that they rallied to the banner of Meyerbeer. They may have encouraged the Jockeys, but it was without doubt the Jockeys, at all three performances, who brought down *Tannhäuser* with their whistles.

[21] In this prediction Minna was right for once. *Tannhäuser* was not again performed in Paris until 1895.

really made fools of themselves for all time, and I could really hate the otherwise so clever, polite, adroit Frenchmen for their mean, disgusting behavior, when in other ways they always have an advantage over the Germans. All musical Christendom, together with the [?] Jewry, is taking revenge on poor Richard. The latter are paying Richard back for his *Judenmusik* [*sic*], of which he spoke in one of his books, with malicious, gloating interest, and they let him suffer cruelly by a mean lack of understanding for his immortal *Tannhäuser*; it is really shocking. Oh, what a terrible pity it is that Richard did not follow the advice you gave him from Schandau and perform *Rienzi*—then the Parisian mob would have been happier and completely satisfied, and Richard would have come away with more glory; and *Rienzi* is really so infinitely beautiful; and none of the operas ever performed in Paris would have come close to it in the solid quality [*Gediegenheit*] of its composition. They would have known who Rienzi was and understood everything in it very well. May this bitter reward which he has just received be a beneficial hint to poor Richard henceforth to follow your advice, my dear Minna."

Two of Wagner's sisters wrote to Minna. Cäcilie Avenarius wrote from Berlin, March 16, 1861 (332 C):

"I have just read in the newspaper that *Tannhäuser* has been performed in Paris and was rejected by the public. To be sure, when I thought of the superficial, frivolous French people I was sometimes afraid whether such a genuine masterpiece as *Tannhäuser* would please the taste of this flighty French mob, but still I must say that the telegraphed news caused me grief and excitement in the highest degree. I can imagine Richard's fury. Richard who on account of this performance has spent such a long time full of the most enormous excitement by spiritual and physical exertion. You, too, my dear Minna, have shared all the exertions of this time, and surely like Richard, you too are touched in the highest degree by the outcome. I will still believe that some opponent or other has been so amiable as to spread some false rumors. But I beg you most URGENTLY to relieve me from this terrible uncertainty, otherwise I shall pine away from the excitement."

Luise Brockhaus wrote from Dresden on March 19 (380):

"MY GOOD DEAR MINNA!

"Encouraged by the friendliness and kindness you showed during our last stay in Paris, and full of gratitude for the delightful hours spent there with you, I urgently beg you to report to me something about the success of *Tannhäuser* by return mail if possible. One reads here so many exaggerated and surely misrepresented things that I was much worried about you and the many troubles necessarily caused for Richard by that performance, and I shall *continue* to worry until you send me some news (which I can't expect from Richard). Even if the reports one reads here—they are incomprehensible to me—should be true (namely, that the opera fell completely flat in Paris), Richard will not be discouraged, for how could he be!! His fame has found full confirmation and masterly justification in Germany—only his health, his present plans might be affected, and therefore I repeat my request that you write me only a few true words about all this, and I assure you in advance of our sincere thanks. Give Richard my warmest greetings and soon relieve your truly devoted sister-in-law from anxious uncertainty—

Luise Brockhaus"

Dr. Anton Pusinelli writes to Minna from Dresden as follows:[22]

"I too am of the opinion that the failure of the opera was chiefly caused by party intrigues; however, I believe that lack of understanding on the part of the French also figured in this. They have revealed their shortcomings and proved that they are not susceptible to what is truly poetic. There are certainly some individuals with greater gifts among them who are responsive to the novelty and beauty of Wagner's work, but the majority remains untouched by it. Nevertheless I trust that Wagner's music has a future there too. For what is really beautiful, great, and genuine cannot for ever be banned and suppressed; it breaks through victoriously; it wins its well deserved recognition and exercises the most powerful influence on the taste of the public and the tendencies of contemporary art and science. The road that Wagner's muse has taken in Germany, where its supremacy is now generally recognized, is significant enough. It was not without struggle that this supremacy was established: here too it met determined opposition in everything that is customary, traditional, old, established; and though from the very beginning it won a popular following and not least the youthful element, this youth was guided much more by a vague feeling, a notion of the deep significance of Wagner's new ideas than by a clear understanding and a conscious judgment. Even Wagner himself went through this process of personal development. He too at first upheld traditional forms; only gradually did he leave the accustomed path and follow new, hitherto unfamiliar trends while he irresistibly drew his compatriots with him.

"I can only approve Richard's having first presented *Tannhäuser* to the Parisians and not *Rienzi,* which many people would have thought better. With the latter he would not have expressed his characteristic trend. If he had had *Tannhäuser* performed later, it would have needed a new start to lead the audience to the right viewpoint. That was one experience here, and it was at first detrimental to *Tannhäuser.* If one gets to know *Rienzi* first, one expects something similar in *Tannhäuser,* and then one feels disappointed and dissatisfied. It is

[22] This letter (388, June 6, 1861) has been published in *The Letters of Richard Wagner to Anton Pusinelli.*

true, when Wagner performed his operas in Dresden for the first time, he himself had not yet chosen a definite direction and could not give more than he just had. But now it is different. Moreover, he was unknown at that time; and now he already carries a famous name, and in Germany, at least, public opinion has decided in his favor. I am glad that in Vienna he found so much distinction, but I assure you that, should he be in Dresden to hear one of his operas, he would be glorified in the same manner. The other day, at the performance of *Tannhäuser,* with Schnorr and Johanna, the applause was so enormous and so unusual that it was meant not as much for the excellent performers as for the creator of the work and was also intended to be a demonstration against Paris."

Pauline Tichatschek in Dresden addressed Minna as *"Meine liebe, liebe, theure Mietz,"* on March 25 (382), and had this to say about *Tannhäuser*: "That you wrote so much about the performance was tremendously interesting, and it can be only intrigue and envy that have caused such troubles; the work will establish itself, we're not afraid of that, if only Richard doesn't lose his patience, that is the main thing. You, poor soul, must have plenty of worries and excitement, but a rest with me will do you a lot of good. [Frau Tichatschek had just invited Minna to visit her in Dresden.] What luck for Wagner that [?] protects him; that's very noble and fine, and it makes me really happy—I can't imagine that Niemann is not altogether excellent, for everybody says that's his best part; he really must have lost much of his voice; that's a great loss for Richard, for if he could have enraptured the audiences as the part demands, the disturbing elements would have felt ashamed and would have finally kept silent." [23]

Wagner was neither deeply upset nor discouraged by all this. The concern for him expressed by his friends in Germany was unfounded, and probably came from the vicious attacks by the Parisian press, in their turn prompting similar reports in the German papers. But Wagner knew, and he took care to point out, that he had in no sense suffered a musical defeat. The French public had shown a disposition to attend and applaud *Tannhäuser,* which after all had proven itself many times over, and was not up for trial. But the French public had not been allowed to hear it. *Tannhäuser* had become a political issue, a factional attack on the Austrian Princess Metternich. Wagner's bitter musical opponents, the Meyerbeer adherents, had been only too eager to support the attack and gloat over the result.

[23] Niemann, writing to a friend, claimed that he had saved his "artistic honor," and in the second and third acts "reduced the hissing, the whistling, and the laughing to silence, and won the loudest applause, not only from the whole of the public, but again and again from His Majesty the Emperor." But any subduing of the audience in the third act was momentary, according to all other reports. In the third performance Niemann simply went down with the rest.

But Wagner's attitude had been resignation when he saw that in spite of his efforts the whole project was on the downgrade, and indifference when it was over. He had embraced the opportunity for a state-supported *Tannhäuser* because he wanted a foothold in Paris, where music could be turned into gold, and because he was given a free hand in casting and *mise en scène,* and a superb orchestra. His immense labor in drilling the artists, singly and together, was a satisfaction so long as it was building up a fine production. But when he returned from weeks of sickness at the end of the year, he found that the participants had lost their enthusiasm and had become stale from over-rehearsal. When at the last rehearsals an incompetent conductor took charge, he knew that the production had lost its integration, its spirit, its power to move an audience.

It had become a lifeless machine which continued to function only because an emperor had so decreed. He wrote to his sister Luise Brockhaus after the debacle: "My sufferings *before* the performance, which I unfortunately could no longer cancel, were far greater than *after* it. The truth is that I am glad to have been prevented by the Jockey Club from getting my work actually heard. I myself could not have listened to it any more!" And to Hans von Bülow, a few days later (April 5, 1861): "As to my latest adventure, I should have been more intimately affected by it if I had been personally more deeply involved in the performance of my work. But I was many miles away, and what took place on the stage and in the orchestra seemed actually to be no concern of mine."

All that could have really engrossed him was the still unperformed *Tristan.* It was *Tristan* which he had first planned to produce in Paris. Theaters in Germany were afraid of it—few singers could even have attempted it. Wagner had written to Liszt from Paris: "*Tristan,* altogether, has become an impossible and a half-shadowy thing" (October 20, 1859). But this was not lack of faith in *Tristan*; only impatience at the half-heartedness of intendants and the sluggishness of Karlsruhe. But a year later, when there was a great commotion around him over the pending *Tannhäuser,* he wrote to Mathilde Wesendonck (December 23, 1860) that all this left him "cold and untouched. . . . I confess now that when I suddenly cast a glance upon my Nibelungs, upon *Tristan,* I start up as from a dream and say to myself: 'Where have you been? You have been dreaming! Open your eyes and see—*this* is reality!' "

≈ XXV ≈

THE "UNPERFORMABLE" *TRISTAN*

"My future is also quite unknown to me: Germany is open
to me, but only now do I actually recognize that I really have
no sanctuary for my art. Where?? That is the question which
still remains completely unanswered."
—Wagner to his friend Mrs. Agnes Street-Klindworth,
August 11, 1860 (349 C).

Wagner posed this question on the strength of the partial amnesty granted
him on July 15, 1860. The question was not to be answered until five years later,
when, through the intervention of a young devotee who happened also to be a
powerful king, *Tristan* was at last produced, in Munich. Until then *Tristan*
awaited a "sanctuary," and Wagner a home anchorage. These were the years
of Wagner's painful but final severance from Minna, of the slow (because often
interrupted) creation of *Die Meistersinger,* of money difficulties due to the fact
that all he had composed in the last fifteen years, including more than half of
the *Ring* and *Tristan,* remained unproduced, bringing him only what he could
collect on their expectations. Letters in this Collection throw fresh light on these
matters, and especially on the protracted but vain attempts of the composer of
Tristan to see his opera through into performance in Vienna or Baden. These
attempts bogged down for want of a tenor with the voice and courage to undertake the title part.

The following letter to Tichatschek shows not only that Dresden coquetted
in 1859 with the unperformed *Tristan* (which Karlsruhe had just side-stepped),
but that Wagner was eager to see it accomplished even without his presence, by
a conference with the *Kapellmeister,* as had happened in the case of *Lohengrin,*
and no doubt with the principals as well.[1] The project came to nothing. Wagner
withheld *Tristan* from Dresden because they would not cancel his indebtedness
on the strength of performances of his early operas, to which they had acquired
the technical rights without fee. Dresden did not hear *Tristan* until the year
after his death, when they capitulated on the financial point.

[1] 337 C (Paris, Oct. 24, 1859).

"My dear Friend!

"I can tell you in a single line how much joy your dear letter gave me. At least it contains something hopeful, while from all sides until now I have had nothing but misfortune, which I anxiously try to conceal from my wife so as not to worry her. Everything will turn out well in the end; I have had too much hardship on top of a hard year.

"Do your best so as to give me courage to live again.

"Your news about Lüttichau delighted me. I have had to give up my plans for Karlsruhe entirely. It is very embarrassing for me from the financial point of view to postpone *Tristan* for such a long time. But if I can safely count upon being called personally to Dresden myself next summer for the performance of my new work, I shall *accept* this first of all. Aside from that nothing would be left to me but to make a contract with Vienna, where (by an especially influential connection) the possibility of safe conduct has been opened to me. At all events I should enjoy the privilege there of having the *Kapellmeister* sent to me (as it was in the case of *Lohengrin*), upon whom I could rely after a meticulous study of the score. Thus I could look forward to a first *Tristan* performance there even *without* a personal invitation.

"However, needless to say, I wouldn't ask anything better than to fight at your side in this last glorious battle, you dear old comrade in arms. Even the voice of Ney is acceptable to me, but she herself only if I can train her *myself*.

"So let's wait and hope.

"Unfortunately, I must urgently repeat my recent request of you.[2] My embarrassment is growing and—until the *Tannhäuser* performance in Paris— there is nothing in prospect for me. Then certainly everything will be easy for me, even the requested repayment of the loan, if the Vienna matter should be delayed. I confess that I have rarely in my life waited for good news with such eagerness. May Heaven help you! I have just written to Hagen. For I shall soon need money for my wife!

"A thousand thanks and greetings from

"Your

RICHARD WAGNER"

On April 15, 1861, three weeks after the abandonment of *Tannhäuser* in Paris, Wagner went to Karlsruhe. Hans von Bülow and, according to the letter following, Alwine Frommann, had heralded his coming. The Grand Duke of Baden was entirely friendly, and, learning that the main problem was to find a tenor and soprano sufficient for the principal parts, he suggested that Wagner engage them in Vienna. Wagner thus had a double incentive for a visit to Vienna: he would hear his *Lohengrin* for the first time, for Heinrich Esser, the conductor of the Vienna Opera, had arranged to perform it in his honor; he

[2] See 337 B, page 160.

would meanwhile appraise Aloys Ander and Frau Dustmann as possible material for *Tristan und Isolde*. The friendliness and acclaim he met in Vienna on the wave of excitement at the *Lohengrin* performance inclined him to revise his first opinion that Karlsruhe would give him a freer hand with *Tristan*, unencumbered by institutional routine. He now felt that Vienna, where competent singers were ready for the asking, and where the stage equipment and orchestra were far superior, was the place for *Tristan*. As it was to turn out, both theaters were to cool before the difficulties of *Tristan* and finally shy away from it altogether.

385 A *(Wagner to Minna, Vienna, May 10, 1861)*

"Dear Mutz:

"Yesterday on Ascension Day I arrived in Vienna at noon, favored by wonderful weather. As I entered Austria, a thick fog arose which finally gave way at dawn, near Linz, to the clearest sky. You know the effect of such enlivening impressions on me! The good Esser and Dustmann [*der Mann der Dustfrau*] met me at the station. In the evening *The Magic Flute* was given, and the director, a kindhearted, crazy Italian, had invited me to his box. For this morning a piano rehearsal is scheduled, for tomorrow an orchestra rehearsal, and on Sunday the *Lohengrin* performance. I am treated with great reverence, and the doormen fell over each other to throw open the door for me. My arrival is said to be generally known here, and I am afraid that Sunday won't pass without much emotion. These, briefly, are the events of my life.

"In Karlsruhe, which I left on Wednesday afternoon, I again found the old pleasant relations. The grand-ducal couple received me immediately on the day of my arrival and eagerly conversed with me for more than an hour: she also told me she has corresponded with Alwine since our last meeting. I have left orders, in anticipation of my return, for finding a suitable apartment. I intend to rent it at once if anything suitable should be available, since renting must be done there four months ahead. In any case, on my return from Paris I shall have something to count on. I am beginning now to see the immediate future more clearly. Now I am in an incredible tension about my *Lohengrin*. So much depends on how I like the singers. Last night Dustmann sang very beautifully: an ample soprano, resonant and full of feeling; expressive face, animated; a figure by no means small, but—an enormous bosom! Ander did not sing.

"Well, my next letter will tell you more definite news."

Returning to Paris, Wagner again journeyed to Vienna in August, and stopped at Weimar, where he heard a four-day music festival, met more people than he cared to, endured the extravagant spoken praise of some poor music, especially by Liszt, and managed to prevent a torchlight procession in his honor. The following two scraps of a letter written to Minna at Soden (they have been clipped off with scissors) tell the story in a few words (385 B):

"MY GOOD MINNA!

"I am still here and won't leave before this noon, because I yesterday slept badly and felt exhausted. . . . I had to fight tooth and nail to put the idea of a torch procession out of the people's heads when they wanted to arrange it for me. . . ."

Wagner reached Vienna by mid-August, when rehearsals were to begin for a production of *Tristan* in early October. But with preparatory rehearsals the obstacles increased. The orchestra players were enthusiastic, Frau Dustmann worked hard at her part, a willing and likely Brangäne was found in Destinn, but Mayerhofer would not accept Kurwenal, and the casting of Tristan remained the real problem. Wagner worked hard to save the project. He not only wanted to experience his latest opera in performance; he also wanted to prevent it from being generally dismissed as unperformable; and what was most pressing—he was in grievous need of the income it would bring. His next letter to Minna naturally hinges on practical living plans. He needs a place he and Minna can call home. He is through with Paris; German cities are half hospitable—he will go where *Tristan* is accepted. *Tristan* needs a home, and that home will be his. Dresden hovers in the background of his thoughts, but Saxony is still barred to him.

He was willing to compromise to save *Tristan* in Vienna. Ander was not the first or last to be fearful of the cruel vocal exactions of the title part. Wagner cut page after page in the third act and even modified the range. But Ander's illnesses, his hoarseness were of mental origin.[3] In despair, Wagner pinned his hopes on Morini, an Alsatian whose real name was Schrumpf—but Morini proved unequal to the part. His thoughts turned toward Schnorr von Carolsfeld, a young tenor who had been praised to him, and Tichatschek, his old stand-by. If he was half-hearted about these prospects, it was because he had never heard Schnorr von Carolsfeld, and Tichatschek was no longer young. But the more immediate obstacle was the Dresden Opera, to which both these tenors were committed.

Wagner's letter to Minna from Vienna on October 3, 1861 (385 C), shows that he is still ready to fall back on Karlsruhe: "I have written to Alwine Frommann urging her to communicate with the Grand Duke of Baden, if only to find out by that roundabout way whether my letter sent to the Grand Duke a month ago safely arrived, and what kind of an answer I am finally to expect." Wagner looks forward "with a peculiar feeling of bitterness" to a silver-wedding anniversary (November 24) without any prospect of a hearth and home they can call their own. Dresden is still in abeyance, although Seebach holds out

[3] Symptoms of insanity increased in his singing. He died on Dec. 11, 1864.

some hopes of an early amnesty for Saxony.[4] "I am taking up Karlsruhe again; now I will and must know what answer the Grand Duke there will give me; I made it very easy for him, and if he doesn't agree with any one of my wishes I know that Karlsruhe will no longer exist for me." Failing this, "only Dresden would remain." Therefore he intends to appeal to Seebach once more in behalf of his wife and their "silver-wedding day."

And so he returns to his Vienna problems:

"O God, how miserable all this is! Here things progress slowly. Ander has wholly regained his voice and is now studying with Esser every day. Next week we are to begin the general rehearsals. I worry about Ander. But I get comfort from some, especially from Laube. They observe that Ander's voice is becoming more dependable after each real illness; previously he was less dependable, and all those who knew him only as he was before—as is the case abroad—are right. After his serious illness two years ago, when people believed he would never recover again, his voice was nevertheless so much strengthened that he has accomplished incredible feats in his repertory since then; he has sung more frequently in a month than he was obliged to, and at last even Tannhäuser, which in the earlier days one did not expect from him at all. His illness this time was a simple cold, with a consequent hoarseness more obstinate in the hot dry summer than in winter. Everything in his case is caused by the nerves. When the weather became cooler, his voice returned and even with a greater range and clarity than before: but now he still has to spare himself. By the way he is a very zealous, goodhearted, and childlike man. All the same, I am pleased that Salvi brought along the new tenor *Morini*. He will appear in the middle of the month, since he first has to learn his parts in German. *Ander,* who happened to hear him in a rehearsal, assures me that he has an excellent voice, is a very cultivated, passionate singer, and will have a great success (which also spurs him on very much). Morini is still young, handsome (almost like Roger), very literate and very *musical,* which is most important for me, for he himself was formerly music director at a church in Paris (like Saint-Saëns), piano and music teacher. Thus I have the splendid plan to coach him on the side in *Tristan* too, which won't be so difficult considering his abilities."

A letter of a month later shows Wagner's increasing disgust, as, in spite of fair words from the opera management, the hopes for *Tristan* did not advance.[5] On the contrary, a hostile element, audible in the Vienna press, began to spread the idea that Wagner had written an opera impossible to perform; while the fee for *Tristan* failed to materialize, Wagner was living at an expensive hotel on funds even more meager than he could usually muster. Not least, as the letter shows, thoughts of another opera were stirring and making him restless. He

[4] The full amnesty did not come until March 28, 1862.
[5] 385 D (Vienna, Nov. 4, 1861).

had visited Nürnberg on his way to Vienna. Soon *Die Meistersinger* would be absorbing him.

"DEAR MINNA!

"Anyone who had to say how I am getting along would have a hard time. Above all he wouldn't know how to begin. Patience is a good thing: I believe I have shown that I have it. But how to manage to hold on to it, I hardly know. Bad luck can be survived—even a great deal of it; but these obstacles to anything and everything I undertake, they persist so long, and finally destroy all courage. I am pestered on all sides by secret and open annoyances. I am in exactly the same situation as a beginner except that I am burdened by a general hatred and envy inspired by my former accomplishments and my fame. Nothing is successful either here or elsewhere. Even Pourtalès doesn't answer me. A visit to Berlin just now would be no help at all; this is the opinion of Alwine Frommann, whom I have consulted. It is more than doubtful whether the Queen would receive me. And what if she did? The Grand Duke of Baden claims that he answered me—he told Frau Frommann so, but I haven't yet received the letter. He intimated only that he doesn't believe he can comply with my requests. I would care little about these questions for the moment if I could only succeed in something here. For a new success would make all further progress easier. I could not have experienced a more unlucky winter than this one as regards the Vienna Opera. Everything is ready and in order, but the tenor question is still entirely unsolved, and 'if' and 'when' are questions which, with the best will in the world, can't be answered. The malicious take advantage of this uncertainty to spread obstructive rumors, and my position for the future as an artist is so bad that there is no prospect for me at any of the theaters. On top of this, the tightness of the financial administration here was reflected in a recent answer to me in the matter of my fees which immediately induced me not to accept a single gulden before the performance. This caused great anger. Only the orchestra stood by me. They recently of their own accord played several fragments of *Tristan*—Dustmann singing—in a private rehearsal; and after one single trial they did it so excellently that the musicians themselves as well as the listeners were sent into the greatest rapture; all of them, and I especially, became convinced that this opera more than all my other ones will succeed even in the first performance.

"The orchestra then urgently asked me to repeat these private rehearsals more often with them. That is fine and shows me who I am and what I accomplish; but all this can't counteract my unlucky star, which opposes me on every side. In the main question, that of the tenor part, everything is still in the dark.

"The worst of it is that this continued ill luck in the end undermines my spirit and health. I can't sleep, and live in a perpetual state of terrible irritation which is especially aggravated by unnecessary argument. I fear a catastrophe. A few months of complete rest and retirement, without special worries, would be the only remedy. From a trip which would again involve much talking I could only expect an increase of my nervous ailment. Deep in my soul I feel urged to forget the whole world for a while and to tackle an entirely new work which by its subject would be a relief. I have plenty of material [*Stoff*]. I have an invitation from the Nakos,[6] who in the winter live on their beautiful estate, with a completely furnished castle—about three railway hours from Vienna. Yesterday also the good Metternich, who in his short visit proved very friendly, surprised me suddenly by the words: 'Dear Wagner, you need rest and distraction. Come with us to Paris for a few months. You will live with us; I am now definitely settled there and nothing will disturb you. Besides, we shall combine with Pourtalès and Seebach, and even from Paris we can at last do something for you in Germany.' I must confess that I was very much touched by the until then rather calm and reserved man. But I feel only perplexed now by everything and I balk at any decision for the moment. Perhaps it would be well to act quickly and accept one of the offered chances—but on the other hand I don't know what a loss it might be for me to leave Vienna entirely for a few months! *For I can't begin again with another theater.* Here is the place where it must be fought out and where I must prove that everything which had been circulated about my new work was false and evil. Thus I am and still remain for the moment—undecided. . . ."

Wagner, at his wit's end for a Tristan, turns to his old friend Tichatschek, in the hope of somehow prying him loose from Dresden.[7]

"DEAREST FRIEND!

"You didn't answer my question about a concert in Vienna. My situation soon changed again. Last Wednesday evening the tenor *Morini* (on whom I had to count in an emergency) sang for the second time, and it turned out that his engagement would be of no use to the theater. To find a way out for Tristan I proposed to the manager to engage you for the three months of your leave—March, April, May. He said that's too late, he wouldn't know what to do until then. Then it occurred to me that Schnorr could be spared in Dresden during the time you are there; the manager requested me to ask him about it immediately. Schnorr now answers me, so far by telegram, that he could not possibly get away for December, January, and February. As I now sit here and ponder my miserable situation, it occurs to me that Schnorr probably could not get away at this time because he has to study something new. In this case, and since he sings your parts in your absence anyway, it seems to me again that *you* might be able to get away more easily. As far as I know, your position in regard to the Dresden management is now freer than usual. On a combination of these

---

[6] Wagner visited the Count Coloman Nako as a possible patron, but was discouraged by the dilettante talk of the Hungarian nobleman and his wife. He was amused when his bland suggestion that he might make his quarters in the palace was received with alarm.

[7] 392 A (Venice. Nov. 11, 1861).

factors I base a new hope that *you* might perhaps find it possible to get away for December, January, and February as an exception (if for a *still* longer period, so much the better!). This would be the most desirable thing for *me*. I hear many good things about Schnorr, also he *already knows* Tristan, which is of decisive importance in my plan to produce the opera as quickly as possible. But even him I have personally neither heard nor seen; and after the numerous disappointments which I've already had no one can blame me if, in the final analysis, I don't *absolutely* trust anyone except an old tried and true comrade in arms. So don't brood any longer, but think over the following:

"I'm not allowed to go to Dresden where there are *two* singers who could sing Tristan. In Vienna I have an excellent Isolde, likewise Marke (Beck)—a superb orchestra, an enthusiastic public. Above all—it has already progressed too far; I cannot go back on it again without confirming the slanderous statements that it is impossible to produce, thus making it infinitely more difficult for me to introduce it at any other theaters. All the other singers here know their parts well enough for the opera to be read in four weeks at the latest if Tristan joins the cast. No singer is more musical than you. I've already made some cuts in the last act: if you can come on December 1st (at the latest), you'll sing Lohengrin a few times this month and/or Tannhäuser, otherwise we'll just rehearse Tristan. You can—if *you* like—then sing what you wish: only, I frankly confess that your engagement would flatter me most if you would agree to sing only Tristan and my operas.

"For heaven's sake see whether you can persuade Lüttichau to do something extraordinary *for my sake* too, just once. My situation is really *terrible,* and all because of the hard-hearted behavior which I still find in Dresden! It is in Lüttichau's power to make up for much that I've suffered and still suffer. You see, there are *two* of you in Dresden for the same part, as far as I know. It must be *possible*! Certainly! Just a little good will and everything is possible! I beg you, try to do it, and let me hear good news quickly! My doctor has forcibly dragged me along on a trip to Venice so that I can pull through. Tonight I'm going back again. Please, as soon as you can give me some hope, send me a telegram to *Vienna, Empress Elisabeth, Weihburg Gasse!*

"I *have to* see SOMETHING succeed once, or I'll go to pieces. If it would only come through you, my old steadfast friend!

"Yours,

RICH. WAGNER"

Going to Paris in December, 1861, according to the intention expressed in his letter to Minna, quoted above (385 D), Wagner, unable to obtain Tichatschek at once, because of his unbreakable guest engagements, induced the Vienna Opera manager Salvi to go to Dresden for the purpose of concluding an arrangement for the following winter. He wrote to Tichatschek: [8]

[8] 392 B (Paris, Dec. 8, 1861).

"MY DEAR OLD FRIEND!

"At last I have another chance to write you a few lines about myself. Perhaps it's already too late, and *Salvi* is already in Dresden. I had promised him to write to you before that. He wanted to come to Dresden *this week* (that would mean about this time), and I was supposed to ask you perhaps to sing Lohengrin for him. I was also supposed to ask you to be kind enough to fix your fee for a six-month engagement (next winter) in advance. Unfortunately, I had no time to do so in the confusion of my trip. Heaven grant that I haven't spoiled anything! For you're my only hope for next winter in Vienna. If this engagement doesn't materialize, I don't see any prospect ahead at all. So—do your best and help me get this important relief!

"That's really all I have to report to you today. My head is whirling; I am sick, without any comfort, until recently always in doubt as to what to do next. Now I want to start a new work; that should distract and console me.

"In the summer I'll see you in any case: we'll make a definite appointment. In the meantime Cornelius is sending you from Vienna the cuts in the third act.

"Thank your good wife cordially for the kind favor, and accept the warmest regards from me, you remarkable and unshakable singer and friend!

"Farewell!

Your old

RICHARD WAGNER"

Wagner had gone to Paris on the invitation of Princess Metternich, expecting to find a rent-free *Asyl* in her apartment for the versification of *Die Meistersinger.* He stopped at Mainz to come to some arrangement with Schott over a languishing *Tristan* or a promised *Meistersinger,* arrived in Paris by the middle of December, where, the Metternichs not being able to receive him, he nevertheless finished the *Meistersinger* text by the end of January. Before going to Paris, he wrote the following note (undated, 411), presumably to Heine in Dresden. He evidently hoped that Salvi would obtain Tichatschek for *Tristan.* But this hope was to be disappointed: Dresden would not release him.

"You will understand, child, that I have already hesitated much too long to carry out my plan. Now that it has been decided this way, I live here as on red-hot coals. It is extraordinarily kind of Tichatschek that he intends to visit me in Vienna, but I can't wait for it. I have to go to *Mainz* to arrange everything with Schott personally, and then at once to Paris: for if my whole plan is not to go askew, I must finish my work as punctually as possible. *Thus*—I'm leaving Vienna *Wednesday* to be at work in Paris by December 1st, at the latest. Tell that to the good Tichatschek. If he insists on seeing me, we'll have to arrange a short meeting on the Rhine next spring perhaps. *Salvi* will be in Dresden on Monday: he should arrange everything with him. I'm not at all in favor of a *short* guest engagement this winter (without *Tristan,* of course) as

Salvi wants it, for then I cannot possibly come back for *Lohengrin* or *Tann-häuser*: if Tichatschek wants to, fine! wonderful! but then he won't find me there. But perhaps it's good that way. I think I'll write to Tschekel tomorrow. That he has been again hearing talk against me I can well imagine: as soon as one associates with certain riffraff, one is always among thieves and rascals. What don't I have to hear and read every day about what I'm supposed to have done or said!! I hope T. knows about it too!"

The following telegram from Wagner to Ludwig Schnorr von Carolsfeld (408 A) was obtained by Mrs. Burrell from the singer's brother. Wagner sends this message from Biebrich to Schnorr in Karlsruhe, May 25, 1862:

"Please get me one ticket for *Lohengrin* tomorrow incognito first or second row left with the greatest discretion."

This telegram throws light upon an interesting incident. Wagner, in search of a tenor for Vienna, and never having heard Schnorr, went to Karlsruhe, where he was to sing Lohengrin. Wagner presents the case in his *Recollections of Ludwig Schnorr von Carolsfeld* that he did not disclose himself to the singer, fearing the embarrassment of an unfavorable impression. The opening phrases of Lohengrin were enough to set at rest his doubts and hesitations. But this telegram shows his memory to have been at fault. His anonymity was evidently on account of Eduard Devrient, the conductor, with whom he had had words about the *Tristan* plans for Karlsruhe. Wagner openly disapproved of Devrient's way of handling *Lohengrin* and naturally would not have liked to be recognized attending a performance of it.

Wagner was visited by Schnorr and his wife at Biebrich in July, when parts of *Tristan* were sung through by the illustrious couple. The tenor's voice and his eagerness, which had not yet reached the point of full understanding, qualified him for the part, so far as Wagner was concerned, as the following telegram (406) from Dresden shows:

*"General Direktion der Königlich Sächsischen
musikalischen Kapelle und des Hoftheaters,*
October 20, 1862, to Wagner in Biebrich:

"[The Management] instructs me, dear sir, herewith to reply to your petition of the 16th of this month, that the leave of absence requested for Herr Schnorr von Carolsfeld must be refused, since it has been decided, with the exception of charity performances and special festivities, henceforth not to grant applications for an extracontractual leave to those company members who are entitled to a leave in their contracts.

DR. JULIUS PABST"

Schnorr von Carolsfeld was indeed destined to be the first Tristan, but not until June 10, 1865, in Munich.

❧ XXVI ❦

THE FINAL SEPARATION FROM MINNA

"Presumably you have now been separated from your husband for a considerable period. Such is the fate of many wives as well as mothers who have as husband or son a great *artiste musicien*."

—Liszt's mother (Anna) to Wagner's wife (Minna),
December 26, 1861 (391).

When Wagner turned his back on Zürich, in 1858, and went to Venice to continue his *Tristan* in solitude, a permanent change took place in his relation to Minna. She was from that time definitely an invalid, to be treated with kindness and consideration, but, except at a distance, a menace to his peace of mind. Wagner craved a home, as always, but except when he had his last fling at Paris, he was long to remain a wanderer, a *juive errand* as Kietz, in his quaint French, once called him, seeking a quiet corner in which to compose, or an operatic center in which to plant himself and his *Tristan*. Thoughts of a home for them both were often mentioned by him, but only once did he attempt such a thing. The *ménage* at Paris was an "arrangement"—a truce on the basis that the least converse meant the least conflict.

After Paris, Wagner mentioned the possibility of an anchorage at Karlsruhe, Vienna, Dresden, but he must have realized what Minna realized (and several times admitted)—that living together on any enduring basis was at an end.

Writing to Kietz from Dresden (393, December 14, 1861) Minna said: "On the 24th of last month I received *congé* for one year from my dear husband. . . . After that year we may possibly meet on the Rhine, where I shall perhaps await his further disposition of my insignificant self." The letter referred to was actually written on the 22nd, but may have arrived on the 24th, and since this was the Wagners' silver-wedding anniversary, Minna evidently took the suggestion at that particular moment as unpardonable. Wagner sent a telegram (389 B) on the anniversary with the message: "Peace, patience!" Wagner had asked for "complete retirement, and concentration of all my powers on a new work" (*Die Meistersinger*).

After visiting Mainz, to see Schott and extract a payment on the prospects of *Tristan,* Karlsruhe, where he accomplished nothing, and (in December) Paris, where he completed the libretto of *Die Meistersinger,* Wagner once more

405

deliberately went into retirement to create. His choice was Biebrich, a pleasant town on the Rhine, where he would be without friends or relatives, unless he should encourage a visit.

"About a week after I had settled down with my newly arrived Erard grand," wrote Wagner in *My Life* (page 813), "Minna suddenly appeared in Biebrich." And after the attempt at a reunion had failed miserably, Wagner wrote to Cornelius (March 4): "While I was sadly trying to install myself in winter quarters here in Biebrich, my wife was appealed to by my straits, and instead of answering me by letter appeared here in my chambers of her own accord." Whether Wagner or Minna was more responsible for this rash step may now be decided: Wagner's letter which Minna did not wait to answer is in the Collection (February 14, 1862, 396 A):

"I intend to move in tomorrow: I expect the grand piano today. So things will be all right once more, and once I am at work I hope soon to forget all the misery of my life. What else is left to me? My wife? Oh, my God! Must I not shudder at the fact that whatever is necessary and good for *me* has just the opposite effect on *her* and thus distresses her? *I* no longer look forward to anything pleasant, and who could say anything certain about whether we would ever enjoy a quiet, congenial companionship? I'm anxious about everything! for I can do nothing more in this world than work out a few good ideas which are still in my head: otherwise everything is meaningless, miserable, hopeless for me. Whether here or there—it's all the same! I tell you this so that you may know for sure what I *don't* want; what I do *want* and *choose* I cannot say exactly. To be left in peace, that's all! Life will be painful and cheerless for me to the grave. It could, of course, be made easier for me, but who would think of it? I am firmly convinced that, whereas I for once, and surely for the last time, express my grief and sadness honestly and openly, you probably believe that I want to say something nasty to you, to insult you—which is not even remotely in my mind! Rather I feel sorry for you, as I do for myself, and I know that you don't live a pleasant life either. It is only this silly nonsense that I hear from time to time about all this being my own fault, etc. I can't stand that any more, and recently I've given the Grand Duke a piece of my mind on the subject. The time will come when people will look back on a life like mine, will realize with shame how thoughtlessly I was exposed to continual unrest and insecurity, and what a *miracle* it is that I have created works like my present one under such conditions. But everyone spends his life thinking only of himself, and looking upon whatever unpleasant things have happened to him as the most important thing. That's why I wish only to remain unmolested: I am completely resigned and can do without everything if only I can work. Therefore I say this to you, good Minna: Think it over! There was a time last year, after you could *not* decide to rent a reasonable apartment somewhere with a room for me as I wished, and after you had again touched on the wretched old chapters which drive me to desperation—a time, then, when I said to myself: For God's sake, don't force anything again! Maybe she'd better live by herself after all, have her social life to which she is fully entitled, and at last lead a congenial life which I can only disturb if I want to persuade her, by force and against the will and encouragement of fate, to live with me again! In the final analysis it would be better if I could live by myself; as soon as I once live at a permanent place, I'll settle down well enough and get along. I've repeatedly discovered how little diversion and company I need; in general I can live all alone and feel no need at all for company; or if I do feel it I only have to mix with people once in order to be happy again when they are gone. How much needless arguing, disturbing each other, etc., would thus be avoided?

"I must leave the decision entirely in your hands! I neither dare to say: Come! nor could I bring myself to say to you: Stay! This is completely *up to you!* But I invite you to think it over thoroughly! You are right: another visit would be the most miserable thing that could happen to us both. You must feel what your heart wants you to do: if you feel nothing which tells you that living with me seems preferable to getting along by yourself, then think it over! I can give you no guarantees other than those I've mentioned to you: I look for nothing more in this world than peace and a mood conducive to work; once that stops I shall die gladly and willingly, for life no longer offers me anything attractive whatever. If you feel, after the great hardships which have depressed you and your heart, that you can devote yourself completely to this my final purpose in life; if you feel that your one mission in life now is to make my life easier, as far as it is in your power, and to preserve it for this my one and only purpose, and if you feel that you can achieve *your* purpose in life only when you provide me with all possible quiet and cheerfulness for my work so that you can say to yourself that *you* too have taken part in my creations—then I say: Come! Everything else will take care of itself! But again: Think it over! If you feel this or that drawback and can't completely dismiss it, then hesitate— at least hesitate! Time can heal that too, if you keep quietly to yourself. But if you don't understand my present state of mind which is completely free, exalted, sad to be sure, but without any ulterior motives; if you think even now that you are reading hidden reproaches in these words which you would have to answer; if you cannot free yourself completely, breathe freely and affection- ately, and judge everything between us to be fine and noble—then you have completely misunderstood this letter, and I believe it would then be better to let time have its way for a while. As I have said: It all depends on you!"

Minna ignored the clear logic of this letter, but she sensed her husband's loneliness and took advantage of the "choice" he gave her. Within a week, without answering, she appeared at Biebrich.

There followed what Wagner called, in a letter to Cornelius (March 4), "ten days of hell." The arrival, at the wrong moment, of a letter from Frau Wesendonck, shortly followed by a delayed Christmas box from her, were enough to start a succession of stormy scenes, in which none of the old recriminations was forgotten. "Incapable of viewing my relation with that lady in any save an odious light," Wagner writes to Cornelius, "she refuses to understand a single explanation, but indulges in that vulgar tone again which makes me lose all self-command." Wagner's version of this untimely coincidence is to be found in his letter to Cornelius, and in *My Life*. Minna's version now appears in a letter to Natalie from Dresden on March 6, immediately after her return: [1]

"Richard had written to me, somewhat ill-humoredly, that he would stay in Biebrich, a terrible provincial town in any case, in order to compose his new opera there undisturbed. But he had nobody, he wrote, who could make his life there more easy and comfortable, he had to borrow a few pieces of furniture, with some trouble, in order to exist; in a word he became very bitter. So I quickly made up my mind to travel to him. Well, that journey is no trifle, especially at this rough season, when you can't get any heated coaches even on this line; and I almost froze to death. I left from here at six in the evening by the shortest possible route and arrived the next day around two o'clock midday in Biebrich. Richard was extremely delighted when I came and almost beheaded me in his joy, and really was good to me. But the next morning at breakfast he received a letter from the Wesendonck and all peace was at an end before I had said a *single* word. He raved and shouted without any reason, telling me that this is not my business, he can correspond with anyone he likes, etc. The next day we traveled from Mainz to Darmstadt with the Schott family, since *Rienzi* with Niemann was performed there, and we returned to Biebrich on the following day. As we were seated at breakfast, another voluminous letter from that hussy the W. arrived. But again I didn't utter a word about it. My Richard, however, started talking himself into a really savage fury, then I only said: 'Well, it is certainly a peculiar coincidence.' Those words he mockingly repeated, as streetboys do. I said that he could abuse me as much as he wished, I wouldn't answer anything; so he actually continued ranting for three-quarters of an hour, until I finally told him that he had no idea of the rights of a wife, which I had certainly never exerted, out of concern for him and out of modesty, and that I would actually have to forbid that correspondence for the sake of what is right and godly, since it evidently had a bad influence on him. All this I calmly uttered, although I was so furious that I almost had a stroke. On the following day the crates with our furniture were opened at the Customs House and repacked; then an official came to me with the information that a box had come in the mail and had been waiting there a few days. With the best intentions, because I knew that R. doesn't like to be bothered with such matters, I had it opened, supposing it to be music, and to pay the duty—but there it was

[1] 361 H.

again from that filthy woman: an embroidered cushion, tea, Eau de Cologne, pressed violets. Now a new scandal was to be expected, nor did it fail to come. I don't want to repeat what I had to hear again, although I begged and implored him not to shame me in front of people—I placed our furniture in Richard's three rooms as quickly as possible, which took five full days and so that on my return trip I had one day each in Wiesbaden, Darmstadt, and Mainz, during this time. Thank goodness that I am back in my peaceful cell with my good Jacquotchen. So I had to assure myself once more that this horrible man has made it impossible for me to live with him; until fate, that is to say bad times, come for him and cure him somewhat."

In a letter to Minna on May 21, Wagner speculates on the strange stories about his conduct which may some day appear in his biography: "Whoever finds your letters to me will see it written down that my wife calls me and my conduct to her 'heartless,' 'brutal,' and 'vulgar.' So that will get into my biography too. Well, I can't stop it."

With the above letter to Natalie, the accusation he anticipated does appear in the record of his life, but in that record there appear letters from Wagner to Minna before and after the event, showing him as patient, forbearing, anxious to make her contented. In the letter of May 21 he proposes to establish her in Dresden, mentioning (perhaps in cajolery) the possibility of joining her there. Ernest Newman is the latest spokesman of the generally accepted point of view among Wagner's biographers that Minna had by this time become "insanely jealous," "incurably suspicious"; that life with her was a sheer impossibility, that he was powerless against her "eternal self-pity and ever-smouldering resentment." Even those who are not ready to go so far as to call her jealousy an "insane obsession" are obliged to admit that Wagner could hardly have done more for Minna. It was natural for her to cling to her increasingly famous husband, begrudge the possession of him by other women, and refuse the divorce, soon afterward proposed, which would have meant giving up what hold she had—this although she admitted to others that living with him had become impossible. What is hardest for us to understand is that Wagner had not long since faced a final break. Both realized that the heart condition of the one and the nervous excitability of the other made it necessary to avoid certain subjects. But Minna could not refrain from speaking her mind, whereupon Wagner's forbearance would vanish in a flash of anger. The worlds of these two touched at no point save in habit, convenience, and a pet parrot.

In the following summer (June 14, 1862), Wagner wrote to Pusinelli, asking him to consult Luise Brockhaus on the subject of a final break between himself and Minna. He evidently felt helpless to face the situation alone and turned for support to his doctor and his sister. He did not mention divorce, but it was plainly in his mind. Pusinelli, evidently grasping what was expected of him (he would hardly otherwise have undertaken so delicate a mission), wrote to Minna and brought her anger upon his own suffering head. She would not—and never did—accept the idea of a legal separation. Pusinelli sturdily took the blame, while Wagner protested: "the. thought of a divorce never entered my head." But in *My Life* years later he wrote that he had asked Pusinelli "to impress upon Minna the necessity for a legal divorce," and this upon the advice of his sister, Cläre. The truth seems to be that Wagner did entertain the idea of legal freedom and the possibility of having an "under-standing companion" (then specifically Mathilde Maier) permanently at his side, but shrank from the effect of any such proposition upon his invalid wife. This only could excuse the following placating letter, with its readiness to use Dr. Pusinelli as his cat's-paw against the fire of Minna's wrath: [2]

"Dear Minna!

"It is pleasing and consoling to me to know that you are now in the magnificent mountain air of Reichenhall, in a new environment, and—as is now the case here—that you are having good weather. Heaven grant that you may find recovery and peace! Think of nothing but yourself and what is pleasing to you. Stop nursing the old wounds! You'll ruin yourself, and I—certainly—cannot bear it any longer! Let our correspondence rather be silent for a while, as long as it cannot be kept completely free of those dreadful relapses. I, at least, can and will no longer answer these.

"It was surely quite natural for me to turn to your doctor for exact infor-mation after you last wrote me of a most serious illness. It was likewise quite obvious to him—who is also our *friend*—that I did not hide my great concern for our common future from him on this occasion: for it is no longer a question here of who is right or wrong, but what can be of the greatest advantage for our future mutual benefit. In his sympathetic zeal Pusinelli went further than I wanted him to: I wanted to hear his opinion, his advice; even though I also advised him to talk this matter over with my sister Luise, who has given me evidence of the greatest good will toward you, this was done merely to hear the opinion of others. Now I have seen that Pusinelli feels just as other people who have also had occasion to observe us: he, too, considers our mutual position far more serious and more in need of a change than it seems to you—even after the most incredible outpourings. Be this as it may, rest assured that I did *not* ask Pusinelli to intervene, but that he did so purely according to his own judgment.

"Now he informs me himself that you interpreted his request to come to Dresden for a consultation as an effort to persuade you to get a divorce. I am sorry that such a painful thought occurred to you, a thought which I never entertained. About this I fervently ask you to calm yourself!

"But I must remind you that, even though you think you must accuse me of having been the sole cause of your sufferings, you still have a duty toward

[2] 402 (Biebrich, June 27 [1862]).

me: to give me some peace or to leave me alone! It cannot go on like this! Since I see that everything I explain to you exactly and in detail gets no consideration from you at all, I cannot and shall not make any more attempts of a similar kind, and I therefore ask you urgently henceforth rather to keep quiet altogether or to limit your remarks solely to that which will always deeply concern me, your health and your present life. I entreat you to abide by this, to stop making these eternal scolding phrases: for no matter how detestable and guilty I may seem to you, it is ultimately my duty to protect myself from needless tortures.

"So I appeal once more to time itself: let peace reign! Old age can aggravate old sores, but it can also eventually remove them—this is what I long for, and I still don't despair!

"I have every reason to abide by my latest plans for settling down. I hope to see you in Dresden late in the fall. May God grant the necessary peace of mind until then!

"And so farewell! Take care of yourself! Enjoy the quiet and the refreshing beauty of your stay and accept the warmest greetings from

"Your

RICHARD"

An exchange of letters in the following August shows how the friendly relations of the two could continue—at a safe distance—and how the creation of *Die Meistersinger* was brought to a complete standstill for several weeks by the bite of a dog. Wagner wrote on August 1, 1862 (306 C): "I can write only a little, and that badly, because Leo has bitten me on the thumb of the right hand; it did not make a big wound, but it has robbed me of the use of the hand for several days because it is just in the joint."

Minna answered from Reichenhall, on August 4 (403): "It frightened me at first that the awful, ungrateful Leo bit you, I hope it won't get bad. I'd rather have taken the bite myself, because such wounds heal quickly with me. The stupid animal doesn't even deserve to be fed scraps of bread as you probably used to do; just be careful with him, you never can trust these old malicious bulldogs. You'd do me a favor if you'd tell me in two words that your poor hand is all right again. Is the friendly light-colored little dog still living? You must feed and pet this friendly little animal all the more."

But in his next letter, on August 7 (396 D), he was forced to dictate to Natalie: "Even though I can't write to you myself, dear Minna, since my finger has been affected again by writing too soon, and has become slightly worse, still I don't want to worry you unnecessarily by leaving you completely without news. The thing is not in the least dangerous, just protracted and tedious, since I have to favor the thumb of the right hand. Don't worry about Leo either, he was not at all mad when he bit me, just frightened because I wanted to have him washed; and these dogs are especially sensitive on the back, as I didn't find out till later." In a letter of September 10 he writes: "Thank God—my finger is all right," but the handwriting is still shaky.

When Wagner went to Dresden for a few days in November, he stayed at the Wolframs', where Minna was. But the meeting was strained and uncomfortable for everyone. Wagner was not to see Minna again. The correspondence continued, but Wagner kept stressing his need for solitude as the score of *Die Meistersinger* approached completion. Suggestions for another meeting were made guardedly, without intent of fulfillment.

From Prague, on February 7, 1863, on the eve of his concert in that city, Wagner wrote Minna (417 A): "I would have telegraphed you to come to the concert tomorrow if I had been in better health. But I am no good to anybody, and must wait for better times." He was to start for St. Petersburg before the end of the month, and return in March in time for *Tristan,* which he expected to be given in Vienna at last.

The next letter we have was written from Vienna on February 12 (417 B). Minna had misinterpreted his remark about not telegraphing her to come to Prague: "You wrong me this time—as you always do—by misunderstanding my clear words. I did not write you that I was too tired to send you a telegram, but too worn out to be of any use to you in a visit to Prague, because I had to withdraw entirely from seeing anyone in order to refrain from too much talk, which will certainly sometime kill me." He will need a tranquil solitude, even in Russia, for which reason he cannot accept the invitation of the von Mecks to stay with them. He cannot face being entertained by, and entertaining, strangers. "God himself could never get me to the Brockhauses in Leipzig again, or anywhere else."

On May 10, in Vienna, having returned from St. Petersburg, he wrote about the payment of various debts, presumably from his Russian earnings. It would seem that Minna had expected him to return by way of Dresden, where she was, but this he had not done (417 C): "You would be wise, dear Minna, no longer to concern yourself with what I do or don't do, considering our present position; only in this way could you contribute to my peace." Later, he writes: "Since I must be near Vienna, I have taken a summer residence in Penzing near by, where I am preparing again for work. I am determined to avoid everyone and everything, and to ward off from the first moment anything which could disturb me in my much needed retirement and quiet for work."

From Penzing he wrote on July 4:[3]

"I have received your letter: it was from your point of view thoroughly kind and just, but it again touched matters into which I can no longer enter, not because I am scornful or obstinate, but because I can stand no more of it! I am suffering from a life sickness [*Lebenskrankheit*] which deprives me of all

[3] 417 D.

my vigor and leaves in its place a perpetual restlessness. This restlessness is multiplied into an all-destroying anxiety, which I unfortunately also feel each time a letter from you arrives. Nothing can cure me of it—but forgetting! I entreat you, have pity on me and make it easier for me to forget. Since I know that this is best, too, for *your* welfare, I implore you, comply with my urgent wish, and let us each find his own peace! Let us wish each other recovery, tranquillity, help in resignation, and let us occupy ourselves with what nature and reason offer to people sick of life—distraction and forgetfulness! Only then is recovery still possible! If you wish to, you may now lead a more pleasant and peaceful life than you led with me in the hard, stormy years of the past. You can do this if you seriously want it, and if success favors my endeavors always fully to care for your needs. . . . But now, dear, good Minna, make all this helpful to yourself, and don't question me any more. I painfully need the concentration of my terribly shattered and ruined mental powers: all my hope rests upon my full ability for work again; if ever I should lose it another time, I most firmly declare that life for me would have no sense or value any longer, and that I would try to end it.

"So be considerate and understanding! I entreat, I implore you, it is now determined by fate that you can contribute to the preservation of my life by that highest consideration for my soul's peace!"

One more reproachful letter made Wagner realize the need for putting an end even to their correspondence. His letter is directed to Natalie, as intermediary: [4]

"DEAR NATALIE!

"This time I am sending the money for Minna to you, asking you to forward it to her at once.

"I had already intended to do so: a letter from Minna which I received today confirms me in it.

"She writes me fairly and justly from her viewpoint; she is even almost gentle and friendly. In the final analysis she is right in everything, as she sees things: but I see them differently, and that's where the misfortune lies.

"Believe me, good Natalie, my heart has been bleeding for years: for I realize clearly and distinctly that I cannot live with Minna any longer. It isn't a question of any blame which I attribute to her nor of any reproach: but experience has shown me that the greatest calamity for us would be to live together again. Despite the fact that I have realized this for some time, I still kept wavering as to how to carry out the bitter resolution. The consideration for her health usually decided the matter, and I avoided final, decisive statements. If I could only hope thus to set matters straight, I would gladly continue that way. But I see that I only prolong *her* torture and thus also mine. In the

[4] 419 (Penzing, June 20, 1863).

end she still keeps clinging to a hope which I cannot fulfill, and she is thereby prevented from leading that kind of life which under these circumstances is the only thing that could bring *her* peace. I used to think that it would be all right if I visited her from time to time: that is what one first thinks of, but it could be done only in the case of quite different, more easy-going people. She has developed a distrust, an uneasy diffidence toward me, which really makes every hour we are together an agony. Despite my best will and my deepest, most sincere pity for her, I feel this so clearly that I always shrink from the thought of visiting her. Certainly I don't hate Minna: I want to do good for her as much as I can; but the difference is too great, and the dissension caused by sad experiences is so obvious that there is no use trying to deceive oneself.

"Therefore, I must now ask myself what further purpose it could serve if I keep the poor woman in a state of uncertainty which tortures both her and me? Even our letters can never be completely harmless: something will always contribute to the misunderstanding and produce statements which are bound to be troublesome. I must seriously believe that it is better to stop writing also. When I say this, you may rest assured that it costs me a terrible inner struggle, and that my heart suffers more from this apparent harshness than all of you probably imagine. Better, though, if I keep my softness for myself: if I revealed it to Minna it would only produce new confusion. My only consolation is that there is no person who knows us both who is not of the opinion that it is better this way for both of us.

"Now Minna also writes me that she wants to give up the large apartment. She should certainly do so, and I shall do what is necessary to give notice for October 1st. Only she should not think of moving into a furnished apartment! If she cannot use some of our things in a smaller apartment, she should give them away or sell them, but always keep what she can use. I also wonder whether it would not be better if she would move to Zwickau near you: there she could live very pleasantly on the money which she will regularly receive from me, and she would have her relatives with her. In Dresden her position toward me would become unbearable for her (I realize that!). She really should start an entirely new life! But it is not proper for me to advise her, least of all to prescribe anything for her: alas! I have to leave it completely up to her how she is going to help herself from now on. The only thing I can contribute is to put an end to the uncertain condition in which she cannot live in peace. She is absolute owner and proprietress of all those things which she at present has with her: she should do with them whatever she likes. If, however, she wants to send me something, I'd like to have the silver laurel wreath and the goblet which were once presented to me; perhaps she would also *share* the silver with me equally, she already left me some of it in Biebrich. I would also ask her for the fire screen, if I did not sincerely consider every emotion as injurious and harmful at this time; but the arrival of this screen would affect me very much.

"Natalie! I'm writing this to you amid bitter tears. Perhaps I should have waited longer; for both of us now have to show the greatest control and calmness.

"But when I thus express, in the form of an *urgent* request, the desire, even the need, of so arranging my dealings with Minna that she won't entertain any more mistaken expectations, I also declare that she shall *always remain my wife. I will never consider divorcing her.* I'll stay by myself, and no one shall take her place.

"Only we can't live together again: it won't work. It won't work! Rather bear everything else than the sad relationship into which we would fall! Let Minna take to heart what I express in this statement, and I hope she will find in it a proof of my true and sincere respect for her.

"My lot is loneliness: my life—work!

"I'm not going to add anything more to this. I know especially that explanations of any kind between me and Minna are completely useless. Here no one is right and no one is wrong: only he would henceforth be wrong who would casually and superficially suggest new attempts to live together!

"Greet Minna for me with a bleeding heart! She should accept the inevitable! It will perhaps be more difficult for me than for her!

"Best regards to you too, dear Natalie, and to the good Tröger and to Charlotte!

"Your
RICHARD W"

Speaking more freely than she could have spoken to Wagner, Minna turned to her old friend Kietz, and described to him her lot in life: [5]

"BEST FRIEND!

"Although uncertain, I shall send this letter where I may expect you to be. If you should already have counted me among the deceased, try in your heart to restore an old friend to life, for—despite everything—I still belong to this earth. If, by the way, I had been able to report something good about myself, you would have received at least a dozen letters from me and requests to take a little trip over here. That would really be a decision for which you should receive a medal at the very least; through days, or weeks, I would tell you my experiences since I last saw you. Of course you would have to do the same, and I can assure you in advance that in me you would have the most intent and sympathetic old friend. But since I have the sneaking suspicion that your

[5] 423 (Dresden, March 28, 1864).

coming may be delayed for a little while longer, I would meanwhile like to know how you are, whether you are married and the father of several dozen children, etc. I ask you to give me some news of yourself *soon*. May you gather from my request that I don't belong to that miserable race of people who trample down the past with their feet and that I always remember dear old friends with a grateful heart, not only those of the *good* old days, but also those of the earliest, really *bad* days. How terrible they were and still how happy compared to the present. How the world was open to us then—what yearnings, what hopes!

"Now everything is closed—desolation, sad and quite miserable, whereas one should really enjoy one's life without cares in one's old age, at least in a quiet, pleasant atmosphere. . . .

"My life here would be quite bearable if I had not lost my health through this grief which Richard so unscrupulously inflicted on me, but this gnaws at my heart and threatens to spread to my chest in addition to my heart ailment; I'm prepared for this. My friends have all remained faithful to me; they are dear and good to me, which acts like heavenly balm on my sore heart. From the King I have received one of the best seats in the theater, which, however, I use rarely because of the frequent repetition in the repertory. In short, they love and respect me, which, as I've already said, sustains me reasonably well under the circumstances. Dresden is beautiful and has grown more than twice as large as when you left it. The Heine family is still living, not exactly in an abundance of health and wealth, but vigorous and active. Their daughter Marie has been married for two years, has the dearest little girl, but the young mother is always sick. But one more thing: every three months I receive a crumb from R's abundance; in accordance with his wish I rented a larger apartment at the time, because he wrote me three years ago he was thinking of living here from time to time, but now I'm renting a few furnished rooms.

"There you have the whole story of my life and suffering from me. Let us just come back to my dear husband in Munich for another moment. You probably read in the papers nearly a year ago about his enormous good fortune; namely, that the young King, who is very musical and at the same time enthusiastic about Wagnerian music, had him located in Zürich and summoned to the court, offered him a life free of worries so that he could work unencumbered; which, however, has not yet materialized. Your fine, dear friend Pecht and some other eccentric, frivolous riffraff move around him so that the papers are making fun of it, as, for example, in the Augsburger *Allgemeine* Nos. 50 and 55. Even *Punsch,* which appears in Munich, reports the funniest absurdities about Richard's life and luxury, which can have very bad consequences, considering German standards. It is true that many small exaggerations are based on envy, but nevertheless I've heard the most fantastic little stories from eyewitnesses, stories which can only be expected of fools, but which must simply be ridiculed by sensible people, and now enough, let us pray for the poor soul of Rumorhäuser,[6] as he is called.

"Forgive me for having been so lengthy and detailed about him and my humble self, but when the heart is full the pen overflows. Now I ask you once more to write *a lot* about yourself, how you live. You have the absolute right to tell me about yourself for at least ten sheets; I'm thirsty and starved. My refreshment here is art, which I prefer even to my dear, friendly families. The King has given me a good seat for my daily use, which makes me very happy. The Wagnerian operas are all in the repertory and are often performed; unfortunately, I can hear them only rarely without getting terribly excited; he was too mean to me. May God forgive him for it and let him prosper! I write to him rarely, he to me even more rarely.

"I haven't heard anything from Paris for a long time; I was, as I said, very ill and stopped writing, one reason being that I know that many people— you are a praiseworthy exception—don't like mournful letters. I haven't seen your brother for a long time, but I know he is causing a stir here as artist. His wife visited me also; she is tall and was very large. In any case you are a happy uncle. Farewell for today; don't become intoxicated too often with the nectar of champagne, then I'll soon see my request fulfilled.

"With a thousand cordial greetings I remain as ever,

"Your old friend

M. WAGNER"

At this point Minna seems to have learned her lesson, and, rather than be cut off from Wagner entirely, kept her own counsel about rumors which may have reached her of his secret connection with Cosima, and to have spared him her complaints and reproaches altogether. We have none of her letters to Wagner after 1863,[7] but a succession of letters from Wagner, keeping her informed of principal events in his strangely developing career, would certainly otherwise never have been written. Since no letters from Wagner to Minna at this time have been published until now, allowing space for considerable speculation as to his treatment of her in her last years, the ten letters and two telegrams in the Collection from the years 1864–1865 are given in full. The first is as follows:[8]

"POOR DEAR MINNA!

"I have just learned from Wolfram, who writes me on a business matter, that there has been another loss in your family, that you are stricken by the death of Charlotte, and that this has left you feeling extremely weak.

[6] The *Punsch,* of Munich, had published a travesty on "The Morning Life of a New-German Composer," giving him this compound name.

[7] Excepting a drafted payment (440) which may never have been sent.

[8] 422 A (Penzing, Feb. 15, 1864).

"Minna, if you could see the many tears I often shed for you, and which at this moment almost prevent me from writing, you would learn what to think of my apparent hardness toward you.

"So much I know: if I come to see you, it could only be to stay with you entirely and without interruption; no other agreement would be feasible. But I can't yet bring myself to make this decision, out of anxiety for you as well as for me. I therefore considered it better to be entirely silent. Should I give you any hope today, as my heart would so much like to do? Life is so grave and terribly hard; who can clearly tell what is the right thing to do? Poor Minna! Fate has linked you to one of the strangest of men. Daily experience makes it ever more clear to me how little I actually am understood, how I stand alone and abandoned by the world! No wonder that you have much to suffer from it. For the present, I feel only one immediate necessity: the most un-heard-of interruptions of all sorts have so delayed my work on *Die Meister-singer* that I feared at the beginning of this winter I should have to stop work entirely. By deciding not to undertake anything else of outward importance this winter, and not to go to Petersburg again, I forcibly compelled myself to tackle my work and to stay with it. I now hope to be able to keep at it un-interruptedly so as to deliver it to the theaters next winter. My internal and external welfare depends on seeing it through. I beg you to contribute to this result by using the utmost patience. You will be able to do it, above all, by your early recovery. Care for your health as much as you can, dear Minna, and think of the joy you would give me and how you would make my life bearable. I'll try to save 100 thr. especially for the care of your health this summer. You may count on it.

"If I had succeeded in securing my livelihood by a fixed income, some share of it would have been allotted to you. Now—more than ever before—everything is fluctuation, insecurity, dependence on good luck—and luck doesn't favor me. Now I'll try to force my luck by this work; unfortunately it demands a good mood which I am losing more and more. When it is finished and life somehow presents a more friendly face, we two shall have another reasonable discussion. Who knows, Minna, what will seem advisable to us then? Perhaps it will be just what we both wish. Certainly! Summon up courage and don't neglect your health! Believe in my most heartfelt assurance that it is only your well-being that I care for.

"My fondest greetings and kisses. If you feel like writing to Chemnitz, tell Wolfram how much I thank him for his letter. Farewell, really well, dear Minna!

"Your

RICHARD"

Minna wrote to Kietz on March 28, 1864: [9]

"Can you imagine, dear friend, that I've lived alone here in Dresden since our separation in Paris: I haven't seen my good, excellent husband for almost two and a half years. He is happy, lives in Munich in the greatest luxury through the young King of Bavaria; he doesn't need me any more. Many people want to console me and think that with such an unbalanced character as Wagner's this good fortune cannot last long, and that through the strange, dissolute life he has been leading for years he has sunk so low as a human being in the eyes of his betters that they would not help him with such enormous sums any longer. If he were then again in great distress, he would come back to me. God knows whether I'll live to see that; and if I do, whether I should still be inclined toward a man who has so deeply and continually insulted me and has done this out of an exaggerated, silly vanity which miserable, slovenly women have awakened in him, whereby he became heartless and mean toward his stupid, *faithful* old companion. Unfortunately, he'll starve as an artist, for he hasn't created anything since he separated from me; his whole life is taken up by insipid, unworthy, superficial trivialities, and this is the most deplorable of all to me, because my vision [*Blick*] for him was very far-seeing; it did not stop at the things in front of him! What a pity, a man so richly endowed by God, in his best years, already ceasing to create when he is still able to enrich the world with many magnificent works, who with a sensible, regulated life, produced the most beautiful works, shaking them out of his cuff, so to speak. These wonderful times are as hard to recapture as one's youthful years."

422 B (*Wagner in Starnberg, May 26, 1864, to Minna*)

"MY DEAR MINNA!

"I have experienced a strange fate. Above all, I am happy that I can do something for you again. You got from Pusinelli and Pauline Tichatschek together 200 thr. in my name: now you are getting 100 thr. more. On the 15th of July you are to get 200 thr. again from Berlin royalties, which this time will amount to a great deal. Thus you are provided for the six months' summer season your regular share of money; and you *must not* give up anything, especially not the *bathing cure*. Do you hear? If necessary, even more money must be procured.

"Greetings to Pusinelli and Pauline. They may still credit their advances to me for a few months. They will get everything back, promptly in October. Be sure not to give them anything from *your* money: otherwise you would make it more difficult for me to support you now. As for the rest, I suppose it will come from God: at least I see that He doesn't abandon me. Pauline may

[9] 423.

have informed you about my misfortune. I had counted on the Moscow concert receipts to provide me for a whole year. Suddenly I found myself without an answer—I waited; finally I missed the time, and when it was too late, I learned that my affirmative letters, where I agreed to come, had been delayed there for six weeks. I really lost my head, and at first I didn't know at all how to make up that heavy loss in my receipts, gave up my Penzing apartment, and looked for a work refuge on the Zürich Lake at the Willes'. There the young King of Bavaria had me searched out and invited me to live near him. He is touchingly devoted to me and my art, and especially wishes me, through his intervention, to perform all my new works quite according to my own intentions. In order to avoid sensation and to ward off envy, I am living quite as a private citizen near him; he pays me a small salary (1,200 gulden) and gives me at any time when I want to make use of it a free apartment near by! By now I am located quite near him in the country, since he lives most of the time in the little Schloss Berg on Lake Starnberg. We meet daily. I behave with great cautiousness, so as not to expose myself to reproach for exploiting the favor of the very young Monarch. So it happens that for the present I can't draw any great advantage from his devotion to me except that I no longer need worry much about my personal needs, that I find rest, and that in the King himself I enjoy a highly inspiring intercourse. All the rest will develop in a good and friendly way.

"But *you* too should be free from worry! Now it will be easy for me to provide you with all you need. Above all, think of your cure and don't forfeit anything to that purpose! Well, courage and patience! Count always on my faithful sympathy. Farewell and now you may sigh with relief!

"Tender greetings from your

RICHARD"

422 C (*Wagner, in Starnberg, June 25, 1864, to Minna*)

"DEAR MINNA!

"You must surely yourself know that your letters have given me a great joy: I heartily thank you for them! If I am not mistaken I detect in them a real note of cheerfulness, which I have so long been missing. Let us do everything to brighten our life: it is so serious, so wretched! I still tremble and shudder when I consider how things could be, had not Heaven so suddenly disclosed that miracle to me and sent me the real savior of my life. Now for the first time I realize increasingly that everything I once began, everything I reluctantly pursued in order to keep myself going (like the intended *Tannhäuser* production and the big London concerts which followed)—these came to nothing, and nothing, actually nothing, materialized. What I have created so far seems too little even to warrant my lifelong support. They again demanded a new opera without considering that I had four works still awaiting a good performance, for which they neither would nor cared to provide the means. So I am always looked upon basically as a vulgar opera composer, not much better than Flotow and Offenbach, of whom they also expect something new every few years—otherwise! . . . How humiliating for me! And how stingy! As if, for instance, Dresden would ever have rewarded me for my *Lohengrin*! Well, the right thing happened at last: that young King loved me for what I am and have achieved; he longed for me and wished that from now on I should live without troubles, contented if I should still find the world worthy to be presented with something. In the year of the first *Tann-häuser* performance that precious reward of my genius was born for me out of the womb of a Queen: in his fifteenth year he attended a *Lohengrin* performance and since then he has been devoted to me, warmly and faithfully. My external relation to him is quite undefined; he is happy to have me near him, is taking care of my living quarters, and has left it to me to arrange with his trusted cabinet-secretary for a salary, which I may draw regularly. On account of the immense sensation which my appointment made, also the dismay and envy, we considered it adequate not to exceed the amount paid by the late King to a poet like Geibel, etc. But I am not restricted, I am only restricting myself so as to keep my relation as pure as possible from the beginning. If I need more it is at my disposal. For the moment, dear Minna, I am happy to be able to take care of you from the plentiful Berlin royalties, without bothering anybody else, and even to pay off the debts incurred on your account. Today I ordered the Berlin Theater to send 400 thr. to your address in Dresden; therefore, you will not only receive the promised 200 thr. to complete your half-year's payment, but also an additional 200 thr. with which I urge you to pay back right away 100 thr. to Pusinelli and as well 100 thr. to good Pauline in my name, with the most hearty thanks. How glad I am to know that you will thus be freed of all care and evil, pressing worries. In the future, I shall always be able to provide you promptly with all you need, since I won't need anything for the rest of my life and so can use my other income elsewhere; in case of need a kindly resource will always be open to me.

"Thus I am gradually recovering too. I needed it after the welcome my German homeland had offered to me on my return: I shall never forget those three years when I could get help only from Bohemia, Russia, Hungary, while in Germany every connection was carefully barred to me. You are fortunate to have been spared much of my bitterness!

"Now I soon expect my young King to come back. I have promised to make music for him in my own way every day. Then I shall really work. In the fall, when the King can attend the theater again, I am first going to arrange a concert performance of my new compositions for him: let's hope that next year we'll achieve *Tristan* with Schnorr. If the singers are available, I'll also perform *Lohengrin* for him. What he most longs for is the *Nibelungen*. He wants to perform the whole work as I originally intended it. Otherwise, I have nothing at all to do with the theater: my position is quite distinguished [*vornehm*], without any title, only personal—

"The dear picture was the first answer to your good, beautiful letter. I hesitated until I had more detailed news about my Berlin receipts. And now I am happy that everything has turned out well. I approve your choice of Tharand. The forest air is very strengthening for the nerves, and it is also true that you, dear good Minna, especially need rest and invigoration. It must come partly from within yourself. Resignation is our lot, forgiveness and lenience our only redemption from pain and passion [*Leiden und Leidenschaft*]. How well I have learned not to attempt the impossible! Forbearance and kindness pave the road in the end to any true peace of mind. . . .

"The memory of Jacquot greatly touches me. My landlord in Penzing, an old baron, has presented me with an old, very beautiful big hound which I have actually brought along with me. It is brown, its name is Pohl, and it is an exceedingly kind, intelligent animal, which I feed for charity's sake. The King had learned about it and wanted me to bring it along. Well, greet Jacquot from me; it is nice to hear from him. Greet old Mathilde too—I see you aren't getting rid of her after all. Greet the Heines, Pusinelli, and Pauline. You shall surely have good news from me soon again.

"Farewell, dear good Minna! Take care of yourself and your returning good spirits; you will so awaken in me joy and fair hopes!

"With all my heart,

Your

RICHARD"

422 D (*Wagner, in Starnberg, September 5, 1864, to Minna*)

"DEAR GOOD MINNA!

"I'm writing you today anyway, although it is a little late and the letter won't leave until tomorrow. I arrived here only today, in order to take care of my catarrh. Yesterday, in Munich, I got your letter which (as you can imagine) gave me much joy; for the last few days I had the letters held in Munich, because I didn't know in the end how long I should be away. I wasn't in Karlsruhe, but Liszt was there, and later on called on me here. I have no use for those music societies, and Karlsruhe, where I had been so long led by the nose, is one of the last places where I would stay to make music. Lately I have often been visiting my young King in Hohenschwangau; he thrives more and more and dearly loves me. My only difficulty is to curb his impatience: he would like to perform the *Nibelungen* as early as this year.

"Although I am not bound by any obligation of service [*Dienstleistung*], I have to yield to his entreaties and give the first performance here of *The Flying Dutchman* at the beginning of October, when he is to attend the theater for the first time since his succession to the throne. The opera has been very carefully prepared and well cast, therefore I also am glad to undertake it. All the further plans are still in God's hands, and one doesn't know whether or not they will come to pass. Actually it is very hard for me now to have dealings with singers, etc. In order not to be forced into anything, I am keeping myself very independent: I am too tired really to desire anything but rest and peace. Anything else I do under compulsion, and in this none will succeed except the young Monarch in his rare love and enthusiasm.

"You seem to have had an enviable time at Tharand. My stay here unfortunately hasn't turned out to be very pleasant, on account of the exceptionally nasty cold and damp weather which has prevailed here since May with only a few short interruptions. I don't yet know where I can be accommodated in the city and I'll probably have to make my camp here for some time to come, which is not exactly one of the most pleasant prospects. I am all the more pleased that you feel tolerably well and seem to be in a good humor; but many desirable things are not my lot, and the thought of working only for my art from now on strengthens me; for this purpose everything has been made easier now.

"As I already cabled to you this morning, accept my most heartfelt wishes for your birthday. The most important of all is reasonable health, which you seem to have somewhat regained recently. If I have contributed to this in any degree, you may well believe that I am pleased about it. May it be preserved for you and strengthened more and more.

"Soon you will hear from me again! Warmest greetings from

"Your

RICHARD"

"(Old Pohl greets Jacquot)

"On the King's orders an excellent, large-sized bust is being made of me in marble. I shall see to it that you get a copy of it later on: this must suffice for my (birthday) present."

422 E *(Wagner, in Starnberg, September 26, 1864, to Minna)*

"DEAR MINNA!

"You have probably recently received 20 louis d'or from Coburg; by the 15th of October I'm going to send you the balance of 140 thr.

"You must understand that I am glad that income from various parts enables me to send you your share undiminished. I have just had another experience of the bad position into which I am often pushed by maliciously invented newspaper reports. It is not only that the crazy exaggeration of my fortunate circumstances results in the most nonsensical claims, as you will see again from the enclosed letter from the good Frau Kriete, but there is a general desire here to lay everything hostile at my door. An official refutation of these silly rumors has been published in the papers here: I send it to you, so that you may be as well informed about my position as Frau Kriete, to whom I beg you to send it. I have made up my mind not to change my modest position in any way, in order to preserve the sympathy and enthusiasm of my young King for my higher goals in art.

"For the present I shall stay here, since the performance of the *Dutchman* has had to be delayed.

"Take care of your health, for thus alone can you assure my happiness; it is what fate has left you to do for me. Believe me and consider that my lot is toil and difficulty until the end of my life, since it is no longer for my *own* well-being that I must work, but for the higher purpose for which I have been put in the world.

"Warmest greetings from your

RICHARD"

422 F *(Wagner, in Munich, October 15, 1864, to Minna)*

"DEAR MINNA!

"I am sending you today the missing 140 thr. as an addition to your quarterly payment. I am sorry that people have been persistently confusing you: not a word of what young Fritz Brockhaus told you did he get from me; if I had said anything of the sort, it would have been a lie, and I don't know why I should tell a lie. I shall no longer try to refute the rumors about myself— because I shouldn't know where to begin. Nor will I exhaust myself with denying gossip: there has been a recent and rather favorable change in my status: I have received the actual commission from the King to finish and to produce the *Nibelungen,* for which purpose I am enabled to dispense with other pursuit of income for three years. It especially occurred to me that I'll be able to send you your quarterly allowance promptly from my income here.

"I shall now really enjoy the salary of 4,000 fl. for three years to come. After deducting your 1,000 thalers from that amount you won't find it extravagant.

"My troubles, which you don't seem to understand, will be great, for dealing with our opera singers and theater folk is to me like delivering myself to intolerable torments. This is really so.

"Lately, by confusing me with a singer by the name of Richard here, the rumor of my fatal illness got into the papers. I received inquiries by telegraph from many parts, etc. Supposing you might be scared too, I have telegraphed you and hope you did not resent it [427 B].

"But for the present I really feel a little exhausted, which is probably due to the very unwholesome climate here. Forgive me for limiting myself to the most necessary things only, and be reassured that my care for your well-being will forever remain to me a dear and sacred duty.

"For the rest, I don't demand anything further from the world except peace and patience so that I may finish my work, since I have now found the good genius who is making this possible.

"Farewell and fondest greetings from your

RICHARD"

422 G *(Wagner, in Munich [21 Briennerstrasse], October 15, 1864, to Minna)*

"DEAR MINNA!

"I beg you to send me here the silver work (laurel wreath and music sheets, etc.) which was once presented to me in Paris, as well as the silver goblet which I was given at the Zürich concerts. I have promised to show them to the King.

"I hope you will comply with this reasonable request. With affectionate greetings,

"Your
RICHARD"

422 H *(Wagner, in Munich, December 20, 1864, to Minna)*

"DEAR MINNA!

"I am sorry that I have kept you waiting for news—even after your reminders—for such a long time. I have had very little time to myself; it is especially the involved correspondence that makes demands on me, and I am trying to relieve myself of this business, which takes all of one's time, so that some may remain for my work. The persistent wrong and stupid news reports about me and my undertakings always seem to be invented especially to disturb me by involving me in corrections and denials. So much is certain: after a life as many-sided as mine, the hard period begins at my age, when one must decide whether to respond to the world's claims, or belong only to one's self. The greatest possible simplification therefore became a necessity to me. Merely to be able to see to it that my works are well produced: how many-sided are the experiments and inquiries it requires! And things always get so extremely difficult. I have no time nor thought left for really comfortable correspondence.

"This in general for your orientation!

"I have duly received all that you sent, and I thank you for them! Just at the time they came I was suffering badly from piles and confined to bed for a rather long time. My first task when I could get out was to see the lawyer whom the Kriete family had directed against me here. Seeing that nobody in Dresden would help me against those demands, I finally found no peace until I had agreed to yearly payments of 200 thr. and interest. Although this put a new stricture on my scarcely balanced budget, I shall always try my best to send you your share regularly. I am glad I can be punctual, especially this time, and send you the quarterly amount before New Year. May you get it in tolerable health and may it contribute somewhat to improve your good humor.

"I'll be glad to hear about the good success of my wishes. Farewell until then, affectionately

"Your

RICHARD"

Two telegrams were sent by Wagner from Munich, in 1864, to Minna in Dresden:

427 A *(September 5)*

"A thousand good wishes, dear Minna, for your birthday. Have been away. Letter follows.

427 B *(October 9)*

"Have just learned that false rumor in the newspapers reports me dangerously ill; so that you won't worry I assure you that I am actually well. Will answer your letter soon.

RICHARD WAGNER"

435 A *(Wagner, in Munich, March 28, 1865, to Minna)*

"DEAR MINNA!

"You will soon receive from Berlin the one and also the other half of the 250 thaler which are due you on April 1st. . . .

"Several references in your last letter lead me to remind you once more of my actual status at present. The King has arranged for my apartment and gives me—for three years—4,000 gulden while I complete the composition of my *Nibelungen*. Out of this annual allowance I am paying you around 1,800 fl. (equal to 1,000 thaler), and in addition 350 fl. (equal to 200 thaler) to the Krietes. The opinion here that this is an enviable income is due to the local standard of living; their exaggeration of it into the legendary was intended to incite public opinion and turn the King against me. The worst consequence for me in all this is that—even though the King, who knew better what is going on, remained quite unconvinced—claims were raised against me from everywhere and from the remotest times. It is possible that as a consequence of this life will be made miserable for me even here, and that I shall ask the King to let me live peacefully on a smaller pension in some hidden corner of the world. You, too, can—in your way and by correctly judging my position—contribute toward protecting me from such a potential change in my way of living.

"What I want is *peace* at all costs!

"With best wishes for your health I remain, with cordial greetings,

always your

RICHARD"

It would be pleasant to report that the status of entirely friendly interchange continued until the end. But the following letters indicate otherwise. A fragmentary draft of a letter by Minna, written in a trembling hand and partly illegible, dated Dresden, July (?) 19, and with no year given, may well be the cause of Wagner's refusal, in the letter which follows it (435 B), to receive further communications from her. It is a pitiable exhibition of her tendency, in spite of her husband's plain speaking of what he could not accept, to say the wrong thing and so force him to close the door of intercourse between them (440):

"My dear good Richard!
"Many thanks for your last letters!
"At the bottom of your heart you are good, after all; I always knew it, it is only from your mind, in which so much beauty and splendor dwells, that also sometimes there comes much harm for those about you—all that shall now be forgiven and forgotten. You should now know that once I have forgiven, never a word about the past has escaped my lips; so shall it be now, but before that I had to unburden myself to you frankly. When you spoke of reunion and seeing each other again—which I no longer believed in seriously—you should have examined yourself so that I could be glad from the bottom of my heart, which I could not quite be in my letters to you, as you can still gather now. From now on I shall strive to kill every disagreeable thought of the past in my mind, and it will be revived only in the case of a renewed offense—against which may the heavens protect me for all eternity! Husband and wife should discuss everything frankly and honestly; they must confess good and bad to each other; they must advise and help one another; in short, there must be sincerity, otherwise no happiness and blessing will dwell in the home. One must have confidence in the other, more so than in strangers. God hears and sees everything, and he often punishes severely those who sow weeds among the wheat. One should not complain behind the back of the other, something that by all saints has never entered my mind. . . . You should at least know me as well as that when you remember that I always keep my word, and that never a word of reproach about it escaped my lips. . . . It all depends from what source the offense stems. But I ask you once again not to believe that I was stirred up by some one or other. I assure you that the whole incident has not allowed me a quiet moment: it has pursued me at night while awake and dreaming, so that I found myself constantly in a feverish state of mind that had a most destructive effect on me; and if I had not still had some strength left, it would be scarcely possible for me still to exist, wherefore I do not care at all for a life full of torment which I don't deserve. This, my good Richard, I have had to tell you frankly and honestly; I hesitated a long time to do so. As you will have seen from my letters, I could never be happy, even when you gave me hope for a reunion or a meeting, a hope which would have made me so happy under different circumstances.

Added to this was what I learned just before my departure—not quite directly—about the horrible insult, those mean reproaches you had uttered about me. I put them with the rest and they grieved me very much. So, my child, it was only natural that I had to talk to you, not excitedly, but quietly, and before I could again put my whole future and life into your hands. As concerns the indirect offenses, they too shall be placed with the rest of the insults; in case there is no repetition, they shall be forgiven and if possible forgotten—"

435 B *(Munich, October 5, 1865)*

"Dear Minna!

"Pardon the delay this time: it shall not happen again. My request was not carried out.

"I have not yet read your letter: since your letter of last spring which depressed me so shamefully, I have decided not to embitter my heart and my memories unnecessarily.

"If you have something to tell me which needs to be taken care of, ask Pusinelli to tell me about it. I shall always do everything in my power to console you.

"Cordial greetings from your

Richard W"

The chorus of slander in Munich, which left no possible weakness in Wagner unexploited, attacked him for neglecting his wife. Her denial, published at the time, is in the Collection. It is in a wavering hand: [10]

 "Honor to the Truth

"As a result of an erroneous report in the *Münchner Weltbote,* I hereby truthfully declare that so far I have received sufficient support from my absent husband, Richard Wagner, to live a decent life, free from care.

Frau Minna Wagner
geb. Planer

"Dresden, January 9, 1866"

Minna's death, on January 25, 1866, followed this by sixteen days. Wagner wrote to Natalie from Geneva on April 2: [11]

"Dear Natalie!

"I thank you for your friendly letters, which I could not answer immediately since I was often delayed. The sad message of Minna's death reached me, as you know, when I was far away: to say anything about it is still impossible

[10] 449.
[11] 453.

for me. I myself live only through the conviction that I am destined to write important works: this alone gives me the strength to bear the disgusting annoyances to which my life is continually exposed and which I'm glad to have kept from Minna in the last years.

"According to what the excellent friend Pusinelli wrote me, it would be advisable for you to furnish a small apartment with the furniture Minna left you and to rent it. As I promised, I shall send you 30 thaler quarterly (this time 6 Napoleons d'or), and begin today. I hope this will make it a little easier for you, since you are modest and unassuming. Besides, life is again being made very difficult for me just now, since I had to decide, in order to get away from the awful disturbances, to live away from my house in Munich for some time, which makes it much more difficult for me to get along; and I don't want to ask for any kind of compensation for this, because this would at once bring new slanders on my head, considering the terrific envy to which I am exposed. Thus I offer you what I can actually spare only by making sacrifices, and I'll be so much the happier if it is of use to you.

"I hope to be able to visit Dresden in the fall: if the matter can wait so long, I should then like to take the necessary steps to get a worthy tombstone for poor Minna; but I'm also prepared to consider any propositions which you might want to make to me before that.

"Try then, you poor, good Natalie, to help yourself through life as well as you can: that you are not without friends you can see in me, and you shall continue to find it so in the future to the best of my ability.

"If Minna has kept my letters, I hope she has not disposed of them, and I should like to get them back into my hands. I should also like to have back our pencil portraits which Kietz once made in Paris.

"Otherwise I claim nothing, unless the deceased may have left something to me personally.

"Farewell, dear Natalie! Let me know where you will be staying and be assured of my continued warm interest. With best regards

from your

RICHARD WAGNER

"Please give my warmest regards to the noble, cherished friend, Dr. Pusinelli."

❧ XXVII ❧

THE GOVERNESS'S DIARY

Susanne Weinert was employed as governess in Wagner's household at the Villa Wahnfried in Bayreuth between July 16, 1875, and April, 1876. During those nine months she kept a diary (493 A) which bears the title: *Im Hause Richard Wagners—Ein Beitrag zum Familienleben des grossen Meisters*. It is fragmentary: the writer herself refers to it not as a *Tagebuch* but as a *Manchmal-Buch*, a notebook with occasional entries. Fräulein Weinert records her impressions of the *Meister* and the family life, as viewed from the nursery. That there could have been much family life to record was hardly to be expected, for these were the months of final intensive preparation for the opening of the Festspielhaus and the introduction of the *Ring* on August 13–17, 1876. Throughout her stay singers were being engaged, drilled at Wahnfried, rehearsed in the theater, entertained, and sometimes cajoled. The vital problems of casting and *mise en scène* were not all: the whole project was in jeopardy; Wagner's visits to Prague, Vienna, and Berlin, here noted, were made in the interest of obtaining funds through concerts. Yet the notebook shows that while the children were for the most part left in the hands of the new governess, they were by no means forgotten.

The following memorandum is appended in the hand of Mrs. Burrell: "Ludicrous Journal of an innocent idiot Governess at Wahnfried, Bayreuth, unconsciously describes the inhabitants to the very Life—all their pomposity, impudence, and impecuniosity." Whatever else her story may be, it is often rambling and inconsequential. It is here condensed to the salient items.

On July 16, 1875, Susanne Weinert entered Villa Wahnfried, "passing through a garden path lined with beautiful white poplar trees. . . . In the middle of the garden a bust of King Ludwig of Bavaria stands on a high pedestal." The front door opens into a small vestibule from which a staircase leads to a wide, bright room, the *Kindersalon*. There is a solemn quiet in the house; even the noise of footsteps is stifled by the soft carpets. The *Kindersalon* serves also as a schoolroom where, sitting at a long table, she would give lessons. Immediately adjacent to the *Kindersalon* is Cosima's boudoir and the so-called *Denkzimmer* (room for meditation). The furniture of the boudoir is "miraculously cosy. . . . Its doors are draped with heavy silk curtains. The room is furnished comfortably and decorated with ornaments whose arrangement and value reveal the taste of the highly cultured lady." The *Denkzimmer* is "particularly cosy in the evening. . . . The gaslight spreads its bright glow over the medium-sized quadrangular room and the red velvet of the *causeusen*. A big round table of ebony stands in the middle of the room. Bookshelves, richly carved, are filled with classic works as well as with children's books. There are also dainty little tables of graceful shape, softly upholstered armchairs, and other chairs with daintily colored silk upholstery." There is a breakfast room on the second floor.

The first floor centers upon the hall which is "surrounded by a gilded gallery. . . . In the middle of the hall stands a grand piano. . . . There are also four sofas covered with black leather. The big room is always comfortably warm owing to the hot-air heating, and is softly lighted by a skylight. . . . Four high folding doors lead to the adjacent rooms: to the vestibule, to the dining room, to Cosima's yellow boudoir, and to Richard Wagner's study, which at the same time serves as the reception room. . . . Each of the folding doors is flanked by dark pedestals, two of which carry the busts of Richard and Cosima Wagner, while the others show the principal characters from Wagner's operas."

Wagner's study is described as follows: "The big room looks upon the garden, entered by a glass door. Close to the window stands Wagner's desk, laden with a number of precious writing utensils, a sacred place for the Wagner family. The floor is covered by a carpet of dark red and black design. A second carpet with a pale, multicolored design is spread over the first. The red-draped walls of this parlor are covered with shelves containing books in precious bindings and arranged with extreme tidiness. The library comprises works of German litera- ture from the earliest beginnings to modern times, the creations of the great men of all countries, of the spiritual fighters within all realms of human knowledge. A precious grand piano stands opposite to the writing desk. The room is filled with rich furniture in informal disorder. In one corner there is an armchair covered with yellow satin, in the other corner a crimson colored *causeuse* into whose soft upholstery one fairly sinks. Opposite to the fireplace there is a charm- ing little sofa covered with silk damask of a colored design, in front of it a small oval table covered by an azure satin cover hanging down almost to the floor. Silver flowers are woven into the cover. Besides there are other little tables, hassocks, chairs of many shapes, a richly gilded table with wonderful exotic plants. From the ceiling hangs a magnificent chandelier which at night spreads its brilliant light over the variegated collection of furniture." The beautiful garden contains a summerhouse, a terrace, and a greenhouse. Susanne Weinert does not describe any of the bedrooms in Villa Wahnfried. She shares her own room with Siegfried, "an angel on earth."

On July 20, 1875, four days after her arrival, the new governess, together with Wagner and the Bülow children, attended a rehearsal of the *Ring* in the Theater. Liszt, Frau von Schleinetz, and other "high-ranking personalities" were present. "The interior of the Theater was still unfinished; there was no scenery on the stage; all over the place were scaffoldings, beams, tools lying around. Then the music, performed by the invisible orchestra, began, and the singers started with their parts. Suddenly Wagner interrupted. With youthful liveliness he jumped over a few steps leading to the pit and, gesticulating, talked to the conductor and the singers."

It will be noted that this account differs with the existing belief that the orchestra was heard for the first time in the new auditorium on the afternoon of August 2. On July 24, a test was made of the opening sets for *Das Rheingold* and *Die Walküre.*

On August 5, 1875, a reception took place at Villa Wahnfried. "Members of society in Bayreuth, Liszt, and Richard Wagner's collaborators" were present. Susanne Weinert mentions particularly Frau Materna, Lilli Lehmann, Herr and Frau Gura, Joseph Rubinstein, Wilhelmj. The governess admired the colorful picture, "the ladies in elegant robes—one of them in a heavy green satin robe— the gentlemen in evening dress or in uniform" (*"die vornehme Welt in Wahrheit und Dichtung"*—the nobility of fact and fiction—so the rather naïve lady writes). "Sitting on a sofa and hidden by an arrangement of flowers," the Fräulein and the children observed the party. The children, particularly Daniela von Bülow, were less impressed by the pompous show and ridiculed the affectation, the gestures, and the dresses of the guests, a criticism which was rebuked by the humorless governess.

A few weeks later, on August 17,[1] Wagner gave a garden party at Wahnfried for the whole of the opera personnel and a few close friends, about 150 in all. "There was a concert and also fireworks. The children, clad in white dresses with bows, attended the feast. In preparation for the party the servants adorned the trees and the bushes with paper lanterns and little flags. Buffets were set up at different places, and in the neighborhood of the hothouse a platform for the orchestra, decorated with plants, had been erected." Susanne Weinert mentions among the guests the banker Feustel, his wife and daughters. Cosima, "in a white dress with precious lace, and Richard Wagner took part in the animated conversation. . . . A torchlight procession was arranged by the younger members of the party; from time to time Bengal fire flashed up. The party ended with a speech by Wagner from the platform. Addressing his guests, he praised the majesty of the art which linked him closely and permanently with its disciples. A triple cheer for the arts and their admirers, accompanied by a roaring flourish of the orchestra, ended the party."

In September, 1875, Richard and Cosima made a trip to Prague. Only the Wagner, not the Bülow, children were included. The trip started at the beginning of September, after September 6, and ended before September 20. Teplitz was one of the places that the family visited on their way to Prague. They stayed at an elegant hotel in Prague, inspected the historical parts of the city and made several excursions to the surroundings. They traveled first class, not without

[1] Ernest Newman (*Life*, Vol. IV, p. 447) reports the date as August 13.

having, on their way back, an unpleasant encounter with a lady who wanted to prohibit the Wagner family from entering her compartment.

A second and more comprehensive journey followed in November and December, 1875. The family left Bayreuth on November 1, stopped at Munich, where they visited the studio of Franz von Lenbach, who had supper with them, and arrived in Vienna on November 5. They left Vienna on December 13.

On November 16 Fräulein Weinert attended the performance of *Lohengrin* at the Hofoper Theater of Vienna.[2] "Richard Wagner and Cosima sat in a box together with Hofoper Manager Jarno"; the governess and the children sat in the next box. Wagner evidently had plentiful objections to the tempi of the performance; "sometimes he wanted to have the tempo slowed up, but sometimes he murmured: *'Elende Bummelei, da macht doch vorwärts!'* (Miserable dragging—hurry it up!)" The opera had an overwhelming success with the public. An enthusiastic audience shouted continuously, "Richard Wagner, Richard Wagner." "The children enjoyed it and whispered, 'How they shout; what a noise!' and they softly imitated: 'Richard Wagner, Richard Wagner!'" Wagner spoke from the stage. "He thanked the Viennese people who had offered him such a friendly welcome and had greeted his *Lohengrin* so favorably. He also thanked the singers who had given their best to perform the opera as the composer wished. . . . Cosima wept after the performance." Fräulein Weinert observes: "She is said to weep at every performance of *Lohengrin.*"

Toward the end of the diary she reports that Richard and Cosima went to Berlin between February 20 and March 22, 1876. This is in accordance with the fact that Wagner was in Berlin to supervise the rehearsals for the performance of *Tristan* on March 20.

Susanne Weinert's duties brought her in close touch with the children. On her arrival, Cosima's five children were at Wahnfried: Daniela von Bülow, already a "self-confident young lady showing a striking similarity to her father, Hans von Bülow" (Fräulein Weinert remarks elsewhere that Daniela has "one blue and one brown" eye); Blandine von Bülow, a "charming little girl" about twelve years of age; nine-year-old Isolde von Bülow, Wagner's natural child, "a frail girl with light-brown hair and with a sort of dreamy expression in her eyes"; Eva Wagner, seven years old, "with dark, roguish eyes which gazed merrily at the world"; Siegfried, six years old, "a beautiful fair boy, a little timid." Daniela and Blandine were only temporarily at Wahnfried; during the greater part of the year they were boarders of the *Luisenstift* near Zwickau (Niederlössnitz). Only the three Wagner children were Fräulein Weinert's permanent pupils.

Interference by the parents with her plans of education is mentioned only

[2] Ernest Newman (*Life,* Vol. IV, p. 460) reports that the performance took place on Dec. 15, 1875. If Fräulein Weinert is correct in her dates, this cannot have been the performance which Wagner attended.

occasionally. At the beginning she had outlined a schedule of instruction which aroused criticism from Cosima in so far as too much time was to be dedicated to religion. Fräulein Weinert ventured to maintain her opinion that the children were deplorably backward "in this science so predominantly important for the establishment of human happiness," whereupon Cosima answered: "Oh, the children will learn that of their own accord later in life" (*Ach, das lernen die Kinder im Leben von selbst*). As Susanne Weinert's views differed so much from those of her mistress, she "canceled one hour a week only."

Regarding musical education, she mentions only the children's singing. On March 25, 1876, a party took place in the big hall. The children played in their room. Suddenly a servant appeared with the summons to sing: *"Fräulein, der gnädige Herr wünscht dass die kleinen Herrschaften auf der Galerie singen möchten."* Quickly the children and the governess hurried to the illuminated gallery, from which they looked down upon the hall crowded with the festively dressed guests. The children began to sing in two parts the song written by Richard Wagner for Cosima's birthday in 1874, with a last verse reading, *"Allerliebste, allerschönste Cosima."* "They got much applause and ran away giggling."

Often, in the presence of guests, Wagner asked the children to sing *"Freude, schöner Götterfunken."* "Then the children crept underneath the grand piano, singing from there, accompanied by Richard Wagner. This always caused much laughter. . . ."

"Every morning before the reading lesson began, the children had dancing lessons and lessons in etiquette with balletmaster Fricke.[3] . . . The children practiced the *Kaiserschritt* (Emperor's step) and the *Promenadenschritt* (promenade step) and learned how to bow to the right and to the left with an amiable smile. . . . Fricke accompanied these exercises by playing the violin."

At the time when the trip to Vienna was planned, Cosima suggested that "the history lessons should deal with the rule of the house of Hapsburg, so that the children would be interested in the Austrian dynasty at the time of their stay in Vienna." Occasionally Richard and Cosima listened to a lesson in geography, when Fräulein Weinert described a trip along the Rhine.

The children's playing was quite normal. There was a big wooden swing in the garden, made for four. The children liked to play with the two big Newfoundland dogs Branke and Marke. The Fräulein mentions particularly a dolls' theater. "The dolls were dressed magnificently, princes and the princesses in silk dresses with trains. . . . The most touching scenes were performed."

The manners of the children toward their parents showed a certain ceremonial respect. "Whenever Cosima entered the room, the children approached her and kissed her hand. . . ." When Richard and Cosima visited the classroom, the children—and the governess too—rose. A quoted remark of Wagner to his daughter indicates a lack of understanding of children: "Eva does not know anything; she is so stupid that I pity her."

[3] Richard Fricke, engaged as choreographer, was then working upon the swimming motions of the Rhine Maidens.

But as a rule the relations between parents and children seem to have been very cordial. This cordiality included the Bülow children; they too were very fond of Richard Wagner. Daniela and Blandine said to the governess: "Oh, our father Richard is unique; we love him so!" When they left for the *Luisenstift,* they had tears in their eyes.

The parents participated in the children's games. "They played hide-and-seek with them; Richard Wagner swung them around in a circle." Wagner particularly liked to play with Siegfried. "When the boy attempted to turn a somersault or a wheel, he helped him. . . . He laid him flat down on the floor," or "Wagner himself lay down, pretending to be Siegfried's riding horse, whereupon Siegfried climbed all over his father." Whenever Wagner's time permitted it, Siegfried was in his study playing around his father's chair. "Often Siegfried climbed on Cosima's knees, kissing her vehemently." Once when the children entered Wagner's study, he warned them jokingly in genuine Saxon dialect to be quiet: *"Na, meine Kudsten, bleibt nur da, seid aber hibsch ruhig, das sag ich Eich, bedankt Eich scheene bei mir, wie sich's gehert. . . . Sehn Se, mei Freilein, ich bin Se a guder Sächse, Se sein doch ooch ene Sächsin"* ("Now, dearest, you may stay, but I must tell you to be nice and quiet, and thank me nicely as you are supposed to. . . . You see, young lady, I am a good Saxon, so you are one too"). Wagner teased his children. He "pulled the children's ears, flipped their noses." Once when a favorite dish of Isolde's was served, he remarked with feigned regret: "Oh, Isolde cannot eat that; the tip of her nose reveals it!" The children teased their father too. One day they pulled their father's hair and cried: "But, Papa, here you have quite greenish hair!" "This new nuance of his hair amused the adults very much; however, it was true: his hair near the temples had a shade of green in it." Then Wagner continued sentimentally: "Oh, children, your poor father is to be pitied; he has such a bad time in this world. Also, Fräulein Weinert is no longer pleased with the world; she pulls quite a solemn face!" The Fräulein protested and the children cried, "But she does not look solemn at all!"

Christmas Eve was celebrated in the usual way. On New Year's Eve, 1876, the German custom of melting lead was observed. Lead is melted and then thrown into cold water. The lead turns into queer shapes whose significance is interpreted by the participants. Richard's piece was interpreted as a butterfly, whereupon he said almost solemnly, "Look, children, the symbol of immortality!" Cosima's piece turned into a little ball, usually interpreted as money. She remarked, "That is not so bad: to have money." "Wagner himself was dressed in his *Meistersinger* costume on this occasion." Another custom was observed: throwing the shoe backward over one's head. "If the tip of the shoe points toward the inside of the house, the owner will remain there during the following year; if it points to the exit, he will leave. . . . Frau Cosima threw her azure satin shoe, Richard Wagner his black velvet shoe, and both pointed to the inside; several other shoes flew through the air. Daniela's little black velvet slipper pointed to the exit." Susanne Weinert, who actually left in the spring of 1876, does not say anything about what happened to hers. Joseph Rubinstein, the only guest, played the piano.

As already mentioned, the Wagner children accompanied their parents on their trips to Prague, Munich, and Vienna. When the parents returned from Berlin, the children met them at the railway station.

Except through the family life of the children, Susanne Weinert had little contact with Wagner himself. Once Wagner dictated a letter to her. At another time she was happy to learn that Richard Wagner gratefully remembered her grandfather, Rector Baumgarten-Crusius of Meissen, who had once been his teacher.

On January 1, 1876, she was present when Wagner said to his children: "Children, just imagine, the King of Bavaria sent a telegram with congratulations for the New Year, and he calls me his beloved friend. Later you will recognize what a famous father you have. And you, you little foolish chap" (he addressed Siegfried), "you do not yet know anything, and nevertheless I set all my hope on Siegfried, that he may sometime follow in my path and continue my work."

Fräulein Weinert had a rather amusing experience on a trip to the stalactite grottos at Muggendorf in the Fränkische Schweiz on August 30, 1875. On this trip she suddenly discovered that she did not have money enough to pay the innkeeper. Daniela von Bülow tried to soften the wrath of the innkeeper by saying: "You don't seem to know that my papa is Richard Wagner, the famous Wagner for whom the new theater at Bayreuth has now been built. You don't need to be afraid; we won't run away, and you will get your money." However, the unimpressed innkeeper answered: "What do I care about your famous papa Richard Wagner; he does not mean anything to me, and the people of Bayreuth may build a theater for him ten times. I want to have my money, whatever your papa's name might be." Did the innkeeper know more about Wagner's financial standing than his children? . . . "Wagner and Cosima were rather amused by the story." [4]

In general Susanne Weinert praises Richard Wagner's "amiability." She also mentions his predilection for "the bridal song from *Lohengrin,* which he frequently sings and plays on the piano."

Once she had the opportunity to look at the material from which Wagner's dressing gowns were made. "In the basement of the house there were large boxes of colored satin, partly pale pink, partly azure, partly green. The housemaid, Asra, a Swiss, told her that she had to make the dressing gowns and pajamas from this material, and she showed Fräulein Weinert a model from which she had to work. This model consisted of a spring-green satin dressing gown decorated with pink bows."

Cosima's personality and the way she dresses are a constant source for Susanne

[4] On the other hand, an innkeeper at Berneck, who had seen Wagner, treated the governess and the children with the greatest respect.

Weinert's admiration. Cosima's "distinguished appearance" impresses her greatly. Her "vivid and large eyes and her spiritual [*durchgeistigtes*], rather pale face reveal at once a woman with a great mind and a worthy companion of the great Master." Repeatedly she mentions Cosima's "beautiful light-brown hair, which was arranged in heavy braids down to her neck. . . . The poise of her head and the graceful way in which she walks made a most dignified impression." In Prague she admires the intelligent manner in which Cosima explains the beauty of the sights to the children and to herself. She praises Cosima's "general knowledge within the different trends of learning, her conversational skill, her way of expressing herself," and concludes, "Frau Wagner is a genius" [*eine geniale Natur*].

Cosima's wardrobe always revealed a "distinguished taste. As a rule her street and traveling clothes were black. At home, particularly for festive occasions, she wore magnificent silk dresses." When Fräulein Weinert met Cosima for the first time, Cosima wore "a simple black dress which by no means impaired her graceful figure." At the garden party of August 17, 1875, Cosima wore a "white silk dress trimmed with precious lace." At another party at Wahnfried she wore "a royal blue [*königsblau*] dress, the tunic of which was interwoven with the most dainty bouquets of flowers. She wore her train with royal grace." The writer mentions several morning gowns, one of them "made of pale green silk interwoven with colored flowers." The other one is "a white satin dressing gown, a former evening dress trimmed with a black-velvet embroidered strip." Dressed in this gown, Cosima "walks through the rooms like a fairy in a fairy tale." At the performance of *Lohengrin* in Vienna, she wore a "magnificent satin robe with an imposing train." When the Wagners had invitations in Vienna, "Cosima put on her most lovely clothes; a light-purple satin robe floated around her slim figure, pearls adorned her beautiful hair, neck, and arms."

Susanne Weinert was very much impressed by "the most delicate courtesy" with which Richard treated Cosima. "With tender politeness Richard offers his arm to Cosima and leads her to the dining table. His eyes sparkle when he calls her 'My dear Cosima' or '*Mein liebes Weibchen.*' It was charming to listen to Cosima's laughter caused by Richard's humorous remarks."

At night Wagner sometimes read aloud from the classics. On September 2 he read scenes from *Hamlet* in his study, where Cosima and Liszt were present. Susanne Weinert listened from the hall.

In a little grove, in the middle of the garden, Richard and Cosima had provided for a place to be buried. One day the children showed her the gray stone slab, simply saying, "This is Papa's and Mama's grave."

She was also much impressed by Liszt during his stay at Wahnfried. She praises his "generosity" and describes him as "a delightful old gentleman whose amiability attracted everybody, including the servants." She admires also "his distinguished demeanor. . . . His relations with his son-in-law were very cordial and confidential, but nevertheless respectful. Each of them recognized the other as the great master within the realm of music. . . . Liszt smiled happily when looking at his daughter. . . . With pride he called her 'My dear daughter,' and he tenderly caressed her cheeks." Fräulein Weinert liked to listen to the fluent conversation of father and daughter in French and was entertained by the remarks which Richard Wagner then made in his not correctly pronounced French. These remarks "always caused amused laughter on the part of Cosima as she nodded to her husband."

The children too liked their *Grosspapa* very much. One night the whole family, *"Grosspapa"* Liszt, Cosima, the three Wagner children, and also the governess danced in the hall to the tune of the waltz from *Der Freischütz* played by Wagner on the piano.

A great number of servants were employed in Wagner's household. There was a valet who also took care of minor money matters in the household, the lady's maid (who accompanied the family on the trip to Vienna), the gardener, the janitor, the chambermaid, and the very influential cook, Victoria. When the family returned from Vienna, all the servants were lined up at the entrance door to welcome the *geehrte Prinzipalität* (the respected superiors), as Fräulein Weinert calls her employers. The way in which the servants addressed the family was very submissive. The valet Georg addressed even the six-year-old Siegfried as "Herr Siegfried."

Further members of the household were the Spitz dog Putzi and the Newfoundland dogs Branke and Marke, the children's pets. Branke was a female dog, her name evidently derived from Brangäne. Despite his name of tragic import, Marke was rather young and merry. Eva said of him, "He laughs all over his face." The neighbors were afraid of them. One Sunday in February, 1876, when the Wagners were in Berlin, they embarrassed Susanne Weinert very much. According to the wish expressed by Richard and Cosima, the dogs were accompanying her and the children on a walk. Suddenly Marke, "the black monster," seized a farmer's hen and killed it. After this the Bayreuthers demonstrated against Richard Wagner's wild dogs. One of the crowd cried, "What would happen to one of us, if he tried to let such beasts run around without muzzles!"

The daily meals in Wagner's household were rather frugal. Thanks to Susanne Weinert, history knows that on September 2, 1875, the Wagners had "veal steak and macaroni for supper." On their journeys they lived luxuriously. In Prague even the children got champagne.

At the end of the diary, Susanne Weinert writes: "Just at this moment Frau Wagner informed me that she would like to have a change and to engage an English governess for the children. This soon brought an end to my activities in Wagner's house."

Appendix A

THE BURRELL COLLECTION

Listed and Described

Appendix A

THE BURRELL COLLECTION

Listed and Described

A "Catalogue of the Burrell Collection" was compiled anonymously, and published in 1929 by the Nonpareil Press in London. In it the items were listed according to date, and their contents briefly indicated. The appendix which here follows preserves for the sake of convenient reference the original catalogue numbering, although its tendency toward alphabetical subdivisions is cumbersome and its chronology not always faultless.

Letters complete or their significant parts are here set forth either in the appendix, or in the body of the book, to which page reference is made. In addition to the letters the Collection contains other manuscripts, printed matter, pictures, literary and musical notations by Wagner. These latter call for extended comment and analysis in a place where further space allows.

1 Mrs. Burrell's book, *Richard Wagner, His Life and Works from 1813 to 1834* (129 pp.).

The title page is inscribed: "Compiled from original letters, manuscripts, and other documents by the Honorable Mrs. Burrell, *née* Banks, 1898."

The book is printed on handmade paper, each page watermarked with a facsimile of Wagner's autograph signature. The pages measure 21 x 27¾ inches. The text is in hand-engraved script characters, the important nouns capitalized. The profuse illustrations are made in heliogravure. The frontispiece reproduces a marble medallion relief of Wagner's head, made in 1881 by Gustav Kietz (506). The book is bound in white half-vellum, and weighs 37¼ pounds. One hundred copies were made for private presentation.

At the end of the text, the heirs of Mrs. Burrell add these words: "Her call to higher Service on June 26th, 1898, prevented its completion and from her Manuscript her Husband and Daughter have now had this first Volume brought out according to her wishes and instructions, as a worthy Foundation for the Monument she had hoped to erect to the Genius of Richard Wagner. Perhaps at some future date the important and interesting collection she made preparatory to this Work, and to which so many nobly contributed of their best may be given to the public."

2 Autograph notes by Mrs. Burrell (15 pp., 1894).

This was evidently Mrs. Burrell's draft for the continuation of her book, based mainly on the results of her visits to Natalie Bilz-Planer at Leisnig. The text is literary in intention. It addresses "the reader," but there are loose ends, points marked "verify" in the margin, and a general disconnectedness. "The extraordinary appearance of these volumes," she writes, referring to her notes, "must be accounted for. Natalie gave us the letters irregularly—at intervals declaring that she had *no more!* We were forced to keep on copying, the task was so enormous; no sooner was a copy book filled than a letter for the very middle of it appeared and had to be inserted."

3 A   Mrs. Burrell, 18 Hôtel du Nord, 32 Unter den Linden, Berlin, August 13, 1890, to Natalie Bilz-Planer at Leisnig (4 pp.).

The letter begins: "Dear Madame! Have you finished a notebook for me yet? If so you could send it to me here. Don't forget the story: *'Klara, du gehst.'* But I would especially like to get the exact anecdote about the chair, which has a bearing on the poem, *'Verzeihung, liebe M.'!!"* (107 A). Characteristically, Mrs. Burrell wants her material in writing. The anecdote about the child Wagner and his sister Cläre was provided by Natalie in 19 A. Mrs. Burrell has heard through Fräulein Kietz that Natalie is considering a move to the Johannis Hospital at Leipzig, with the help of the Wagner Society.

3 B   Natalie Bilz-Planer, Leisnig, August 25, 1890, to Mrs. Burrell in Berlin (4 pp.).

Natalie addresses Mrs. Burrell as "dear, revered, gracious lady!" The letter reveals that Mrs. Burrell has written twice since August 13; she is evidently impatient for memoranda. These Natalie agrees to provide, but since she trusts no one to take her notes from dictation, she will write them herself. Natalie tells of the superintendent of the institution and her "rough pack" (*rohe Sippschaft*), who count on her death so that they may divide her belongings.

4   Natalie Bilz-Planer, Leisnig, October 25, 1891, to Mrs. Burrell (page 8).

5   Natalie Bilz-Planer, 42 Wartburgstrasse, Dresden, 1892, to Mrs. Burrell.

Natalie has just had a visit from Mrs. Burrell, her "honored, chivalrous husband," and her "sweet and charming daughter." It has been a "glorious ray of sun" in her lonely life. Their departure has been the "fading of a blissful dream," and the awakening has made "barren reality twice as dull and dreary." She emphatically denies having sold a Wagner letter of any length to the "peddling Jew Thürmann." [1] This dealer had extracted from her no more than "two or three small notes of a few lines each," and of no significance. If he has anything more, he must have obtained it "by some sly act of theft."

6   Copy of baptismal certificate:

"ERNESTINA NATALIA

"illegitimate daughter of Herr Ernst Rudolph von Einsiedel, royal Saxon Guard Captain, and of the single Christiane Wilhelmina, legitimate daughter of Herr Gott-

---

[1] This was Hugo Thürmann, a schoolmaster at Lauta, near Marienberg.

lief *Planert,* Mechanic, both of Evangel.: Luther. creed, was born on the 22d Febr., 1826, in Dresden and was baptized on the 28th of the same month.

Baptismal witnesses were:

"Jungfrau Christiane Charlotte Planert, sister of the child's mother
"Herr Johann Gottlob Grossmann, citizen and gilder
                    "and
"Jungfrau Christiana Rosina, Herr Gottlieb Waange's, wineshop-keeper, leg. daughter, all of them Evang. Luther. creed.

"This is testified by the parish register of the Kreuz Church in Dresden according to No. 167 of the year 1826.

"Dresden the 13th of July, 1891
"Evang. Luth. Parish—Office of the Holy Cross
"D. Dibelius
"Consistorialrath and Superint.
"Parish book . . .

[Stamped]
"Kirche zum Heiligen Kreuz, Z. Dresden, No. 631"

The date of the copy shows that Mrs. Burrell did not first learn about Natalie's illegitimacy from *My Life* (in 1892), as has been stated. Natalie knew nothing about it until her old age, and it is plain that Mrs. Burrell did not tell her. Friedrich Herzfeld, in *Minna Planer und ihre Ehe mit Richard Wagner,* relates that Frau Planer and Minna, fearing the wrath of Gottlief Planer, removed themselves from his sight before the birth of the child, and led him to believe, as long as he lived, that Natalie was his own daughter. If they succeeded in this incredible piece of deception, the secret may have been confined for many years to the baptismal witnesses, Minna's mother, and Wagner himself. In Wagner's last known letter to Natalie (463 B, October 7, 1869), he signs himself "your true brother-in-law." There is no intimation in the writings of Natalie that she knew the truth. Yet in 1887, Cosima wrote to Natalie about the care of "the grave of your mother" (8 C).

That "Ernestina Natalia" was named after her father, Ernst, would indicate that at the time of baptism Minna had not dismissed him from all consideration. The spelling "Planert" is not a disguise; it occurs in one of her theater bills of this period (33).

7   Photograph taken late in life of Natalie Bilz-Planer. (See facing page 7.)

8 A   Cosima Wagner, Bayreuth, November 13, 1886, to Natalie Bilz-Planer.
"DEAR NATALIE!

"I was very sorry to learn that the small monthly installments have not been paid out to you for some time. But I was so busy this summer that you must excuse me.

"As for the letters of Herr Ritter, I no longer have them at hand, and regret that I cannot comply with your request. As before, my dear Natalie, I admonish you to be patient, although I can very well imagine how hard life may be for you. If I could help you, be assured that I would do so; you may be convinced of that. But as matters stand now I can only advise you to win the friendship of those around you by small gifts here and there, and by not thinking the worst of them, even if their behavior is not in keeping with what you may call decency. May your health return, and if it comforts you to know that my warm sympathy is not wanting, be assured of it and accept my heartfelt good wishes.

"Yours

C. WAGNER"

8 B   Cosima Wagner, Bayreuth, December 20, 1886, to Natalie Bilz-Planer.
"MY DEAR NATALIE!

"Since you prefer not to have the Christmas gift I had suggested, I have arranged to have a small amount of money sent to you. Buy with it whatever gives you pleasure, and I shall be most happy to have given you at least one enjoyable moment. You are not wrong in your remarks about the Protestant and Catholic Churches. But I have known very sympathetic good Protestant ministers too, and I had hoped that you might have found such a one in Leisnig as a support to you.

"Let's hope, too, for a change in the hearts of those about you, my dear Natalie, for that is possible in everyone. Write me every month; I shall always answer, and if sometimes my answer is short, it will be because my time is scarce. Even today I have not much time, but I send my warmest wishes for the holiday, and assure you of my true faithfulness.

"Your friend,

C. WAGNER"

8 C   Cosima Wagner, Bayreuth, July 31, 1887, to Natalie Bilz-Planer.
"MY GOOD NATALIE!

"Warmest thanks for your inquiry! I can't complain about health, even though the course of events is not without sorrow and care for me too. I should like to recommend to you this one thought when you are in trouble: Nobody is spared, each of us has to suffer and the idea that any of us is better off than the rest is only an illusion. And if I may add some advice to that recommendation, I would say: Don't mind too much the weaknesses and faults of the others. Our race is anything but good, but let's at least be lenient. Besides, I repeat what I once advised you: Make a small gift now and then to the people around you. You will receive another small present along with these lines, and I would be glad if you could win over your associates by an invitation or some other amenity. If it were in my power I would take you out of that institution which you dislike so much; but I really can't, and I have to restrict my sympathy to the small sum I have sent.

"Having learned that the grave of your mother has been damaged by the weather, I saw to its restoration, and trust you will be satisfied.

"Unfortunately I can't send you the music you want, I do not have it and would not know how to procure it here.

"Now, goodbye, dear Natalie, God be with you, and give you the power to endure. We all need it; and the worse people are, the more unhappy they are, of that you may be sure. Best greetings from your

C. WAGNER"

9 Gustav Kietz to Mrs. Burrell, Dresden, December 27, 1891 (Wintergartnerstr. 3).

Gustav Kietz, the brother of E. B. Kietz, acknowledges payment for the letters he has sent, and "guarantees" that she is now "in sole possession of the complete collection of Wagner's letters to my brother and that those letters have never been copied, or been in other hands." (Page 86.)

10 A Genealogical list of Wagner's forebears as drawn up by F. A. Herrmann at Leipzig for Mrs. Burrell, together with copied birth and baptismal dates.

B D. Pank, in Leipzig, November 29, 1894, to Mrs. Burrell (letter accompanying above).

Herr Pank makes this interesting remark about the wedding date of Wagner's mother and her first husband: "That the date of the wedding day of Carl Friedrich Wilhelm Wagner and Johanna Rosina Pätz was June 2, 1798, is an invention. There is nothing about it in the Leipzig church register." Newman names this date as "probable." Yet the absence of an official record, together with the period of exactly nine months between this date and March 2, 1799, the birthday of their first born, Albert, looks like a piece of speculation, both arbitrary and dubious, on the part of Glasenapp, who was first responsible for the statement.

11 Copies from the birth, marriage, and death certificates of Wagner's eighteenth century ancestors.

12 Copies of birth certificates of Wagner's family. (As in the cases of 13 and 14, only those dates are here given which do not agree with the generally accepted record.)

The birth date of Carl Friedrich Wilhelm Wagner, father of the composer, was June 17, 1770, according to the baptismal certificate. (Newman gives June 17 or 18.)

13 Copies of marriage certificates of Wagner's family.

The marriage of Wagner's brother Karl Albert to Elise Gollmann of Mannheim took place in Augsburg, on August 12, 1828.[2]

The marriage of Ludwig Geyer and Johanna Wagner took place, according to the certificate, on August 28, 1814 (not August 14, as stated elsewhere).

14 Copies of death certificates of Wagner's family.

The death of Carl Friedrich Wilhelm Wagner, the composer's supposed father, occurred on November 23, 1813 (not November 22, as stated).

[2] But their daughter Johanna was born on Oct. 13, 1826.

15   Letter from Ludwig Geyer, Dresden, January 14, 1814, to Frau Carl Friedrich Wilhelm Wagner.[3]

"CHERISHED FRIEND!

"From the bottom of my heart I thank heaven for Albert's recovery and for the peace which this joyous hope restores to your soul. Poor good woman! Heaven has certainly chosen you for suffering, but it has at least lent you the strength to endure it; and your joy in knowing that your prayer for Albert's life has been answered must be truly comforting and uplifting. I have, indeed, felt the terrible experience with you, for were Albert my own son he could not be closer to my heart, and so I wish you and myself and Albert good fortune in the newly won life, the value of which has been enhanced for all of us.

"Your kind solicitude for me and my health merits my cordial thanks; but praise God! I am well, as are all of us here, and only my daily duties at the theater and the memorizing of several difficult parts could allow me to lapse into the discourtesy of leaving a letter unanswered; and now don't think ill of me again, but forgive me with kindness and forbearance. I've long owed Herr Regis an answer; he received it a short time ago, and he will not have failed to report to you that I've thought of you as always.

"It appears that you are to keep your apartment? If you have reliable and good tenants and if Schindler lowers the rent a bit, I believe it will be the best thing for you; but, my dear friend, now I also ask you for some advice. It happens to be my brother's fate to have to fight for the fatherland, and at this moment he is probably already before Magdeburg, where his regiment has been ordered; my mother, whom for various reasons I cannot send to my sister on account of my brother-in-law, is coming to me by Easter at the latest, and it is my duty not to fall behind my brothers and sisters who have so far done more for her than I have. Under these circumstances a small household is probably most practical for me, since my mother, who is used to activity, would soon be borne down by oppressive idleness, and a so-called bachelor's household would seriously threaten my budget. My mother could bring along the most necessary items, such as beds, kitchen utensils, etc.; now if I could find a nice little apartment with two rooms, bedroom, kitchen, etc., it would be very nice. Something of that sort can be had on a monthly basis too, and would you then be good enough to give a little time to this matter, or to tell some one else about it? The apartment on the bridle path I don't find suitable for this purpose, but don't tell Stallmeisters about it yet, and give me your advice without any hesitation. You will be very much satisfied with me when I tell you that I have no more debts at all; outside of the balance of the tailor's bill of 10 thaler, 19 groschen, which will be wiped out with 8 thaler, I can now take a free breath. For the children, too, everything has been paid up; tomorrow Julius will get a braided coat, a cap,

[3] This letter from Ludwig Geyer to Wagner's mother (then widowed two months) was published, in the original German only, in Mrs. Burrell's book (1), together with three others (of Dec. 22, 1813, Jan. 28 and Feb. 11, 1814) which Mrs. Burrell had been allowed by Cäcilie to see and copy. (Page 11.)

and a jacket, not new of course, but still good for the winter. The children are all well. Tomorrow I shall submit a letter to the Freemason Lodge on behalf of Julius. To those faithful souls, Jettchen and Luischen, kindly express my wish: to be as high in their esteem as they are in mine. The Cossack's wildness can be nothing else than divine; for the first window he smashes he shall have a silver medal.

"God keep you! To all friends and to my Albert a greeting and kiss from your ever faithful friend

GEYER

"The Seconda has urgently reminded me to return the cut copy of the book of *Nathan* which I brought along to Leipzig last year, please look for it right away and send it by the next mail. You did not write anything either about Schletter's picture." [4]

16 No number listed in catalogue.

17 Adolph Wagner, in Leipzig, June 19, 1816, to Dr. A. Brockhaus in Altenburg. A brief note, showing autograph of Wagner's uncle.

18 The part of Apollo in a play, *Der Parnass,* by Ludwig Geyer, in his own manuscript. It is dated "February 9, 1821—Wednesday, at three o'clock in the afternoon—reading rehearsal at Geyer's." Mrs. Burrell has written on an attached slip (dated Dresden, August 7, 1894): "This role is in the handwriting of Ludwig Geyer—written for the joint birthday anniversary of Gustav Zocher and Theodor Hell. Given to me by Frau Baumgarten, daughter of the former, who was christened the same day." [5] Theodor Hell was the pen name of Hofrath Winkler, associated with Geyer as intendant of the theater in Leipzig, and later associated with Wagner in the same capacity in Dresden.

In the play, which is in rhymed verse, and humorous in style, Apollo consults the Muses on the prowess of these two men: Theodor Hell is finally appointed "Vice Director" of the Muses, and Gustav Zocher their "Counsellor in Good Taste."

19 A Natalie Bilz-Planer, in Leisnig, to Mrs. Burrell.
"Notations" (*Aufzeichnungen*), in two installments, the first postmarked December 11, 1890. (Pages 12–14.)

19 B Natalie Bilz-Planer, in Leisnig, to Mrs. Burrell.
Letter postmarked February 17, 1891.

20 Clippings from Dresden newspapers (1892–1898), paragraphs about Wagner: notices of performances, anniversaries, deaths, publications.

21 MS statement by H. Löscher, sexton, with stamp of the Kirche zum Heiligen Kreuz, Dresden, July 13, 1891.

[4] This postscript would throw doubt upon the supposition that the Seconda theatrical troupe were *not* in Leipzig in 1813, but in Teplitz, where Frau Wagner visited Geyer with the infant Wagner. (See Ernest Newman, Vol. III, App. I.)
[5] Mrs. Burrell prints the text of this part in her book.

"It is here testified that Richard Geyer was confirmed in this church, on Easter, 1827, according to the registry." (See page 12.)

22 Letter from Natalie Bilz-Planer to Mrs. Burrell in Paris (postmarked Leisnig, November 25, 1890).

Natalie effusively thanks Mrs. Burrell for the receipt of 300 marks. She has also received some writing paper. She encloses a Wagner letter and promises some anecdotes. She explains that the signature to the *Leubald* MS (23) consisted only of the initials R. W.; that this signature has been torn off and may have drifted into the hands of a dealer.

23 *Leubald, Ein Trauerspiel,* by Richard Wagner (1825, 56 MS pp.). (Page 14.)

24 A Letter from Thekla Pfeiffer-Sipp, daughter of Robert Sipp, to Mrs. Burrell (dated Leipzig, May 6, 1890), with added lines by Robert Sipp.

B Beginning of a letter from Thekla Pfeiffer-Sipp to Mrs. Burrell (dated Leipzig, September 10, 1890).

C Letter from Robert Sipp to Mrs. Burrell, with added lines by his daughter (probably late 1890; page 15).

D Newspaper paragraph about Robert Sipp (probably 1899).

E Letter from Robert Sipp's daughter (remarried: the signature is Thekla Löhrmann) to the daughter of Mrs. Burrell (then deceased). The letter is inscribed: "L. Zohlis, January 23, 1900."

F Fragment of a letter from the same (evidently 1900).

25 Rosalie Wagner, Prague, February 5, 1827, to Hofrath Winkler in Dresden.

Wagner's sister, the talented actress, addresses with great cordiality on his birthday the theater secretary whom she had evidently known well as a family friend in Leipzig (see also 18).

"My Honored, Most Cherished Friend:

"Even though I have so far failed to fulfill the pleasant obligation of writing you something about my life and artistic activity here, I cannot possibly let pass the anniversary of the *ninth of February,* a day so dear to all of us, without giving you at least a small token of our inmost sympathy and our ever grateful feelings, and joining your intimate and close friends in the most cordial welfare and good fortune which you so richly deserve. That I can unfortunately do this only from a distance saddens me deeply, and never has the thought of being away from the place where I grew up and where I spent the greater part of my life grieved me more than at this moment; for what happy and sad memories are associated with the remembrance of your goodness and sincere friendship for our family, images pleasant and serious, appear before me at each vivid recollection; and how saddened I am to think that fate begrudged me the opportunity to remain longer in the circle of my friends, but put me in a wholly strange place and among people who can in no way compensate the lack of true and long friendship; people to whom I can never become closely attached and from whom I'll probably never have any token of friendship and sympathy to hope for or to expect, such as I have received innumerable times from you, my most cherished friend. . . ."

Rosalie, however, expresses herself as quite contented with her treatment at the theater in Prague, except from over-rigorous local stage censorship, which "prevents many of the better, interesting plays from being performed." She attaches a list of twenty-one leading feminine parts, apparently a partial list ("etc." is written at the end) of what she had acted in Prague. They include Gretchen in *Faust*, Ophelia in *Hamlet*, Portia in *The Merchant of Venice*, Fenella in *Die Stumme von Portici*. She classes herself as a "sentimental lover" (*sentimentale Liebhaberin*).

26 A, B   Two letters, probably drafts, from Rosalie Wagner in Leipzig, August 6 and September 23, 1833, addressed to L. von Alvensleben. In the first, she asks the editor of the *Allgemeine Theater Chronik*, in Leipzig, for "a few lines" in order to make a favorable impression on the critics at Magdeburg, where she is about to begin a guest engagement. She states that she is to appear in Magdeburg in some of her "better parts"—"Gretchen in *Faust*, Gabriele, Marianne in *Geschwister*," etc.

The second letter, evidently addressed to the same critic, is a polite acknowledgement of the notice asked for.

27   Note from Rosalie Frey-Marbach to Mrs. Burrell, dated Charlottenburg, August 31, 1895.

The daughter of Rosalie sends a specimen of her mother's writing, clipped from a diary, and "dedicates" it to Mrs. Burrell.

28   Note from Johanna Jachmann-Wagner at Charlottenburg, October 27, 1891, to Mrs. Burrell.

Wagner's niece, once an opera singer, sends the clipped signature of her father, Albert Wagner, to be added to the photograph of him which she has already sent.

29   Specimen of the handwriting of Ottilie Brockhaus, Wagner's sister (end of a letter, with signature, dated Leipzig, July 14, 1873).

30   A photograph of Minna in middle age, holding her cocker spaniel (Peps or Fips?). A silhouette and a pencil drawing which the catalogue identifies as of Minna's mother and father.

31   Certification from the Evangelist-Lutheran Church at Oederan, July 26, 1890, of the birth of Minna as "Christiane Wilhelmine Planer" on September 5, 1809, at Oederan, and her baptism on September 6, 1809.

Certification from the Evangelist-Lutheran Church in Dresden, July 26, 1890, of her death as "Frau Wilhelmine Wagner," on January 25, 1866.

32 A   Printed playbills of the Eumorphia Theater, Dresden. Pencil marks evidently indicate parts in which Minna Planer appeared:

November 28, 1831: *Die Schuld* (tragedy by Adolph Wüllner) (Elvira, wife of Hugo, Count of Derindur).

December 8, 1831: *Die Schweizerhütte am Rheinfall* (comedy by Franul von Weissenthurn).

Die Helden (comedy by Marsano) (Julie, a young widow).

January 16, 1832: *Die Benefiz-Vorstellung Posse* (after the French by Th. Hell) (Gambasuella, a famous dancer).

May 21, 1832: *Die Engländerin* (comedy by Fr. v. Weissenthurn (Fanny Klappland, an English girl).

March 29, 1832 (wrongly catalogued as of Dessau [34]): *Die Erbschaft* (Kotzebue) (Madame Dahl, a widow).

Allen ist geholfen (Holtei) (Gertrude, wife of Caspar Brendel).

B   Four MS poems, addressed to Minna Planer by anonymous admirers.

Blossoms woven into a wreath for the New Year, 1833, by Ch. A. C.

Thirteen lines of verse, the last four in French.

"Longing" (*Sehnsucht*) (five verses).

To Mina [*sic*] P . . . . r. (Page 20.)

33   Printed playbill of the Hoftheater in Dessau, November 7, 1832.

First performance of *Richards Wanderleben*, comedy in four acts, freely adapted from the English by G. Kettel. "Dem. Planert" [6] is cast as Sophie Hainfeld, *Herrnhuter* and niece of a ship's captain.

34   R. Atmer, in Dessau, December 26 [1832] to Minna.

"FRÄULEIN PLANER:

"Member of the Theater in Magdeburg

"ESTEEMED FRÄULEIN!

"In answer to your letter I am asking whether you would be willing or able to obtain a release from your present contract for the month of February or a little later, in which case I should like to sign an agreement with you for a longer term. Let me know in any case whether you are ready for an engagement with me and what your conditions are. Be so kind as to indicate the roles in which you would like to star and name as many roles as possible. I hope you are able to fix the time of your guest appearance in February quite to your liking. For this month and perhaps for the beginning of March I could manage (after knowledge of your repertoire) to let you appear in several roles in quick succession. I should appreciate an early reply and remain, sincerely yours,

R. ATMER"

35 A   MS poem addressed "to Fräulein Planer (as Sena in *Solomon's Judgment*, February 12, 1833)" and inscribed "Dessau, February 14, 1833."

---

[6] See 6.

The poet describes the actress as depicting a faithful wife and mother. Each of the three verses bears the refrain *"Er liebt mich noch!"*

B　MS part—prologue to above. An apostrophe in verse to Prussia and its king.

C　"Management, Royal Court Theater, Gotha, December 23, 1833
　　"To Demoiselle Planer
　　　"Member of the Civic Theater
　　　　"Magdeburg
　　"If you, Fräulein Planer, would be ready to accept an engagement at this Court Theater, I ask you to inform me about the conditions under which you would be willing to star.

v. Manstein"

D　"Management, Royal Court Theater, Coburg, November 13, 1834,
　　"To Demoiselle Planer
　　　"Member of Civic Theater
　　　　"Magdeburg
　　"Since I have had no reply to a letter sent to you on the 15th of October, I fear that you did not receive it and therefore I renew my proposition to you: Would you accept an engagement at this Court Theater and under what conditions?

v. Manstein"

36　Postcard certification, Rudolstadt, September 10, 1891,
　　"Herr W. Burrell
　　　"Bad Ems, Pariser Hof
　　"Theater Director Bethmann in Rudolstadt engaged in 1834: Wilhelmine Planer as actress, Richard Wagner as music director.

H. Hesselbarth
Royal Kapellmeister"

37　Natalie Bilz-Planer to Mrs. Burrell, Leisnig, September 30, 1891.
　　Natalie acknowledges the receipt of 600 marks and "again" sends "three love letters." She writes that Minna's "first feelings for Richard were compassion with his loneliness, because his family, and especially his sister, had deserted him. Out of this feeling of sympathy, love grew by degrees. But Richard often put her love to a hard test by his unspeakable, groundless jealousy and his often arrogant manner, which hurt her so bitterly that, in spite of her fervent compassion, she was ready to give up his acquaintance. But her true loving heart, her sympathy for the lonely man, prevailed."

38　MS poem, two sides of a page, unsigned and incomplete. It is headed "The Thirteenth of July" and praises the charms of Minna, with classical allusions, as first beheld by the poet twelve months before. The catalogue states that "the writing is almost certainly R. W.'s." The present editor submits that while similar, it is not identical, that Wagner was never addicted to classical allusions, least of all in connection with Minna, and that his first encounter with her, at Läuchstadt, seems definitely to have taken place, not on July 13, 1834, but at the end of the month!

"The Thirteenth of July
    "To M. P.
    "Twelve months ago it was—I wandered in pensive gloom. I cared not whether a zephyr whispered or a storm assailed my grave thoughts. The flower smiles whether Phoebus shines in his grandeur or mists and clouds pile into threatening shapes.

"And behold! as I wandered in somber mood between double rows of plane trees, heart filled with doubts, how then could I foretell a favorable fate!? So near, so near, ah! Suddenly there appears a girl possessing every charm in which I find delight! The soul's treasure is told in her glance!

"From her little head to the tips of her feet I beheld the glorious girl. A mouth! as Venus could have had, alluring to tenderest kiss! The eyes! a reflection of all that is good and lovable, of chaste sweetness born of earthly magic, enkindling earthly bliss.

"A harmony! everything so splendid, so beautiful, created only for love and delight!! Away, Philosopher! You will never understand the use of the Stoic's arms. *Here* your beginnings come to *naught*; one would move body and soul to still ardent desire, to achieve *here* the happiness of Minna!!

"And *quickly*—on the instant—I turn to her, moved by an inspiration to follow. Magnetic power seizes me. Keenly hoping and speechless, I reckon neither cause nor consequence. Only a *single* thought, only to embrace *her,* the object of hope and longing" [The page ends here.]

39 Early map of Dresden and engraving of the Königliche Schauspielhaus, destroyed by fire in Wagner's boyhood.

40 A Dr. Strecker in Mainz, September 17, 1896, to Mrs. Burrell in London.
    Dr. Strecker is of the firm of Schott's Söhne in Mainz. He promises to deliver the "Batz-Voltz Collection" to her in London through "our representative, Mr. Volkert." The letters of Wagner to his business agents are in this Collection.

B (Enclosed in A) Hand copy of a letter addressed to music dealers Schott's Söhne at Mainz, Leipzig, June 15, 1832.[7]
"Dear Sir!
    "I am sending you herewith a score for piano, two hands, of Beethoven's Symphony No. 9, which you had last year and sent back to me on account of having too many manuscripts. I am again putting it at your disposal to use as you may see fit, at any time. I ask no fee, but if you would make me a gift of music in return, I should be grateful. May I therefore request through Herr William Härtel, Beetho-

---

[7] This letter is published in the collection of Wilhelm Altmann.

ven's 1) Missa Solemnis (D major) orchestra and piano score, 2) Beethoven's Symphony No. 9 full score, 3) *idem*: 2 quartets, score, and 4) Beethoven's Symphonies arranged by Hummel? The sooner you could fill this request, the happier I should be.

"Your faithful servant
RICHARD WAGNER"

41 Overture in D minor, in autograph, signed "Richard Wagner," and dated September 2, 1831 (38 pp.).

Wagner alludes to this overture of his eighteenth year in *My Life*. He wrote it under the eye of his teacher, Theodor Weinlig, in Leipzig, and succeeded in getting it performed at the Gewandhaus concerts on December 5, 1831. It "clearly showed the influence of Beethoven's *Coriolanus* Overture," writes Wagner. The catalogue traces the history of the MS: "At the end is a signed inscription by Louis Schindelmeïsser, a friend of R. W. It is dated 'Darmstadt, Oct. 23, 1859,' and states that R. W. had given it to him, and that he was giving it to Ernst Pasque. And enclosed is a letter from Carl Meinert, dated April 26, 1896, stating it is in his collection, and offering it to Mrs. Burrell."

42 Programs of three concerts at the Leipzig Gewandhaus, at which music by Richard Wagner is included.

Sixteenth subscription concert, February 23, 1832: "*Ouverture, von Richard Wagner.*"

Concert by Matilde Palazzesi, April 30, 1832: "*Ouverture von Richard Wagner* (*neu*)."

Twelfth subscription concert, January 10, 1833: "*Symphonie, von Richard Wagner* (*neu*)."

Presumably the Overture is the one in D minor (41). The Symphony is described in *My Life,* page 71.

43 Autograph of "*Sonate in B dur für das Pianoforte, von Richard Wagner.*"

This sonata was composed in 1831 (see *My Life,* p. 68), and published by Theodor Weinlig. Mrs. Burrell notes that she compared the MS with the printed sonata and found it "perfect."

44 MS score of Wagner's Overture to Raupach's *König Enzio* in a four-hand piano arrangement.

The catalogue calls it an "autograph musical MS with title page in R. W.'s own handwriting." The manuscript is dated 1832. Wagner refers to this Overture in *My Life,* page 70, where he admits the influence of Beethoven. The full score, edited by Felix Mottl, was published in 1908 by Breitkopf and Härtel.

45 Autograph of *Die Feen.*

A Prose sketch (of 18 pp.) entitled *Dialoge zu der Oper: Die Feen.*

B　Musical sketch, with text, on three staves: Trio from Act II, *"O Grausame"* (6 pp.).

C　Scene and air, on two staves (6 pp.); orchestral parts (43 pp.).

This once belonged to Tichatschek, according to a notation by Mrs. Burrell, who also writes: *"Die Feen* was written in 1833, when R. W. was 20 years old, and is his first complete opera. (Grove, p. 582: 'I had borrowed the plot from a dramatic fairy tale by Gozzi, and called it *Die Feen.'*) This set of MSS. enables us to follow his opera in the course of construction, from the framework of the plot, to the orchestration. It enables us to see how well at this early age and almost in boyhood R. W., had studied and mastered the art of opera."

46　Programs for three concerts at the Gewandhaus, Leipzig:

Concert by Elisabeth Fürst, April 10, 1834. *"Ouverture zur Oper: 'Die Feen', von Richard Wagner (Neu)"* is listed, but a slip announces the substitution of an overture by B. Romberg.

Subscription concert, April 2, 1835: *"Ouverture zu Columbus, von R. Wagner (Neu)."*

Concert by Livia Gerhardt, May 25, 1835: *"Ouverture zu Columbus, von R. Wagner (Neu)."*

47　Autograph musical sketch for Wagner's opera *Das Liebesverbot*, on two staves (30 pp.).

The music is in Wagner's hand. The text, which is in French, is in a different hand. The catalogue notes: "In two places are half-pages of autograph music which are sketches for *The Flying Dutchman* and *Rienzi*. On the outside is an autograph note signed by Jos. Tichatschek stating the music was written by R. W. and handed over to him. According to Bertling, the dealer who acquired this ms from the Tichatscheks—and sold it to Mrs. Burrell, [the words] were put in by Tichatschek. These French words no doubt came from the translation into French made by Dumerson in Paris, 1839 or 1840. (See *My Life,* p. 212.)

"This ms falls into three portions: (1) The *Cavatine de Claudio* both in tenor and in soprano keys . . . *'Du kennst'* to *'auf ihren Mut.'* The music is, in fact, unpublished. . . . (2) Trio from 2nd Act, from *'Wie glücklich'* to *'gar noch aus.'* The Dorella in the German text is Florette in this version. (3) *Chant de Carneval,* written both as a duet for two pianos and as a song for Lucio in 2nd Act. Words correspond only very roughly to German text from *'Ihr junges Volk'* to *'zur Lust.'* . R. W. calls the *Chant de Carneval* 'my beautiful *Chant de Carneval'* in *My Life.* It was extensively pirated during his life.

"*Das Liebesverbot* was R. W.'s second complete opera, composed from 1834 to 1836, between his 21st and 23rd year."

48 Note to Dem. Planer, member of the Civic Theater in Magdeburg, from Schwerin, January 25, 1835.

"Much honored Demoiselle!

"In case you would be ready to accept an engagement at the Court Theater here, I ask you kindly to send me your conditions and a list of your roles. Should you wish a guest appearance in advance of the engagement, be good enough to communicate to me your conditions for this as well. Respectfully looking forward to your reply,

Faithfully yours,
HOFFMANN *Ober-Regisseur"*

49 Wagner, at Reichels Garten, Leipzig, Care of Rosalie Wagner, May 6, 1835, to Fräulein Minna Planer at the Theater, 3 Engelstrasse, Magdeburg. (Page 25.)

50 Wagner, in Leipzig, May 10, 1835, to Minna, address as above. (Page 26.)

51 Wagner, in Leipzig, May 25, 1835, to Minna at Äussere Rammische Gasse, Dresden. (Page 27.)

52 A Draft of a letter from Minna (dated August 24) to an unnamed person. (Page 29.)

B Draft of a letter (undated) from Minna to Director Bethmann of the Magdeburg Theater. (Page 28.)

53 Wagner, at Magdeburg, November 4, 1835, to Minna at the Kronprinzen, Königstrasse, Berlin. (Page 31.)

54 Wagner, November 5, 1835, to Minna, addresses as above. (Page 33.)

55 Wagner, November 6, 1835, to Minna, addresses as above. (Page 35.)

56 Wagner, November 7, 1835, to Minna, addresses as above. (Page 36.)

57 Wagner, November 8, 1835, to Minna, addresses as above. (Page 37.)

58 Wagner, November 9, 1835, to Minna, addresses as above. (Page 39.)

59 Wagner, November 10, 1835, to Minna, addresses as above. (Page 39.)

60 Wagner, November 11, 1835, to Minna, addresses as above. (Page 40.)

61 Wagner, November 12, 1835, to Minna, addresses as above.

This letter, together with a silhouette of Minna referred to, is missing in the Collection.

62 L. Wolff, Prompter, Royal Court Theater in Berlin, November 26, 1835, to "Dm. Planer, Stadttheater, Magdeburg."

"Esteemed Fräulein!

"Although I called twice at your apartment during your stay here, I had to miss the pleasure of making your personal acquaintance to bring to your attention an opening for some one from another town. I am therefore writing and I look forward to an early answer. Would you agree to an engagement at a very well established Court Theater? What would be your conditions and at what time could you start the engagement?

"I should like to add that the security of the theater at which a vacancy for your roles exists is well known and that the theater is rightly considered among the best. If you are interested in making a change, please communicate your conditions by return mail, so that I may attend to the matter at once.

"Respectfully looking forward to your reply,

Faithfully yours,

L. WOLFF."

63 A MS text of a prologue, *Germania*—evidently a working part of Minna's, with certain words underlined to indicate stress in delivery. At the top is written:

"Saturday, March 30, 1833
"Eve of the Birthday of
"Her Royal Highness, the
"Frau Duchess Maria
"Germania
"Prologue by Alpin
"Spoken by Dem. *Planer"*

Under this is written: "(*on the program*)," as if the speaker were being careful about her rights. The four verses declaim the expected birthday compliments, royal adulation, and patriotic sentiments. The performance was at the theater in Altenburg.

B Printed program for the above, in which the line "*gesprochen von Dem. Planer"* duly appears. The prologue is followed by *Je toller, je besser!* a "comic opera" in two acts, with music by Méhul.

64 Correspondence between Minna Planer and theatrical directors (1834–1836).

A Minna Planer, Magdeburg, December 27, 1833, to an unspecified theater director, stating her conditions. She will not accept guest appearances, but only a year's engagement at 600 thaler, plus traveling expenses. She expects the leading tragic and young heroine parts. She asks for an answer by return mail.

B F. Anhold, Brandenburg, January 16, 1834, as also in the letters following, presumably to Minna. He would like her for guest appearances at her convenience. "If you have not since changed your mind, I would consider myself fortunate if you would support my institution with your splendid talent."

C   Ludwig Meyer, regisseur of the Bremen Stadttheater, May 20, 1834. He offers leading parts in comedies, secondary parts and alternate leading ones in dramas, at Bremen or Oldenburg, as she prefers.

D   Carl Schätze, *Schauspieldirektor* at Lübeck, September 16, 1834. He offers guest appearances preparatory to a permanent engagement. "Your talent, known to me, leaves me no doubt that you will be successful with the public here, since it is a cultivated one."

E   Ringelhardt, in Leipzig, December 23, 1834. He wishes an appointment in Magdeburg, to negotiate an engagement.

F   Anton Hübsch, director of the Königsberg Theater, July 23, 1835, to "Fräulein Planer."
   "I take the liberty of inquiring whether you are now inclined to accept an engagement here. Remembering that when I was fortunate enough to meet you in Magdeburg a year ago, you were not disinclined to begin negotiations with me, I have the more reason to expect an agreement with you now. I could also offer an engagement to your sister for small singing roles and chorus."

G   Mühling, theater director at Aachen and Cologne, Aachen, August 19, 1835. He offers an engagement at a monthly salary of 49 reichsthaler, expenses paid, for leading tragic and light juvenile parts. He asks for an immediate reply, with list of her roles.

H   Director Bode, Bernburg, August 31, 1835. He offers a yearly engagement, to begin within three months in Dessau, and would like to receive her conditions.

I   F. Anhold, Bremen, September 18, 1835. He would like her conditions for becoming "a splendid acquisition for my stage through your youth, beauty, and talent."

J   The "*Königliche Preuss. Commissionsrath, Eigenthümer und Director des Königlichen Theaters*" in Berlin, M. Cerf, October 4, 1835.
   Cerf, in Berlin, takes a far more independent tone. The letter is written in another hand, and without salutation:
   "I beg to reply to your friendly letter of the 25th of last month that I shall hasten your guest appearances as much as possible; but I cannot consent to the interim of a week fixed by you, because unforeseen obstacles could easily cause a prolongation of that period. I must also stipulate that after you have finished starring as a guest you begin your engagement here at once, if it is demanded by me. The salary wished by you, which I certainly am not willing to increase, includes all the other advantages offered by the engagement at my theater. As to the selection of the 3 roles, we had better leave it until your arrival here.

Respectfully signed

M. CERF"

K M. Cerf, Berlin, October 19, 1835.

Written in another hand, without salutation:

"I have until now been vainly awaiting your arrival; since I do not wish to be kept in this uncertainty any longer I beg you to notify me by return mail whether or not and when I may count on your coming to Berlin."

L Anton Hübsch, Königsberg, March 6, 1836:

"Last year I took the liberty of offering you an engagement at the theater here, and since I have heard that your engagement in Magdeburg expired on the 1st of May, I now put the humble question whether you are willing to accept an engagement here and beg you to indicate to me your honored conditions."

65 Contract between Anton Hübsch of the Königsberg Theater and Minna Planer (dated March 28, 1836).

Minna is engaged for a year at a salary of 700 reichsthaler. She is required to play the first tragic lover parts, youthful heroine parts, and to appear in comedies. She must travel with the company when ordered.

66 Playbill of the theater in Altenburg, May 18, 1836.

The piece is *Aline, or Altenburg transported,* magic folk opera in three acts by Bäuerle, music by W. Müller. This would refer to the Königsberg troupe.

"Dem. Planer" is cast as the "Fairy Lissa, divine protectress of the country."

67 Wagner, in Berlin, May 21, 1836, to Minna at the Königsberg Theater ("to be called for"). (Page 43.)

68 Wagner, in Berlin, May 23–27, 1836, to Minna. (Page 45.)

69 Wagner, in Berlin, May 29–June 1, 1836, to Minna. (Page 50.)

70 Wagner, in Berlin, June 3–4, 1836, to Minna. (Page 53.)

71 Wagner, in Berlin, June 5–21, 1836, to Minna. (Page 56.)

72 Wagner, in Berlin, June 22–26, 1836, to Minna. (Page 67.)

73 Wagner, in Königsberg, August 7, 1836, to Heinrich Dorn, music director at Riga.

This letter is published in Wilhelm Altmann, *The Letters of Richard Wagner,* also Kapp and Kastner, *Richard Wagners Gesammelte Briefe.*

74 *Unterhaltungsblätter,* Königsberg, November 5 and 23, 1836. Newspaper containing a poem, and an article on Minna Planer as an actress.

75 Receipt for purchase of wedding ring at Königsberg, November 23, 1836: "*11 Reichsthaler 11/3/4.*"

76 A   MS poem addressed to "Fräulein Minna Planer on the occasion of her marriage with the music director, Herr Richard Wagner."

The poem, in four verses, is dated Königsberg, November 24, 1836. The actress is praised and felicitated in florid and adoring phrases: "Wander through life, fair artist, while Art and Love strew flowers before thee; thou mayest still long delight Königsberg by thy talent while the Graces hover over thee."

B   Note from Natalie to Mrs. Burrell, dated Leisnig, July 24, 1890.

Natalie encloses the above poem, together with a clearer copy she has made of it, "being afraid that your kind, dear eyes would prefer not to read our German script." She explains that the poem was received by Minna after her performance of Fenella in *Die Stumme von Portici,* on the eve of her wedding. On that occasion Richard conducted for the first time in Königsberg; it was a special favor to him, although he was not yet employed."

77   MS directions for the silent part of the Dumb Girl in Auber's *Die Stumme von Portici.* This was apparently Minna's working part, inherited from a "Madame Müller" whose name on the first page replaces another which has been inked out.

78   Copy of *Königsberger Heiraths-Anzeiger* (Wedding Bulletin), November 24, 1836.

The editor is August Koch. Richard and Minna Wagner, the "happy couple," are felicitated.

79   Pink satin handkerchief on which is printed an anonymous poem to "Fräulein Minna Planer, on the celebration of her wedding with Music Director Richard Wagner." These handkerchiefs were distributed to each guest at the reception.

80   Letter from Otto Heese, bearing seven signatures of his family, from Magdeburg, October 24, 1836, to Wagner and Minna.

Heese was evidently Wagner's landlord at Magdeburg. He has asked the "cantor" to send Wagner a certificate (birth?) which Wagner has requested. He congratulates the couple and relates at length the news of the neighbors in his community.

81   Oil portrait, 20" by 16", of Minna Planer, painted in 1836, by Otterstedt. (See facing page 18.)

82   Letters from Natalie Bilz-Planer at Leisnig to Mrs. Burrell.

A   Leisnig, September 19, 1890. Natalie mentions the portrait of Minna (81), which Gustav Kietz has had restored. "If God had bestowed as many high gifts of the mind on me as on you, gracious lady," she writes, "I would write Minna's memoir—but not as a sister—that would spoil everything" (implying prejudice). The letter lapses into denunciation of the "frivolous, low egotism of other women," which "inflicted untold tortures upon poor Minna."

B   Natalie's written certification that the portrait of Minna, which Mrs. Burrell wishes to buy, is genuine and "true to nature."

C   Leisnig, October 12, 1890. Natalie states three times that the portrait has never been "copied or photographed." She berates Kietz's daughter for "inventing the unfounded lie" that she has entertained two dealers and contemplated selling the picture. She neither has received nor will receive them. She believes that her notes will be used verbatim by Mrs. Burrell, for she asks her to attribute them to "an old friend," instead of a "sister," so that they may seem unbiased.

83   Printed "Prologue" in verse by Dr. A. Schreiner, delivered on New Year's Day, 1837, on the Königsberg stage by Madame Wagner.

84   Wagner, in Berlin, June 20, 1837, to Minna, Care Frau Mechanikus Planer, Äussere Rammische Gasse 211, 2nd floor, Dresden. (Page 77.)

85   Wagner, in Riga, September 9, 1837, to Amalie Planer. (Page 81.)

86   No number listed in catalogue.

87   Wagner, in Riga (undated), to Minna in Dresden. (Page 79.)

88   Listed as "missing" in catalogue.

89   Registered letter from Natalie Bilz at Leisnig (dated November 24, 1892) to Mrs. Burrell at Mentone. (Page 10.)
    The first part of the letter, after complaints about her ill health, is devoted to the Richard-Minna-Mathilde triangle, and certain anonymous letters to Minna which Natalie (of course with no justification) would like to attribute to Mathilde Wesendonck. On the envelope Mrs. Burrell has noted: "Only about anonymous letters to Minna, maligning Richard; trying to get Minna to divorce him. That Richard was in Dresden without meeting or visiting Minna trying to get Louisa and Pusinelli to persuade her to consent to a divorce." Natalie writes:

"As for the base anonymous letters where the poor good Richard is so infamously besmirched in regard to Minna and doubtless outrageously slandered, and where his actions and way of living are immensely exaggerated, nobody but poor Minna and I ever saw those horrible letters, because Minna, after reading them, immediately burned them to ashes in the stove. Though not believing that Richard really could forget himself and become so far involved, her already sore heart suffered the deepest mental agonies so that each of these vile letters made her ill for many days; and the poor tormented heart beat so heavily that she had to wear an ice pack day and night in order to alleviate the palpitations and the pains, although the ice would melt in a few minutes, and the pack become quite warm. One couldn't empty and refill it quickly enough. What she suffered by that devilish, infamous malice cannot be described. And do you realize, honored lady, the purpose of that inexcusable evil and mental torment inflicted upon Minna, and why one dragged poor Richard in the dust before her, absolutely without justification? They tried to induce Minna to divorce him so that on top of all the heart pangs inflicted on her for the benefit of others, they could put the burden of shame upon her for having divorced Richard, and so publicly expose her as a vulgar woman unworthy of Richard. That was the devilishly concocted intrigue of those shameful, shameless anonymous letters, and that was their purpose with Minna.

"Well, my lady, your pure noble mind could not imagine, nor find it possible to imagine, such a devilish wickedness committed against Richard and Minna, and so effectually contrived to tear them apart by force. And Minna in her unspeakable sorrow and anguish of heart considered Frau Wesendonk,[8] that cold slippery serpent, as the diabolical instigator of all this, until she bitterly, with streaming eyes, accused her before God. And if all those nasty incriminations and reports about Richard could have been true, it was certainly the sole fault of that disloyal, coquettish, heartless creature Mathilde, who pulled Richard down from the path of honor and duty and manly self-esteem, and exposed him like a rudderless vessel to the winds and waves of seduction. While Minna was not induced by all those well contrived slanders to abandon duty and honor and divorce him, their success was all the greater in persuading Richard to a divorce, for they wanted to snatch away from the poor hard-pressed Minna her last advantage: to be, and to be called, Richard's wedded wife. She was *supposed* to and *had* to bear the disgrace of being a divorced wife after twenty-four years of marriage. Richard himself was in Dresden at his sister Luise's home without having visited Minna; he wanted Luise to persuade Minna to consent to Richard's divorce; he even went with her to Pusinelli so that he also might induce Minna to agree to a divorce.[9] I really can't understand how Richard, after twenty-four years of happy marriage, could bring himself to inflict upon his old faithful wife, who had willingly borne grief, sorrow, and want with him, such a disgraceful, hard action, denying every sentiment in favor of another woman; especially since he knew Minna's ailing condition and had even learned from Pusinelli that she had to be spared any strong excitement, and that her heart complaint was so serious that any moment her sudden death by heart attack could be expected. How Richard must have been stirred up and incited against poor Minna, that every feeling for her could be extinguished by force, and changed into hatred and callous cruelty! Indeed, most honored lady, that celebrated, lamblike, sweet little friend, the charming Mathilde, was careful not to tell you of all those diabolical deeds so efficiently and slyly inflicted upon Minna, in her efforts not to tear from her own head the crown of her matchlessness before your eyes. And such a contemptible shameless creature dares speak only scornfully about Minna and at her expense exculpate her own vile deeds. Oh, this infamy is too base! But the worst of all is that when such a poisonous reptile defiles Minna, she is accorded firm and unshakable belief, as to an evangel. And do you know what Minna's immense crime

[8] Sometimes so spelled.
[9] This of course is untrue (see page 409).

actually was?—that she was an obstruction to the desires and aims of that selfish, scheming person and that she lived too long to suit these people. She should have favored the long-cherished wishes and ambitions of that beautiful lady, and should have had enough sense to oblige her by emptying a whole bottle of digitalis instead of taking a drop of it. Minna, not being conscious of any guilt toward Richard and having been a loving, sympathetic, and faithful wife throughout all those long years, of course firmly rejected the unfair, heartless, and rude demand that she comply with a divorce from Richard; since she also knew from Pusinelli himself that a long life was no longer in store for her and that she might die suddenly at any moment from a heart attack, and so she did not agree with the suggested divorce. No fair-thinking man, especially if he knew her more intimately, could have blamed her for not having accepted the disgrace of dying at last as a divorcée, so as perhaps to save the honor of another woman."

The second part of this letter is concerned with the separation and attempted reconciliation of Richard and Minna in the summer of 1837. Since Natalie was a direct witness of this, her testimony on this subject should be more reliable and valuable. This is quoted on page 75.

90   Richard Wagner to members of the orchestra at Riga. MS letter, signed September 11, 1838. (Page 341.)

91   Four printed programs of the Stadttheater at Riga; "Madame Wagner" is separately announced in large type in each, with a triple star.

"April 8, 1839
   "Die Schauspielerin von Venedig, drama in four parts by G. Harris
   *** Katharina—Madame Wagner, in leading guest role"

"April 11, 1839
   "Preciosa, das Zigeunermädchen, romantic play in four acts, with choruses by
      P. A. Wolff, music by Carl Maria von Weber
   "*** Preciosa—Madame Wagner as guest"

"April 14, 1839
   "Maria Stuart, tragedy in five acts, by Schiller
   "*** Maria—Madame Wagner as guest"

"April 18, 1839
   "Christinens Liebe und Entsagung, play in two acts, adapted by Theodor Hell
   "Die Helden, play in one act, and in Alexandrines, by Wilhelm Marsano
      "*** Christine ⎱
      "*** Julie   ⎰ Madame Wagner in final guest role"

When in the spring of 1839 Wagner faced joblessness, and a load of debt which would have made it impossible for him to leave Riga except by stealth, Minna emerged from her retirement to make four "guest" appearances at the theater, her actual farewell to the stage. It was the money thus earned, together with the proceeds of a benefit concert, that enabled the penniless pair to make their way to London, and eventually Paris.

92 Memorandum: *Thetis,* arrived in Thames Aug. 12–13, 1839; arrived at Gravesend Aug. 12, 1839, from Pillau; captain's name, Wulff.

93 Receipted bill charged by the Hôtel Meublé of M. Furgault, 3 rue de la Tonnellerie, Paris, to "Monsieur Wagner" for October, 1839. The charge is 50 francs for the *chambre garnie,* 45.45 for food, wine, wood, and candles. Wagner has described this, his first abode in Paris, as "positively degrading" in location, and only redeemed by a bust of Molière in front with the inscription: *"Maison où naquit Molière."* Dr. Hans Kristeller contributed the information in 1935 that "this is an unfounded tradition," although the bust then still adorned the house at what was then rue du Pont Neuf in the old Quartier des Halles, now largely demolished.

94 MS note from Heinrich Laube, in Paris, to "Mdme Wagner," Hôtel Molière. The note postpones an intended visit.

95 A List of furniture by Wagner. Mrs. Burrell writes: "This furniture is of Riga bedroom, sold to get money to go to Paris." It includes "grand piano, my bedstead with board and mattress, my mahogany dresser, closet with mirror, trunk, remainder of brown and green curtains, box of kitchen utensils, frame for my working table, leg of the dressing table, mirror from the dressing room. So!! Some of the pictures."

95 B Notes (*Aufzeichnungen*) by Natalie Bilz (unsigned and undated). (Page 82.)

96 Miscellaneous memoranda by Mrs. Burrell, apparently taken down from a conversation with Natalie.

These furnish a few helpful scraps of information about the Wagners in Paris, and their falling out with his sister, Cäcilie Avenarius. Since Natalie, by her own statement, joined the Wagners in Paris after they had broken relations with the Avenariuses, she must have learned the climactic interchange of high words by hearing it freely gone over in the Wagner household.

"Natalie says she arrived November, 1840 & found them rue du Helder, that the '*brouille*' with Cäcilie had already taken place."

"Natalie was in the crowd with Richard and Minna in the Champs Elysées when Napoleon's [——?], the *brouille* was at its height '*ganz frisch.*'"

"Cäcilie: 'It won't do, Minna, for your Richard to keep borrowing money from Avenarius.'"

"Richard: 'You frightful old gossip; come, Minna, we'll have nothing more to do with such relatives.'"

"Probably happened in summer 1840. Reconciliation must have been in summer or autumn 1841."

". . . happened before this, before Natalie arrived, then there was no talk of friendship."

"Richard met Avenarius' errand boy in the street and he said,

'Monsieur Wagner, a little son has arrived at the Avenarius house.' Richard and Minna sent their congratulations in the New Year of 1841, Natalie met Cäcilie for the first time then, she never reciprocated the visit."

97 Photograph of drawing of Minna by Kietz, made in Paris, in 1840. Indicated in the catalogue as "missing."

98 Notations by Mrs. Burrell, in pen and pencil, evidently the result of conversations with Natalie. They concern various points about Minna: her early career, her first meeting with Wagner, incidents during their married life.

"Fräulein Minna Planer (Wilhelmine) first appeared on the stage in Dresden (in a *Gesellschaftstheater*) under Herrn Ziegenhorn. Freiberger Platz. Her first role was Lady Milford in *Kabale und Liebe*—Tieck and Theodor Hell were present. She was at once engaged for Dessau (or Altenburg), Natalie cannot remember which.

"Frau Clementine Stockar Escher was the sister of the *Bundes-Präsident* in Switzerland, Alfred Escher.

"Fräulein Natalie Planer was present when the portrait was painted. She was engaged in Magdeburg and guested in Rudolstadt. The whole company guested together.

"Hotel Molière two floors facing the street. There his wonderful Newfoundland dog was stolen from him. On their famous sea trip to London he saved many human lives (he was called Rover). His brother-in-law, Cavalry-Captain von Meck, a Courlander, had presented it to him.

"Fräulein Amalie Planer, leading singer in Riga, married name—Frau von Meck. Amalie's voice was an alto, she sang Romeo and all the alto parts.

"Helder '16,' 3 stories.

"Rue Jacob in the rear, 2 stories. Kietz was in the next house so that he could call him—Kietz, Kietz.

"Minna left Königsberg. Richard was so jealous, he couldn't stand seeing her on the stage. She guested another time to raise money for the trip to Paris (guested as Frau Kapellmeister Wagner).— Did Natalie join them? No.

"Thürmann! Thürmann, a schoolteacher, asked Natalie to lend him the Tragedy, he had it for two days, tore off the signature and date [see 23]. . . .

"R. W. First picture. January 58—Left Zürich for Paris. Minna left from Zürich for the hydropathic establishment Brestenburg. 6 weeks. Then to Zwickau Dr. Tröger, *almost all the summer*. From there to Dresden and then the picture was taken. Late fall 1859. The second photograph in winter last days of December '65 or first days 1866. Died January 25, 1866.

"Letters, notes."

(See also pages 18 and 73.)

99 Natalie Bilz-Planer to Mrs. Burrell (undated). (Pages 73 and 76.)

100 Notes from Wagner, in Paris, to E. B. Kietz, 1840.
A June 3. (Page 86.)
B October 23. (Page 87.)
C October 25. (Page 87.)

101 Note from Wagner, October 19, 1840, to E. B. Kietz. (Page 87.)

102 Two pages of scribbled memoranda by Wagner.

103 Newspaper clipping (*Dresdner Nachrichten*) without date, but referring to Dresden Hoftheater in 1841.

104 Notes from Wagner, in Paris, to E. B. Kietz, January, March 24, April 5, 7, May 1, July 5, 8, October 13, 19, 1841. (Pages 93–96.)

105 Wagner, 25 rue du Helder, Paris, March 27, 1841, to Ferdinand Heine, Marienstrasse 16, Dresden. (Page 98.)

". . . As Kietz told me repeatedly, you would like to hear my opinion about Berlioz and the newer tendencies in French music as related to him. I intend to write about this shortly for the *Abendzeitung*. Therefore permit me to say a few words about the personal impression which my acquaintance with Berlioz has made on me. The first of his works I heard was his *Romeo and Juliet* Symphony, in which the tastelessness of its extreme economy has repelled me violently from his genius as a musician. I see the matter as follows: Berlioz stands among the Frenchmen so entirely *alone* that, lacking any congenial foundation, he is forced to feel his way about in a fantastic maze, thus very much hampering the beautiful development of his enormous powers, perhaps making it even impossible. He has been and remains an isolated phenomenon, but he is French in the full sense of the word. We Germans are fortunate, for we have our Mozart and Beethoven in our blood and we know how to let our pulse beat. But Berlioz has no predecessor and is doomed to a perpetual fever. Nevertheless, we Germans are doing him an injustice which cries to heaven when, without the slightest reason, we dismiss him as a charlatan. On the contrary his outward expression is in rare harmony with his inner genius. What he gives, he gives from his innermost soul; he consumes himself and is the only French composer who after his success has not become overbearing. He has a highly poetical nature, and this is all the more remarkable as he is otherwise an absolute Frenchman who can express himself only in the utmost extremes. It was only recently that I formed my opinion about Berlioz, actually only some three months ago, when I heard his *Symphonie Fantastique*. At the same time I found out that the tempting possibilities of the orchestra for which he composes present a considerable justification for his eccentric means of outward expression. Involuntarily he felt tempted to lead instrumental music into virtuosity. In another way Vieuxtemps does this too, although he started from the other extreme. He reduces virtuosity, and if I am to judge Vieuxtemps's later work as I foresee it, it will be of the same type, and his triumph will consist in *leading music back* to its true state of chaste beauty. However, Vieuxtemps will never do a work of pioneering and enlarging. His achievements will always have a negative value only. He lacks the necessary passion to be creative; although only twenty years of age, he is an adult already: he was never young. The realm of vision [*Ahnung*] is unknown to him; he sees flat daylight about him and therefore he cannot feel the ecstasy of warmth. However, thus he *must* be in order to accomplish the task which he has clearly perceived and which he performs with a full, calm consciousness. Such natures must be considered as wise gifts of Providence, and must be all the stronger, as they have to counteract fervor. Vieuxtemps's name is extremely characteristic. His last concerto is beautiful and would give me still more satisfaction if I had felt more intensity in his motives. You have nothing to fear from the influence of Berlioz' music on him, for Vieuxtemps is matured and conscious of himself. Anyway, you perhaps imagine the Parisian excesses to be more bewildering and tempting than they are. As I said, Berlioz stands completely aloof, and the worst thing here is the terrible superficiality to which everybody bows who wants to please the public. Each one sacrifices his deeper worth and grows shallow in conviction. And yet I am ready to confess that the dramatic music of the French is far superior to that of the Germans. To my dismay I recently came across a few German operas by Reissiger, Lobe, etc. Is it possible that German composers have gone so far astray in their views about singing and melody as to believe they are furthering the need for melody by using the most common, conversational phrases such as 'How are you?' 'Where do you come from?' for the purpose of certain thematic enlargements, supposed to maintain an ostensible flow of music, where short, vigorous strokes are called for by nature? Of course the melodious outpourings are according to what one would expect: what we so adequately call 'dawdling' [*Nölerei*] results from this, and real singing [*canto*] becomes bawling [*Singerei*]. Yet dramatic truth remains far remote from this; and though the French are often trifling with their thousand coquettish nuances, still they always know how to finish at the right spot by a short stroke where a drawn-out passage is not called for. But I see that I am going on endlessly. Pardon my chattering! I am one of those who always imagine that their opinion has been asked for and so I ramble on with unrequested answers."

106 Notations by Mrs. Burrell from conversations with Natalie, and sketches of the flat in the rue du Helder, in Paris. (Pages 85, 88.)

107 A Wagner—MS poem and drawing for Minna. (Page 91.)
   B Caricature of Minna by E. B. Kietz. (Page 92.)
   C Natalie, Leisnig, May 9, 1891, to Mrs. Burrell.
   She identifies A and relates incidents of the Paris days. (Page 91.)

108 Number not listed in catalogue.

109 Small piece of paper with memoranda by Wagner. On one side is an accounting with his lodger Brix, at Meudon. On the other side is a list of payments for hack work done for Schlesinger (the Brix memorandum fixes the time as 1841 [10]):

> " 500 fr. *für Cornet*
> "1150 fr. *Favorita*
> " 300 fr. *Partitur*
> " 200 fr. *Guitarrero*
> " 200 fr. owed
>
> ———
>
> "2350 fr.
> " 30 fr. *Ouverture Guitarrero*"

110 Autograph poem by Anders, Bellevue, September 5, 1841, addressed to Minna.

111 Autograph poem from Wagner, September 5, 1841, to Minna on her birthday. (Page 94.)

112 Draft of letter (undated) by Wagner for Minna, addressed to Theodor Apel. (Page 89.)

113 Full orchestral score of Senta's Ballad from *Der fliegende Holländer,* in Wagner's hand (20 pp.). Acquired from Tichatschek, it bears his signature.

114 Page of sketch for *Der fliegende Holländer,* in Wagner's hand, on two staves.

115 Pocket notebook worked in beads, given to Wagner by Minna. Indicated as "missing."

116 Letter (undated) from Wagner, in Paris, to Ferdinand Heine in Dresden. (Page 100.)

117 Note dated "Paris, April 7, 1842."

"May this pin bring you, my dearest, many faithful, happy greetings from a distant friend. I shall envy it its position. I send once more a cordial farewell.

WISCZENDORF"

118 Invitation (MS).

"Herr and Madame Wagner are cordially invited for dinner Saturday evening, the twenty-first, at 3 o'clock

MADAME SCHROEDER DEVRIENT [*sic*]

"Thursday, 19th"
[No year given]

119 Wagner, in Dresden, May 12, 1842, to E. B. Kietz in Paris. (Page 164.)

[10] See *My Life,* 232; Newman's *Life,* Vol. I, p. 291.

120   Wagner, in Schönau, near Teplitz, June 13 to July 1, 1842, to E. B. Kietz in Paris. (Page 169.)

121   Prose sketch for *Tannhäuser*, entitled *Der Venusberg*, June 2–8, 1842, Schreckenstein bei Aussig.

Wagner wrote in *My Life* (page 270): "Here [at Aussig] I sketched in my notebook the detailed plan of a three-act opera on the *Venusberg*, and subsequently carried out the poem of this work in strict accordance with the sketch I then made." This is the notebook referred to; the text is hastily scrawled but with few corrections, ten pages in pencil, fourteen in ink. The characters are given, the scenes indicated, the dialogue sketched in brief.

122   Prose sketch of *Tannhäuser*, as copied from Wagner's script (121) by Mrs. Burrell.

123   Wagner, in Dresden, September 6–20, 1842, to E. B. Kietz in Paris. (Pages 103, 136, 171.)

124   Printed program of a concert at the Leipzig Gewandhaus, November 26, 1842.[11] Included on the program are two arias from *Rienzi*, one sung by Madame Schroeder-Devrient, one by Tichatschek.

125   Wagner [in Dresden], December 13 [1842], to Minna [in Zwickau?]. Wagner is short of money and has been trying to raise some. He sends 2 thaler, hoping it will get Minna "as far as Chemnitz." He continues:

"God! I am very depressed: often when I am alone I am seized by the same anxiety as when we were still without any prospects. Nothing, nothing gives me pleasure. I intended to be very diligent during your absence: Heavens! I don't feel like working at all and I hate the empty apartment. I dine usually with Heine—but have been once with Tichatschek and once at home. Today I am to dine with Fischer: shortly I will go to the old folks. Besides, on one evening I was with Mad. Weber. What a pitiful life this is! Without Mienel and without Pabs! Yes, laugh; I rather feel like crying! *The Flying Dutchman* is progressing well—it is certain in any case to be given on the second of the Christmas holidays: [12] *Die Jüdin* has been put aside for it. Although we've not yet had many rehearsals for it, the main thing is that Mad. Devrient is learning it beautifully. She sings the Ballad without any hesitation. *Rienzi* may be given on Sunday too—Devrient, by the way, is the same slut [*Sauluder*] as ever. Nobody ever knows what to expect from her. Only in the *Dutchman* has she surprised me by knowing her job."

126   Reminiscences (autograph MS), by Frau Marie Schmole, of Wagner in Dresden, sent in four installments from Dresden, the first undated, the others April 6, May 19, June 9, 1895. The enclosing envelope is postmarked July 12, 1895. (See Chapter XI.)

[11] The catalogue wrongly gives "May."
[12] The first performance took place on Jan. 2, 1843.

127   MS Sketches for *Rienzi*.

    A   Prose sketch (8 pp.).

    In *My Life* (p. 176), Wagner tells how at Blasewitz, near Dresden, where in July, 1837, he had attempted a reconciliation with Minna, he read Bulwer-Lytton's novel *Rienzi,* and while with his sister, Ottilie Brockhaus, in August, he worked out "a scheme for a grand opera under the inspiration of this book."

    B   Poem of *Rienzi*. Rough copy on fourteen large pages, closely written, with stage directions. Signed: "Riga, 24 July to 6 August, 1838—Richard Wagner."

    C   Fair copy of the *Rienzi* text, made at Riga (45 pp.).

    D   Text of *Rienzi,* translated by Wagner into French in his own hand (43 pp.).

    Before his first visit to Paris (from Riga) in 1839, Wagner dreamed of a production of *Rienzi* in Paris, in French. He engaged a teacher of French; but since he could hardly have mastered the French language in the four weeks before him, he "utilized the hours of the lessons in order to obtain from him, under the pretense of receiving instruction, an idiomatic translation of my *Rienzi* libretto." The translation is fairly creditable, considering the circumstances. But it is neither "idiomatic" nor correct.

    E   Short score of *Rienzi* (162 pp.), dated as follows: Act I, at the beginning, "July 26 to August 7, 1838," and at the end, "Riga, December 6, 1838." Act II, at the beginning, "February 6, 1839," and at the end, "Riga, April 9, 1839, Richard Wagner." Act III, at the beginning, "Paris, February 15, 1840," and at the end, "July 7, 1840, Richard Wagner." Act IV, at the beginning, "July 10, 1840," and at the end, "August 29, 1840." Act V, at the beginning, "Paris, September 5, 1840," and at the end, *"Ende der Oper,* Paris, September 19, 1840, Richard Wagner." The Overture is dated at the beginning, "Paris, October 23, 1840."

    This shows that Wagner began to compose Rienzi a year after he had first sketched his prose outline; that the actual composition (not including the full orchestration) occupied about two years and three months; of this time the last three acts, written in Paris, occupied eight months of continuous work. The full score was completed less than a month after the Overture, on November 19, 1840.

128   Wagner, in Dresden, June 5, 1843, to E. B. Kietz in Paris. (Page 177.)

129   Letter (undated) from Wagner to Minna.

"For You Alone

    "Above all, my good Minna, a few lines for you alone. What you write me about Mother grieved me much: you are the last one in the world who should have to suffer from her pestering. Luise, when I saw her here, told me about it; she mentioned that Mother is full of praise for you, but added that however you should treat her, getting around her as best you could, you could not possibly stand it for any length of time, even if you were an angel of patience. I almost reproach myself bitterly that I have to leave you alone with her so long. I knew all this, of course, but I have come to feel so much above Mother's naggings that they no longer impress me, and every moment I say and think to myself: 'Say whatever you want! You are an old sickly woman! I can't *educate* you any more, so I'll try to bear with you, *because* you are my mother, who I know dearly loves me! But I sh . . . [*sic*] on your wisdom,' etc. If she ever goes too far and I am not in the humor to control myself, I fly out at her and she gives in. This is the way with old women! So for a long time I have not minded being pestered by her. But in your case it is different. You, my dear wife, ought to be treated with a special forbearance. You should be spared every possible annoyance, because in the first place you deserve every consideration, and in the second place you would be more injured than anyone else by rough treatment, for very obvious reasons. Indeed it is a bitter sorrow to me to know that you and your health are subjected to so much, and every additional day which you spend under such conditions is a reproach to me. That is why I am very much put out about your staying away so long. Therefore only on your own account, and for the sake of your health, which is important to me above everything else, I earnestly beg you, my dear wife, to accept *my* point of view about my mother. Think about her as I do, as I have just told you, and remember that I punish her by paying no attention to her allusions and silly teasing. This is the main point and the whole reason. Since Heaven has willed that we are to live so close to my mother (which was truly none of my doing), you will have a new claim to my gratitude by continuing to nurse her—in spite of your reluctance; if she doesn't respond with the gentleness which is due you, hers will be the greater fault, and in the future we shall be less to blame if we avoid her as much as possible. The fourteen days here in Dresden will be easier for you when *I* shall be present. Well, my good child, I am grateful to you for your goodness and let me beseech you not to yield to your anger and to watch your health as the most important of all.

"Your

RICHARD"

130   Draft of a reply by Wagner to a critic of *Rienzi* (undated). (Page 104.)

131   (Missing in Collection) Engraving of Wagner from a drawing by E. B. Kietz, as published in the *Zeitung für die elegante Welt* in 1843.

132   Wagner, in Dresden, February 26, 1843, to E. B. Kietz. (Page 178.)

133   Wagner, in Dresden, April 8, 1843, to E. B. Kietz. (Page 178.)

134   Wagner, in Dresden, May 29, 1843, to Minna in Schönau, near Teplitz.

"MY DEAR MIENEL!

"If all the letters I have been writing to you in imagination had really been put down on paper, I could now send you quite a nice package of them. Only this morning have I felt recovered; for the last few days I have been in a frightfully uneasy state. After you had left and I finally lost sight of you, I could do nothing but wonder again and again where you might be by now: the weather was so uncertain!

At every gust of wind, at every spurt of rain, I thought of you, angry that I had let you start off on such a nasty day—when the sun appeared again and everything cleared up, I was happy again and pondered: Well, she will enjoy the view after all! If I couldn't find comfort in the thought that you went to a nice place, *only* for your recovery and health, and that I really had to thank God, who made it so easy for me to do something for your well-being, then I could become melancholy by brooding over past trips, etc., and this always fills me with painful anxiety. I can't make myself believe that when you leave me this time it is only a proof of how things are going with me now. The day after you had gone I couldn't bear staying at home; I got anxious and worried; I ran from one place to another; lunched at Engel's, and went to Heine's in the afternoon. Imagine whom I ran across there in the garden! The old Schröder and both her daughters, Schmidt and Gerlach; we all felt embarrassed when we saw them, and especially the unhappy Müller,[13] who unintentionally became involved in it. No one found a word to say, and finally I fell into my ironical mood and broke out with a lot of crazy stuff at which they all had to laugh. For which Müller was grateful to me. But that situation made me decide to be a recluse from then on and to avoid all such trouble in the future. In the evening I attended the Liedertafel and thanked them for their serenade. On Sunday I didn't leave the house until six o'clock. I wrote a very polite note to the Fürstenaus, who had invited me three times, saying that I was indisposed, had caught a cold, etc. I had my dinner brought up. But my work wouldn't progress; I was out of humor and distrait. So I started out for a lonely walk to the Grosse Garten in the evening, and this did me a lot of good. I now know what to do to adjust myself to where I am and especially to find the mood which is now so necessary for efficient work after so long an interruption. I have to avoid distraction as much as possible and go for many walks ALONE. I won't go often to the Schuster *Häuschen* with Heine and Müller; I told them so. When I take a walk with anybody else, I belong to him more than to myself; and just now this is a hindrance and a disadvantage. After my walk I dropped in to the theater for a moment, went home, and was in bed before ten. The best part of that was that I felt fresh and alert as early as four o'clock this morning and could work so easily that I had finished my task before eight o'clock; now I can also write to you too, and it is not yet nine. At twelve o'clock I have a rehearsal of *The Huguenots,* which is to be given tomorrow; then I am asked to dinner at Heine's; then I will take quite a walk alone; I shall think of you and my work, and with God's help tomorrow morning at four o'clock more inspiration will come to me. So I must endure your absence as best I may, and so you may always have some idea of what I am doing and pursuing.

"But now tell me a great deal about yourself, too, dear little wife! How you and mother liked the trip, etc. Today the weather is fine and reminds me of your morning promenade and that view over the Turna'schen Garten which must be at its most beautiful by now. Oh, if you only like it and recover! I hope you will write

[13] This would be Lieutenant Hermann Müller, recently the lover of Madame Schroeder-Devrient, later a fellow water-curist with Wagner.

a lot to me; it may become part of your amusement. How is Schlankelino, Kara-scholino, Scharmentino, Pebsino? What does he say about not having my nightshirt any longer? Do the Teplitzers like the beautiful Juniper dog? [14] How does he get along with Turk? I hope you soon will give me full information about these weighty items!

"Above all, be cheerful! You have good reason for it now, and you may thank the good God who is now so well disposed toward us! Goodbye, my good dear wife of my heart! Give my best greeting to Mama; how pleased the good old lady will be to do so well again! Goodbye, goodbye! And think of me as I always think of you, with love, with true love!

"Your

RICHARD

"Schröder, etc., left for Teplitz today. I hope you will keep clear of them."

135 Saxon passport for Minna Wagner, issued in Dresden, May 23, 1843, for a journey to Teplitz and Prague. Minna gives her age as twenty-eight.

136 A Wagner, in Dresden, June 11, 1843, to Messrs. Sturm & Koppe, in Leipzig:

"ESTEEMED SIRS:

"On account of the attention drawn to it by Herr Kapellmeister L. Spohr, a performance of my opera *The Flying Dutchman* in Cassel on the 5th inst. had an extraordinary success. Therefore, I am asking you to oblige me by making a full report about it in your widely-read *Theater-Chronik*. In asking for this I need not mention that I shall repay the cost involved—after the notice has appeared.

"With highest esteem,
Your most devoted
RICHARD WAGNER
Royal Saxon *Kapellmeister*"

B Wagner, in Dresden, October 24, 1843, to Messrs. Sturm & Koppe in Leipzig.

"In answer to your honored letter of the 23d inst., inquiring about the fee for the score and book of my opera *The Flying Dutchman,* I wish to state that I got from Kassel for that opera 20 friedrichsdor, from Riga 15 friedrichsdor, and now from Prague, 100 thaler. From these figures will you be good enough to determine how high the fee should be for a theater of second rank. I think 10–12 louis d'or will not be too much, since the copying of a score in this case would cost me almost as much as the fee.

"I also take this occasion to remark that I should like to leave to you the accept-ance of orders for my operas, although I don't deem it necessary to bother you with the full commission, since I myself have a permanent and generally known residence

[14] Wagner writes *"Wacholderhund,"* a possible word play on *Wachtelhund,* a hunter spaniel.

and therefore—should the situation arise—would expect you to draw your commission only from the theaters which apply to you.

"Will you also kindly tell me where and when I have to pay for my subscription to the *Theater-Chronik*.

"With highest esteem,
Your most devoted
RICHARD WAGNER"

137 Wagner, in Dresden, June 18, 1843, to Minna at Schönau.

"MIEZEL, MIEZEL!

"Something else has arrived! A letter from Riga from Hofmann in which he writes as follows:

" 'I deem it my duty to report to you that your great tone creation *The Flying Dutchman* has been performed here on the 22nd of May (Old Style) with great success.

" 'On the 25th it was repeated with the same success and the next performance is to be in Mitau,' etc.

"With this he enclosed, besides the program—a printed notice from the *Zuschauer*—which I am going to send to the *Theater-Chronik* and wherein my inspired, stupendous, rapturous creation is praised and also the performance greatly extolled. You too will read all this later on; now I am to use it for other purposes.

"Miezel, Miezel, is this not splendid, even if only for the fact itself? O God, the clock is just striking the quarter! This morning I have a rehearsal of *Die Jüdin* at eight o'clock. Now, what do you think? What do you say to my Dutchman? Doesn't he behave well? Greetings to Mama! Excuse my terrible rush but I am writing five letters along with this! Farewell, my most, most good, good little wife [*Weibel*].

"Your
MÄNNEL"

138 Wagner, in Dresden, June 26, 1843, to Minna at Schönau.

After a misunderstanding about Natalie, Wagner has learned from Tröger in Zwickau that she arrived there a week before and is with them, "healthy, happy, and cheerful." Wagner urges Minna to join him for the *Singfest*. She would leave Teplitz on July 5th; he would return with her on the 9th. He tells her about warm reports from Cassel on the second performance of *The Flying Dutchman*.

139 Wagner, in Dresden, July 18, 1843, to Joseph Tichatschek at Breslau.

Wagner congratulates his friend on his success at Breslau. He is about to leave for Teplitz the following day, to stay there until mid-August, when, he hopes, "the Italian tempest will have subsided. You ought to see Reissiger's face!!"

140   Wagner, in Dresden, September 6, 1843, to Johann Kittl, director of the conservatory at Prague.

"MY DEAR FRIEND HANS:

"To avoid falling again into the system by which we have continued to love each other, but meanwhile haven't heard from or seen each other for eight long years, I am starting now to defy the distance and to renew our friendly intercourse. If we always report in brief what we have to say, we shall always find time for what is to be told.

"This time, I have only to express to you my greatest and most enduring joy about our last visit together: rest assured that your deeply valued friendship, so warmly evident in all that you did, made me and my wife genuinely happy. We are thinking with true and deep emotion of our visit to Prague. And since we have resumed, so let us continue; isn't that right, dear old Hans?

"I am now waiting to hear whether you are gradually getting used to the routine of your new vocation, what your mood is, and how your prospects in *certain* matters are developing.

"I am still living in great external discomfort, and it will be a month before our household arrangements are in order; until then, work is not to be thought of. But when we are in order, will you come to us? Herr von Walkersdorf has just been with me, and says he has supplied you with an opera text by Dr. Strauss. Do you like it? I have not yet got around to writing to the poet of this opera text, offered to me and destined for Meyerbeer. Shall I do this in your behalf, or is it no longer necessary?

"The Viennese have now definitely ordered a grand opera from me for 1844–45; I am busy working out my conditions and the outline of a subject. Now you know in brief what has happened, and when the moment comes you may answer me just as briefly.

"Give my wife's best regards and mine to Herr Hoffmann and Berra; our cordial thanks for their offered friendliness! And you, my old friend, goodbye! Stay well and cheerful! That is of the greatest importance. Also remain fond of me! Adieu! Many hearty greetings from my wife.

"Your
RICHARD WAGNER"

141 A   Two autograph notebooks by Marie Schmole, entitled *"Wagner als Königl. Kapellmeister"* and covering the years 1843–1846. (See Chapter XI.)

B   Undated letter from Frau Schmole in Dresden to Mrs. Burrell. She remarks: "A few days ago, Frau Kriete-Wüst's [15] daughter told me that she had found some songs in Wagner's hand among the music of her late mother, which the Master had

---

[15] Wagner became indebted to the actor Kriete through his Meser publication venture in 1853. Kriete's wife was the former Henriette Wüst, who sang Irene in the original *Rienzi*.

written for his friend, the artist. One of the songs, *"Dors, mon enfant,"* may have been written for Frau Kriete's little daughter, therefore about 1845. Frau Müller wanted to bring the songs occasionally to my husband, for his kind inspection." But *"Dors, mon enfant"* was one of three songs written in Paris and published there in 1840; *"Dors, mon enfant"* was reprinted in the magazine *Europa* in 1841.

C Letter from Frau Schmole, in Dresden, August 27, 1895, to Mrs. Burrell. A brief letter accompanying the notes. She apologizes for the delay in completing them, because of "many interruptions."

142 Wagner, in Dresden, January 30, 1844, to Karl Gaillard in Berlin. (Page 108.)

143 Autograph MS of the "short" score of *Tannhäuser* (129 pp.). Only the overture is missing. The instrumental score is written on two staves, the instrumentation occasionally indicated, with additional staves for the vocal parts (which are always included).

At the beginning is written "Composition sketches of *Tannhäuser*: to the best of friends, Gustav Schmidt, in remembrance, Zürich, Feb. 26, 1855, Richard Wagner." The end of the first act is inscribed "January 27, 1844"; at the beginning of the second act is written "Fischer's Weinberg, Sept., 1844"; at the end of Act II, "15 October." At the end of the third act Wagner has signed his name, and added "Sunday, 29 December, 1844." These dates agree with his description in *My Life*. (It was after this that he wrote the overture; he completed the full score on April 15, 1845.) An alternative close to the opera is dated April 30, 1847. The published close of the full score draws upon both closes and omits about four pages of the alternative sketch.

The catalogue traces the history of this manuscript: "R. W. gave it in 1855 to Gustav Schmidt; he was *Kapellmeister* at Darmstadt, and a friend of Liszt. It passed to his widow, Emilie Schmidt. Her son-in-law, a lawyer, Dr. Sieger, sold it on her behalf to Bertling, the dealer, on July 29, 1894. Enclosed is a signed declaration on the subject by Dr. Sieger. Bertling sold it to Mrs. Burrell on July 31, 1894."

144 An autograph part (bass trombone and ophicleide) for the *Tannhäuser* overture. According to the catalogue: "Mrs. Burrell acquired this from Natalie."

145 Letter from Dr. Ferdinand Jolly, in Grimma, February 1, 1844, to Wagner.

Dr. Jolly reminds the "highly honored *Kapellmeister*" of their acquantance fourteen years before, while Wagner was studying at Leipzig. He is sending his "Saxon song, *Ein Kleeblatt,* hoping that you may find it worthy of a fitting musical investiture, produced by your rich talent."

146 Wagner, in Hamburg, March 17, 1844, to Minna in Dresden. (Page 114.)

147 Gasparo Spontini, in Berlin, November 2, 1844, to Wagner in Dresden (in French). (Page 218.)

148 Birthday letter from Frau Johanna Geyer, Wagner's mother, in Leipzig, November 24, 1844, to her daughter Cläre Wolfram. The writing is infirm. (Frau Geyer was sixty-nine.) Cläre was born on November 29, 1807.

"My dear Clärchen!

"Tomorrow is your dear birthday! Unfortunately I can't come to see you. Utter a small wish and I shall be delighted to fulfill it. Be happy tomorrow and continue to love your

Grandmother"

149 Wagner, in Dresden, December 18, 1844, to E. B. Kietz, 30 rue des Petits Augustins, Paris. (Pages 136, 180.)

150 Signature, on a visiting card, of Carolina von Weber, widow of Carl Maria von Weber.

151 Printed *Tagebuch* of the Royal Saxon Theater in Dresden for the year 1844 (twenty-seventh season).

This book lists in order of rank the full staff of the Hoftheater, including the singers, actors, musicians, and guest artists, and a full list of performances. Under *"General-Direction"* Herr Wolf Adolph August von Lüttichau heads the list as *Geheimer Rath und General-Director der Königl. musikalischen Kapelle und des Hoftheaters."* Carl Theodor Winkler is *"Vice-Director und Secretair, Hofrath."* The resident personnel of actors and singers lists fifty-three names, under which are included: Wilhelm Fischer as *"Sänger und Schauspieler, Regisseur der Oper und Chordirektor,"* Ferdinand Heine as *"Schauspieler und Costümler,"* Joseph Tichatscheck (*sic*) is called *"Kammersänger,"* as is also Johann Wächter (whose address shows him to have lived on the ground floor of Ostra-Allee No. 6, where Wagner occupied the second floor).

The chorus shows eleven tenors, nine basses, twelve sopranos, eight altos, and two assistants; the ballet, twenty names and three solo dancers. The *Königliche Kapelle* lists six under the heading *"Kapellmeister,"* in this order: K. G. Reissiger, Richard Wagner, August Röckel (*Musikdirektor*), Carl Lipinski (*Concertmeister*), Franz Morgenroth ("the same"), and Franz Schubert (*Vice-Concertmeister*). There are fourteen violins, four flutes, three oboes, four clarinets, three bassoons, four horns, four violas, four cellos, four double basses, four trumpets, three trombones, one tympanist, one harp, and eighteen *"aspiranten"* (presumably the wind players were used in relays to balance the strings).

The list of operas and spoken dramas shows a year-round activity, with only occasional blank nights. Operas are generally alternated with plays, which in turn range from the classical pieces of Schiller, Goethe, Shakespeare to light comedies, ballets, and farcical pieces (*Possen*) with music interspersed. The operas listed are twenty-nine in number. Conspicuous are *Der fliegende Holländer,* which had its first performance on January 2, and was three times repeated. *Rienzi* was given in two parts on January 23–24, February 12–19, March 28–29. The first part was given on

November 22, but the single evening's performance was reverted to on November 19, 26, and December 10. Other operas, in the order of performances for each, were as follows: Weber's *Der Freischütz* (11), Lortzing's *Czar und Zimmerman* (8), Rossini's *Wilhelm Tell* (8), Donizetti's *Lucia di Lammermoor* (6), Donizetti's *Lucrezia Borgia* (6), Gluck's *Armide* (5), Spohr's *Jessonda* (5), Meyerbeer's *Die Hugenotten* (4), Halévy's *Die Jüdin* (4), Auber's *Die Stumme von Portici* (4), Bellini's *Norma* (3), Boieldieu's *Die weisse Dame* (3), Donizetti's *Linda di Chamonix* (3), Auber's *Fra Diavolo* (3), Lortzing's *Der Wildschütz* (3); the following were performed twice—Mozart's *Don Juan* and *Figaro*, Bellini's *I Capuletti ed i Montecchi*, Marschner's *Der Templer und die Jüdin* (after *Ivanhoe*), Meyerbeer's *Robert der Teufel*; the following had each one performance—Weber's *Euryanthe*, Beethoven's *Fidelio*, Rossini's *Der Barbier von Sevilla*, Bellini's *La Sonnambula*, Rossini's *Otello*, Boieldieu's *Johann von Paris*. Thus it will be seen that the ten evenings devoted to *Rienzi* (complete or in part) were exceeded only by *Der Freischütz*, while the *Dutchman* held a middle ground.

152 Engraving of Carl Maria von Weber, with a dedication to "the esteemed widow of the immortal master" and the engraved signature of F. Heine.

153 Wagner, in Dresden, June 5, 1845, to Karl Gaillard [in Berlin]. (Page 153.)

154 Photograph (autographed) of Johanna Wagner (Wagner's niece) in the part of Phèdre (according to catalogue). (See facing page 381.)

155 Letter from Johanna Geyer in Leipzig, August 15 [1845?], to Minna.

Mrs. Burrell has noted: "The mention of the bracelet fixes the date. It is the bracelet for Johanna Wagner after the first performance of *Tannhäuser*. The mother had come over from Leipzig for the performance, in October, 1845." The mother, still in Leipzig, evidently anticipates the *Tannhäuser* première in her reference to Richard's "success in all his enterprises."

"MY GOOD MINNA!

"Again I want to give you my most heartfelt thanks for your love and thoughtfulness during my stay with you. It is my sincere desire that you soon may give me a chance to return your kindness! My dear Hermann, Ottilie, and the children were waiting for me in my room which the dear good children had decorated *beautifully* with *flowers* to welcome me. The *grandmother* was merry and happy among her children and dear grandchildren! Until now I have not done any kitchen work; this noon I'll eat with Julius in their home and there I'll drink your health; motherly greetings and a kiss to my good old Richard! His success in all his enterprises makes me happy.

"In a few days Heinrich is to leave for Paris with his wife. I am enclosing my payment! If only I could add another hundred. I will see Julius about the bracelet. Farewell and always keep a little of your affection for me.

MOTHER J. GEYER

"Butter costs 4 good groschen a piece. It is very expensive here."

156 Autograph text of *Lohengrin* (1845), including scenic instructions and pencil sketches for each act. Printed text for the first performance (at Weimar) in 1850. Bound in one volume with printed cover and title page.

In *My Life,* Wagner relates that only a few weeks after the first performance of *Tannhäuser,* he had "worked out the whole of the *Lohengrin* text" (p. 394). He left the libretto with Louis Spohr to read (p. 406), and also read it to groups of friends. It was from this manuscript that he must have read.

The following description, which may have been taken from Mrs. Burrell's notations, is quoted from the catalogue: ". . . the most authoritative—and, apparently, the only text—of the libretto of *Lohengrin.* This set of documents shows the minute care R. W. lavished on every detail of an opera production—down to the use of capital letters in the books of the words.

"In the manuscript poem R. W. has written and signed a few lines as to use of type in printing it. Von Zigesar, the Intendant at Weimar, has written in the names of the stage manager, decorator, the chief mechanician, and directions about printing, namely, to print the portions struck out in the ms.

"A number of stage directions in the text of the poem have been struck out. It is conjectured that the reasons for these instructions and alterations are as follows:

"In 1850, R. W., living in exile in Zürich, could not come to Weimar. He, therefore, sent written instructions for the scenery and decorations. He had got a ms. of the poem and sent it to von Zigesar to have the book of the words for the first performance printed from it; hence his few lines as to the use of type in printing it. But R. W. had used this same ms. to have the words put in the musical score and, when so doing, had struck out, for convenience, a number of stage directions. A comparison of the ms. with the published musical score shows this to be the case. Hence the deletions in the text of the poem. But he wanted these stage directions restored in the book of the words. Hence von Zigesar's directions about printing, namely, to print the portions struck out in the ms."

157 MS part (first violin, first desk) of the opening page of the *Lohengrin Prelude.* "Mrs. Burrell acquired it from Natalie Planer and dated it 1847."—Catalogue.

158 Wagner, in Dresden, February 1, 1846, to E. B. Kietz, 30 rue des Petits Augustins, Paris.

Although Gustav Kietz stated in writing to Mrs. Burrell (9) that the letters from Wagner to his brother which she obtained from him were all unpublished, this letter has proved an exception. It first appeared in the *Münchner Nachrichten* on February 13, 1908, and was reprinted (in German) in the Kapp and Kastner Collection. (Page 182.)

159 Wagner, in Dresden, May 20, 1846, to Franz Liszt. (Page 116.)

160   Draft of a contract for a loan to Wagner by the Dresden Court Theater Pension Fund. It is drawn up in two handwritings, not Wagner's, and it is neither dated nor signed.

In 1845, Wagner's indebtedness at Dresden became insupportable and threatened a public scandal. Pressed on all sides, he borrowed or attempted to borrow from everyone he knew, thus transferring his obligations from those creditors who were pressing him to friends who would not. When Mme. Schroeder-Devrient put his IOU for 3,000 marks into the hands of a lawyer, he had no choice but to go to Lüttichau, his employer as Intendant of the Royal Theater, "make a clean breast of everything, and beseech him to intervene for me, and if possible to obtain a royal advance that would enable me to clear my position, which was so seriously compromised" (*My Life*, p. 404).

The result of this appeal was a loan from the Theater Pension Fund, made in August, 1846. This draft shows the amount as 5,000 thaler, at 5 per cent interest, to be repaid in ten annual installments of 500 thaler. Listed as security was a life-insurance policy, publication rights in his three operas to date, and a third part of his salary as Royal *Kapellmeister*.

161   Wagner, in Vienna, July 18, 1846 [1848], to Minna. (Page 222.)

162   Photograph of Wagner, taken in Vienna. (See facing page 223.)
Mrs. Burrell dates this photograph as of 1848, from his summer visit to Vienna in that year; the compilers of the catalogue are inclined to place it at a later date, "1863 or thereabout," because he looks "older."

163 A   Notebooks of Marie Schmole. (Ch. XI.)

B   Frau Schmole in Dresden, February 20, 1896, to Mrs. Burrell. She has been studying Praeger's book to revive her memories of the revolutionary days. She has consulted the daughter of Fischer, "confirmed everything about which I made inquiries, including Fischer's hatred of Röckel." Wagner's letters to Fischer had come into the hands of Fischer's young grandson (her son), and she did not know how they had years later fallen into the possession of Cosima Wagner. "The 'little Natalie,'" says Frau Schmole, "really writes very confusedly, and, much as I hate to say so, I fear there is no place in which she will feel well! Though she now signs herself as 'Frau Bilz,' she is still a genuine old spinster. . . . Whether the best furniture of the 'poor seduced Richard' could bring her much is doubtful. It has lost too much of its presentability. The poor little old woman is to be pitied, for she won't find any peace in this life!"

164   Printed full score of Gluck's *Iphigenia in Aulis* (Le Marchand, Paris), with corrections and additions by Wagner for his use as the conductor's working score.

A typed notation, with corrections in ink by Mrs. Burrell, corresponds exactly to the description of this number in the catalogue. It is here quoted verbatim: [16]

"At least 200 pages of this musical text [298 pp.] have undergone alterations and comments in his hand, and on practically every page he has written musical indications and instrumental directions; in nine places he has inserted small pieces of paper with more considerable alterations. But it is his own additions in his own hand which are of the highest interest: they occupy no less than 40 folio pages, including 8 complete pages that constitute a new close to the opera.

"This Wagnerian version of *Iphigénie* was first performed on February 22 or February 24, 1847,[17] at Dresden, R. W.'s niece Johanna taking the leading part. It was frequently performed in Germany during his lifetime.

"A pianoforte arrangement of it, which is a very abbreviated version of R. W.'s work, was published by R. W. A version of some sort was printed for the purposes of production at the Königsberg Stadt Theater in 1854, and a copy is in the Oesterlein Museum at Eisenach (Museum catalogue). The authors of this Catalogue have not had the opportunity to compare this document with the printed book at Eisenach. . . .

"This is the book he got from Paris and worked on, and is the only authoritative text."

165 Supplement of the *Dresdner Anzeiger und Tageblatt,* June 15, 1848. Article entitled "In What Relation Do Public Endeavors Stand to Royalty?" and signed on June 14 by "a member of the Vaterlandsverein."

This is the anonymous article by Wagner which he delivered to the Vaterlandsverein as an oration before its publication. The excitement caused by this paper is described by him in his autobiography (p. 439 *et seq.*). There are English translations in Praeger (p. 156) and the *Prose Works* (Vol. IV, p. 136). Ellis there states that, unable to obtain the original publication, he had used a reprint by Wilhelm Tappert, of 1883.

166 Wagner, in Dresden, July 3, 1848, to Karl Gottlieb Reissiger. (Page 221.)

167 Wagner, in Dresden, August 25, 1848, to J. Tichatschek.

"GOOD DAY, DEAREST FRIEND!

"God knows where these lines will reach you! But if they reach you may they call out to you as if with my voice: "Stay away no longer and return as soon as

[16] It cannot be ascertained, except in a few instances where scribbled notations have survived, how much of Mrs. Burrell's actual research was used in the compilation of the catalogue. This note, and others which describe musical scores, indicate her painstaking methods.

[17] Ernest Newman gives February 22, Loewenberg (*Annals of Opera*), Feb. 24. Wagner's detailed account of his revision will be found in his *Life,* pp. 408–410. It has frequently been used by European theaters, notably Vienna (1867), Strassburg (1900), Berlin (1914), Zürich (1936). Wagner further revised the overture with an ending for concert purposes (Zürich, 1854), and this version has become standard for concerts. See "Gluck's Overture to Iphigenia in Aulis" in the *Prose Works,* Vol. V.

possible!" Riedel's opera has now been put on the shelf, and Lüttichau wants to have my new opera as soon as possible. Your absence is now all that prevents me from beginning with the studying. As soon as you come and still feel the old desire, then we shall start!

"Counting on seeing you soon I shall write only these few lines, but I greet you with a joyful heart!

"Adieu! Your

"RICHARD WAGNER"

168 Song *"Wann? Wo? Wie? Duett aus Stadt und Land,"* for two voices, "Apolonia" and "Sebastian," with piano accompaniment, composer unspecified. It is listed on the title page as the last in a collection entitled *Helikon,* and published by the Heinrichshofen Musikalienhandlung, Magdeburg, 1848. Mrs. Burrell has written the name of Wagner after this song, on the evidence of Adolf Hofmeister's *Handbuch der musikalischen Literatur* (1844–1851, page 276).

169 Otto Richter, in Dresden, February 28, 1895, to Mrs. Burrell.

Dr. Richter, royal councilor at Dresden, sends a report on a manuscript copy of Wagner's *Plan for the Organization of a German National Theater for the Kingdom of Saxony.* This was the script which was read and considered, for there are penciled remarks by Reissiger, Devrient, Heine, and others, and a retort to these remarks by Wagner himself. This paragraph Dr. Richter copies. The text had been published in the *Gesammelte Schriften,* in 1871, but without these added notations, and with certain omissions. Mrs. Burrell evidently obtained copies from these pages in the manuscript, or was allowed to see them, for she has written out the disparities in her own hand, by comparison with the published version; she has also copied a penciled notation at the end of the manuscript, written by Kammermusikus Julius Rühlmann:

"This plan of reorganization outlined by Richard Wagner in 1848–1849 has been copied word for word by several Dresden copyists according to the author's manuscript. It served as material within the General Management of the Dresden Hoftheater for the various opinions which the Management requested from Kapellmeister Reissiger, Herr Ed. Devrient, Ferdinand Heine, and others. These opinions are also kept in the Dresden archives. This copy carries the marginal notes written in pencil by the above-mentioned experts.

"Other copies have been submitted for consideration and decision to the *Landtag* of Saxony and the Ministry Oberlander (1849) [18] as well as to the *Reichstag* of Vienna (1849). However, this step had no result, since the outbreak of the revolution made any further action impossible in Vienna and Dresden.

"Abstracts from this copy were published by the late Kammermusikus Th. Uhlig in the *Neue Zeitschrift für Musik,* Vols. 34 and 35 (1851). The words *'vide,'* 'beginning,' 'end,' etc., and the red crosses are in his handwriting.

"A complete print of the manuscript, omitting pages 86 and 87, where Wagner

[18] This and the next date should be 1848.

added his marginal notes, is published in *Gesammelte Schriften und Dichtungen* by Richard Wagner, second volume, publishers F. W. Fritzsch, 1871, pages 307–359.

"Signed in good faith,

JULIUS RÜHLMANN

Royal Saxon Kammermusikus"

170   Wagner, in Dresden, March 3, 1849, to Intendant von Zigesar of the Theater at Weimar.

Wagner had every reason at this time to be warmly disposed toward Weimar. His discontent with conditions at the Dresden Opera had become acute and disposed him to look elsewhere. Meanwhile, Liszt at Weimar having conducted the first production of *Tannhäuser* outside of Dresden on February 16, Wagner had had enthusiastic reports from Liszt and his superiors. He had received letters from Zigesar and from Eduard Genast, the regisseur of the Ducal Theater. A career in Weimar was open to him.

Wagner, unable to attend the first two performances of *Tannhäuser* at Weimar, obtained leave to attend the third in May. The outbreak of the insurrection in Dresden at the beginning of that month sent Wagner to Weimar, but for other reasons.

"HIGHLY VENERABLE SIR!

"I have just received your very friendly letter, for which I extend my warmest thanks. The extraordinarily generous gift which you sent me from your exalted sovereigns and their affectionate tributes which, coming from the same source, accompanied the gift—both give me proof of the unusual interest which I was so fortunate as to awaken in the gracious donors. Be good enough to believe my sincere and cordial assurance that that which has now come to me in and from Weimar has made on me an indescribably encouraging and uplifting impression: it would take too long to tell you specifically the source of the deep dejection which has burdened my mind, especially in all that has concerned my art undertakings; it may suffice to tell you that by now I had resigned myself to meeting no further interest in my endeavors. For the first time in years I am given courage by you and my friends in Weimar to hope again; for the last few weeks I have been feeling cheerful, serene, and peaceful. Please accept the great share of gratitude due you, and the assurances of my deep indebtedness for your good will and the fine way in which you have carried it out.

"As for the high sovereigns who on their part too have remembered me in such an unexpectedly generous manner, and have so surprisingly rewarded my small merits, please assure them that my heartfelt joy over this kindness will remain as a most thankful remembrance; I sincerely wish that I may have the chance soon (I hope, in the month of May) to repeat these sentiments in person and by word of mouth. Moreover, most honored sir, I too look forward to the opportunity of cultivating your acquaintance more closely; this will be made possible in the near future by the visit to Weimar which is being planned with loving care. You have taken on my case with so much warmth that I should like to show you in return my warmest response.

"May I ask you then to keep me favorably in mind until that time and accept again my assurance that it is a long time since anything has so truly pleased and refreshed me as the success in which you have played so important a part.

"With the greatest respect and reverence, I remain,

Most faithfully yours,

RICHARD WAGNER"

171 *Die noth:* manuscript revolutionary poem, dated March 30, 1849, unsigned but in Wagner's hand. (Page 223.)

172 Wagner, in Eisenach, dated only "Wednesday morning," but certainly May 16, 1849, to Minna. (Page 229.)

173 Wagner, in Weimar, May 14 [1849], to Minna at Chemnitz (addressed care of Heinrich Wolfram). (Page 226.)

174 Wagner, in Weimar, May 18, 1849, to his "brother-in-law" Heinrich Wolfram. (Page 231.)

175 From Wagner, in Weimar, May 19 [1849], to Minna Wagner (enclosure). (Page 232.)

176 Wagner, in Magdala (near Weimar), May 22 [1849], to Cäcilie Avenarius in Leipzig. (Page 236.)

177 Wagner in Rorschach, Switzerland, May 31 [28, 1849], to Minna. The letter is an enclosure, with a note to Eduard Avenarius, and message from Cäcilie to Minna. (Page 236.)

178 Wagner, in Paris, June 4–5, 1849, to Minna in Leipzig. (Pages 242, 266 n.)

179 Wagner, in Paris, June 8, 1849, to Minna in Leipzig. (Page 245.)

180 Wagner, in Zürich, Tuesday, June 26 [May 29], 1849, to Minna (enclosure). (Page 237.)

181 Wagner, in Zürich, July 10, 1849, to Natalie in Dresden. (Page 248.)

182 A Minna, in Chemnitz, July 18, 1849, to Wagner in Zürich. (Page 251.)
   B Minna, in Chemnitz, August 3, 1849, to Wagner in Zürich. (Page 255.)
   C Minna, in Chemnitz, August 11, 1849, to Wagner in Zürich. (Page 259.)

183 Wagner, in Zürich, July 23, 1849, to Minna in Chemnitz. (Page 253.)

184 Franz Liszt, in Weimar, July 27, 1849, to Minna. (Page 255.)

185   Draft, undated, in Wagner's hand, for a letter from Minna to Bookseller Heinrich Brockhaus, Leipzig

This letter refers to an unpleasantness that had arisen over Wagner's library, which Minna had left for "safe custody" with Heinrich Brockhaus to prevent it from being seized by her husband's creditors after his flight from Dresden in 1849. Heinrich, who was the brother of Wagner's brother-in-law Hermann Brockhaus, had, according to Wagner, "insisted on looking after them." But when Minna asked "this kind friend to send her the books, he replied that he was holding them as security for a debt [19] of 1,500 marks that I had contracted with him during my troubled days in Dresden." Wagner's indignant protest, which Minna presumably copied and sent, was of no avail. Since he was unable to repay the loan, some of his choicest books were lost to him forever.

"Most honored Sir:

"When, in 1849, in that period of my misfortune during the breakdown of our domestic life, you offered to keep the library of my husband, it was done with the assurance that you were doing so with only the most friendly intention to save the book collection—so costly to my husband—from a threatened seizure by the Court. Now my husband informs me that you intimated to an intermediary some time ago that you are considering keeping the library as a pledge or compensation for a former loan given to him. Since I was the one who delivered these books to you with a quite different understanding, I should regret having deprived my husband of his particularly treasured possession by having put my trust in you while you really intended to indemnify yourself in this way. That is why I consider it my duty humbly to submit the question to you whether you really meant to take advantage of my great distress and of our need for saving our small possessions. This would mean that you wanted to be reimbursed as the only one among several others, at a time when even the least creditor felt obliged to renounce his demands. Considering your means and the character of your relation to my husband, that loan so decidedly had the meaning of friendly help that I, like my husband, never supposed that you could press the payment so crudely, especially when the personal circumstances of the debtor are so desperate. So I beg you to tell me frankly what I am to expect of you in this matter, and whether I must confess to my husband that my own ill considered step caused him this great loss. For this affair concerns only me. Your claim on my husband is a different case.

"If you can't make up your mind to cancel his debt, you are indeed at liberty to come to an understanding with him about a repayment presumably indispensable to you. Considering your favorable financial position and remembering the time when you helped out my husband with the loan in question, you could follow the procedure of other much less affluent creditors, who, on account of the unusual circumstances and the exceptional position of my husband in life and art, canceled his debts.

[19] *My Life,* page 316.

"I have only wished to make you understand that until now I have considered myself personally responsible to my husband for the preservation of the collection of books which are in your keeping. Awaiting your friendly decision, which may clarify your present as well as your former intentions, I am with greatest respect,

Faithfully yours,

M. W."

186 Wagner, in Zürich, November 19, 1849, to Ferdinand Heine in Dresden. (Pages 261–262.)

187 Wagner, in Zürich, December 4, 1849, to Ferdinand Heine in Dresden. (Page 267.)

188 Photographs of Ferdinand Heine and his daughter, Frau Marie Schmole, with a signed certification by her of the authenticity of the former, dated Dresden, August 5, 1894. (Facing pages 263 and 120.)

189 Wagner, in Enge, near Zürich, to Joseph Tichatschek. (The catalogue states: "presumably Autumn, 1849.") (Page 150.)

190 Natalie, in Dresden, December 19, 1899, to Miss Burrell (Raphaela).

This letter, according to Miss Burrell's (?) notation on the envelope, is an acknowledgement of the receipt of 200 marks, and shows that after Mrs. Burrell's death, Natalie continued to contribute items and received payment for them. She here offers the possibility of a "drawing by Kietz in Paris, at the beginning of 1840." This letter speaks of August Röckel as Wagner's "evil spirit," his "deceitful corrupter, who, under the jesuitic pretext of friendship, was Richard's greatest enemy." Like Frau Schmole (141 A), she accuses Röckel of involving Wagner in debts to discharge his own. The letter is otherwise an exhibition of fawning flattery.

191 Pamphlet, *Der Aufruhr in Dresden am 3, 4, 5, 6, 7, 8, 9, 1849 Mai*, by Q. Carl Krause, 1849.

According to the catalogue, this is the "account by eyewitness of the Dresden Revolution in May, 1849. There are notes on it in ink by Mrs. Baumgarten, who was also an eyewitness. She procured the book and made the notes at the request of Mrs. Burrell."

Frau Baumgarten was the daughter of Gustav Zocher, an early friend of the Wagners. Mrs. Burrell has made the following notation, mostly in German, as if from Frau Baumgarten's dictation:

"The Baumgartens lived in the Neumarkt. Salomonis apothecary, second (third) floor, at the corner of the present Landhausstrasse, then Pirnasche Strasse, next to Hotel de Saxe, corner of Moritz-Str., Hotel de Rome, then small Schuhmacher Gasse, wherefrom most shooting came. Frau B. first saw from her window a young miner, then an old one in the same miner attire; he stood on the pedestal of a lamp post opposite to her and addressed the crowd. The people went to get the key from the town hall to the town-council house in order to collect arms there. One cortege from the town hall marched past her. An athlete in gray dress with a red feather on his hat carried the sabre aloft with the key attached to it. They found no weapons there and then marched in anger to the armory. She heard the first shot and soon afterward she saw a big crowd surrounding an open van pulled by proletarians, a corpse half-naked lying there on his stomach so that the bloody wound was visible; thus the corpse of the same old gray-haired miner who shortly before had harangued the crowd was exhibited.

"Schwarzburg Rudolstadt's hearse was the very first carriage crossing the bridge after the revolution.

"Commander of the Communal Guard Charles Napoleon Lenz married to Medizinalrath Baumgarten's sister, lived 1st floor, corner of Altmarkt & Wildsdruffer Strasse, Pariser Meds Geschäft. Ground floor was 'Löwenapotheke' Besitzer Otto Schneider. When the victim of the first shot was drawn past dead on a *Leiterwagen,* lying on his face, Schroeder-Devrient called out of the first-floor window '*Rächt Euch an der Reaction*'; the insurgents took it to mean the contrary, rushed up and threw all the '*Waaren*' [merchandise] out of the windows, and made a barricade of them in the Wildsdruffer Strasse.

"Kampische Gasse is right, but on the old map it is Kamische Gasse."

192　Draft of a petition by Minna (undated) to the King of Saxony.

Woldemar Lippert (*Wagner in Exile*) identifies this petition with Minna's visit to Dresden in October, 1854. She went from Weimar, probably on the advice of the Grand Duke, and without Wagner's knowledge, in her efforts to find some way to enable her husband to visit Berlin and so make possible the long-planned and long-desired production of *Tannhäuser* there. The petition was refused. The continuing hostility of the Saxon Court toward Wagner is seen in a secret communication from Privy Councilor Körner to the Munich Chief of Police on January 16 of that year, that if Wagner should appear there, as reported, he was to be arrested at once. Nor did the accession of King Johann improve Wagner's case.

"Most serene and gracious Sir and King!
"Your Majesty!

"Encouraged by your Majesty's widely known generosity and mildness, I come from a great distance humbly to implore your Majesty's mercy and forgiveness for an exile whose creations once enjoyed the good graces of your Majesty; and so the wife of the exiled Richard Wagner dares ask your Majesty as a protector of art and science to bestow mercy on an erring artist who, hampered in his labors by the impossibility of hearing his newer works, is deeply depressed. .

"Would your Majesty bestow mercy and forgiveness on my husband, the misled Richard Wagner, and enable him to attend the performances of his works, promoting thereby his further creative labors by your Majesty's mercy and generosity?

"With troubled heart I venture a humble petition and implore pardon from your Majesty for a guilty misled man who is atoning *heavily* by the banning of his art.

"To her most judicious and gracious King there appeals with trust and confidence your Majesty's most humble servant,

MINNA WAGNER"

193 Natalie Bilz-Planer, in Leisnig, August 4, 1891, to Mrs. Burrell at Bayreuth.

Natalie, extolling Minna as Wagner's protecting angel and savior, claims that she saved him three times from arrest, at the Kreuzkirche tower in Dresden, at Chemnitz, and in Weimar.[20] She thus saved him for the world, for if he had been imprisoned for years, like Röckel, he would have died or gone mad, and his music dramas would never have been written.

"I must tell you about another small experience. A little while ago I was unexpectedly called to Waldheim; it was my first visit to the town. There I saw the horrible penitentiary with its high, surrounding walls set on top with fragments of sharp glass to prevent escape. I must confess that a cold shiver came over me at the sight of that sinister black edifice with its strongly iron-grilled little windows, and the thought came to me that Richard barely escaped being imprisoned there, where, beyond hope and pity, he would have pined away, and would have died or gone insane if Minna had not saved him by her love and faithfulness. (While I was looking at that strange edifice, quite stunned, and absorbed in recollections, a soldier gruffly asked me what I was staring at—whether I had somebody inside). I silently admired Minna's courage, when out of genuine love and friendship and warm sympathy for Röckel's poor wife, living in Weimar with the children, she had traveled to Waldheim to comfort her, and had entered that horrible grave of living humans to see Röckel there and find out how he was doing, in order to give a message to his poor wife. She herself told me how she trembled with pity and inner agitation when she heard his step, wishing she could have met him at some other place than that house of horror, and when she saw him the tears flowed down her cheeks in spite of herself. But he looked well and was happy that she had thought of him and his wife."

194 Alwine Frommann, in Coblenz, July 3, 1850, to Minna in Zürich. (Page 299.)

195 Pen-and-ink sketches by E. B. Kietz (page 488): Four unidentifiable heads, and a caricature of Wagner seated at ease in a cart drawn by human figures; a woman in housewifely garb, presumably Minna, stands behind him, holding the reins.

196 Wagner, in Mulhouse (postmark, January 30, 1850), to Minna. This note, written en route to Paris, is no more than the reassurance of safe progress in his journey.

197 Wagner, in Paris, February 6, 1850, to Franz Liszt [in Weimar]. (Pages 273, 277.)

---

[20] However, it appears from Wagner's own accounts that while Minna's anxiety may have had a certain restraining influence. Wagner's caution in extremity, plus sheer good luck, had more to do with it.

(195)

198   Wagner, in Paris, February 9, 1850, to Franz Liszt in Weimar. (Page 137.)

199   Daguerreotype of portrait of Wagner by E. B. Kietz, the portrait made for Jessie Laussot. Missing in the Collection.

200   Photograph of daguerreotype (199).

201   Jessie Laussot, in Bordeaux, March 6, 1850, to E. B. Kietz in Paris. (Page 278.)

202   Jessie Laussot, in Bordeaux, April 7, 1850, to "Frau Minna Wagner, Zürich" (not postmarked). (Page 279.)

203   Wagner, in Paris, to E. B. Kietz in Paris.
   A   February 13, 1850. (Page 183.)
   B   April 9, 1850. (Page 183.)
   C   April 14, 1850. (Page 183.)
   D   April 25, 1850. (Page 286.)
   E   April 25, 1850. (Page 287.)

204   Wagner, in Paris, April 16, 1850, to Minna in Zürich. (Page 281.)

205 A   Wilhelm Baumgartner and Jakob Sulzer in Zürich, April 21, 1850, to Wagner in Paris (copy by Natalie). (Page 285.)
   B   Wagner (undated, but in the summer of 1850) to Wilhelm Baumgartner in Zürich (not postmarked). (Page 298.)

206   Letter from Natalie Bilz-Planer, in Leisnig, April 24, 1893, to Mrs. Burrell.

Natalie acknowledges the receipt of 160 marks. She can well understand her benefactor's satisfaction "in receiving Richard's letter sent to you, although your noble heart will have surely perceived that Richard's behavior was not so noble." This would be 214. She indulges in her usual vilifications of Mathilde Wesendonck, Cosima, and "that devil, Rökel [sic]." She looks forward to a monumental, exculpating biography of Minna by Mrs. Burrell. Mrs. Burrell's imputation that the letters she has sent have been marked by other hands or even been in other hands has wounded her deeply. She encloses two newspaper articles which she considers a noble vindication of Minna. They are by Ludwig Hartmann, in the *Hamburger Signale*: "*Wie Wagner war*" (September 20, 1892) and "*Nochmals R. Wagners erste Frau*" (January 5, 1893). (Page 286.)

207 A   Wagner, in Geneva, May 4, 1850, to E. B. Kietz in Paris. (Page 287.)

   B   Wagner, in Zürich, July 7, 1850, to E. B. Kietz in Paris. (Page 308.)

   C   Wagner, in Zürich, September 14, 1850, to E. B. Kietz in Paris. (Pages 309, 331.)

"MOST EXCELLENT FRIEND KIETZ!

"What more can one ask? To provide the subject, in the blackest period of one's life, for such an amusing, colorful portrait as I succeeded in doing for you, that is really sufficient! Your superb portrait which I shall keep as a sacred relic will henceforth serve as my model. I now live in the firm intention, as often as I can remember it and control myself, to direct and see everything in such a way that I can laugh about it. The horse- and cowtails [21] shall contribute their bit to strengthen me in my purpose! Be assured that your letter also made me and my wife very happy. I should have written to you right away, but many things interfered, chiefly the performance of my *Lohengrin* in Weimar. You recall that in Montmorency I gave you a letter containing a message for Liszt: acting on that letter Liszt—as I did not learn until much later—had the score sent to him from Dresden and proceeded to perform it. This took place on August 28. . . .[22]

"Otherwise I'm now very poor again, since I can no longer accept the assistance which was offered to me earlier—as you know. The Ritters themselves are not wealthy enough to help me completely. I have now received a fee from Weimar. That's all. For the rest I no longer have much joy in life, and that is most sensible in my position. Otherwise it is very nice here, and I prefer Zürich to anywhere else: also I have friends here who are very fond of me.

"The most useful thing I can still do is actually—to write. Recently I was again inspired to do so, and I wrote a long essay entitled "Judaism in Music." It will appear shortly in the Leipzig *Neue Zeitschrift für Musik* under a pseudonym, K. Freigedank, because I had to be wary of using my real name and making the whole thing a personal issue from the start. Tell Anders to see where he can get the paper: I

[21] The horsetail is a Turkish symbol of authority. See also 207 D.
[22] See p. 331.

think it will interest both of you. Now I'm sending you and Anders each a text of my *Lohengrin*. There were awful misprints in it; I have corrected the most important ones very neatly. For Anders I'm also enclosing the paraphrase of Beethoven's Ninth Symphony which he wanted. I hope you'll send it to him soon and give him the messages in this letter. Next time I'll write to *him,* and he should then do the same for you. So give my best regards to Anders. Minna sends regards to both of you— Don't forget Semper— Farewell and write soon.

                                                                    YOUR RICHARD W."

D   Caricature in water color by E. B. Kietz showing Wagner as a Turk with horse- and cowtails suspended from his head (referred to in 207 C). Also a visiting card with this message: "Richard Wagner has the honor to present to Herr Meyerbeer the Herren Schletten and Groll who were recommended to him from Cassel by Herrn Spohr."

208   Draft of a letter from Minna, in Zürich, May 8, 1850, to Wagner. (Page 289.)

209   Mrs. Ann Taylor, in Bordeaux, May 8, 1850, to Minna in Enge (near Zürich). The letter is in French. (Page 292.)

210   E. B. Kietz, in Paris, May 27, 1850, to Minna in Enge. (Page 294.)

211   Minna, in Zürich, June 12, 1850, to E. B. Kietz in Paris. (Page 295.)

212 A   (Undated) Natalie to Mrs. Burrell.
    Natalie states that she is sending "a few notes," some love poems to Minna from her admirers, and some drawings by Kietz, "lightly sketched in his gay, artistic mood, all of them glorifying Richard's fame to come." (These should be 207 D.) She also writes: "The fact that the Bordeaux affair became so well known in Dresden was probably the fault of the old maid to whom Minna had confided her sorrow and grief and who unforgivably, under the seal of secrecy, made it widely known in Dresden." She writes: "From the Bordeaux time, when Richard wanted to go away with Jessie and leave Minna, never to see her again, dates the marriage proposal which Minna received from Dresden, by which she felt herself deeply insulted and humiliated, and over which she shed hot tears. I doubt whether this admirer ever got an answer from Minna." (Page 297.)
    B   An unknown admirer in Dresden, June 12, 1850, to Minna (the letter referred to in A). (Page 297.)

213   Wagner, in Paris (undated, but certainly June, 1850), to Minna in Zürich. (Page 300.)

214   Copy by Natalie Bilz-Planer of 213.
    Mrs. Burrell has made the following notation on the first page: "Copy by Natalie Bilz-Planer of a letter written by Richard Wagner to his wife, Minna, about the Bordeaux affair with Madame Jessie Laussot, née Taylor. 1850." Mrs. Burrell

has begun to write "Natalie believes the original letter . . . with the huge pack she sent" . . . Later she has crossed out "believes" and substituted "found," adding, "I have it." The catalogue says: "Natalie at first gave Mrs. Burrell copies only, declaring she had not the original; she suspected her to be an agent of Cosima Wagner; later she gave her the original."

215 Receipt for three months' rent (50 gulden) from "Mdame Wagner, from Dresden," signed by Widow Hirzel Bürklé, Enge near Zürich, July 1, 1850.

216 Mrs. Ann Taylor (undated, but probably of July, 1850) to Minna (in Zürich). Unlike 209, this letter is in German. (Page 307.)

217 Program of the Société Sainte-Cécile, Paris, Sunday afternoon, November 24, 1850. This is announced as the opening concert. M. Seghers is the orchestral director. The closing number is announced as follows:

"7. *Ouverture de l'opéra Tannhäuser de R. Wagner, exécutée pour la première fois à Paris.*" (See page 137.)

218 Wagner, in Zürich, December 13, 1850, to E. B. Kietz in Paris. (Page 138.)

219 Jessie Hillebrand (née Taylor), in Florence, January 7, 1888, to Mrs. Burrell. (Page 275.)

220 Wagner, in Enge, May 10, 1851, to Intendant von Zigesar at Weimar.

Liszt's "success with *Lohengrin,*" wrote Wagner (in *My Life,* p. 561), "gave him confidence in his ability to execute a yet more hazardous undertaking, and he invited me to set my poem of *Siegfried's Death* to music for production at Weimar. On his recommendation, the manager of the Weimar theater, Herr von Zigesar, offered to make a definite contract with me in the name of the Grand Duke. I was to finish the work within a year, and during that period was to receive a payment of fifteen hundred marks." Later he writes: "The fresh green and early spring flowers of May acted as a cheerful stimulant on my mental condition. I now conceived the idea of the poem *Young Siegfried,* which I proposed to issue as a heroic comedy by way of prelude and complement to the tragedy of *Siegfried's Death.*"

The following letter is Wagner's offer of his new, May-conceived idea to von Zigesar:

"ESTEEMED SIR!

"It may not have happened for a long time, and it is less likely to happen again, that the head of any theater makes an offer to a creative artist of just my kind, as you have done. While no theater can be found which, even equipped with the best means, would perform one of my dramatic works, you not only undertake that task, not only sacrifice time and money, without assurance or hope of any gain or even costs, but you yourself invite me to deliver to you new works which nowhere else would even be considered, and along with this you offer me a financial aid enabling me easily to devote myself to my artistic work, a money offer which the best endowed art institute would not or could not afford for that purpose. I considered this act as such an extraordinary one, that I wish to express to you first of all my most sincere joy that such a thing can be possible in these times, even regardless of the fact that *I* am the one to whom this has happened.

"Permit me at this point to refer to something that may enlighten you about my attitude. In my essays, and even recently in a book, which is to appear under the title *Opera and Drama,* I have elaborately expatiated on the subject of art and its relation to life. I have been able to do this only by establishing an ideal which I consider attainable for mankind. The artist or man who never gets to the point of pursuing an ideal contrary to the prevailing standards, an ideal in which the noblest ability of his spirit appears as the desire of his soul, will never progress a single step beyond the commonplace. Only by the strength of that ideal does he gain the power to rise above the usual level and to take part in what we call an advance, or a progressive development. In order to establish that ideal in its unmistakable purity, I must free it from any influence of present reality: for this reason I must first of all deny that reality, reveal it as futile, before I gain the ground on which my ideal can be conceived, and conceived in such a way that in my conviction of its existence I now find power and courage to take the next step toward attaining my ideal, that is, to create something new.

"Whenever in real life I get in immediate touch with existing reality, I should have to remain a most incapable man if I did not strive for a possible success in such a way as to attain it. Thus I must deny existing reality only in the sense of laying hold upon it with the most noble intention, that is to say, with an intention which, derived from my ideal, overcomes the existing reality by ennobling and exalting it.

"So I beg you: Don't consider anything I say about reality as an insult to you or anybody else, even if it seems to reflect upon a position like yours; for, as soon as I approach the actuality of the moment, I may attack a position in a generalized way without in the least losing sight of the fact that such a position, when filled by a man of noble intentions, is the only means of achieving something useful at the present time.

"If I ever had any doubt about this, then *you* would be the man to remove that doubt for good, and therefore I ask you: consider this warm expression of my respect for you as completely sincere and unqualified.

"To come to the point, I have to communicate the following to you: in any case I would have turned to some comprehensive work of art, even under the most distressing conditions; the incentive for it had come from our friend Liszt. My deliverance from this distress is something for which I heartily thank you. But along with this an idea had already come to me through an intuition which shapes the character of my prospective work in such a way as to facilitate its performance on the stage and to insure its success with the public. The more the thought of seeing my *Siegfried's Death* performed on the stage occupied my mind, the more distinctly I faced the difficulties it would present to our singers, unused to such a task, and to the public, unused to such a plot. This I considered as a threat to its success, nay even to the possibility of a performance. But at the very same time my fantasy became engrossed in another plot (which is in a very desirable preparatory relationship to *Siegfried's Death*: It is the lighthearted and almost popular plot of a *Young Siegfried*. At this time I can only indicate to you the following details about the advantages of that plot.

"*The Young Siegfried,* which is most lighthearted, engaging, and warm in character (qualities, of course, not taken from the *Nibelungenlied*), contains the conquest of the Nibelungen hoard and Brünhilde's awakening as its principal moments. Little or almost no knowledge of the myth need be presupposed on the part of our public for the understanding of that plot; rather do they become acquainted with the plot itself in its most popular features, without any need of deep or coordinating thought, but in a playful way, so to speak, as children learn by a fairy tale. After a performance of this lighthearted drama (which by the way is a complete unit in itself), the audience immediately senses conditions extremely important for a ready understanding of *Siegfried's Death* (a complete unit again)—and that second, more serious drama, performed later on, will make such a definite impression as could hardly be attained now without the first one. When both dramas have been performed in the specified order, each of them can be given at any time you like or is possible. Another important advantage, however, is that the singers in *Young Siegfried,* which is much closer to their present customary routine, are naturally educated for *Siegfried's Death* and thus are made able to sing it. We only have to be concerned about one thing, that is, an amiable, fresh, and slender tenor!

"I hope to write my poem, for which I am now concentrating my thoughts, in June, and to start with the music in July. By the 1st of July next year, in any case, everything—poem and music—of *The Young Siegfried* will be in your hands.

"Now I beg you, dear sir, to accept the assurance of my most sincere and cordial thanks for your successful care for me, and know that I shall never cease to be most respectfully your

very faithful

RICHARD WAGNER"

221   Wagner, in Zürich, to E. B. Kietz in Paris.
  A   May 2, 1851. (Page 184.)
  B   July 2, 1851. (Page 184.)
  C   October 24, 1851. (Page 185.)
  D   December 5, 1851. (Page 186.)
  E   December 17, 1851. (Page 186.)

222 A   Wagner, in Saint Gallen, July 5, 1851, to Minna in Enge (Zürich). (Page 310.)
  B   Wagner, in Engelberg, August 3 [1851], to Minna in Enge (Zürich). (Page 311.)

223   Wagner, in Albisbrunn, to Minna in Zürich.

Undertaking a water cure in Albisbrunn (near Zürich), Wagner sought to expel all traces of poison through his pores by an appalling regimen which left him in an acute state of "irritability and overwrought nerves."

A   September 23, 1851.

Writing "a few words," Wagner is solicitous about the health of his wife and urges her to "remain quiet" and avoid "excessive activity."

B   September 26, 1851.

Wagner is bored. He greets his wife affectionately and hopes that she will join him on Sunday.

224   Wagner, in Albisbrunn, to Minna in Enge (Zürich), 1851. (Pages 311–312.)

A   (Undated).

B   September 17.

C   November 2.

225   Number missing in catalogue.

226 A   Wagner, in Albisbrunn, November 14, 1851, to Minna in Enge (Zürich).
Wagner still writes in a domestic vein. He is longing for the comforts of home.

B   (Dated only "Monday.")

Wagner has gained vigor and muscularity—he signs himself "your Hercules." He hopes to return home on the following Sunday, but his treatments must continue there. He wishes to have a bathtub installed—an upright variety where he can be immersed in a standing position, up to his neck—"with a certain amount of inundation" of the floor round about.

227 A   Color print of Johanna Jachmann-Wagner as Ortrud.

B   Letter from Johanna Jachmann-Wagner, in Hohen Aschau, September 15, 1891, to Mrs. Burrell.

Wagner's niece writes a polite note, confirming December 26, 1836, as the date on which she sang Salomé under the theatrical director Bürgel, according to information obtained in Würzburg. The date, which finds Johanna as a little girl of eight, on the "Second Christmas Holiday," seems to define the occasion.

C   Letter from Frau Jachmann-Wagner, September 15, 1891, to Mrs. Burrell. She wishes the correct address in order to send a photograph. "I still live in the marvelous musical memories of Bayreuth—this Parsifal—nothing superior exists for me. . . . Circumstances have brought me nearer to you too, dear Mrs. Burrell, and I hope it may always remain so." Mrs. Burrell at one time took singing lessons from Johanna.

228   Wagner, in Zürich, to E. B. Kietz in Paris.

A   February 24, 1852. (Page 187.)

B   March 8, 1852. (Page 188.)

C   March 20, 1852. (Page 188.)

D   April 3, 1852. (Page 188.)

E   May 2, 1852. (Page 189.)
F   May 28, 1852. (Page 189.)
G   September 7, 1852. (Page 191.)

229 A   Wagner, in Interlaken, July 11, 1852, to Minna in Zürich. (Page 313.)
    B   Wagner, in Lugano, July 21, 1852, to Minna in Zürich. (Page 313.)

230 A   Wagner, in Zürich, August 11, 1852, to Ferdinand Heine in Dresden. (Page 139.)
    B   Wagner, in Zürich, September 11, 1852, to Ferdinand Heine in Dresden. (Page 141.)

231 (Undated.) Natalie Bilz-Planer, in Leisnig, to Mrs. Burrell. (Page 316.)

232 Letter from Natalie Bilz-Planer, in Leisnig, January 18, 1891, to Mrs. Burrell.
Natalie writes that Minna perpetually dissuaded Wagner from writing "so many books" which created enemies and were maliciously interpreted, instead of "creating high, noble, wonderful, great and splendid, immortal masterworks." Mathilde, on the other hand, "in order to flatter her way into his favor, pronounced his books incomparable." Minna likewise advised against the choice of *Tannhäuser* for the "frivolous French," and urged *Rienzi,* which would gratify the "Frenchman's desire to be amused, and offered action and spectacle." Afterward, when it was too late, so writes Natalie, Wagner acknowledged that she had been right.

233 Photograph of Miss Röckel, sister of August Röckel. The catalogue dates the photograph as of 1852, "by the style of dress." "Educated in England," says the autobiography, "she married the actor Moritz whom I had known from my earliest youth."

234 ' Christine Planer, in Dresden, December 4, 1853, to Natalie Planer.
The grandmother of Natalie, duly keeping up the lifelong deception, s.gns herself as "Your faithful mother—Christine Planert" (note use of the earlier spelling of her name). It is an affectionate letter, expressing her satisfaction that Natalie is to return to the Wagners, after a separation.

235 Wagner, in Zürich, February 5, 1853, to Raymond Härtel.
Wagner writes that *Lohengrin,* which the firm of Breitkopf and Härtel are to publish, will be ready by Easter.

236 Printed invitation to a reading of the *Ring des Nibelungen,* Zürich, February 12, 1853 (missing in the Collection).

237 Wagner, in Zürich, 1853.
Draft of an essay proposing the establishment of a permanent orchestra by the *Allgemeine Musik Gesellschaft* in Zürich. (Page 343.)

238 Water-color portrait of Wagner by Frau Clementine Stockar-Escher, in 1853. (This portrait was reproduced. It is missing in the Collection.)

239 Natalie Bilz-Planer's voucher for the authenticity of the above portrait, for which "Wagner himself sat every morning."

240   Wagner, in 1853, in Zürich, to E. B. Kietz in Paris.
    A April 2. (Page 194.)
    B June 6. (Page 195.)
    C November 7. (Page 196.)
    D November 30. (Inquiry about Lindemann.)
    E Undated. (Page 196.)

241 A Engraved invitation from Wagner, Zürich, April 18, 1853, to singers to take part in the chorus in concerts of the "next month."

B Printed program (16 pp.), with texts and explanations of numbers to be performed at concerts on May 18, 20, and 22, in Zürich. In a foreword Wagner explains that because of the present impossibility of giving full stage presentations of his operas in Zürich, he is presenting in concert form scenes which will give a preliminary idea of these works, with descriptions which will lead to their understanding. There accordingly follow the text or description of each number (except the opening one—Peace March from *Rienzi*). They include: Senta's ballad and Sailors' Chorus from *The Flying Dutchman* (texts); the Overture (which he calls "The Dutchman's Voyage"); the Entrance of the Guests into the Wartburg, with chorus, the introduction to Act III, Pilgrim's Chorus, and overture from *Tannhäuser* (the overture he entitles "The Venusberg"); the Prelude to *Lohengrin* (which he calls "The Holy Grail"), followed by the Men's Scene and Bridal Procession, the Introduction to Act III, and the Bridal Chorus. (The descriptions of the *Tannhäuser, Lohengrin,* and *Flying Dutchman* overtures are included in the *Prose Works,* Vol. III.)

242 Wagner, in Zürich, June 30, 1853, to Wilhelm Fischer in Dresden.

This letter is missing in the Collection, but there is a letter from Otto Lessmann, in Charlottenburg, December 31, 1884, to Mrs. Burrell, offering the letter, which he has acquired from Fischer's son. Lessmann gives a résumé: Wagner sends Fischer specifications for his change in the final scene of *Tannhäuser,* written on separate sheets, with alterations in the text. "He orders these altered texts forwarded to different theaters."

243 Engraving of Wilhelm Fischer. (See facing page 100.)

244 Explanation by Wagner of his overture to *Tannhäuser,* printed in Zürich (undated). A slight amplification of the explanation in 241. (This appeared in the *Neue Zeitschrift für Musik,* January 14, 1853.)

245 Mathilde Wesendonck, in Ems, July 4, 1853, to Minna. (Page 362.)

246 A Wagner, in Saint-Moritz, postmarked July 20, 1853, to Minna. (Page 317.)
    B Wagner, in Saint-Moritz, August 2, 1853, to Minna. (Page 317.)

C   Wagner, in Berne, August 25, 1853, to Minna. (Page 317.)
D   Wagner, in Geneva, August 27, 1853, to Minna. (Page 318.)

247   Caroline Uhlig, in Dresden, August 17, 1853, to Minna in Zürich.

The widow of Wagner's friend Theodor Uhlig, who had died in Dresden, January 3, 1853, wishes to correspond with "Frau Wagner," whom she has never met, as one "who was close to my unforgettable husband." This "closeness" is attested by the names of her children. She writes that "little Siegfried now walks all by himself," and "Elsa, when she sees the picture of your dear husband, asks when they are to see Uncle Wagner again." (See also 271 and Appendix B.)

248   Wagner, in Spezia, September 5 [1853], to Minna. (Page 318.)

249   Plaster medallion of Theodor Uhlig, modeled in 1853 from memory by Gustav Kietz, according to a notation by Mrs. Burrell, and given to her in 1890. "He said Uhlig looked like St. John, and carried his head heavenward."

This medallion is missing from the Collection.

250   Countess von Broel in Broelberg, October 7, 1853, to Minna.

Mrs. Burrell notes: "An actress who had acted with Minna." She was also a collector of pets and had sold a parrot cage to Minna. The letter consists of advice on the care of parrots.

251   Wagner, in Zürich, October 31, 1853, to Ferdinand Heine in Dresden. (Page 332.)

252   Wagner, in Zürich, November 19, 1853, to Natalie Planer in Leipzig.

DEAR NATALIE!

"We hear that you've left Bachmann's and accepted a job in the Hôtel de Pologne. We don't approve of that at all, and I especially consider it unsuitable. If you need a *good* home, I now offer you one. It is with *us* in Zürich. *Minna* has become very sickly, and I'm seriously worried about her; for that reason I intend to make things in the house as easy for her as possible: she must no longer touch anything and must always remain quiet, otherwise we have much to fear for her. I'm therefore absolutely determined to take someone into the house who—with a cook—will look after the household, keep everything in good order, keep the seamstress busy, supervise the laundry, in short do everything *Minna* herself did up to now. But it would be really terrible if we should take a strange person into the house while you, our own relative, have to work in a hotel. I have enough confidence in you to believe that you—if you make it a point of honor—can do just what is necessary in our house. Therefore I'm offering you the position—with Minna's approval—and under the following conditions: You'll receive a yearly salary of *200 francs,* and of course the appropriate presents as a member of the family. You'll get the room next to our bedroom, with the bed as it is. Otherwise you can do with your time what you like so long as you keep up the household in the way Minna has kept it up to now.

"If you agree to this, I'd like you to start on *New Year's* day at the latest: but then I'll also ask you to hire a good servant in Leipzig or in Dresden and to bring her along; we've already spoiled Cathrine so much that she is no good any more. Perhaps you've met a good maid: whatever she asks she'll get; I'll immediately send traveling money for the both of you. You must do everything possible to get a good maid.

"First answer me at once so that I'll know whether to look around elsewhere or not.

"Minna sends you her best regards! Farewell!

Your
Richard W."

253   Wagner, in Zürich, December 17, 1853, to Joseph Tichatschek in Dresden. (Page 152.)

254 A   Wagner, undated letter to an unspecified correspondent. (Page 142.)
   B   Caricature from the *Kladderadatsch*, Berlin, 1856. (Page 144.)

255   Notation in German by Miss Lermonda Burrell, daughter of Mrs. Burrell, taken from Natalie's dictation, according to the catalogue, as "a description of Wagner's style of dressing at Zürich." (Page 310.)

256   Two sets of autograph copies of the letters from Wagner to Theodor Uhlig (August 9, 1849, to December 24, 1852).
   The copies are in the hand of Uhlig's daughter Elsa. The first set is bound in cloth and has been inscribed on the flyleaf: *"Eigentümerin: Elsa Uhlig, 1886."* In the back is pasted a clipping, *"Ungedruckte Briefe Richard Wagners,"* signed O. F., probably from the *Allgemeine Musikzeitung,* 1885. The second set is stitched in four paper covers. (See Appendix B.)

257   Autograph certification in the hand of Elsa Uhlig.

"The undersigned herewith certifies that the letters directed by Richard Wagner to her father, Theodor Uhlig, originals of which have been for many years in the possession of the former's widow, Cosima Wagner in Bayreuth, have only three times been reproduced in word-for-word copies, one copy of which once came into the possession of Herr Nikolaus Oesterlein in Vienna and from him went to Eisenach together with the rest of the Wagner collection, while the two other copies are here and will be sold by me today to the firm Richard Bertling in Dresden. One of these two copies, in stiff covers, was once made for the writer of the letters and was returned to the undersigned, when the originals were transferred to the possession of the Wagner family.

Elsa Uhlig

"Dresden, 10th of September, 1897"

Enclosed is a specification of the copies and accompanying letters (258–262) drafted by the dealer, R. Bertling, as acquired by Mrs. Burrell.

258   Cosima Wagner, in Bayreuth, June 2, 1879, to Fräulein Elsa Uhlig in Dresden. (Page 608.)

259   Cosima Wagner, in Bayreuth, June 16, 1879, to Fräulein Elsa Uhlig in Dresden. (Page 609.)

260   Daniela von Bülow, in Bayreuth, March 4, 1883,[23] to Fräulein Elsa Uhlig in Dresden.

"DEAR FRÄULEIN!

"Accept the expression of our heartfelt thanks for your sympathetic words, in the name of our still ailing mother, Frau Cosima Wagner.

"Respectfully,

DANIELA VON BÜLOW"

261 A   Fräulein Eva Wagner, in Bayreuth, November 6, 1885, to Fräulein Elsa Uhlig in Dresden. (Page 609.)

B   Fräulein Eva Wagner, in Bayreuth, January 21, 1886, to Fräulein Elsa Uhlig in Dresden. (Page 609.)

262 A   Cosima Wagner, in Bayreuth, May 22, 1891, to Fräulein Elsa Uhlig in Dresden. (Page 609.)

B   Cosima Wagner, in Bayreuth, May 26, 1891, to Fräulein Elsa Uhlig in Dresden. (Page 609.)

263   *Allgemeiner Polizei-Anzeiger* (Police Gazette) of Saxony, 1851 and 1853.

In the earlier issue Wagner is listed among criminals wanted as "No. 190— Wagner, Richard, *Kapellmeister* from Dresden. Age, 38 years; middle stature, brown hair. Posted by the police deputation of Dresden May 16, 1849."

The issue of 1853 publishes a lithograph portrait of Wagner (first posted in 1849).

264   Wagner, in Zürich, May 1, 1854, to Hans von Bülow.

"DEAR HANS!

"The theater management in Wiesbaden write that they have been trying in vain to get the piano score of *The Flying Dutchman* from the music shops.

"Make this known as from me either by an order from my creditors, the lawyer Pleissner, or Hiebendahl or Kriete, who may take Meser to task only in case of some carelessness on his part, or have them arrange for a new edition in case the old one is sold out. And for heaven's sake have them set to work with a will.

"When am I to get news of you? Lazybones.

R. W.

Answer quickly!"

[23] Richard Wagner had died February 13.

265 A Wagner, in Zürich, June 3, 1854, to E. B. Kietz in Paris. (Page 197.)
B December 7, 1854. (Page 198.)

266 Draft by Wagner of an appeal from Minna to Botho von Hülsen. It is undated, but the catalogue gives August, 1854. (Page 145.)

267 Wagner to Minna, 1854.
A From Seelisberg, September 12, to Zwickau (postmarked Zürich, September 13).
B October 15 (no address given). (Page 320.)

268 Letter from Wagner, in Zürich, February 4, 1855, to Karl Franz Brendel.
Wagner asks the editor of the *Neue Zeitschrift für Musik* in Leipzig to do him the favor of sending a copy of the new second edition of *The World as Will and Idea* by Schopenhauer (published by Brockhaus) to his friend August Röckel in prison at the Schloss Waldheim.

269 Joseph Tichatschek, in Dresden, February 5, 1855, to Wagner in Zürich. (Page 152.)

270 Wagner, in London, March 5, 1855, to Minna in Zürich. (Page 349.)

271 Caroline Uhlig, in Dresden, March 10, 1854, to Minna in Zürich.
The widow of Wagner's friend Theodor Uhlig still bemoans her loss and worries about the upbringing of her small children. She has been left poor. Siegfried, who is beginning to walk, points with interest to the picture of his godfather, Wagner. (Page 608.)

272 A Printed program of a Philharmonic Society concert, in London, March 26, 1855, "Conductor, Herr Richard Wagner," offering Weber's Overture *"Der Frieschütz"* (*sic*), an air from Cherubini (Mrs. Lockey), Mendelssohn's Violin Concerto (Mr. Blagrove), Selections from *Lohengrin,* and finally, Beethoven's Choral Symphony, No. 9. Texts are included.
B Printed brochure (8 pp.) in English, translation of Wagner's analysis of Beethoven's Ninth Symphony, "written at Dresden in 1846."

273 Wagner in London, 1855:
A To Minna, in Zürich, April 5. (Page 349.)
B To Minna, in Zürich, May 11. (Page 355.)
C To Minna, in Zürich [undated]. (Page 352.)
D To an unnamed friend, June 16. (Page 357.)
E To Minna, in Zürich [June 26]. (Page 359.)

274 Letter from Wilhelm Fischarch, in Dresden, April 20, 1855, to Minna in Zürich.

Addressing her as "Dear, honored friend," Herr Fischarch apologizes for his delay in answering her letter about her husband's pardon.

"I wrote to our *Geheimrath* very soon after the receipt of your letter and asked him whether he had spoken to His Majesty. He answered me that it is very difficult, and no fitting occasion for it has as yet presented itself, but as soon as it is possible he will not let it slip by. In Geheimer Hofrath Zenker all of us have lost a good champion; he knew the theater conditions exactly, which knowledge we now very much lack. Everything goes strictly according to law and the established rules, which is at times quite difficult in our business. It is the same way with Richard's affair. In the meantime don't lose hope: strict as our King is in the letter of the law, he is just and lenient also; only he cannot pardon Richard alone—there can only be a general amnesty, which will certainly take place soon. I hope that the performance of *Tannhäuser* [will take place] in Berlin next fall, for on Wagner's order from London I sent the score to Herr v. Hülsen several weeks ago. A certain party will then, I hope, no longer spitefully object to the local performances, and this will finally contribute to the complete forgiveness of past sins."

The writer hopes that "Richard may return from London loaded down not only with honors, but also with English pounds."

275 Minna, in Zürich, 1855, to Wagner in London.
A April 25 (draft, finished in pencil). (Page 352.)
B May 4 (uncompleted letter). (Page 355.)

276 Wagner, in London, 1855, to E. B. Kietz in Paris.
A April 27. (Pages 348, 353.)
B June 21. (Page 358.)

277 Otto Wesendonck, in Zürich, May 19, 1855, to Wagner in London. (Page 356.)

278 Mathilde Wesendonck, in Zürich, January 19, 1855, to "Herrn and Frau Wagner." Acceptance of an invitation. (Page 361.)

279 Elise Schlik, in Prague, January 2, 1855, to Wagner. (Page 146.)

280 Note (without salutation or signature) identified by Mrs. Burrell as "Roeckel to Richard, January 1, 1855." This would have been Eduard, the brother of August, who was a music teacher at Bath, and friendly to Wagner on his English visit.

"The poet Puttlitz much regrets not having met you in my home; he was a great admirer of yours in Magdeburg and always rushed to the theater as a *Primaver* [senior student]; when Minna played he raved about her."

281 Wagner at Saint-Moritz, July 27, 1855, to Minna in Zürich. (Page 321.)

282 Letter from Alwine Frommann, in Schwalbach, August 3, 1855, to Minna.

"Although I am in Schwalbach, dearest Minna, you see this vignette [letterhead] of Schlangenbad, because I sat there and waited four weeks for *Lohengrin*! At last it was performed as a benefit for Kapellmeister Hoegen on the 25th, when I had taken my last bath and sailed on the wings of the wind to Wiesbaden. Although I had applied a long time before, I got only a poor ticket, but still a *ticket* in the overcrowded house where at last I again had the opportunity of hearing this music; sometimes it was indifferently, sometimes well done; at least Herr Perritti knew *what he was singing*. In spite of a poor chorus and other shortcomings, I was most deeply struck; and wherever I go, the impression still resounds in my soul. You know that some details of it are not according to my taste—I even am impudent enough to think that Richard, if he could hear it, would change or *abbreviate* some of it; but what are these little particles of dust compared with the marvelous impression of the whole and the *heavenly* details? No, I cannot tell you how full I am of it! Last Sunday it took all my strength not to go to the repetition, but I *had to resist*. I am longing for it again. But honestly, at the same time I learned to prize the Berlin Opera in spite of all its deficiencies. The basic elements, a good orchestra and good chorus, are worth something after all. There was also little poetic expression here in Wiesbaden, and orchestra and chorus were often horribly false. It is true, the best should be still better, but, as I said, to *sing* and to *play* in *tune* is not half bad!

[She describes the vicissitudes of the cure, in bad weather]

"In Schlangenbad there was infamous music, but when they played something from *Tannhäuser,* on my request, tears of joy filled my eyes. What magic sounds and ideas Richard possesses, to weigh me down and at the same time exalt me! But even with this mangling, and still they say there is no melody—no music!!

"They played nothing from *Lohengrin*; "that is too debatable and not for every-body"—Poor Richard, *Tannhäuser* is for everybody! . . . In Jena I saw *Liszt* when he conducted a concert. He was *amiable toward me,* but a slight veil hung between us; still I was very glad to see him. . . ."

283 Franz Lachner, in Munich, August 13, 1855, to Wagner. (Page 147.)

284 Frau Christine Planer, in Dresden, December 3, 1855, to her "children" in Zwickau.

Minna's mother writes of the father's impending death; a postscript to the letter tells that he has died that afternoon. According to a notation on the letter, he was born August 2, 1770, and so was eighty-five years old. She writes: "If I may only live quietly in your dear, faithful care, and end my days among you." And at the end of the letter: "I will now take care of myself for a short while, and then I will hasten into your dear arms; I know I am welcome."

285 Verse by Otto Wesendonck (?), September 25, 1855. (Page 363.)

286 Hans von Bülow [in Berlin], December 24 [1855], to Wagner.

Bülow was laboring in many ways in behalf of the *Meister,* as this letter shows. He was making a four-hand arrangement of the *Faust* Overture, and was to conduct it at the *Verein* concerts of Julius Stern in February. He was sparing no pains to further the chances of *Tannhäuser,* which Berlin was to hear at last: he paid a claque out of his own pocket, and despite his promise to Wagner to keep out of the newspapers, was to berate the "amusement-seeking" Berlin public for not understanding *Tannhäuser.*[24]

Liszt was in Berlin for the sake of appearances. He was entertained, even lionized, but had no further finger in *Tannhäuser* than parts of two piano rehearsals; and when he conducted a program of his own music at Stern's concerts on December 6, the critics all leaped upon him. All of them, Kossak and Rellstab included, despite Bülow's hopes here expressed, did the same with *Tannhäuser.* This in spite of a lavish production, a good cast, commendable handling by Dorn, and a public which, if they were not quite clear as to what *Tannhäuser* was all about, came in large numbers and were impressed. As Liszt expressed it, the applause was great, with only a "tail" of opposition, which gradually "curled itself into a cipher."

"HONORED FRIEND!

"Many thanks for the beautiful Christmas present with which you've made me very happy; I only regretted that none of the works carried the signature of the giver; for this I should have been especially grateful.

"But now I have to justify myself against your reproach that I did not answer you in detail. I wrote to you on *November 4* and on *November 11.* I can give the exact dates because since Berlin I've kept a record of all letters, those received and those sent. It seems that the second letter did not reach you. The arrangement of the *Faust* Overture is finished—I've followed your directions wherever possible. Liszt's presence necessitated such an endless amount of writing, running about, etc., that I had to stay in bed for eight days, sick from exhaustion and exertion. The Conservatory demanded that I make up for lost time, and so it is only now that I have the chance to make a neat copy. This could not be taken care of by a copyist because of the necessity of choosing between the variously arranged versions to which a great many individual passages gradually forced me. By New Year's you shall receive the fair copy which I promised.

"The first performance of *Tannhäuser* definitely takes place on Friday, January 4.[25] The King has personally attended to the scenery and costumes with special interest. All of us live in the greatest excitement because of it. I've given up my journalistic profession—mainly on your advice; actually nothing came of that but the most incredible exasperation and indignation of the entire Philistia. The reviewers have taken their revenge on Liszt; but the Liszt concert thus has beautifully paved the way for the success of the opera—just as the recent fiasco of the *Heinrich* Overture of Joachim had a most beneficial effect on your *Lohengrin* excerpts.

"The *Faust* Overture is not scheduled to be performed until the first concert of the second cycle—fortunately, Stern has realized that he does not understand it and cannot conduct it, and therefore he has given it to me. I don't think I've told you

[24] Berlin *Feuerspritze,* January 14 (see *Bayreuther Blätter,* 1901).
[25] The first performance in Berlin actually took place on January 7.

yet about my success as conductor and expressed my thanks to you for your previous efforts which you so unselfishly made.

"At the final concert of the first cycle the *Corolian* [*sic*] Overture will be played in order to soothe somewhat the aroused tempers and maliciously to provoke them to renew their subscriptions for the new concerts. I presume that you will permit me to reprint your program notes on the overture? It seems to me that this will also have a useful influence upon the *Faust* Overture. In Cologne and Leipzig, orchestra, conductor, and public seem to have made fools of themselves; I hope things will turn out better here.

"A few performances of *Tannhäuser* will help considerably. Kossak will probably switch to your side. Liszt personally has had a good influence on him. He'll be the more inclined to do it because, in view of my withdrawal, he has the chance to enter into lone opposition against all the remaining critics, something which he usually enjoys doing.

"Rellstab has been somewhat intimidated by me through a personal provocation, which he has evaded. Altogether the matter is not as bad as it appears on the surface. I hope to report to you soon about other things which concern me and which will probably interest you too, since you unwittingly played the main part in them.

"My address at present is: Wilhelmstrasse No. 49, since Liszt's daughters, who worship you, live with my mother, and there is no more room for me.

"Give my best regards to Carl [Ritter]—I'll answer him at New Year's. His letter to Joachim was forwarded to Hannover, where J. is at present spending a few months, on the day and hour it was received. Liszt is coming here for the first performance in order to pay Hülsen a courtesy. That Dorn is conducting is relatively fortunate. T. [Taubert] is too big a rascal, although Johanna denies it.

"Have you read Raff's pamphlet (*The Wagner Question*), and briefly what do you think of it?

"Once more, a thousand thanks. Take care of yourself!

                                        "Always
                                            your
                                    Hans v. Bülow"

287   Wagner to Minna (undated—the catalogue says "about 1855").
    A short note of greeting. He has received 1,000 francs from Frau Ritter and has heard from Liszt that *"Rienzi* can't be performed this winter."

288   "Praeger's Book"—notes by Natalie Bilz-Planer.
    These comments on Praeger's *Wagner as I knew him,* fifty-two pages of manuscript (undated), were written, according to the catalogue, "at Mrs. Burrell's request." A copy of the book in German translation is included. Mrs. Burrell would have been likely to send the book to Natalie on its appearance, in 1892, for her correction, and perhaps for what memories it might stir up. The book did not please Natalie. She makes a few minor corrections, but for the most part uses the text as a

point of departure for statements of her own—statements which show an even greater power of creative imagination than the since-discredited author himself. According to her, Mendelssohn did not carelessly misplace the score of the early symphony sent to him in Leipzig by Wagner, but did away with it in a spirit of "ugly envy," seeking thus "to discourage him" and "break the wings of his spirit." With "craft and cunning," this "slippery, subtle, sly Jew" committed the "infamy" in London of "deliberately disfiguring and mutilating" the score of the *Tannhäuser* Overture so that it was "hissed down at the performance and couldn't be finished." This information she claims that Wagner had from "the good, true Luders and Sainton" when he went to London and conducted the overture himself.[26]

Natalie extols Minna's "goodhearted" mother as the sympathetic friend of Wagner, and attacks Wagner's own mother for having treated her son with "blunt indifference from his first adolescence." Statements of this sort cannot claim further space here. They prove nothing except the personal bias of the writer. The bulk of this memorandum is concerned with Minna. Natalie is incensed that Praeger should "pass over in silence" so many of Minna's virtues. Natalie suspects the "influence of Mathilde and Cosima" here. But Praeger, on the contrary, met and took a special liking to Minna; he is kind and generous in his book, giving her at least her due place in Wagner's career.

289 Note from the Princess Karolyne Wittgenstein to Minna (by hand, undated). A note of thanks for flowers received on her departure.

290 Note from Emma Herwegh [1855], to Minna. "Emma," as she signs herself, is short of cash and wishes to borrow a few francs.

291 *Der Baldur-Mythos,* by Mathilde Wesendonck, poem (12 pp.), dated March 27, 1875, printed in Dresden. A presentation copy to Mrs. Burrell.

292 Mathilde Wesendonck, in Paris, January 11, 1856, to Minna in Zürich. (Page 364.)

293 Gottfried Semper, May 24, 1856, to Wagner. Semper is offended because, asked to a tea at the Wagners' without his wife, he had found other wives present. He was willing to overlook such omissions in the past when he was socially noticed on account of his title of *Hofrath,* and not for

---

[26] Mendelssohn conducted the *Tannhäuser* Overture in Leipzig in 1846, with complete incomprehension, to judge from the confused impression it seems to have made. Lindpainter introduced it to London at a concert of the New Philharmonic Society a year before Wagner's visit—May 1, 1855. It was no doubt poorly performed, at a time when Wagner's music was still an enigma to uninitiated conductors, Mendelssohn included. The London press was hostile—but the London press was then consistently hostile to Wagner. That the music made some impression on its audience is indicated by additional performances at Jullien's concerts. That Mendelssohn had any hand in a London performance, or sabotaged the parts, is of course pure fantasy.

personal reasons. Frau Wesendonck has erred on this point. But now he expects equal consideration for his wife. He concludes tartly:

"My view of women is about the same as yours, but I honor in them the husbands to whom they belong if they are my friends. Besides, my wife is as harmless as anyone could be, nor is she more stupid than another, although she has never learned stilted phrases about art, and in her modesty is not inclined to loud protestations of delight in a work of art which pleases her."

294   Wagner, in Mornex, 1856, to Minna.
    A June 18.
    B June 28.
Wagner, seeking relief from erysipelas, has found a retreat in a pension in this mountain resort near Geneva. He is contented with his cure, and finding rest and quiet. He reads, sits in the garden, or takes a mountain walk. His dog Fips seems to be his principal company.

295   Wagner, in Mornex, June 27, 1856, to Tichatschek. (Page 154.)

296   Telegram from Wagner, in Saint Gallen, November 26, 1856, to Minna in Zürich.

    "I'm not coming until seven-thirty, as you did yesterday."

297   Josef Tichatschek, in Dresden, December 20, 1856, to Wagner. (Page 155.)

298   Tax demands on Wagner for 2,000 francs for the year 1857 (dated Enge, September 10, 1857).

299   Natalie Bilz-Planer, in Leisnig, September 27, 1891, to Mrs. Burrell (registered letter).
    Natalie says that even while the Asyl was being prepared for the Wagners, close to the "magic palace" of the "arch she-devil [Oberteufelin] Helene Mathilde Wesendonck," Minna sensed that it was an "unlucky house, destined for misery and confusion."

300 A   (Undated.) Wagner to Minna.
    Wagner sends some money, in a note of greeting, and signs himself her "Geldmann."
    B   Wagner in Zürich, December 30 [1851], to Kietz. (Page 187.)

301   Cäcilie Avenarius, in Berlin, January 7, 1858, to Wagner in Zürich.

    ". . . Though many years have passed, my dear, best brother, since I have written to you, you must still believe that I have never ceased and will never cease to cling to you with all my heart, with unfailing eagerness. I lead here a somewhat prosaic and very quiet life, mostly among people whose ideals and ways of life are different from what I have been used to. But I should be ungrateful if I did not respond to the friendly attitude with which we are surrounded; and if I did not try to adjust myself to those to whom I owe much, and who are well inclined toward my husband and so also toward me. But at the same time I am often inwardly disconsolate, for among my associates I have almost no one who really shares our spirit and our ways of thought. So I am devoting my holiest, most beautiful hours to the thoughts of you, my splendid brother; I am reading the letters you wrote to Rosalie and mother in the old days, and I am reading the letters which I myself was happy enough to get from you, and then in my mind I go back again to those times when we were together in childhood as well as later on in Paris and Bellevue. How marvelous, too, for me, were the days when we could visit you in Dresden from Leipzig. Oh, what beautiful times those were! I could even despair at the thought that you are now *so far* away from us; for a journey to Zürich requires much planning. I must give my husband the credit for having urged me each year to visit you in Zürich, but I frankly confess that I was deterred by the expense, for it seemed extravagant in our circumstances to spend so much for my personal pleasure; it was not only this, but also the thought of being away from the children, since I was never able to leave them in good hands, for they are still tiny and helpless, and having once come to you I would hate to go away so soon again. . . . But this is certain, my best beloved brother: I will soon come to you if you want me. I must try to make it possible some time, for I should not like to die before seeing you once again and pressing you to my faithful, sisterly heart. In Leipzig, by association with your admirers, I kept on living mentally with you; but here such a privilege is cut off from me; I don't see anybody except people who neither know nor understand you well. . . . How will it be with *Lohengrin?* Is that also soon to be performed in Berlin? Who is to sing, and especially to act, the part of Lohengrin, I don't know; for although Formes has a good tenor voice, he is, after all, a little runt of a fellow, a poor actor, and without even a spark of spiritual understanding, so that his Tannhäuser is really offensive to me. I now hear and see very little of the theater, although it gives me the greatest pleasure.

"Unfortunately, I don't see any more of Albert and his family. I waited every day for a visit from Albert last fall, when I knew that the Wagners were back from their traveling, but neither he nor anyone of his family turned up. Then I learned through my sister-in-law, Louis's wife, that Johanna had been talking to her in the most disgraceful way, accusing me of a lot of things about which I know nothing whatever, even today. Presumably it had something to do with her intentions of marrying—I confessed to her, face to face, not behind her back, that I am not happy about it and can see no happiness in it for her. I told her this in no spirit of malice, but with hot tears of deepest sympathy; she herself was much moved by them. In a word, however the situation may be now, it is based on gross misunderstanding which could soon be corrected if I could see Albert. But I am so indignant at the vulgar way Johanna dared assail her father's sister that I'll have nothing to do with her and all the others and I'll not take the slightest step toward clearing things up.

Albert is a good fellow, but he is so henpecked by the females that he himself is no more accountable for his actions; otherwise, I should have been doubly offended that he can permit such vulgar babble; it is this that makes my husband so angry about Albert. When I first moved here, I had looked forward to seeing Albert; he was, after all, a member of our family here in the strange city, and when he sometimes talked to me about my father I felt much attracted to him; but I soon realized that an intimate association with the Wagners was not possible here, since you couldn't ever visit them at any other time than four o'clock in the afternoon. But sometimes it became five or half past five o'clock, before one could make that formal visit, and no sooner were you there than all of them ran off to the theater and we had to leave too. At that time they were very spoiled people, but they too perhaps will at some time experience the dark side of life. I am convinced even now the Wagners are having their troubles, since Johanna's voice has lost much of its metallic power; indeed her most beautiful tones, in the low and middle range, have begun to fail in vigor and resonance, although she tries to make up for it by her fine acting and is still even today the most interesting personality on the Berlin stage.

". . . Don't take it amiss that I have bothered you with such a long letter—but I thought you would like to hear about us and, besides, it is such a delightful feeling to speak to my most beloved and dearest brother again. If you want to give me great happiness, use a leisurely hour to write a letter to me, tell me how you are doing and what your dear good wife does, about whom I have heard that she is unfortunately not well at all. I am very anxious to hear from you. Hans Bülow has been here once, but he didn't meet me and never came again. I simply don't care much about Bülow, but how I would have welcomed the chance of getting news of you, my dear one! So I bid you a very tender farewell, darling brother, remain good to me, for I shall never stop loving you.

"Your faithful

CÄCILIE

"Heartiest greetings to your wife from me and Edward."

302 A   Wagner, in Strassburg, January 15, 1858, to Minna in Zürich. (Page 147.)
   B   Wagner, in Paris, January 29, 1858, to Minna in Zürich. (Page 321.)
   C   Wagner, in Zürich (according to catalogue, April 17, 1858), to Minna in Brestenberg. (Page 323.)
   D   Wagner, in Zürich, April 29, 1858, to Minna [in Brestenberg]. (Page 324.)
   E   Wagner, in Zürich, May 19, 1858, to Minna in Brestenberg. (Page 325.)
   F   Wagner, in Zürich, July 1, 1858, to Minna [in Brestenberg]. (Page 326.)
   G   Wagner, in Zürich, July 11, 1858, to Minna in Brestenberg. (Page 327.)
   H   (Undated) Wagner to Minna. (Page 325.)

303   Wagner to Kietz at Epernay, 1858.
   A   Zürich, January 12. (Page 199.)
   B   Zürich, January 14. (Page 200.)

C Paris, January 22. (Page 200.)
D Paris, February 1. (Page 200.)
E Brestenberg, May 8. (Page 201.)
F Venice, October 18. (Page 202.)

304 Wagner, in Zürich, March 16, 1858, to an unknown benefactor.

"Highly honored Sir!

"I thank you cordially for your continued considerate kindness toward me. Your last letter was forwarded to me several days ago from Paris, which I left some time since, and because I gather from it among other things that some money has again been deposited with you for me, I make bold to ask you to send me this small amount also. Unfortunately, I can always use money! If any more arrives for me— and may your kind messages hold this prospect—I ask you to continue to send it to me; for the time being I'm staying in Zürich again.

"Since our friend Liszt will already have arrived at your house by now, give him my warmest regards and tell him how much I envy you for having him with you. I'm too wretched to write much about it! I should be the more cheered when I hear so many gratifying things about him and his activities, and I hope that I may have induced you, honored sir, if he should not have the time to write—to do so.

"When I try to express in some measure my gratitude for your great favors, I can only refer to him [Liszt]. I asked you for these favors in his name, and may he now personally reward you for them; it is, unfortunately, completely beyond my power to reciprocate!

"With the friendliest regards and the assurance of my most grateful consideration,
I remain
your
most devoted
Richard Wagner"

305 Emilie Heim, in Zürich, March 30, 1858, to Minna Wagner in Dresden. (Page 322.)

306 Wagner, in Zürich, April 7, 1858, to Mathilde Wesendonck (by hand). (Page 369.)
The full text in the original language is here given:

"Madame Mathilde Wesendonck

"Soeben aus dem Bett.
"Morgenbeichte.

"Ach, nein! nein! nicht den De Sanctis hasse ich, sondern *mich,* dass ich mein armes Herz immer wieder in solcher Schwäche überraschte!— Soll ich mich mit meinem Unwohlsein, meiner daraus genährten Empfindlichkeit und Gereiztheit entschuldigen? Wollen versuchen, wie es geht. Vorgestern Mittag trat ein Engel zu mir, segnete und labte mich; das machte mich so wohl und heiter, dass ich am Abend ein herzliches Bedürfnis nach Freunden empfand, um ihnen an meinem inneren Glücke Antheil zu gönnen; ich wusste, ich wäre recht lieb und freundlich gewesen. Da höre ich, dass man in Deinem Hause meinen Brief sich nicht an Dich abzugeben getraute, weil De Sanctis bei Dir sei. Dein Mann blieb derselben Ansicht. Ich wartete vergebens, und hatte endlich das Vergnügen, Herrn v. Marschall zu empfangen, der sich den Abend bei uns niederliess, und mich durch jedes seiner Worte mit einem schrecklichen Hass auf alle De Sanctis's der Welt erfüllte. Der Glückliche—der hat sie jetzt mir fern gehalten! Und durch welche Gabe? Nur durch ihre Geduld. Ich konnt' es ihm nicht verdenken, es mit Dir so ernst zu nehmen; ein jeder nimmt es ja so ernst, der mit Dir zu thun hat! Wie ernst nehm' ich's doch! bis zur Qual für Dich! Aber warum pflegt sie diese pedantische Fessel? Was bedeutet ihr das Italienische? Nun, darauf konnt' ich mir bald antworten. Aber je besser ich's konnte, desto verdriesslicher ward ich auf den Lästigen; er verschwamm mir im Traum mit Marschall, und hieraus bildete sich für mich eine Gestalt, in der ich alles Elend der Welt für mich erkannte.— So ging's die Nacht fort. Am Morgen ward ich nun wieder vernünftig, und konnte recht herzinnig zu meinem Engel beten; und dieses Gebet ist Liebe! Liebe! Tiefste Seelenfreude an dieser Liebe, der Quelle meiner Erlösung! Nun kam der Tag mit seinem üblen Wetter, die Freude auf Deinen Garten war mir versagt; mit der Arbeit wollt' es noch nicht gehen. So war mein ganzer Tag ein Kampf zwischen Missmuth und Sehnsucht nach Dir; und wenn ich mich so recht herzlich nach Dir sehnte, kam mir immer unser langweiliger Pedant dazwischen, der Dich mir raubte, und ich konnte mir nicht anders gestehen, als dass ich ihn hasste. Ach, ich Armer! Ich musst' es Dir sagen; das ging nun einmal nicht anders. Aber recht kleinlich war es doch, und ich verdiente dafür eine gehörige Strafe. Welche soll es sein?— Nächsten Montag komm' ich nach der Stunde zum Thée, und will den ganzen Abend recht liebenswürdig mit De Sanctis sein, und französisch sprechen, dass alle ihre Freude dran haben sollen.—

"Was war das gestern einmal wieder für ein dummer Göthestreit? Dass Göthe für die philisterhafte Accomodation an die Welt hergerichtet werden konnte, beruht zwar schliesslich auf dem Misverständnisse des Dichters; dass es aber doch geschehen *konnte,* hält mich in wachsamer Bedenklichkeit gegen ihn, und namentlich gegen seine Ausleger und Zurechtmacher. Nun, weisst Du, liess ich auch gestern alles gelten, und namentlich Deine grosse Freude am Faust; aber endlich immer wieder hören zu müssen, der Faust selbst sei der bedeutendste Menschentypus, der bisher von einem Dichter geschaffen, das machte mich—(sehr thörichter Weise!)—bös. Ich kann hierüber bei den meinigen keine Täuschung bestehen lassen. Fausts Weltverzweiflung beruht im Anfange entweder auf Welterkenntniss,—dann ist er erbärmlich, wenn er sich beim Wechsel in die verachtete Welt mit grossem Aufwand hineinstürzt, und zählt in meinen Augen zu jenen Menschenverächtern, die dennoch ihr ganzes Leben über keinen Ehrgeiz kennen, als die Menschen zu täuschen und sich von ihnen bewundern zu lassen;—oder aber, und so wird's sein,— Faust ist eben nur phantastischer Gelehrter, und die eigentliche Welt hat er noch gar nicht durchgefühlt; dann ist er eben nur krüppelhaft unentwickelt, und man mag es gut heissen, dass er in die Lehre der Welt geschickt wird. Da wäre es denn nun aber besser, er lernte wirklich, was zu lernen ist, und zwar bei der ersten, so schönen Gelegenheit, der Liebe Gretchens. Ach, wie glücklich ist da aber der Dichter, als er ihn aus der Seelentiefe dieser Liebe heraus hat, um ihn eines schönen Morgens die ganze Geschichte spurlos vergessen zu lassen, damit er nun die eigentliche grosse Welt, die antike Kunstwelt, die praktisch-industrielle Welt, mit möglichsten Behagen vor seiner recht objectiven Betrachtung *abspielen* lassen könne. So heisst dieser Faust für mich eigentlich nur die versäumte Gelegenheit; und diese Gelegenheit war keine geringere, als die einzige des Heiles und der Erlösung. Das fühlt auch der graue Sünder schliesslich, und sucht das Versäumte recht ersichtlich durch ein Schluss-tableau nachzuholen,—so ausserhalbliegend, nach dem Tode, wo's ihn nicht mehr genirt, sondern nur recht angenehm sein kann, von dem Engel an die Brust genommen, und gar wohl zu neuem Leben geweckt zu werden.— Das heiss' ich nun Alles recht gut, und Göthe bleibt mir immer gleich gross als Dichter, denn er bleibt immer wahrhaftig, und kann nicht anders; auch mögen die Leute das Objectiv nennen, nämlich wenn das Subject nie dazu kommt, das Object, die Welt, in sich auf-zunehmen (was nur durch thätigstes *Mit*leiden geschehen kann), sondern dafür sich einzig das Object vorführt, betrachtend sich darin versenkt, durch Anschauung, nicht durch Mitgefühl (denn dadurch würde er die Welt selbst—und dieses Weltwerden des Subjects ist eben Sache des Heiligen, nicht des endlich zum Philistervorbild gewordenen Faustdichters); endlich freut mich auch immer wieder an Göthe, dass er das Missliche seines Treibens immer fühlte, und doch kein Behagen dabei fand, dass er sich das grosse Mitleiden so angelegentlich vom Halse hält,—und, wie gesagt, mir ist Göthe ein Naturgeschenk, durch welches ich die Welt erkennen lerne, wie durch wenig andre. Er that was er konnte, und—Ehre ihm!— Aber aus seinem jämmerlichen Faust einen edelsten Menschentypus machen zu wollen? Das kommt daher, dass es der Welt Angst wird, wenn es an die Tiefe des grossen Problemes des Daseins geht; wie lieb ist's nun den Leuten, dass der Faust da endlich abspringt, und sich entschliesst, da er nun doch einmal von der Welt nicht lassen will, sie zu nehmen wie sie ist. Ja, wüsstet Ihr nur, dass er von da an auch nur noch den Mephistopheles zum Führer hat, und macht euch darauf gefasst, ewig von dem Lügengeiste gequält zu werden, nachdem euch die holde Erlöserin, das herrliche Gretchen, schmerzlich erhoben den Rücken gewandt hat. Das wusste Göthe wohl; aber Ihr sollt's auch wissen!—

"Was fasle ich da für dummes Zeug! Ist's die Lust, allein zu reden, oder die Freude, zu Dir zu reden?— Ja, zu Dir! Aber sehe ich Dein Auge, dann kann ich doch nicht mehr reden; dann wird doch Alles nichtig, was ich sagen könnte! Sieh, dann ist mir Alles so unbestreitbar wahr, dann bin ich meiner so sicher, wenn dieses wunderbare, heilige Auge auf mir ruht, und ich mich hinein versenke! Dann giebt es eben kein Object und kein Subject mehr; da ist Alles Eines und Einig, tiefe, unermessliche Harmonie! O, da ist Ruhe, und in der Ruhe höchstes, vollendetes Leben! O Thor, wer sich die Welt und Ruhe von da draussen gewinnen wollte! Der

Blinde, so hätte er Dein Auge nicht erkannt, und seine Seele nicht in ihm gefunden! Nur Innen, im Innern, nur in der Tiefe wohnt das Heil!— Sprechen und mich erklären kann ich auch gegen Dich nur noch, wenn ich Dich nicht sehe, oder Dich nicht sehen—darf.—

"Sei mir gut, und vergieb mir mein kindisches Wesen von gestern: Du hast es ganz richtig so genannt!—

"Das Wetter scheint mild. Heut' komm' ich in den Garten; sobald ich Dich sehe, hoffe ich einen Augenblick Dich ungestört zu finden!—

"Nimm meine ganze Seele zum Morgengrusse!—

"d. 7ⁿ April 1858." [27]

307 Minna to Mathilde Wesendonck; draft for a letter (undated but obviously 1858. (Page 374.)

308 Princess Karolyne von Wittgenstein, April 23, 1858, to Minna.
The Princess expresses concern for "Frau" Minna's health, advises her to forgo a water cure, and cordially invites her to visit Weimar in Germany—the "homeland." "The *Meister* Liszt will be here, and you could surprise us so pleasantly with your visit."

309 Cläre Wolfram, in Chemnitz, June 3, 1858, to Minna. (Page 372.)

310 Wagner's signed, autograph manuscript, July 17, 1858, giving authorized cuts in *Rienzi*. (Page 117.)

311   Alwine Frommann to Minna.
A Jena, August 4, 1858, to Zürich.

Alwine Frommann, impecunious but helpful to Wagner through her employment as reader to the Princess Augusta of Prussia, was, by the evidence of these letters, devotedly attached to Minna. Addicted, like the Wagners and many of their friends to cure resorts, she has been trying Schwalbach and Schlangenbad, and is here content to "stay quietly" in her "little corner." She is genuinely concerned for Minna's health:

". . . I have certainly written to Richard in annoyance. He wrote with the best intention that I shouldn't miss any *entertainment* in his home, but owing to my ailing and nervous state I felt thoroughly offended and wrote that it would be an unbearable thought to me to go to a home where you are not present, and that my visit is meant just as much for you as for him. I also believed, since he wrote from Brestenberg, that you might have added a word about your wishing me to come, although you were away and five days were too short for such a trip. As it appeared later, I would not have been able to come anyway. So let's drop this. Give Richard many thanks for his letter on *Tristan and Isolde* in regard to the Grand Duchess.

[27] The date is not in Wagner's hand.

Well, if she and our Grand Duke should some day be rulers of Saxony! In Wiesbaden I at least heard *The Flying Dutchman* after having waited a long time for an opera, and there and then I was inspired with faith in Richard's music. It's important that he is not dismayed by *such* performances!!! The chorus is distinguished by singing permanently *forte* and out of pitch. The singers sang like bad Italians with stage effects—but since they did it in love and good faith, it was effective in a certain sense, although the Dutchman was in the costume of an Italian bandit and acted accordingly.

"I felt again what a divine spark must be in an opera which is not entirely ruined by such a performance; it even brought more response than the *Tannhäuser,* for instance, in Berlin. I am very anxious now to hear about the impression *Lohengrin* made in Vienna—let's hope also in Berlin? . . .

"I imagine that the Bülows are with you by now and am glad about it for Richard's and your sake. Many greetings to both of them and Richard. I must close, since I am not allowed to do too much writing (but I have partly finished my work after all) and I embrace you in spirit with warm wishes for your health and would like to say much which I don't say. God be with you!

ALWINE"

B   From Jena, August 9, 1862, to Reichenhall.

A chatty, inconsequential letter about cures and relatives.

C   From Berlin, April 12, 1863.

Since at this point Wagner and Minna had made their final parting, Alwine's letter shows her divided but continuing loyalty to them both:

"Unfortunately, dearest Minna! I can't tell you anything about Richard. Perhaps you will hear more. I don't see the Bülows because I am very busy, and she doesn't receive any visitors yet.[28] Your letter greatly afflicted me; the story about the cake is *so sad* and *so true* and so like my own experience! The renting of rooms is like any other profession; it ties you down; you can trust only a reliable friend; but I am very sorry that your dear visit here had such bad consequences for you! Your sweet bouquet has arrived and I felt *much* honored. Life is not easy, and three times more difficult *for you*. But there is no help, you have to see it *through*. How hard it became for me to accustom myself, after a regular, leisurely, and secure existence, to the earning of every penny, since I didn't want to become a burden to my brother, who had six children and his own worries. One of my hardest privations was the impossibility of making presents any longer; for many years I would not think of allowing myself the slightest extravagance, and even now I have to remind myself to be sensible; now the presents of the Queen which enable me to make gifts on my part are twice as much in value to me. As to your worries about the royalties, you may be reassured—Richard has long forgotten it nor has he done anything

[28] Cosima's daughter Blandine was born on March 20.

about them, but at that time it was better than nothing. Nor can you count on the 1000 th. with any certainty; this is one of those ideas which are always popping up in his mind, and which he imagines he can carry through.

". . . Richard has to care for you since you are entitled to it and are sick at that, but I want to advise you after all not to count on him too much, for his intentions are usually more generous than his ability to carry them out. But if he can give so much, save it, dearest, for the time when things become more hard for him; for considering his uncertain way of living, everything is chance and change.

". . . Getting older takes away so many of my friends, and one gets used to bearing privations with more humility when the powers of enjoyment are also decreasing, and a small corner, music, nature, and a few friends hold everything we can still give and enjoy. Be sure to write me soon, dearest, whether you have rented your room again, whether you feel all right, whether you were attracted by the theater. Is Frau Heber engaged? To be brief, everything which concerns you and interests me. My most heartfelt wishes are with you. My lilac tree is getting green, and likewise all the bushes in the Tiergarten; how beautiful Dresden must be! My dear Dresden, where I would like to live!

"Your

ALWINE"

D   Berlin, April 21, 1865.

This letter is largely a report of the anti-Wagner agitation already buzzing in Munich.

". . . I expected news from Munich; two cousins of my sister-in-law finally wrote at length about the newspaper articles, one letter to a friend here, the other to Jena to my sister-in-law. They are daughters of Prof. Thiersch, relatives of Liebig, both clever and very cultured, quite without personal relations with Richard; and they write that there was no definite reason or fact, but an intrigue, the causes and purpose of which they reveal by giving the names of the main persons involved who stirred up the affair and made use of it; Richard had offered them the reason for their lies by his whole behavior and proceedings. Almost all prominent strangers who had been called to Munich had similar experiences—Thiersch, Liebig, Heine, etc., all of them had to run the gantlet as a punishment when the King called out the aliens. Besides, I saw acquaintances who have a brother there, and got several details, e.g., that the *carpets,* since they were fixed to the floors, had to be *rented* together with a house from a baronet So and So; besides that, Wagner's dinners are very simple (he had eaten there). To be brief, the newspaper slander was more beneficial to him than *detrimental* in the city, and they could only wish that he himself would not act so as to injure himself in one way or another. The Queen and her court are quite against R., and many people believe they are serving her by intriguing against him.

"In any case it is fortunate that his malicious opponents cannot have the satisfaction of frustrating his plans from the very beginning; apart from what we already know, it would have been too bad for the sake of his works, if his musical enemies had triumphed. I have misgivings about *Tristan*; for much as I am convinced that there are divine passages in it, I have no liking for the plot, which, strange to say, had so often been used in the past.

"Here, *Rienzi* with Niemann was supposed to be given. But I don't know how matters stand since De Ahna, who was supposed to sing Adriano, fell seriously ill. It would be too bad if the performance had to be canceled. They ought to engage Johanna for this part and for Ortrud, for yesterday a terrible Azucena from Breslau sang in *Il Trovatore*. Niemann, though his limitations are known, is greatly appreciated and, considering the scarcity of tenors, is important for his ability to fulfill his role and not to become Herr Niemann in between. Recently *Cosi fan tutti* [*sic*] was given with somewhat altered text. What an abundance of charming ensembles! The arias are not very important, but some solo dances would be suitable in the kissing scene—of course, national dances with national melodies. Is Tichatschek in good voice again? I hope so; and when are the Schnorrs coming again?"

E   Berlin, December 4, 1865.
A short note; Alwine is grateful to Minna and Heine for some good turn they have done her.

F   Fragment (undated) containing nothing of consequence.

312   Wagner, in Zürich, August 9, 1858, to Joseph Tichatschek. (Page 155.)

313   Natalie Planer, in Zwickau, August 4 [1858], to Minna in Zürich.
This is the earliest autograph letter of Natalie in the Collection. She tells of the floods which have ravaged Zwickau, but her main object is to learn the details of the Wesendonck affair, broached in a "brief allusion" by Minna. Minna seems to have been extraordinarily uncommunicative. The storm, having broken four months before, had by this time run its course. On the very day of this letter, Wagner wrote to Liszt of his intention presently to leave Zürich, "never to return." Minna's answer to the following letter was to go to Zwickau:

"My dear good Minna:
"From your letter of July 27 I learned to my great regret that according to the brief allusion in your letter something rather bitter and harsh must have happened to you again, which makes me rather worried about you, my dear good Minna, and which I therefore regret with all my heart. Please, dear good Minna, give me your confidence again, and tell me, if it does not affect you too much, the details of the sad event which you merely hinted at in your letter. Has Richard perhaps got mixed up in debts or political affairs, or could that Bordeaux catastrophe have repeated itself? Charlotte too asks you to acquaint us with the exact circumstances, for Charlotte also sympathizes most warmly! and begs you to come to us in Zwickau; we shall take real care of you.

". . . Once more, my good dear Minna, accept from Tröger and myself the most heartfelt, sincere, and cordial sympathy, and be sure that we shall keep the strictest silence about everything you will tell us about the things that have happened to you, and that the request about more exact details is born of our sorrow and fondest sympathy for you, my dear heart, Minna; I have shared with you, dear Minna, many gloomy things that have befallen you, and have then always felt the most sincere compassion for you, you good Minna, so be convinced of that again, and believe me that I should be far happier if I could have turned this misfortune away from you."

314 Telegrams from Wagner to Minna in Zürich, August, 1858.

These five telegrams, sent in the course of a week while Wagner, having left Minna, was making his way to Venice, shows his anxiety for her health.

A Geneva, August 18, 6:15 P.M.

"Calm! Calm! Patience and courage! If you would only give in to me this time, leave duties to friends, and take a trip very soon! During the trip you will at once feel better. Vaillant says so too. It's hot here. Can't decide anything definite yet. Write soon or simply wire me tomorrow. Good night! RICHARD"

B Geneva, August 18, 8:00 P.M.

"How did you come through yesterday? Well? I'm tolerably well. Still uncertain. WAGNER"

C Geneva, August 20, 11:11 A.M.

"Sent letter to you yesterday. Keep up your courage. Be sensible. The end is soon. God be with you on your journey. RICHARD"

D Geneva, August 24, 2:10 P.M.

"Going to Italy tomorrow. Write to you today. Write to me general delivery Venice. RICHARD"

E Lausanne, August 26, 9:45 A.M.

"On my journey. Send you warm greeting. Just wrote a letter to you, Venice Monday. RICHARD"

315 Minna, Zürich, August 24 [1858], to Wagner. (Page 375.)

316 Frau Elise Fries-Steiner in Zürich, September 2, 1858, to "Frau Musikdirektor Wagner"; forwarded to Zwickau.

Frau Fries-Steiner was the wife of the first oboe of the Zürich orchestra, of whom Wagner thought highly.

"DEAR FRAU WAGNER.

"Since I shall unfortunately not be able to visit you once again before your departure, I want to express my thanks to you once more in writing for the nice souvenir which you sent me and which will always remind me of your kindness toward me. That I feel deeply about your tragic fate you must surely believe me; that's why I wish with all my heart that the future will turn out to be happier for you than you imagine it at this moment, and that you may still have happy days to look forward to. To be sure, you will always look back with sadness to the time you last spent in Zürich; but time, even if it does not heal your grief, will certainly alleviate it.

"Farewell then, my dear, esteemed Frau Wagner! Do not leave Zürich in too embittered a mood; for I assure you that everyone who knows your fate has sincere compassion for you. My dear husband also sends his deepest regrets and his best wishes. Even when far away, think of your sincerely loving and and devoted

FRAU ELISE FRIES-STEINER

"If I can be of any service to you at all or perhaps get you something, even if you are away, I ask that you use me as you see fit; I shall always be glad to be at your disposal."

317 A   Minna, in Zwickau, September 11 [1858], to Frau Cosima von Bülow.
    The von Bülows, not long married, had visited the Wagners at Zürich.

"MY DEAR FRAU VON BÜLOW!

"Accept my heartiest thanks for your kind and friendly lines, which reached me in the midst of my work, or rather amidst the despoiling of our pretty little home in Zürich. If this were in the slightest degree my fault, I would be inconsolable for life. Since a week ago, sick and much depressed, I have been sitting in the home of my sister and brother-in-law Dr. Fried. Tröger. Being an excellent physician, he examined me the day after my arrival and found at once the reason of my illness. Now I am under his care but have to stay here for at least four weeks if any good is to come of it.

"But I must refuse with thanks your friendly invitation, my dear Frau Cosima. Besides all the troubles which I had to go through just before leaving Zürich, the exertions made me worse and so thoroughly depressed that I would expect only relatives to receive me in their home. Therefore I shall not go to Dresden until November, although the Tichatscheks have repeatedly invited me to come to them at once. My nerves are so shattered that I am unable to listen to music, least of all that of Wagner, which I before had loved more than anything else in the world. You have perhaps heard directly from my husband that he is in Venice with Ritter; he writes that he likes it very much and has sent me as a birthday present a map of that water-bound city, along with a tiny Venetian gondola. May he long enjoy it there, and may the new impressions inspire him in his work, from which he has been kept for such a shamefully long period.

"Pardon me, my friend, and remember me to your husband!
"The most cordial regards and kisses to you

from your faithful

MINNA WAGNER"

B   The gondola mentioned in the above letter (missing in the Collection).

318   Frau Julie Ritter, in Tharand, October 30, 1858, to Minna in Berlin.

"HONORED LADY

"Your esteemed lines have helped me out of an embarrassing situation; your husband had written to me to address the money to you in Zwickau, but at the same time I heard here by chance that you were at present in Berlin—thus it was very pleasant for me to see my doubts removed and to find out with certainty where you were staying.

"After subtracting an advance payment, the money amounts to 270 thaler, which are herewith enclosed.

"We heard with pleasure that you are thinking of spending some time in Dresden, where it will be a pleasure for us to see you again after so long.

"My daughters send their best compliments.

"Respectfully yours,

J. RITTER"

319   Wagner [in Geneva, August, 1858] to Minna [in Zürich]. (Page 328.)

320   Emma Herwegh, in Zürich, September 29, 1858, to Minna in Zwickau. (Page 329.)

321   Wagner, in Venice, to Minna, 1858.

A   October 10.

A reference to Tröger, and to Dresden as a prospect for Minna, indicates that she is still at Zwickau.

"O YOU WICKED WOMAN!

"I shall be really happy when I know that you are resting in Dresden. Really being by oneself is so good and necessary for both of us. I feel it myself in every unnecessary word I have to utter. But how much more in your case! That you'll stay with the Rottdorfs again is really not without significance: it was a good idea on your part. The little house has a friendly and yet lively location, and only pleasant memories can become associated with it. Really, you good poor Mutz, I don't blame you if you consider the short time we lived there as your happiest. See that you find rest there, relaxation for your overexerted energies; live in memories, refresh the present with them, and so strengthen yourself for a quiet, even—I dare prophesy it to you—happy future as the end of our long life of wandering. You'll feel at home with our old faithful acquaintances; I wrote to Papa Fischer yesterday and sent greetings to the *Oberseergasse*. I also wrote to Frau Ritter to receive you hospitably. Eventually you'll also bring yourself to go to the theater, and even to see my operas. Then they shall no longer be memories, but harbingers of an early and better future. I now have the peace and quiet to take stock of myself, fully and decisively, and my future is decided in so far as I have only one more wish in my life which I intend to strive for: artistic activity. Never again shall I decide to accept a permanent position; but, as soon as I'm pardoned by an amnesty, my aim will be to settle down, however modestly, with you and my little household spirits [*Hausko-boldchen*] in a large city of Germany where there are good and sizable artistic forces with which I can perform my works from time to time. Then perhaps I'll be more sociable than I ever was because I shall have become very quiet and given up all demands on people. It is then only a matter of which city is selected—Berlin, Vienna, or Dresden. This I must as yet leave undecided. But such a city it must be. Now, in solitude, I still want to complete my new work: it shall and will prepare the way for my permanent return to Germany: by the middle of next year, God willing. Until then, my good Mutz, get a good rest; take care of yourself, and— please! please! don't leave anything undone to make yourself comfortable. I'll gladly provide for everything you need. If Frau Hänel must be paid at once, do so; it is all right. Frau Ritter is sending you—the end of this month, I think—a thousand francs. I don't attach any importance to the babbling of Frau Elise; here it isn't a matter of the Wagner parasite, but of the Ritter family with their mother at the head who feels honored and happy to be able to serve me. To be sure, it will stop some day, but, according to her express desire, not until a pension of at least an equal amount will be paid me: for they see for themselves that, despite my receipts, I need something steady, permanent. In general, don't let any side influence you with any coaxing or persuading: be assured that no soul living on earth is friendlier to you than your husband! Believe this firmly and surely!— And have confidence in the good Pusinelli: I have great respect for his friendly concern and his knowledge. I shall write to him that he should take you completely under his wing so that I'll find a really healthy and invigorated wife when I knock on the little cottage of happiness in Dresden where we want this time to embark upon an untroubled, peaceful old age. Yes, yes!— I know what I still have to do in this world: no one shall suffer on my account, and my art shall edify and uplift every one.

"Now don't forget to write to Frau Ritter (Zwingerstrasse 3), where you'll be staying at the end of the month; for I've already written to her to send the money to Zwickau. Then, when you go to Dresden, be sure to take Jacquot along, you heartless woman! Travel *first* class, and then you'll be able to find a place for the bird!

"Bülow's address is: Anhaltstrasse No. 11. About myself I'll write you more the next time. The grand piano has been here for three days and gives me great happiness. Unfortunately, I had to post a bond of 258 francs in Zürich, besides the freight, in order to be able to bring the instrument back again free of duty. But now I have given orders to have this permit set aside since I am not seriously considering taking the grand back to Switzerland. The money will be put to some other use.

"I have not made any money here so far, but I have received various promises for *Rienzi* so that I'll soon be in a position to send money to Zürich. But—as I said— about myself some other time. Give my best regards to Cläre and Wolfram, and my best wishes to the young couple. More for them too, the next time! For today, fare-well, good dear Minna! Be calm!

"YOUR RICHARD"

B   November 20.

"MY DEAR MINNA!

"Tomorrow morning Karl [Ritter] is leaving for a visit to Dresden in order to congratulate his mother on her birthday on the 25th of this month. You can well imagine that I am taking the opportunity to congratulate you on our wedding day— even though you've had a lot of trouble with your bad husband. Karl has promised me to arrive on the 24th, if possible, and to go to see you at once in order to bring you my wedding gifts. Take them also for Christmas presents. It is very difficult here to send anything, and every time it takes a thousand errands and export duty on top of it. Karl shall smuggle it out. May God give him his blessing for it.

"Well, then, a coat, all my own choice, specially made and the material selected. I hope it will take your fancy. You can't imagine anything more substantial and fine, and yet it looks discreet. The hood looks very nice; but you can also take it off if it is too hot for you; for that reason it is merely attached. It looks very well even without a hood.

"And now the black satin dress I owe you—this time turned out to be a little more substantial than its predecessor. *This* I shall never ask to use as lining for a dressing gown.

"Well, if only I've done it the way you want it. At least, dear Mutz, recognize the good will to make you happy. Don't spoil this hope for me and accept the presents in good grace!

"Karl has found a photograph which also shows my palace [photograph enclosed]. You will see my three windows and the bay window quite distinctly. Watch it sometimes, and I'll be looking out of it.

"—Today, on St. Mark's Square, a man again offered me a beautiful little dog. Only with difficulty could I part from it, and already the idea occurred to me to ask Karl to take it along for you. But it would sadden me too much to cause the good faithful Fips grief through such an addition to the family: certainly he would grieve if he were to get a successor in the house. As far as I'm concerned, I miss a little dog very much; and if for any reason I had believed or feared that I would not be coming back to you in the near future, I would have bought the little fellow for myself today. But you can see from that, dear Minna, how definitely I hope and how firmly I assume that I'll be with you again beginning next summer; *for that very reason* I'm not getting a dog so that Fips won't be unhappy.

"I have nothing more to say to you today except that my recovery has been progressing rapidly. I'm in a really excellent mood for composing, and therefore I'm taking as good care of myself as I can in order to preserve it; for so much now depends on the completion of my work, in fact, the entire change in my existence. With *Tristan*—as you know—I return to Germany.

"So take good care of yourself too; that's the most important thing with which you can make me happy. Pusinelli wrote to me giving me exact information about your illness and also an extraordinarily comforting consolation and real assurance, so that I see how understanding and sincerely concerned he is about your recovery. Be sure to follow his directions obediently! I entreat you!

"And if you want to give me a present too, then get me—at Kressner's—*genuine Parisian* snuff, two pounds. And you could also give me a nice cigar case for small cigars, as I always smoke them. Karl will bring it along.

"And now write soon; keep yourself quiet, have hope and confidence!

"Accept a thousand greetings and congratulations from your

RICHARD

"Karl is also bringing you the score of my *Rheingold*. You should keep it for the time being until I write you where you should send it."

321 C   December 20.

Minna has been short of funds and has offended Wagner by the way she has referred to it. Wagner, still concerned about her health, gives her instructions about how to take care of herself, also describing ailments of his own.

". . . Just be patient, my good Mutz! The worst is certainly behind you! If you don't improve noticeably in the course of the next summer, the two of us will look for a really beautiful, mild climate for the winter, for the Dresden climate doesn't seem to be the right one either. I liked Dresden for your sake, especially because I knew that you like it, that acquaintances and diversions would best help you get over the present difficult time. Now you'll want to and have to stand it there a while longer; you won't find things much better anywhere else either, unless we go straight to Palermo. But only one thing—for God's sake don't deprive yourself of anything; rather let me know at the right time what you need, and don't let yourself be urged by me so that you have to come around with a lament like that!

"Now something more about the future, which my last letter especially—as I confess—treated perhaps somewhat excitedly. The clipping you enclosed today was very pleasing to me, and I do believe that there's something to it. One must not expect much, in fact almost nothing; but one must not close the door entirely on good fortune and see everything black. Thus I received a letter a few days ago from Ed. Devrient in which he reports to me that he wishes to give *Tristan* on the birthday of the Grand Duke, on the 5th of September. (What do you say to that?) I should give my consent so that the Grand Duke may take all the steps necessary to effect my visit to Germany at this time. I wrote to him immediately to approach the Grand Duke most urgently in my name in order to find out whether I would get the permission or not. I shall first wait for this, and take further steps according to what I hear. If the G. D. receives the definite confirmation from Dresden, I admit that for the time being I would be satisfied. Once I am in Karlsruhe, I'll manage the rest soon; from there I would probably go to Dresden to settle the whole matter—if it should still be necessary. But if the G. D. receives a definitely negative answer, I'll then be free to start the matter in the way I discussed recently and to go to the Minister of Justice, in which case I would only have to apply for safe conduct to Dresden and back again in order to be able to choose exile in case I am convicted and sentenced to a disgusting prison term. . . .[29]

"As for you, my good Minna, I don't want you to get any more excited about the matter; for it is, after all, exciting for you too. I don't want you to go to the minister yourself: I feel myself how violently your heart would beat. That is to be avoided. Have a little more patience, dear Mutz. It will all come out all right, one way or the other, and in any case we'll have each other again in the summer and I hope we will know then *where* to make our nest. Now be a little carefree. Above all, wish me undisturbed health so that I can finish *Tristan*. Everything now depends on that, and therefore I must make every effort not to be impeded in that by anything. When that is completed, the world will suddenly look quite different for both of us. Today I had to laugh. The Breslau director informed me of the success of *Rienzi* at his theater and added the urgent *request* to let Breslau have the *first* performance of *Tristan*. That is now the *sixth* theater which wants this honor: Karlsruhe, Weimar, Munich, Prague—and Vienna. *Lohengrin* is to be produced in Berlin the beginning of January. We'll see. Don't you want to go there to see it? But—not third class, please!—"

D   December 25

"Well, you good Mutz? I kept thinking that I would get a letter from you yesterday or today. Has my letter before last about the amnesty matter given you much trouble? Has it worried you? I can almost believe so when I remember that I didn't quite accept your advice. But to me the matter has a very ugly appearance: I confess that it fills me with terrible bitterness when I think about the hardheartedness and petty smallmindedness with which this king treats me after I wrote to him and finally to his son in such a way that it should have moved or even shamed him. I openly confess to you that I am disgusted to the depths of my soul by the thought that he paid no attention to me at all, that I did not get a word in reply, and that one expects me to endure with my spirit unharmed the whole dishonorable unpleasantness of two months of examinations, confrontations, and investigations just to show that I did not hold myself above any other shyster or bankrupt lawyer who at that time played the revolutionist. Can you blame me for that? Isn't it a low trick which they want to play on me, and isn't it worth while assuring myself first whether I'll really accomplish anything by it? I'm repeating these arguments to you once more in order to inform you about my mood because it might otherwise grieve you that I was not better prepared to act eagerly on your reports. On the other hand, it is certain that the matter must be decided within half a year. I just can't leave my poor wife without a definite domestic conjugal shelter. No! By then we must know exactly *where* we're going to settle down; and in order that it may last for the rest of our lives everything must be definitely decided by the authori-

[29] The end of the page is cut off (a scissors cut). Could this mean the removal, by Minna or Natalie, of an additional reference by Wagner to his Paris imprisonment. (See page 88.)

ties. Just let me finish *Tristan* first, because too much depends on that, and a new interruption to which I'm now so sensitive could easily be fatal to its completion. But wait, perhaps the rotten thing will come out all right after all. These days, I suspect, the Grand Duke of Baden will consult Dresden again: if there is a trace of nobility in this King, everything combines to induce him to be considerate toward me. In this respect the enclosed notice about a performance of *Lohengrin* in Vienna which, as you can gather from it, the entire Austrian court and Prince Albert of Saxony attended was not unimportant to me. The paper was sent to me from Hamburg (*Theaterzeitung*), and I cut out the clipping for you. In a Dresden paper the *beginning* would surely look quite good.

"Well—just let us wait for what the new year brings to us poor, sorely-tried married people. I don't mean by that that I want to give up my intention of writing the letter to the Minister of Justice. On the contrary, I consider it very important. But I hope I'll soon get news from Karlsruhe and can then make better arrangements, all according to what the success is there. Then I'm thinking of asking the minister, with all the persuasiveness at my command, simply for an endorsement of my earlier petition to the King for a pardon, that is, for his support of a full amnesty. Only if this should once more fail completely, would I ask for safe conduct in order to undergo the examination in Dresden. So—doesn't it *have* to succeed? Don't you think so too?

"Courage then! A little more patience—and good hope!

"Now I still have something extraordinary to tell you about. Well—an offer for an engagement in New York [Neuyork]. Through a perod of eight months beginning next September an excellent opera enterprise is to be established there, and my operas are to be produced for the Americans with fabulous magnificence. Johanna is inclined to accept the offer also. I should merely send my conditions. God, how I have waited for this happiness! In the meantime, however, I'll have to see that I can gain some advantage from it so that they get the operas properly through me and I get something substantial out of it. If I were to reject it outright, that, too, would be cut off. So I explained that they should surely realize that only the assurance of very considerable advantages and the acquisition of a small fortune could induce me to assume the difficulties of such an engagement; that's why I first awaited a definite explanation as to what guarantees they could offer me? Now I shall see what they answer. If they are nice about it, I'll pretend to be very happy; but I'll make it clear that unfortunately the doctor has forbidden me to make the trip to America and to stay in New York. Then I'll catch them with the fee for the operas and recommend Klindworth to them. You see what a trickster I am! Perhaps I'll also use this offer to scare the Saxon Minister of Justice and to make it clear that, if they don't pardon me, I'll be forced to leave Europe forever though Germany is the natural soil for my art. We'll soon see!

"Now, my good Minna, you have nothing, nothing further to do than to take very good care of yourself, to live on schedule for your health, so as to give me the great, deep, and fervent happiness of finding you somewhat improved and recovered, quiet and at ease, when we finally have each other again. Then you shall have my best and most loving care and affection as long as I live!

"My leg is better after all; [30] today I walked for nearly an entire hour. I can certainly speak of luck: foreigners, especially those accustomed to mountain air, are here by the sea—you heard correctly—exposed to very bad and lingering ulcers. So I'm completely quiet and happy. Now I'll probably soon get news again about how you are. O God! if it is only good news. That always makes me very happy and serene!

"Farewell! Sleep! Sleep well! And always trust your good

RICHARD

"Your quite extraordinarily good portrait is lying on my left as I write. It always looks at me so goodheartedly and softly, so questioningly, and a little worried— No, Minna! Don't worry. Everything is all right! Be happy!

"Well, I hope Christmas has brought you a little something from me. May you have very little need for the night lamp. But if you do need it when you wake up, just think: he is, after all, a good fellow! Then you'll fall asleep again soon. I've also been very sleepless lately. I haven't been able to sleep any night before two or three o'clock in the morning. Yes, yes!—"

322 Adelheid Marschall von Bieberstein, in Zürich, November 3, 1858, to Minna in Dresden.

Marschall von Bieberstein had been a schoolmate of Wagner, a fellow revolutionary in Dresden, and, later, a fellow exile in Zürich. Frau von Bieberstein commiserates Minna, hopes for a reconciliation between the Wagners, and envies her her return to Dresden. The most interesting part of this letter is a reference to Mathilde Wesendonck, to whom the writer had paid a "condolence visit" on hearing of the death of her small son Guido:

". . . Frau W. received me, and—I say it in all sincerity—I felt compassion when I saw the deterioration and deathly pallor of this young woman in the midst of her luxurious surroundings. She was deeply shaken and dissolved in tears—we only talked about the momentary grief, and, explaining her sorrow, she mentioned the *storms* of last summer. She reproached me for having stayed away so long and added that recently she has not visited any of Wagner's friends on principle so as not to be suspected of drawing them into her circle. I left with a very gloomy impression of her and had the feeling that there is no real happiness on earth, for where it could be so, people violently plunge themselves into ruin. All talk has been silenced—your lovely little villa looks down into the valley dark and empty—at one time they were saying that the Köchlys who had to leave Flora behind would move in—but it doesn't seem to be true. The death of the child now gives the W.'s the most natural cause to withdraw entirely for this winter, and this is in accord with their feelings in any case."

[30] In his last letter he had complained of a swollen vein.

323 Wagner, in Venice, December 9, 1858, to Natalie.

"DEAR NATALIE!

"I thank you very much for the message, and answer you at once so that you can order the night lamp and clock immediately. Have the words *'Er ist doch ein guter Mann'* engraved around the clock or at least in such a way that it can be seen by the light of the luminous dial. That will give the poor woman pleasure when she cannot sleep at night. I'll send you *10 thaler,* and you'll shortly get the money from Berlin, where I'll give orders also to send it to Fräulein Rottorf. If it should not arrive in time for the clock, ask Fräulein Rottorf to lend you the money.

"Furthermore, I ask you to let me have frequent news—secretly—about Minna's condition. I'm very much worried about her, but hope for improvement when she adjusts her mind to some degree. For God's sake, avoid everything that might irritate her in the least. I, too, am firmly resolved to do that. Do the right thing, and I shall not fail you! Goodbye!

"Your
RICH. WAGNER"

324 Hermann Müller, Schanzengraben, December 29, 1858, to Minna in Dresden.

The following letter shows that Hermann Müller, a fellow revolutionist of Wagner, and a co-patron of water resorts, was Minna's friend as well:

"MOST HONORED FRIEND!

"I received your cordial lines on Christmas eve in the home of Frau v. M.; how could I better express the joy which you gave me than by thanking you for them still in the old year, even on the threshold of the new one.

"Both of us during these holidays have lived more in the recollection of bygone times than in the present, though you who have suffered for several years may have had more peace of mind this season than last Christmas on the Lake of Zürich. I need scarcely assure you how aware I am in these days of the friendship and kindly care with which you knew how to bring some happy moments to the unhappy exile in the great Christian Festival of Peace. In the last year my associations have been confined to the few families known to you because of the almost complete cessation of other relations; your departure left a great void in my life. The dear good Frau v. M. now means 'Zürich' for me.

"So you may not wonder, dear friend, when I tell you that I am about to weigh anchor and to move to Berne as General Secretary of the East and West Railways.

". . . Communicate this news to the Heines, Tichatscheks, and to all the old friends, please, who have not yet entirely forgotten the 'red miller.' [31]

". . . I only wish that I could have enjoyed *Rienzi* together with you. I can imagine that the Tichatschek of today behaves quite differently from the one of 1842. These must have been evenings abundant with wonderful recollections for you.

[31] Hermann Müller.

Maybe we both had tears in our eyes, for how much from the memories of sixteen years passes through our vision!"

325   [Minna] in Chemnitz, October 28 [1858], to Wagner.
       This letter, unsigned, is probably a draft.

"DEAREST RICHARD!

"This will be my last letter to you from here. A week from today I shall be traveling to Dresden with dog, bird, and Natalie, whom I expect here next Tuesday with Jacquot, and we shall immediately move into my little flat with the old Fräuleins Rottdorf, 9 Marienstrasse, which suits me very well. Good Pauline Tichatschek wrote me a few days ago that she had my little apartment fixed up quite prettily; she had had it supplied with all necessary implements for my convenience, even with some kitchenware, which I probably shan't need, since I don't care to do any cooking for myself alone. I was really very pleased with the good lady; at least one person cares for me. I shall see whether I may keep the furniture during my stay there, for it would, of course, save me great expense if I needn't have my things brought from Zürich. I had written to Pauline Tichatschek that I would have my belongings sent, and forced her to betray the surprise she had prepared, which made me very sorry for her sake.

"I was pleased and surprised to receive such a quick answer to my letter; here I must be considerably closer to you than in Zwickau, for there I often received your letters only on the sixth day, while here they come on the fourth day. The dear lady also wrote me that the forgotten 50 louis d'or would be sent to you from Hanover; the intendant and the musical director were present again at the ninth performance, for which no tickets could be obtained after ten o'clock in the morning. The directors would be real fools if they should throw away their chance of good profits by not performing *Rienzi*. You are right to tease me about it; with my extreme modesty I really felt funny myself on mentioning the gift of *Rienzi* only jestingly, so I was glad that you took it that way; I'll not do it again.

"And now, my dear Richard, your enclosure to Clärchen and the threat to write to Mathilde oblige me to assure you most solemnly that the good creature is innocent; she does not know anything about the last affair; she had written to me while I was still in Zürich, quite shocked, and with the most fervent sympathy for us, whether it was true that we were going to be divorced (from which may God ever protect me) because you wanted to marry a rich and very courted baroness; a certain Frau Kälberle, who had spent the summer in Zürich, had spread this pretty news in Dresden. I wrote at once to Mathilde that nothing of this ugly gossip was true, which made her most happy; she knows nothing more, so she will be very astonished to get a letter from you. Anyhow, my dear Richard, you must not imagine that the true reason for your departure from Zürich is not known; don't consider what I tell you about this matter as a reproach; I myself appear to people far more quiet than I am inside: at the utmost a tremor may be perceived in my voice, but certainly I shall not give away anything; even to Clärchen I would not have admitted anything if she had not already known everything before my arrival. Her eldest son had brought the pretty tidings from the singing club; I had to tell you this in answer to your unjust accusation, though I should have liked to keep it from you. Some day, when the time comes, I shall tell you the news from Dresden, but as you will see it did not come from Mathilde at all. Believe me, I have no external cause to tear my wounds open; people see that quite well and avoid talking about it. These [wounds] bleed freely in any case; they were too deep; you may even believe that I pray God to make me forget them, but unfortunately it has been in vain so far; when once they shall have healed I also shall be saved. You have made me very miserable by all the offenses and insults which I have had to suffer on account of your liaison. You know very well that no word against you nor anything had passed my lips as to *that former* Bordeaux affair, but then I was not made to suffer as much as during the last one."

326 Mathilde Wesendonck, in Berlin, May 13, 1891, to Mrs. Burrell in Paris.

This letter (written in German) is a sample (the only one in this Collection) of a long correspondence between the two ladies. Literary and musical subjects drew them together. The English lady was in worshipful awe of the inspirer of Isolde, although she was tactful and reticent about direct questions on Mathilde's relations with Wagner. She called her *"Freudenbringerin."* The correspondence ceased not long after this date because of Mrs. Burrell's failing eyesight and her neuralgic attacks.

Mathilde here writes on the subject of her eyes:

"So you have had trouble with your eyes? But you must protect and take care of those dear, precious eyes as you would a jewel, they must see as brightly and clearly as they always have, a reflection of your very own nature and being!" Mathilde mentions a talented new conductor from Darmstadt, just now busy rehearsing a new performance of *Lohengrin*—Felix Weingartner.

"Siegfried Wagner," she writes, "is studying here in Berlin at the Polytechnikum and visits me often. His judgment is far ahead of his age; I find his manner most agreeable; we understand each other. He will interest you too!"

327 Natalie Bilz-Planer, in Leisnig, March 2, 1891, to Mrs. Burrell.

This is a description of Minna's mistreatment at Zürich during the Wesendonck crisis, the illness for which Wagner sent her to Brestenberg, and her visit to Zwickau following this. The letters in the Collection within this period, including some by Minna herself, show Natalie's account to be full of exaggerations and misstatements. She writes that Wagner was habitually in a "good humor" until he paid a call upon the Wesendoncks, whereupon "he became despondent—and showed an extravagant feeling of unhappiness." This "sudden change" worried Minna. "Even his two Swiss friends,[32] so faithful and self-sacrificing in times of need, who helped Richard so readily when he came to Zürich as a poor refugee, and who provided him with the

[32] Sulzer and Baumgartner.

means for his livelihood in the kindest and noblest manner—even they noticed this very strange behavior, for it often happened that they called for us and went along to the Wesendoncks. The older one especially, who, as an intelligent and highly educated young man, held the highest honorary post as state official of the Canton of Zürich, had specially kept an eye on Richard as well as on Mathilde. For it was this young man who said at the time, after the Bordeaux love affair which was comparable to a champagne intoxication, that at Wagner's age [33] it is unfortunately to be feared that such a love affair will be repeated far more intensely and seriously." These two saw through Mathilde as a "scheming, flirtatious creature," thereby causing Wagner to drop them in a "rough and unfriendly manner." On moving to the Asyl, Wagner "banished Minna from his bedroom for the first time in their twenty-two years of marriage." Mathilde, wearing a "charming, elegant morning suit," often visited Wagner in his upstairs apartment, while the servants observed and Minna rested on her "dignity and pride." Coached by Mathilde, Wagner said to Minna, "in the roughest and rudest manner: 'We must separate; Mathilde will no longer tolerate that we stay together'" [!]. Natalie continues: "If I'm not mistaken,[34] Richard left Zürich after this almost brutal, heartless declaration, leaving Minna in this terrible emotional upheaval to move from the unhappy house, to give up the whole household, and to have the furniture packed up and stored in order to go to the sanatorium at the water resort of Brestenberg on the advice of Dr. Rahn, who was the friend and family physician of the Wesendoncks and who made Minna sick with medicines." The coachman who was to drive her to the station, according to Natalie, locked her up in his house instead, until she had paid from her meager purse 400 francs which he claimed Wagner owed him. Natalie attacks not only the Wesendoncks' doctor (who "had no idea what was wrong with Minna, treating her for consumption one day and gout the next") but the Brestenberg doctor, who all but killed her, in her advanced heart condition, "with ice-cold applications." "Cruel and unscrupulous," he dismissed her, in a really critical condition, from the hospital, so that Charlotte's husband, receiving her in Zwickau, pronounced him "either an unmitigated jackass or an irresponsible, incapable, ignorant scoundrel who only takes people's money." It is easy to believe almost anything about the ineffectuality of doctors in that era of violent treatments, but that the latter one acted in bad faith is an unfounded charge; the implication that Wagner abandoned her indifferently to her fate is manifestly untrue.

328 A   (Undated) Otto Wesendonck, to Wagner.
    The Wesendoncks' son Guido was born in 1852.

"DEAR FRIEND!
    "On my way back from your house last night I asked myself whether or not you've accepted the role of godfather.

---

[33] Wagner was then thirty-six; at the time of the Wesendonck crisis he was forty-four.

[34] She was not only mistaken but had her sequence of events quite jumbled, as she could have seen by examining the letters in her possession.

"Since you express certain reservations which seem to yield only to considerations of friendship, I had to conclude that you would not like to accept the role which I mentioned— In such matters there can be no half-coercion & your freedom of conscience must remain intact. Therefore you'll surely understand that today I'll ask an oldtime friend of the family to be godfather to our Guido; I'm certain of his consent.

"I hope that you'll be well enough to attend the christening from the beginning or to come afterward. Well—I'll visit you soon again to see how you are.

"Your
OTTO WESENDONCK"

B (Undated).

"DEAR FRIEND!

"It is a long time since I visited you on your sickbed. It has not been ill will. Various matters have not left me the time. Furthermore, I've had a toothache for three days & tomorrow I'll get fixed up & my poor little wife is still suffering from eye trouble—just like a hospital! And then the weather! But patience; things will get better without the need of waiting at the Frankfurt Bundespalais *without an umbrella* until they come out and proclaim President Liberty—Heine's joke, not mine.

"Everything is upside down, even the paper.

"Well, get better, or else . . .

"Sleep well.

"Your
OTTO WESENDONCK"

"Saturday night"

329 A Telegram from Wagner, in Venice, January 1, 1859, to Minna in Dresden.

"Warmest good wishes. Your letter on New Year's Eve brought great happiness. Much worried before because no news. Soon everything will be fine. Health, well-being, hope, confidence. RICHARD"

B Telegram from Wagner, in Lucerne, May 1, 1859, to Minna in Dresden.

"Still no letter! Do you blame me for worrying? Answer what is the matter with you. Twenty words prepaid. RICHARD"

330 Wagner, in Venice, February 15, 1859, to Tichatschek. (Page 157.)

331 S. de Charnal, Paris, April 2, 1859, to E. B. Kietz in Epernay. (Page 202.)

332 Cäcilie Avenarius to Minna.

A Berlin, April 10, 1859, to Dresden.

In a long and affectionate letter, Cäcilie reproaches her sister-in-law for neglecting to write. "Since we have known each other through such a long period of years," she says, "and have gone together through so many phases of life, I think we should cling to each other more and more closely; for the remaining years of our lives are getting less and less—death may come and separate us forever." Later she writes: "I read in the newspapers that Richard is again in Switzerland—but I didn't know any details, I didn't even know where he is living until I got your letter today. So he is in Lucerne. Well, he might like it better than Venice. In that heavenly region he will probably feel as happy as possible. Of course I did not get another letter from Richard as I have not yet thanked him for his last dear letter. At that time he wrote me that he did not think you were going to choose Paris as your future residence as he *hated* Paris. Now, after all, you have decided to do so. O God, it makes my heart quite sad to see you going away so far, but, on the other hand, Paris has for me an infinite charm; for although linked with much struggling the time of my stay in Paris was the most beautiful in my life, and still today, with all my beautiful recollections, I am attached to Paris just as to a dearly loved person. Certainly much has changed since I have been away from there. My youth has gone; [35] our former friends are no longer there. . . . However, I should no longer care about it if I had not the marvelous prospect of being with you both again during our old age, at the place where we were brought together as quite young couples. How nice it was to live together at Bellevue! Good God, what we have experienced since then! Do you remember when we went to Meudon in the mornings to buy meat? Oh, I don't want to think at all of the unpleasantness which country life has had for me, for these remembrances make me quite sad." She closes: "Give my cordial greetings to the good Mathilde. I am looking forward very much to seeing her too. Also give my greetings to sister Natalie, who probably also will go to Paris again. How she will be looking forward to it, for she raves so much about Paris. Now farewell, my dear, good Minna, and keep loving your

old

CÄCILIE."

B   Berlin, August 17, 1859, to Schandau.

Again Cäcilie is offended at not having heard from Minna. She has this to say about her brother: "Where is Richard now? I can't imagine him as still in Lucerne; he could never stand staying in one place so long, away from his home. What about Paris? Or is Richard going to America?"

C   Berlin, March 16, 1861, to Paris. (The envelope is addressed care "Monsieur Richard Wagner.") (Page 391.)

D   January 16, 1863, to Dresden.

Cäcilie begins by saying: "I belong to those absolutely sincere and honest human beings who cannot speak or act except as prompted by their innermost conviction. To trim one's sails to the wind as some of my sisters do; to be nice to someone for

[35] Cäcilie was then forty-four.

this or that reason, even though he is not to my liking, only in order to attain some ends which are desirable for me—such behavior is strange to me." The object of her disapproval is her sister Cläre Wolfram, who has apparently swallowed her scruples about her brother's conduct because of the radiance of his fame. She, as well as the Brockhaus family, so Cäcilie has learned from Minna, have "competed in kissing the dust off his feet." Cäcilie is also jealous because, immediately after she had warned Minna against Cläre, Minna received her in her house during Wagner's visit in November, 1862.

". . . I must say quite frankly, my dear Minna, this has shaken my confidence in you to some extent. As to Cläre I cannot be deceived any longer; I got to know her thoroughly. Of course, she wanted to see RICHARD *by all means. Thereupon* she did everything necessary to attain her end. Surely I too would have liked to see Richard again after a separation of fourteen years, and after having loved him honestly and sincerely from childhood on; but never will I betray my pride and the innermost self-respect which every honest person must preserve under all circumstances, even though one's heart suffers painfully. Never would I force myself upon my brother, who evidently does not want to have anything to do with me. On receiving the brief news of his coming, I might have gone to Leipzig or Dresden. I have friends in Dresden, too, who would have liked to put me up for a few days, but as he did not think it worth while to express the desire to see me again by *one* written word, I have let this *good* chance go by without taking advantage of it."

E Berlin, March 10, 1863.
    Cäcilie, always sensitive, was ready to be offended with Minna for not having written. She had concluded that "you just didn't want to have me in Dresden." She is still not on speaking terms with Cläre Wolfram. Having fallen out with her sister-in-law, Emma Avenarius, she has made peace with her. She is newly offended with her brother Richard, who has spent two days in Berlin, and has not come to see her. "I myself no longer expect anything from Richard, but I cannot deny that when on my birthday [February 26] my son brought me this news through Albert, I felt completely ashamed before my husband and children, who all know too well with what an amount of love and devotion I have been attached to Richard." Her husband and sons are planning a trip to Russia, and she urges Minna to come and stay with her immediately and in the summer. Her sons and their friends make the household spirited and youthful. "Oh, yes, dear Minna, I could wish with all my heart that you had a son or a daughter. They link us so nicely with life and its interests! If you had a beloved child, everything would be different."

F Berlin, October 15, 1863.
    This letter opens, like all the others, with a reproach because Minna has neglected to write. Cäcilie clings to her as one lonely woman to another. She finds herself lonely and depressed, although she has four sons, a loyal husband, and an active home: "I too feel terribly low in spirit and body, and after my heart cries out con-

vulsively for some warm feminine heart to cling to for understanding." She finds little comfort in her brothers and sisters. "You know, Minna, sometimes I am overcome with a terribly sad feeling, also a frightful rage when I ponder what a *disloyal lot* my family is. I really have the need deep down in my soul to love my brothers and sisters since they are the living memories of my deceased parents. But is is impossible; again and again I am made to realize that they have no heart for anything but egotism and vanity. Luise [Brockhaus] is still the one who gets the most attention, as she lives under the best financial conditions." She is offended with Albert, who has not come to see her for months. "How soothing it would be for me to speak with him of our parental home, since he knew my father better than I did, as I was only six years old when he died." For Albert's daughter Johanna, she has little use. "It is the same with Ottilie— How much I love Ottilie, but does she ask for me?" As for Richard, she has had a talk with him, but she cannot accept him apart from Minna. "To *you*, my Minna, he should turn his heart again; that is all I desire and claim from him. Therefore I was most agreeably impressed by what you told me about his last letter. O God, perhaps he will really return to you definitely and at last find with you again what he has lost on his meandering paths of life. Oh, if only I could see you two reunited *for good!*" She contemplates visiting Minna. "Whether during my stay with you Richard will come or not remains to be seen; I should feel quite queer in his presence, as he never took any notice of me. The only reason why I would forget my own self entirely would be to try to do everything I possibly could to bring him to his senses and to an understanding; he may then do with me whatever he likes. If Cläre learns that R. is coming to Dresden, she will thrust herself upon you again. Well, that is your affair! To begin with, I don't believe he will go to Dresden at all, for he changes his plans every moment."

G   Cäcilie Avenarius [in Berlin], October 22, 1864, to Minna in Dresden.
   Cäcilie writes as follows about Wagner:

". . . Many thanks for your news concerning Richard. I am happy to know that he is not ill, although many things you told me about his life and doings did not exactly please me: for instance, that the Bulow [*sic*] flock will now also settle in Munich. To this extent I share your feeling that his star will fade again soon, for these people definitely contribute only to his immoral conduct and to his misfortune. I also heard from Albert how much R. is endangering his position in Munich by his excessively arrogant behavior; all musicians and members of the orchestra are said to hate him. And this certainly is very bad. However, his arrogance will become still more unbalanced through the influence of the Bülows, who support him in his attitude. Bülow himself is such an impudent fellow too—I could never stand this fellow. May Heaven grant that the happy relations with the young King last a long time. If not, what will then become of Richard? A little while ago, when I sat down to write, it slipped out—for I am ashamed to tell it to other people—that Richard has been twice in Berlin without calling on me. This news made such a terrible impression on Marie [36] that she became deathly pale and started violently, exclaiming: "That is not true, that is impossible," and I regretted deeply having said anything. For now he is judged from *this* side too, and it hurts to see a brother whom you once loved so ardently, now also condemned by such impartial good people. Richard's remark that you should turn to friends in order to increase your income is an impudence which I cannot characterize by words. Tell me, dear Minna, do you never write to him any more? He should give you a reasonable excuse; he himself should understand your painful situation. Yes, yes, his heart seems to be dead. What a pity for him, for once he had such a good, gentle heart. I always remember your life in Paris at that time and your charming life in Dresden. Nothing else has destroyed his noble feelings as much as these frivolous Bülow people and finally the nefarious loose women. How he used to detest such a dissolute crowd, and now? Since the letter I once wrote to him in *your* interest, I have never written to him again. I am entirely through with him, and if I heard today that he were in Berlin, I would not move one step—this I owe to myself; and I also gave up interfering for your sake, for I see that it would be no longer of any use. But now enough about Richard. It is always the same theme with its hundred variations, and it remains always the same old story."

H   Berlin, October 30, 1863.

Cäcilie is indignant over stories which have come to Minna from some "Russian ladies" about Wagner's behavior in St. Petersburg, where he has been conducting. She has had a specific denial from her sister-in-law, Marie Avenarius, who has stayed in the same hotel, and who has spoken to the landlord. "According to information from these people, Richard was then *quite alone* and was glad and happy to rest in his room for hours by himself, and without any human being; he is said to have been often indisposed, and to have looked upon the solitude of his room as the greatest benefit." Albert has had it "from a very reliable source that Richard is much too exhausted to look for relationships with such bad women."

I   Berlin, February 1, 1865, to Dresden.

Cäcilie has been seriously ill and is writing from her bed. The letter is occupied only with her illness.

J   Charlottenburg, April 28, 1865, to Dresden.

Cäcilie is still convalescent: she has gone to Charlottenburg to regain her strength. There is only this mention of Wagner: "Think of yourself always—of *yourself only* and *your health*; do not think of Richard; let him do as he pleases. I have kept my word and have never again written to Richard since the letter I wrote on *your* behalf. Our Richard [her son] went to see him in Munich and heard a part of *Tristan,* which was being rehearsed there."

[36] Cäcilie's sister-in-law, Marie Avenarius.

333   Wagner to Minna, 1859.

A   Lucerne, May 2.

"You thoroughly bad woman!

"To have to take abuse even by telegraph when worrying about one's wife! Well, anyway, I was very glad to hear from you yesterday before going to bed, and I had no regrets about the money since I could count on a letter today with certainty. You know, of course, that I wrote to you just two weeks ago today and that I received no answer to this letter. This worried me, good Mutz. But now it's all right and—sensible. Moreover—just try to imagine a little my situation here! I see and speak to literally no one except the servants. If the weather were always nice and if I could take excursions which I had anticipated and which I had definitely counted on, everything would be fine, for then I would hope to have a clear head for work, and that would make me forget all that's amiss. But the devil brings in one fog after another: I have not been able to take any long trip without uncertainty; it's weighing me down like lead, and when I look around I don't even have a little dog to talk to! Sometimes the mouth needs a bit of exercise too! So I live only on what the mail brings me. Your letters are always so welcome, for first of all they entertain me; 2, they make me happy with good news about your condition, and 3, through their whole tone they now give me the calm and the hope which I need so very badly in our old age. (I'm getting shamefully gray-haired!) If you now suddenly stop writing—with your health still so deeply affected—I shall quickly begin to worry; I am easily thrown into a bad humor. Well, all this will soon come to an end. Today Liszt sent me his *Dante* Symphony—hell—purgatory—and paradise. Well! I thought to myself: you've endured hell; the purgatorial year is approaching its end, so paradise must be at hand!—Amen!

"Your letter has put me into a better humor once more, as you see. During all of last week I was quietly desperate, and my only thought was to start out for Paris, because I didn't think I could stand it any longer under these conditions. I thought I'd at least let Kietz chat with me in the evenings! Now I hope once more to stay here until I've finished *Tristan*. In the end I would after all greatly regret it if I were to plunge into the sea of houses and deny myself the invigorating effect of the Swiss air. So I want to leave it completely up to good weather and the progress of my work; I'll also leave it to news from Paris whether anything substantial will develop there for next winter. In the meanwhile there has been news from *America*. It is really quite acceptable: the manager wants to limit my engagement to only *three* months, during which I should conduct only *my* operas and concerts; for that they've guaranteed me 20,000 francs and a benefit concert for from 10,000 to 15,000 francs. Free trip both ways. I'd get off with two months less and, after all deductions, I'd still have my 30,000 francs left. What do you think? The manager is coming to Europe in three weeks and will visit me personally. So I'll postpone my decision until then. The guarantee of the money would be taken care of. My opinion is that, if nothing definite happens in Paris, I'll have to accept Newyork [sic] for three months after all, for—money; we must have money, plenty of money, if we are to feel comfortable in Paris; and even if I have good prospects for a nice income, it is still a good feeling to have a small amount of capital around and gradually to replace with the earnings what is used for living expenses. Of course, I would rent the larger apartment permanently in the fall, so that you can await me there in comfort; and I consider America merely as an excursion. If Paris materializes, so much the better; then I wouldn't even leave at all. In the meanwhile let things take their course. Moreover, I have received letters from no one; but the 'profit' which you dreamed I received has actually come in: the Vienna Choral Society sent me another ducat. (Don't you still have the first one?)

"Your news about Karl suddenly enlightens me. Imagine: since I left Venice I have not been able to get a line out of him. I wrote to him three times and finally reminded him in no uncertain terms. God knows whether he ever got my last letters at all. Don't they know *when* he left there? It is so typical of him that he didn't utter a sound. Still, Emilie and his wife must have received my last warning letter. But what confusions! Did the two just go to Venice on impulse?

"As far as the damned war is concerned, I think that those fellows started it only because of my crate of books. That's still standing in Venice. Just yesterday, stupid blockhead that I am, I wrote to Karl that he should take the *Siegfried* sketches out of it and keep them so that they at least won't get lost with it. It is really awful, and I am so unlucky with such things these days. All I've gotten back are my cigars from last year: they are pretty old by now!

"When you told me about Tichatschek I was much pleased: it merely confirms my opinion of this superficial person in whose faithfulness I don't put too much stock, for in the final analysis he doesn't know anyway what he has in me, and if Bärenmaier [Meyerbeer] should come he'll be just as enthusiastic about him. No: no more intimacies; I'll get away as best as I can from all these back-slapping friendships which finally bring me only painful disagreements; on the other hand I whisper to you to become very sociable. This should be quite easy in Paris; I'll gather together a cozy little crowd (Germans, of course) for whom I want to be at home every evening as long as the strict lady of the house does not chase us to the devil. Dinner parties in Paris are out; but sitting around in the evening does not cost much, and it will do me good to relax at night by talking. I have everything in hand now, and if I don't expect too much intelligence, which I certainly won't in such company, it will be very easy for me to gather a congenial circle around me, whereas on the other hand I should not be obligated in any way. These advantages can be found in a metropolis like that, and in that respect Paris is unique. You can have everything, but you can also withdraw from everything. All you have to do is to be in a comfortable situation and not to count definitely on a goal to be achieved in Paris. Neither of these conditions shall apply to us. On the whole I always consider Germany and the German theaters as the basis of my position as well as of my work; I have really found out to my great satisfaction what it can offer and I always find out more. Berlin, for example, will never stop sending me a nice annual income;

so far, at least, it has brought me something every three months. Thus I can be a completely free man in Paris, can let everything come to *me,* and don't have to compromise in the least—which will also keep my social position very independent. If they let me wait too long there and don't perform anything by me, and if my reserve funds run out eventually, I'd go to Newyork for three months to reestablish the equilibrium. In our old days, then, you shall still have the opportunity to keep the home congenial, and for that you shall be absolute mistress.

"In my fortunate position *as German exile* nothing stands in my way, even in case of war, and I believe, I believe—Paris now will become the *quietest* and *safest* place in the world for a *long* time. So much I must confess, that Louis Napoleon has handled things with devilish cleverness this time; he has extremely favorable chances, in every respect, even as far as Germany is concerned (if they wanted to *attack* him from there—for *he* won't attack there now), and, in any case, this war firmly establishes him in France. The people are like that. The Germans had better look out, and if they should get really whipped, I should not know whether to cry or laugh; at most I should feel sorry for Nepomuk! I really don't know why I should get enthusiastic about the German Confederation; I'm glad that several princes are favorably disposed toward me; it is the more shameful that they don't have the energy to help me out decently. God bless them all!

"I have lost all patriotism under such miserable circumstances, and see nothing which could give me any enthusiasm. This way I hope to live very peacefully and undisturbed in Paris!

"Well, now I have at least used my pen, if not my mouth: but that shall soon happen again too. Now—put the purgatorial summer to good use! Get really well and find some bodily recovery. The rest will then come out all right, and before the end of the summer you'll enter Paris victoriously, as German Empress! —And Fipps as head court factotum [*Oberhofscherrwenzel*]! For the others we'll also find accommodations! For today, then, best regards and a most cordial farewell from

ME"

B   Lucerne, August 6, to Schandau.
    "Just now—at half past four—dearest Minna, I have written the last note of *Tristan!*

"May he rest in peace, and she too! [*Ruhe er sanft, und sie auch!*]"
"Today is supposed to be the first performance of *Lohengrin* in Dresden. If it takes place it would be a very strange and unexpected coincidence.[37]
"Well, be that as it may: I am to be congratulated, and you will surely not be the last one to do it.

[37] The first Dresden performance of *Lohengrin* actually took place on this date, with Tichatschek, then fifty-two, in the title part.

"Now I want first to loaf a few days and—write letters. If the weather stays fine, I'm thinking of climbing Mount Pilatus. The French ambassador (a *new* one) is again making difficulties for me because of my passport. He tells me that he has first had to report to Paris about it. So I don't yet know exactly when I can start the trip. Before that I'll write to you again, that's understood, and that'll be a real letter. I'm expecting a letter from you which, I hope, is already on the way. You can write to me about this letter and about *Lohengrin* to *Lucerne*: if I should finish everything and leave earlier I'll still get the letter. I hope to meet *Devrient* in Strassburg; if the Grand Duke were at home and available, he would have made it possible for me to spend a day in Karlsruhe. All that is now uncertain. Eventually it is important to me to be able to form some opinion of the artistic forces there. And in October?? Well, let us hope for the best, especially that I'll experience the joy of finally seeing you somewhat healthier and in good spirits. About Paris the next time. For today nothing is certain except that *Tristan is finished*! This was in my power; but the mean hearts of certain potentates unfortunately aren't in my power.

"Well, I can at least say to myself that I'm doing what is mine to do.

"Goodbye! Dearest good Minna! Now I'll gradually breathe more easily and look ahead to see what life has in store for us! Farewell, and accept my best and dearest regards!

"Your

RICHARD"

C   Paris (avenue de Matignon, Champs Elysées), September 13, to Schandau.

"DEAREST MINNA!

"Here I am, moved in again—only to move out in four weeks. I confess I am completely dizzy with this eternal packing and unpacking and moving.

"Even today I can write you only a very little, for I've just gotten around to it—after unpacking—and then I want to hurry out to get you a draft for 200 thaler. It must get to the post office in time. And then I'll have to write to everyone to whom I made known my new address yesterday (Lucerne and Leipzig), because I found out today that I wrote one *r* too many, which could easily cause confusion. The name is Matignon—*not* Martignon. Be sure to remember this.

"Now for my adventures in brief. I was pleased most of all to see Sulzer, whom I visited in Winterthur. His boy is *splendid*, the image of his father. He gives him great joy. I could not yet judge the smallest—a little girl. He seemed very well and in good humor and promised me to come to Kalrsruhe. In Zürich I took care of my business with Heim. The store has been sold to the railroad, but our things will remain undisturbed until I send for them. But if they are left there any longer they should be opened up and aired, because otherwise they would be injured by the dampness. But I think we'll soon have them sent. I found the Herweghs in the same old predicament: they were supposed to move and had no other quarters yet, so there was much excitement. But I just rushed through there and hurried to Strassburg to wait for Devrient, who finally had to notify me by letter that his opera manager had become sick and he had to direct the rehearsals of the new Coburg opera for him, so he could not come. As soon as I get a chance I'll arrange everything with him by letter.

"Here I have not yet seen anybody, but I've just rested and become excited all over again, and looked for a furnished room for myself. I found one which is very pleasantly situated and also—relatively—cheap, because as yet there are no outsiders here. That's why I got it for only *one* month; because after that it will be rented only for the whole winter, and then—*terribly expensively* so that I've immediately given up the thought of living with you in a furnished room. On the other hand I have hopes of finding an *unfurnished* apartment which is not exorbitant; and anyway, since this is the renting season, we can do nothing but rent something of this sort, since we can't count on Karlsruhe without sufficient guarantees. Therefore I'll look around; I think Mad. Herold should be quite helpful in this matter. Although I'm still very much dazed, I have the feeling that we'll like it. The nearness of the Champs Elysées is invaluable for walks and for Fipps. No rough pavement—little noise. Well, we shall see. And more about this soon.

"What I wanted to ask you: make an intensive search for a decent young girl (who also speaks French) as companion and nurse for you. It means everything to me to make your life easy and painless, and I'm glad to see that I'll have the means for it. For my sake do everything possible to find a woman like that who is agreeable to you: I shrink from no sacrifices for this—this time I have received no answer *at all* from Moudin about poor Nette (!). But I found out from Heine that my friend, Professor *Fröhlich* in *Berne,* has an institute just like it. I'll go to him now and can be pretty sure to receive a favorable reply from him. That is very agreeable to me.

"Well, now—here is a draft for 200 thaler. My good Minna, I think you'll get along with this until we meet again. Make everything easy and comfortable for yourself. But if this should not be sufficient either, I'll have more ready. I simply want you to have everything: this makes me happy!

"I'll answer your letter more fully the next time. Now I'll await your Strassburg letter which will be forwarded to me here.

"An affectionate farewell for today: be assured of my unalterable, most loving care, and make me happy with encouraging news about your condition!

"Adieu, good Mutz!

"Your

Richel

"Dear Minna! I write this postscript at Rothschilds'. They issue no drafts, but listen:

"You only have to go to *Kaskel* and identify yourself, then you'll get 200 thaler. *Whenever* you want. So do it!"

334   Adelheid, Marschall von Bieberstein, Zürich, May 20, 1859, to Minna.
   This Zürich friend of the Wagners sends news and gossip about the neighbors.

Of Wagner she writes: "Of course you know better than I that he is living in Switzerland again, and even lately visited Zürich incognito, in lordly fashion. We recently read some notices about him in the Lucerne paper, and I have heard that Herr Wsdk [Wesendonck] is now suffering from an excessive enthusiasm for him, a proof at least of what an enchantment his wife is able to achieve. We, as well as the rest of Zürich society, have seen nothing of the W'sdk couple for months on end; and their villa increasingly exudes an air of petrified aloofness." She concludes: "You may be sure that I shall always feel the same way toward you. Faithful devotion to my friends is perhaps my best virtue, among a thousand failings."

335 Hans von Bülow, in Berlin, August 24, 1859, to an unspecified publisher (written in French).

"Sir,
"It is very kind of you to want to arrange for my return to Paris. As for us, I would ask for nothing better than to follow your advice and to go there at the beginning of the musical season, but I'm afraid that my work will not permit me to do so. At this moment I'm chained to the office, where I'm working like two negroes to do the piano score of the new opera by Mr. Richard Wagner, *Tristan und Isolde,* which the composer has promised to present for the first time at the grand ducal theater at Karlsruhe during the month of October. The task is sufficiently complicated not to be entrusted to another musician less familiar with the intentions of the composer, and since he is in a hurry my fingers are becoming numb from handling the pen; later I must have the necessary time to limber them up again on the piano before turning them loose on the beautiful pianos of a Pleyel or an Erard. Permit me therefore, sir, to give you a definite reply in about six weeks, during which period I shall be better able to arrange my plans of campaign and winter quarters, while always thanking you for your offers. In any case I shall not fail to go to Paris at a less impossible date than that of my first trip. As for my competition with Mr. Leopold de Meyer—I hope to be as little embarrassed by it as he is about me. Our 'styles' do not in the least challenge each other—I would rather say that they are almost mutually exclusive. Mr. de Meyer plays Italian transcriptions, Austrian polkas inimitably well, and he recalls that golden age of piano virtuosity which now has but very few representatives—whereas my youth belongs essentially to the iron age of virtuosity, in which one no longer has faith in the possibility of monstrous receipts, of ovations in the form of poetry and flowers, etc., but in which one holds simply and modestly to the interpretation of the classic and modern masters with what intelligence and technical cleanness one may command. Mr. de Meyer is a Bacchus, I am merely a mortal; he can claim to be king of the piano, I am satisfied to be agent of the masters who have composed for this instrument.
"I must also thank you, sir, for sending your periodical (in the last issue I noticed with pleasure that Mr. Roche is following in the footsteps of a Commettant and a Chadeuil) as well as the kind translation of the brochure which treated my skirmishes with the Commettants and the Chadeuils of the Berlin press. My only fear

is that it may have given Parisian readers that ultra-German impression toward which Mr. Roche so cleverly applies his bassoon 'Frantz' in the concerto by Octave Jonathan. Finally—your intention, sir, to publish these fragments is certainly very kind toward me, and be assured of my sincere gratitude. I learned with pleasure the other day that *Le Siècle,* which has not deigned to knock me as pianist, has vigorously applauded me as author. Yes, sir, it is I, as author of a democratic-Bonapartist pamphlet, who have caused a fuss in the Berlin press, where I attacked their myopic absurdities of reading 1859 for 1813 and failing to distinguish a III from a I. You know that I am a Bonapartist, not although, but because, I am a revolutionary, and that I consider the genius of Emperor Napoleon III the most brilliant and the only actually possible incarnation of the great French Revolution. I do not concede that it has been interrupted, and I believe it is destined to overthrow, either peacefully or violently, the old political system piece by piece. Mazzini is, to me, a medieval aristocrat who cultivates the anachronism of the conspiracies of the old Italian republics, a ghost of the fifteenth century who understands absolutely nothing about Napoleonic, that is to say democratic, ideas. Do you want me to send you my pamphlet, which indeed could well be published in Paris under my name? My brother-in-law Daniel has just translated and delocalized it (it is addressed particularly to the democratic and non-Socratic Prussians): it is entitled *Critical Essay on the Emperor Napoleon III, Designed to Combat the Blind Prejudices of German Democracy*—naturally, a less Germanic title would have to be found. Could you, sir, perhaps suggest a method by which a German copy could be sent to the Tuileries? If not, never mind.

"If you meet Berlioz, please put me at his feet by telling him that I adore him with all my heart. If you see any other 'illustrious people,' that is to say, the less illustrious ones, kindly remember me to them, if they have a memory.

"Accept, sir, the assurance of my most sincere consideration.

HANS DE BULOW"

336   Emilie Heim, in Rheinfelden, September 20, 1859, to Minna.

Frau Emilie Heim assures Minna of her loyalty: "You bad, dear woman, how could you possibly think I'm angry with you? What reason could I have to think of you with anything but friendship and faithfulness?" She says of Wagner: "We know from a letter from your husband that you're going to meet him this fall in Karlsruhe for the performance of his new opera. Unfortunately, I can stay here only until the end of October, and *Tristan* will surely not go on the stage until November; otherwise I would certainly visit you on this occasion. How much I should like to see you—but it will be too late!" She and her husband met the Grand Duke at Mainau in Lake Constance, and received his assurance that he would do everything in his power toward an amnesty for Wagner.

337   Wagner to Tichatschek, 1859.

A Lucerne, September 3 (incomplete). Published, in 1883, in the German press. (Page 158.)

B   Paris, October 19. (Page 160.)

C   Paris, October 24. (Page 395.)

D   Paris, December 24. (Page 379.)

E   Paris, December 26. (Page 381.)

338   Wilhelm Fischer, in Dresden, September 21, 1859, to Minna.

Fischer, with a polite note to the "esteemed *Frau Kapellmeisterin*" (the title itself, in 1859, is a polite gesture), sends a copy of the *Leipziger Zeitung* supplement to Wagner at the request of Appellationsrath Einert, of Leipzig.

339   Wagner, in Paris, 1859, to E. B. Kietz at Epernay.

A   October 10. (Page 203.)

B.   October 12. (Page 203.)

C   October 20. (Page 204.)

D   December 31. (Page 204.)

340   Cosima von Bülow, in Berlin, to Minna in Chemnitz.

The letter is undated, but the contents fix the period as the autumn of 1858. Cosima, married a year to Hans von Bülow, has visited the Asyl with him in August. Still shy about approaching Wagner, she can also still turn to the afflicted Minna in friendly sympathy. The first performance of *Lohengrin* in Berlin took place on January 23, 1859. Johanna Wagner as Ortrud, by the way, in spite of Cosima's fears, was to be one of the successful features of that production:

"Dear Frau Minna!

"In spite of the wrong address I received your dear letter and I would have answered earlier if I had not been ill, and if I did not have to run about so much these days. I appeal once more to your usual kindness and implore you not to doubt, in spite of my delay, that I enjoyed your lines very much, and welcomed them because they proved to me that you had not quite forgotten the 'Fräulein.' You don't mention your health. Are you not better? Has the heart palpitation not improved? I should be very happy to know that you are in good health. Poor Frau Frohmann [*sic*] lies sick in bed and sees no one but the doctor, so that I couldn't bring her news from you; however, you have very likely written to her too. As for my old gray dress, I am pleased, dear lady, that you made good use of it; I didn't think it would serve a better purpose than dusting the stairs or something of that sort, and so I am very proud that it will still function as a dress. The clock arrived safely. You ask about *Lohengrin,* and I should like to give you some precise answer, but we don't know at all when the performance will be, whether in the beginning or end of

November or even in December. Yesterday I heard Johanna in the *Vestale* and I was terrified; she looked splendid in her Roman costume but she couldn't produce any tone at all and I was in despair about how she will sing Ortrud.

"But it is possible that she was in an especially bad voice on that evening. At least I hope so. You very likely know that Taussig [*sic*] is here; he arrived quite unexpectedly and is probably going to spend a few weeks in Berlin. We have had no news from Richard for a long time; I should have liked to write him; every moment I think of doing it and then again I lose my courage. I am silly enough to be still shy toward him. Now I have bored you long enough; don't be angry with me, dearest Frau Minna, accept my best wishes, and my apologies for all the trouble we have continued to cause you since our departure, and permit me to kiss you a thousand times. Hoping that you won't spend all the time in Dresden but will also move to Berlin, I am

Cosima v. Bulow"

"Hans sends a thousand greetings, hoping with me that you will visit us. Be lenient with my horrible German."

341   Alwine Frommann, in Berlin, November 8, 1859, to Minna.

Frau Frommann gives Minna, about to join Wagner in Paris and set up a ménage there, some kindly advice about extravagance in entertaining guests. She suggests that if the house is too large Minna may find some "German ladies," and take them in as boarders.

342   Wagner, in Paris, November 8, 1859, to Ferdinand Heine.

This letter, addressed to Heine, and headed: "To the memory of Our Beloved Fischer," was written on the news of the death, within a short time, of both Louis Spohr and Wilhelm Fischer. The sentiments are personal, as if intended for the friends of Fischer, including Heine. The letter was evidently also intended for publication, and duly appeared in the Dresden *Constitutioneller Zeitung,* November 25, 1859. According to the catalogue, Mrs. Burrell obtained the manuscript, and also a copy of the *Zeitung,* from Frau Marie Schmole, Heine's daughter.

"I am moved by the death, almost at the same time, of two worthy, highly venerated old men. The loss of one concerns the whole musical world, which mourns *Ludwig Spohr*. I leave it to that world to estimate what an abundant power and noble productivity is lost to us by the Master's death. It reminds me, to my sorrow, that now the last has gone of the line of genuine serious musicians whose youthful days were directly illuminated by the radiant sun of Mozart, and who with inspiring fidelity nurtured the light they received as Vestals nurture the pure flame entrusted to them, and who preserved it against all the storms and winds of life on their chaste hearth. Their sublime duty kept these *men* pure and noble, and if I with *one* stroke of my pen had to put down what has impressed me so unforgettably about Spohr, I would say: He was a serious, honest master of his art; the foundation of his life was his faith in his art; his best impulse sprang from the strength of that faith. And that solemn faith kept him free from any personal narrowness; whatever he failed entirely to understand he left aside as strange to him without hating or persecuting it: this was considered as coldness and harshness; but whatever grew understandable to him (and a deep fine feeling for all beauty could surely be assumed in the creator of *Jessonda*) was unreservedly and zealously loved and protected by him, as soon as he recognized it in one thing: seriousness, seriousness in Art. And this was the tie that bound him to the recent endeavors in art even in his old age. They might have become alien to him but never hateful. Honor to our Spohr! Veneration for his memory! Faithful regard for his noble example!

"At the news of his death it was almost only the happy recollection of my former personal contact with Spohr which prevailed with me as a melancholy, yet joyous memory; but that chord of merely human sympathy was brought to painful resonance when I learned of the death of our beloved Fischer. Here the respect for the modest comrade in art could be entirely absorbed by the feeling of sorrowing devotion to the dear human friend. And yet when one death followed the other so quickly, I had to recognize such a close kinship in the nature of the two deceased ones, that they almost merged into one for me. The memory of the famous, highly respected Master will be commemorated far and wide, and in a better way than by my humble word: but the eulogy of this splendid, vigorous, extremely lovable old man, of our dear Fischer, is to be spoken by myself, and I should like to do it for the much smaller circle of *his* friends. And how easy will the task become to me, how few words are needed to praise this outstanding man to those who knew him: since he was no creative artist he could not become renowned far and wide, but was known only to those who stood close to his personal work, to his professional activity, to his unmatched friendship. And I gladly speak to those who want to become aware of what they lost in Fischer, by telling them what I lost in him.

"It will now soon be twenty years since I applied to him from Paris, whence even now I am sending my last messages; then I begged him to take under his protection my *Rienzi* which I had submitted to the Dresden Opera. His answer disclosed some sort of hesitation; doubtful about the reason and origin of his scruples, I finally started out for Dresden myself and quickly learned the origin of the scruples named by Fischer, when, welcoming me, he rose joyfully and embraced me, then still a stranger to him, with exuberant tenderness. I never will forget this act of kindness: it was the first, the very first encouragement, the first expression of enthusiastic sympathy to cheer the entirely helpless, unknown, needy, and hard-pressed young artist on his path in life. It is you, my friend, who knows this, and I need not remind you of the part you took in that heartening encouragement. This was the basis for the gradual sweeping away of all those scruples. The growing and enthusiastic interest of our Tichatschek in his task and in the whole work soon extended to all those called to participation, a thing which hardly ever happens in these times of ours, and with our reserved attitudes; and the Dresden public, happily prepared by the miracle of that warmest sympathy of all artists for the work of an entirely unknown artist, boldly adopted me as its favorite on the stormy night of the first *Rienzi* performance.

"Then our Fischer grew more and more content, and as in tender awareness of having been the first to recognize me, and of having been the incentive for my success, calmly fixed his clear, friendly eye on me as if to say: 'Well, I knew it would turn out this way!'

"From now on I was his joy. My aspirations, my creative work, were his delight; my need was his pain, my attainment his success. With more zeal and eagerness than anyone else, he exceeded himself when it came to assisting me in some especially difficult problems. When I had succeeded in what I had audaciously demanded—what a joyful smile radiated from his face! What he was capable of achieving, to what level his performances as the choral director were rising, and how they were made memorable in the history of art—this we all of us learned when he accomplished the incredible task and drilled his chorus in Bach's motet, *Singet dem Herrn*. He did it in such a way, and the performance of the singers was so absolutely secure and masterly, that I was induced to have the first part of the motet sung at a really fiery pace which, as you know, scared the critics to death, since, owing to its harassing difficulty, it is always performed in the most cautious *moderato*. The popular success of Beethoven's Ninth Symphony was made possible, in my belief, through the presentation by the chorus, which was of the confident boldness I had intended, but which could be realized only through Fischer's accomplishment as a choral conductor—and this was absolutely unique in my opinion.

"This and many similar achievements put Fischer's name squarely among those who have promoted the correct understanding of sublime masterworks in the history of art. The fact that his merits remain unheeded only justifies my stronger emphasis in mentioning them. And so we may further remark that achievements, seldom credited to their source, are the result of unspeakable drudgery and worries. How often did I pity the poor man when he had to meet my drastic demands by his own despair. Good singers would fall ill, the best ones were dismissed because their demands for higher pay had been refused, the rest were overtired, or disabled by excessive work, or not available because of other duties. And he was a considerate man who never liked to let things come to a breach, but mediated and tried to make the best out of mediocre material. There we sometimes came to blows, and the firm one got excited against the stormy one, and the fight grew all the more violent because he really wanted just what I wanted. And then we went ahead after all. God knows how, but we succeeded. And then the joy, the reveling in reconciliation!

"Thus our work in art and our friendship was an ever merging and reviving unity; and I may publicly celebrate the companion in art by praising the friend.

"What kind of trouble the poor man had with me! Prudent and realistic in his practical appreciation of the happenings in this world—how deep was the grief, the pain, he suffered for me when I was torn away from him. Fate drove me so far away. Only a few months ago I had hoped to see him again. But now I shall never again be able to press his hand. If there was anything that could endear that rare man to me more than our association had done, it was our separation. In his first letter to me in my exile, his sorrow and love showed as in bright flame: the intimate *du* which I once had proposed to him and which the strange man had refused on account of our official relations, he now offered me in ardent devotion; the father lovingly embraced the beloved lost son. Once I was his joy, but now I was his care! And how he cared for me! When the unexpected miracle happened, and my operas began to spread across Germany with suddenly increasing popularity, his 'care' gradually changed to 'taking care'; and when the young man failed, the vigorous old man stepped in, eased me of all my burdens, watched the copying and arrangements of my scores, wrapped them up, corresponded, pushed ahead or stopped—for the sake of my peace—so that I might work again and devote myself to my art. Now I succeeded again and how delighted he was! But that joy was forever dimmed to him. When would he see me once more? Would he ever? At last, when all his hope vanished, he wanted to start out himself, to come and visit me at the foot of the distant Alps. Then illness prevented him: his savings had to be used for a cure, the plan to see his friend had to be abandoned. Having confidently expected to see him, I now learned of his fatal illness and was able only to—write to him. He died—and my letter failed to reach him.

"Now my home has become much more alien to me; but you live quite close to me, dear friend, in my heart, where I carry you around with me, and no exile can separate us again.

"There are not many men like him left in this world, for he was such a rare man. If the artist is permitted to draw forth that man into the public view as a friend, I do it only to show in him also the deserving, serious companion in art. He bequeaths to his sorrowing heirs a certain treasure which, pathetic in its origin, offers rich reward to aspiring musicians. When Fischer retired to his little room from the toil of his duties, the worries of his profession, the cares of friendship, for a few quiet hours of recreation, I often found him there absorbed in a project which he undertook for his own diversion: with his neat hand he copied all kinds of rare and precious musical works, especially works in many vocal parts, and of the older masters who to most people were hardly known by name. To my wondering smile he answered that this was his way of filling his time pleasantly, and learning while enjoying himself. For if you are not able to create such works yourself, nothing would be better than copying them; in that way you study them in a thorough way you could hardly do otherwise. And this man came to the theater in his age of early adolescence, became an actor, won the impassioned favor of the Leipzig public as a bass buffo, but this didn't suffice him; he was more attracted by serious art: so he developed his musical knowledge, became choral director in addition to his position as an actor, again acquired high fame as such, and kept studying in order to preserve himself for decisive and important participation in the solution of the most serious and bold tasks of art, and above all to preserve a free and open understanding of every advance, every development of the older music. Thus he was able to extend a noble and fearless welcome to works of mine which were met with doubt and dis-

trust by the critics, though he did this only after hesitation and friendly head-shak-
ings. His understanding of them came quite spontaneously by practical participation
in the performance of the doubted work, thus gaining faith through love.

"Truly, it is a comfort that such men exist! It is a priceless boon to have met
such a man! It is a deep grief to lose him.

"And so I have dared to put our dear Fischer beside the much honored Spohr.
Death united both for me and involuntarily merged them into one: the significance
of their actions makes them appear equal to me. What places one in the forefront
by his works and fame I should like to bestow upon the other; if I should follow the
dictates of my heart I would yield to him all my achievements as an artist, if I did
not deem them too slight. Thus I prefer to bridge the distance by my full gratitude
and love.

RICHARD WAGNER."

343   Dr. Anton Pusinelli, in Dresden, November 15, 1859, to Wagner.

This letter has been published in *The Letters of Richard Wagner to Anton
Pusinelli,* translated by Albert Lenrow.

344   Itemized account (12 pp.) by the Tapissier Churnis, in Paris, for the decoration
of Wagner's house in the rue Newton, October, 1859. There are about 150 items,
ranging to 80 francs. Wagner wrote in *My Life* about this episode: "I was reproached
with a love of luxury." This is evidence that the reproach was just.

345   Photograph of Minna Wagner and Natalie Planer, taken, according to a notation by Mrs. Burrell on a scrap of paper, on November 15, 1859. Mrs. Burrell, noting that Natalie gave her the picture in July, 1890, copied the inscription where
Fräulein Natalie Planer is referred to as *"Ihre Schwester,"* but these two words have
been heavily crossed out.

The photograph is missing in the Collection.

346   Visiting card of "Richard Wagner, 16, rue Newton, Champs Elysées."

347   Wagner, in Paris, to Joseph Tichatschek in Hamburg.

A   March 23, 1861. (Page 389.)

Wagner writes of the *Tannhäuser* scandal in Paris, and compares his friend to
"the shrinking coward who runs around howling that he ruins his voice with my
Tannhäuser. You can well imagine how I feel." Wagner is delighted to hear good
reports about Tichatschek's health and voice. "Since Heaven wants to preserve you
for me so wonderfully that I'm to find you in good shape when I return to Germany,
we'll still accomplish something at which everybody will be amazed!"

B   July 21, 1860.

348   Anna Liszt, in Paris, to Minna in Paris.

A   March 26, 1860.

B   September 7, 1860.

Friendly notes from the mother of Franz Liszt. In the first she writes of her intention of visiting Minna in her "grass-widowhood," and adds, later: "How are you, dear Madame? Do you get good news from your husband; if the weather is as nasty in Brussels as it is here, it may make a bad impression on him because he is so nervous." In the second letter she speaks of her granddaughters, "Madame de Bulow" and "Madame Olivier."

349   Wagner, in Paris, 1860, to Mrs. Agnes Street-Klindworth.

This was the daughter of Karl Klindworth whom Wagner had met in London. Frau Street-Klindworth had entertained Wagner during his visit to Brussels to give concerts the previous month.

A   April 14.

". . . The piano score of *Tristan* should be finished soon now: you and the young Kalerginska will soon get the whole business. It won't make you very happy: the music is grayish [*gräulich*], I tell you that confidentially. Fortunately, however, you are—as Liszt's pupil—a good pianist in any case: the arrangement by Bülow will then at least entertain you; to me, undisciplined pianist that I am, it simply remains a riddle because it is so pianistic.

"Heaven knows when I shall ever hear this music which I like so much— despite the fact that it is so monstrous! That's the only thing I care about, nothing else in Paris. Your father probably knows about it already, but doesn't want to tell me. Surely the tyrannical Saxon minister has answered by this time? I have finally met Prince Metternich. I liked him pretty well: he expressed hopes for me on the part of the Saxon government; Seebach told him so. If there should still be insurmountable obstacles, he thought he could give me hopes for Vienna. It all sounded very promising. What I liked most was that he expressed some misgivings [*Bedenken*] about my music: I assured him that nobody had more misgivings about that than I. I haven't seen the Princess again. As for Herr Münch, I have been able to present myself twice only by way of my card.

"Since Papa surely can do everything (why would he be sitting in Brussels otherwise?), let him straighten out the Dresden trouble [*Misere*] as soon as possible. I'll have to be able to go to Germany soon in order to look around for a birthplace for *Tristan*. That happens to be a matter of the heart, and matters of the mind can be taken care of clearly and successfully only when the heart is satisfied. So if Papa wants the Parisians to see an intelligible *Tannhäuser,* he'll first have to help me to bring out *Tristan*. The rehearsals here can't really get started before the middle of September. But in Vienna or elsewhere I can bring out *Tristan* in the beginning of August: how easy would my job of civilizing the Parisians then become! Papa should consider that and should straighten out everything quickly.

"I'll write to him soon. Give him my most cordial regards for today and tell him he is really a wonderful papa. Since I have no children, I look upon myself as having only an uncle's place in the world. But to you I want to be a real friend even if you don't say much to me. But when you do say something to me, let it always be as sincere and fine as in the last letters: then I understand, feel ennobled, strengthened and uplifted; then I smile, and say to myself: 'Well, things must be going well again for a change.'

"A thousand fervent regards from your

RICHARD WAGNER"

B   May 22.

". . . I cannot yet say anything definite about my future for the summer. Next month I shall definitely hear from v. Seebach, who is returning from Dresden, what I have to expect in the matter of my amnesty. If everything turns out favorably, I want to do all I can to produce *Tristan* in Germany (Vienna or Dresden) before the *Tannhäuser* rehearsals start in Paris. Then—goodbye Switzerland! And you would have to come to Dresden or Vienna if we are to meet. If nothing should come of that (do you wish it so?), then a trip to Switzerland will be my only relaxation this year, and then we shall talk it over thoroughly."

C   August 11.

"You really are kindness personified, dearest friend! I do not deserve your leniency. That you continue to think of me faithfully and graciously shows you to me in an ever finer light. Many thanks! continue to be good to me, and perhaps you'll never regret it.

"But I have the feeling that you can't really imagine the actual character of my troubles; it seems as if you were guessing sometimes too high, sometimes too low. First of all strike out every obstructed ambition; assume also that, when I perform my *Tannhäuser* here, it will take place only because I expect to get a truly inner satisfaction out of the accomplishment and the results of the performance. Nothing in the world, not even the most urgent consideration for my economic position, could bring me to see this through if I had to expose myself to the least disfigurement, or make any compromise whatsoever. This way I shall not be subjected to any conflict with myself.

"But let me be silent about all this today. Enough that, since I left you in Brussels, I have been so depressed by worries that I—frankly speaking—could not give vent to my feelings, and that demonstrations of enthusiasm especially affected me with incredible bitterness. This has now cleared up a little, and I can at least occupy my mind again with cares of a nobler sort, as used to be the case. Still, you can easily imagine my situation if I must forgo all relaxation from without during the entire summer; and the Bois de Boulogne is my only refuge in nature during the few sunny hours which we have these days! But I'm just about to make momentary use of the favor of the King of Saxony—probably already known to you—by going to the Rhine for a few days in order to look up the Princess of Prussia in Coblenz, with whom I need to have a personal discussion in order to determine once and for all how far I can rely on this lady, that is, how far she is able to understand what this is about. At that time I shall also call for my wife in Soden. Altogether I can devote only five or six days to this.

"Your visit to Liszt made me very happy: that was the way to do it! You describe him to me as everybody describes him. His grief—for whom is it intended? I feel he has really only *one* thing about which to grieve, and that is his intangible dependence on a woman who is doing him unbelievable harm. But nothing would betray the fact that he grieves about that; he is merely becoming embittered over the harm which that relationship causes him without wanting to admit the reason. Now we are all in trouble: we cannot help him, not even console him; our contacts must be kept almost superficial; we have to be diplomatic, and to pretend not to know this or that, etc.— What can we do? I feel very much constrained toward him: I cannot be frank without hurting his feelings, and how easily he is offended these days.[38]

"I can't think of a visit to Germany until the second half of the winter: then I'll visit Liszt first. He surely may not and will not come to you in Brussels. My future is also quite unknown to me: Germany is open to me, but only now do I actually recognize that I really have no sanctuary for my art. Where?? That is the question which still remains completely unanswered.

"You seem to have become stronger, for which I'm happy; in any case you have a good outlet for many a heartache—you can still interest yourself seriously and wholeheartedly in politics. I have not been able to do so for a long time: I have no more taste for the changing forms of world conditions, since I can no longer feel that the basic character of the world is at all affected by them; thus I lose a fascinating and—diverting interest, whereas perhaps I have the sole advantage of recognizing the character of the world in the apparently most insignificant individual happenings of life; and this all the more definitely as the essence of the world, in its greater expanses of time and space, often becomes indefinite and unrecognizable so that we think we're seeing realities where there is actually nothing but deceptive cloud formations.

"But I don't want to argue with Papa; on the contrary, I send him my love through you. I am infinitely glad to see you again: you may believe that! And many thanks and a faithful return of your friendship

R. WAGNER"

[38] Julius Kapp quotes a remark from the Collection catalogue about this letter: "R. W. deplores this dependence on a woman who does him only harm"; he misreads this as referring to Wagner and Agnes Street-Klindworth instead of to Liszt and his Princess. The astonishing result is that one more is added to *The Women in Wagner's Life* (p. 152), for he concludes: "The lovely Agnes, who was perpetually changing her lovers, seems to have harnessed Wagner also to her love-chariot." It is too bad that he could not have seen these entirely innocent letters of Wagner to the daughter of his friend.

350   The Countess Hacke, Zürich, August 17 [1860], to Wagner [in Baden-Baden].

Wagner relates in *My Life* (p. 749) how, arriving in Baden-Baden, he availed himself of a letter of introduction from Count Pourtalès to make himself known to Countess Hacke, lady-in-waiting to the Crown Princess of Prussia. "After a little delay, I duly received an invitation to meet her in the Trinkhalle at five o'clock." This is the invitation referred to:

"SIR—

"I request that you be in the Trinkhalle at half past four, where Her Royal Highness, the Princess of Prussia, will go to speak with you.
                                "Respectfully
                                                    A. GRÄFIN HACKE
"Zürich, August 17"

351   Olga von Meck, in St. Petersburg, December 9/21, 1860, to Minna.

The young daughter of Amalie, Minna's sister who married the Russian officer Carl von Meck, in 1839, writes to her "own dearest Aunt." She tells that her family have bought a house, into which they are about to move, and she describes the house. She inquires about the health of her uncle, having read in the papers that he was sick.

352   Ludwig Schindelmeisser, in Darmstadt, October 18, 1860, to Wagner in Paris.

The *Kapellmeister* at Darmstadt tells his friend that the production of *The Flying Dutchman,* contemplated for Darmstadt, cannot be achieved immediately. He writes with great interest of the coming performance of *Tannhäuser* in Paris. (Page 382.)

353   Hans von Bülow, November 11 [1860, to Wagner].

"HONORED FRIEND!

"Today I have been able to finish only half of the arrangement. Don't take it badly, I really could do no better. My Jewish conservatory director scheduled the students' examinations a week earlier than they had been previously planned. So I have plenty to do to shield the conservatory from blame, for I was much opposed to the ostentation of advancing the examination dates just now.

"The arrangement of the *Faust* Overture in its old form was not my doing; I obtained it from Uhlig, and later on I left it with the Ritters. It was not practical but it might have facilitated my work. I hope to handle the score in such a way that you won't have to complain about an abundance of misplaced reverence.

"If you really want to give me a return present—let us rather say, if you wish to give me joy—present me with your essays, which I don't own and which I keep drawing from the lending library—an occupation economically unfavorable. Or give me another copy of *Der Ring des Nibelungen,* since my once well bound book is completely spoiled with being read, a permanent practice of my so-called friends. Are you now quite well again? Liszt is to leave from Weimar on the 25th—his concert is scheduled here for the 6th of December. On the 15th he is supposed to conduct the second subscription concert in Hanover.

"Joachim is here; he *never* got a letter from you, which would have given him the chance and joy of an answer. He was in Zürich in July and stayed there for a few days, expecting you, and finally he had to return.

"I heard infamous things about Dorn concerning *Tannhäuser*. But he won't get off so easily. Yesterday I wrote him an externally very harmless and enormously polite letter from which he however—and only he himself—may and must gather that I know him. I believe that on reading it he won't blush, but grow pale.

"Frau Frommann is awfully anxious and excited about the 'Event of the 15th of December,' the preliminary date of the first performance. If only she would succeed in getting the Princess of Prussia to that performance!

"Taubert would be in truth—better. But I remind you of a nice song which you once sang to me and Karl in Zürich on the melody:

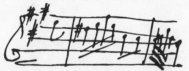

and this after all is fitting to all the mess here too.

"Yours faithfully

Hans v. Bülow"

354 Rehearsal notice, addressed to Wagner, for *Tannhäuser* at the Théâtre Impérial de l'Opéra, called for 1:30 P.M., October 3, 1860.

355 Photograph, according to Natalie's inscription, of the French translator of *Tannhäuser*. This could be Roche, or Nuitter, who collaborated with him.

356 Manuscript of certificate of honorary membership, conferred upon Richard Wagner on the occasion of the hundredth anniversary of the Musical Society of Riga. Four members of the board express the desire "that you may henceforth preserve your devotion and loyalty proven in the past."

357   Natalie Planer, in Zwickau, to Minna.

A December 25, 1860.

Natalie describes at length a family Christmas celebration and thanks Minna effusively for her gifts. The letter ends with these remarks about Wagner:

"Do not lose the hope for happy, intimate, lovely days; Richard will again be, as in former happy times, your good, faithful, attentive, congenial Richard-man [*Richard-Mann*], as you often called him in peaceful, happy times, and in his renewed love and openheartedness you will soon have forgotten the sorrow he has inflicted on you, and Richard will feel ashamed for having so misjudged and offended his faithful, loving companion. It cannot be otherwise—his inherent good heart could not so deny itself. The disposition and character of one who is graced with such a splendid genius can never become as warped as in another prosaic human being. There is still a noble foundation, and the man inspired by noble music will find himself again, and with a strong arm save himself and you, dear woman offended in her holiest rights, from moral ruin. Certainly, dear Minna, that's what will happen, his intoxication will pass and, uplifted and reformed, he'll come back to you. Have courage and step boldly into the future: subdue fate with your strong spirit; don't let yourself be subdued by it; have faith in God; nothing is impossible for His wisdom and omnipotence. And now accept my most fervent parting kiss in the old year as a seal of my eternal gratitude. I wish you, with all my heart, a kiss of peace and happiness for the years to come. Farewell, then, and a happy New Year, with many affectionate greetings,

"YOUR LOVING NATALIE"

B   April 23, 1861.

Natalie tells Minna that she is taking four language lessons, two music lessons, one arithmetic, and three drawing lessons a week, at a minimum cost, which she specifies. Her expenses include a few textbooks, and presents to the Trögers and others where necessary: "I'm almost stingy, and save wherever I can," she protests in answer to Minna's reproach that she is not a good manager of her funds. She further assures Minna that she has not "fanned the flames of the Trögers' domestic discord." She writes: "In your next to last letter you advise me to get married. Are you really serious, my dear good Minna? Would you be satisfied if a man with a position should turn up? There is no prospect of that now, but the same thing that happened to that old woman with the winning ticket could perhaps happen to me." She fears that her looks are fading, asks for a remedy for wrinkles, "especially in the forehead," and finds that white hairs are appearing among her "red ones." She reflects upon the condition of her supposed sisters, Amalie and Charlotte, and decides that Amalie "shines with her Herr von Meck," and that Charlotte, "in spite of all discord at home," has kept her "pretty, dark hair," and is free of wrinkles. She would exchange faces with her, but "her figure is too stout for me." Natalie concludes: "I never count myself as among the élite, but as better off than any of you who have won a big prize in the marriage lottery. . . . I'll certainly work hard to make a living as an old maid, because I probably won't get a man now. Today an acquaintance of mine was married to a man who amounts to nothing, and depends on the grace of his parents-in-law, all this just to have a man."

358   Pauline Tichatschek, in Frankfurt, December 8, 1860, to Minna in Paris.

The wife of Tichatschek writes affectionately to Minna. She has just visited the Brockhaus family at Neustadt. "I made them tell me a lot about you; she said that she is very sorry for you, since life with Richard must be hard, but you must have patience with him since he can't live without you." She continues, apparently referring to Luise Brockhaus: "I don't agree that you should tell everything to your sister-in-law. How can you assume that the sister will say you are right? Have you not learned, after many years of suffering and enduring, how cold those people are? You will have to bear your troubles alone, and only a fellow sufferer like me can realize the torments which destroy life—and so, my beloved Minna, we are united for our whole lives." Her meaning becomes clear as it appears that her husband, her "Tichy," is running after a dancer. Pauline has no alternative but to accept the situation in bitter silence. The letter is otherwise filled with the people and doings of the theater world. Wagner's niece Johanna Jachmann is included in the gossip. She has found her husband with a chambermaid and is said to be about to divorce him.

359　Dr. Adam Tröger, in Zwickau, to Minna.

A　December 26, 1860.

The letter bears the salutation "Dearest sister-in-law and sister!" and is signed "Tröger and wife." The spelling often lapses into the Saxon dialect. This letter consists of Christmas messages and thanks for a clock which Minna has sent.

B　August 10, 1864.

Another letter of gratitude for a birthday gift to Charlotte. But he adds: "The way Richard behaves toward you is disgraceful, I should not like to do a thing like that, for it is a sin; but the punishment, I hope, will not fail to come." Both are pleased with Natalie, still living with them. In Charlotte's absence she has supervised the renovation of the house.

360　Fr. Dingelstedt, Intendant of the Hofkapelle and Hoftheater at Weimar, December 30, 1860, to Wagner.

"This is to convey, venerable Master, the news of the great success of *Rienzi,* which has been performed on our stage on the 2nd and 3rd holiday [39] and which has been placed on the repertory for the 6th of the coming month. I enclose a program as well as two modest critical essays of the small local daily and close with the cordial wish that the 'Tribune of Weimar' may be a forerunner in miniature for the 'Minnesinger of Paris.' [40]

"In sincere admiration

Your devoted

FR. DINGELSTEDT"

[39] December 26 and 27.
[40] The *Tannhäuser* première in Paris was then expected momentarily.

361   Minna, in Paris (excepting D), to Natalie Planer in Zwickau.

A   May 8, 1860.

Minna is unable to send payment for Natalie's lessons because her husband is short of money, but hopes to send 200 francs soon. She urges her to be industrious and neat, and not run around looking like the "sloppy sluts" [*schnepprigen Schlumpen*] of Zwickau. Natalie is being primed for a position as governess. She must be able to teach "the elements of the various subjects, especially music, drawing, French, history, etc." It will require "good manners," appearance, and the "ability to move about in good society." Minna cites a governess then in Paris, Fräulein von Meysenbug (Minna spells the name Meysenburg), whose mistress, the English Mrs. Schwabe, the Wagners have met. "As a rich Englishwoman," remarks Minna, "she will not escape from Richard's hands unfleeced." Minna has been urged by her sister-in-law, Cläre Wolfram, to receive the daughter "Röschen" in Paris. Minna is reluctant but fears to offend the mother. She remarks of the impending *Tannhäuser*: "God, if this opera will only be a success—let's hope so."

B   May 23 (1860).

Natalie is to receive the money promised in the earlier letter. Zöllner, the theater manager in Brünn, has had the "fortunate idea" of mounting *Tannhäuser,* and will send the fee of 10 louis d'or directly to Zwickau. Minna complains of an expensive ménage and unsatisfactory servants in their Paris house.

C   June 26, 1860.

The money expected from Brünn has not been forthcoming. Wagner has written Zöllner and his Dresden publisher Müller about it. Minna has reduced the staff of house servants. "Richard is often in the most terrible financial difficulties. . . . He knows, as I wrote him, how to start on a high level and end on a low one." Their staff of servants must be reduced. She is about to go to Soden on July 2, alone, for a four weeks' cure. She has discouraged the advent of Röschen, and thereby made Cläre "deeply offended" and "quite angry." She adds a postscript: "Jacquot still calls every morning—'Natalie make coffee!' It is sweet."

D   Soden, July 14 [1860].

Wagner has had 30 thaler sent to Natalie and Minna advises her to hold it against future embarrassment, instead of frittering it away, for "it is *very* hard to send money." She concludes: "I miss the dog and Jacquot greatly, not so much Richard."

E   February 10 [1861].

Minna has found through Frau von Szemere a position for Natalie with an English family, to teach a twelve-year-old girl. Her lack of knowledge of English will not stand in her way—this circumstance will compel her pupil to learn French or German. Since Natalie is already able to play sonatas by Beethoven and Schumann (Minna writes *"Bethhofen und Schuhmann"*), she should be able "to communicate this to others by teaching." She has told Frau von Szemere that Natalie speaks "well and fluently" (!), for she has heard that to impress English people "one must pretend to have swallowed knowledge by the spoonful."

F　Paris, March [April?] 5, 1861.

Minna is impatient with Natalie because she is still in the preparatory stage: "Will you ever become independent or do you want to remain perpetually an overgrown child, and continue to have lessons for years?" Money is still a problem; Minna is sending a promissory note which she holds. Natalie may have to borrow on it if she cannot collect at once. She describes the *Tannhäuser* scandal. (Pages 378, 390.)

G　Paris, April 18, 1861.

Natalie is still a financial burden. Minna writes: "It is still uncertain where we are going to go, perhaps to Karlsruhe, where Richard is now staying for a few days, or to Weimar, or even to Frankfurt. You need not tell anything about this to anybody."

H　Dresden, March 6, 1862.

After relating her stormy encounter with Wagner at Biebrich in the previous month (see page 408), Minna discusses Natalie's future: "If your Türk hasn't proposed to you by the fall, he *never* will do it. In that case come to me and everything will be all right. You make too much of a few friendly words, as was also the case with . . . [?]. But they don't always mean anything. They are never really serious —they do nothing but chatter in order to find out how it stands with the money. You are too old after all for T., and it is no great fortune to get a man with a salary of 320 thr. You are far from understanding how to make ends meet with your money. But if you love him, you would learn this too. Don't be so prudish, my good Natalie. Don't make such ugly faces, otherwise you won't even get that poor wretch. I could manage a small marriage portion. . . ." (Page 9.)

I　April 18, 1862.

Still miserable from her Biebrich experience, Minna would like to turn to Natalie for comfort. "I have nobody near me to talk things over with reasonably and calmly. You, my dear Natalie, are the only one who could compensate me for all the distress I am meeting on my rough path of life. You could have borne and shared so much with me—" But Minna is unable to confide wholeheartedly in Natalie; the grudging tone returns: "By your lack of experience, your stubbornness and harshness, you have always estranged yourself from me and preferred to make friends with my maids instead of me, because I mistakenly tried to correct what the good mother and late sister [41] had spoiled in you." Minna warns Natalie not to interfere if Tröger casts his eyes about for another wife. If he should court Natalie, Minna would not favor the idea, for Natalie "would not be amiable enough to hold a man permanently: that goes with the sort who has no brains but is naturally attractive." She should rather make herself useful and pleasant around the house, in the hope that he may not try to get rid of her.

"You are a good girl, don't misunderstand me, but unfortunately you have the wrong idea about the attitude of men toward a girl when it comes to showing their honest intentions, and so, in the long run, you have missed out. It is certainly a great misfortune for you, my good child, that you never listened to my advice, never obeyed it, and always looked upon me as your *enemy*." She continues to reproach her for her "unfriendliness," "slovenliness of dress," and "irritability." [42] (Page 9.)

J   Dresden, April 23, 1862 (addressed to a "most honored friend," unspecified).
Minna is writing to a friend in Zürich, to renew past memories. Speaking of her heart trouble, she mentions her intention to take a cure at Schandau in the following month. "At the beginning of September, Wagner expects me in Strassburg in order to travel to Paris with me, where he plans to settle again for good. But I could not safely guarantee that news." Where she goes is a matter of indifference to her, but she would like "peaceful solitude," where she may be spared the company of silly women who "even here envy me the possession of a great artist." She would rather have them envy the man than the artist. She then relates her version of the Asyl crisis (see page 376).

K   (Undated) Minna to Natalie.
Since Minna has just visited Zwickau, after the death of her sister Charlotte, this letter is probably of 1862. There has been an unpleasant property altercation, and Tröger has tried to get from her a written statement renouncing further claims. Natalie is to remain as his housekeeper. Minna gives her routine instructions, with more unflattering advice about her conduct and appearance.

362   Photograph of Minna, taken in Dresden, according to a notation in Natalie's hand, in 1851.

363   Photographs of Cläre Wolfram and Cäcilie Avenarius, Wagner's sisters, late in life, and given to Mrs. Burrell by Natalie.

364 A   "Richard Wagner," pamphlet (16 pp.) by Champfleury, published in Paris, 1860.
Although Champfleury was not a musician (he was a painter and sculptor), he

[41] Natalie's "sister" Charlotte had recently died, leaving her alone with Tröger, the husband.
[42] These letters confirm Wagner's statement in his autobiography that Minna and Natalie were constantly quarreling, that dictation from the mother was not taken in good part by Natalie, who looked upon her as an overdemanding sister.

felt called upon to defend Wagner in this brochure. The article was reprinted in Champfleury's book *Grandes figures d'hier et d'aujourd'hui* (1861).

B *Les Concerts de Paris—Revue de la Saison Musicale de 1860* (3 pp.), published in 1860.

365 Filled-in notifications for *Tannhäuser* rehearsals, addressed to Wagner by the Théâtre Impérial de l'Opéra, 1861.

A January 2: one o'clock
B January 12: one o'clock—chorus
　　　　　　seven o'clock—orchestra
C January 15: one o'clock (2nd act)
D January 20: 7:15 (first two acts—singers—chorus)
E January 26: 12:45 (chorus—1st scene and 3rd act)
　　January 27: 7:30 (orchestra)
F January 28: one o'clock (chorus—Act III, scene 1)
G January 29: seven o'clock—full rehearsal

366 Lithographed invitation to Wagner for the opening of the salons of the *Cercle de l'union artistique,* February 1, 1861. Signed by Prince Poniatowski, president of the committee.

367 E. B. Kietz, in Epernay, January 18, 1861, to Wagner in Paris. (Page 204.)

368 The director of the Théâtre Impérial de l'Opéra, February 25, 1861, to Wagner (letter in French):

"MONSIEUR ET MAÎTRE:
"I received your letter at a quarter past three; there are absolutely no box seats left; I am sending you an orchestra seat, and the director of the opera wants me to inform you that his box is always open to you. Accept, sir, my sincerest compliments."
[Signature illegible]

369 E. Cormon, stage manager of the Théâtre Impérial de l'Opéra, "Thursday, 7 o'clock," to Wagner. (Page 389.)

370 Wagner in Paris, January 22, 1861, to E. B. Kietz. (Page 207.)

371 Princess Metternich, January 30, 1861, to Wagner. (Page 383.)

372 Dr. Anton Pusinelli, in Dresden, to Minna. (These letters have been published in *The Letters of Richard Wagner to Anton Pusinelli.*)

A January 31, 1861, to Minna in Paris.
Dr. Pusinelli has been concerned, as other friends have been, about Wagner's illness. There have even been rumors in Dresden, he says, about brain fever, mental derangement, and the like. He frankly mentions Minna's "pathological irritability"

as well as Wagner's temperament. He prescribes pills for Minna and warns her "against opium." He is apprehensive about the pending production of *Tannhäuser* in Paris and reassures Wagner that the discriminating minority of the present will be the majority of the future. He gives his personal opinion that *Lohengrin,* among the four of Wagner's operas then being given in Germany, is "the most homogeneous and clear work of art."

B   September 4, 1861, to Minna in Weimar.

He tells Minna of the sudden death, from cerebral hemorrhage, of his son Eric, Minna's godchild.

C   August 17, 1862, to Minna in Reichenhall.

Pusinelli had already mentioned to Minna the idea of a divorce, thereby incurring her anger. Now with what tact he may he again brings up the unhappy subject. He courageously takes the responsibility for first broaching it. He repeats what by now the two of them have recognized: that they must live apart. Any attempt to live together could only be injurious to both of them. A divorce, however, which would have meant giving over Wagner to another woman, was an idea Minna refused, then or ever, to accept.

373   *Tannhauser, opéra en trois actes,* printed text in French, Librairie Théâtrale, 1861.

374   Frau Marie Niemann, in Paris, January 2, 1861, to Wagner. (Page 387.)

375 A   Photograph of Wagner (missing in the Collection).

B   M. Fillon, Paris, February 3, 1901, to Mrs. Burrell. A verification that this photograph was taken in 1861, by Pierre Petit in Paris.

376   Minna in Paris, 1861, to E. B. Kietz at Epernay.
A   February 1. (Page 383.)
B   February 13. (Page 385.)
C   February 19. (Page 385.)

377   Albert Niemann, in Paris, February 20, 1861, to Wagner. (Page 387.)

378   G. Cormon, Paris, to Mme. de Szemere. (Page 389.)

379   G. Cormon, in Paris, to Mme. de Szemere.

Undated, but anticipates the *Tannhäuser* production. Mme. Cormon writes: "My husband would have answered himself but he is entirely occupied with the remarkable work of your friend, on which he means to spare nothing. For me this great artistic event is a real occasion, and although I have not the privilege of knowing Mr. Wagner, my whole sympathy is with him and I hope his success is epoch-making."

380   Luise Brockhaus, in Dresden, March 19, 1861, to Minna in Paris. (Page 391.)

381   Passport of Minna from Saxony to Paris, dated March 16, 1861.

382   Pauline Tichatschek, in Dresden, March 25, 1861, to Minna in Paris. (Page 393.)

383   Karlsruhe, April 20, 1861.

"The undersigned herewith notifies Herr Richard Wagner that His Royal Highness the Grand Duke wants to speak with him on Sunday at half past eleven.

v. REISCHACH
Ober-Ceremonienmeister"

384   Visiting card of Gräfin von Pourtalès, née von Bethmann-Holweg. Mrs. Burrell writes: "This is the Countess Pourtalès who took Wagner into the Embassy for several weeks in Paris to prevent his being put in prison for debt." It is unfortunate that Mrs. Burrell did not particularize, or quote her source. It is certainly true that Wagner was extremely short of funds in Paris at this time, having derived nothing but trouble from his *Tannhäuser* experience. He has written of the convenience of being harbored in the Prussian Embassy while his quarters were denuded of furniture in the process of moving. But of actionable indebtedness there is no hint in the considerable correspondence of this period.

385   Wagner to Minna, 1861.
   A   From Vienna, May 10. (Page 397.)
   B   From Vienna, August 9. (Page 398.)
   C   From Vienna, October 3. (Page 398.)
   D   From Vienna, November 4. (Page 399.)

386   Wagner to the *Wiener Presse,* May 18, 1861, copy by Minna. (Page 339.)

387   Malwida von Meysenbug (undated, but presumably May, 1861) to Minna. (Page 338.)

388   Dr. Anton Pusinelli, in Dresden, June 6, 1861, to Minna in Paris. (Page 392.) (Published in *The Letters of Richard Wagner to Anton Pusinelli.*)

389   Telegrams of greeting, the first a birthday congratulation from Wagner to Minna.
   A   September 5, 1861, Vienna to Weimar.
   B   November 24, 1861, Vienna to Dresden.

390   Leopoldine von Szemere [Paris], November 16 [1861], to Minna in Weimar.
   Frau von Szemere relates small news about friends and her children. One remark is an indication of how gossip travels: "I hear from Vienna that *Tristan und Isolde* is said to be beautiful, but surpasses the capacity of the singer."

391   Anna Liszt, in Paris, December 26, 1861, to Minna in Zwickau (forwarded from Weimar).

Liszt's mother writes: "My dear friend, may you be spared in the coming year from the many troubles which you have had to undergo in the present one. May God grant you good health; then you will again enjoy happy times. Presumably you have now been separated from your husband for a considerable period. Such is the fate of many wives as well as mothers who have as husband or son a great *artiste musicien.*"

392   Wagner to Joseph Tichatschek [in Dresden].
   A   Venice, November 11, 1861. (Page 401.)
   B   Paris (19 Quai Voltaire), December 8, 1861. (Page 403.)

393   Minna, in Dresden, December 14, 1861, to E. B. Kietz. (Pages 207, 364, 405.)

394   Pauline Viardot to Wagner (note by hand, undated).

The mention of Saint-Saëns indicates the year 1860, when the twenty-five-year-old composer astonished Wagner by his ability not only to play the piano from score, but to play the new, unknown, and strange *Tristan* "by heart." Wagner has mentioned gatherings at the house of Pauline Viardot, when, in the presence of Berlioz, *Tristan* was read, Wagner taking the male parts with too much warmth for comfort, Mme. Viardot-Garcia singing the female parts with too little.

"Luck is decidedly against us. No rehearsal is possible today. I sing Orphée tonight, and at the time Saint-Saëns can come I shall be at table.

"We have arranged a meeting at my house tomorrow at a quarter past one for him and Reichhardt, if you can be there. Most sincerely

                                                            PAULINE VIARDOT
"Sunday"

395   E. B. Kietz, in Epernay, January 26, 1862, to Minna in Dresden. (Page 209.)

396   Wagner, in Biebrich, 1862, to Minna.
   A   February 14. (Page 406.)
   B   March 25.
Wagner's instructions to Minna about his amnesty in the following letter were his last. Full pardon and permission to return to Saxony came three days later:

"DEAR MINNA!

"Here is the letter to the King which you requested. May it have the expected success! It is written just the way you wanted it: it was finally possible for me to find the briefest and most appropriate expression for my points:

"1. Dresden theater. 2. Your health, and the residence in Dresden necessary for it. 3. Reference to Pusinelli's statement (which is available if needed).

"If it all depended on hearing from me, it will surely not fail to be successful this time.

"I have been in a very bad humor these days. It is probably because nothing pleasant happens to me any more, hardship and worry keep torturing me. If I don't finish my projected opera by next winter, I really shan't know what to do. Nothing cheers me up or inspires me to work. There are always futile and disagreeable things which pursue a person into his very solitude.

"Whoever wishes me well now, should only wish that I'll soon enjoy my work. God grant that nothing more will interfere with it, not this or the other thing, but that I can enjoy peace and quiet for once! Amen!"

C August 1. (Page 411.)
D August 7. (Page 411.)
E September 10 (to Zwickau).

Wagner is distressed at not being able to send Minna expense money punctually. He has been in Frankfurt negotiating to conduct *Lohengrin,* and hoping "to win a rich man over to my cause."

397 Telegram from Friedrich, Grand Duke of Baden, in Karlsruhe, March 7, 1862, to Wagner in Biebrich.

"Thank you very much for your letter. Will you read your work to us Sunday the 9th? Please reply."

Wagner had moved to Biebrich at the end of February, with the intention of composing *Die Meistersinger*. He read the text to the Duke on the date specified.

398 Minna, in Dresden, March 8, 1862, to Frau Schott. The letter is a copy, made by Dr. L. Strecker, of the publishing firm of Schott and Sons.

Minna writes in great friendliness, urging Frau Schott to visit her in the autumn. She has had her photograph taken and sends a copy, although "it is serious and gloomy, like my whole life." She also writes: "Frau von Bülow, daughter of Liszt, wrote to me last week that she wants to live in Biebrich with her husband next summer, which will please my husband very much. You will find in Frau von Bülow a kind, intelligent lady, who will surely visit you often."

399 Wagner, in Biebrich, March 26, 1862.

The letter is evidently addressed to Mrs. Street, the daughter of Wagner's friend Klindworth. He bemoans the ill luck which has prevented him from visiting Liszt at Weimar and the recipient in Brussels. He suggests that she visit him instead. "I have finally settled down (alone) in two finely situated small rooms close to the Rhine in a makeshift arrangement, and I am now awaiting the visit of my Muse into whose arms I may finally throw myself once more! Come and visit me some time, with or without Papa; I need something human, friendly! Bring it to me!"

400   Three telegrams from Wagner to Minna in Dresden, 1862.

A   Biebrich, May 20.

"Can't make the trip. Don't expect me. Letter follows."

B   Leipzig, October 31.

"I'll try to spend a few days in Dresden. We'll see. Letter follows."

C   Vienna, November 24.

"Believe me, dear Minna, I think of you, even if anxiously. Hope for good news!"

401   Cosima von Bülow, in Berlin, May 27, 1862, to Minna.

Cosima writes at Wagner's request, to advise Minna about the accommodations at Reichenhall. She and Hans are to join Wagner at "Bieberich" in July: "I want to get away earlier, for Richard writes he is very lonely, but I cannot leave my little girl for so long."

402   Wagner, in Biebrich, June 27 [1862], to Minna. (Page 410.)

403   Minna, in Reichenhall, August 4 [1862], to Wagner—unfinished letter. (Page 411.)

404   Minna, in Zwickau, September 11 [1862], to Cosima von Bülow.

The first page of a letter which may have been rewritten. Minna says that she had arrived a week before at her sister's "with servant, dog, and bird." Charlotte and her husband, Dr. Tröger, hardly recognized her, on account of her illness. She has put herself in his care.

405   Cläre Wolfram, in Chemnitz, October 17, 1862, to Minna in Dresden.

This loyal sister-in-law addresses her "dear, good Minel" affectionately. She is planning shortly to visit her in Dresden. She is not on speaking terms with Cäcilie, but expects to see Luise. She writes: "Well, my dear Minel, are you really at peace? I had a real shock when I read your letter. To have to procure 300 thr., and a *woman* at that, and not to know from where! You really are a genius too! I would have given up, for I would not have got it; truly you have a real spirit of enterprise. Richard could seek among a thousand and not find your equal—I would certainly have given you the money if I had had it, for you keep your promise when it comes to paying back." She concludes: "I thank God that you are at peace—you have obtained that peace by hard fighting."

406   General Management of the Royal Saxon Music Kapelle and the Hoftheater, signed by Dr. Julius Pabst, October 20, 1862, to Wagner at Biebrich.

Refusal of leave of absence for the tenor Schnorr von Carolsfeld. (Page 404.)

407 Minna, in Chemnitz, October 26 [1862], to Natalie in Zwickau.

Minna, visiting her sister-in-law Cläre, in Chemnitz, is soon to return to Dresden, where Frau Tichatschek has been kind enough to have her apartment painted and the floor polished. Minna, who has been in Zwickau and who has evidently left her dog and parrot there, directs Natalie to come to Chemnitz with the pets. She says in a postscript: "I'm trembling quite a bit again, you can see that in my handwriting." It is indeed observable.

408 A Dr. Schnorr von Carolsfeld, in Dresden, July 21, 1894, to Mrs. Burrell.

The brother of the famous tenor answers Mrs. Burrell's inquiry by saying that Ludwig's widow, Malvina, possesses the letters and telegrams of Wagner to her husband. She has made known ten pages of them in the *Deutsche Revue,* Breslau and Berlin, October, 1883 (Vol. 1, No. 10). "These form the end of a rich correspondence carried on for years always in pursuit of one aim—the performance of the work deemed impossible to perform—*Tristan und Isolde.*" Dr. Schnorr, however, has found among his papers three telegrams which he copies in his letter. The first, from Biebrich to Karlsruhe, May 25, 1862, asks for one ticket "incognito" for *Lohengrin* on the following day, "with the greatest discretion." The second, from Frankfurt-am-Main, September 5, 1862, asks Frau Schnorr von Carolsfeld in Dresden to come and sing Ortrud on the following Wednesday. The third, from Vienna, November 25, 1862, says: "Everything in order and accepted. Letter on the way. Take care of May too." (Page 404.)

B Additional note, July 23, 1894, giving dates of telegrams, omitted in the earlier letter.

409 Program of a concert at the Gewandhaus, Leipzig, November 1, 1862, given by Wendelin Weissheimer. The program, opening with the Prelude to *"Die Meistersinger zu Nürnberg (neu)"* by Richard Wagner, ends with the Overture to *Tannhäuser,* each conducted by the composer. Wagner's friend Weissheimer arranged this concert for the performance of his own music. Leipzig, hostile to Wagner, turned out in small numbers but encored the *Meistersinger* prelude and remained to give Wagner an ovation at the end of the concert.

410 J. Bürde-Ney, November 7, 1862, to Minna.

Letter of regret from the singer because "today's rehearsal and tomorrow's opera make it impossible to accept your husband's kind invitation." Wagner was visiting Dresden for a few days—his first visit since his hasty departure thirteen years before. It was a gloomy return, like that of Rip Van Winkle, with the added strain of the last meeting with Minna. Wagner read his *Meistersinger* to a few friends, and it was to this meeting that he may have invited Frau Bürde-Ney, with an eye to the future.

411 Undated note by Wagner. There is a penciled notation in another hand, "Addressed to Heine." The catalogue attributes this note to 1862, but the text places it in 1861—probably November. (Page 403.)

412 Copy of title page of five songs by Wagner, as made by Dr. L. Strecker from the original manuscript in the possession of B. Schott, Söhne, Mainz.

Fünf
Dilettanten-Gedichte
für Frauenstimme
in Musik gesetzt
von
Richard Wagner
1. *Stehe Still*
2. *Der Engel*
3. *Schmerzen*
4. *Im Treibhaus*
5. *Träume*

413 Telegram from Wagner, in Vienna, January 1, 1863, to Minna in Dresden.

"Can only telegraph. Second concert given. Splendid success. Third on the 11th. Happy New Year.   RICHARD"

Three concerts, consisting mostly of Wagner's unperformed *Ring* and *Meistersinger* music, were given in Vienna, on December 26, January 1, and January 8. At the second (according to *My Life,* page 847), the attendance was small but the applause prolonged.

414 Amalie von Meck, in St. Petersburg, January 3, 1863, to Minna in Dresden.
Minna's sister has heard of Wagner's impending visit to conduct in St. Petersburg. Knowing that Minna is "unhappy," she warmly urges that, for the sake of the change, and to see once more this branch of the family, she journey to St. Petersburg with Richard.

415 J. Bergmann, in Prague, January 31, 1863, to Minna in Dresden.
Bergmann was a businessman of Prague and an admirer of Wagner (who had tried to borrow from him). In response to Minna's inquiry, he tells her that Wagner is to conduct a concert in the first week of February. People are in high expectation of it, and a banquet is being arranged in his honor. Wagner conducted on February 8 and took away 1,000 florins, which compensated in part for his losses from the three Vienna concerts just before.

416 Marie Wolfram, in Leipzig, to Minna.
A January 31, 1863.
The mother-in-law of Cläre Wolfram writes affectionately: "Has your august master written to you? Or is Wagner again at fault? *He* probably won't come to Dresden for a long time. I even believe that is the best, you faithful good soul, for your peace, for what can you do with a heartless and unscrupulous man? It is impos-

sible to meet him with warmth and love, for you would have to face being repulsed. Therefore it is better that he should stay where he is until he understands."

B   May 22, 1863.

Frau Wolfram urges Minna to take a cure in the coming summer. She will later come to her and nurse her—give her an "after-cure." She still hopes that there may be "a lasting reconciliation between you two. Could not Frau Avenarius influence him? I would have appealed to his conscience. He can't be entirely without feeling!"

417   Wagner to Minna, 1863.
   A   Prague, February 7. (Page 412.)
   B   Vienna, February 12. (Page 412.)
   C   Vienna, May 10. (Page 412.)
   D   Penzing, July 4. (Page 412.)
   E   Karlsruhe, November 20.

Wagner had just given two concerts in Karlsruhe, on November 14 and 19, after two in Prague—a concert in Breslau was to follow on December 6. These concerts, undertaken for the need of money, aroused great enthusiasm but brought little return. He writes that he is "absolutely exhausted." He is going to Löwenberg, where a concert is planned for December 1st. "On the way there I shall see you in Dresden, though for a short time only."

418   Photograph of E. B. Kietz, inscribed to Minna, and dated "Paris, June 8, 1863."

419   Wagner, in Penzing, June 20, 1863, to Natalie Planer. (Page 413.)

420   Cäcilie Avenarius, in Berlin, to Minna.
   A   September 29, 1863.

Cäcilie, protesting her love for Minna, wants to know "what your relations are with Richard at present. Of him I know nothing in God's wide world, for even if there has been something about him in the newspapers—I have read no newspaper all through the summer. I still think with much grief of your last letter, so unhappy and so perturbed."

B   December 4, 1864.

Cäcilie has visited Minna "a year ago," which would be after the previous letter: "The days I spent with you were so beautiful, so cozy and enjoyable—I shall always remain grateful to you for them. It is true, the fact that Richard stayed away and did not write cast a dark shadow over those days; however that was only one shadow beside much beautiful sunshine. I promised you at that time once again to write to Richard in your interest and only at your request. At least I have honestly fulfilled my promise and have also honestly kept my word in that I have not answered his letter and have never again written to him. . . . Is Richard writing to you oftener now? Now and then I have heard about him indirectly; he seems to be the man of the day in Munich."

421   Cäcilie Avenarius, in Berlin, to Minna, 1864.

A   February 1.

Cäcilie sympathizes with Minna in the loss of her sister Charlotte. "What will become of Natalie now?" she asks. "I dare say she will stay with the brother-in-law and will keep his household for him, for she has now reached the age where, in my opinion, nothing objectionable could be found in it." (Natalie was thirty-eight!) She does not believe, as Minna does, that Richard will come to Berlin in April; although he has written to her (Cäcilie) and asked to stay with her. She writes "you yourself said in your last letter—'In the state in which Richard now is I do not care too much about living with him; it is extremely dangerous, what did he offer me while we lived together,' etc. *He* himself says in *his* letter that he still requires the greatest consideration and indulgence, and that he would therefore not be able to extend them to others! This is an endless and discouraging theme, with all its variations, so that one can hardly imagine any solution satisfactory to both."

B   October 30.

Letter about her family, water cure, and so forth. She has read in a news dispatch from Munich that Richard is ill and she is alarmed.

422   Wagner to Minna, 1864.
A   Penzing, February 15. (Page 417.)
B   Starnberg, May 26. (Page 419.)
C   Starnberg, June 25. (Page 420.)
D   Starnberg, September 5. (Page 421.)
E   Starnberg, September 26. (Page 423.)
F   Munich, October 15. (Page 424.)
G   Munich, October 15. (Page 425.)
H   Munich, December 20. (Page 425.)

423   Minna, in Dresden (16 Porges Strasse), March 28, 1864, to E. B. Kietz. (Pages 415, 419.)

424   Wagner, in Mariafeld (Canton Zürich), April 25, 1864, to Pauline Tichatschek. (Summary and extracts from this letter are given by Altmann, German edition, quoted from the Catalogue of Bertling, 1890.)

425   Heinrich Wolfram, in Chemnitz, May 27, 1864, to Minna in Dresden (Walpurgis Strasse).

Wagner's brother-in-law tells Minna of the recent death of his son, Fritz, from pneumonia. He asks her to inform "our sister-in-law, Cäcilie of this misfortune; you realize that neither I nor my wife can take the opportunity to write to her personally, and still I should not want to leave her uninformed. Perhaps this sad event will bring the hearts of the two sisters closer to each other, for misfortune sometimes reconciles the bitterest enemies, so why not two sisters who have always been so close."

426 Luise Brockhaus, in Dresden-Neustadt, August 26 [1864], to Minna in Tharand.

Luise Brockhaus, who signs her Christian name as "Louise," and calls herself "your loyal and affectionate sister-in-law," asks "do you have news of your husband —and how is he?"

427 Telegrams, Wagner, in Munich, 1864, to Minna in Dresden.
A September 5. (Page 426.)
B October 9. (Page 426.)

428 MS dated Munich, November 27, 1864.

"To be inserted in the *Allgemeine Zeitung*:
"To the increasing number of written inquiries concerning an *opera school* opened in Munich under my direction, I must reply that newspaper reports concerning such an undertaking are erroneous.

RICHARD WAGNER"

429 [Alwine Frommann], in Berlin, December 28, 1864, to Minna.
A letter of thanks (incomplete) for a Christmas gift.

430 Frances Flaxland, in Paris, June 15, 1864, to Minna, in Dresden.

The wife of Wagner's Paris publisher writes in French. She has gone to Dresden to reach an understanding with Müller, who claimed the rights of publication for France, which Wagner had since sold to Flaxland. For the consideration of 6,000 francs, Müller has relinquished the French rights for *The Flying Dutchman, Rienzi,* and *Tannhäuser.* This, she trusts, will be a reassurance to Wagner, as forestalling future lawsuits.

431 Police card for residence in Dresden by Minna for the year 1866.

432 Ludwig Schnorr von Carolsfeld, January 9, 1865 (according to the catalogue, addressed to Kammermusikus Julius Rühlmann, president of the Musical Society of Dresden).

Schnorr thanks the recipient for a score which he will study while confined to his room.

433 Hans von Bülow, in Munich, January 12, 1865 (to Kammermusikus Julius Rühlmann of the Dresden Tonkünstlerverein, according to a notation by Mrs. Burrell).

Von Bülow asks for the return of Wagner's manuscript "Fragments of a Draft for the Reform of the Theater in the Kingdom of Saxony." The King "wishes to obtain a complete collection of all manuscripts written by Wagner." Von Bülow wishes the Tonkünstlerverein could "transplant itself" to Munich, where there is plentiful opportunity for awakening and reform. "The world would be perfect if Ludwig II held the throne in Dresden, or if the vocal and instrumental personnel of Dresden were employed in Munich. However—it is idle to argue with fate. Besides, this fate has really done something extraordinary in relieving the great *Meister* from the terrible confusion of his recent past. Professor Semper, who a short time ago was received by the King, got the definite assignment to build the Nibelungen Theater. So the prospect is fair and assured."

434   Telegrams from Wagner in Munich, 1865, to Minna in Dresden.
  A February 15.

"Be completely reassured. Envy, stupidity, and slander got hold of something they could not understand and used it to report falsehoods about me. Since there has been not the slightest cause for change in my relations, I am happy to enjoy now as before the full favor of my sublime protector, for the world will soon have the best proof, and thus I am too proud to refute that lying correspondence.

RICHARD WAGNER"

  B October 5.

"Have just mailed what is required.

RICHARD"

435   Wagner, in Munich, 1865, to Minna.
  A March 28. (Page 426.)
  B October 5. (Page 428.)

436 Hermann Müller, in Zürich, April 17, 1865, to Minna in Dresden.
  The Zürich friend thanks Minna for an embroidered pillow and wishes her restored health from a pending cure at Tharand. "I follow with interest the fluctuating life of your husband, which now goes on in Munich, at least so far as one can learn from here through the public press. And from a distance it has seemed to me that the favor and bounty bestowed on the composer by the youthful King has aroused a great deal of characteristically Bavarian envy. Unfortunately, certain leanings of Wagner toward extravagance may have furnished a welcome pretext for the circulation of all sorts of monstrosities against him, giving little weaknesses the aspect of great follies."

437 E. B. Kietz, in Epernay, April 4, 1865, to Minna. (Page 210.)

438 Richard Avenarius, in Zürich, May 1, 1865, to Minna.
  The son of Cäcilie, who has just arrived in Zürich with introductions to several of her friends, expresses his thanks.

439 Copy of will of Minna Wagner, dated May 11, 1865. The copy is certified by the Dresden District Court, June 3, 1867.

"Since I leave no descendants qualified to be my heirs, especially as a result of the unconditional waiver of all claims to my eventual inheritance, I hereby designate my beloved sister, Natalie Planer, as heir to my entire estate, whatever it may consist of." She directs that Natalie give Luise Brockhaus an oil portrait of her husband, Cläre Wolfram two engravings and a small, green easy chair, Cäcilie Avenarius a "good, embroidered pillow, an engraving of a dog and a cat."

A waiver, evidently intended to be signed by her husband, is unsigned.

The designation of Natalie as her "sister" shows that she risked invalidating her will in order to keep her secret from Natalie and the world, even after her death.

440 Minna, in Dresden, July 19 [?, possibly 1865] to Wagner. (Page 427.)

441 Hans von Bülow, in Munich, June 2, 1865, to "Herr Friedel."

Herr Friedel, apparently a friend of the Schnorrs, has asked for a manuscript score of Wagner's *Huldigungsmarsch* for Musikdirector Pohl. Bülow tells him that the rough manuscript sketch would be of no use to him. Franz Schott, in Mainz, has published it, but it is hard to get anything, even a letter, out of Schott. Frau Schnorr has been recuperating from an illness at Reichenhall, but is expected back for the *Tristan* rehearsals "at the beginning of next week." He signs himself: "*Tristan* conductor, now as always, despite the lies spread by the Augsburg *Allgemeine Zeitung,* Berlin, etc."

442 Pauline Tichatschek, in Dresden, July 22, 1865, to Minna in Tharand.

A chatty, inconsequential letter. She intends to send a "first payment" when she can extract it from her husband. She relays the current talk about Schnorr's sudden death. "It is terrible, such a sturdy fellow [*Knast:* a log of oak wood]! The poor parents! It is really heartrending; two days before his death, all his hair was cut off, and he is said to have roared like a lion; three people held him, so furiously did he rage!!! The doctors say he died of *Triestan* [*sic*]."

443 This number does not appear in the Collection.

444 [Minna],[43] in Dresden, December 16, 1865, to Cäcilie Avenarius.

Minna addresses "My good, beloved Cäcilchen!" She looks back on breaks in their friendship, "imposed on us by gossip," and hopes henceforth to be "happy in your love." She has been too sick even to walk any distance. "Yesterday I had a letter from Cläre in which she notifies me that Richard sent her his bust, which she wets with tears when she looks at it. A very short time ago I had a long letter in which she properly attacked him. Well, that is her lack of character—a favorable wind, a letter from him, and she changes at once to the other side. I completely understand that Richard, considering his follies, needs more than one defender. Maybe he sent his bust to you too? Write if I guessed correctly!" She concludes: "The smudge is Jacquot's footprint, he is naughty, and without shame."

[43] The letter is unsigned. The catalogue attributes it to Natalie, an obvious error.

445   Cläre Wolfram, in Chemnitz, November 6, 1863 (misdated in the catalogue, 1865).

The letter is about a young actress (unnamed). It has nothing of consequence.

446   Alwine Frommann, in Berlin, December 30, 1865, to Minna.

A New Year's greeting. She remarks that she is converting the queen's presents into rent, which she "needs more."

447   A. de Gasparini to Léon Leroy.

A, B   Two notes, scarcely legible, the first dated *"Jeudi,"* the second, *"26 Août,"* written in French, concerning the correction of an article: music is also involved. Léon Leroy was the editor of *La France Musicale,* Gasparini a Wagner devotee.

448   Newspaper clipping of a poem on Wagner by Georg Herwegh, Wagner's Zürich friend. It is quoted from the Vienna *National-Zeitung.* It deals humorously with Wagner's Munich experiences, and Mrs. Burrell accordingly dates it as of 1865.

449   Written statement by "Frau Minna Wagner, *geb.* Planer," Dresden, January 9, 1866, refuting the "erroneous report" in the *Münchner Weltsboten* that she has not received "sufficient support" from her husband. (Page 428.)

450   (Undated), Luise Brockhaus to Minna.

"Through Madame Tichatschek I have heard, dearest Minna, that you are ill again; is this the case? Please let me know in a few words how you are; if you cannot write yourself, your sister will perhaps be kind enough to inform me. With warmest greetings and best wishes I remain—your devoted sister-in-law,

LUISE BROCKHAUS"

451   Photograph of the tombstone of Minna, in Dresden.

452   Cäcilie Avenarius, in Berlin, January 30, 1866, to Natalie Planer.

A letter of condolence, on the death of Minna. Cäcilie wants to know how she died, how Natalie found her, and every particular of the funeral: "Who put her in the coffin, and what did she wear besides the white jacket and the morning cap?—O God, my dear Natalie, I should like to ask you a thousand questions; every detail, even the smallest one, is of the greatest interest to me."

453   Wagner, in Geneva (Les Artichauts), April 2, 1866, to Natalie Planer. (Pages 7, 428.)

454 Wagner, in Lucerne (Schweizerhof), April 5, 1866, to Franz and Anna Mrazek. (An abstract of this letter is given by Altmann.)

Wagner sends instructions to his servants:

"DEAR FRANZ AND DEAR ANNA!

"We are going to stay away longer. Soon I'll write you more exactly how we want everything taken care of: don't dig any more in the gardens than is necessary, so that nothing may be destroyed. The lawn we'll leave for next year.

"For today I merely wanted to ask you please to send me quickly the things listed on the note. You list everything

"*as used furniture*
"*dishes and clothing*
"Address it to
"*Verena Weidmann,*
"Villa *Triebschen near Lucerne,* Switzerland.

"I'll ask Herr Mathieu to be kind enough to help you.

"As I said, within the next few days I'll let you know more exactly how we want everything done. Just keep being faithful and economical; it won't hurt you. If Anna didn't have the children, I would have both of you come here for the summer. Well, may God keep you in good health!

"Affectionately,

RICHARD WAGNER"

455 A Wagner, in Geneva (undated, but the contents place it in the new year of 1866), to Anna Mrazek in Munich.

"DEAR ANNA!

"Have Herr Mathieu open for you the big desk in my study downstairs: then with the enclosed key you will open the upper drawer (or *Schubladel*) on the right or perhaps the one in the middle; in one of those there should lie another little key; you will take out that one. Then have the bookcase opened for you; there you will open the top drawer (*Schubladel*) on the left with the key previously found; you will find there a music portfolio which is filled with music (both written and blank music sheets); this portfolio consists of a volume of music and a bookbinding of dark-blue morocco leather; on the back is written: '*das Rheingold.*' Should this portfolio not be in the left drawer, then it will be in the one to the right; you will find the proper key in the left drawer. Should the portfolio not be in there either, then it must be in one of the inner lower drawers; you will find the key for those also in the upper left-hand drawer: there you will open both doors and pull out the left-hand drawer. Should the portfolio not be found there either, the ——— [*sic*] must have taken it! Now try whether you can find the thing!

"Franz and Vreneli [servants] send their best regards: on New Year's Eve we drank to your health and to that of your children. I hope that you will soon join us, at any rate before Easter; right now you should be glad to stay in peace and comfort with the children.

"Farewell, and try to manage it all nicely. If Herr Porges is still there, have him help you in your search. But don't tell the Frau Baronin [Cosima von Bülow] of this request to you.

"Adieu and good health!

"Your

R. WAGNER

"Have Herr Mathieu pack the portfolio and send it to me at the following address: *Richard Wagner, Campagne des Artichauts, Genf.*"

B Wagner, in Lucerne, August 16, 1866, to Franz and Anna Mrazek [in Munich].

"DEAR FRANZ AND DEAR ANNA!

"I herewith inform you that I have decided to relinquish my house and estate in Munich to His Majesty the King with my most devoted thanks, since I have no intention to dwell in it any longer. Therefore I ask you to clear the house of all the furniture in the course of the present month. You should also remove all the carpets and have Herr Mathieu pack them all carefully together with all my other belongings. For the present I should like to ask Herr Mathieu to rent an empty storeroom for me which will not cost too much and where for the moment all these things may be stored as my property until I dispose of them further. I should like to ask Herr Mathieu to supervise the careful storage of this furniture against due remuneration for him. You should try to sell, at the best possible price, the flowers, camellias and roses, which I had purchased and which could not very well be transported, and then take the proceeds into account for me. Some things, however, should be sent me by freight to Lucerne at once; namely, the following: my two beautiful wardrobes, also the other wardrobes; all we possess in the way of beds and bedsteads. Also Vreneli's things. Also the beautiful things which stood on the marble box in my study downstairs; in short, all that is precious. Also all the dishes. However, you should sell the ordinary kitchenware, as that will not be worth transportation. You can also bring along your children's beds. For the situation is this: This winter I do not want to establish myself here completely, as various installations and reconstructions would be necessary in the house in which I live now, all of which would bother me right now far too much and which would interrupt my work. This I want to avoid. Therefore I shall postpone the complete *new* installation till next spring; and so I cannot use all my furniture right now, as I shall leave several rooms unoccupied during the winter.

"You two with your children will manage to find some kind of home already furnished: so what you don't really need you could store temporarily through Herr Mathieu in Munich; it would only be a burden here. Should I change my opinion about this within the next days, I shall inform you of it by telegram.

"For the moment just act according to my instructions: should I want EVERY-

THING at *once,* that could be easily done, once everything is packed. Now you have time till September 1. Then, when everything is cleared, you will get ready for the trip and will come to Lucerne, where for the moment we shall not yet be installed and lodged quite according to our wishes, but where from then on we shall be able to be together again. Before that you will well air and fumigate the house, above all, the top floor. Then Franz will call upon Herr Hofsecretär Hofrat von Hofmann, and will ask him on my behalf to name somebody to whom you can turn over the house and the premises. When you deliver the music book for the King to the Prince Taxis, you can tell him at once about the arrangements made by me. Do not forget anything necessary! And take good care of everything. Soon we shall see each other again!

"Let Franz draw the salary on September 1. I think you might arrive here around the 3rd. Vreneli will write you about it all again!

"Now God be with you! Farewell! Kindest regards to Herr Mathieu.

"Your
R. Wagner"

C   Wagner (probably autumn, 1867), to Franz and Anna Mrazek [in Munich].

"Dear Frantz [*sic*] and dear Anna!

"I send you my best regards and am glad that the perseverance of the Frau Baronin [Cosima] will help you to a job after all! Soon I hope to see you again.

"For today I have a request for Frantz. A trunk full of things which I bought in Paris on behalf of the Frau Baronin will shortly arrive at the address of Frau Anna Mrazek in Munich. Here are the keys for it. Let Franz arrange it all nicely and deliver the trunk to the Frau Baronin. Franz might try to get the money for the expenses, freight and customs duty. I am sorry that the allowance is already here. If Franz has not enough money he should borrow it from Herr Mathieu until the 1st of next month.

"Well then, children! Get it well done! And keep fond of me. For Christmas I'll give you presents!

"Kindest regards, also for your children!

"Cordially,
your friend
Rich. Wagner

"I hope that when I come to Munich Anna will be able to serve me."

456 A   Clara Wolfram, in Chemnitz, August 17, 1866, to Frau Eichberger.

Frau Eichberger was the wife of Joseph Eichberger, a *Heldentenor* of Wagner's time, and herself a singer. Clara Wolfram would like to intercede for her with Wagner, but, except that he is "wandering from one place to the next" in Switzerland, she does not know where to reach him.

"I don't really know how he could withdraw even more into seclusion and scare away the kind, young monarch; warnings such as you gave me he has surely heard from his own friends already. Also I'm firmly convinced that he has *never* discussed politics with the young king nor even made his influence felt in that respect; on account of the very great affection of the monarch people have become jealous, and these have made him into a political figure. Incidentally, this perhaps excessive enthusiasm on the part of the young king is less harmful and less destructive than if our crown prince, because of a great friendship with the Emperor of Austria, should make himself, his house, and, what is far worse, perhaps the whole country, unhappy. This is between you and me, but the feeling for our royal family is not very great either at the moment.— It seems very strange to me that my brother is supposed to be indirectly at fault for the defeat of Bavaria! Because these people are unbelievably *lazy,* they try to justify themselves by hurting others with lies and intrigues. The Bavarians are mean people; who knows if the young king does not suffer enough from that and the very lies and slanders, which that pack [*die Bande*] attributes to my brother and which the young king through his connection with him must recognize as such, tie him ever more closely to the latter. Enough, I am very, very sick this summer, and get excited even when I think of these things; spare me any further discussion of them. My brother sent me his bust several months ago. I haven't even written to him after that because I must always avoid any excitement and there are many things I have against him. If you know the place where a letter would reach him, please write me, and I shall try to find the quiet to write to him and remind him of the welfare of the young king. But I wouldn't blame him very much if he stayed in Switzerland, that's where he was before the young King became aware of him."

B   Jenny Heuberg-Eichberger, in Weisser Hirsch, July 26, 1895, to Mrs. Burrell. The daughter of Joseph Eichberger, the singer, tells how her parents were friendly with Clara Wolfram.

457   Wagner, in Lucerne, to Natalie Planer, 1867.
   A   April 24.
   Wagner has asked Dr. Pusinelli to see to a tombstone and the care, in other respects, of Minna's grave. "Everything should be cared for in a dignified and adequate manner. . . . I don't restrict the cost, so long as necessary and fitting details are looked out for." He has asked his friend because he is unable to go to Dresden just then. "I also appreciate your doubly proved loyal and understanding attitude. I am certainly happy to be somewhat helpful to you for now and later. The last time I had the money sent through the housekeeper, since I myself would have got around to it too late. Farewell and thank you for your faithfulness. I am to go to my young King at Starnberg Lake at the end of May for a few months; for the rest I shall keep my actual residence near Lucerne for many years to come."

   B   September 28.
   Wagner requests a fire screen, embroidered by Minna, as a keepsake. It bears

the pattern of a falcon and was copied by her, for their Dresden quarters, after the "former one." [44]

C October 21.

Wagner has received the screen and asks for the stand that goes with it. Natalie has refused to accept payment for it. He would like to make her a present. He has not been inclined to talk about Minna's death with anyone, although he is convinced of Natalie's sincere feelings on the subject. "I am living in complete retirement, and never speak about my past. Working—that is my main concern."

D November 13.

Wagner is worried because the stand has not yet arrived.

E November 18.

The screen stand has arrived. He gives further instructions about Minna's grave, Pusinelli to pay out any expenses, in his name. He signs himself "your brother-in-law."

F December 21.

Wagner is sending a Christmas gift. He is packing "to go to Munich for some time." Letters should be addressed care of Hans von Bülow, 11 Arcostrasse.

458 Wagner, in Lucerne, December 14, 1867, to an unnamed correspondent.

"Most honored friend!

"Kindly look for my dressing gowns in your clothes closet. If they are not there, they must be somewhere else: they are not here either.

"Thanking you for the kind inquiry—your most sincerely devoted

Richard Wagner"

459 Wagner, in Triebschen, Lucerne, February 22, 1868, to E. B. Kietz. (Page 213.)

460 Wagner to Natalie Planer, 1868.

A Munich, March 28.

Wagner apologizes for not writing oftener, and makes the lapse apparent by thanking her for a Christmas present! "Perhaps I'll go to Dresden next autumn, although I never really hear anything pleasant from there."

B Lucerne, June 26.

Wagner sends "the small quarterly allowance" and protests at the expensive presents she is sending him. "I have just undergone much strain and excitement and am glad to have arrived here again in my peace and quiet. You'll hear and read a lot about it. Always think kindly and well of your

old Richard W.

"Cordial regards to Dr. Pusinelli; that he could not come grieved me very much; for one *cannot* re-live this!"

[44] This might be the vulture emblem, referring to Ludwig Geyer, which appears on the title page of *My Life*.

C   Lucerne, July 31.

"DEAR NATALIE!

"Your letter and your news made me very happy. It is really fine that you are going to be married: accept my cordial wishes and return in kind the friendly message of your fiancé. Let me know the day of your wedding and tell me what you would most like to have in the way of a small wedding gift. On the whole, I may assume that through Minna's inheritance you've acquired not inconsiderable household effects with which you can establish yourself comfortably. I shall continue to the best of my ability the allowance which I have been sending until now, even after your marriage.

"But now I ask a favor of you:

"Ask at the Arnold bookstore whether they would be willing to lend you—*for me*—the volumes for 1841 and 1842 of the *Abendzeitung* for a short time; they contain essays of mine which I now need.

"If not, look for the best *old* lending library in order to hunt up the same volumes there for a fee: at the same time I should like to get the same volumes for 1841 and 1842 of *Lewald's Europa* from the lending library.

"If you can take care of this for me, I should be very pleased.

"At the same time you could perhaps have someone announce in a Dresden newspaper that my demands for the *Meistersinger* about which there is so much clamor are limited only to the *royalties* as they already exist in other theaters, and to the guarding of my work against mutilations such as are current in Dresden too.

"Now farewell and let me soon hear good news from you again.

"With cordial regards, your

RICHARD W."

D   Lucerne, October 10.

Wagner thanks Natalie for the fulfillment of his commissions. "I really intend to visit Dresden soon again. Could you ask my sister, Luise Brockhaus, whose address I never know exactly, whether I could stay with her, since I don't like to stay at a hotel—wishing to remain unnoticed." He signs himself, as in several earlier letters, "your brother-in-law."

E   Lucerne, November 27.

Wagner would like returned to him a "small Chinese *Buddha,* a kind of gold-plated idol, enclosed in a small shrine of black wood, with doors that open." It was a present to him from the Countess d'Agoult. If Minna has given it away, he will be willing to pay "whatever is necessary" to get it back. "Except for my incomparable friend, Pusinelli, I have heard nothing very wonderful about the one-time Dresden acquaintances of Minna and myself," whereby he anticipates difficulties.

"But I do ask in *all seriousness* for my *letters to Minna.* No disposition of any kind can be made of such letters: as long as the recipient was living they belonged to her, she could keep them or destroy them. If Minna has definitely and demonstrably done the latter with my letters, I have, of course, nothing to say against it: but if she has kept them, they necessarily revert to the sender, and in case Minna should have given these letters away, I shall fight this illegal action with every legal means, if this should be necessary, and insist on the surrender of the papers. Only, it would be nice if you would give me information about this and help me in every way you can to get the letters back; in any case I claim them as *my* property."

461 A   Wagner, in Lucerne, October 16, 1868, to Joseph Tichatschek in Dresden. (Page 161.)

B   Wagner, in Lucerne, December 22, 1868, to Joseph Tichatschek in Dresden. (Page 162.)

462   Receipt, signed by Wagner, for books, borrowed from the State Library in Dresden, dated October 23, 1868.

These are evidently the books for which he asked Natalie in 460 C.

463 A   Wagner, in Triebschen, February 6, 1869, to Natalie Bilz-Planer.

"I was very glad," Wagner writes, "that no misuse was made of the letters which could find protection only in *my* hands." He has received the Buddha he asked for. However, he has had a notification from the Dresden Library that the volumes of the *Abendzeitung* and the *Europa*, borrowed for him by Natalie, have not been returned. He wonders whether she is at fault. He adds: "Did you manage to see *Die Meistersinger?* It is supposed to have gone very well."

B   Wagner, in Triebschen, October 7, 1869, to Natalie Bilz-Planer.

"DEAR NATALIE!

"I'm sorry to have left you in uncertainty about myself for some time. I've had to experience many unpleasant things; also, because of various changes in my circumstances, I find myself forced to tell you that I'm really no longer able to send you the regular allowance as I did when you were alone [single]. Let me, however, assure you of my help in an emergency; I can propose to help you only in those cases as much as is possible, since my regular income is not nearly sufficient to take care of my likewise regular, most immediate obligations. This will soon become quite apparent to you. But to show you that I continue to think of you, I'll tell you that recently I took the first opportunity to send you a small, but supplementary sum. The Chemnitz Theater must pay me ten louis d'or for *Rienzi,* which is scheduled to be given: I have directed that this be sent to you, and for that purpose I have given Kapellmeister R. Schöneck in Chemnitz your address. Should they delay the matter too long from there, I advise you to go to Wolfram and ask him to remind Kapellmeister Schöneck, or the manager, Langer himself, to fulfill his obligation. Be sure to give your exact address.

"May you thus recognize my good will always to prove my faithfulness and interest in you! I also thank you for the last present from you to reach me, and wish above all that you may continue to be happy and content in your marriage. Give my best regards to your dear husband and always keep in your kind memory your true

brother-in-law,
RICH. WAGNER"

464   Wagner, in Lucerne, to Franz Mrazek, 1869.
A   February 26.
Messages about small errands and payments.

B   March 25.
Packing instructions.

C   April 14.
Wagner orders cigars, and asks Franz to send him the cup painted with the Flying Dutchman, which he received from the King on his birthday two years before.

465   Wagner, in Lucerne, March 29, 1869, to E. B. Kietz. (Page 215.)

466   Photograph of E. B. Kietz, taken in his old age. (See facing page 165.)

467   Wagner, in Lucerne, to Franz and Anna Mrazek, 1870.
A   January 25.
There are instructions about paying bills. He writes: "Herr Richter is well: he is in Brussels, producing *Lohengrin* in French in the big theater there, and seems to be content."

B   April 22.
There is more evidence that Franz keeps his accounts for him.

468   Heinrich Laube, in Leipzig, April 12, 1870, to Herr Hohmann. Laube acknowledges a letter and would like to see him.

469   Wagner, in Triebschen, May 21, 1870, to E. B. Kietz. (Page 216.)

470   Wagner, in Lucerne, 1870, to G. A. Bonfantini in Basel.
A   June 17.
Writing to the printer of *My Life* (the letters are all in French), Wagner is returning proofs "with many corrections." He understands that second proofs will be sent "when necessary." "I shall also send you the first proofs of the new manuscript."

B July 7.

"I am herewith returning the corrected proofs.

"You can very easily hire a German compositor for your work. In the agreement we concluded, everything depends on the strictness with which you can watch that no proof and certainly no copy slip out among the public, since I am bearing the expenses of printing fifteen copies of this autobiography with the sole purpose of avoiding the possible loss of this single manuscript and of putting them into the hands of faithful and responsible friends who must keep them for a distant future. I could make a lot of money, instead of spending it for this printing job, if I wanted to sell this manuscript to a publisher for publication. Thus, the first basis for our agreement is the greatest discretion on your part. You must know whether you can entrust the work to a compositor who understands German perfectly, since the essential point is to watch only that neither the manuscript nor a page of the printed material be removed, which will be prevented if you scrupulously destroy every corrected proof, and if you comply with our agreement conscientiously and don't prepare more than the fifteen copies we agreed on which should be sent to me immediately after they are printed. You know that of the first four sheets I have received only a *single* copy. Besides, pages 65 to 96 are missing from the manuscript which was returned. Would you please see whether Mr. Nietzsche doesn't have them."

C September 1.
In correcting proofs, Wagner notes that a page of the second proofs is missing.

D September 3.

"I think that at the end of this year we'll come to the end of the *first* volume of our manuscript, for which you will still have nearly 100 pages of manuscript.

"Next year we'll be busy with the second volume, which will be followed by a third. You see that it is a sufficiently extensive enterprise.

"It would be agreeable to me to straighten out the accounts with the end of the first volume; I'll be at your disposition any time you need me."

E October 12.
Wagner returns corrected proofs. He is "in perfect accord" with the financial arrangement, and is ready "to send money, if you need some."

F October 21.
Wagner sends the remaining MS for Volume 1. He explains that there are two more volumes to follow.

G November 21.

"Here are the proofs. For the title I ask you please to remove the name of your printing establishment, since that would give my manuscript the character of a publication, which I want to avoid by all means. Instead of that you will put the coat of arms at the place I indicated in the proof. If you show a little ambition (even flattering to me) to be known by my descendants as the printer of my autobiography, you will be asked to indicate it at the bottom of the last page of the volume in small type—as is the custom elsewhere."

H November 26.

Wagner asks him to put the name of the firm on the last page. He appreciates Mr. Bonfantini's offer "not to make an extra charge for corrections."

471   Wagner, in Lucerne, June 10, 1870, to E. B. Kietz. (Page 216.)

472 A Wagner, in Lucerne, August 21, 1870 [to G. A. Bonfantini].

Instructions to set up and print 120 copies of the announcement enclosed. The announcement, in Wagner's hand, reads:

"We hereby have the honor to announce our marriage, which took place on August 25 of this year in the Protestant Church, in Lucerne.

Richard Wagner

Cosima Wagner née Liszt"

B The above announcement, as printed. It is addressed to Frau Natalie Bilz, Niederneuschönberg bei Olbernhau, Saxony, and postmarked August 27.

473 A Certification of baptism, dated Lucerne, October 13, 1892.

"Helferich Siegfried Richard Wagner, born in Triebschen, Lucerne, June 6, 1869, baptized September 4, 1870.

"Parents: Wilhelm Richard Wagner, composer from Leipzig, and Franziska Cosima née Liszt

"Witnesses: His Majesty King Ludwig II of Bavaria, and Countess Caroline Waldbott-Bassenheim of Bavaria

The local clergyman: D. Altherr."

B Hand-copied certification of marriage.

"On August 25, 1870, in the Protestant Reformed Church in Lucerne the marriage was consecrated of:

Wilhelm Richard Wagner, composer from Leipzig, residing in Triebschen near Lucerne

marital status: widowed, former wife Mina [*sic*] Planer † in Dresden, 1866, born in Leipzig on May 22, 1813

son of Friedrich Wagner, police actuary, and of Johanna née Pertz, and

Franziska Cosima née Liszt, from Berlin, residing in Triebschen near Lucerne

marital status: divorced from Hans v. Bülow—born in Como on December 25, 1837, daughter of Franz Liszt, composer from Reidling [*sic*] (Hungary), and Countess d'Agoult née Flavigny

The local clergyman
D. ALTHERR"

C   Rosalie Frey-Marbach, in Charlottenburg, February 4, 1896, to Mrs. Burrell. Frau Frey-Marbach was the only child of Wagner's sister Rosalie Marbach. She married F. L. D. Frey, an actor, on April 5, 1875. She refers to "the grandfather's children's play" and expresses doubt about the intention of Mrs. Burrell to dwell upon an item in her biography "in which Richard had only a silent part." Her doubts extend to Mrs. Burrell's plan to include "only unpublished material" in her book. Is this principle "not too rigorous," and would it not entail "disturbing omissions"? Frau Frey-Marbach has read the biographical portions of the recently published book by Houston Stewart Chamberlain, and in it she has found many "deeply disturbing things"—especially "what Chamberlain says about poor Johanna! How can he dare to say of such a great artist who has done such magnificent things in Wagnerian parts, that the poet has 'remained' completely foreign to her?! What does Ch. know about that?! He did not fulfill my request to soften the harsh judgment of the brothers and sisters, but he did add several things which are perhaps supposed to do so, but which don't achieve that purpose. It is really gibberish what he says about that; one sentence nullifies what was said in the preceding one. To judge by all this, it seems to me that the entire book was most strongly influenced by Cosima and that only *those* people are praised in it who have found favor in Cosima's eyes. I was really angered by the manner in which Ch. mentions her marriage with Wagner. Instead of merely alluding to the weaknesses sensitively and gently, he glorifies the immorality and speaks of 'heroism of the heart which taught this great woman to follow a higher duty.'— If Ch. thinks he is honoring W. with that and winning sympathy for him, he is very much mistaken. In reference to what he says about Aunt Cäcilie, I have written to my cousin Ludwig Avenarius (the lawyer), have enclosed the letter I wrote to Chamberlain in which I expressly emphasized that Cäcilie always felt great love and admiration for her brother, and helped him as best she could when he was in Paris. Thus I hope to have justified myself to my cousins; let them now do what they want in the matter."

474   Cosima Wagner, in Lucerne, September 6, 1870, to E. B. Kietz in Zürich. (Page 217.)

475   *Mein Leben* (My Life). Copy, unbound and uncut, of Wagner's privately printed autobiography (first three parts). This was the copy which the printer in Basel, G. A. Bonfantini, secretly struck off for himself, when he printed eighteen copies for Wagner, between 1870 and 1875. It was purchased by Mrs. Burrell from his widow, Thekla Bonfantini Stuckert, on October 1, 1892.

Wagner, having distributed copies confidentially to his friends, recalled them, and probably destroyed most of them. No human eye outside of Bayreuth had the privilege of further acquaintance until 1911, when *My Life* was at last delivered by Wagner's widow to the publisher for general consumption. But until then Mrs. Burrell, and her heirs after her death, possessed Wagner's closely guarded text in the stolen book. Mrs. Burrell's posthumous book on Wagner (1) reproduced the title page and first page of the introduction, but quoted not a word of the text proper. In 1911, the usefulness of the original book thus became one of comparison with the printed text for evidence of what changes Cosima may have made before releasing it. Cosima was freely accused, by some who could not know what she had done, of tampering with the text. It was also said that Nietzsche, who saw the original corrected proofs, read as the opening sentence, "I am the son of Ludwig Geyer." But the original MS of this page shows no such statement. Julius Kapp, in 1930, not having access to the copy in the Burrell Collection, was allowed to examine a copy inscribed to Liszt. He found the opening page to be exactly as it had been published, and alterations through the three volumes few, unimportant, and not unjustified.

These three volumes carry Wagner's account of his life to 1861. A fourth volume was subsequently written (and printed in 1881, before Wagner's death), carrying the story to the intervention of King Ludwig in 1864. This volume, which Cosima had even been accused of writing herself, proved almost identical in publication.

The name of the printer on this original copy appears, according to Wagner's instructions (470 G) only at the end of the text of each volume: *"Basel: Druck von A. G. Bonfantini."* (Pages 2, 11.)

476   Cläre Wolfram, in Chemnitz, November 8, 1871, to "Frau Jenny" [Jenny Bürde-Ney?].

Cläre "often visits" her sister Luise, and Cäcilie whom she is trying to console for the loss of her son Max. "Frau Jenny" has asked for an autograph of Wagner; Cläre has long owed him a letter: she will write him.

477   MS verses, with melody, in Wagner's hand. According to the catalogue, the song is addressed to Kraft, the proprietor of the Hôtel de Prusse, in Leipzig, April 22, 1871. (Published in the *Monthly Musical Record,* April 1, 1883.)

"To be sung with the greatest vivacity—

"1. Many words are spoken, but few deeds performed;
   The Hotel Eden is made a Paradise—
   Not by words, but by Kraft." [45]

"2. What avails me the hospitality of my own town?
   My dwelling and delight [46] I owe
   to my noble host, Herr Kraft."

[45] *Kraft* (strength).
[46] *Wohn und Wonne.*

"3. For him who served me well my song resounds;
   A song of his arts, the glorious [47] host—
   Long live Kraft."

478   Wagner, in Lucerne, July 20, 1871, to Joseph Tichatschek. (Page 162.)

479   Notes from Cosima Wagner [to Bonfantini, 1871].
   A   June 6.
   B   June 12.
   C   July 5.
   Cosima, in her husband's name, asks for proofs, sends manuscript sheets, and asks for the return of manuscript for correction by him.

480   Wagner, in Lucerne, March 14, 1872, to Herren Batz and Voltz.
   Beginning the year previous, Wagner entrusted his business affairs, in particular the arrangement with opera houses and the collection of fees, to the Mainz firm of Batz & Voltz. As will be seen, while relieving him of a considerable amount of the nuisance of correspondence and financial dealings, these partners brought him petty worries—even distrust.
   This letter concerns performances of *Die Meistersinger* and fees from Mannheim and Dessau. Wagner is concerned over a new copyright law, in effect January 1, 1871, whereby printed music not bearing a clause about copyright and rights of performance could be performed without the consent of the author.

481   Wagner, in Lucerne, 1871, to A. G. Bonfantini (in French, except D which is in German).

   A   March 28.
   Wagner is leaving for Germany on April 15, to return about May 15. His writing will have to be interrupted for this period.

   B   April 7.
   He acknowledges proofs and sends more manuscript. He will continue to work until his departure April 15.

   C   June 5.
   He is still receiving proofs and sending more copy.

   D   September 13.
   Further instructions about proofs.

   E   October 16.
   Wagner is resuming his letters in French, because even though *"la correspondance française ne soit pas mon fort,"* nevertheless he can be more clearly understood. Manuscript, he insists, must be insured in sending, for safety; not proofs, because

[47] *Ruhmreich* (rich in fame) suggests RUMREICH.

they are replaceable. Yet they should be securely sealed against inquisitive eyes. He is fatigued by the preparation of his collected writings for publication in Leipzig.

482   Wagner, 1872, to Voltz and Batz.

A   Bayreuth, June 9.
Wagner will be glad to see the addressee (unnamed), but not before Thursday.

B   Bayreuth, June 14.
Wagner addresses C. F. Meser, as purveyor of music to the Saxon Court, and asks that the bearer (Voltz?) be permitted to examine contracts with his firm.

C   Bayreuth, June 15.
Wagner instructs the firm of Breitkopf & Härtel, in Leipzig, to inform the bearer, Carl W. Batz, about the composer's rights in *Lohengrin* and *Tristan*.

D   Mid-June [?].
Wagner warns his agent that since the King of Bavaria has the sole right to performances of his operas in Munich, without fee or royalty, he should leave that territory alone.

E   Bayreuth, August 18.
Wagner is weary of a dispute with the theater at Chemnitz. He would like to drop past claims but restrict right of further performances of his works there. He orders from Voltz "a barrel of good Médoc for my table."

F   Bayreuth, August 21.
Wagner encloses a letter to Wolfram concerning his Chemnitz dispute. Since he can now take no further step without suing his brother-in-law for exceeding his instructions, Wagner prefers to drop the matter altogether.

G   Dresden, July 29.
Franz Plätner (acting for C. F. Meser) writes instructions for sending scores of *Tannhäuser* to dealers in Berlin, Paris, and London, with warning about performance rights. Wagner has written a provisional endorsement at the top of this letter.

H   Wagner, in Hanover, December 6, 1872, to Voltz.
Wagner must pay 3,000 francs, by the 20th of the same month, to Madame Charlotte Charlton, purveyor of *"confections et nouveautés,"* in Milan. He asks Voltz to "make this payment and then to charge me for it together with the other expenses at the end of the winter when, as I hope, everything favorable has been realized." This lady, adds Wagner, "provides my dear wife's clothing, with the payment for which I am a little in arrears."

I   Bayreuth, December 18.
Wagner would like his agents to furnish 1,500 francs, "chargeable against next spring," to "cover some debts in Lucerne which have turned up recently."

"At the present moment," he adds, "I am in the situation of the Russian criminals who have been sentenced to 200 lashes and who after the first 100 lashes are led away to get healed until they have recovered enough to stand the remaining hundred."

483   Wagner, in Bayreuth, August 22, 1872, to A. G. Bonfantini (in French).

"DEAR MONSIEUR BONFANTINI,

"For the moment we are at the end of the manuscript, and I cannot fix the exact time when the work will be taken up again. Let us now see whether the remaining manuscript gives you enough to make up a third volume; I would like to finish it here, which seems very convenient if we get almost to the 300th page.

"Your very devoted
RICHARD WAGNER"

484   Wagner, in Bayreuth, 1873, to A. G. Bonfantini (in German).

A   January 12.

The following letter is cited in the catalogue as an indication that, 15 of the 18 copies Wagner here orders to be printed having been delivered to him, "the copy in this Collection is one of the three that were left over." But 484 E shows that Wagner has received all 18 copies. (It should be remembered that the first two volumes only were then completed; another would follow.)

"MOST ESTEEMED SIR!

"I am and shall remain so extremely busy that I cannot think of continuing our work at the present time.

"Would you be so kind as to have the last 11 pages printed, also, in addition to the other already finished sheets, and the whole sent to me in 18 copies, as agreed upon; we might have the last page, in connection with what is to follow, reset later.

"At the same time kindly send an accounting of what I owe and pardon the inconvenience I have caused you.

"Respectfully yours,
RICHARD WAGNER"

B   February 10 (in German).

Wagner apologizes for further delays.

C   February 27 (in German).

Having gained additional leisure time, Wagner would like "to continue dictating his life—if possible up to the completion of the third volume. Now I should prefer to have you finish the complete printing of this volume, if I did not fear that you would suffer loss under the changed conditions."

D   July 29 (in French).

Wagner asks him to figure the probable number of printed pages which will result from the setting of the manuscript in hand.

E   November 10 (in German).

"DEAR SIR!

"I ask you once more whether you are willing to print the third volume of *My Life* in full. The manuscript contains additional material for about 100 printed pages. As for the price, you would charge a correspondingly increased fee. The last proof which I received from you contains three blank pages; if it were possible to continue printing on these, I would send back to you the 18 copies; if not, we could cut through this sheet, and take up the page which has been begun with a new sheet.

"Above all, I am concerned about the discretion which you have maintained so well in your printing office.

"Awaiting your kindly reply, I remain respectfully yours,

RICHARD WAGNER"

485   Meta Feustel, in Bayreuth, September 28, 1888, to Mrs. Burrell. The wife of Friedrich Feustel, the banker, writes a friendly letter, enclosing a letter from Wagner to her husband (486) as evidence of the generosity of the *Meister*.

486   Wagner, in Bayreuth, January 2, 1873, to Friedrich Feustel.

"MY DEAR FRIEND!

"How am I to thank you for all the good you are constantly doing for me? Just tell me that!

"So I thank you now again for taking care of my poor finances, which, considering all the details, surely is often troublesome! As a reward for your sympathetic efforts, I express the hope that one day my affairs will bring both you and me satisfaction and joy through good prosperity.

"For the time being I still find myself in such an exceptional situation that good may probably be expected from a calmer future. My immediate needs and the sacrifices which I still have to face are met by the encouraging prospects of not inconsiderable revenue from the management of my theatrical enterprises. Above all, that well known lawsuit is nearing victory, as I have gathered from official communications; and I hope it will give you some satisfaction that soon you may see my finances in an honorable state again.

"However, friend, I really cannot accept that you continue to credit interest at a rate of 4 per cent to my account! I know from experience that nowhere do they compute it so favorably within a current account. Won't you rather distribute this surplus accrued by your exaggerated generosity among the young men of your office who have so much trouble with my affairs?"

487   Wagner, in Bayreuth, to Voltz and Batz, 1873.

A   February 16.

Wagner has settled with the Milan dressmaker. He writes: "May Justitia bless the Leipzig suit," but at the same time, "See to it that I remain entirely spared from all vexations from directors and courts, and that on the other hand I am provided with an enormous amount of money at the end of March."

B   March 20.
Wagner asks for "an especially generous sum at the end of this month, since my needs at that time will amount to 5,000 francs."

C   March 26.
There has been a plan from him to conduct in London, but a change in dates would book him for Cologne on the 23rd and London on the 25th—a sheer impossibility.

D   March 29.
Wagner has expected the 3,000 francs intended for the Milan creditor, but only 2,000 have been forthcoming; whereas Wagner is embarrassed because he owes his banker all of the 3,000 francs, and now he can pay neither.

E   March 29.
Wagner is ready to give up the idea of conducting in London, on the advice of Dannreuther. "The road there is peculiar, and productive only if entered rightly."

F   April 15.
There is more about London: "In no case would I go to London to conduct there in person." He looks for favorable results from a dispute with the Mainz Society.

G   May 5.
Wagner addresses Voltz as follows:

"I have come to the following decision in regard to *Tristan*.

"I authorize you to deliver *Tristan und Isolde* also to the theaters but *only* on condition that the same royalties be paid by the theaters in question, not only for that opera, but for all my former operas from the day of signing the contract.

"I don't believe that Mannheim and Wiesbaden, which now are in question, will be able to perform the *Tristan* in such a way as to make it quickly into a repertory opera; if royalties are to be paid for this opera, but not for my previous operas, then it is with certainty expected that *Tristan* will be completely neglected and put on the shelf, while my older works, now as ever, will be given for nothing. Therefore I intend to stick to this condition consistently. If they won't agree to it, it is all right with me.

"How is our trial going on? When will the disputed receipts arrive, by which I could—if not build—at least equip my house? It seems to me that everything is dragging.

"Well, God protect us! Greet Herrn Carl W. Batz

"Yours truly

RICHARD WAGNER"

H Wagner needs more money for the furnishing of his house. He believes that it should be forthcoming because of having won the suit against Director Haase.

I Contract (dated January 4, 1860) between Wagner and G. Flaxland, on the French and Belgian property and performance rights of *Tannhäuser, Lohengrin,* and *The Flying Dutchman.* A copy in the hand of Cosima. The text is in French. An added elucidation of the clauses, in German, is begun in the hand of Cosima and dated by her "Bayreuth, June 24, 1873." The paragraph is completed and signed by Wagner.

"Contract between Herr Richard Wagner and Herr Flaxland [in French]. The undersigned, Mr. Richard Wagner, musical composer, and Mr. G. Flaxland, publisher, both living in Paris, have agreed upon the following:

"Mr. Richard Wagner surrenders to Mr. Flaxland all property rights, for France and Belgium, to the following three operas: *Tannhäuser, Lohengrin,* and *The Flying Dutchman.* Mr. Richard Wagner agrees to have translations made of these three operas at his own expense and to send them to Mr. Flaxland in the course of the present year. At the same time he will give him title to the property rights to these translations signed by the translators (for France and Belgium) as soon as the translation of these three works, or of one of them, has been completed. Mr. Flaxland agrees to publish editions of them with piano accompaniment. The edition of these scores for voice and piano shall constitute the only obligation for Mr. Flaxland. The other editions shall be left to the discretion of Mr. Flaxland. The German text of *Tannhäuser* and *The Flying Dutchman* only can be published by Mr. Flaxland. If Mr. Richard Wagner makes any changes in, or additions to, the music or the words of these operas, these changes or additions shall with full right [*de plein droit*] become the property of Mr. Flaxland.

"As price for these three operas Mr. Flaxland agrees to pay Mr. Richard Wagner the sum of 3,000 francs in cash, plus 250 francs per performance, beginning with the sixth, to the amount of 4,000 francs for each opera. These performances shall take place in Paris in a French opera house and in French.

"Mr. Richard Wagner agrees not to authorize any manager from the provinces to produce his operas unless the orchestral score shall have been bought directly from Mr. Flaxland.

"Made in duplicate in Paris this 4th of January 1860."

[Signatures follow]

"It can be clearly seen from this that Herr Flaxland obtained the property rights to the work (*Tannhäuser*) plus its newly added scenes and changes only for France and Belgium, since '*de plein droit*' is to be interpreted to mean that he would not have to pay me anything more for it (namely, the new scenes), but that he in no way obtained these 'pour tous pays' (for all countries), and the works themselves for France and Belgium only. This had to be noted in anticipation of certain loopholes.

RICHARD WAGNER

"Bayreuth
24 June, 1873"

J   June 30.

Addressing Herrn Voltz, Wagner speaks with admiration of his partner, because of the winning of the lawsuit against Haase. "The prospect of thus gaining a not inconsiderable fortune" makes it impossible for Wagner to await this result "with calm." Under present circumstances he is forced "to look forward with agonized impatience to the realization of the expected gain. The hopes and prospects opened to me by you and Herrn Batz just a year ago induced me then to acquire the plot of land and to carry through the definite building of a house, although the estimates exceeded the capital placed at my disposal. Those estimates were overstepped by the laying out of a garden and by some supplementary construction, and therefore I was forced in advance to give up the idea of contracting a mortgage; but at the same time I depended entirely on the realization of the prospects then offered by you, so far as the inside furnishings were concerned. At present I can't give the slightest further order for such furnishings, and therefore am put in many ways in a very awkward, almost shameful position.

"So I maintain that after the great success of your endeavors you could render me now no greater favor than to raise by yourself the thr. 5,000 which you could place at my disposal right away, and for which I would give over to you my receipts as they pass through your hands until my liabilities, plus interest, are cleared."

K   July 2.

Wagner has been warned by Feustel that Haase, having appealed the case, can do it a second time, thus delaying the verdict and enabling him to continue performing Wagner's operas while his money could not be touched. Wagner suggests putting a claim on Haase's income.

L   August 15.

Wagner presses his "most honored friends" to fulfill their promises.

M   September 27.

Wagner urges a clear statement of his financial prospects, especially as regards the Leipzig suit against Haase. The lack of any definite information "leaves me in a truly shameful financial embarrassment, from which I must certainly free myself."

N   October 14.

"DEAR HERR VOLTZ!

"Try this one: for the performing rights of *Iphigenia*, nothing at all, but royalties from my older operas.

"Or else—demand for *Iphigenia* what you think appropriate; I suggest a heavy fee, for that opera will hardly be given often.

"Best regards,

RICH. WAGNER"

O   October 17.

"DEAR SIRS!

"I can't refrain from emphatically reminding you of the importance for me of being kept posted promptly and accurately about the state of my affairs,

"Therefore I ask you:

"1. What was the result of the Berlin Conference in the case of the three Court theaters?

"2. The Haase affair was supposed to be decided in the latter part of this month, whereupon—presupposing a favorable decision—you planned to offer as a compromise an after-payment of the royalties. How does that stand?

"What concerns me is the question of giving or not giving the necessary orders for the interior furnishing of my house.

"With the best regards,

faithfully yours,

RICHARD WAGNER"

P   November 23.

"I see that we always live *in spe* and never arrive *in rem*. If the Haase Compromise is to bring only 50 thlr. pr. performance as after-payments, the expected results from this lawsuit dwindle to a minimum.

"What I liked most was that you hold out to me the hope of a settlement—or clarification—about those two main items by the end of the year. I find it difficult to postpone the equipment of my house until then."

488   Wagner, in Bayreuth, to A. G. Bonfantini, 1874.

A   January 17 (in German).

A batch of proofs has been lost in the mails. Wagner urges Bonfantini to send all proofs under seal, because in Germany—particularly in Bavaria—every official in the postal service knows me too well."

B   February 5 (in French).

Wagner wants the first proofs returned with the revised proofs, so that he may check them against his own corrections.

C   June 29 (in German).

Wagner is enclosing the "lost pages" with "small corrections" and asks Bonfantini to add these pages to the third volume. He is grateful for Bonfantini's "discretion."

489 Wagner, in Bayreuth, 1874, to Voltz and Batz.

A March 31.

Wagner has been waiting for two months for news from them about "compensation from the Prussian Court theaters, as well as the Leipzig Haase affair. Do you consider me indifferent on this point?" Although he has been receiving half-yearly reports and payments, he cannot wait, and considers the point "pedantic." "I now need much money, in spite of Schott, since I am about to move into my house."

B April 9.

Wagner has offended their "self-esteem" by his "joking bad humor." He promises to "refrain from such utterances in the future." He is still waiting for a settlement from the three Court theaters and Haase: "Frankly, it was on the prospects of extra income that I undertook to equip my house." He is not anxious to have an immediate visit from his agents, since this house is not yet presentable.

C April 12.

Encouraged by a report of increase in his income, Wagner instructs his agents to pay 2,100 francs to Jacob Stocker in Lucerne. The furnishing of his estate is progressing, but is proving expensive. He would like them to visit him "one of these days."

D April 15.

A note on the payment of an obligation to Crevelli in Lucerne.

E April 25.

He has been in the process of moving, but has found his notes and so lists for them the dates of first performances of his operas.

F June 26.

Wagner has obtained a flat fee of 1,000 florins for *The Flying Dutchman* at Pesth through the conductor Richter, and expects the same for *Rienzi*, an extraordinary amount. This is a direct, friendly arrangement, and his agents are not to interfere.

G June 30.

Wagner protests that his agents have no right to a commission from his Pest deal, but sends "in any case," 250 florins from the 1,000 he received. He will need a secretary and manager for the *Nibelungen* performances. He is expecting help from Professor Wilhelmj.

A fragment of a letter (a copy) is dated Paris, June 30, 1874. The writer states that *"Lohengrin* will certainly be performed in London in the following season, with Albani as Elsa and Nicolini as Lohengrin. Wagner may expect royalties, although *Lohengrin* is in 'public domain.' "

H July 11.

Wagner, in answer to questions by Herr Voltz, states that he has had no payments from Copenhagen for about three years, also that *Rienzi* for Pesth has gone no further than the copying of the score.

I July 15.

Wagner is indignant, on receiving a payment from his agents, to find that they have deducted 250 florins for a Pest fee which has not yet been received. He is also indignant that they have charged a commission against a Stockholm "honorary fee" which is "outside of our agreement." He expects both amounts returned to him.

J July 18.

Wagner yields on his agents' claims of commission from Stockholm (which has offered to pay them), and Pesth as well.

K July 27.

Wagner sends to Voltz a letter he has just received from Copenhagen, which is dated July 24, and signed by Hornemann and Ersler, music agents. This letter asks for the right of performance for *Tannhäuser* 1,000 francs, the fee for which *Lohengrin* and *Die Meistersinger* were given at the Royal Theater, "with great success."

L August 4.

Wagner has heard that Herr Voltz has collected a payment for himself for granting the right of performance of Wagner's operas in Berlin and Wiesbaden. "I would be embarrassed," he writes Batz, "to inquire of him personally about such unheard-of things and therefore I request you to tell me confidentially whether there is any truth in these accusations."

M September 19.

Wagner needs 1,000 florins before the end of the month. "Where is Herr Batz hovering (jokingly meant) for the time being?"

N September 25.

Wagner confirms his telegraphed order to pay 901 gulden to Carl Giani in Vienna.

O September 26.

Wagner has just received 1,000 florins from Pest for the performance of *Rienzi*, and agrees to his agents' fee.

P (Undated.)

Wagner protests against sending money back and forth, "like an errand boy." Evidently enclosed is a letter from Zulauf at Kassel, who sends the fee of 141 reichsthaler, 20 pfennigs, for the performing rights of *Iphigenia in Aulis*, in Wagner's adaptation. He is communicating with Wagner directly, because Voltz has expressed himself as "unauthorized" to make the terms.

Q   October 26.

Wagner questions the right of Voltz and Batz to a 25 per cent commission on returns "which automatically and by standing custom come to me from well established Court theaters." They have no claim on indefinitely continuing royalties. Wagner grants their just expectation of such commissions to date, especially since they have been put to considerable expense, but wishes an adjustment of his contract for the future.

R   December 7.

Wagner does not intend to dispense with the services of Voltz and Batz. He is drawing a new agreement for their consideration.

S   December 15.

Addressing Herr Voltz, Wagner writes that although he has "clearly and firmly" presented his reasons for changing their contractual relations, Herr Batz especially has paid little attention to him. "Since I see now that my actions and assurances have failed to drive Herr Batz from his entrenched position, behind which he taunts me with distrust, etc., I now consider it best not to carry on further negotiations in person, but to leave them henceforth entirely to my lawyers."

T   December 22.

Wagner, addressing Herr Voltz, awaits "your counterproposals in your last friendly letter as a basis for further profitable relations between us."

U   Letter in another hand (a lawyer?) undated, addressed to Herr Carl Voltz and Herr Carl W. Batz, and signed by Wagner.

"I am answering together your two letters of the 19th inst. Having carefully read them, I am not persuaded to relinquish my demands to exclude the Frankfurt payments to date and the Hamburg payment, which incidentally should have been excluded last quarter.

"All your explanations are untenable in view of the simple fact that you received money for me in Frankfurt, that the earned sums are unconnected with the result of the suit, but that I got no more than 300 th. as a result of those receipts; doubtlessly the Hamburg money had also been due last quarter. But since I don't like carrying on such correspondence as is now taking place, I am giving you a respite until the 29th inclusive to settle in fairness those items including interest on deferred payment, otherwise I will resort to the law. As to your claims for Dresden and Vienna, you may make a statement for me. Prove them by the correspondence between us, and tell me at what time and with whom you negotiated on my behalf.

"I want this all the more because on the occasion of our last negotiations in Vienna the people in authority absolutely denied having communicated with you on my behalf, and even from Dresden I haven't yet had the slightest proof that you acted at any time in my special interest and still less that was there any good result for me.

You may safely refrain from doing this, for in Dresden you would quite fail to accomplish anything. As to the change in our intercourse emphasized by you, you may see the cause in yourself alone. Recalling your way of acting I realize that your deeds and words have little in common. On your last visit here we agreed to a new contract. The wording had been put down exactly according to the suggestion of Notary Skutsch. You left for Munich, intending to stop here on your return in order to sign the contract—but instead you returned to Wiesbaden, you didn't conclude the prepared contract, and you had the courage to submit a countercontract which quite offends my honor and would bring me to a disgraceful dependence on you. After that development of things and the so demonstrated character of my relations with you, only a strictly businesslike status between us is still possible, and this without dissertations on the sacrifices you have made, and how you have favored me over other composers; this appears to me as absurd. Also, any attempt to make others responsible for the changed situation, or to speak of tricks and the like, I shall look upon as childish as well as offensive. The breaking of your word caused the present situation. No sophistry or accusations of other people can change this. I don't find among my papers the requested letters from Frankfurt-on-the-Oder and Halle-on-the-Saale, which won't surprise you since you know that I don't keep them on file; so you may also find it correct that from now on my correspondence with you will be carried on through people experienced in business. But I am sending along some items belonging to you which I found on that occasion.

"In regard to my relations with Fürstner, to whom I submitted only a counter-bill, the enclosed note which I want you to publish in theater journals, will give you satisfactory information. My negotiations with that gentleman will be most clearly recognized by the two letters which I once communicated to you and whose return I must now request.

"Respectfully,

RICHARD WAGNER"

490   Cosima Wagner, Bayreuth, July 8, 1874 (to Bonfantini).
A note in French, ordering the printing of calling cards.

491   Wagner, in Bayreuth, 1875, to Voltz and Batz.

A   February 5.
Wagner has received recently a draft for a new contract, which he rejects, as they have rejected his own legally drawn agreement. However, in consideration of their "practical" and "energetic" administration of the estate, he is willing to return to the first contract, with a supplementary provision.

B   June 17, 1875.
Authorization, written and signed by Wagner, for Carl W. Batz to act on his behalf in Russia, "as he deems necessary."

C   October 15, 1875.

The letter is drafted by another, presumably a lawyer, and signed by Wagner. Wagner complains about various charges. He demands money due him from Frankfurt, "in cash and by return mail."

492   Wagner, in Bayreuth, April 4, 1875, to A. G. Bonfantini.

Wagner apologizes for the delayed payment of 180 francs. He has been "very much satisfied" with Bonfantini's work.

493 A   Diary of Susanne Weinert, governess employed by Cosima Wagner at Wahnfried, July 16, 1875, through April, 1876. (Ch. XXVII.)

Written in ink, on 92 ruled sheets, with minor corrections in another hand. An occasional change to the past tense indicates that the manuscript may be a copy, by the writer or another. According to the catalogue, it was acquired by Mrs. Burrell from Frau Baumgarten.

B   Application by Fräulein Susanne Weinert, April 1, 1893, for financial support; addressed to Marie Tittmann Foundation, Dresden, with accompanying letters.

C   Letter of recommendation by Cosima Wagner, May 15, 1876:

"I herewith certify that Fräulein Susanne Weinert has been in my home as a teacher from August, 1875, until May, 1876, and that she has distinguished herself by her conscientiousness, her knowledge, and her modesty. Fräulein Weinert leaves my home because I wish to have an English governess for my children in the future."

494   Eleven envelopes, addressed to G. A. Bonfantini in Basel, in Wagner's hand. The envelopes are empty. Mrs. Burrell's written comment is: "The letters belonging to these envelopes are missing. I do not think Mrs. Bonfantini had them." The catalogue adds: "Presumably these letters contained some indications of the contents of the book, and were accordingly destroyed." Wagner's precautions about his copy and proofs support this. The Bayreuth postmark does not give the year.

495   Wagner, in Bayreuth, 1876, to Voltz and Batz.

A   April 5. (The enclosure referred to is not in the Collection.)

"DEAR HERR VOLTZ!

"The enclosure I herewith am sending you again draws my attention to a matter which I still cannot understand. You will still have to convince me of the 'imaginary' character of my claims. I continue to rely on your honesty, which I have never for a moment doubted. On the other hand, some interpretations of your rights and claims still do not make sense to me.

"Concerning *Tristan und Isolde* I authorize you to deal with all *municipal theaters* as my agent, receiving a commission of 25 per cent. This relationship shall last for *twenty years*; after that all rights shall revert to me or my legatees.

"Sincerely yours,

RICHARD WAGNER"

[Notes in Voltz's handwriting:]

"Belongs to the negotiations which precede the agreement of 1880, etc.

"Proposal rejected as it would change the agreement of 1873."

B　April 10.

"DEAREST HERR VOLTZ!

"As to the *Iphigenia,* you are bothering me quite unnecessarily, particularly at the present moment. *Iphigenia* is and remains a matter of *very* small importance which will hardly yield any essential profits, as the *Iphigenia* performances will be only a luxury of some very few theaters.

"By the way, my original score has remained in Dresden: you can best trace it with *Tichatscheck's* [*sic*] help. For present uses, Härtel's copy has been arranged by Tichatscheck on the basis of my original score. He gave it me as a gift. I gave it to Härtels, so that they could make further copies and use them in case orders should they come in.

"I shall be very much pleased with your visit!

"Yours,

RICHARD WAGNER"

C　April 16.

Inquiry about revenue from Cologne and the right to perform *The Flying Dutchman* at Salzburg.

D　June 22.

"MOST ESTEEMED HERR VOLTZ!

"I enclose a paper that Herr Batz sent me. I see from it that you did not inform him about my wishes concerning our further relations such as I had expressed to you previously.

"You know that, highly as I esteem the merits and the outstanding abilities of your partner, it has become unbearable for me through his behavior and the tone sometimes adopted by him, to enter into any, even written communications with him, neither can I appoint a substitute for these relations which he tries to re-establish again and again, otherwise I would expose each of my friends to a treatment from Herr Batz which one simply cannot tolerate. As a proof of this, his recent activities as 'representative' of my administrative committee [*Verwaltungsrat*] are still fresh in my memory; now he still wants to get some rights of patronage [Bayreuth subscriptions] or other awards for this alleged 'activity,' though his behavior actually could consist in nothing but—maybe unintentional—scaring off. All this seems to prove that he has no idea with whom he is dealing.

"This irreparable personal situation is all the more disagreeable as I had quite a need for the professional knowledge and skill of Herr Batz in order to arrange my property-right relationships more thoroughly. Last spring I believed that I could discuss many of these things with you; since, as it happens, you are connected with Herr Batz, I hoped you would bring all these arrangements to a speedier fulfillment, but you did not come! At the present time it is impossible for me to concern myself about anything aside from the preparation of my performances; as to the right to perform my compositions in concerts, I must also postpone my decisions for the time being. For this reason I wanted Messrs. B. Schott's Söhne to rely on that clause [Contractual?] and go ahead with my claims.

"This time I ask you, dear Herr Voltz, to make a clear and final statement about the use of that disputed Frankfurt revenue, at the end of the current quarter. It is impossible to keep this item undecided any longer. I ask you earnestly to get this business over with.

"If you want to attend the performance of my Festival Plays, I shall get a seat for you, though we are now forced to reserve all seats for sale. Therefore I just wondered why my friends and those who are linked with my affairs could not also make an effort and buy a seat. *I myself* have enough expenses for the undertaking, and as I shall never get one groschen of profit out of this business, I wonder why it should be I who must distribute gifts.

"Apart from that, please consider my very shaky health and be so kind as to spare me any bickering and the like.

"Kindest regards,
yours,
RICHARD WAGNER"

E July 15.

"DEAREST HERR VOLTZ!

"I again miss the item concerning *Cologne,* particularly the one of last March, as to which I inquired last time. You wrote me that you had received it in April, only *after* you had sent me the current revenue for the first quarter of the year.

"Have there been no further performances of my operas in April and in the following months?

"I hope for an immediate explanation as to this.

"A permanent seat for all three performances will be reserved for you as my confidential business agent [*Geschäftsvertrauten*], and you will find the tickets ready for you on your arrival.

"Kindest regards,
yours,
RICHARD WAGNER"

F   Florence (Hotel New-Yorck), December 6.
Wagner asks for an advance of 2,000 gold francs.
Voltz (?) has noted, "Russia receipts."

496   Receipts, signed by Wagner to Carl Voltz.

A   April 16, 1876. For first quarter, 6,308 marks.

B   October 15, 1876. For third quarter, 2,365 marks.

C   December 18, 1876. Drawn on a Florence bank—2,000 gold francs.

497   Wagner, in Bayreuth, 1877, to Voltz and Batz.

A   January 2.
Wagner asks for duplicate of receipts lost in the mails.

B   January 17.
Wagner writes to Voltz: "What strange people you gentlemen are! So, a good, lasting, and friendly understanding with us is not worth anything to you? All that can be said for the present is that the apparently good business keeps up the understanding."

C   April 26.
Writing to both agents, Wagner objects to their having "accepted commissions for a number of technical collaborators in the performance of last year's stage festival at Bayreuth." He hopes that Herr Brandt will be consulted by other theaters, notably Leipzig, for stage sets. The Brückners would probably be entrusted with the making of the stage decorations, Hofmann would be consulted as the originator. "I would not advise the use of Prof. Döpler's sketches for reasons which will be well known to Herr Döpler." (The letter, written by Cosima, is signed by Wagner.)

D   December 8.
Wagner asks for an advance of 1,000 marks, 500 francs of which are to be sent to Mme. Judith Gautier, "That lady is buying Christmas presents for the household on my behalf."

498   Receipts, signed by Wagner, to Carl Voltz, 1877.
A   January 15, for last quarter (of 1876), 2,879 marks.
B   April 15, for first quarter, 4,450 marks.
C   July 1, drawn on a Mainz bank, 4,000 marks.
D   July 15, for second quarter, 1,134 marks.
E   October 15, for third quarter, 1,325 marks.
F   Bank deposit slip, April 13 (Mainzer Volksbank), 4,450 marks.

499   Wagner, in Bayreuth, 1878, to Carl Voltz.

A   January 17.
Wagner encloses receipts.

B   June 22.
Wagner asks for a 1,000 franc advance, to be sent to Jacob Stocker in Lucerne.

C   Wagner writes on a letter from Theodor Wünzer, in Darmstadt:

"Dear Herr Voltz! Please consider this matter as part of your business, and arrange it accordingly."

The letter inquires about Wagner's arrangement of Gluck's *Iphigenia in Aulis* for performance at the Hoftheater in Darmstadt.

D   November 6.
Wagner instructs Voltz to pay 1,000 francs to Jacob Stocker.

E   Addressing both "gentlemen," Wagner inquires about "scores delivered to Breitkopf und Härtel in 1870–1872."

500   Receipts, signed by Wagner, to Carl Voltz, 1878.

A   January 16, for fourth quarter (of 1877), 3,143 marks.

B   January 16, for one performance of *Iphigenia* in Hamburg, 180 marks.

C   April 16, for first quarter, 5,915 marks.

D   July 14, for second quarter, 2,924 marks.

E   October 15, for third quarter, 1,437 marks.

501   Wagner, in Bayreuth, 1879, to Carl Voltz.

A   January 1 (by exception to both "gentlemen," Voltz being sick).
Wagner orders 3,262 francs from his next quarterly payment to be sent to Mr. Félix Preveté, in Paris.

B   July 9.
Wagner orders 1,000 marks sent to Jacob Stocker.

C   October 13.
Wagner misses the receipts from Hamburg in the last quarterly payment and is restive at having to wait three more months for them.

D   October 17.
Wagner apologizes for his impatience in the previous letter and asks that 1,500 marks in advance of the next quarter be sent to Professor Gedon, in Munich.

E   (December).

Wagner knows nothing about the "Petersburg story." He would like it publicly denied. He is to leave for Italy on December 26.

F   December 28.

Wagner, still in Bayreuth, asks Voltz to take care of the enclosed letter from von Rudolphi, intendant of the theater at Brunswick. Rudolphi has inquired about the arrangement of *Iphigenia.*

502   Receipts, signed by Wagner, to Carl Voltz, 1879.

A   January 11, for fourth quarter (1878), 123 marks.

B   April 17, for first quarter, 4,065 marks.

C   July 16, for second quarter, 3,711 marks.

D   October 15, for third quarter, 1,380 marks.

503   Wagner, in Posilipo, Naples, 1880, to Carl Voltz.

A   February 4.

Wagner, signing the letter only, apologizes for "inflammation of the eyes." He has heard that the Municipal Theater in Leipzig is considering *Tristan.* He asks Voltz to make terms for royalties of "at least 10 per cent," using, if possible, the opportunity to get "some advantages for my older operas."

B   April 18.

Wagner's last quarterly payment has been delayed in forwarding. This was "unpleasant for me, because, just at this moment, I had to ask my local banker for a renewal of my credit, as on the whole my finances are rather low at present."

He has been approached by the Leipzig management regarding *Tristan,* which he was unwilling to allow without his personal supervision. Meanwhile they have embarrassed him by not applying to his constituted agents, Voltz and Batz.

C   May 8.

"Royalties bring next to nothing—last year I got a total of 200 marks. I am of the opinion that you should try to get something worth while for *Die Meistersinger*— and not spend too much money on lawsuits." On the back of the letter—

"I have just had an idea! Tell them that *I* oppose the deal because everywhere I have had the experience that my more recent works, for which *royalties* must be paid, are neglected in favor of the older ones for which no royalties are due, so that the former are performed only rarely, whereas *Tannh., Lohengr., Fl. Dutchman,* are constantly played. Witness for this is also Schwerin, where my *Nibelungen* have been entirely disregarded, whereas, etc. The same thing would happen to *Die Meistersinger.*"

504   Wagner, in Bayreuth, 1881, to Carl Batz.

A   April 24.
Wagner urges an agreement, even involving compromise with the theaters at Stuttgart and Schwerin. The latter is considering *Die Meistersinger,* and the Grand Duke of Mecklenburg is very friendly.

B   June 2.
Wagner considers that Batz is throwing away money after "unsuccessful lawsuits."

C   July 2.
Wagner has asked Herr Feustel to draw up a new contract to be patterned after the original one.

D   July 18.
Claar, in Frankfort, is ready to sign an agreement to produce *Der Ring des Nibelungen.*

E   (Undated.)
Wagner writes that his wife would be honored to receive Frau Batz at Wahnfried, at four o'clock.

505   Wagner, in Bayreuth, 1882, to Carl Batz.

A   May 7.
Wagner wishes a conference with Voltz and Batz.

B   May 15.
Wagner has negotiated with Herr Franck [48] for *Tristan* and the *Meistersinger* on a basis of 10 per cent royalties. He has no control over his older operas.

C   May 18.
In a friendly tone, Wagner urges Batz to come to Bayreuth and discuss a new contract.

506   Marble relief of Wagner by Gustav Kietz.

507   Photograph of Cäcilie Avenarius, taken in her old age (1890).

508 [49]   Letter from the Ministry of Saxony to Wagner (undated, name not legible).

[48] Manager of the Drury Lane Theater.
[49] This and the remaining fifteen items in the catalogue were evidently put at the end because they were undated and considered unplaceable. The present editor hazards dates (specific or approximate) for nine of them.

"Sir—

"You will find me tomorrow at eleven o'clock at the Ministry of the Interioɪ [?] —— Street,

"Very respectfully yours

—— [?]"

The letter is addressed to 16 Walpurgisstrasse, which would indicate November, 1862, when Wagner was in Dresden for a few days. He had obtained his full pardon in March.

509 Alwine Frommann (undated, to Minna).

The content indicates 1862, the year of the final separation of Wagner and Minna.

"... *Oh what a pity about his noble, rich talents*—later he will surely return to you—!—don't let yourself die—learn again and start something—anything—some work, a job—be courageous—God gave you a strong heart and let us see to it that we never stand *beneath* our fate—yours is so hard, so terrible—I shudder. Dear Minna, I know that you love me; prove it to me, take up an honest fight—*worthy of yourself*—against these heavy odds. I am sending you what I have here and what I would take from you without a word if the situation were reversed; unfortunately it is so little! But you know that I wish it were thirty times as much! You must not take it amiss *that I dare this*; my heart bleeds.

"I shall write within the next few days. May God strengthen you."

510 (Undated.)

Machinka Schubert, wife of the Dresden concertmaster, invites the *Frau Kapellmeister* to visit her.

511 (Undated.)

Machinka Schubert sends Minna tickets for a "quartet evening" by her husband.

512 (Undated), Anna Liszt to Minna.

Liszt's mother accepts an invitation to dinner with the Wagners. A reference to Mme. Olivier indicates Paris, 1860 or 1861.

513 Franz Liszt, postmarked Coblenz, August 18 (no year), to Belloni.

Liszt tells his secretary that he is going to the recital of *"le petit* Rubinstein" the next day.

514 (Undated), Pauline Tichatschek to Minna [in Dresden].

Frau Tichatschek cannot visit Minna because her husband has typhoid fever.

515 Cläre Wolfram, Hilbersdorf, May 26 (no year given), to Minna.

Cläre's daughter, Marie, is about to be married. She discusses wedding plans and presents.

516   (Undated), Wagner to Minna.

A A note, addressed "Madame" and signed "Monsieur," evidently left for Minna in the second Paris period, as he went to dinner with the "Ambassador and his wife." He intends to "walk around a bit and work up appetite," so that he may repay himself for the cost of the "white cravat."

B Karlsruhe, May 24 [probably 1861].
Wagner, returning from Vienna, writes Minna in Paris, the letter to precede his arrival by "twenty-four hours."

C Unsigned penciled note.
"Foolish Girl [*Thörigte Bubin*]:
"Tomorrow I am going away, because you don't catch any more flies for me."

D (The contents indicate Brussels, March 28, 1860; cf. published letters to Minna.)

"I am worried that I received no letter from you today. Could my last letter— of Monday—have been lost? However that may be, I at least hope that no accident has prevented you from writing to me.
"I just want to tell you briefly that today I have the second and last concert, and will arrive *tomorrow* evening in Paris. Make sure that I find you well; that is the main thing. All the rest will be all right now!"

E Probably October, 1851.
Wagner, in Albisbrunn, is returning and asks Minna to meet him at Wildegg.

F A few lines, apparently enclosing a bill, which Wagner expects Sulzer to take care of (evidently from Zürich).

G Wagner is evidently returning from Albisbrunn (November 23, 1851). Minna has been offended by some remark, and he tries to joke her out of it.

H July 5 (evidently Zürich, 1854, when Minna was at Seelisberg).
Wagner is shortly to undertake an excursion.

Appendix B

COSIMA'S BLUE PENCIL

The Uhlig Letters, As Written

Appendix B

COSIMA'S BLUE PENCIL

The Uhlig Letters, As Written

Much has been said about the excessive zeal of Cosima Wagner in editing her husband's letters for publication. The compilers of the catalogue of this Collection made the statement in their preface that "Wagner was set to work to recover the stores of letters that his profuse pen had scattered everywhere in Germany." These letters were "drastically rehandled and reshaped" in publication. The accusation is not specific, nor do the accusers name cases when they tell us that "stores of letters . . . were more or less cooked by his family, in many a volume," and that the "Wahnfried strong box" was "an incinerator as well." Such charges are for the most part necessarily guesswork, because the cataloguers could have had no access to the originals at Bayreuth for comparison. There was one collection of letters, and one alone, on which they could have spoken with authority—the letters of Wagner to Theodor Uhlig. For the Burrell manuscripts contain copies of these letters made from the originals before they were edited at Wahnfried for publication.

Wagner in the first years of his exile (1849–1852) wrote to no one as freely as to his friend Theodor Uhlig, violinist of the Court Orchestra at Dresden. He stood on no ceremony with Uhlig, as with Liszt. Uhlig was younger than Heine or Fischer (he died on January 3, 1853, in his thirty-first year) and, unlike them, he was sympathetic to Wagner's hotheaded political views. Unlike Kietz, he was a composer and writer, and stood on Wagner's level as an intellectual companion. He had the degree of devotion requisite for admission into Wagner's intimate friendship. This relationship is evident in the letters to Uhlig in their published form. The unexpurgated texts now reveal that Wagner went a good deal further in unburdening himself when Uhlig, and Uhlig alone, was his audience.

Uhlig's daughter Elsa, years after her father's death, made copies of these letters and sent them to Wahnfried. Later sending the originals, she was careful to make and keep another set of copies. The first set was duly returned to her when the originals were received. She thus possessed two sets of copies, which Cosima used every effort to induce her to destroy. But she kept and eventually sold them. They thus fell into the hands of Mrs. Burrell. As they now come to light, they afford a line-by-line comparison of Wagner's original text with the text which appeared in publication from Wahnfried in 1888, and in English two years later. We can look over the shoulder of Cosima (her husband perhaps at her side, for before his death he had a say in the matter), as she deletes passages on page after page, crossing out anything from a name or an expletive to an entire letter. Only 23 out of 93 letters were allowed to appear intact.

These suppressions and alterations are here reproduced complete, their position indicated so that the reader who so wishes may fit them into the gaps of the printed English text. He may then decide for himself whether Cosima went too far. Of course, she may have been restrained by the consciousness that Elsa Uhlig held the trump card of possible exposure; aside from this, she was obliged to protect the privacy of living individuals mentioned, tempted to shield the good name of her husband, and moved to respect his explicit wishes on the subject. Cosima's responsibilities as editor, torn between what conscientious love of truth she may have possessed and her human affections and loyalties, were, to say the least, unenviable. There was much in these letters to invite censorship. A detailed examination of what she did to them should expose the depth of her perfidy, if such it can be called.

It should be noted that these letters brim with remarks about people who would have been deeply and needlessly offended. Wagner is annoyed for the moment with a publisher, a relative, a benefactor, and relieves his feelings in language colorful to the point of obscenity, delivered as between two men when they are by themselves. The name of Jessie Laussot could hardly have been allowed to appear—that affair was still quite unknown to the public. Frau Julie Ritter and her son Karl must have presented to Cosima a delicate case. Restive at being constantly beholden to the good lady for her bounty, Wagner speaks in momentary pique; his quarrel with Karl and their separation had strained his relations with the family. His free discussion of Karl's character would have been inconceivable in the public print: the fact that Karl had homosexual tendencies and was a problem to friends and relatives in itself forbade that. The removal of allusions to Hans von Bülow, then a young admirer of Wagner and not even yet Cosima's fiancé, is less defensible, but also less important. The elimination of Wagner's still violent revolutionary remarks reflects Cosima's consistent effort to minimize his part in the Dresden uprising. Of those who come in for sharp remarks, suppressed by Cosima, Liszt, Pusinelli, Tichatschek, Frau Ritter, and Albert Wagner had died when the letters appeared in 1888—but members of their families were still living.

The history of the Uhlig correspondence, in brief, is this: After Uhlig's death, in the new year of 1853, Wagner wrote two (since published) letters of consolation to the widow, in the second of which (March 17, 1853) he remarked: "Regarding my letters to my dear friend, may I ask you—if you do not wish to destroy them—to guard them carefully to yourself? They concern no one else, they are for the most part of an extremely confidential nature, and there is much in them which no one but Theodor himself could have really understood." On August 17, 1853 (247), and March 10, 1854 (271), Caroline Uhlig wrote to Minna. She was evidently poor. Her children were named, in true Wagnerian loyalty, Elsa and Siegfried. Siegfried was Wagner's godson. Elsa received from Wagner, on December 12, 1878, a request that she make and send him copies of his letters to her father. In a letter to Elsa dated June 2, 1879 (258), Cosima writes that she has received copies of some of the letters. The Uhligs have expressed the intention of bequeathing the originals to Wagner's son Siegfried. This does not please Cosima, who, in a letter on June 16 (259), refers to "the restoration of the original letters to my husband" as a "first intention," which she hopes can "still be realized."

In 1882 Elsa, according to her own account (256), gave over five of the letters, keeping no copy because of their "confidential" character. These letters were to be published by Cosima, but only in a fragmentary form. It was after Wagner's death that the remainder of the originals were also sent, Elsa receiving in return her manuscript copies which Wagner had had bound. But Elsa, taking no chances, had meanwhile made an additional set of copies for herself. (She even mentions a third copy.)

On November 6, 1885 (261 A), Elsa Uhlig received a thinly veiled warning from Cosima's daughter Eva. Three letters of Wagner had appeared in the *Allgemeine Musikzeitung*—two addressed to Elsa's mother in 1853, and one to herself in 1878. They were harmless enough, but they established a precedent in the publication of Wagner letters. There was evident anxiety at Wahnfried that Elsa might continue. Eva asks her "not to divulge anything further of the letters which are in our possession." Still another letter from Eva, dated January 21, 1886 (261 B), shows that Elsa has retorted in open defiance. The time for plain speaking was at hand. And so we have this battle cry from the namesake of one Wagnerian heroine to the namesake of another: "Since Mama's request to you, worthy Fräulein, as presented by me not to publish the letters has had your answer that no consideration would prevent you from publishing them, Mama has had no recourse but to take legal steps." This seems to have quieted Elsa.

Three years later the letters were officially published. But apparently Elsa was not satisfied with what had been done to them, and let it be known that if she was not ready to defy Wahnfried, she might still deliver her copies to those more courageous than herself. Cosima was newly alarmed and again took pen in hand. She advised Elsa (262 A, May 22, 1891) to compare her own copies with the printed version— she would observe that "the motive which controlled me corresponds to the spirit of your father no less than the point of view of my house, and you will therefore find that to deliver the material into strange hands is out of the question." What Cosima calls the "intimate details" which she has eliminated "are not to be seen by strange eyes—not a single one." There can be no question of publication, she reminds Elsa—"we alone are entitled to that." Cosima's wish is to protect her "against undesirable pressure," and to assure her that in the letters as published she has a "permanent remembrance" of her father. The "destruction" of the copies will "prevent indiscretions which would have deeply offended his closest friends." Four days later (262 B) Cosima's uneasiness has increased. She lists the publications to date of matter by or about Wagner, to show that all has been told. She concludes: "I hope I am mistaken in my misgivings that there is something here that bodes no good, but I thought I had better warn you!" and as a final postscript: "I repeat my advice that you destroy the copies."

Again, Elsa was momentarily quieted, but not convinced. She not only kept her copies, but eventually (in 1897) she took the step Cosima had dreaded. Whether it was the call of truth or the need of money we cannot know, but she sold two sets of the copies she had made to a dealer, Richard Bertling, in Dresden. A third copy, according to her own certification (257), went to Nikolaus Oesterlein, and thence to his Wagner Collection at Eisenach.[1] Mrs. Burrell evidently lost no time in acquiring the two copies thus thrown on the market.

The five letters which Elsa had not copied are accordingly missing in the set of copies which went to Bayreuth and was returned in bound form. In her own private set of copies, these five letters do appear, but not in their original text. Under the first of them (44) she has written: "This letter is copied from the printed collection. It is very much shortened by the editor. The original was returned to R. Wagner in 1882, no copy having been made because of its extremely confidential character [*übergrosse Vertraulichkeit*]. The same is the case with letters 47, 80, 83, 84." This creates a confusion of numbering in the cloth-bound manuscript copies as compared to the numbering in publication.

The comparison of the copied text with the published one (in the English version [2]) is now presented.

First, the names which have been replaced by a single letter are restored: [3]

Letter *X* means:

Meser in letters 30, 32, 35, 44, 53, 57, 63, 68, 74, 76, 77, 79, 81, 87, 88, 89;
Brendel in letters 42, 49, 59, 69;
Tichatschek in letters 82, 86;
Jessie Laussot in letters 5, 6;
Bülow in letter 40;
Wigand in letter 20;
Eisold in letter 2.
In letter 50, paragraph 3, *X* means *Lüttichau*; in paragraphs 5 and 6 *X* means *Meser*, and in paragraph 7 it means *Brendel*.
In letter 54, paragraph 5, *X* means *Meser*; in paragraph 10, *Wigand*.

Letter *A* means:

Avenarius in letters 23, 26, 41, 42, 43, 44, 45.

[1] The cataloguers of the Burrell Collection did not find this copy in the Collection at Eisenach.
[2] *Richard Wagner's Letters to Uhlig, Fischer, and Heine,* translated by J. S. Shedlock, 1890.
[3] These cryptic initials sometimes replace names where the remarks are harmless—the persons mentioned would have remained identifiable to those who knew them—rightfully obscure to the stranger who had no concern with such personal matters.

Letter *B* means:

Brendel (sometimes *Br*) in letters 34, 39, 59, 72;
Bülow in letters 37 and 57.

Letter *D* (also *E. D.*) means:

Eduard Devrient in letters 51, 56, 57, 63, 67, 72, 81.

Letter *K* means:

Karl Ritter, in every case except the following:
Koehler in letters 59, paragraph 15, and 63, paragraph 6;
Krebs in letter 88;
Kummer in letters 14, paragraph 8; 63, paragraph 16; 64, paragraph 3; 65, paragraph 2.

Letter *L* means:

Lüttichau in letters 7, 8, 25, 33, 53, 56, 88, 89;
Löwe in letter 62 (cf., however, 85, where *L* means *Lump,* or scoundrel).

Letter *P* means:

Paez in letters 5 and 6;
Planer in letter 45;
Portius in letters 31, 40, 44, 46, 49.

Letter *R* usually means:

Ritter (cf. below). However, it also means:
Röckel in letters 32, paragraph 3; 36, 51, paragraph 2; 53, paragraph 4; 58, paragraph 9; 82;
Räder in letter 53, paragraph 10;
Reissiger in letters 67, 88, paragraph 6; 89.

With one insignificant exception (21, P.S.) all references to the full name of the Ritter family, which at the time of Richard Wagner's greatest need gave him financial support for years, were suppressed. Forty-five of the published letters are subject to alterations and omissions in the mention of this family. The letter of April 28, 1852, between 61 and 62, dealing with relations to the Ritter family exclusively, was suppressed completely. The following enumeration quotes the letters involved:

5, 7, 11, 14, 16, 17, 19, 20, 22, 24, 26, 27, 30, 35, 37, 39, 40, 41, 42, 43, 45, 48, 49, 51 (paragraph 12), 52, 53 (paragraph 15), 54, 55, 56, 57, 58 (paragraphs 1 and 4), 59, 60, 61, 62, 63, 65, 71, 72, 77, 83, 86, 88 (paragraph 5), 90, 91.

Karl Ritter specifically is stricken from 41 letters:

3, 5, 6, 7, 9, 10, 13, 14 (paragraph 4), 14 (paragraph 10), 16, 17, 18, 24, 30, 32, 33, 34, 35, 37, 38, 39, 40, 42, 45, 46, 48, 49, 50, 51, 52, 53, 54, 57, 62, 63 (paragraph 10), 64, 65, 77, 81, 85, 90. The omitted letter of April 28, 1852, also refers to Karl Ritter.

Omitted parts reveal Wagner's extremely radical attitude in matters of religion and politics at that time. Up to 1852 and 1853 Wagner is a revolutionary and a socialist of the most radical type. He wants the capitalist society to be destroyed and believes its end to be quite near. He considers 1852 as the year for the revolution (14, 53). He mocks Uhlig for believing that the Royal Saxon orchestra will still exist at his friend's death, so that he would get a pension from the King (14). He predicts that the future revolution will be much more radical than all preceding revolutions; its program will include the burning of Paris (18). He mentions a revolutionary conspiracy between himself and his friends Karl Ritter and Herwegh (49). His *Nibelungen* is a genuine revolutionary conception. His theater of the future is to be the theater of the revolution. Only the generation after the revolution will understand him and his art (43). His sympathies are entirely with his revolutionary friends, particularly with Röckel.

LIST OF ALTERATIONS AND OMISSIONS

By comparison with *Richard Wagner's Letters to Uhlig, Fischer, and Heine,* translated by J. S. Shedlock (1890).

(The numerals at the left refer to the paragraphs in each letter as published. The restored passages are here given in italics.)

LETTER 1

Paragraph 3. After: "At the beginning of the winter I shall go again to Paris to have something performed and to put my opera matter into order":
But it is here [in Zürich] *that I really intend to establish my home.*

4. Instead of: "I beg you to get the score [*Lohengrin*] from the Dresden theater in order to continue the piano version":
I beg you to get the score which I have sold to the Dresden Theater, etc.

6. H. means *Hiebendahl.*

7. A. means *Augusta.*

LETTER 2

8. After: "I desire to escape from the Parisian opera scheme into which I so unwillingly entered":
The one who brought me into this conflict is Liszt alone; this modern worldling

[Weltkind], *who has his excellent qualities, is so fond of me that he would like to prepare for me an enormous, universal Parisian success.*

9. After: "So I shall be right, even if no idler take notice of me":
Therefore, I have no faith in my Parisian opera! But my wife must know nothing of this.

12. After: "the roughest fellow":
Eisold.

14. H. means *Hiebendahl.*

LETTER 4

Postscript: *Read my letter to Schirmer: It is written badly and with repugnance. However, I should like somebody to know about its contents and its character. Do not believe that I consider Schirmer as dishonest, but he does not understand me. He answered my first letter by asking me to write an opera for the wedding of Prince Albert and thus to reconcile myself with prevailing conditions. That man has good intentions, but it is quite likely that with all his good will he might put me in a position which would look like asking for an amnesty or something of the sort. That would be just what I need! Although my letter is rather confused, I still think it suffices to make clear to you that, God knows, to strive for an amnesty would be my last intention.*

LETTER 5

1. Instead of: "The news from X":
The news from Frau Laussot in Bordeaux.

1. After: "While I was expecting news":
from Bordeaux.

LETTER 6

3. After: "In no way has any change in my plan been made, so far as it depends upon myself, but only delay in carrying it out so far as it depends on others":
In other words, I have not had any news from Bordeaux up to now.

3. After: "The sum notified by you":
from Bordeaux.

3. Instead of: "as a letter was owing from me":
as I owed her a letter.

LETTER 8

9. F. v. L. means *Frau von Lüttichau.*

LETTER 9

Undated in publication. Actually dated *Februrary 24 to March 10, 1850.*

2. After: "Spyri, a young lawyer":
clumsy [tölpisch].

2. Instead of: "He [Alexander Müller] has become somewhat inaccessible to new ideas":
somewhat obtuse and inaccessible to new ideas.

5. F. L. means *Frau Laussot.*

5. After: "a detailed letter the content of which will be communicated to you":
by this excellent friend.

5. After: "a journey southwards":
of my friend.

5. After: "a journey southwards":
touching Bordeaux.

7. Instead of: "the great sweet-smelling drain":
the great sweet-smelling sewers of Paris.

Between 7 and 8 the following paragraph is missing:
Do you actually believe the Minister of Justice of Saxony could be so mean as to ask for my acquittal in connivance with the Court, whereas poor devils like Herz are sentenced to fifteen years of hard labor? Neither can I imagine such a degree of wickedness, nor will the Court and Lüttichau be so stupid, seriously to consider recalling me to my former position. Even if both were true, I would show generosity toward these scoundrels by refusing to accept the acquittal as well as my former position. Thus their meanness and their stupidity would lack any apparent success in the eyes of the mischievous world. This surely does not ask for any further explanation. Neither am I willing to act carelessly, for without doubt I am now better protected than under the cover of the favor of the Court of Saxony which one day might become damned oppressive to me.

LETTER 10

3. After: "From the only other quarter whence I learn something about you":
from Bordeaux.

5. After: "I start off":
to Bordeaux.

Between 5 and 6:
If you plan to write soon to such an inconsistent man as I am, please put the letter into an envelope addressed to Mad. Jessie Laussot, 26 cours du 30. Juillet à Bordeaux: thus it will certainly reach me.

7. After: "I am all confusion about my hasty departure":

The benevolence I am enjoying now—now, just now, delights me. How much I pity you all for not having the chance to be as happy as I am!

A letter dated April 15, 1850, was published in *Die Sonne*, Leipzig, February, 1933. It does not appear in this Collection.

LETTER 11

Letter 11 is written from Bordeaux on March 26, 1850. The official edition mentions the date only and omits the place.

1. Instead of: "[I received] your last [letter] of all today":
your last one to Bordeaux today. Jessie is just writing to the Ritters. I use this opportunity to enclose a few lines for you.

3. After: "I have a yearly maintenance":
from Frau Laussot.

3. Instead of: "As I read your last, enclosed letter by the fireside . . . I threw this letter into the bright chimney fire!":
As I read your last, enclosed letter in the presence of my friend by the fireside, I got so fearfully out of temper that I had to stop reading aloud the letter of my best friend. Otherwise the philistine treatment of the financial problem would have offended this affectionate woman. Now Jessie wanted to read the letter herself, but I, embittered and angered by your unworthy joy over my maintenance, threw this letter into the bright chimney fire.

4. E. means *Emilie.*

7. After: "I have already a lady violin-pupil for you":
Frau Laussot.

8. Instead of: "Greetings to Elsa Marie":
Greetings from us to Elsa Marie.

LETTER 12

Between 3 and 4:
Don't write or send any money to Sulzer, send it to Wilhelm Baumgartner, *music teacher, Rennweg, Zürich. This one is closer to my wife, and I am afraid she would not be equally pleased with Sulzer's mediation.*
Postscript: The letter "K." is no abbreviation. It is used as a poste restante address.

LETTER 13

The salutation is not: "Dear Friend," but:
Dear Karl!

3. After: "Whether Brendel will have the courage . . . I know not":
If he is afraid, he is an ass! This must be made clear to him.

6. M. means *Meyerbeer*.

8. W. The abbreviation appears in the original text.

LETTER 14

4. Instead of: "Well, I read the notice of my last work":

Well, I read the review of my last work in the Berliner Abendpost *written by the young Bülow. He at least has still the fresh susceptibility of youth. I thought he would follow my ideas more definitely. He does not criticize my ideas, but when reference is made to sculpture, suddenly the reviewer notices that the author now lacks his otherwise so praiseworthy clarity, and that he seems to proclaim the down-fall of sculpture.*

5. After: "Dearest, confess that we are both crazy":

Indeed, I understand that a periodical can be edited with a little more decency and a little less dirtiness!

8. S. means *Sascha* (Alexander Ritter?).

8. After: "I will guarantee you a good subscription list":

So far as your financial situation is concerned, let me show you first the present dark side of it: With that poor salary of yours, you have to play the violin in the orchestra. In doing this, you are doomed. You are no free, happy man. Second: Do you really think that, if God grants you a long life, you will actually receive this salary for a long time to come? Do you seriously believe that the Royal Saxon orchestra will exist longer than you will be alive? Do you imagine that your wife would ever get a pension from a Royal Pension Fund? Dearest, such dreams may be dreamed by those who look neither right nor left, but who continue to live in their pleasant court habits like cattle. But it would not reveal a very shrewd intelligence of yours if you should conceal from yourself that this mad system is galloping to its death. Compared with you, I feel as if I were in Abraham's lap. Keep the year 1852 in mind! If in December, 1852, you are still getting your salary, grass will grow from my desk.

9. After: "I only know the Saxon exiles":

your relative Hitzschold *at the head of them.*

10. Instead of: "K. gives me much pleasure . . . confidence":

Karl gives me much pleasure. Sometimes I have to fight against certain traits of his character. However, this is a very easy task for me, as I give him the most un-restricted freedom as far as important matters are concerned. In this way—to my satis-faction—I always succeed in making him choose the sensible decision by himself. His gifts are extraordinary. He grasps everything extremely quickly. Whenever he has drunk a little or when we are alone on a walk, he expresses the most amiable confidence.

LETTER 15

6 begins as follows:

There were symptoms of manifold character which made me recognize soon that I as a bona fide reformer had been entirely mistaken in assuming a favorable attitude from the people in authority. I learned that, in those regions whence we trusting people were accustomed to get decisions and regulations, the presentation and recognition of facts, the consideration of common higher needs is of no value at all. Everything depends solely on the question how far personal interest is involved. In this dominating clique of privileged persons, there is only one goal that matters: the maintenance of the privilege.

7. After: "to offer himself as a sacrifice":
how sweet is the reward of a supreme sacrifice in Court [Oberhofopfer].

LETTER 16

2. Instead of: "I have become surety . . . at the theater here":
I have become surety for Karl's music-directorship at the theater here (probably Bülow will participate in the conducting too).

2. After: "Brendel . . . places his paper at my disposal":
This paper is real filth [ein rechter Dreck], *however* faute de mieux *I accept.*

LETTER 17

3. After: "My friendly intendant at Weimar (a thoroughly good soul":
even though very narrow-minded).

3. Instead of: "Every day I must . . . conduct the orchestra myself, as X. is not getting on very quickly":
Every day I must . . . conduct the orchestra myself, as Karl is not getting on very quickly. Bülow arrived here the day before yesterday. Bülow's narrow-minded and cruel father had tried to prevent him by force from seeing me here at Zürich. With the help of Karl I have at once abducted him from his father. With Bülow things will go faster.

LETTER 18

3. After: "Liszt's . . . striving . . . to . . . kindle . . . the fire of my fame touches me deeply":
however also appears to be rather amusing.

7. Instead of: "You know X. wished to become musical director":
You know Karl wished by all means to become musical director.

7. After: "I declined the offer":
however, I induced him to employ Karl at a salary of 80 gulden, of course with me as a surety.

9. After: "the institution . . . can only be maintained in this manner":
I hope to be able to retire from this job, thanks especially to Bülow's decisive talent.

Between 13 and 14:
However, it is just against these causes that the real spirit of revolution rebels. There is no need for any metaphysical enlightenment to recognize these causes. What is necessary is only to annihilate this misleading culture and to replace it by the consideration of a quite simple, natural need. What actually is the essence of socialism? Those who preach socialism already begin to misinterpret it by their endeavors to organize. Its sole content is to eliminate luxury and want. Therefore it is not necessary to teach the people, they need only be told: You are right! And surely the people themselves become more and more conscious of this, since they have recognized that unfortunately they had placed their confidence in leaders. *Isn't it quite necessary for them to look at the* political *nonsense in order to know what they have to expect from politics? There has never been a period of history better suited for the riddance of wrong ideas with lightning speed than the present reactionary era! Do you actually believe that people will still fight* for politics? *You certainly must believe it, for you have remarked that you could foresee a victory of the revolution only by a new alliance between constitutionalists and democrats. I tell you—not a single hand will be raised for democracy, because every political revolution has become altogether impossible. In politics men do not need any further enlightenment. Everybody* knows *about the dishonesty of our political conditions. Only the fact that the social question is hidden behind the political problem gives everybody the cowardly courage to tolerate these conditions. There is no longer any other movement than the radical social movement, but this is quite different from what our socialists imagine: everything else remains weak and entirely inefficient. Now you ask me: But where are those who shall achieve this necessary revolution? I don't see anything but the most miserable men, philistines and cowards, in my own environment, and even in the lower spheres I don't see anything but apathy and a state of mind like that of a beast of burden!*

Dearest Uhlig, remember the day during the Dresden revolt when you met me in the Zwinger promenade. Anxiously you asked me whether I was not afraid that, under most favorable conditions, the revolution would lead to the rule of the mob. You had been terrified at the aspect of those men for whom you now seem to look in vain! These men were still dominated by the bonds of politics; they still glanced respectfully at the higher political goals which they considered embodied in their leaders. They were not yet what they actually are, they did not act as yet as they really will act. They obeyed where they should have acted. All this degraded them and made them appear to you like fellows who got intoxicated by political brandy and who shouted along the streets which they perhaps might have set on fire with all the regal pomp of beautiful Dresden, if they only would have been allowed to act according to the fury that was in their hearts. I have seen these people again in Paris and Lyons, and I know now the future of this world. Up to now we know the reaction of enslaved human nature only as crime *which rouses our repugnance and horror: if now robbers and murderers set a house on fire, we are right to consider this as base and disgusting; but what will be our impression when the enormous city of Paris is burned to ashes, when the firebrand spreads from city to city, when, with wild enthusiasm, we ourselves set these uncleanable Augean stables on fire, in order to create healthy air? With complete soberness of mind and without any deception I assure you that I do not believe in any other type of revolution than that which starts with the burning down of Paris. There will not again be merely the fight which happened in June* [1830], *for man has come to regard himself as holy; the holes in which they turn to beasts are no longer sacrosanct. Are you terrified? Think about it honestly and deeply—there is no other conclusion! Strong nerves will be needed, and only real men will survive, that is to say: those who have become men only by privation and by supreme horrors. You ask whether the results will be helpful? Let us first see how we shall find ourselves after this fire-cure: perhaps I would be able to envision this future. I could even imagine how here and there an enthusiast would call together the survivors of our old art and would ask them: Who would like to help me perform a drama? Only those would answer who were really willing, for now there would be no longer a possibility to make money by that. And those who would gather would use a quickly erected wooden building in order to show the people what art is. In any case, everything will develop very quickly, for, you see, there is no question of a gradual progress: Our savior destroys everything that is in our way with lightning speed! When? I don't know, for such a revolution is not planned. I only know that the next storm will surpass all the preceding ones just to the same degree as the revolutions of February, 1848, surpassed the expectations of 1847. There is only one further step to be made, and this step is imperatively necessary.*

LETTER 23

1. Instead of "A. will in any case assist us":
Avenarius, to whom for several reasons I cannot offer the manuscript personally, will in any case assist us.

4. After: "despicable":
like the fool Brendel.

4. Instead of: "the other paper":
Brendel's paper.

4. Instead of: "the *Rheinische Zeitung* is, in fact, a musical paper of the day. I understand that you must now continue to write in a musical paper":
I was not seduced by this. However, it made me think again about the reason why the Leipziger Musikzeitung *is served in Paris by an entirely incompetent and unqualified man. The* Rheinische Zeitung *is in fact a musical paper of the day; the* Leipziger Zeitung *is simply a worthless sheet* [ganz einfach ein Luderblatt]. *I understand that you must now continue to write in this paper.*

6. After: "Consider again the matter of extracts from my manuscript for Brendel's [4] paper":

Would it not be too ridiculous to see the content of these same extracts afterward attacked by Herr Brendel in the same paper? And would I not be absolutely crazy if I should argue with Herr Brendel? Should I come down to such a low level?

LETTER 24

Between 6 and 7:

I had to give up entirely the intention to use Liszt as a mediator between me and the Court of Weimar, so far as my Siegfried *is concerned: nothing suitable would result from that.*

7. After: "you will probably not insist on my withdrawing my opinion":

concerning Brendel and his periodical. Such dirty tricks [Schweinereien] *can only happen under the leadership of such a dumbhead and wretch* [Ho...sch...s (*sic*)]. *I ask you again: Don't mention me in this paper; write good essays on music and ask for a good payment—excellent! But I should not like to have this ridiculous paper considered as my standard-bearer. Can you blame me for that?*

LETTER 26

Between 6 and 7:

I have heard horrible things about the "human" qualities of Krebs.[5]

LETTER 27

2. Instead of: "I was informed":

Bülow informed me.

LETTER 30

(September 2, 1851: undated in published editions.)

2. After: "I cannot get on at all with men":

—and—a woman!—Yea, a woman!—

Between 3 and 4:

As far as Dresden is concerned, there is still another point to be considered: I can and must no longer have anything to do with this Court mob [Hofgesindel]. *They shall know that I do not belong to them in any way—and apart from that—this whole gossiping place* [schwabblige Nest]!

[4] Franz Brendel, editor of the *Neue Zeitschrift für Musik* in Leipzig, was opening his columns to Wagner, Uhlig, and Bülow at this time. Wagner found his support stronger in loyalty than in understanding.

[5] Reissiger's successor as Kapellmeister at Dresden.

4. F. means *Fürstenau*.

6. After: "a bath in the lake, or a hip-bath":
The clysterpipes agree with me very well.

LETTER 32

2. After: "my two other operas":
edited by Meser.

2. After: "sacrifice of one single family":
which up to now is by no means rich.

2. Instead of: "Of all persons in the world he is the least fit for such a business":
Among all music dealers in the world he is the least fit for such a business, and, if one would distill the quintessence of the most damned timid [scheissängstlichsten], *the most unreliable, the most cowardly philistine, one would get just: Meser.*

Between 2 and 3: [6]
Now Pusinelli!— I too am sorry about the development of the relations between me and Pusinelli: but for reasons other than those which he would understand: and that is just the bad part of the story. A man who refers to his services rendered, to his "proven delicacy," and who asks for gratitude for that, asks in truth and in full consciousness for a self-deception: how easy would it be for me to provide him with this deception by sending him a letter full of assurances! Just by refusing to act in this way, I prove that I at least respect him more than he seems inclined to respect himself. This unhappy man would be satisfied if I should listen to his repeated admonitions, if I should finally assure him that his services rendered and his delicacy obliged me to be grateful to him. And all this though he once clearly stated that I had been mistaken as to the character of his friendship, that in this friendship he would not be able to follow me further than to a certain point which was determined by the limits of his nature, that he was by far weaker and more dependent on prejudices than I believed, that he therefore could not follow me and that I should leave him alone. A man who is pretty clear about his relations to me now deliberately ventures to ask for a proof of his weakness and to remind me of this. How extremely easy would it be for me to give him this proof. Unfortunately, however, I have chosen truthfulness for my religion: I am no longer able to lie intentionally; I cannot testify to Pusinelli that he put me under obligation to be grateful to him, as he caused me only bitter and disgusted feelings, which he confirms more and more. I confess: there is a tragic conflict at the basis of this antagonism, a conflict which grieves me too at this moment, thus as it has always grieved me. If I feel pains, then Pusinelli may feel them too: he may feel them vehemently and strongly, this alone can free him from the pettiness of his character. If he does not know me at all, then his judgment about me is his affair only. However, if he still knows me, then he must understand that I could no longer fulfill his wish. The more pain this

---

[6] This paragraph is published in the Pusinelli correspondence (pp. 37–39).

causes him, the closer we will approach each other, and with greatest joy I shall then shake his hand again. Why cover superficially what can be healed only from its root? Is it my task to spread such ointments? It was the worst time of my life, when I was still shrewd enough to do so. Again: How easy would this be for me now! What am I when I refuse it?— Ungrateful? Be it so!

3. After: "Could not Schulz procure him Feuerbach's lectures on the nature of religion":
and apart from that cold clysterpipes?

Between 6 and 7:
I had to send a terrible letter to Karl recently.

LETTER 33

2. After: "to be brief":
(His late Majesty, the King of Prussia) [7] *No fear.*

2. After: "Lieutenant Müller taking the waters with me":
Karl being there too—crazy fellow—Homo Lin. IV 36.

2. After: "go on":
Wishing to spank J. J. Weber's rear.

2. Instead of: "why the Court and L.?":
why the Court and Lüttichau? Better to chase them away!

LETTER 34

2. Instead of: "You already know that Müller is here":
You already know that Karl and Müller are here. Karl is in no good condition, it is a pity. If anything could help him, it would be a complete water cure. Fortunately he has firmly made up his mind to take this cure.

LETTER 35

(Albisbrunn, October 12, 1851: undated in published editions.)

2. Instead of: "such a man as X":
such a brute as Meser.

5. After: "Why the deuce are you suddenly concerned about my money affairs":
Listen, there is one thing I warn you about: beware of any correspondence with the Wagner family in Berlin! [8] *This might easily become dangerous:* For not only would I never take a dime from them; *he who negotiates with them will have damned poor thanks from me (this only by the way!).*

[7] *Allerhöchstselig":* Frederick Wilhelm III of Prussia (1797–1840) is said to have expressed himself in this abrupt way. Wagner's letter is a humorous imitation of this type of language.

[8] Albert Wagner.

6. After: "not worth the trouble":
"800 thaler Tietz [?]"—a chambermaid—this was done by Meser's lawyer, without my request.

6. After: "All the same to me":
Florian Schulze and Röckel, sorry I heard about them.

8. After: "With Brendel—all right!":
Shit! ["Scheissdreck"]—Fischer—ass!

Postscript 1. After "Albisbrunn":
Don't refer to Meser again.

Postscript 1. Instead of: "Müller sends":
Karl and Müller send greetings.

<h2 style="text-align:center">LETTER 36</h2>

(Albisbrunn, October 14, 1851: undated in published editions)
11. Initials R., W. also in original text (meaning: *Röckel, Waldheim*).

<h2 style="text-align:center">LETTER 37</h2>

Between 1 and 2: [9]
Therefore let us proceed to the main point at once, and split up the collective phrase: "The Wagner family" into its component parts, so that we can understand each other better about the whole. Johanna is a good girl, though with a lack of character and highly dependent on others. However, I like her. Franziska seems to me to be very efficient, she loves and understands me. I remember Marie as a gifted, but spoiled, light-minded, and rather impertinent girl. The mother of these three daughters has become really repugnant to me: She is a "play-actress mother" [Komödiantenmama], who is able to store a lot of poison within herself in order to give it forth at a suitable moment. For this purpose she uses her husband, my brother: He is a gifted man with great artistic instinct, but effeminate, weak and dependent and thoroughly depraved by this permanent comedian business. He accused me in his letters to Switzerland of not being practical enough in composing my operas, as I did not sufficiently consider the small theaters and the demands of the singers; chiefly, however, he blamed me for having let myself be allured by the scoundrel Röckel and thus having lost my good job at Dresden. To sum up: Do you mind my confession that this whole family is absolutely indifferent to me, with almost the only exception of Franziska, of whom alone I should like to hear more? However, this indifference had to turn into something else after the following complications had occurred: After you had met Johanna at Soden, my wife got news from my sister at Chemnitz that she was so happy to hear that Johanna (that is to say, the Wagner

[9] This passage was quoted by Julius Kapp and Hans Jachmann, *Richard Wagner und seine erste "Elisabeth"* (1927).

family) now had decided to do something for me; probably we would already have received a letter from her. Thus Johanna had already informed other members of my family that she was going to support me now (by the way, neither a letter nor anything else has arrived). When I met Karl at Albisbrunn, he told me that his mother had written to him and had invited him to come to a family gathering in Berlin. I confess my weakness in having been suddenly surprised by this news, particularly by the choice of Berlin as a place. I assumed that the Wagners had approached the Ritters for the purpose of a common *financial support to be granted to me, and that consultations concerning this subject would take place in Berlin. This assumption tortured me to such an extent that it made me sleepless, and I at once asked Karl urgently to write to his family and to express my feelings toward them, emphasizing that I would not accept the slightest sum from the Wagner family. A common action by the Ritters and the Wagners in my favor, already the thought that they were consulting about my situation and my future, could make me so unhappy that I would even have to abandon the thought of accepting any help from the Ritters. Must I give you still more details why I don't want to have anything to do with the Wagner family and why that suspected common action would have made me furious? I expect not!* [10]

2. Instead of: "look at the others and look at the R.s.":
Look at the Wagner family *and look at the* Ritters.

Between 2 and 3:
How deeply I am already hurt that there must now be discussions about me and my relations with the Ritter family in the presence of a new member.

LETTER 38

3. Instead of: "illusions":
court illusions.

10. After "I wrote":
with Karl.

10. Instead of: "the miserable business":
the trouble with the Wagner family.

LETTER 39

The letter begins as follows:
Let me first set the Meser [11] *affair straight. De facto, I am no longer the owner of*

---

[10] See p. 143.

[11] Hopeful about a quick popular success for *Rienzi* and *The Flying Dutchman*, and still more hopeful about the pending *Tannhäuser*, Wagner entered in 1844 into an agreement with the Court music publisher, C. F. Meser, which was to include the publication of these operas in full score, arrangements, or selections, the composer to furnish the capital

the compositions published by Meser. I should be able to draw revenues from them only after all my Dresden creditors would have been repaid from this source. Regarding the whole situation and the authority granted by me to Judge Schirmer, this alone is the source from which they can get a repayment of their loans. Solely in the interest of my creditors, the publishing of my three operas Flying Dutchman, Tannhäuser, *and* Rienzi, *is being continued at present. If any change of this business takes place, this would primarily affect the interests of my creditors only. I am interested in so far as I must wish to see my debts gradually paid back as much as possible. Among these creditors Meser is the one most interested. He has done the work without compensation up to now, has himself made advances in cash, and has also vouched for loans of other persons. This affair becomes a burden for Meser only, because he does not possess the financial means necessary to render the business profitable. Hence he wants to sell it in order to get his money back, and he wants my consent for such a sale. I, on my part, declared that I have no right to grant such a consent, that I can only attribute this right to my creditors. Therefore I advise that Judge Schirmer, to whom I gave a power of attorney concerning these matters, should ask my creditors about their decision. Whatever they decide is all right with me. However, I wish to point out that the sale of the publishing business and of the publishing rights, so far as the three operas are concerned, would be disadvantageous to my creditors, for the following reasons: Considering the present scope of the circulation of my operas, we cannot expect that right now a buyer would offer a sum which would leave any profit to the creditors. After the sale, however, all hope of ever receiving anything would have disappeared, as I probably should never again become able to acquire property. I must be content to earn a scanty livelihood with the help of some friends. However, it is by no means impossible that gradually my operas will win that degree of lively interest which would lead to an improvement of the business and finally to ample profits. Considering the possibility of such a development, it would be the true interest of the creditors to preserve the ownership of this business. If they have this intention, they surely cannot force Herr Meser to continue under oppressive conditions. They could enable him to continue more willingly by simply offering him the—so I am informed—moderate means which are necessary for a more energetic management. The interest of the educated public in my operas is now growing. It would be necessary to avoid every stagnation*

(by borrowing), Meser to have 10 per cent of the profits. The operas did not become popular as expected, Wagner's indebtedness became acutely embarrassing, and the unsuspecting Meser found himself in control of a venture which meant for him much trouble and no appreciable return. As before and afterward, the success which Wagner anticipated for his works was far too slow in arriving. When Wagner wrote to Uhlig about Meser, he was alarmingly hounded by his creditors, while the plodding publisher, instead of keenly following up the advantage of Wagner's now increasing fame, was content to jog along and take no hazards. Wagner's impatience with Meser at the time is surely understandable. But compare these with his equable remarks in *My Life,* and his letter to Dr. Pusinelli of 1853 (No. 7 in the published letters to his friend) in which he speaks of Meser's "great tribulations," is reluctant to lose his services, and objects to nothing except that he had "carried on the management of the business with too little energy."

in business, to make new shipments of my works to music dealers in Germany, and above all to interest the public by frequent advertisements in the best known newspapers. It would, in my opinion, be in the best interest of my creditors to regard the matter in this way and to make its continuation possible. But whatsoever they decide, I again declare that I will agree with their decision. Dear friend, be so kind as to inform Judge Schirmer *about this on my part. . . . Now only a line or two.*

LETTER 40

2. Instead of: "He does me no harm":
It does not do any harm, neither to me nor to Karl.
3. Instead of: "X. wrote in detail to me yesterday":
Bülow wrote in detail to me yesterday: hence there is harmony again in Weimar! Good for them!

LETTER 41

4. After: "You are the right sort of chap!":
I should like to have a complete *copy of Bülow's retort* [Antikritik].

LETTER 42

4. After: "I think of carrying it out in my own manner":
Therefore I shall have to sever relations with Weimar (this remains between us two).

Between 7 and 8:
Recently I wrote a long letter to the Ritters concerning Karl. Health is the main problem with him. Apart from this I do not worry about him. He knows what he wants. I should be very glad if Mama Ritter would also come at the same time. In this case there might possibly be some results.

LETTER 43

6 reads correctly as follows: [12]
I can think of a performance only after the revolution. Only the revolution can provide me with the artists and the listeners. The coming revolution must necessarily put an end to the whole of our theater enterprises. *All of them must and will perish. This is inevitable. From the ruins I shall* then *find those whom I need. Then I shall erect a theater on the banks of the Rhine and issue invitations to a great dramatic festival. After a year's preparation, I shall produce my complete work in a series of four days: with this I shall make the men of the revolution recognize the* meaning *of their revolution according to its most noble contents.* That audience *will understand me; the present one cannot.*

[12] This passage was published in the *Bayreuther Blätter*, 1892.

LETTER 44

Since the original letter was not copied by Elsa Uhlig, the full text is unascertainable.

1. H. (Elsa Uhlig inserts "Hitzschold.")

LETTER 45

Between 2 and 3:
Tell her [Frau Ritter] *also that she must cease worrying about Karl. Everything that depends on his health is in very good shape with him: He alone has a thoroughly concentrated, conscious, by no means vague and unclear view about the duties in a higher and more reasonable sense now imposed on the Ritter family, if, to a considerable extent, they want to make use of the fortunate opportunity offered to them. What he has in mind not only bespeaks enthusiasm and the worthiness of his point of view—it is very intelligent, more so, more prudent than the timid caution which for unknown reasons seems to have paralyzed the otherwise energetic Frau Ritter. If she neither wants nor is able to believe me, then—as soon as her health permits—she should make it possible to come and visit us here. I would like so very much to have her taken away from Dresden with its frenzied tea parties* [theekannenschwitzenden Dresden]. *Enough of that for today.*

LETTER 46
(Zürich, November 29, 1851: published editions have November 28.)

9. H. means *Hähnel.*
9. After: "redeemed":
through Karl Ritter.

Between 10 and 11:
It is rather tiring for us that Emilie hesitates so long. Müller wrote to me about Karl yesterday. The day's talk at Albisbrunn dealt with the fact that Karl had twice raised his voice at table, and this in order to answer a French gabbler [Heuler—Bramarbas?] *in rather a rude and sarcastic way.*

LETTER 47
(Full original text not known.)

LETTER 49

Between 9 and 10:
Well, Karl leaves here on Tuesday *in order to see his mother! I am very happy about this decision, for I very well understand our friend's longing for her son. Just before his departure Karl wavered. He was afraid of the journey on account of his*

health. The fur gave him new courage. Treat Karl in the right way—it is worth the effort to coax something out of him [etwas aus ihm loszulockern]. *Pure gold comes to light from this inaccessible mine* [diesem verschlossenen Schacht]. *If only his health were more stable! However, this too will be better next spring and next summer.*

After 12, before: "So farewell for today":
Recent political events have exercised a strong, but only a contributory influence. For now only this: Yesterday, on December 17, 1851, a decision was reached by me and Herwegh in the presence and with the participation of Karl which in my opinion can become the starting point of a new turn in world history. We have promised each other to use all our energy and all our conviction and means of persuasion for the purpose of making our decision known in wider and wider circles, so that, as we hope, our plans will materialize in a not too distant future. From now on, except when I am writing poetry or composing, I shall concentrate my entire literary activity on this. The goal is throughout a positive and practical one, and of unlimited logical consequence. At the same time it is a goal which no reactionary power in the world will be able to hinder.

12. After: "So farewell for today":
Karl will have much to tell you.

LETTER 50
(Zürich, December, 1851: undated in published editions.)

9. After: "I am well":
To be sure, Karl, who left yesterday morning, would like to have me appear rather ill.

LETTER 51

2. W. means *Waldheim.*

9. After "have somewhat disposed me in his [Brendel's] favor":
If this man could only know what really matters. I believe he has not the slightest notion.

After 12:
I expect to have a letter from Karl tomorrow. I hope he has arrived safely.

LETTER 52

Between 1 and 2:
Bülow goes so far in his impoliteness that he has made no answer to two letters, although the second included some urgent requests. Thus I always feel like a beggar who runs after everybody to get a pfennig. With Karl this is different. He nourishes

his great grief within himself, complaining about his stomach, which has been spoiled by his predilection for the confectioner's shop. He has no time to worry about the small matters which foolishly afflict my situation. Sometimes he does what he can. After three weeks of absence from me he finally writes twenty-one words, really one word for every day! Oh, these unhappy Ritters, what bad luck they have!

4. Instead of: "the whole world is full of fools":
the whole world is full of nasty cowards [Scheisskerlen].

Between 4 and 5:
Be sure to give my kindest regards to my niece Johanna, Emilie's beloved friend. Oh, if she would put in a word for me. Ask her quite urgently; she will certainly do so, the good girl. Tell her how badly off her poor devil of an uncle is! She has now the full power to help me toward recognition, for I learn to my greatest satisfaction that a Prussian prince [13] *is her lover and has already done much for her, and her contract; perhaps, if she is very obliging to him, and if her Mama does not object, she might also achieve something for me! Oh, how happy I should be, how delighted the Ritters would be to sit in Berlin at a* Tannhäuser *performance which I should have made possible by my shrewdness and a little bit of compromising!!*

7. Instead of: "Why do I not rather imitate my lady S.?": [14]
Why do I not rather imitate the Stoics?

LETTER 53

(The copies show the date, Zürich, January 22, 1852.) [15]

6. A. H. means *August Hitzschold*.

Before 8:
(V) I had not exactly intended to give the score of Tannhäuser *simply to Bülow; it should be given to Weimar in general. If, however, Bülow would like to have the score for himself, and if he wants to arrange the Weimar score accordingly, then, for God's sake, let him consider the matter as though it had been given to him under the aforementioned condition. You can transmit this statement to him now, and accordingly he may claim the copy for himself.*

[13] Evidently Prince Georg, youngest brother of Wilhelm I, a very artistic man.
[14] The German editor was needlessly cryptic, reducing the harmless *"die Stoiker"* to *"die S."* The translator was thus led further astray.
[15] A postscript to this letter reads: "53 [!] December, '51 (I shall continue in the *coup d'état* month until the desired 1852 really comes)." Wagner elucidates this in *My Life,* p. 578. Having prophesied to Uhlig momentous world events in 1852, he suggested jokingly that the two continue to date their letters "December, 1851," the month of the *coup d'état* of Louis Napoleon in Paris, not recognizing that 1852 had arrived until it was justified by the expected fulfillment.

8. Instead of "(V)":

(*VI*)

9. After: "Now about your godfather [16] affair":

It is a shame that you have to have your child baptized. If you want to diminish the humiliating effect of this action, as far as a symbolic meaning is concerned, and if you think . . .

9. After: "Will you inoculate him with the poison of":

religion and of.

Between 13 and 14:

If Karl would once write to me a proper letter, this would be a great joy to me! Certainly!

LETTER 54

6. After: "humbug!":

I am often overcome by the desire to write to Frau Ritter once again; sometimes I feel so monstrously ungrateful toward her! Without this generous woman I should be the most miserable human being. All imagination, all thinking balks at the prospect of what I should now be without her. I can have no other conception of it than the most horrible one. And yet there is a spirit of dissatisfaction in me, which, as though I were to annihilate myself, incites me to turn against my most beloved, even against this woman. I believe the reason is that she is so far away from me and that she insists on keeping this distance. If she would live close to me, if I could live in intimate personal relations with this family, I believe the painful dissatisfaction would disappear! Hence I hope that my wish may be fulfilled, for otherwise everything that the Ritters do for me begins to make me uneasy. Don't laugh, sometimes I feel like being "paid" for the Tannhäuser. *This is the cursed suspicion of the proletarian against the capitalist. But greet . . .*

6. After: "greet the ladies today in your heartiest manner":

From Karl –––– [The five dashes are in the original].

7. Instead of: "it was already a reproach to me that":

Frau Ritter already blamed me for taking no pleasure in it

3. (Postscript) X. X. means *Franz Abt.*

LETTER 56

8. F. means *Freytag.*[17]

Between 12 and 13:

Oh, if it were only May! But no, leave the swamp to the frogs! If one could only

---

[16] Wagner became godfather to Siegfried Uhlig.

[17] Gustav Freytag, editor of the *Grenzboten*, hostile to Wagner; subsequently better known as a novelist.

get some news from R. [Röckel] *I always forget to ask Bülow to go to see Frau Röckel at Weimar; she must have letters from him. Please don't forget to ask Bülow for this. As I hear from Schwerin, Franziska Wagner is still there. She attends the* Tannhäuser *performances but never dreams of sending me a few lines about it. A strange family! I am happy that the Ritters like her so much.*

16 reads correctly as follows:

Some new acquaintances have forced themselves on me: the men are highly indifferent to me, the women less so. A rich young merchant, Wesendonk [18]—*the brother of the Reichstägler—settled down at Zürich some time ago, and in great luxury. His wife is very pretty and seems to have caught some enthusiasm for me after having read the preface to the three operatic poems. Thus it is with some Swiss families of the aristocracy here (I refer only to the women, for the men are horrible). I am astonished . . .*

16. After: "There will be no scandal":
this time!

LETTER 57

6. After: "I would go straight to Paris and see him":
I advise Karl urgently to go to Paris soon and to consult with Lindemann thoroughly. I give the same advice to Kummer.

6. Instead of: "Tell all this to the R.s, however":
Tell all this to the Ritters, to Karl and to Kummer.

Between 8 and 9:
I was very much amused about Bülow's having become a martyr for the sake of Fräulein Sonntag. I have already consoled him on this subject. The report of the Deutsche Allgemeine Zeitung *about the Sonntag incident and its remark that Bülow's essay had caused general indignation in Leipzig also is scandalous. He who feels indignation about this essay deserves a special thorough castigation from you.*

13. After: "If I could only have a pleasant journey this summer to Italy":
The Ritters could help me toward that if they decided to spend a little more money on me. They certainly would do so if they knew how few years I still have to live and how soon they would therefore be freed from the burden of my existence!

LETTER 59
(Zürich, March 23, 1852: undated in published editions)

4. Instead of: "united income of a family":
total income of the Ritter family.

Between 4 and 5:
As a whole I am a little sorry about the philistine character of this family, and

---

[18] Sometimes so spelled.

honestly less for my own sake (for truly I have no reason for any complaint) than in their own interest.

6. Instead of: "this G-to-E-string being":
this G-to-E-string beast.

8. After: "beg you to ask him":
preferably through Bülow.

14. Starts:
The song by Bülow (enclosure) did not satisfy me.

LETTER 60

3. Instead of: "persons like Rietz":
crooks like Rietz.[19]

3. Instead of: "perhaps the Leipzig folk will henceforward":
But the Leipzig folk may henceforward kiss my tail [mich im Arsch lecken].

LETTER 61

Between 1 and 2:
If I again propose to the Ritters that they settle in Switzerland, it may be in my interest, but almost solely to the extent that I identify their interest with my own. Your news about the theater enthusiasm of the Ritters made me very sad. I must recognize the fact that in their situation they have no chance to amuse themselves in any other way; the unfortunate thing is that they do not have the energy to change this situation.

LETTER —

(The following letter, which appears in both copies, was entirely omitted in publication, and has no number.)

Zürich, April 28, 1852

Dear Friend:

The decision of Frau R. [Ritter] that the 75 thaler should be considered as an advance on the next annual payments has hurt me very deeply! Just now, in my present situation, a stab through the throat would not have caused me so much pain as this cruelly pedantic step! However, I had not approached Frau Ritter, but Karl, in order to get the additional payment. In the end, Frau Ritter may be right; however, she should have arranged it in another way. I therefore appeal again to Karl. I speak no more of his offers for similar cases when I prepared performances, etc. I know that these former promises are no longer valid, but I am still definitely of the opinion that I am not asking too much if in this unique case, which will never and in no way be repeated, I beg Karl and his sisters to bring a sacrifice that cannot be

---

[19] Julius Rietz, *Kapellmeister* at Leipzig.

too great a burden for them. Each of them has an income of 1,300 thaler annually, whereas I, who have to take care of five persons, am entirely unable to bear such a loss. I demand from Karl that he take care of these special expenses, and HOPE *that he has still enough sympathy for me to consider the sacrifice I ask for as bearable. It is true, I could not believe that the Ritter family's interest in my doings has dropped so low that they, as I see now, do not understand at all what is at stake. What I ask for is their support for a renewed attempt to come again into some comforting contact with the life of our time, that they support me to such an extent that in trying this I do not succumb under the burden of the pettiest worries. Assuming that my relations to the Ritters were still better, I finally had—on my own account—called for some additional orchestra players—violinists and cellists—so that I now have incurred a debt of 100 thaler. Please approach Karl at once—by the mediation of Bülow —and urge him to settle this business of the 100 thaler quickly. I really should be punished too severely if I should miss this amount of my next payment. In fact, I thought it would be an evidence of my unchanged friendly feelings, of my respect for Karl when I unconditionally counted on him so far as this sacrifice is concerned. If he were petty in this matter, it would be just terrible; then I would again have to consider a complete change in the conditions of my life. I beg you to settle this matter as far as it can be done under the present circumstances: actually my whole mood very much depends on this affair. Please tell me how Karl behaved, I* must *know this.*

How sad all this is:—

Just now I have again suffered terribly. Today the Dutchman *will be performed for the second time. At the first performance—on Sunday, April 25—at the beginning the main singer became hoarse: that was lovely! Finally he merely squawked. However, today the house will again be filled. Further performances will take place on Friday and Sunday. Today I cannot write anything more—I am finished from anger and fright! Perhaps I will be quiet enough to write a letter tomorrow!*

Farewell, dearest friend!

Your

Richard Wagner

LETTER 62

Between paragraphs 3 and 4:

As to the whole business I was actually thinking of Karl, whom in so far I still consider as one who understands me. Therefore it is only he that I am approaching. What I wrote to you about him the last time must stand; he must and will help me out. I hope he will not spend all his money with the confectioner who, as Kummer tells me to my horror, unfortunately is again very much in Karl's favor.

Paragraph 4 begins as follows:

But kind greetings to the Ritters from me and do your best to calm them. They will never hear of any further financial extravagances *of mine. On that they can rely. I certainly* . . .

Postscript: Instead of: "he is a Jew!":
Löwe is a Jew!

LETTER 63

6. W. means *Wauer*.

9. Before: "What have I to do with such a man":
If you are able to make Eduard Devrient confess that he gives up his belief in God and the immortality of the soul, I will trust him; if not, all his knowledge and endeavors must have this one goal only, to maintain the belief in God and in the continuance of the soul after death.

9. After: "what sincerity is there in him but his cowardice":
and weakness? Ask everybody with whom you want to have a discussion whether he believes in God and immortality. From his answer you will also learn whether he fits into our artistic program.

11. After: "My surroundings are ofttimes very painful to me":
In times like the recent one I unfortunately have no support at all from my wife: she feels absolutely like the modern public; there has often been terrible quarreling and anger. That was the last thing I needed, besides all my other troubles!

Between 15 and 16:
As to the Ritters we agree. Already for a long time I have had the idea that they have avoided being close to me, being afraid that they would be imbued by me with a view of life and, according to it, induced to practices which they now consider as onerous and inimical to their "happiness." Strangely enough, this fear seems also to have taken hold of the Kummers as well.

Between 16 and 17:
I am glad to hear that Karl was, or is, still in love: this is the best news I could learn about him. I hope you have arranged my business with him, and he will prove to be generous.

LETTER 64

Between 2 and 3:
At the same time I got a letter from Karl. The statement concerning the 300 thaler is correct in so far as Frau R. already deducted the advanced 100 thaler. In his letter Karl cancels the promise he gave to you, to refund the 100 thaler to me within two months if possible: This is the reason why he did not want you to write about it to me; he wanted to avoid false hopes. Apart from this, he advises me to approach Liszt or some rich Zürich lady, and prescribes some underlined phrases which I should

use for this approach. If you see Karl, give him my greetings, tell him: Everything is all right. I thank him for his advice; I accept it all the more easily because I hope that this gift has not caused him any great effort.

Apart from this, I beg you urgently, dear friend, never to remind me again of my financial relations with the Ritters. By trying to forget I can perhaps regain the equilibrium of mind which I need in order to be able to bear my dependence upon them.

LETTER 65

Between 1 and 2:

What touched me most in your letter was your report about Karl. I foresaw this development of his. It is true that a man of his type would have needed a particular energy directed toward life if such a close relationship as his and mine had brought him more harm than good. If Karl had that amount of necessary energy, he would, on leaving me, have jumped into life head over heels in order thus to become that *which I can no longer become.*

[There follow in the copy of the letter three lines carefully covered with ink in order to make them illegible. Some words can be deciphered: *Feel . . . what is to be said . . . if only now . . . contain . . .* The letter continues as follows:]

The independence which he strives for, and which is not sufficiently vigorous and free to push him inevitably away from me into life, goes only so far as to make him feel his past dependence upon me as an oppressive fetter. He is conscious only of this fetter, not of the incentive I gave him, and thus his whole search for independence consumes itself in the sole effort to get rid of me. He believes that if he should succeed in that, he would also presumably be a mature man. His enthusiasm for me, so far as it was a mere matter of feeling, was one-sided. This I could not help realizing from his effeminate tendency toward mysticism. I also was amazed to learn in Bordeaux that his enthusiasm had been, so to speak, kindled by the women. But how is it possible that a young man who is actually in harmony with me could have behaved so impertinently toward me before his last departure from Zürich? The reason of his behavior was that I seriously blamed him for striving, with clever zeal, to make the acquaintance of a fortuneteller woman! Aware of his weakness—he always spoke here of shooting himself—he saves himself by considering my view of the present situation as exaggerated, particularly as far as art is concerned; for if anyone will admit that my judgment is right, he is lost unless he has the energy to do battle for it to the death. The weak personality who wants to avoid this battle, who wants to live "awhile," finds a way out by saying that the situation is actually not so bad. If he really persuades himself that this is true, he can easily coddle himself.— Now, many things could be said on this subject. Only one further point: I am not so sad about the fact that Karl wants to free himself from me, for some day this would have to happen—but it gives me pain to see him do it in such a cowardly fashion, behind my back, that he loses the nobility of his mind, and that this liberation will be of no use to him. Nevertheless, I will not give up hope and I will always believe that eventually he will accomplish at least something. *If he should ever do this, if he should ever take an active part in anything, I should be entirely reconciled with him, even if he persevered in keeping away from me!*

2. After: "Hahn considers his case a very bad one":
So that I was shocked to hear how easily Dr. Schulze took his case recently.

6. Instead of: "the notice of Cellini":
Bülow's essay on Cellini.

7. After: "By no means bad":
I have told them that I would not accept any medals.

7. Instead of: "Yet it must some day come to a stop even with you":
Yet one of these days things must improve with you. This playing in the orchestra must come to an end!

LETTER 67

The letter begins as follows:
"Elih! Elih! lama asabtani [sic]*!" That is, in German: Uhlig! Uhlig! You are a God-damned fellow* [ein Herrgottssakramenter]*!*

2. After: "I am in daily expectation of an answer from him":
These Weimar people are miserably slow in answering.

2. After: "news of the Ballenstädt musical festival":
This Bülow (Herr von—) has not written to me for three months. Now I will no longer bother him.

4. M. means *Meyerbeer.*

13. After: "if you knew what I have now planned in my mind for him":
In the first act of the Valkyrie *he* [Siegfried] *is conceived almost before the eyes of the public. How Siegfried will enjoy seeing how he was made: I should like to see his expression!*

14. After: "the last would be unbecoming treatment":
by His Majesty.

15. After: "Opera and Drama":
As he is so repentant, give him [Reissiger] *a slap on his fat mug for me* [Gib ihm doch was von mir auf sein Fettmaul!].

LETTER 70

8. After: "And so I have written to my wife to come with Peps":
It is funny—whenever I want to have something alive around me, I always have to rely on these two.

LETTER 71

2 and 5. W. means *Wirsing.*

LETTER 72

Between 4 and 5:

If I seriously consider the realization of this project [buying a place in the country], *there is only one thing about which I must be entirely sure beforehand—namely: Will the Ritter family be able and will they continue to be so attached to me that for the rest of my life I can expect the annual payments which I am now getting from them? I don't know how Frau Ritter and her children feel about that. Do they think in terms of some temporary support only? Or are they ready to make me a sharer in a certain part of their income for the rest of my life? I suppose that no real decision has been made with regard to this matter, but that they are leaving it to the development of my financial situation whether they continue with their support or whether they cancel it. It would be well if they could be thoroughly informed that I shall* never *again be in a situation which would enable me to live without a fixed annual amount of aid, for a change could only be attained by accepting a permanent job, a decision which, I hope, none of my friends will urge me to take. My remaining income will always be of such a casual type, it will be so uncertain and so variable in time and size, that I shall never be able to consider it as a fixed amount which would guarantee a living. Apart from that, the cancellation of the annual payment would deprive me of any possibility of realizing the plan of a place in the country which is so necessary for me. For these reasons it is extremely important for me to know definitely how the Ritters feel about this; and therefore I beg you, dear friend, to arrange a serious conversation with Frau Ritter, as I consider negotiations in this way, through a mutual friend, as more delicate and proper than a direct approach. As for me, the Ritters certainly have only the one desire to ease my troubled life as far as possible. Therefore they certainly have not thought of conditions and clauses, and I can look forward to a comforting answer. On the other hand I consider it my duty to say that, if ever my financial situation should change in such a way that I could do without or reduce the annual payments without any danger to me, I would certainly of my own accord stop any further sacrifices by the Ritter family. Shall I add to this the consolation, sad for you all, that, without doubt, I have only a few more years to live. Thus I shall be a burden to my friends for not too long a time.*

7. W. means *Wirsing*; S. means *Gustav Schmidt*.[20]

14. After: "On my return Brendel's paper made me quite sad again":

Finally there appears a more comprehensive and reasoned essay—acoustical letters! I have already written to Bülow to ask Brendel whether he might not want letters.

15. Instead of: "I wish you would send a line or two to your friends, at your leisure, begging them":

I wish you would send a line or two to Bülow, at your leisure, asking him and Liszt.

[20] Wirsing was the theater director at Leipzig, Gustav Schmidt *Kapellmeister* at Frankfurt, Uhlig was acting for Wagner in projects for the production of *Tannhäuser*.

16. Instead of: "As regards friendship":
As regards your break with Bülow.

LETTER 74

Between 4 and 5:
If Brendel fails with his periodical, he deserves this fate. Hardly anybody has acted in a more irresponsible way! First to raise the highest expectations, and then to become definitely colorless, *that is too much.*

LETTER 75

4. After: "A second [copy of the score of *Lohengrin*] I think of presenting to Robert Franz, and will send it to you to see that he gets it":
As to the third, I still am in doubt whether I shall give it to Bülow or to Julius Schäffner; I don't know whether Bülow much cares for it. I should like to prove to Schäffner that I have been pleased with his good will and his zeal.

LETTER 76

4. Instead of: "I should indeed be sorry for some persons":
I should indeed be sorry for Tichatschek, Frau Devrient, and even for Johanna.

Between 7 and 8:
*What advantage do my creditors expect to draw from the favorable **development** of Tannhäuser? I had drawn their attention to my copyrights in the operas. If they do not cooperate now, if they do not appoint a manager to conduct the business, and if they do not take the necessary steps in order to secure the means for a vigorous handling of the enterprise, they deserve to lose everything. I beg you, go to see Schirmer, prepare with him a meeting of my main creditors, discuss the situation with them—Pusinelli and Kriete—personally, and try to induce the unlucky creatures to advance the necessary amount for the costs of a sufficiently large edition of Tann-häuser (particularly of the single numbers). Apart from that they should enable Meser to arrange comprehensive shipments on order. The handling of this business is really too irresponsible. Ask the creditors for a power of attorney so that you can supervise and direct Meser, and do this for the sole reason that you cannot bear to watch any longer the present way of doing business. If in the present favorable state of affairs my creditors cannot get their money from the proceeds of the sale of my opera scores, they deserve to lose it.*

LETTER 77

Between 2 and 3:
I do not like Karl's having the Lohengrin *score copied for himself. I did not care for the expenses of 15 thaler. In any case I consider Karl's sacrifice as most super-fluous—for him and for me. Please cancel this!*

Between 3 and 4:

Nor am I pleased that you have arranged my personal affair with Karl. *The person who is concerned is Frau Ritter only, not that childish fellow.*

Today is my wife's birthday: of course we will drink chamgagne. You may imagine how happy I shall be!

LETTER 78

1. W. means *Wirsing.*

1. Instead of: "I am getting in a rage with this director: he does not answer at all":

I am becoming furious with this swine of a director: the beast does not answer at all.

LETTER 79

2. Instead of: *"So far my brother!":*
So far my famous brother in Christo!

LETTER 80

(Since the original letter was not copied, the full text is unknown.)

LETTER 81

3. After: "had my brother":
(I wish he were in heaven!)

4. Instead of: "if a certain person happened to read my pamphlet":
if Tichatschek happened to read my pamphlet.

6. Instead of: "W.":
the cad Wirsing.

6. After: "I am much in debt, too, with my establishment here":
for Karl's subsidies are insufficient, as he knows very well.

6. After: "I am condemned . . . without money":
Do I enjoy any love?

LETTER 82

1. Instead of: "the Leipzig S——":
the Leipzig filthiness [Schweinehunderei].

4. After: "How surprised would the intendant now be to learn of this suppressed passage through a public paper!":
It is true, my brother was silly and a coward. However, this might appear more hostile than I had really meant it to be, for my real aim was to show my brother my disgust for him.

6. After: "the camp of Israel":

This Liszt is almost crazy! The demon of outward success confuses him again and again.

LETTERS 83 AND 84

(Since the original letters were not copied, the full texts are unknown.)

W. (Elsa Uhlig inserts: *Wirsing*).

LETTER 85

3. Postscript: After: "my indifference":

Believe me. I most bitterly repent my humiliating submissive flattery toward Tichatschek. How mean was my whole behavior toward this childish fool! As I saw that the stupid boy did not understand me, I had to treat him like a raw egg, had to flatter and to praise him in order to keep him in good spirits. I had to prostitute myself. How mildly did I still treat this stubborn fellow in my last essay!

3. Postscript: Instead of: "I have arrived at a ——— completely":

I have arrived at a mood of complete indifference [l.m.A. means: *leck mich am Arsch*].

3. Postscript. L. means: *the scoundrel* [*den Lumpen*].

5. Postscript. After: "a heavy blow to me!":

Recently Karl sent me a few lines asking me to send him his suitcase. It has been done. Please ask him whether he also wants to get back the music which was not in the suitcase but with me. In this case I will send it back separately. Why don't you tell me anything about his play? [21] *I should have been interested in it. He, of course, does not mention it with one syllable. I should have liked to know something about the plot!*

LETTER 86

2. After "Don't be uneasy about my present money wants":

What good were councilors of the Government, particularly if they are ministers of finance, as now Sulzer, if they would not lend money?

3. S. means *Steche*.[22]

4. After: "which Tichatschek never liked":

because he had to learn it anew and never was able to master it properly.

13. After: "Frau Ritter, of course, had written to me":

a rather insignificant letter, however, as always.

[21] *Alkibiades.*
[22] A lawyer who represented Wagner in Leipzig.

5 and 6. H. means *Heine.*

5 and 6. F. means *Fischer.*

7. Instead of: "whether this then was a ———?":
whether this then was dog manure?

14. W. means *Wirsing.*

L~~ETTER~~ 89

6. H.s means *Härtels.*

6. After: "I spared no pains to put before":
these cowards [Hosenscheissern] *my whole intercourse with Wirsing, Rietz, etc.*

6. Instead of: "W.'s shabbiness":
Wirsing's shabbiness.

L~~ETTER~~ 90

This letter begins as follows:
Dearest Theodor:

Today I am expecting a letter from you. I will hurry to answer you. So as not to forget too much, I should like to thank you in advance for the great trouble you took to provide me with a copy of the Alkibiades. *This showed again your devotion to me.*

As to Karl's drama, your remarks represent the most justified criticism, of which I approve absolutely. Karl is for me rather a tragic character. Uncertainty of himself and prematurity of development [Frühgereiftheit] *are combined within him, thus forming an extremely disagreeable mixture. The main feature of his character is weakness* [Schwäche], *and his essential activity consists in forcing this weakness to as much strength as possible. His Alkibiades actually is the freshman who has become snobbish before having enjoyed life, who wants to appear as a graduate student and instead immediately becomes a philistine! Now I can understand why you did not want to write me about the play. The feelings and thoughts which it rouses are of such a disagreeable and embarrassing type, and certainly these impressions are only increased by the recognition of many features of great gifts and talent. I too will now be silent about it, as you originally wanted to be silent, and for the same reasons. Nevertheless, I am surprised that the play will not be performed. However, Karl seems to have quickly overcome this disappointment.*

Appendix C

LETTERS NOT INCLUDED IN THE
BURRELL COLLECTION

Appendix C

LETTERS NOT INCLUDED IN THE BURRELL COLLECTION

C 1   Wagner, in Zürich, December 28, 1852, to Otto and Julie Kummer.

Otto Kummer was first oboist at Dresden. He married Julie Ritter, the daughter of Frau Julie Ritter, Wagner's benefactress, herein mentioned. Because of the instability of Otto, Wagner was not happy about his engagement to the young Julie. Karl and Emilie were Julie's brother and sister:

Zürich, December 28, 1852

"Dear Otto!
"Dear Julie!

"How to begin? I feel as if I had to speak before a public meeting. Well! Today I had set out to write to both of you (by 'you' alone, you might have thought that the letter was addressed to one of you only), but unluckily I have just had a very bad night and am out of sorts. What can I do? I'll write all the same! But—what? I don't know yet. About the weather. Don't imagine you alone have beautiful weather. Even here it's so warm and bright that we almost should have liked to go to the Rinderknecht. A few times we were in the country and planted potatoes there. I then took occasion, too, to finish my *Nibelungen.* Now I feel uncertain whether to shoot myself or not. My wife thinks I'd better not, for everything is all right. What is your opinion? In the Reich they perform *Tannhäuser* now and then. People write about it to me (but not Emilie). In Breslau, Schwerin, and Weimar they're even going to give *The Flying Dutchman* very shortly. Here I 'give' nothing but myself, and nobody wants him—not even myself. The cock [1] no longer crows here—he is now changing Tiefenau to a paradise. Frau Wesendonck has returned ill from Lyons; he has grown still more blond.

"In January I plan to read the *Nibelungen* in four evenings. Would you like to be invited? We haven't yet exchanged presents, though I have paid many bills. It shall be done at New Year's—I am anxious to know whether I'll get a silk nightshirt. But I've some heavy forebodings. O God, if I only had plenty of champagne, what more would I need to be happy? For I am your 'fatherly' friend, I know you are well cared for, as I am myself. Is Ottoschka to marry soon?

"Tomorrow I'll write to 'your' mother too. But then I shall be serious, and hope

[1] Probably a pun on Dr. Hahn.

645

I shall have had a good sleep. That news about Uhlig's illness is true, but he is said to be better. Mama Julie promptly and elaborately answered my anxious inquiry. I would say Mama is better than all of you! I hope to see Karl in that world where it is to be hoped we'll both wear some laurels upon our brows. Since Emilie will visit you in the spring, I assume that you will all arrange to return without passing through Zürich—maybe I won't be in Zürich any longer myself. Probably I'll accept a Napoleonic job as *Kapellmeister*. I trust you have had enough of my news by now. You would be amazed to hear how much can happen to me here in Zürich. Every day I have joy, profit, and delightful stimulation, in spite of the fact that the Fräuleins Welcker are not here to coax some pensioned-off fiddler to play. All I miss is Herr Kuenzi from Berne. I don't know him at all and have had no chance yet to inquire about him. Give him my best regards. Minna embroiders, Natalie sews, Peps snorts—everybody is all right and sends greetings. If you were here on New Year's Eve you would get some presents, but as you are not you'll get nothing. I wish you a happy New Year, to Otto marvelous health, to Julie a quantity of Bayer-Devrient in Dresden, to Ottoschka an efficient housewife. May God the infinitely kind and powerful guard and protect you. Amen! I can say no more.

> "Your most devoted
> RICHARD W."

C 2　Wagner, in Zürich, August 15, 1854, to Otto Kummer.

"August 15, 1854

"MOST HONORED OTTO THE GREAT!

"I congratulate you on your improved health. That you follow the water tap [water cure] needs must bear fruits. It's fine that you will play the violin again, since a good violinist is surely needed everywhere, especially in Zürich, at least if I conduct a symphony. But whether you are well paid for it, that is a different question. It wouldn't be advisable to seek a job at the theater here for the winter. It is miserable and the pay is poor. It would amount to no more than the six or seven concerts of the Musikgesellschaft, and due to the poor financial circumstances of that society I couldn't promise you much, of course, perhaps 200–300 francs at the most. Besides this there might be an extra fee for a solo performance, and that is all. So if you want to earn anything like your Dresden salary, the prospect is bad. The same is true for the whole of Switzerland. People live mainly by giving lessons, and I don't think you would feel like doing that. However, if you wouldn't mind accepting a position for this amount, try it for the following winter, when I, too, will end by being involved. So let us both wait for the time when something really efficient will happen for the building up of the orchestra. And we shall have it. Who knows whether, within two years, I myself will not take the theater in hand in order to educate the personnel to my purposes. Then you must join up. You may also count upon it that even in the winter after next the theater will have improved. Thus if you would chance with me an improvement in the musical conditions here, you are heartily welcome. I

should like to have you, for I am fond of you. Since the Ritter family shows a lean-
ing toward Switzerland, it would be only logical if the head of the family should do
the same. Karl is going to settle here, so why not the whole *Rittertum* [2] at once?

"I am a bad man. I should have written you long ago. I am so extraordinarily
well that, with all the comforts of life, I don't know what to do with them. In order
not to succumb entirely to the delights of my existence, I am working like a fool—I
make the most of every moment. Even Emilie shouldn't miss Emil Devrient here. I
would play her a comedy, even in a beautiful wig. A thousand greetings to the dear
Ritter family and to all who belong to them.

> "Your
>
> RICH. WAGNER"

C 3 Wagner, in Seelisberg (November 3, 1855), to Madame Léonie Praeger [in
London].

Wagner writes in French, at length, and in jocular fashion, to the French wife
of Ferdinand Praeger. (The manuscript was presumably placed on the market by
Praeger.) The language, while neither idiomatic nor correct, is extremely fluent.
Praeger claimed that Wagner could easily out-talk Berlioz in his own tongue. The
letter appears, with translation, in Praeger's *Wagner as I knew him,* pp. 277–283.

C 4 Wagner, in Venice, September 3, 1858, to Heinrich Esser in Vienna. (Page 334.)

C 5 Wagner, in Venice, November 11, 1858, to Heinrich Esser in Vienna. (Page
335.)

C 6 Wagner, in Paris, September 27, 1859, [to Heinrich Esser in Vienna]. (Page
336.)

C 7 Wagner, in Vienna, May 16, 1861, to Herr Stürmer. (Page 339.)

C 8 Wagner, in Munich, October 6, 1866 [to an unnamed correspondent].

A notation on the back of the letter names Julius Fröbel as the addressee.
Wagner had established Fröbel in Munich as an editor and a sort of political spokesman; the fact that he had been active as a Dresden revolutionary did not exclude him
from the King's favor, although he was looked at askance by the Court officialdom.

"MOST HONORED FRIEND!

"I beg to send you—in a copy which is unfortunately defective—two memoirs
which I have written—as a kind of most confidential communication—for the King
of Bavaria. If you don't mind, I ask you to read them in detail. In this way you could
accomplish something that nobody but you could be called upon to do. In a few days
I hope to be in Vienna for a day and to see you then for an extensive talk. I'll send
ahead my treatises. About them as well as about my journey to Vienna I beg you to
be absolutely silent. Until I have the pleasure of seeing you—

> "With best regards, faithfully yours,
>
> RICHARD WAGNER"

[2] A pun on "knighthood."

C 9   Wagner, in Lucerne, August 16, 1866, to Heinrich Esser [in Vienna].

This letter is additional proof of the general usefulness of Wagner's friend, as arranger and go-between as well as conductor and coach.

"MY DEAR FRIEND!

"Forgive me for not telling you about all the various accidents that have steadily harassed me since we last met. It may suffice to announce that by complete retirement I have been able to master my emotions again, that I am working hard to finish my *Meistersinger* and hope to achieve this aim by the end of the coming winter. So I am already making plans for this work, and especially the arrangement of the piano score. After several attempts I have come to the following decision: Fr. Schott shall first publish—together with the orchestra score—a real piano score for practical use with all the indications for the singers, etc. (at a low price).

"This score must not be arranged by any piano virtuoso, but rather by you, dearest friend, for you seem to me to be the most fitting man for such a task. In the some way that you arranged *Tristan und Isolde* for the piano rehearsals, *Die Meistersinger* arrangement ought to be outlined from the beginning. There would be no point in including all the middle parts, etc.: it should merely give the less skilled conductors, singers, stage managers, etc., an easily playable score, for the purpose of coaching, accompanying, etc., with an indication of the figurations in accordance with the formulas for a simple accompaniment. This method may be explained on the title page, so that the apparent incompleteness in the rendition of the score may be justified from the start. It may depend then on the work's success whether later a second more pianistic score should be published, for which Bülow, who would be the most suitable man, would need considerable time. Therefore I ask you to declare yourself ready to undertake this and to notify Herrn Schott about it. I can't send the score to you yet, of course, nor to Herrn Schott, until I get a correct copy of it. For that part of the original manuscript which was in the hands of the printers was returned to me in such a carelessly soiled state that I could not bring myself to expose my manuscripts to a similar treatment in the future. So I need a very intelligent, entirely musical copyist. If you know one among your numerous younger or other needy musicians of Vienna who would be suitable for this job, a man whom you could recommend for it, you would oblige me very much. So I would take him as my assistant, first for half a year for board and salary (probably in my Lucerne flat for this winter) in order that he may accomplish this difficult copying correctly under my supervision. I should like to learn his terms. The arrangement would begin in October.

"Now, a word for Matheus *Salvo—venia!* [3] Your excellent, though always sleepy opera director let me know sometime ago that he may possibly produce my opera *Rienzi* in the coming season, and that he would like occasionally to learn my terms for remuneration from this opera. Since I happened to read again recently in the

[3] A pun on Matteo Salvi, manager of the Vienna Opera. The Latin phrase means "with your permission."

Viennese papers that preparations are indeed being made in the opera house to perform my *Rienzi* next November, I beg to request of you that you notify Director M. Salvi that if I am to consent to the performance of my five-act opera *Rienzi* in the present old opera house, before payment of the expected royalties, then the same conditions should be granted to me which were previously given by Herrn Eckert for *Lohengrin*. This time, however, with the special proviso that the amount of 2,000 gulden convention currency, which I got at that time, be remitted instantly with a good draft for 5,000 francs. Having concrete reasons for insisting on this demand, I wish that the honorable administration would decide right away whether it would rather give up the idea of performing my opera or yield to my conditions. The score and book of words are to be had from C. F. Meser, Court Music Shop (H. Müller) in Dresden on simple payment of the cost. Well, dear Esser, be kind enough to let me have an early answer to my request. One word more about *Die Meistersinger*: Having planned this work in order to save myself from a miserable world of experience, I finally succeeded in finishing it in order to keep myself alive by this same occupation. The work gives me a final immense satisfaction; this month I hope to finish the second act. It will be the means of leading me back to the world again. I count with certainty on my most popular success from this work, and am reckless enough to promise you some exhilarating amusement from it if you would like to read it. Now farewell. Greetings to Vienna and its dear Jews. Keep yourself in good health and convey my best regards to your wife. Heartily your grateful friend—

RICHARD WAGNER"

C 10 Wagner, in Triebschen (Lucerne), October 25, 1869 [to an unnamed correspondent].

The context indicates the ever obliging Esser.

"DEAR FRIEND!

"I don't feel well these days, I am quite out of humor, and so I'll reply to your nice and confidential letter with only what is most necessary. First of all there is the arrangement of *Rheingold* and *Walküre* ordered by you. You certainly don't need the score for this. The difficulty with Klindworth's piano arrangements is that while they make it easy for the musician to grasp the structure of the score, on the other hand they presuppose that the pianist knows the method of modern piano playing, that he knows how to make the notes sound. You will surely understand what I mean. Anyway, by using this very clearly outlined arrangement your work will be facilitated considerably. Well, good luck and some pleasure too! I was quite touched by your conscientiousness about the newspaper story. Indeed, I had simply trusted your word, and I felt no grudge against you on account of it. You may have realized from your own report how one has to shut oneself off from the world, especially nowadays, when the press nuisance exposes one's naked body in the streets. I no longer write anything about myself to anybody and have made up my mind to be strictly silent about my personal affairs. But I have to put up with the fact that just this may give rise to any desired interpretation. On the other hand, I shall also see to it that the true circumstances of my life and experience do not remain unknown to my really sympathetic friends. I have reached as far as the forty-ninth year of my life in my very conscientious, and at the same time strict and detailed autobiography.[4] Parts of it I shall have published before long. As for *Die Meistersinger*—it will fare as God pleases. I have lost all desire to have any part in such productions. The people gobble up whatever comes along—good performances and bad. Anything goes, but I don't want to know about it. In Vienna it might go well; perhaps it only needs my assistance. But Vienna too has become repugnant to me. I suffered a lot there, and now as a reward your Jews and heathens are dragging me through the mud as if I were there for no other purpose. Dearest, count yourself fortunate that you have no further traffic with any opera theater. No one can get the better of this monster. Anyone who deals with it for any length of time becomes bogged in its mire. This was the bitter feeling I had when I believed you were acting under Dingelstedt's influence. But, not another word about this! Keep well, and you may still derive some joy from your life and work.

"With warmest greetings—

RICHARD WAGNER

"One more favor! Could you get me six boxes of Faber's tooth powder? You can't send it collect from Austria to Switzerland. But I'll send you or Faber the amount some time, if I know how much. Don't be angry!"

C 11

Copies of two letters in photostat (presented by Carl Engel). Each is addressed to Herrn Pütterich, in Munich. Wagner (in Triebschen, January 9, 1870) acknowledges the receipt of a mirror and orders a frame according to earlier specifications. Cosima (in Triebschen, January 26, 1870) sends embroidery and satin to be mounted.

C 12   Wagner, in Lucerne, March 19, 1870 [to an unnamed correspondent].

The addressee could be Johann Franz von Herbeck, who was the *Kapellmeister* at the Vienna Opera.

"MY DEAR SIR:

"I still owe you my thanks for your news and only regret that your telegram caused us great excitement. But your last detailed telegram reassured me completely. The more favorable my impression of the matter became according to this telegram, the more strange it seemed to me that I have heard nothing yet about more performances of *Die Meistersinger*. In the repertory of a whole week there were no *Meistersinger*. What is the reason of it? Tell me frankly about this. Not a single letter came from Vienna. The alarming reports which caused my telegram were conveyed to me via Munich by a friend. Why do the performances now stop? Seeking an explanation, I begin to think that the management has recognized the weakness of the cast and is trying to improve it. It seems to me that I was wrongly informed

---

[4] "*Mit meiner sehr gewissenhaften, aber ebenso genauen und ausführlichen Selbstbiographie.*"

about the Beckmesser (Campe) about whom you had already told me. About the unsuitability of Fräulein Ehnn there unfortunately seems to be general agreement. Why did they select such an unsympathetic person for the part of Eva? Also, her singing is said to have made an unpleasant effect, especially in her part of the Quintet in the third act. Could something not be done about this?

About Beck, whom I heard two years ago in Munich, I know that he became unable to perform the part of Hans Sachs. He became rough, stiff, and unteachable, which I much regretted since I thought a great deal of him. Maybe even he should soon be taken out. All these questions occupy my mind a great deal. Do you understand now how important it is to me to get a clear reassuring report, especially from you, for you seem to be in agreement with me on this question! I hope you decide on this, and so oblige me again.

"With highest regards,

RICHARD WAGNER"

C 13   Wagner, in Lucerne, May 24, 1870, to an unnamed correspondent.

"DEAR SIR:

"Although it gives me some trouble to look through analytical treatises on my own works like the kind presented to me, I could not help recognizing at first glance that you have accomplished something highly commendable and useful. But I must at once confirm your doubts, whether you would succeed in a correct identification of the themes (*Themata*) without consulting the score. So I want to help you do this, since your work really interests me and it is so promising. As I am out of touch with the board of management of the Hoftheater, I can't refer you to it directly and ask you therefore to apply, on the strength and by the use of this letter, to the Court Secretary Hofrath L. Düfflipp, the only one of my sincere and not uninfluential friends left in Munich. In this way you may get the recommendation to the board of management needed for access to the score of *Das Rheingold* for the time required.

"With the best wishes for a good success, I remain

"Faithfully yours,

RICHARD WAGNER"

C 14   Wagner, in Lucerne, March 4, 1872, to Edward Dannreuther [in London].

"DEAR HERR DANNREUTHER!

"You were already known to me before you approached me recently in such a pleasant manner. My best thanks for your good success, which was due to your own merit only. Indeed my hopes are centered in a new generation, now that the reasons for the decadence of the old one have become all too clear to me. But that new generation must develop just as you do, that is, music must extend far beyond simple 'music-making' and include all its profundity. Try to get the incomparably beautiful essay of my young friend Professor Nietzsche in Basel. Its title is *The Birth of Tragedy from Music*—Leipzig, published by E. W. Fritzsch. Such a work inspires great hopes for the future and may even be highly regarded among English authors, though I do not really know what music may do to them. But they have a good classical education, are serious and thoughtful, a condition no longer to be found in Germany, as you know, except perhaps with Moltke.

"My wife well remembers the *Meistersinger* evening in your company, and returns your greeting. I shall be glad to hear from you soon again. . . .

"Faithfully yours,

RICHARD WAGNER"

C 15   Wagner, in Lucerne, April 11, 1872 (to an unnamed correspondent).

"DEAR FRIEND!

"I wonder why I haven't heard anything from you in regard to J. J. Weber's [5] objections, and so nothing at all recently. My letter to Weber, since then, crossed the enclosed one from him to me. As you may see from this document, he pretends never to have been informed by you as to the complete editions of my writings and poems, and to learn now by chance only that this edition should contain the *Ring of the Nibelung* too. If he is right, I would certainly have to protest that you didn't straighten out this matter on taking over the publishing concern. As you reported to me at that time that Weber would make no objections, owing to your talk with him on that point, I had to believe that he had renounced his copyright. Since then I pleaded earnestly in my last letter to him to forgo his claims for the future, telling him emphatically that the exploitation of that contract, to the effect that he arbitrarily would decide about new editions without consulting me, and thus prevent future editions desired by me, would be disgraceful and infamous. In case he should now behave in such a dishonest way, I request you to approach my old friend, the lawyer Pehschke (my Leipzig 'Patron'), and ask him in my name to take the matter in his hands, warn J. J. Weber (after examination of the contract) of its infamy, in a friendly manner, and urge him not to take advantage of it. If this does not help, Herr Pehschke ought to look for possible legal protection against the execution of this contract, and accordingly demand from me power of attorney for judicial proceedings against J. J. Weber. On this occasion Herr Weber's nice behavior toward me in regard to *Judaism in Music* may become the topic of conversation. This with my best and faithful regards to my old friend, whose *Gretchen at the Spinning Wheel* (or was it a different girl?) I still remember. The printing now doesn't seem to get on well. Does J. J. Weber obstruct everybody? Nice fellows, these publishers!

"May God protect you from becoming like them. This as a greeting from your

R. WAGNER"

C 16   Wagner, in Bayreuth, October 20, 1875, to Georg Unger.

Wanting the tenor, Georg Unger, for Siegfried in the pending first production of the *Ring,* Wagner arranged for him to take vocal studies under Julius Hey (whom Wagner thus refers to as Don Basilio) in Munich, and subsequently to coach with Wagner himself at Bayreuth in the acting of the part. This involved releasing

[5] Leipzig publisher of the *Ring* libretto.

him from an existing contract with Scherbarth, the opera director at Düsseldorf, which release Wagner was to accomplish.

"BEST HERR UNGER!

"Don't worry—carry through unswervingly what is due to yourself and your art! No wavering now!

"To get an honorable release from Dir. Scherbarth would be nice, I myself have even tried it, appealing to his sense of honor as an artist, his human reasonableness; of course he replied that these things don't concern him as director of a theater and he can't agree with my demands. Thereupon I bluntly answered that it would be more reasonable to agree, for if he doesn't release you voluntarily it would have to be against his will. We would then await his complaint and defend ourselves against him; but if he should behave decently, with the real purpose in mind, you would surely show yourself grateful toward him, which wouldn't be difficult for you as a singer of great reputation. When he saw that he could not achieve anything in this way, he decided to warn you through a lawyer, and your answer was just right. What now remains to be done about Scherbarth? It will be difficult for him to declare you simply as a contract breaker; if he takes some vicious action, I shall be there to enlighten the public. I think, however, he won't miss the occasion to trim himself up and to parade before his public with our correspondence. That would be very good indeed, and would leave me little more to say. Neither your relation to me nor to Scherbarth can hurt you. Until you take a fixed engagement again, he won't be able to extort many fines and the like from you. What would be needed at once must be provided by me. So you may await the next development confidently. If it comes to a lawsuit, well, all the better. It will take its time; it can't turn out absolutely unfavorable for us; and by the time a decision has been reached, your engagement will have ended and you will have become Siegfried. Don't bother with anything in the world but your studies, which should bring you joy, honor, and glory. The Düsseldorfer may meanwhile have his beard shaved: [6] it may be a misfortune for him, but who is without misfortunes?

"On my journey to Vienna I shall reach Munich on the 30th of this month, at night, and stay there for one day (31st). My friend Hey will be kind enough to provide lodging for me for twenty-four hours in the Hotel Marienbad (Jahreszeiten is situated too openly on the street near the theater, etc.). I need two rooms each with one bed, and two rooms each with two beds (children and governess), also two servants' rooms for valet and parlormaid. Don't tell anybody else about my arrival, especially from the theater. You will also get to know Seidl in time, but it would be advisable to procure a good pianist in Munich. We will talk about it. Now keep up your courage and feel as safe as in Levi's (I should say Abraham's) bosom. Greet and praise in my name the excellent Basilio, Meister Hey! *Auf Wiedersehen!*

"Yours very truly

RICHARD WAGNER"

[6] A pun on *Barthscheren–Scherbarth.*

C 17   Wagner, in Bayreuth, June 20, 1875 (to an unnamed correspondent).

The singer addressed has identified herself on the back of the letter as Frau Sara Wolf-Oppenheimer (she did not appear in the first *Ring* production).

"HONORED FRAU!

"I have learned through my wife, who just saw her father, Franz Liszt, in Weimar about it, that owing to a visit of your husband and the conversation which then took place I had mistakenly believed you to be prevented (in a strict sense) from attending this year's rehearsals in Bayreuth. I thought I had to put up with the inevitable and to dispense with your visit next month. But if the reason should be not so imperative as I thought, I must assure you that only reluctantly would I resign myself to it, and that you therefore would highly delight and oblige me by joining all our artists as early as July, so that no breach would prevent their cooperation. Begging you to convey my best regards to your husband, I remain,

"Yours sincerely

RICHARD WAGNER"

C 18   Wagner, in Florence, December 11, 1876 [to an unnamed correspondent].

"DEAREST PROTECTOR AND FRIEND!

"How you put me to shame! God knows I had forgotten the holy Francis—to my great disgrace. Now your friendly reminder reached me very late, too, and by this delay you might have guessed already that this time we shall be considered to have arrived too late for the saint. Now I've spent my whole 'American trip' fee [7] in Italy; besides, many a thing could be found in antique shops which delighted and satisfied my wife. I myself was quite occupied by the most unpleasant worries and experiences in regard to my 'national' undertaking, etc., and so I almost never found the peace of mind to enjoy what I saw.

"Now we are to return to the cold and snow which will make us akin to you in Neulenzbach. There we expect, according to our request, friendly news from you again. With most cordial greetings, your most faithful

RICHARD WAGNER"

C 19   Wagner, in Bayreuth, January 5, 1877, to Herrn Fritzsche.

"DEAREST MR. FRITZSCHE:

"Make me a present of another half-dozen of the single pamphlet *The Purpose of Opera*. In return you'll get a new article shortly, containing the photograph of a distinguished musician whom I want to recommend to the German musical world.

"With kind regards, faithfully yours,

RICHARD WAGNER

"I've a wonderful story for Tappert to be used by him. I should appreciate seeing him. He could put up in my home."

[7] The reference is to the $5,000 he was paid for his "American Centennial March."

C 20   Wagner, in Bayreuth, April 7, 1877, to Edward Dannreuther [in London].

Wagner wrote this letter shortly before going to London to conduct a summer festival of excerpts from his operas in the Albert Hall, a venture intended to bolster the Bayreuth project. Wagner's apprehensions about the London managers Hodge and Essex were not unfounded. The affair, financially speaking, was a failure.

"Dear Herr Dannreuther!

"Best thanks! Herr Schlesinger has already been written to. Richter will go to London today. Hodge and Essex give me a lot of trouble. Their management of business is petty, and unsafe for me. I have no payment from them yet. I hardly mention any guarantee, but only expenses that I have to meet from my own pocket. All those engaged by them complain that they remain without contract protection on their part (H. and E.). First they approach the best musicians of Berlin, Vienna, Munich, etc., then they declare they are too expensive for them. You, my dear, may know whether you can do without the Germans or not. If this is possible, I agree! For to get to London from here is no trifle. Probably Wilhelmj put his shoulder too strongly to the wheel in the beginning. The retreat is unpleasant now. Would you be kind enough (I can't speak English and my wife is away) to demand categorically from Hodge and Essex (1) that Frl. Exter and Fr. Waibel get half of the stipulated reimbursement of £50 each as an advance? This therefore means for each lady 500 marks, both together 1,000 marks, to be sent forthwith to Professor J. Hey, 34 Adalbertstr., Munich, for payment to both. (2) To the bass singer, Chaudon, 500 marks to be sent instantly 16 Johannistr., Cöln a/Rhein, demanded in advance. (3) The excellent harpist, royal chamber musician, August Pombo, Hochbruckenstr. 2, Munich, would like to come to London along with them, expenses only for traveling; 500 marks ought to be granted and half of it (250 mk.) to be sent to him. He is excellent and very important.

"I am glad about Seidl and Fischer! Kind regards to them.

"With me so much is going on that it is hard to keep my countenance. How loathsome that I have to interfere in affairs like those today. And to bother you on top of it! Forgive me and remain favorably inclined to

yours faithfully,

Richard Wagner"

C 21   Wagner, in Ems (Villa Diana), June 23, 1877 [to an unnamed correspondent].

Dr. August Förster had negotiated with Wagner for a production of the *Ring* at Leipzig, thereby involving both the composer and himself in a dispute with the Bavarian Monarchy, which had rights of ownership.

"Honored Friend!

"I foresaw in the long run what now is happening and wanted to avoid it because all public declarations are loathsome to me. In this way, as I now learn, I have enabled Dr. Förster to pretend he has broken with me. After all, this turn of affairs means nothing to me—but if you want closer information, ask Dr. F. for my letters, especially the last ones from Bayreuth and the two last ones from London. More about this another time! Best regards. Faithfully yours,

RICHARD WAGNER"

C 22   Wagner, in Bayreuth, November 25, 1877 [to an unnamed correspondent].

Wagner is evidently addressing Robert Prölss, the author of *Geschichte des Hoftheaters zu Dresden.*

"DEAR SIR!

"The *History of the Court Theater in Dresden* was just delivered to me. Considering your unmistakably favorable attitude toward my artistic achievements, I regret that in regard to my character you were now and then led into error, that is, inexact statements from the Archives of the Court theater, the only available source to you. So I found on page 536 that I declared myself to be honored to be employed as music director with 1,200 thaler as salary. My carefully kept diary, however, tells me that I never competed for a position in Dresden. When, upon the refusal of the job as music director, a position as conductor was offered to me, I accepted, only after strong persuasion through the widow of C. v. Weber. What you may gather from politely phrased letters can't count very much to one who knows. Besides, as to page 543, I am sorry I have to confirm the literal utterance of the late H. v. Lüttichau, according to my diary. 'If Reissiger should take a trip to a watering place and die, in Karlsbad for example, then we would solemnly bring back his corpse to Dresden.' Lüttichau was not falsely charged by me.

"The letter of mine printed on pages 546 and 547 was caused by the great excitement which Herr Ed. Devrient (whose name is mentioned in a letter) stirred in me by bringing a communication from Lüttichau. He had to report to me that a deputation of the royal orchestra had addressed Lüttichau to demand my removal, whereupon L. reprimanded those gentlemen and refused their unfair demands. Of course I was touched by L.'s action as much as I was taken aback by the reputed attitude of the orchestra. But it happened that my emotion didn't last. For later Hofrath Winkler put it on record—but in a strangely inexact way—and afterward I learned, also by a deputation of the orchestra, that they had not petitioned for my removal but, on the contrary, for apology that they didn't respond to the call of the Court authorities to demand my dismissal.[8] This, of course, entirely changed the view of the matter. The demand that I should keep my position only after having come to an arrangement with my creditors was neutralized by them, for they now desisted from their demands for an immediate payment. This happened in consideration of the fact that their loans were not squandered but used for my three operas *Rienzi, Holländer,* and *Tannhäuser,* published by myself. My agent [*Commissionär*][9] at the time and his successor did a good business with them, whereas I myself had to keep paying until only recently. This incidentally!

"I communicate this to you without any further intention. I only wanted you to

[8] *Cf. My Life,* pp. 448–449.   [9] C. F. Meser.

know those things which you couldn't know. I also ask you not to make this public in any way whatsoever. In regard to my *Life*, I have provided that after my death it may be presented to the friends of my art for their clear understanding, corroborated by numbers and names.

"Sincerely yours
RICHARD WAGNER"

C 23   Wagner, in Bayreuth, February 2, 1878 [to an unnamed correspondent].

"DEAREST FRIEND!

"I think you are connected with a music lending library? Would you be so kind as to procure for me Brahms's Symphony [10] in orchestra and piano score for a short time on guarantee of the fees required? I'm not learning anything any more of what happens in the world and here you can't get such a thing. Continue being good to me and before I die you'll get from me something nice for your music publication. I now still continually need as much money as possible, for I have to cover so many expenses. The first act of *Parsifal* is composed.

"Faithfully yours,
RICHARD WAGNER"

C 24   Wagner, in Bayreuth, July 10, 1882 [to an unnamed correspondent].

"DEAR FRIEND!

"It amuses me to have the Berlin *Blatt* controlled on certain matters. Here again is a notice, not a word of which is true. This seems especially impudent, considering the tone of assurance, as from a close friend. To a plot, outlined more than twenty-five years ago, I had given the name *Die Sieger*. Since undertaking *Parsifal*, I entirely abandoned the Buddhistic project (related in a weaker sense to *Parsifal*), and I have never since then had it in mind to do anything with it, much less to read it aloud.

"Yours truly,
RICHARD WAGNER"

C 25   Wagner, in Venice, December 17, 1882 [to an unnamed correspondent].

"DEAR FRIEND!

"Yes! You may announce it. You will receive a letter containing the story of my symphony performed fifty years ago for the first time in the *Schneiderherberge* of the Euterpe in Leipzig. And at Christmas it will be performed again here for the first time in Venice, on the occasion of my wife's birthday. By the way, in France they want to edit a translation of my published essays. I find it so risky that I can view it only as the foolhardy enterprise of some enthusiastic friends. If they want to risk this, they may do it. I for one make no terms, and I think you won't either.

"Best regards,
RICH. WAGNER"

[10] This may have been the Second Symphony, which was finished in the year previous.

INDEX